TABLE OF CONTENTS

PRACTICING TO TAKE THE GRE® GENERAL TEST

The General Test is intended to measure verbal, quantitative, and analytical skills. Although a brief review will not dramatically change the abilities you have acquired over years, use of this book may help you evaluate your ability level and identify areas for further study before you take the General Test.

This practice book contains the six GRE® General Tests that were given at GRE test centers in June 1990, December 1990, February 1991, June 1991, December 1991, and February 1992 and an additional special full-length test with questions, answers, and explanations. The tests are complete except for the single section of trial questions in each test that was not counted in the scoring. The location of the nonscored section varies from test to test. The order of the verbal, quantitative, and analytical abilities sections may vary; therefore, when you take the General Test to earn scores, you may find that these sections are not in the same order as they appear in these tests.

The practice book also contains detailed descriptions of the nine general types of questions used in the General Test and suggested strategies for answering them. Forty-eight sample questions with explanations illustrate these strategies.

On the following pages are suggestions for the use of this practice book. To obtain maximum benefit, try the following:

- Take the first test, score it, and compare your scores with the scores of other people who took the test by referring to the table on page 160.
- Read the practice material on pages 8-43.
- Then work through the test with explanations.
- Take the second test, score it, and compare these scores with your scores on the first test to note your improvement and/or any persistent areas of weakness.
- Review again the sample questions and explanations related to the areas where you have answered questions incorrectly. This will help guide you to further study.
- When you are ready, take the third test. The scores you earn on this test are good estimates of what your performance might be if you take the General Test under standard conditions in the near future. If you believe you need more practice, take any or all of the remaining tests.
- Be sure to observe the time limits for each section.

4

The OFFICIAL Guide

We prepare the tests— let us help prepare you!

GRE®

PRACTICING to Take the *General* TEST

9th Edition

The *Only* Guide Containing *Actual* GRE General Tests

Look what you'll get . . .

★ Six Actual GRE General Tests
plus one additional test complete with explanations

★ The Math Review
to familiarize yourself with the mathematical skills needed for the GRE

★ Test-taking Strategies
and information on how the test is developed

Published by Educational Testing Service
for the Graduate Record Examinations Board

The Graduate Record Examinations® Program offers a General Test measuring developed verbal, quantitative, and analytical abilities and Subject Tests measuring achievement in the following 16 fields:

Biochemistry, Cell and Molecular Biology	Economics	Literature in English	Political Science
Biology	Education	Mathematics	Psychology
Chemistry	Engineering	Music	Sociology
Computer Science	Geology	Physics	
	History		

The tests are administered by Educational Testing Service under policies determined by the Graduate Record Examinations Board, an independent board affiliated with the Association of Graduate Schools and the Council of Graduate Schools.

The Graduate Record Examinations Board has officially made available for purchase a General Test practice book. The Board has also made available for purchase practice books for 15 of the 16 Subject Tests each containing a full-length test. No practice book is currently available for the Biochemistry, Cell and Molecular Biology Test. The Subject Test practice books and *Practicing to Take the General Test* — 9th Edition may be purchased by using the order form on page 511.

Individual descriptive booklets for the General Test and all 16 Subject Tests are available free of charge. The booklets contain sample questions and descriptions of each test. The *GRE Information and Registration Bulletin* is also available free of charge. You may request copies of the *Bulletin* and descriptive booklets by writing to:

Graduate Record Examinations
Educational Testing Service
P.O. Box 6014
Princeton, NJ 08541-6014

Practice materials are developed to familiarize examinees with the types of questions they will see on actual GRE tests and to help them estimate their performance. The materials consist of previously administered paper-and-pencil tests. Differences in the number of items and the actual format of the test may be found. Questions in this practice book are presented in a different format from that used in the Computer-Based Testing (CBT) Program.

USA: 0-446-39469-6
CAN: 0-446-39470-X

TEST-TAKING STRATEGY

Your test-taking strategy may affect your scores. In preparing to take the General Test, it is important that you become thoroughly familiar with the directions in the practice tests because they are the same as those in the actual test. You have probably taken tests that contain questions similar to those found in the verbal and quantitative sections of the General Test. The question types found in the analytical section may be less familiar. You are strongly urged to review the directions for these questions and to work through some of the practice questions, particularly if you have not encountered questions of this type before. The same is true for any of the verbal or quantitative question types that are not familiar to you. Research suggests that practicing unfamiliar question types results in improved performance and decreases the likelihood of inaccurately low scores. You should still read the directions for each group of questions carefully during the actual test administration.

Work as rapidly as you can without being careless. Check frequently to make sure you are marking your answers in the appropriate rows on your answer sheet. Since no question carries greater weight than any other, do not waste time pondering individual questions you find extremely difficult or unfamiliar.

You may find it advantageous to go through a section of the General Test a first time quite rapidly, stopping only to answer those questions of which you are confident. Then go back and answer the questions that require greater thought, concluding with the very difficult questions, if you have time.

Your scores on the General Test will be determined by the number of questions for which you select the best answer from the choices given. Questions for which you mark no answer or more than one answer are not counted in scoring. Nothing is subtracted if you answer a question incorrectly. Therefore, to maximize your scores, it is better for you to guess at the answer than not to respond at all.

Some sections of the General Test contain test questions with four response options (A through D). All GRE answer sheets contain response positions for five responses (A through E). If an E response is marked for a four-option question, it will be ignored. That is, an E response for a four-option question is treated the same as no response (omitted).

During the actual administration of the General Test, you may work *only* on the section the supervisor designates and only for the time allowed. You may *not* go back to an earlier section of the test after the supervisor announces, "Please stop work" for that section. The supervisor is authorized to dismiss you from the center for doing so.

PROCEDURES FOR PRACTICING

To get an idea of your performance at this time, before further review, take the first practice test under conditions that simulate those at an actual test administration and evaluate the results.

Allow 30 minutes to complete each section of the test. Work on only one section of the test during each 30-minute time period. Do not go back to a previous section or work on a subsequent section. (If you do so at an actual test administration, you may be dismissed from the test.) Once you have completed the third section of the test, you may take a 10- to 15-minute break.

Do not use books, compasses, rulers, slide rules, calculators, (including watch calculators), pamphlets, protractors, highlighter pens, stereos, or radios with headphones, watch alarms (including those wth flashing lights or alarm sounds), dictionaries, keyboards, or paper of any kind, since you will not be permitted to use them at a test center.

When you are ready to begin the test:

- Remove an answer sheet from the back of this book.
- Read the back cover of the test book (page 159) and complete the identification portion of the answer sheet.
- Note the time and begin testing.

Once you have completed the test, determine your score and evaluate your performance, following the procedures outlined in the following two sections. If you find you are not doing well on any of the question types, review the relevant sample questions and explanations. Once this process is completed, review the full-length test with explanations. The explanations provide a basis for the underlying logic of the correct or best answer choices. Rationales are provided for all possible answer choices for the analytical and verbal tests. For the quantitative tests, the best answer choices are accompanied by solutions or quantitative explanations. When you are ready, take the second test following the same procedures as you did with the first. Repeat the process of scoring and evaluation to determine if your practice proved beneficial. If you still note weaknesses, review again those sample questions and explanations and undertake whatever further study and review you consider necessary. When you are ready to take the third test, again try to simulate actual testing conditions. Take the test, score your answer sheet, and convert the scores. These scores are good estimates of what your performance might be if you take the General Test in the near future. If you believe you need more practice, take any or all of the remaining tests.

Research on the General Test shows that scores often rise by 20 to 30 points as a result of taking the test more than once, although scores of some examinees do decline. The possible significance of this finding is tempered by the observation that repeaters are typically a self-selected group who believe that repeating the test will increase their scores. However, by preparing to take the General Test as suggested here, you may be able to do better than you would if you took the test without any initial preparation.

HOW TO SCORE YOUR PRACTICE TEST

On the page following each test is a list of the correct answers. Match your answer to each question against the answer given in the list, crossing out questions you answered incorrectly or omitted. For test GR90-16, add the number of your correct answers in Sections 1 and 5 to obtain your raw verbal score, in Sections 2 and 4 to obtain your raw quantitative score, and in Sections 3 and 7 to obtain your raw analytical ability score. For test GR91-17, add the number of your correct answers in Sections 3 and 7 to obtain your raw verbal score, in Sections 2 and 5 to obtain your raw quantitative score, and in Sections 1 and 6 to obtain your raw analytical ability score. For test GR91-18, add the number of your correct answers in Sections 1 and 4 to obtain your raw verbal score, in Sections 2 and 5 to obtain your raw quantitative score, and in Sections 3 and 6 to obtain your raw analytical ability score. For test GR91-19, add the number of your correct answers in Sections 3 and 6 to obtain your raw verbal score, in Sections 1 and 5 to obtain your raw quantitative score, and in Sections 2 and 4 to obtain your raw analytical ability score. For test GR92-1, add the number of your correct answers in Sections 2 and 4 to obtain your raw verbal score, in Sections 3 and 6 to obtain your raw quantitative score, and in Sections 1 and 7 to obtain your raw analytical ability score. For test GR92-2, add the number of your correct answers in Sections 1 and 4 to obtain your raw verbal score, in Sections 2 and 6 to obtain your raw quantitative score, and in Sections 3 and 7 to obtain your raw analytical ability score. In the conversion table for each test, you will find the scaled scores that correspond to your raw scores on the test. Convert your raw scores to scaled scores.

EVALUATING YOUR PERFORMANCE

To evaluate your performance, you may compare your scaled scores with those of others who have taken the General Test at GRE test centers between October 1, 1985, and September 30, 1991. The score conversion tables on pages 161, 264, 311, 355, 401, and 449 indicate for each scaled score shown, the percentages of examinees who earned lower scores. For example, in the table on page 161, in the percent column next to the verbal ability scaled score 460 is the percent 45. This means that 45 percent of the examinees tested between October 1985 and September 1988 earned verbal ability scores below 460. For each score you earned on this practice test, note the percent of GRE examinees who earned lower scores. This is a reasonable indication of your rank among GRE General Test examinees if you follow the test-taking suggestions in this practice book.

The P+ number to the right of each correct answer is based on the percent of examinees who actually took that edition of the test and answered the question correctly. (This percent, however, has been adjusted so that it is an estimate of the P+ that would have been obtained if all examinees tested in a recent three-year period had had the opportunity to answer the question.) This information enables you to see how other examinees performed on each question. It can also help identify content areas in which you need more practice and review.

It is important to realize that ability patterns differ for people who have different interests and experience. The second table on page 499 shows you the average scores for people in various categories of intended graduate major fields. You can see that those whose interests lie in the physical sciences, which are highly mathematical, generally have relatively high scores in quantitative ability, whereas those interested in the humanities generally have relatively high verbal scores. Find the major field category most closely related to your career goal to see how your performance compares with that of others who are striving for similar goals.

ADDITIONAL INFORMATION

If you have any questions about any of the information in this book, please write to:

Graduate Record Examinations
Educational Testing Service
P.O. Box 6000
Princeton, NJ 08541-6000

TEST PREPARATION MATERIAL

Purpose of the GRE General Test

The GRE General Test measures certain developed verbal, quantitative, and analytical abilities that are important for academic achievement. In doing so, the test necessarily reflects the opportunities and efforts that have contributed to the development of those abilities.

The General Test is only one of several means of evaluating likely success in graduate school. It is not intended to measure inherent intellectual capacity or intelligence. Neither is it intended to measure creativity, motivation, perseverance, or social worth. The test does, however, make it possible to compare students with different backgrounds. A GRE score of 500, for example, has the same meaning whether earned by a student at a small, private liberal arts college or by a student at a large public university.

Because several different forms (or editions) of the test are in active use, all students do not receive exactly the same test edition. However, all editions measure the same skills and meet the same specifications for content and difficulty. The scores from different editions are made comparable to one another by a statistical procedure known as equating. This process makes it possible to assure that all reported scores of a given value denote the same level of developed ability regardless of which edition of the test is taken.

Since students have wide-ranging backgrounds, interests, and skills, the *verbal sections* of the General Test use questions from diverse areas of experience. The areas range from the activities of daily life to broad categories of academic interest such as the sciences, social studies, and the humanities. Knowledge of high school level arithmetic, plane geometry, and algebra provides adequate preparation for the *quantitative sections* of the test. Questions in the *analytical sections* measure analytical skills developed in virtually all fields of study. No formal training in logic or methods of analysis is needed to do well in these sections.

How the Test is Developed

The General Test is composed of questions formulated by specialists in various fields. Each question is reviewed by several independent critics and revised if necessary. New questions are pretested in actual tests under standard testing conditions.

Questions appearing in a test for the first time are analyzed for usefulness and weaknesses; they are not used in computing scores. Questions that perform satisfactorily become part of a pool from which a new edition of the General Test will be assembled at a future date. Those that do not perform well are discarded or are rewritten to correct the flaws and tried out again.

When a General Test has been assembled, it is reviewed by other subject matter and test specialists from inside and outside ETS. After any problems raised in these reviews have been resolved, the test goes to a test editor, who may make further suggestions for change. Individual test questions and the test as a whole are reviewed to eliminate language, symbols, or content considered to be potentially offensive or inappropriate for major subgroups of the test-taking population, or serve to perpetuate any negative attitude that may be conveyed to these subgroups.

All reviewers except the editors, copyreaders, and proofreaders must attempt to answer each question without the help of the answer key. Thus, each reviewer "takes the test," uninfluenced by knowledge of what the question writer or test assembler believed each answer should be. The answer key is certified as official only after the reviewers have agreed independently on the best answer for each question.

The extensive procedure described above has been developed to assure that every question in the General Test is appropriate and useful and that the combination of questions is satisfactory. Even so, the appraisal is not complete until after the new edition has been administered and subjected to a rigorous item analysis to see whether each question yields the expected results.

This analysis may reveal that a question is ambiguous, requires knowledge beyond the scope of the test, or is inappropriate for the total group or a particular subgroup of examinees taking the test. Answers to such a question are not used in computing scores.

Description of the General Test

In this description, several examples of each type of question included in the verbal, quantitative, and analytical measures of the GRE General Test are discussed, and explanations of the correct answers are provided.

Verbal Ability

The verbal ability measure is designed to test one's ability to reason with words in solving problems. Reasoning effectively in a verbal medium depends primarily upon the ability to discern, comprehend, and analyze relationships among words or groups of words and within larger units of discourse such as sentences and written passages. Such factors as knowledge of words and practice in reading will, of course, define the limits within which one can reason using these tools.

The verbal measure consists of four question types: analogies, antonyms, sentence completions, and reading comprehension sets. The examples of verbal questions in this section do not reflect precisely the difficulty range of the verbal measure. A greater number of difficult questions than would be encountered in the test have been included to provide practice in approaching more complex verbal questions.

Analogies

Analogy questions test the ability to recognize relationships among words and the concepts they represent and to recognize when these relationships are parallel. The process of eliminating four incorrect answer choices requires one to formulate and then analyze the relationships linking six pairs of words (the given pair and the five answer choices) and to recognize which answer pair is most nearly analogous to the given pair. Some examples of relationships that might be found in analogy questions are kind, size, contiguity, or degree.

Some approaches that may be helpful in answering analogy questions:

- Before looking at the answer choices, try to establish a precise relationship between the words in the given pair. It is usually helpful to express that relationship in a phrase or sentence; for example, the relationship between the word pair THRIFTY : MISERLY could be expressed as "to be *miserly* is to be *thrifty* to an excessive degree." Next, look for the answer choice with the pair of words whose relationship is closest to that of the given pair and can be expressed in a similar fashion.
- Occasionally, more than one of the answer choices may seem at first to express a relationship similar to that of the given pair. Go back to the given pair and try to state the relationship more precisely or identify some aspect of the relationship between the given pair of words that is paralleled in only *one* answer choice pair.
- Remember that a single word can have several different meanings. If you are unable to establish a relationship between the given pair or to find a parallel relationship among the answer choice pairs, check to be sure you have not overlooked a possible second meaning for one of the words.
- *Never* decide on the best answer without reading *all* the answer choices. If you do not read all the answer choices, you may miss an answer choice that would have appeared superior to the choice you made or might have prompted you to reevaluate your understanding of the question.

■ Practice recognizing and formulating relationships between word pairs. You can do this with the following sample questions and with the analogy questions in the practice test in this booklet.

Directions: In each of the following questions, a related pair of words or phrases is followed by five lettered pairs of words or phrases. Select the lettered pair that best expresses a relationship similar to that expressed in the original pair.

1. COLOR : SPECTRUM :: **(A) tone : scale (B) sound : waves (C) verse : poem (D) dimension : space (E) cell : organism**

The relationship between *color* and *spectrum* is not merely that of part to whole, in which case (E) or even (C) might be defended as correct. A *spectrum* is made up of a progressive, graduated series of colors, as a *scale* is of a progressive, graduated sequence of tones. Thus, (A) is correct. Here, the best answer must be selected from a group of fairly close choices.

2. ABDICATION : THRONE :: **(A) paradox : argument (B) competition : match (C) defeat : election (D) bequest : will (E) resignation : office**

The relationship between *abdication* and *throne* is easy to perceive and only the correct answer, (E), expresses a similar relationship. (C) is incorrect because *defeat* is not voluntary, as are *abdication* and *resignation* and because *election,* the process of attaining a particular status, is not parallel to *throne* and *office*.

3. DESICCATE : MOISTURE :: **(A) pulverize : dust (B) varnish : deterioration (C) shatter : shards (D) bend : contents (E) darken : light**

To *desiccate* an object is to cause it to dry up by depriving it of *moisture.* Among the answer choices, only (E) has a similar relationship between its two words: to *darken* an object is to make it darker by depriving it of *light*. In the other four choices, the first words, *pulverize, varnish, shatter,* and *bend,* are parallel to *desiccate* in that they describe actions that alter the condition of an object, but the second word is not something of which an object is deprived as a result of the action the first word describes. In (A) and (C), the second words, *dust* and *shards,* are the results of pulverizing and shattering, respectively. *Deterioration* in (B) may be prevented through varnishing, and *contents* in (D) bears no relationship to bending that resembles the relationship between *desiccate* and *moisture*.

4. HEADLONG : FORETHOUGHT :: **(A) barefaced : shame (B) mealymouthed : talent (C) heartbroken : emotion (D) levelheaded : resolve (E) singlehanded : ambition**

The difficulty of this question probably derives primarily from the complexity of the relationship between *headlong* and *forethought* rather than from any inherent difficulty in the words. Analysis of the relationship between *headlong* and *forethought* reveals the following: an action or behavior that is *headlong* reveals lack of *forethought*. Only answer choice (A) displays the same relationship between its two terms.

Antonyms

Although antonym questions test knowledge of vocabulary more directly than do any of the other verbal question types, the purpose of the antonym questions is to measure not merely the strength of one's vocabulary but also the ability to reason from a given concept to its opposite. Antonyms may require only rather general knowledge of a word or they may require one to make fine distinctions among answer choices. Antonyms are generally confined to nouns, verbs, and adjectives; answer choices may be single words or phrases.

Some approaches that may be helpful in answering antonym questions:

- Remember that you are looking for the word that is the most nearly *opposite* to the given word; you are *not* looking for a synonym. Since many words do not have a precise opposite, you must look for the answer choice that expresses a concept *most nearly* opposite to that of the given word. For this reason, antonym questions are not measures of rote vocabulary knowledge; rather, these questions ask you to evaluate shades of meaning and the interaction of meaning between words.
- In some cases more than one of the answer choices may appear at first to be opposite to the given word. Questions that require you to make fine distinctions among two or more answer choices are best handled by defining more precisely or in greater detail the meaning of the given word.
- It is often useful, in weighing answer choices, to make up a sentence using the given word; if you do not know the precise dictionary meaning of a word but have a general sense of how the word might be used, try to make up a phrase or sentence with the word. Substituting the answer choices in the phrase or sentence and seeing which best "fits," in that it reverses the meaning or tone of the sentence or phrase, may help you determine the best answer.
- Remember that a particular word may have more than one meaning, so if you are unable to find an answer choice that appears opposite to the given word, examine all the words for possible second meanings.
- Use your knowledge of root, prefix, and suffix meanings to help you determine the meanings of words with which you are not entirely familiar.

Directions: Each question below consists of a word printed in capital letters followed by five lettered words or phrases. Choose the lettered word or phrase that is most nearly *opposite* in meaning to the word in capital letters. Since some of the questions require you to distinguish fine shades of meaning, be sure to consider all the choices before deciding which one is best.

5. DIFFUSE: (A) concentrate (B) contend (C) imply (D) pretend (E) rebel

The answer is (A). *Diffuse* means to permit or cause to spread out; only (A) presents an idea that is in any way opposite to *diffuse*.

6. COINCIDENCE: **(A) depletion (B) incongruity (C) pessimism (D) ill fortune (E) lack of ideas**

One meaning of *coincidence* is being in harmony or accord; another is corresponding in nature, character, or function. *Incongruity,* the correct answer, means lack of harmony or lack of conformity. Answer choice (D) may seem plausible at first glance since a *coincidence* of events is often a pleasant chance occurrence ("good luck" as opposed to "bad luck"), but careful reflection reveals that a *coincidence* is not necessarily a positive phenomenon.

7. MULTIFARIOUS: **(A) deprived of freedom (B) deprived of comfort (C) lacking space (D) lacking stability (E) lacking diversity**

Multifarious means having or occurring in great variety, so the correct answer is (E). Even if one is not entirely familiar with the meaning of *multifarious,* it is possible to use the clue provided by "multi-" to help find the right answer to this question.

8. PARSIMONIOUS: **(A) initial (B) vegetative (C) prodigal (D) affluent (E) impromptu**

The answer to this question is (C); *parsimonious* means frugal to the point of stinginess, and *prodigal,* which means extravagant to the point of wastefulness, is the only answer choice opposite in meaning. At first, answer choice (D), *affluent,* may seem plausible in that it may be thought that wealth is an opposite concept to frugality — but it is well known that not all wealthy persons are generous.

Sentence Completions

The purpose of the sentence completion questions is to measure the ability to recognize words or phrases that both logically and stylistically complete the meaning of a sentence. In deciding which of five words or sets of words can best be substituted for blank spaces in a sentence, one must analyze the relationships among the component parts of the incomplete sentence. One must consider each answer choice and decide which completes the sentence in such a way that the sentence has a logically satisfying meaning and can be read as a stylistically integrated whole.

Sentence completion questions provide a context within which to analyze the function of words as they relate to and combine with one another to form a meaningful unit of discourse.

Some approaches that may be helpful in answering sentence completion questions:

- Read the entire sentence carefully before you consider the answer choices; be sure you understand the ideas expressed in the sentence and examine the sentence for possible indications of tone (irony, humor, and the like).

- Before reading the answer choices you may find it helpful to fill in the blanks with a word or words of your own that complete the meaning of the sentence. Then examine the answer choices to see if any of them parallels your own completion of the sentence.

- Pay attention to grammatical clues in the sentence. For example, words like *although* and *nevertheless* indicate that some qualification or opposition is taking place in the sentence, whereas *moreover* implies an intensification or support of some idea in the sentence. Pay attention also to the style of, and choice of words in, the sentence; sometimes determining the best answer depends in whole or in part on considerations of stylistic consistency among the parts of the sentence.

- If a sentence has two blanks, be sure that *both* parts of your answer choice fit logically and stylistically into the sentence. Do not choose an answer on the basis of the fit of the first word alone.

- When you have chosen an answer, read the complete sentence through to check that it has acquired a logically and stylistically satisfying meaning.

Directions: Each sentence below has one or two blanks, each blank indicating that something has been omitted. Beneath the sentence are five lettered words or sets of words. Choose the word or set of words for each blank that *best* fits the meaning of the sentence as a whole.

9. Early ------- of hearing loss is ------- by the fact that the other senses are able to compensate for moderate amounts of loss, so that people frequently do not know that their hearing is imperfect.

(A) discovery . . indicated
(B) development . . prevented
(C) detection . . complicated
(D) treatment . . facilitated
(E) incidence . . corrected

The statement that the other senses compensate for partial loss of hearing indicates that the hearing loss is not *prevented* or *corrected*; therefore, choices (B) and (E) can be eliminated. Furthermore, the ability to compensate for hearing loss certainly does not facilitate the early *treatment* (D) or the early *discovery* (A) of hearing loss. It is reasonable, however, that early *detection* of hearing loss is *complicated* by the ability to compensate for it. The correct answer is (C).

10. The ------- science of seismology has grown just enough so that the first overly bold theories have been -------.

(A) magnetic . . accepted
(B) fledgling . . refuted
(C) revolutionary . . analyzed
(D) predictive . . protected
(E) exploratory . . recalled

At first reading, there may appear to be several answer choices that "make sense" when substituted in the blanks of the sentence. (A) and (D) can be dismissed fairly readily when it is seen that *accepted* and *protected* are not compatible with *overly bold* in the sentence. The sentence yielded by (C) is logically more acceptable but not as strong as the sentences yielded by (B) and (E). Of these two latter choices, (B) is superior on stylistic grounds: theories are not *recalled* (E), and *fledgling* (B) reflects the idea of growth present in the sentence.

11. If her characters are still being written about as unfathomable riddles, it is to be attributed more to a human passion for ------- than to dubious complexities of her art.

(A) conundrums (B) platitudes (C) scapegoats (D) euphemisms (E) stereotypes

The answer to this question is (A). While any of the answer choices may be argued to be an object of human passion, only *conundrums* enables the sentence *as a whole* to acquire a coherent meaning. It is necessary, in choosing an answer, to complete the sentence in such a way as to make clear why the writer's characters are seen as *unfathomable riddles*. A human penchant for *conundrums*, or puzzling questions whose answers can only be conjectural, will account for this.

Reading Comprehension

The purpose of the reading comprehension questions is to measure the ability to read with understanding, insight, and discrimination. This type of question explores the examinee's ability to analyze a written passage from several perspectives, including the ability to recognize both explicitly stated elements in the passage and assumptions underlying statements or arguments in the passage as well as the implications of those statements or arguments. Because the written passage upon which reading comprehension questions are based presents a sustained discussion of a particular topic, there is ample context for analyzing a variety of relationships; for example, the function of a word in relation to a larger segment of the passage, the relationships among the various ideas in the passage, or the relation of the author to his or her topic or to the audience.

There are six types of reading comprehension questions. These types focus on (1) the main idea or primary purpose of the passage; (2) information explicitly stated in the passage; (3) information or ideas implied or suggested by the author; (4) possible application of the author's ideas to other situations; (5) the author's logic, reasoning, or persuasive techniques; and (6) the tone of the passage or the author's attitude as it is revealed in the language used.

In each edition of the General Test, there are two relatively long reading comprehension passages, each providing the basis for answering seven or eight questions, and two relatively short passages, each providing the basis for answering three or four questions. The four passages are drawn from four different subject matter areas: the humanities, the social sciences, the biological sciences, and the physical sciences.

Some approaches that may be helpful in answering reading comprehension questions:

- Since reading passages are drawn from many different disciplines and sources, you should not expect to be familiar with the material in all the passages. However, you should not be discouraged by encountering material with which you are not familiar; questions are to be answered on the basis of the information provided in the passage, and you are not expected to rely on outside knowledge, which you may or may not have, of a particular topic. You may, however, want to save for last a passage that seems particularly difficult or unfamiliar.

- There are different strategies for approaching reading comprehension questions; you must decide which works most effectively for you. You might try different strategies as you do the reading comprehension questions in the practice test in this booklet. Some different strategies are: reading the passage very closely and then proceeding to the questions; skimming the passage, reading quickly through the questions, and then rereading the passage closely; and reading the questions first, then reading the passage closely. You may find that different strategies work better for different kinds of passages; for example, it might be helpful with a difficult or unfamiliar passage to read through the questions first.

- Whatever strategy you choose, you should analyze the passage carefully before answering the questions. As with any kind of close and thoughtful reading, you should be sensitive to clues that will help you understand less explicit aspects of the passage. Try to separate main ideas from supporting ideas or evidence; try also to separate the author's own ideas or attitudes from information he or she is simply presenting. It is important to note transitions from one idea to the next and to examine the relationships among the different ideas or parts of the passage. For example, are they contrasting? Are they complementary? You should consider both the points the author makes and the conclusions he or she draws and also how and why those points are made or conclusions drawn.

- You may find it helpful to underline or mark key parts of the passage. For example, you might underline main ideas or important arguments or you might circle transitional words that will help you map the logical structure of the passage (*although, nevertheless, correspondingly,* and the like) or descriptive words that will help you identify the author's attitude toward a particular idea or person.

- Read each question carefully and be certain that you understand exactly what is being asked.

- *Always* read all the answer choices before selecting the best answer.
- The best answer is the one that most accurately and most completely answers the question being posed. Be careful not to pick an answer choice simply because it is a true statement; be careful also not to be misled by answer choices that are only partially true or only partially satisfy the problem posed in the question.
- Answer the questions on the basis of the information provided in the passage and do not rely on outside knowledge. Your own views or opinions may sometimes conflict with the views expressed or the information provided in the passage; be sure that you work within the context provided by the passage. You should not expect to agree with everything you encounter in reading passages.

Directions: The passage is followed by questions based on its content. After reading the passage, choose the best answer to each question. Answer all questions following the passage on the basis of what is *stated* or *implied* in the passage.

Picture-taking is a technique both for annexing the objective world and for expressing the singular self. Photographs depict objective realities that already exist, though only the camera can disclose them. And they depict an individual photographer's temperament, discovering itself through the camera's cropping of reality. That is, photography has two antithetical ideals: in the first, photography is about the world and the photographer is a mere observer who counts for little; but in the second, photography is the instrument of intrepid, questing subjectivity and the photographer is all.

These conflicting ideals arise from a fundamental uneasiness on the part of both photographers and viewers of photographs toward the aggressive component in "taking" a picture. Accordingly, the ideal of a photographer as observer is attractive because it implicitly denies that picture-taking is an aggressive act. The issue, of course, is not so clear-cut. What photographers do cannot be characterized as simply predatory or as simply, and essentially, benevolent. As a consequence, one ideal of picture-taking or the other is always being rediscovered and championed.

An important result of the coexistence of these two ideals is a recurrent ambivalence toward photography's means. Whatever the claims that photography might make to be a form of personal expression on a par with painting, its originality is inextricably linked to the powers of a machine. The steady growth of these powers has made possible the extraordinary informativeness and imaginative formal beauty of many photographs, like Harold Edgerton's high-speed photographs of a bullet hitting its target or of the swirls and eddies of a tennis

stroke. But as cameras become more sophisticated, more automated, some photographers are tempted to disarm themselves or to suggest that they are not really armed, preferring to submit themselves to the limits imposed by premodern camera technology because a cruder, less high-powered machine is thought to give more interesting or emotive results, to leave more room for creative accident. For example, it has been virtually a point of honor for many photographers, including Walker Evans and Cartier-Bresson, to refuse to use modern equipment. These photographers have come to doubt the value of the camera as an instrument of "fast seeing." Cartier-Bresson, in fact, claims that the modern camera may see too fast.

This ambivalence toward photographic means determines trends in taste. The cult of the future (of faster and faster seeing) alternates over time with the wish to return to a purer past — when images had a handmade quality. This nostalgia for some pristine state of the photographic enterprise is currently widespread and underlies the present-day enthusiasm for daguerreotypes and the work of forgotten nineteenth-century provincial photographers. Photographers and viewers of photographs, it seems, need periodically to resist their own knowingness.

12. According to the passage, the two antithetical ideals of photography differ primarily in the

(A) value that each places on the beauty of the finished product
(B) emphasis that each places on the emotional impact of the finished product
(C) degree of technical knowledge that each requires of the photographer
(D) extent of the power that each requires of the photographer's equipment
(E) way in which each defines the role of the photographer

The answer to this question is (E). Photography's two ideals are presented in lines 6-10. The main emphasis in the description of these two ideals is on the relationship of the photographer to the enterprise of photography, with the photographer described in the one as a passive observer and in the other as an active questioner. (E) identifies this key feature in the description of the two ideals — the way in which each ideal conceives or defines the role of the photographer in photography. (A) through (D) present aspects of photography that are mentioned in the passage, but none of these choices represents a primary difference between the two ideals of photography.

13. According to the passage, interest among photographers in each of photography's two ideals can be described as

(A) rapidly changing
(B) cyclically recurring
(C) steadily growing
(D) unimportant to the viewers of photographs
(E) unrelated to changes in technology

This question requires one to look for comments in the passage about the nature of photographers' interest in the two ideals of photography. While the whole passage is, in a sense, about the response of photographers to these ideals, there are elements in the passage that comment specifically on this issue. Lines 18-20 tell us that the two ideals alternate in terms of their perceived relevance and value, that each ideal has periods of popularity and of neglect. These lines support (B). Lines 21-22 tell us that the two ideals affect attitudes toward "photography's means," that is, the technology of the camera; (E), therefore, cannot be the correct answer. In lines 43-46, attitudes toward photographic means (which result from the two ideals) are said to alternate over time; these lines provide further support for B. (A) can be eliminated because, although the passage tells us that the interest of photographers in each of the ideals fluctuates over time, it nowhere indicates that this fluctuation or change is rapid. Nor does the passage say anywhere that interest in these ideals is growing; the passage *does* state that the powers of the camera are steadily growing (lines 25-26), but this does not mean that interest in the two ideals is growing. Thus (C) can be eliminated. (D) can be eliminated because the passage nowhere states that reactions to the ideals are either important or unimportant to viewers' concerns. Thus (B) is the correct answer.

14. Which of the following statements would be most likely to begin the paragraph immediately following the passage?

(A) Photographers, as a result of their heightened awareness of time, are constantly trying to capture events and actions that are fleeting.
(B) Thus the cult of the future, the worship of machines and speed, is firmly established in spite of efforts to the contrary by some photographers.
(C) The rejection of technical knowledge, however, can never be complete and photography cannot for any length of time pretend that it has no weapons.
(D) The point of honor involved in rejecting complex equipment is, however, of no significance to the viewer of a photograph.
(E) Consequently the impulse to return to the past through images that suggest a handwrought quality is nothing more than a passing fad.

Answering this question requires one to think about where the discussion in the passage as a whole is moving and in particular where the final paragraph points. The last two paragraphs discuss the effect of the two ideals of photography on photographers' attitudes toward the camera. The final paragraph describes two such attitudes, or trends in taste (one in which the technology of today's camera is valued and one in which it is seen as a handicap), and tells us that these two attitudes alternate, with the second currently predominating. (B) and (E) can be eliminated because they both suggest that the first attitude will prevail, thus contradicting information in the last paragraph. (A) is not connected in any way to the discussion of attitudes toward the use of the present-day camera and so is not a good choice. (D) appears related to the previous material in the passage in that it discusses the second attitude; however, it introduces an idea — consideration of the viewer — that has not been developed in the passage. (C), the correct answer, is superior not only because it comments on the second attitude but also because it reiterates the idea that neither attitude will prevail. (C) is strengthened through its stylistic relation to earlier elements in the passage: the use of the word *weapons* recalls the references in lines 31 and 32 to photographers as *armed* with cameras.

Quantitative Ability

The quantitative sections of the General Test are designed to measure basic mathematical skills, understanding of elementary mathematical concepts, and ability to reason quantitatively and to solve problems in a quantitative setting. The mathematics required does not extend beyond that assumed to be common to the mathematics background of almost all examinees. The questions include three broad content areas: arithmetic, algebra, and geometry. Although a question in these areas may be posed in either English or metric units of measure, neither the knowledge required for converting units in one system to units in another system, nor the ability to convert from one unit to another in the same system, is tested. If an answer to a question is expected to be in a unit of measure different from the unit in which the question is posed, a relationship between the units is provided unless the relationship is a common one, such as minutes to hours.

Arithmetic

Questions classified as *arithmetic* include those involving the following topics: arithmetic operations (addition, subtraction, multiplication, division, and nonnegative powers) on rational numbers, estimation, percent, average, interpretation of graphs and tables, properties of numbers (such as those relating to odd and even integers, primes, and divisibility), factoring, and elementary counting and probability.

Some facts about numbers that might be helpful. An odd integer power of a negative number is negative, and an even integer power is positive; for example, $(-2)^3 = -8$, but $(-2)^2 = 4$.

Squaring a number between 0 and 1 (or raising it to a higher power) results in a smaller number; for example, $\left(\frac{1}{3}\right)^2 = \frac{1}{9}$, and $(0.5)^3 = 0.125$.

The sum and product of even and odd integers will be even or odd depending on the operation and the kinds of integers; for example, the sum of an odd integer and an even integer is odd.

If an integer P is a divisor (or a factor) of another integer N, then N is the product of P and another integer, and N is said to be a multiple of P; for example, 3 is a divisor (or a factor) of 6, and 6 is a multiple of 3.

A *prime* number is an integer that has only two distinct positive divisors, 1 and itself; for example, 2, 3, 5, 7, and 11 are primes, but 9 is not a prime because it has three positive divisors: 1, 3, and 9.

The sum and product of signed numbers will be positive or negative depending on the operation and the kinds of numbers; for example, the product of a negative number and a positive number is negative.

For any two numbers on the number line, the number on the left is less than the number on the right; for example, $2 < 3$ and $-4 < -3$.

The radical sign "$\sqrt{\ }$" means "the nonnegative square root of." For example, $\sqrt{0} = 0$ and $\sqrt{4} = 2$.

If n is a positive integer, then "x^n" denotes the product of n factors of x; for example, 3^4 means $3 \cdot 3 \cdot 3 \cdot 3 = 81$.

Note also that $3^0 = 1$, and that division by zero is undefined; that is, $\frac{5}{0}$ has no meaning.

Algebra

Questions classified as *algebra* include those involving operations with radical expressions, factoring and simplifying algebraic expressions, equations and inequalities, and absolute value. The skills required include the ability to solve first and second degree equations and inequalities, and simultaneous equations; the ability to read a word problem and set up the necessary equations or inequalities to solve it; and the ability to apply basic algebraic skills to solve unfamiliar problems. In general, the algebra required does not extend beyond that usually covered in a first-year high school course, and it is expected that examinees will be familiar with conventional symbolism, such as:
$x < y$ (x is less than y), $x \neq y$ (x is not equal to y),
and $|x|$, which is equal to x if $x \geq 0$ and $-x$ if $x < 0$; for example,
$|8| = 8$ and $|-8| = -(-8) = 8$. Nonstandard notation is used only when it is explicitly defined in a particular question.

Some facts about algebra that might be helpful. If $ab = 0$, then either $a = 0$ or $b = 0$; for example, if $(x-1)(x+2) = 0$, it follows that either $x - 1 = 0$ or $x + 2 = 0$. Therefore, $x = 1$ or $x = -2$.

Adding a number to or subtracting a number from both sides of an equation preserves the equality. Similarly, multiplying or dividing both sides of an equation by a nonzero number preserves the equality. Similar rules apply to inequalities, with the exception that in the case of multiplying or dividing by a *negative* number, the inequality reverses. For example: multiplying the inequality $3x - 4 > 5$ by 4 yields the inequality $12x - 16 > 20$. However, multiplying that same inequality by -4 yields $-12x + 16 < -20$.

The following rules for exponents are useful. If r, s, x, and y are positive integers, then

(a) $x^r \cdot x^s = x^{r+s}$; e.g. $3^2 \cdot 3^4 = 3^6 = 729$

(b) $x^r \cdot y^r = (xy)^r$; e.g. $3^4 \cdot 2^4 = 6^4 = 1,296$

(c) $(x^r)^s = x^{rs}$; e.g. $(2^3)^4 = 2^{12} = 4,096$

(d) $\frac{x^r}{x^s} = x^{r-s}$; e.g. $\frac{4^5}{4^2} = 4^3 = 64$

Geometry

Questions classified as *geometry* include those involving the following topics: properties associated with parallel lines, circles and their inscribed and central angles, triangles, rectangles, other polygons, measurement-related concepts of area, perimeter, volume, the Pythagorean Theorem, and angle measure in degrees. Knowledge of simple coordinate geometry and special triangles such as isosceles, equilateral, and $30^\circ - 60^\circ - 90^\circ$ triangles are also tested. The ability to construct proofs is not measured.

It is expected that examinees will be familiar with the conventional symbolism used in elementary geometry, such as the following: $\|$ (this means *is parallel to*), $\perp$ (this means *is perpendicular to*), and

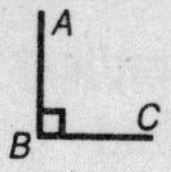

A, B, C (this means that $\angle ABC$ is a right angle).

Some facts about geometry that might be helpful. If two lines intersect, the vertical angles are equal; for example, in the figure

y°, x° , $x = y$.

If two parallel lines are intersected by a third line, some of the angles formed are equal; for example, in the figure

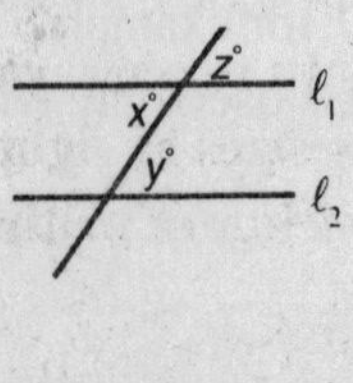

z°, x°, y°, ℓ_1, ℓ_2 where $\ell_1 \| \ell_2$, $y = x = z$.

The number of degrees of arc in a circle is 360; for example, in the figure

if x = 60, then the length of arc ABC is $\frac{60}{360}$ of the circumference of the circle.

The sum of the degree measures of the angles of a triangle is 180.

The volume of a rectangular solid or of a right circular cylinder is the product of the area of the base and the height; for example, the volume of a cylinder with base of radius 2 and height 5 is $(2^2)(5) = 20\pi$.

The square of the length of the hypotenuse of a right triangle is equal to the sum of the squares of the lengths of the two legs.

The coordinates of a point (x,y) give the location of the point in the coordinate plane; for example, the point $(2,-3)$ is located in the fourth quadrant 2 units to the right of the Y-axis and 3 units below the X-axis.

The sides of a $45^\circ - 45^\circ - 90^\circ$ triangle are in the ratio $1{:}\ 1{:}\ \sqrt{2}$, and the sides of a $30^\circ - 60^\circ - 90^\circ$ triangle are in the ratio $1{:}\ \sqrt{3}{:}\ 2$.

Drawing in lines that are not shown in a figure can sometimes help in solving a geometry problem; for example, by drawing the dashed lines in the pentagon

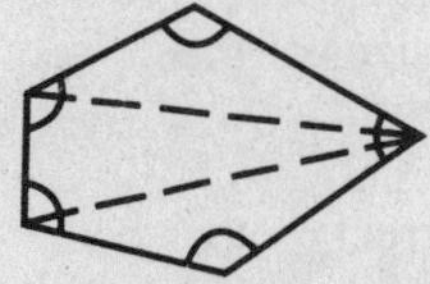

, the number of degrees in the pentagon can be found by adding up the number of degrees in the three triangles.

The quantitative measure employs three types of questions: quantitative comparison, discrete quantitative, and data interpretation. Pacing yourself on all of these question types is important. Do not spend an excessive amount of time pondering over problems you find difficult. Go on to the next question and, if time permits, come back to the difficult questions when you have completed the section.

The following information on numbers and figures applies to all questions in the quantitative sections.

Numbers: **All numbers used are real numbers.**

Figures: **Position of points, angles, regions, etc., can be assumed to be in the order shown, and angle measures can be assumed to be positive.**

Lines shown as straight can be assumed to be straight.

Figures can be assumed to lie in a plane unless otherwise indicated.

Figures that accompany questions are intended to provide information useful in answering the questions. However, unless a note states that a figure is drawn to scale, you should solve these problems NOT by estimating sizes by sight or by measurement, but by using your knowledge of mathematics.

Quantitative Comparison

The quantitative comparison questions test the ability to reason quickly and accurately about the relative sizes of two quantities or to perceive that not enough information is provided to make such a decision. To solve a quantitative comparison problem, you compare the quantities given in two columns, Column A and Column B, and decide whether one quantity is greater than the other, whether the two quantities are equal, or whether the relationship cannot be determined from the information given. Some questions only require some manipulation to determine which of the quantities is greater; other questions require you to reason more or to think of special cases in which the relative sizes of the quantities reverse.

The following strategies might help in answering quantitative comparison questions.

- Do not waste time performing needless computations in order to eventually compare two specific numbers. Simplify or transform one or both of the given quantities only as much as is necessary to determine which quantity is greater or whether the two quantities are equal. Once you have determined that one quantity is greater than the other, do not take time to find the exact sizes of the quantities. Answer and go on to the next question.
- If both quantities being compared involve no variables, then the correct answer can never be (D), which states that the relationship cannot be determined. The answer is then reduced to three choices.
- Consider all kinds of numbers before you make a decision. As soon as you establish that quantity A is greater in one case while quantity B is greater in another case, choose answer (D) immediately and move on to the next comparison.
- Geometric figures may not be drawn to scale. Comparisons should be made based on knowledge of mathematics rather than appearance. However, you can sometimes find a clue by sketching another figure in your test book. Try to visualize the parts of a figure that are fixed by the information given and the parts that are collapsible and changeable. If a figure can flow into other shapes and sizes while conforming to given information, the answer is probably (D).

Directions for quantitative comparison questions and some examples with explanations follow.

Directions: Each of the following questions consists of two quantities, one in Column A and one in Column B. You are to compare the two quantities and choose

A if the quantity in Column A is greater;
B if the quantity in Column B is greater;
C if the two quantities are equal;
D if the relationship cannot be determined from the information given.

Note: **Since there are only four choices, NEVER MARK (E).**

Common Information: **In a question, information concerning one or both of the quantities to be compared is centered above the two columns. A symbol that appears in both columns represents the same thing in Column A as it does in Column B.**

	Column A	Column B	Sample Answers
Example 1:	**2×6**	**$2 + 6$**	● Ⓑ Ⓒ Ⓓ Ⓔ
Examples 2-4 refer to ΔPQR.	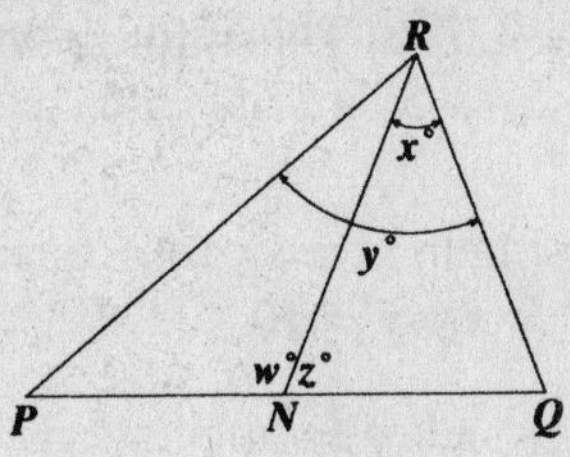		
Example 2:	**PN**	**NQ**	Ⓐ Ⓑ Ⓒ ● Ⓔ **(since equal measures cannot be assumed, even though PN and NQ appear equal)**
Example 3:	**x**	**y**	Ⓐ ● Ⓒ Ⓓ Ⓔ **(since N is between P and Q)**
Example 4:	**w + z**	**180**	Ⓐ Ⓑ ● Ⓓ Ⓔ **(since PQ is a straight line)**

	Column A	Column B
15.	**9.8**	**$\sqrt{100}$**

$\sqrt{100}$ denotes 10, the positive square root of 100. (For any positive number x, $\sqrt{x}$ denotes the *positive* number whose square is x.) Since 10 is greater than 9.8, the correct answer is B. It is important not to confuse this question with a comparison of 9.8 and x where $x^2 = 100$. The latter comparison would yield D as the correct answer because $x^2 = 100$ implies that either $x = \sqrt{100}$ or $x = -\sqrt{100}$, and there is no way to determine which value x actually would have. However, this question asks for a comparison of 9.8 and $\sqrt{100}$, and $9.8 < \sqrt{100}$ for the reasons previously given.

	Column A	**Column B**
16.	$(-6)^4$	$(-6)^5$

Since $(-6)^4$ is the product of four negative factors and the product of an even number of negative numbers is positive, $(-6)^4$ is positive. Since the product of an odd number of negative numbers is negative, $(-6)^5$ is negative. Therefore $(-6)^4$ is greater than $(-6)^5$ since any positive number is greater than any negative number. The correct answer is A. Do not waste time determining that $(-6)^4 = 1,296$ and that $(-6)^5 = -7,776$. This information is not needed to make the comparison.

$$x + y = 10$$
$$x - y = 2$$

17.	$x^2 - y^2$	**19**

Since $x^2 - y^2 = (x + y)(x - y)$ and, from the information given, $(x + y)(x - y) = 10 \cdot 2 = 20$, which is greater than 19, the correct answer is A. The two equations could be solved for x and y, giving x = 6 and y = 4, and then $x^2 - y^2$ could be computed, but this solution is more time-consuming.

18.	**The area of an equilateral triangle with side 6**	**The area of a right triangle with legs $\sqrt{3}$ and 9**

The area of a triangle is one-half the product of the lengths of the base and the altitude. In column A, the length of the altitude must first be determined. A sketch of the triangle may be helpful.

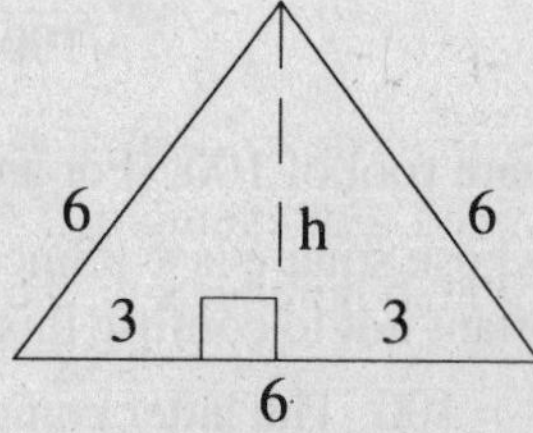

The altitude h divides the base of an equilateral triangle into two equal parts. From the Pythagorean Theorem, $h^2 + 3^2 = 6^2$ or $h = 3\sqrt{3}$. Therefore the area of the triangle in column A is $\frac{1}{2} \cdot 6 \cdot 3\sqrt{3} = 9\sqrt{3}$. In column B, the base and the altitude of the right triangle are the two legs, and therefore the area is $\frac{9\sqrt{3}}{2}$. Since $9\sqrt{3}$ is greater than $\frac{9\sqrt{3}}{2}$, the correct answer is A.

Column A	Column B

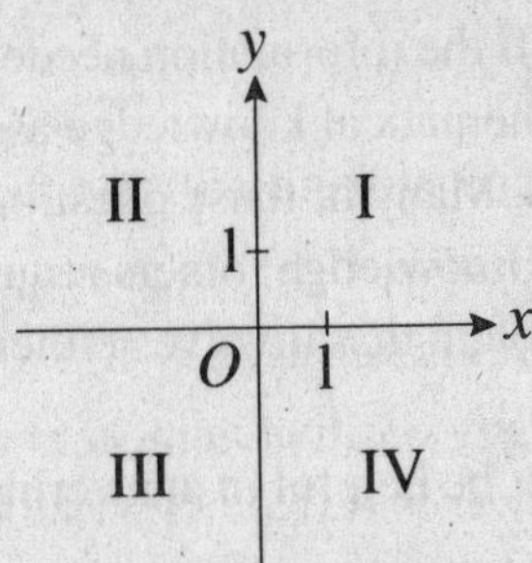

A point (x,y) is in region III.

19. **x** **y**

From the fact that point (x,y) is in region III, it is clear that x and y are both negative. However, since the location of the point within the region is not known, the relative sizes of x and y cannot be determined; for example, if the point is $(-3,-6)$, $x > y$ but if the point is $(-6, -3)$, $x < y$. Thus the answer is D.

$$(273 \times 87) + q = 29,235$$
$$(273 \times 87) + p = 30,063$$

20. **p** **q**

It is not necessary to do a lot of computation to solve this problem. The sum of a number and q is less than the sum of the same number and p. Therefore $q < p$, and the answer is A.

$$x^2 = y^2 + 1$$

21. **x** **y**

From the given equation, it can be determined that $x^2 > y^2$; however, the relative sizes of x and y cannot be determined. For example, if $y = 0$, x could be 1 or -1 and, since there is no way to tell which number x is, the answer is D.

Discrete Quantitative

Each discrete question contains all the information needed for answering the question except for the basic mathematical knowledge assumed to be common to the backgrounds of all examinees. Many of these questions require little more than manipulation and very basic knowledge; others require the examinee to read, understand, and solve a problem that involves either an actual or an abstract situation.

The following strategies might be helpful in answering discrete quantitative questions.

- Read each question carefully to determine what information is given and what is being asked.
- Before attempting to answer a question, scan the answer choices; otherwise you may waste time putting answers in a form that is not given (for example, putting an answer in the form $\frac{\sqrt{2}}{2}$ when the options are given in the form $\frac{1}{\sqrt{2}}$ or finding the answer in decimal form, such as 0.25, when the choices are given in fractional form, such as $\frac{1}{4}$).
- For questions that require approximations, scan the answer choices to get some idea of the required closeness of approximation; otherwise, you may waste time on long computations when a short mental process would be sufficient (for example, finding 48 percent of a number when taking half of the number would give a close enough approximation).

Directions for discrete quantitative questions and some examples with explanations follow.

Directions: Each of the following questions has five answer choices. For each of these questions, select the best of the answer choices given.

22. The average of x and y is 20. If z = 5, what is the average of x, y, and z?

(A) $8\frac{1}{3}$ (B) 10 (C) $12\frac{1}{2}$ (D) 15 (E) $17\frac{1}{2}$

Since the average of x and y is 20, $\frac{x+y}{2} = 20$ or $x + y = 40$. Thus $x + y + z = x + y + 5 = 40 + 5 = 45$ and therefore $\frac{x+y+z}{3} = \frac{45}{3} = 15$. The correct answer is D.

23. Several years ago, Minnesota produced $\frac{2}{3}$ and Michigan $\frac{1}{6}$ of all the iron ore produced in the United States. If all the other states combined produced 18 million tons in a year, how many million tons did Minnesota produce that year?

(A) 27 (B) 36 (C) 54 (D) 72 (E) 162

Since Minnesota produced $\frac{2}{3}$ and Michigan $\frac{1}{6}$ of all the iron ore produced in the United States, the two states together produced $\frac{5}{6}$ of the iron ore. Therefore the 18 million tons produced by the rest of the United States was $\frac{1}{6}$ of the total production. Thus the total United States production was $6 \cdot 18 = 108$ million tons, and Minnesota produced $\frac{2}{3}(108) = 72$ million tons. The correct answer is D.

24. Into how many segments, each 20 centimeters long, can a segment 5 meters long be divided? (1 meter = 100 centimeters)

(A) 20 (B) 25 (C) 45 (D) 50 (E) 80

Using the given information that there are 100 centimeters in a meter, it can be determined that there are 500 centimeters in 5 meters. The number of segments, each 20 centimeters long, into which a 500-centimeter segment can be divided is $\frac{500}{20} = 25$. The answer is B.

25. If $\frac{x}{3} - \frac{x}{6} + \frac{x}{9} - \frac{x}{12} = 1 - \frac{1}{2} + \frac{1}{3} - \frac{1}{4}$, then x =

(A) 3 (B) 1 (C) $\frac{1}{3}$ (D) $-\frac{1}{3}$ (E) –3

This problem can be solved without a lot of computation by factoring $\frac{x}{3}$ out of the expression on the left side of the equation $\frac{x}{3} - \frac{x}{6} + \frac{x}{9} - \frac{x}{12} = \frac{x}{3}(1 - \frac{1}{2} + \frac{1}{3} - \frac{1}{4})$ and substituting the factored expression into the equation, obtaining $\frac{x}{3}(1 - \frac{1}{2} + \frac{1}{3} - \frac{1}{4}) = 1 - \frac{1}{2} + \frac{1}{3} - \frac{1}{4}$. Dividing both sides of the equation by $1 - \frac{1}{2} + \frac{1}{3} - \frac{1}{4}$ (which is not zero) gives the resulting equation, $\frac{x}{3} = 1$. Thus x = 3 and the answer is A.

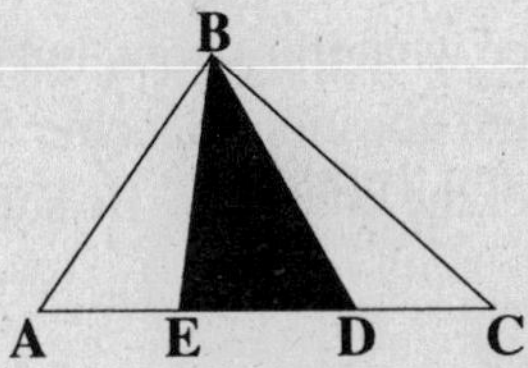

26. In the figure above, if AE = ED = DC and the area of the shaded region is 5, what is the area of ABC?

(A) 10 (B) 12.5 (C) 15 (D) 20 (E) 25

In this geometry problem, the shaded triangular region has a base that is $\frac{1}{3}$ the base of ΔABC and has the same height as ΔABC. Therefore, the area of the shaded region is $\frac{1}{3}$ the area of ΔABC, and hence the area of $\Delta ABC = 3(5) = 15$. The answer is C.

27. Joan earned twice as much as Bill, and Sam earned $3 more than half as much as Bill. If the amounts earned by Joan, Bill, and Sam are j, b, and s, respectively, which of the following is a correct ordering of these amounts?

(A) $j < b < s$ (B) $j < s < b$ (C) $b < j < s$ (D) $b < s < j$
(E) It cannot be determined from the information given.

From the first sentence the following two equations can be written: $j = 2b$ and $s = \frac{1}{2}b + 3$. The first equation implies that j is greater than b ($j > b$). The second equation, however, does not imply anything about the relationship between s and b; for example, if $b = 2$, $s = \frac{1}{2}(2) + 3 = 4$ and $s > b$ but if $b = 8$, $s = \frac{1}{2}(8) + 3 = 7$ and $s < b$. Thus E is the best of the choices given.

Data Interpretation

The data interpretation questions, like the reading comprehension questions in the verbal measure, usually appear in sets. These questions are based on data presented in tables or graphs and test one's ability to synthesize information, to select appropriate data for answering a question, or to determine that sufficient information for answering a question is not provided.

The following strategies might help in answering sets of data interpretation questions.

- Scan the set of data briefly to see what it is about, but do not attempt to grasp everything before reading the first question. Become familiar with it gradually, while trying to answer the questions. Be sure to read all notes related to the data.

- If a graph has insufficient grid lines, use the edge of the answer sheet as a grid line to help read more accurately.

- When possible, try to determine averages by visualizing a line through the important values and estimating the midpoint rather than reading off each value and then computing the average. Remember the average must be somewhere between the least value and the greatest value.
- If a question is too long and involved to take in at one time, break it down into parts and substitute the values from the graph for each part. Then reread the question and attempt to answer it.
- If the numbers are large, estimate products and quotients instead of performing involved computations.
- Remember that these questions are to be answered only on the basis of the data given, everyday facts (such as the number of days in a year), and your knowledge of mathematics. Do not make use of specific information that you recall that may seem to relate to the particular situation on which the questions are based unless that information is derivable from the data provided.

The directions for data interpretation questions are the same as those for the discrete questions. Some examples of data interpretation questions with explanations follow.

***Questions 28-30* refer to the following table:**

PERCENT CHANGE IN DOLLAR AMOUNT OF SALES IN CERTAIN RETAIL STORES FROM 1977 TO 1979

Store	Percent Change From 1977 to 1978	Percent Change From 1978 to 1979
P	+10	–10
Q	–20	+9
R	+5	+12
S	–7	–15
T	+17	–8

28. In 1979 which of the stores had greater sales than any of the others shown?

(A) P (B) Q (C) R (D) S
(E) It cannot be determined from the information given.

Since the only information given in the table is the percent change from year to year, there is no way to compare the amount of sales for the stores in any one year. The best answer is E.

29. In store T, the sales for 1978 amounted to approximately what percent of the sales for 1979?

(A) 86% (B) 92% (C) 109% (D) 117% (E) 122%

If A is the amount of sales for store T in 1978, then 0.08 A is the amount of decrease and A – 0.08 A = 0.92 A is the amount of sales for 1979. Therefore the desired result can be obtained by dividing A by 0.92 A, which equals $\frac{1}{0.92}$ or approximately 109%. The best answer is C.

30. If sales in store P amounted to \$800,000 in 1977, what did the sales amount to in that store in 1979?

(A) \$727,200 (B) \$792,000 (C) \$800,000
(D) \$880,000 (E) \$968,000

If sales in store P amounted to \$800,000 in 1977, then in 1978 they amounted to 110 percent of that; i.e., \$880,000. In 1979 sales amounted to 90 percent of \$880,000; i.e., \$792,000. Note that an increase of 10 percent in one year and a decrease of 10 percent in the following year does not result in the same amount as the original amount of sales because the base used in computing the percents changes from \$800,000 to \$880,000. The correct answer is B.

Questions 31-34 **refer to the following data.**

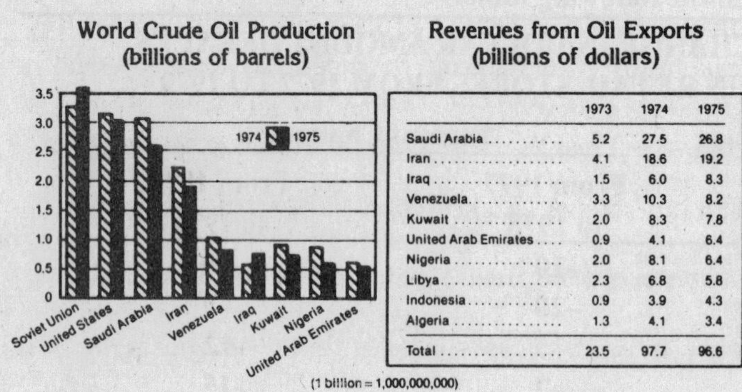

Revenues from Oil Exports
(billions of dollars)

	1973	1974	1975
Saudi Arabia	5.2	27.5	26.8
Iran	4.1	18.6	19.2
Iraq	1.5	6.0	8.3
Venezuela	3.3	10.3	8.2
Kuwait	2.0	8.3	7.8
United Arab Emirates	0.9	4.1	6.4
Nigeria	2.0	8.1	6.4
Libya	2.3	6.8	5.8
Indonesia	0.9	3.9	4.3
Algeria	1.3	4.1	3.4
Total	23.5	97.7	96.6

(1 billion = 1,000,000,000)

Note: Drawn to scale.

31. How many of the countries shown produced more crude oil in 1975 than in 1974?

(A) None (B) One (C) Two (D) Three (E) Four

To answer this question, one needs only to examine the bar graph that deals with production and count the number of countries for which the solid bar is taller than the lined bar. The Soviet Union and Iraq are the only such countries; therefore, the answer is C.

32. In 1974, for which of the following countries were revenues from oil exports most nearly equal to 20 percent of the total for all the countries listed?

(A) Iran (B) Iraq (C) Kuwait (D) Saudi Arabia (E) Venezuela

For this question, only the table is needed. Since 20 percent of the total (97.7) is a little less than 20, and 18.6, the revenue for Iran, is the only 1974 entry that is a little less than 20, the answer is A.

33. The country that had the greatest percent decrease in crude oil production from 1974 to 1975 had how many billions of dollars of revenue from oil exports in 1974?

(A) \$27.5 (B) \$18.6 (C) \$10.3 (D) \$8.1 (E) \$4.1

This question requires the use of both the bar graph and the table. From the bar graph, it can be seen that there are seven countries that had a decrease in production; however, it would be very time-consuming to compute all of the percents. If the percent decrease is to be the greatest, then the difference between the two bars must be larger in relation to the height of the lined bar than any of the others. Some countries, such as the United States and United Arab Emirates, can be ruled out because the heights of the bars are so nearly the same. Venezuela and Kuwait can be ruled out because they have smaller differences but taller lined bars than Nigeria. Iran can be ruled out because it has about the same difference as Nigeria but a much taller lined bar. That leaves only Saudi Arabia and Nigeria and one would suspect that the ratio of the difference to the height of the lined bar is smaller for Saudi Arabia. A quick check shows that $\frac{0.5}{3}$ is less than $\frac{0.2}{0.9}$ and, therefore, Nigeria had the greatest percent decrease. From the table, Nigeria had 8.1 billions of dollars of revenue, and the best answer is D.

34. Which of the following can be concluded from the data?

I. In 1974, Iraq exported four times as many barrels of oil as in 1973.
II. In 1974, Iran exported three times as much oil as Iraq.
III. In 1975, the combined crude oil production of the Soviet Union, the United States, and Saudi Arabia was more than half of the total production of all nine countries shown.

(A) I only (B) II only (C) III only (D) I and II (E) II and III

In this question, you have to decide whether each of three statements can be concluded from the data. Statement I cannot be concluded since no information is given about numbers of barrels exported in either year or about revenue per barrel in any given year. Although Iran's revenue in 1974 was approximately three times that of Iraq, no information is given about the cost per barrel in each of the countries; therefore, Statement II cannot be concluded. Note that it cannot be assumed that the price per barrel is the same in Iran and Iraq (although it might seem to be a reasonable assumption on the basis of outside knowledge) because no such information is provided in the data. In 1975 the combined production of the Soviet Union, the United States, and Saudi Arabia was about 9 billion barrels. Iran's production was about 2 billion and the remaining 5 countries produced less than 1 billion each, giving a total of less than 7 billion barrels for these countries. Therefore Statement III can be concluded, and the answer is C.

Analytical Ability

Each analytical section includes two kinds of questions:

- analytical reasoning questions in groups of three or more questions, with each group based on a different set of conditions describing a fictional situation, and
- logical reasoning questions, usually with each question based on a separate short prose passage, but sometimes with two or three questions based on the same passage.

These sections of the General Test are designed to measure the ability to think analytically. Analytical reasoning questions focus on the ability to analyze a given structure of arbitrary relationships and to deduce new information from that structure, and logical reasoning questions focus on the ability to analyze and critique argumentation by understanding and assessing relationships among arguments or parts of an argument.

The directions for all the questions in the analytical ability sections are the same and are as follows:

Directions: Each question or group of questions is based on a passage or set of conditions. In answering some of the questions, it may be useful to draw a rough diagram. For each question, select the best answer choice given.

Analytical Reasoning

Analytical reasoning questions test the ability to understand a given structure of arbitrary relationships among fictitious persons, places, things, or events, and to deduce new information from the relationships given. Each analytical reasoning group consists of (1) a set of about three to seven related statements or conditions (and sometimes other explanatory material) describing a structure of relationships, and (2) three or more questions that test understanding of that structure and its implications. Although each question in a group is based on the same set of conditions, the questions are independent of one another; answering one question in a group does not depend on answering any other question.

No knowledge of formal logic or mathematics is required for solving analytical reasoning problems. Although some of the same processes of reasoning are involved in solving both analytical reasoning problems and problems in those specialized fields, analytical reasoning problems can be solved using knowledge, skills, vocabulary, and computational ability (simple addition and subtraction) common to college students.

Each group of analytical reasoning questions is based on a set of conditions that establish relationships among persons, places, things, or events. These relationships are common ones such as temporal order (X arrived before Y but after Z), spatial order (City X is west of point Y and point Z), set membership (If Professor Green serves on the committee, then Professor Brown must also serve), and cause and effect (Event Q always causes event R). The conditions should be read carefully to determine the exact nature of the relationship or relationships involved. Some relationships are fixed or constant (The second house on the block belongs to P). Other relationships are variable (Q must be assigned to either campsite 1 or campsite 3). Some relationships that are not given can be easily deduced from those given. (If one condition about books on a shelf specifies that book L is to the left of book Y, and another specifies that book P is to the left of book L, then it can be deduced that book P is to the left of book Y.)

The following strategies may be helpful in answering analytical reasoning questions:

- In general, it is best to answer first those questions in a group that seem to pose little difficulty and then to return to those that seem troublesome. It is best not to start one group before finishing another because much time can be lost later in returning to an analytical reasoning group and reestablishing familiarity with its relationships. Do not avoid a group merely because its conditions look long or complicated.

- In reading the conditions, do not introduce unwarranted assumptions; for instance, in a set establishing relationships of height and weight among the members of a team, do not assume that a person who is taller than another person must weigh more than that person.

- Since it is intended that the conditions be as clear as possible, avoid interpreting them as if they were designed to trick you by means of hidden ambiguities or other such devices. When in doubt, read the conditions in their most obvious, common-language sense. This does not mean, however, that the language in the condition is not intended to be read for precise meaning. It is essential, for instance, to pay particular attention to function words that describe or limit relationships, such as *only, exactly, never, always, must be, cannot be,* and the like. The result of the thorough reading described above should be a clear picture of a structure of relationships, including what kind or kinds of relationships are involved, who or what the participants in the relationships are, and what is and is not known about the structure of the relationships. For instance, at this point it can often be determined whether only a single configuration of relationships is permitted by the conditions or whether alternatives are permitted.

- Many examinees find it useful to underline key points in the conditions or to draw a simple diagram, as the directions for the analytical sections suggest.

- Even though some people who solve analytical reasoning problems find diagrams to be helpful, other people seldom resort to them. And among those who do regularly use diagrams, there is by no means universal agreement on which kind of diagram is best for which problem or in which cases a diagram is most useful. Therefore, do not be concerned if a particular problem in the test seems to be best approached without the use of diagrams.
- Each question should be considered separately from the other questions in its group; no information, except what is given in the original conditions, should be carried over from one question to another. In many cases a question will simply ask for conclusions to be drawn from the conditions as originally given. An individual question can, however, add information to the original conditions or temporarily suspend one of the original conditions for the purpose of that question only.

Sample Questions with Explanations

Questions 35-36

A half tone is the smallest possible interval between notes.
Note T is a half tone higher than note V.
Note V is a whole tone higher than note W.
Note W is a half tone lower than note X.
Note X is a whole tone lower than note T.
Note Y is a whole tone lower than note W.

35. Which of the following represents the relative order of the notes from the lowest to the highest?

(A) X Y W V T (B) Y W X V T (C) W V T Y X
(D) Y W V T X (E) Y X W V T

The answer to this question can be determined by reading the six given statements and understanding the relationships among them. The relationships may be clarified by drawing a simple illustrative diagram:

T
V
X
W
Y

The diagram shows the relative order of the notes; since the question asks for the order from the lowest note to the highest, the correct answer is (B).

36. Which of the following statements about an additional note, Z, could NOT be true?

(A) Z is higher than T. (B) Z is lower than Y. (C) Z is lower than W.
(D) Z is between W and Y. (E) Z is between W and X.

Since W and X are a half tone apart, and since a half tone is the smallest possible interval between notes, Z cannot be between W and X. The best answer is therefore (E).

Questions 37-39

F, H, I, J, K, L, M, and N spoke, but not necessarily in that order. Only one person spoke at a time.
F spoke after L and took more time than H.
I spoke before M and after H, and took less time than K.
J spoke after N and before H, and took less time than N and more time than K.
N spoke after F and took less time than H.

37. Of the following, which spoke first?

(A) H (B) I (C) J (D) L (E) N

38. Of the following, which took the most time?

(A) F (B) H (C) J (D) K (E) N

39. Which of the following must be true?

(A) F was the second speaker and gave the third lengthiest speech.
(B) H spoke before I and took more time than N.
(C) I spoke last and gave the shortest speech.
(D) J spoke after M and took less time than F.
(E) N spoke after L and took more time than F.

These questions may be answered by making two lists of the speakers, as follows:

Order of appearance: L F N J H I M
Length of speech: F H N J K I

From these two lists the answers to all three questions emerge. The answer to 37 is (D), to 38 (A), and to 39 (B). For question 39, it is necessary to note that although (A) could be true, there is insufficient information provided to establish that it must be true.

Questions 40-42

To apply to college a student must see the school counselor, obtain a transcript at the transcript office, and obtain a recommendation from Teacher A or Teacher B.
A student must see the counselor before obtaining a transcript.
The counselor is available only Friday mornings and Tuesday, Wednesday, and Thursday afternoons.
The transcript office is open only Tuesday and Wednesday mornings, Thursday afternoons, and Friday mornings.
Teacher A is available only Monday and Wednesday mornings.
Teacher B is available only Monday afternoons and Friday mornings.

40. Maria, a student, has already seen the counselor and does not care from which teacher she obtains her recommendation. Which of the following is a complete and accurate list of those days when she could possibly complete the application process in one day?

(A) Friday (B) Monday, Wednesday (C) Monday, Friday (D) Wednesday, Friday (E) Monday, Wednesday, Friday

To complete the application process in one day, the student has to obtain a transcript and a recommendation on the same day. This will be possible on Wednesdays, when both the transcript office and teacher A are accessible, and on Fridays, when both the transcript office and teacher B are accessible, and at no other time. The only other day that a teacher recommendation can be obtained is Monday, but on Mondays no transcripts can be obtained. Thus, the correct answer is (D).

41. John, a student, completed his application procedure in one day. Which of the following statements must be true?

I. He obtained his recommendation from Teacher A.
II. He obtained his recommendation from Teacher B.
III. He completed the procedure in the morning.

(A) I only (B) II only (C) III only (D) I and III only (E) II and III only

If a student completed the entire application procedure in a single day, that day must have been a Friday. It could not have been a Monday, since on Mondays neither counselor nor transcript office is accessible. It could not have been either a Tuesday or a Thursday, because on neither of these days would a teacher have been available for a recommendation. And it could not have been a Wednesday because on Wednesdays one cannot see the counselor before obtaining a transcript. Now, given that the student in question must have done everything on a Friday, I must be false since teacher A is not available on Fridays, II must be true since teacher B is both available on Fridays and the only teacher to be so available, and III must also be true since on Fridays all of the relevant business can only be conducted in the morning. Therefore, the correct answer is (E).

42. Anne, a student, has already obtained her transcript and does not care from which teacher she obtains her recommendation. Which of the following is a complete and accurate list of those days when she could possibly complete the application process?

(A) Friday (B) Monday, Wednesday (C) Monday, Friday (D) Wednesday, Friday (E) Monday, Wednesday, Friday

If the student has already obtained her transcript, she must have seen the counselor, too, since seeing the counselor must precede receipt of a transcript. This means that obtaining a recommendation from a teacher is all that is left to do. Since it does not matter which teacher the recommendation is from, the application process can be completed on any day that either teacher A or teacher B is available. Those days are Monday, when both are available, Wednesday, when A is available, and Friday, when B is available. The correct answer, therefore, is (E).

Questions 43-44

A farmer plants only five different kinds of vegetables — beans, corn, kale, peas, and squash. Every year the farmer plants exactly three kinds of vegetables according to the following restrictions:

If the farmer plants corn, the farmer also plants beans that year.
If the farmer plants kale one year, the farmer does not plant it the next year.
In any year, the farmer plants no more than one of the vegetables the farmer planted in the previous year.

43. Which of the following is a possible sequence of combinations for the farmer to plant in two successive years?

(A) Beans, corn, kale; corn, peas, squash
(B) Beans, corn, peas; beans, corn, squash
(C) Beans, peas, squash; beans, corn, kale
(D) Corn, peas, squash; beans, kale, peas
(E) Kale, peas, squash; beans, corn, kale

Options (A) and (D) are not possible because corn appears as a vegetable without beans in a given year. Option (E) is not possible because kale appears in two successive years. Option (B) is not possible because two vegetables are repeated in two successive years. Option (C) contains a possible sequence of combinations.

44. If the farmer plants beans, corn, and kale in the first year, which of the following combinations must be planted in the third year?

(A) Beans, corn, and kale
(B) Beans, corn, and peas
(C) Beans, kale, and peas
(D) Beans, peas, and squash
(E) Kale, peas, and squash

Beans, peas, and squash are planted in the second year, since kale cannot be repeated two consecutive years and since corn cannot be repeated without repeating beans (only one vegetable can be repeated in consecutive years). In the third year, corn and kale must be planted (only one of the second-year vegetables can be repeated). Beans are planted whenever corn is planted, so (A) is the correct answer choice.

Logical Reasoning

Logical reasoning questions test the ability to understand, analyze, and evaluate arguments. Some of the abilities tested by specific questions include recognizing the point of an argument, recognizing assumptions on which an argument is based, drawing conclusions and forming hypotheses, identifying methods of argument, evaluating arguments and counterarguments, and analyzing evidence.

Each question or group of questions is based on a short argument, generally an excerpt from the kind of material graduate students are likely to encounter in their academic and personal reading. Although arguments may be drawn from specific fields of study such as the humanities, social studies, and the physical sciences, materials from more familiar sources such as political speeches, advertisements, and informal discussions or dialogues also form the basis for some questions. No specialized knowledge of any particular field is required for answering the questions, however, and no knowledge of the terminology of formal logic is presupposed.

Specific questions asked about the arguments draw on information obtained by the process of critical and analytical reading described above.

The following strategies may be helpful in answering logical reasoning questions:

- The passage on which questions are based should be read very carefully with close attention to such matters as (1) what is said specifically about a subject, (2) what is not said but necessarily follows from what is said, (3) what is suggested or claimed without substantiation in what is said. In addition, the means of relating statements, inferences, and claims — the structure of the argument — should be noted. Such careful reading may lead to the conclusion that the argument presented proceeds in an unsound or illogical fashion, but in many cases there will be no apparent weakness in the argument. It is important, in reading the arguments given, to attend to the soundness of the method employed and not to the actual truth of opinions presented.
- You should determine exactly what information the question is asking for; for instance, although it might be expected that one would be asked to detect or name the most glaring fault in a weak argument, the question posed may actually ask for the selection of one of a group of other arguments that reveals the same fault. In some cases, questions may ask for a negative response, for instance, a weakness that is NOT found in an argument or a conclusion that CANNOT be drawn from an argument.

45. If Ruth was born in New York State, then she is a citizen of the United States.

The statement above can be deduced logically from which of the following statements?

(A) Everyone born in New York State is a citizen of the United States.
(B) Every citizen of the United States is a resident either of one of the states or of one of the territories.
(C) Some people born in New York State are citizens of the United States.
(D) Ruth was born either in New York or in California.
(E) Ruth is a citizen either of the United States or of Sweden.

The question here is which of (A) through (E), if true, would guarantee that Ruth cannot have her birthplace in New York State without being a United States citizen. Since, crucially, the relationship between birthplace and citizenship is at stake, any statement that concerns itself with birthplace alone, like (D), or citizenship alone, like (E), or with the relationship between residence and citizenship, like (B), will be unsuitable for providing any such guarantee. This leaves (A) and (C), both of which deal with the relationship at issue here. Of these, (C) makes the weaker claim: It leaves open the possibility that there might be people born in New York State who are not United States citizens, and it leaves open whether or not Ruth is one of those people. (A), on the other hand, rules out any possibility of anyone being born in New York State and yet not being a United States citizen. Therefore, (A) rules out that possibility for Ruth also, and (A) is thus the correct answer.

46. Therapists find that treatment of those people who seek help because they are unable to stop smoking or overeating is rarely successful. From these experiences, therapists have concluded that such habits are intractable and that success in breaking them is rare.

As surveys show, millions of people have dropped the habit of smoking, and many people have successfully managed a substantial weight loss.

If all of the statements above are correct, an explanation that resolves their apparent contradiction is provided by the hypothesis that

(A) there have been some successes in therapy, and those successes were counted in the surveys
(B) it is easier to stop smoking than it is to stop overeating
(C) it is easy to break the habits of smoking and overeating by exercising willpower
(D) the group of people selected for the surveys did not include those who failed to break their habits even after therapy
(E) those who succeed in curing themselves do not go for treatment and so are not included in the therapists' data

If, as (E) suggests, those who can succeed on their own do not seek treatment, it is quite understandable why therapists do not encounter them as patients. Thus the restricted group of patients they see would lead them to the conclusion they draw. At the same time, (E) is consistent with the survey results. Therefore, (E) is the correct answer.

(A) is incorrect. Even assuming that (A) is true, no light is shed on why successes should be so rare in therapy, and yet, if the surveys are to be believed, so common overall.

(B) is incorrect. Since the comparative strength of habits is not an issue in the therapists' findings or the surveys, it cannot have anything to do with the apparent contradiction; consequently, information about it cannot help resolve that contradiction.

(C) is incorrect. If (C) were true, the survey results would appear rather unremarkable, but the therapists' findings would be baffling. The apparent contradiction would not be diminished but underscored.

(D) is incorrect. The survey results as reported focus on the number of people who have successfully broken a habit, not on the proportion of those trying to break their habits who succeeded. (D) pertains only to the latter and so is essentially irrelevant.

47. The greatest chance for the existence of extraterrestrial life is on a planet beyond our solar system. After all, the Milky Way galaxy alone contains 100 billion other suns, many of which could be accompanied by planets similar enough to Earth to make them suitable abodes of life.

The argument above assumes which of the following?

(A) Living creatures on another planet would probably have the same appearance as those on Earth.
(B) Life cannot exist on other planets in our solar system.
(C) If the appropriate physical conditions exist, life is an inevitable consequence.
(D) More then one of the suns in the galaxy is accompanied by an Earth-like planet.
(E) It is likely that life on another planet would require conditions similar to those on Earth.

In stating that planets may exist that are similar enough to Earth to make them suitable for supporting life, the author implicitly rules out planets dissimilar to Earth as likely to support life. The assumption underlying the argument is that life on another planet is likely to require conditions similar to those on Earth. Therefore, (E) is the correct answer.

(A) is incorrect. The argument assumes nothing about the appearance of extraterrestrial life.

(B) is incorrect. The statements in the argument imply that it is relatively unlikely that life exists on other planets in our solar system, but those statements make no assumption that absolutely rules out the possibility that such life exists.

(C) is incorrect. Although the argument takes it for granted that there is the greatest chance for life when physical conditions are appropriate, it leaves open the possibility that no life will exist even with appropriate conditions.

(D) is incorrect. The argument grants that it is possible that more than one of the suns in the galaxy is accompanied by an Earth-like planet, but it does not assume that there are actually any such suns.

THE NEW GRE COMPUTER ADAPTIVE TEST (CAT)

Over the past five years, the GRE Board has been conducting research on new directions in testing in order to help graduate programs identify talent in new ways. The first step in this new direction came in October 1992 when the GRE Program began administering a computerized version of the traditional form of the General Test through the Computer-Based Testing (CBT) Program, a development that enabled the GRE Program to offer greater testing and score reporting flexibility.

The second step came during the 1993-94 testing year with the introduction of a new version of the General Test known as the "Computer Adaptive Test" or CAT. In an adaptive test, the selection of questions is tailored to an examinee's ability level in each of the three standard General Test measures (verbal, quantitative, and analytical). Initially, an examinee is presented with questions of average difficulty. Thereafter, the computer selects questions based upon 1) the difficulty level of the questions answered correctly and incorrectly, 2) question types, and 3) coverage of specific content.

Introduction of the CAT marks only the beginning of several planned changes in the GRE General Test designed to improve assessments of the abilities of potential graduate students.

It is expected that by 1997, a completely modular computer-delivered test will replace the traditional paper-and-pencil version of the General Test. The new General Test will likely consist of revised versions of the current verbal, quantitative, and analytical measures as well as a mathematical reasoning measure and a writing measure. The phase out of the paper-and-pencil program will begin with the elimination of the February 1995 administration. In 1995-96 it is likely that only two paper administrations will be offered.

Advantages of the CAT

From an assessment standpoint, the CAT provides precise information about an examinee's abilities using fewer questions than the traditional General Test because questions are tailored to an individual examinee's ability level.

Other advantages for an examinee include convenience and flexibility of scheduling an appointment to test, year-round testing, immediate knowledge of scores, and faster score reporting service.

CAT Strategies

1. Use the tutorial to learn how to interact with the computer.

- The tutorial teaches you how to use the features of the computer system to your advantage. You will find the system very easy to use, even if you have no prior computer experience.

- The ability to type is not necessary to take the CAT. The tutorial shows you how to use a mouse to click on the appropriate area of your screen.
- Take all the time you need with the tutorial *before* you begin the test — even if you feel quite comfortable using computers; there might be differences between the adaptive test software and the software you normally use.
- You may return to any part of the tutorial, even after you begin work on the test sections, by clicking on the "Help" box at the bottom of your screen. However, any time you spend on the tutorials *after* you have begun a test section will reduce the amount of time available for work on that section.
- Some questions, graphs, or passages are too large to appear completely on the computer screen. In that case a "scroll bar" appears to the right of the material and the word "Beginning" appears on the information line at the top of the screen. These are your cues to scroll for more information.
- During the tutorial, make sure you learn how to scroll both slowly (line by line) and quickly (page by page) so that you can move to areas of text at the speed you desire.

2. Answer at least the minimum number of questions required to get a score.

- The directions at the beginning of each test section specify the total number of questions in the section, the time allowed for the section, and *the minimum number of questions that must be answered in order to receive a score for that section.* If you do not answer the minimum number of questions, or if you exit the section before time expires and have not answered all the questions, you will receive No Score (NS) for that section.
- Pay particular attention to the information concerning the exact minimum number of questions you must answer in order to receive a score. *The minimum number may vary from section to section, and from one test administration to the next.*
- If you forget the minimum number of questions required to receive a score, review the appropriate directions by clicking on Help and then on "Section Directions."

The table that follows shows a typical CAT. Individual CAT sections may vary by a few questions. The total amount of time allowed for work on each section is adjusted so that the average time per question is about the same, regardless of the number of questions in that section.

TYPICAL CAT

	Number of Questions	Time	Minimum Number of Answers Required for a Score
Verbal	30	30 min.	24
Quant.	28	45 min.	23
Analy.	35	60 min.	28

3. **Maximize your score through effective time management.**

- Answer as many questions as you can in each section. If time expires and you have already answered the minimum number of questions required for a section, you *will* receive a score for that section.
- The more questions you answer after careful consideration, the more likely your reported score will accurately reflect your true ability.
- The amount of time remaining for each section is displayed on the information line at the top of the screen. Clicking on the "Time" box at the bottom of the screen will turn the time information off or back on again. Check the time remaining regularly to be sure you are making good progress through the test.
- Once you begin a section, section time runs continuously until you leave the section. This is true even if you click on Time to hide the time information or click on Help in order to review section directions or any part of the tutorial.
- Budget enough time for each question so that you will be able to complete the test with several minutes to spare. Once you have answered the minimum number of questions to earn a score, you might want to slow down to maximize use of the remaining time.
- There is a one-minute break between each test section. You will be informed by an on screen message of the availability of a 10-minute break midway through the testing session. Section timing will *not* stop if you take an unscheduled break. You might want to replenish your supply of scratch paper during each break.

4. **Answer each question in the order it is presented to you.**

- You cannot move on to the next question before you answer the question that appears on your screen, and once you answer a question and confirm your response, you cannot return to that question.
- Answer each question by clicking on the oval next to the answer choice you select. You can also answer a question by clicking on any part of the text of an answer choice. Complete your answer by clicking on "Next" and then "Answer Confirm."
- You can change your answer any time before confirming it by clicking on a different answer choice.

5. **Use effective strategies when guessing at answers.**

- The only way to continue your test when presented with a question you find too difficult is to guess at the answer (by eliminating as many answer choices as possible).
- If section time is about to run out *before* you have answered the minimum number of questions required to earn a score, you should consider guessing at the few remaining questions needed. Otherwise, you will not receive a score for that section.

- Guessing at random *after* you have answered the minimum number of questions required could *reduce* your score. Once you have answered the minimum number of questions, you should answer each remaining question only after you have carefully considered it.
- Don't worry about getting too many hard questions as the result of a lucky guess, or too many easy questions as the result of an unlucky one. The computer will adjust its selection to guide you back to questions at an ability level appropriate for you.
- The difficulty of each question selected for you depends on your performance on preceding questions and on factors such as coverage of specific content areas.

6. **Understand the implications of exiting a section or quitting the test.**

- You may click on the "Section Exit" box at the bottom of your screen if you do *not* wish to receive a score for a given test section. Once you exit a section, you cannot return to it.
- If you click on Section Exit and exit a section before you have answered all of the questions in that section, you will *not* receive a score for that section.
- Click on the "Test Quit" box at the bottom of your screen *only if* you decide to end your testing session. If you quit the test, you will not receive a score for any section, even for those sections you have already completed.
- If you mistakenly click on Test Quit or Section Exit, you will be given the opportunity to reverse or confirm your decision.
- You may take the CAT no more than one time within any six-month period. This is true even if you ended your testing session by clicking on Test Quit. You may take the paper-and-pencil General Test at any or all of the announced administration dates.

How Is the CAT Scored?

In a paper-and-pencil version of the GRE General Test, examinees receive one raw score point for each question they answer correctly, whether the question is easy or hard. An examinee's score is based only on the number of questions answered correctly.

In the GRE CAT, an examinee's score is based on the performance on the particular questions that are presented by the design of the test. The test design factors that influence which questions you will be presented include: 1) the difficulty level of the questions answered correctly and incorrectly, 2) question types, and 3) coverage of specific content. This allows the computer to give you questions that are appropriate for you and to ensure that the overall test content meets the specifications for the General Test. In the GRE CAT, the examinee gets more credit for correctly answering a hard question than for correctly answering an easy question. Your final score will reflect the overall level of knowledge you have demonstrated for the content areas being tested.

The computer does not always select a harder question when you answer a question correctly and an easier one when you miss it. This is because the test design includes several factors other than how hard the questions are.

MATH REVIEW
for
Practicing to Take the
GRE®
General Test

MATH REVIEW

This review is designed to familiarize you with the mathematical skills and concepts likely to be tested on the Graduate Record Examinations General Test. The text includes many examples with solutions, and there is a set of exercises at the end of each section. The following material, which is divided into the four basic content areas of arithmetic, algebra, geometry, and data analysis, is not intended to be comprehensive. It is assumed that certain basic concepts are common knowledge to all examinees. Emphasis is, therefore, placed on the more important skills, concepts, and definitions, and on those particular areas that are frequently confused or misunderstood. If any of the topics seem especially unfamiliar, we encourage you to consult appropriate mathematics texts for a more detailed treatment of those topics.

ARITHMETIC

1.1 Integers

The set of *integers, I*, is composed of all the counting numbers (i.e., 1, 2, 3, . . .), zero, and the negative of each counting number; that is,

$$I = \{\ldots,\ -3,\ -2,\ -1,\ 0,\ 1,\ 2,\ 3,\ldots\}.$$

Therefore, some integers are *positive*, some are *negative*, and the integer 0 is neither positive nor negative. Integers that are multiples of 2 are called *even integers*, namely $\{\ldots,\ -6,\ -4,\ -2,\ 0,\ 2,\ 4,\ 6,\ \ldots\}$. All other integers are called *odd integers*; therefore, $\{\ldots,\ -5,\ -3,\ -1,\ 1,\ 3,\ 5,\ \ldots\}$ represents the set of all odd integers. Integers in a sequence, such as 57, 58, 59, or $-14,\ -13,\ -12,\ -11$, are called *consecutive* integers.

The rules for performing basic arithmetic operations with integers should be familiar to you. Some rules that are occasionally forgotten include:

(i) Multiplication by 0 always results in 0; e.g., $(0)(15) = 0$.

(ii) Division by 0 is not defined; e.g., $5 \div 0$ has no meaning.

(iii) Multiplication (or division) of two integers with different signs yields a negative result; e.g., $(-7)(8) = -56$, and $(-12) \div (4) = -3$.

(iv) Multiplication (or division) of two *negative* integers yields a positive result; e.g., $(-5)(-12) = 60$, and $(-24) \div (-3) = 8$.

The division of one integer by another yields either a zero remainder, sometimes called "dividing evenly," or a positive-integer remainder. For example, 215 divided by 5 yields a zero remainder, but 153 divided by 7 yields a remainder of 6.

$$\begin{array}{r} 43 \\ 5\overline{)215} \\ \underline{20} \\ 15 \\ \underline{15} \\ 0 \end{array} = \text{Remainder} \qquad\qquad \begin{array}{r} 21 \\ 7\overline{)153} \\ \underline{14} \\ 13 \\ \underline{7} \\ 6 \end{array} = \text{Remainder}$$

In general, when we say that an integer N is *divisible by* an integer x, we mean that N divided by x yields a zero remainder.

The multiplication of two integers yields a third integer. The first two integers are called *factors*, and the third integer is called the *product*. The product is said to be a *multiple* of both factors, and it is also *divisible* by both factors. Therefore, since $(2)(7) = 14$, we can say that

2 and 7 are factors and 14 is the product,
14 is a multiple of both 2 and 7,
and 14 is divisible by both 2 and 7.

Whenever an integer N is divisible by an integer x, we say that x is a *divisor* of N. For the set of positive integers, any integer N that has exactly two distinct positive divisors, 1 and N, is said to be a *prime*. The first ten primes are

2, 3, 5, 7, 11, 13, 17, 19, 23, and 29.

The integer 14 is not a prime because it has four divisors: 1, 2, 7, and 14.

1.2 Fractions

A *fraction* is a number of the form $\frac{a}{b}$, where a and b are integers ($b \neq 0$). The a is called the *numerator* of the fraction, and b is called the *denominator*. For example, $\frac{-7}{5}$ is a fraction that has –7 as its numerator and 5 as its denominator. Since the fraction $\frac{a}{b}$ means $a \div b$, b cannot be zero. If the numerator and denominator of the fraction $\frac{a}{b}$ are both multiplied by the same integer, the resulting fraction will be equivalent to $\frac{a}{b}$.

For example,

$$\frac{-7}{5} = \frac{(-7)(4)}{(5)(4)} = \frac{-28}{20}$$

This technique comes in handy when you wish to add or subtract fractions.

To add two fractions with the same denominator you simply add the numerators and keep the denominator the same.

$$\frac{-8}{11} + \frac{5}{11} = \frac{-8+5}{11} = \frac{-3}{11}$$

If the denominators are *not* the same, you may apply the technique mentioned above to make them the same before doing the addition.

$$\frac{5}{12} + \frac{2}{3} = \frac{5}{12} + \frac{(2)(4)}{(3)(4)} = \frac{5}{12} + \frac{8}{12} = \frac{5+8}{12} = \frac{13}{12}$$

The same method applies for subtraction.

To multiply two fractions, multiply the two numerators and multiply the two denominators (the denominators need not be the same).

$$\left(\frac{10}{7}\right)\left(\frac{-1}{3}\right) = \frac{(10)(-1)}{(7)(3)} = \frac{-10}{21}$$

To divide one fraction by another, first *invert* the fraction you are dividing by, and then proceed as in multiplication.

$$\frac{17}{8} \div \frac{3}{5} = \left(\frac{17}{8}\right)\left(\frac{5}{3}\right) = \frac{(17)(5)}{(8)(3)} = \frac{85}{24}$$

An expression such as $4\frac{3}{8}$ is called a *mixed fraction;* it means $4 + \frac{3}{8}$. Therefore,

$$4\frac{3}{8} = 4 + \frac{3}{8} = \frac{32}{8} + \frac{3}{8} = \frac{35}{8}.$$

1.3 Decimals

In our number system, all numbers can be expressed in decimal form. A decimal point is used, and the place value for each digit depends on its position relative to the decimal point. In the number 82.537,

"8" is the "tens" digit; the place value for "8" is 10.

"2" is the "units" digit; the place value for "2" is 1.

"5" is the "tenths" digit; the place value for "5" is $\frac{1}{10}$.

"3" is the "hundredths" digit; the place value for "3" is $\frac{1}{100}$.

"7" is the "thousandths" digit; the place value for "7" is $\frac{1}{1000}$.

Therefore, 82.537 is a quick way of writing

$$(8)(10) + (2)(1) + (5)\left(\frac{1}{10}\right) + (3)\left(\frac{1}{100}\right) + (7)\left(\frac{1}{1000}\right),$$

or 80 + 2 + 0.5 + 0.03 + 0.007.

This numeration system has implications for the basic operations. For addition and subtraction you must always remember to line up the decimal points:

$$\begin{array}{r} 126.5 \\ +\ \underline{68.231} \\ 194.731 \end{array} \qquad \begin{array}{r} 126.5 \\ -\ \underline{68.231} \\ 58.269 \end{array}$$

To multiply decimals, it is not necessary to align the decimal points. To determine the correct position for the decimal point in the product, you simply add the number of digits to the right of the decimal points in the decimals being multiplied. This sum is the number of decimal places required in the product.

$$\begin{array}{rl} 15.381 & \text{(3 decimal places)} \\ \times\ \underline{.14} & \text{(2 decimal places)} \\ 61524 & \\ \underline{15381\ } & \\ 2.15334 & \text{(5 decimal places)} \end{array}$$

To divide a decimal by another, such as $62.744 \div 1.24$, or

$$1.24\overline{)62.744}\ ,$$

first move the decimal point in the divisor to the right until the divisor becomes an integer, then move the decimal point in the dividend the same number of places;

$$124\overline{)6274.4}$$

This procedure determines the correct position of the decimal point in the quotient (as shown). The division can then proceed as follows:

$$\begin{array}{r} 50.6 \\ 124\overline{)6274.4} \\ \underline{620} \\ 744 \\ \underline{744} \end{array}$$

Conversion from a given decimal to an equivalent fraction is straightforward. Since each place value is a power of ten, every decimal can be converted easily to an integer divided by a power of ten. For example,

$$84.1 = \frac{841}{10}$$

$$9.17 = \frac{917}{100}$$

$$0.612 = \frac{612}{1{,}000}$$

The last example can be reduced to lowest terms by dividing the numerator and denominator by 4, which is their *greatest common factor*. Thus,

$$0.612 = \frac{612}{1{,}000} = \frac{612 \div 4}{1{,}000 \div 4} = \frac{153}{250} \text{ (in lowest terms)}$$

Any fraction can be converted to an equivalent decimal. Since the fraction $\frac{a}{b}$ means $a \div b$, we can divide the numerator of a fraction by its denominator to convert the fraction to a decimal. For example, to convert $\frac{3}{8}$ to a decimal, divide 3 by 8 as follows.

$$\begin{array}{r} 0.375 \\ 8\overline{)3.000} \\ \underline{2\,4} \\ 60 \\ \underline{56} \\ 40 \\ \underline{40} \end{array}$$

1.4 Exponents and Square Roots

Exponents provide a shortcut notation for repeated multiplication of a number by itself. For example, "3^4" means (3)(3)(3)(3), which equals 81. So, we say that $3^4 = 81$; the "4" is called an *exponent* (or power). The exponent tells you how many factors are in the product. For example,

$$2^5 = (2)(2)(2)(2)(2) = 32$$
$$10^6 = (10)(10)(10)(10)(10)(10) = 1{,}000{,}000$$
$$(-4)^3 = (-4)(-4)(-4) = -64$$
$$\left(\frac{1}{2}\right)^4 = \left(\frac{1}{2}\right)\left(\frac{1}{2}\right)\left(\frac{1}{2}\right)\left(\frac{1}{2}\right) = \frac{1}{16}$$

When the exponent is 2, we call the process *squaring*. Therefore, "5^2" can be read "5 squared."

A *square root* of a positive number N is a number which, when squared, equals N. For example, a square root of 16 is 4 because $4^2 = 16$. Another square root of 16 is –4 because $(-4)^2 = 16$. In fact, all positive numbers have two square roots that differ only in sign. The square root of 0 is 0 because $0^2 = 0$. Negative numbers do *not* have square roots because the square of a real number cannot be negative. If $N > 0$, the positive square root of N is represented by $\sqrt{N}$, read "radical N"; the negative square root of N, therefore, is represented by $-\sqrt{N}$.

Two important rules regarding operations with radicals are:
If $a > 0$ and $b > 0$,

(i) $\left(\sqrt{a}\right)\left(\sqrt{b}\right) = \sqrt{ab}$; e.g., $\left(\sqrt{5}\right)\left(\sqrt{20}\right) = \sqrt{100} = 10$

(ii) $\dfrac{\sqrt{a}}{\sqrt{b}} = \sqrt{\dfrac{a}{b}}$; e.g., $\dfrac{\sqrt{192}}{\sqrt{4}} = \sqrt{48} = \sqrt{(16)(3)} = \left(\sqrt{16}\right)\left(\sqrt{3}\right) = 4\sqrt{3}$

1.5 Ordering and the Real Number Line

The set of all *real numbers*, which includes all integers and all numbers with values between them, such as 1.25, $\frac{2}{3}$, $\sqrt{2}$, etc., has a natural ordering, which can be represented by the *real number line*:

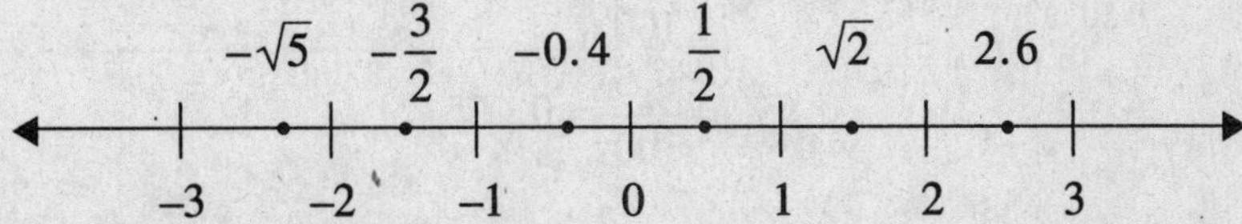

Every real number corresponds to a point on the real number line (see examples shown above). The real number line is infinitely long in both directions.

For any two numbers on the real number line, the number to the left is *less than* the number to the right. For example,

$$-\sqrt{5} < -\frac{3}{2}$$

$$-1.75 < \sqrt{2}$$

$$\frac{5}{2} < 7.1$$

Since $2 < 5$, it is also true that 5 is greater than 2, which is written "$5 > 2$." If a number N is *between* 1.5 and 2 on the real number line, you can express that fact as $1.5 < N < 2$.

1.6 Percent

The term *percent* means *per hundred* or *divided by one hundred*. Therefore

$$43\% = \frac{43}{100} = 0.43$$
$$300\% = \frac{300}{100} = 3$$
$$0.5\% = \frac{0.5}{100} = 0.005$$

To find out what 30% of 350 is, you multiply 350 by either 0.30 or $\frac{30}{100}$,

$$30\% \text{ of } 350 = (350)(0.30) = 105$$

or

$$30\% \text{ of } 350 = (350)\left(\frac{30}{100}\right) = (350)\left(\frac{3}{10}\right) = \frac{1{,}050}{10} = 105$$

If a quantity *increases* from 200 to 250, the *percent increase* is found by dividing the amount of increase, 50, by the smaller of the two given numbers:

$$\frac{50}{200} = 0.25 = 25\%$$

If a quantity *decreases* from 500 to 400, the *percent decrease* is found by dividing the amount of decrease, 100, by the larger of the two given numbers, 500:

$$\frac{100}{500} = 0.20 = 20\%$$

1.7 Ratio

The ratio of the number 9 to the number 21 can be expressed in three basic ways:

$$9 \text{ to } 21,\ 9{:}21, \text{ and } \frac{9}{21}$$

Since a ratio is in fact an implied division, it can be reduced to lowest terms. Therefore, the three ways above could also be written:

$$3 \text{ to } 7,\ 3{:}7, \text{ and } \frac{3}{7}$$

The ratio of the number of months in a year (12) to the number of minutes in an hour (60), in lowest terms, is,

$$1 \text{ to } 5, \text{ or } 1{:}5, \text{ or } \frac{1}{5}.$$

1.8 Absolute Value

The *absolute value* of a number N, denoted by $|N|$, is defined to be N if N is positive or zero and $-N$ if N is negative. For example,

$$\left|\frac{1}{2}\right| = \frac{1}{2},\ |0| = 0, \text{ and } |-2.6| = -(-2.6) = 2.6$$

Note that the absolute value of a number cannot be negative.

ARITHMETIC EXERCISES

(Answers on page 61)

1. Evaluate:

(a) $15-(6-4)(-2)$

(b) $(2-17)\div 5$

(c) $(60\div 12)-(-7+4)$

(d) $(3)^4-(-2)^3$

(e) $(-5)(-3)-15$

(f) $(-2)^4(15-18)^4$

(g) $(20\div 5)^2(-2+6)^3$

(h) $(-85)(0)-(-17)(3)$

2. Evaluate:

(a) $\frac{1}{2}-\frac{1}{3}+\frac{1}{12}$

(b) $\left(\frac{3}{4}+\frac{1}{7}\right)\left(\frac{-2}{5}\right)$

(c) $\left(\frac{7}{8}-\frac{4}{5}\right)^2$

(d) $\left(\frac{3}{-8}\right)\div\left(\frac{27}{32}\right)$

3. Evaluate:

(a) $12.837+1.65-0.9816$

(b) $100.26\div 1.2$

(c) $(12.4)(3.67)$

(d) $(0.087)(0.00021)$

4. State for each of the following whether the answer is an *even* integer or an *odd* integer.

(a) The sum of two even integers

(b) The sum of two odd integers

(c) The sum of an even integer and an odd integer

(d) The product of two even integers

(e) The product of two odd integers

(f) The product of an even integer and an odd integer

5. Which of the following integers are divisible by 8 ?

(a) 312 (b) 98 (c) 112 (d) 144

6. List all of the positive divisors of 372.

7. Which of the divisors found in #6 are primes?

8. Which of the following integers are primes?
19, 2, 49, 37, 51, 91, 1, 83, 29

9. Express 585 as a product of primes.

10. Which of the following statements are true?

(a) $-5 < 3.1$

(b) $\sqrt{16} = 4$

(c) $7 \div 0 = 0$

(d) $0 < |-1.7|$

(e) $0.3 < \frac{1}{3}$

(f) $(-1)^{87} = -1$

(g) $\sqrt{9} < 0$

(h) $\frac{21}{28} = \frac{3}{4}$

(i) $-|-23| = 23$

(j) $\frac{1}{2} > \frac{1}{17}$

(k) $(59)^3(59)^2 = (59)^6$

(l) $-\sqrt{25} < -4$

11. Do the indicated operations.

(a) $5\sqrt{3} + \sqrt{27}$

(b) $(\sqrt{6})(\sqrt{30})$

(c) $(\sqrt{300}) \div (\sqrt{12})$

(d) $(\sqrt{5})(\sqrt{2}) - \sqrt{90}$

12. Express the following percents in decimal form and in fraction form (lowest terms).

(a) 15% (b) 27.3% (c) 131% (d) 0.02%

13. Express each of the following as a percent.

(a) 0.8 (b) 0.197 (c) 5.2 (d) $\frac{3}{8}$ (e) $2\frac{1}{2}$ (f) $\frac{3}{50}$

14. Find:

(a) 40% of 15

(b) 150% of 48

(c) 0.6% of 800

(d) 8% of 5%

15. If a person's salary increases from $200 per week to $234 per week, what is the percent increase?

16. If an athlete's weight decreases from 160 pounds to 152 pounds, what is the percent decrease?

17. A particular stock is valued at $40 per share. If the value increases 20 percent and then decreases 25 percent, what is the value of the stock per share after the decrease?

18. Express the ratio of 16 to 6 three different ways in lowest terms.

19. If the ratio of men to women on a committee of 20 members is 3 to 2, how many members of the committee are women?

ANSWERS TO ARITHMETIC EXERCISES

1. (a) 19
   (b) -3
   (c) 8
   (d) 89
   (e) 0
   (f) 1,296
   (g) 1,024
   (h) 51

2. (a) $\frac{1}{4}$
   (b) $-\frac{5}{14}$
   (c) $\frac{9}{1,600}$
   (d) $-\frac{4}{9}$

3. (a) 13.5054
   (b) 83.55
   (c) 45.508
   (d) 0.00001827

4. (a) even
   (b) even
   (c) odd
   (d) even
   (e) odd
   (f) even

5. (a), (c), and (d)

6. 1, 2, 3, 4, 6, 12, 31, 62, 93, 124, 186, 372

7. 2, 3, 31

8. 19, 2, 37, 83, 29

9. (3)(3)(5)(13)

10. (a), (b), (d), (e), (f), (h), (j), (l)

11. (a) $8\sqrt{3}$
    (b) $6\sqrt{5}$
    (c) 5
    (d) $-2\sqrt{10}$

12. (a) 0.15, $\frac{3}{20}$
    (b) 0.273, $\frac{273}{1,000}$
    (c) 1.31, $\frac{131}{100}$
    (d) 0.0002, $\frac{1}{5,000}$

13. (a) 80%
    (b) 19.7%
    (c) 520%
    (d) 37.5%
    (e) 250%
    (f) 6%

14. (a) 6
    (b) 72
    (c) 4.8
    (d) 0.004

15. 17%

16. 5%

17. $36

18. 8 to 3, 8:3, $\frac{8}{3}$

19. 8

ALGEBRA

2.1 Translating Words into Algebraic Expressions

Basic algebra is essentially advanced arithmetic; therefore much of the terminology and many of the rules are common to both areas. The major difference is that in algebra variables are introduced, which allows us to solve problems with equations and inequalities.

If the square of the number x is multiplied by 3, and then 10 is added to that product, the result can be represented by $3x^2 + 10$. If John's present salary S is increased by 14 percent, then his new salary is $1.14S$. If y gallons of syrup are to be distributed among 5 people so that one particular person gets 1 gallon and the rest of the syrup is divided equally among the remaining 4, then each of these 4 people will get $\frac{y-1}{4}$ gallons of syrup. Combinations of letters (variables) and numbers such as $3x^2 + 10$, $1.14S$, and $\frac{y-1}{4}$ are called *algebraic expressions.*

2.2 Operations with Algebraic Expressions

Every algebraic expression can be written as a single term or a series of terms separated by plus or minus signs. The expression $3x^2 + 10$ has two terms; the expression $1.14S$ is a single term; the expression $\frac{y-1}{4}$, which can be written $\frac{y}{4} - \frac{1}{4}$, has two terms. In the expression $2x^2 + 7x - 5$, 2 is the *coefficient* of the x^2 *term,* 7 is the coefficient of the x *term,* and –5 is the *constant term.*

The same rules that govern operations with numbers apply to operations with algebraic expressions. One additional rule, which helps in simplifying algebraic expressions, is that terms with the same variable part can be combined. Examples are:

$$2x + 5x = (2 + 5)x = 7x$$

$$x^2 - 3x^2 + 6x^2 = (1 - 3 + 6)x^2 = 4x^2$$

$$3xy + 2x - xy - 3x = (3 - 1)xy + (2 - 3)x = 2xy - x$$

Any number or variable that is a factor of each term in an algebraic expression can be factored out. Examples are:

$$4x + 12 = 4(x + 3)$$

$$15y^2 - 9y = 3y(5y - 3)$$

$$\frac{7x^2 + 14x}{2x + 4} = \frac{7x(x + 2)}{2(x + 2)} = \frac{7x}{2} \quad (\text{if } x \neq -2)$$

Another useful tool for factoring algebraic expressions is the fact that $a^2 - b^2 = (a+b)(a-b)$. For example,

$$\frac{x^2-9}{4x-12} = \frac{(x+3)(x-3)}{4(x-3)} = \frac{x+3}{4} \quad (\text{if } x \neq 3)$$

To multiply two algebraic expressions, each term of the first expression is multiplied by each term of the second, and the results are added. For example,

$$\begin{aligned}(x+2)(3x-7) &= x(3x)+x(-7)+2(3x)+2(-7)\\ &= 3x^2-7x+6x-14\\ &= 3x^2-x-14\end{aligned}$$

A statement that equates two algebraic expressions is called an *equation*. Examples of equations are:

$$\begin{aligned}3x+5 &= -2 && \text{(linear in one variable)}\\ x-3y &= 10 && \text{(linear in two variables)}\\ 20y^2+6y-17 &= 0 && \text{(quadratic in one variable)}\end{aligned}$$

2.3 Rules of Exponents

Some of the basic rules of exponents are:

(a) $x^{-a} = \frac{1}{x^a}$.

Example: $4^{-3} = \frac{1}{4^3} = \frac{1}{64}$.

(b) $(x^a)(x^b) = x^{a+b}$.

Example: $(3^2)(3^4) = 3^{2+4} = 3^6 = 729$.

(c) $(x^a)(y^a) = (xy)^a$.

Example: $(2^3)(3^3) = 6^3 = 216$.

(d) $\frac{x^a}{x^b} = x^{a-b} = \frac{1}{x^{b-a}}$ $(x \neq 0)$.

Examples: $\frac{5^7}{5^4} = 5^{7-4} = 5^3 = 125$, and $\frac{4^3}{4^8} = \frac{1}{4^{8-3}} = \frac{1}{4^5} = \frac{1}{1{,}024}$

(e) $\left(\frac{x}{y}\right)^a = \frac{x^a}{y^a}$ $(y \neq 0)$.

Example: $\left(\frac{3}{4}\right)^2 = \frac{3^2}{4^2} = \frac{9}{16}$.

(f) $(x^a)^b = x^{ab}$.

Example: $(2^5)^2 = 2^{10} = 1{,}024$.

(g) If $x \neq 0$, then $x^0 = 1$.

Example: $7^0 = 1$; (0^0 is undefined).

2.4 Solving Linear Equations

(a) One variable.

To solve a linear equation in one variable means to find the value of the variable that makes the equation true. Two equations that have the same solution are said to be *equivalent*. For example, $x+1=2$ and $2x+2=4$ are equivalent equations; both are true when $x=1$.

Two basic rules are important for solving linear equations.

(i) When the same constant is added to (or subtracted from) both sides of an equation, the equality is preserved, and the new equation is equivalent to the original.

(ii) When both sides of an equation are multiplied (or divided) by the same constant, the equality is preserved, and the new equation is equivalent to the original.

For example,

$$
\begin{aligned}
3x-4&=8\\
3x-4+4&=8+4 \qquad &\text{(4 added to both sides)}\\
3x&=12\\
\frac{3x}{3}&=\frac{12}{3} \qquad &\text{(both sides divided by 3)}\\
x&=4
\end{aligned}
$$

(b) Two variables.

To solve linear equations in two variables, it is necessary to have two equations that are not equivalent. To solve such a "system" of simultaneous equations, e.g.,

$$
\begin{aligned}
4x+3y&=13\\
x+2y&=2
\end{aligned}
$$

there are two basic methods. In the *first method* you use either equation to express one variable in terms of the other. In the system above, you could express x in the second equation in terms of y (i.e., $x=2-2y$), and then substitute $2-2y$ for x in the first equation to find the solution for y.

$$
\begin{aligned}
4(2-2y)+3y&=13\\
8-8y+3y&=13\\
-8y+3y&=5 \qquad &\text{(8 subtracted from both sides)}\\
-5y&=5 \qquad &\text{(terms combined)}\\
y&=-1 \qquad &\text{(both sides divided by } -5)
\end{aligned}
$$

Then -1 can be substituted for y in the second equation to solve for x.

$$
\begin{aligned}
x+2y&=2\\
x+2(-1)&=2\\
x-2&=2\\
x&=4 \qquad &\text{(2 added to both sides)}
\end{aligned}
$$

In the *second method,* the object is to make the coefficients of one variable the same in both equations so that one variable can be eliminated by either adding both equations together or subtracting one from the other. In the same example, both sides of the second equation could be multiplied by 4, yielding $4(x+2y)=4(2)$, or $4x+8y=8$. Now we have two equations with the same x coefficient:

$$\begin{aligned}4x+3y&=13\\4x+8y&=8\end{aligned}$$

If the second equation is subtracted from the first, the result is $-5y=5$. Thus, $y=-1$, and substituting -1 for y in either one of the original equations yields $x=4$.

2.5 Solving Quadratic Equations in One Variable

A *quadratic* equation is any equation that can be expressed as $ax^2+bx+c=0$, where a, b, and c are real numbers ($a \neq 0$). Such an equation can always be solved by the *formula*:

$$x=\frac{-b\pm\sqrt{b^2-4ac}}{2a}$$

For example, in the quadratic equation $2x^2-x-6=0$, $a=2$, $b=-1$, and $c=-6$. Therefore, the formula yields

$$\begin{aligned}x&=\frac{-(-1)\pm\sqrt{(-1)^2-4(2)(-6)}}{2(2)}\\&=\frac{1\pm\sqrt{49}}{4}\\&=\frac{1\pm 7}{4}.\end{aligned}$$

So, the solutions are $x=\frac{1+7}{4}=2$ and $x=\frac{1-7}{4}=-\frac{3}{2}$. Quadratic equations can have at most two real solutions, as in the example above. However, some quadratics have only one real solution (e.g., $x^2+4x+4=0$; solution: $x=-2$), and some have no real solutions (e.g., $x^2+x+5=0$).

Some quadratics can be solved more quickly by *factoring*. In the original example,

$$(2x^2-x-6)=(2x+3)(x-2)=0$$

Since $(2x+3)(x-2)=0$, either $2x+3=0$ or $x-2=0$ must be true. Therefore,

$$\begin{aligned}2x+3&=0\\2x&=-3\\x&=-\frac{3}{2}\end{aligned}\qquad\text{OR}\qquad\begin{aligned}x-2&=0\\x&=2\end{aligned}$$

Other examples of factorable quadratic equations are:

(a) $x^2 + 8x + 15 = 0$

$(x+3)(x+5) = 0$

Therefore, $(x+3) = 0;\ x = -3$

or $(x+5) = 0;\ x = -5$

(b) $4x^2 - 9 = 0$

$(2x+3)(2x-3) = 0$

Therefore, $(2x+3) = 0;\ x = -\frac{3}{2}$

or $(2x-3) = 0;\ x = \frac{3}{2}$

2.6 Inequalities

Any mathematical statement that uses one of the following symbols is called an *inequality*.

$\neq$ "not equal to"
$<$ "less than"
$\leq$ "less than or equal to"
$>$ "greater than"
$\geq$ "greater than or equal to"

For example, the inequality $4x - 1 \leq 7$ states that "$4x - 1$ is less than or equal to 7." To *solve* an inequality means to find the value or values of the variable that make the inequality true. The approach used to solve an inequality is similar to that used to solve an equation. That is, by using basic operations, you try to isolate the variable on one side of the inequality. The basic rules for solving inequalities are similar to the rules for solving equations, namely:

(i) When the same constant is added to (or subtracted from) both sides of an inequality, the direction of inequality is preserved, and the new inequality is equivalent to the original.

(ii) When both sides of the inequality are multiplied (or divided) by the same constant, the direction of inequality is *preserved if the constant is positive*, but *reversed if the constant is negative*. In either case the new inequality is equivalent to the original.

For example, to solve the inequality $-3x + 5 \leq 17$,

$-3x + 5 \leq 17$

$-3x \leq 12$ (5 subtracted from both sides)

$\frac{-3x}{-3} \geq \frac{12}{-3}$ (both sides divided by -3, which reverses the direction of the inequality)

$x \geq -4$

Therefore, the solutions to $-3x + 5 \leq 17$ are all real numbers greater than or equal to -4. Another example follows:

$$\frac{4x+9}{11} > 5$$

$$4x+9 > 55 \quad \text{(both sides multiplied by 11)}$$

$$4x > 46 \quad \text{(9 subtracted from both sides)}$$

$$x > \frac{46}{4} \quad \text{(both sides divided by 4)}$$

$$x > 11\frac{1}{2}$$

2.7 Applications

Since algebraic techniques allow for the creation and solution of equations and inequalities, algebra has many real-world applications. Below are a few examples. Additional examples are included in the exercises at the end of this section.

Example 1. Ellen has received the following scores on 3 exams: 82, 74, and 90. What score will Ellen need to attain on the next exam so that the average (arithmetic mean) for the 4 exams will be 85 ?

Solution: If x represents the score on the next exam, then the arithmetic mean of 85 will be equal to

$$\frac{82+74+90+x}{4}.$$

So,

$$\frac{246+x}{4} = 85$$

$$246 + x = 340$$

$$x = 94$$

Therefore, Ellen would need to attain a score of 94 on the next exam.

Example 2. A mixture of 12 ounces of vinegar and oil is 40 percent vinegar (by weight). How many ounces of oil must be added to the mixture to produce a new mixture that is only 25 percent vinegar?

Solution: Let x represent the number of ounces of oil to be added. Therefore, the total number of ounces of vinegar in the new mixture will be (0.40)(12), and the total number of ounces of new mixture will be $12 + x$. Since the new mixture must be 25 percent vinegar,

$$\frac{(0.40)(12)}{12+x} = 0.25.$$

Therefore,

$$\begin{aligned}(0.40)(12) &= (12+x)(0.25)\\ 4.8 &= 3+0.25x\\ 1.8 &= 0.25x\\ 7.2 &= x\end{aligned}$$

Thus, 7.2 ounces of oil must be added to reduce the percent of vinegar in the mixture from 40 percent to 25 percent.

Example 3. In a road rally competition, Jeff and Dennis drove the same course at average speeds of 51 miles per hour and 54 miles per hour, respectively. If it took Jeff 40 minutes to drive the course, how long did it take Dennis?

Solution: Let x equal the time, in minutes, that it took Dennis to drive the course. Since distance (d) equals rate (r) multiplied by time (t), i.e.,

$$d = (r)(t),$$

the distance traveled by Jeff can be represented by $(51)\left(\frac{40}{60}\right)$, and the distance traveled by Dennis by $(54)\left(\frac{x}{60}\right)$. Since the distances are equal,

$$\begin{aligned}(51)\left(\frac{40}{60}\right) &= (54)\left(\frac{x}{60}\right)\\ 34 &= 0.9x\\ 37.8 &= x\end{aligned}$$

Thus, it took Dennis approximately 37.8 minutes to drive the course. Note: since rates are given in miles per *hour,* it was necessary to express time in hours (i.e., 40 minutes equals $\frac{40}{60}$, or $\frac{2}{3}$, of an hour.)

Example 4. If it takes Machine A 3 hours to produce N identical computer parts, and it takes Machine B only 2 hours to do the same job, how long would it take to do the job if both machines worked simultaneously?

Solution: Since Machine A takes 3 hours to do the job, Machine A can do $\frac{1}{3}$ of the job in 1 hour. Similarly, Machine B can do $\frac{1}{2}$ of the job in 1 hour. And if we let x represent the number of hours it would take for the machines working simultaneously to do the job, the two would do $\frac{1}{x}$ of the job in 1 hour. Therefore,

$$\frac{1}{3}+\frac{1}{2}=\frac{1}{x}$$

$$\frac{2}{6}+\frac{3}{6}=\frac{1}{x}$$

$$\frac{5}{6}=\frac{1}{x}$$

$$\frac{6}{5}=x$$

Thus, working together, the machines take only $\frac{6}{5}$ hours, or 1 hour and 12 minutes, to produce the N computer parts.

Example 5. At a fruit stand, apples can be purchased for $0.15 each and pears for $0.20 each. At these rates, a bag of apples and pears was purchased for $3.80. If the bag contained exactly 21 pieces of fruit, how many were pears?

Solution: If a represents the number of apples purchased and p represents the number of pears purchased, two equations can be written as follows:

$$0.15a+0.20p=3.80$$
$$a+p=21$$

From the second equation, $a=21-p$. Substituting $21-p$ into the first equation for a gives

$$0.15(21-p)+0.20p=3.80$$
$$(0.15)(21)-0.15p+0.20p=3.80$$
$$3.15-0.15p+0.20p=3.80$$
$$0.05p=0.65$$
$$p=13 \text{ (pears)}$$

Example 6. It costs a manufacturer $30 each to produce a particular radio model, and it is assumed that if 500 radios are produced, all will be sold. What must be the selling price per radio to ensure that the *profit* (revenue from sales minus total cost to produce) on the 500 radios is greater than $8,200 ?

Solution: If y represents the selling price per radio, then the profit must be $500(y-30)$. Therefore,

$$500(y-30)>8,200$$
$$500y-15,000>8,200$$
$$500y>23,200$$
$$y>46.40$$

Thus, the selling price must be greater than $46.40 to make the profit greater than $8,200.

ALGEBRA EXERCISES

(Answers on page 73)

1. Find an algebraic expression to represent each of the following.
   (a) The square of y is subtracted from 5, and the result is multiplied by 37.
   (b) Three times x is squared, and the result is divided by 7.
   (c) The product of $(x+4)$ and y is added to 18.

2. Simplify each of the following algebraic expressions by doing the indicated operations, factoring, or combining terms with the same variable part.
   (a) $3x^2 - 6 + x + 11 - x^2 + 5x$
   (b) $3(5x-1) - x + 4$
   (c) $\dfrac{(x^2+9)-25}{x-4} \quad (x \neq 4)$
   (d) $(2x+5)(3x-1)$

3. What is the value of $3x^2 - 7x + 23$ when $x = -2$?

4. What is the value of $-7x^3 + 6x^2 - 11x + 1$ when $x = \dfrac{1}{2}$?

5. Use the rules of exponents to simplify the following.
   (a) $(n^5)(n^{-3})$
   (b) $(s^7)(t^7)$
   (c) $\dfrac{r^{12}}{r^4}$
   (d) $\left(\dfrac{2a}{b}\right)^5$
   (e) $(w^5)^{-3}$
   (f) $(5^0)(d^3)$
   (g) $\dfrac{(x^{10})(y^{-1})}{(x^{-5})(y^5)}$
   (h) $\left(\dfrac{3x}{y}\right)^2 \div \left(\dfrac{1}{y}\right)^5$

6. Solve each of the following equations for x.
   (a) $5x - 7 = 28$
   (b) $12 - 5x = x + 30$
   (c) $5(x+2) = 1 - 3x$
   (d) $(x+6)(2x-1) = 0$
   (e) $x^2 + 5x - 14 = 0$
   (f) $3x^2 + 10x - 8 = 0$

7. Solve each of the following systems of equations for x and y.
   (a) $x + y = 24$

   $x - y = 18$

(b) $3x - y = 20$

$x + 2y = 30$

(c) $15x - 18 - 2y = -3x + y$

$10x + 7y + 20 = 4x + 2$

8. Solve each of the following inequalities for x.

(a) $-3x > 7 + x$

(b) $25x + 16 \geq 10 - x$

(c) $16 + x > 8x - 12$

9. Solve for x and y.

$x = 2y$

$5x < y + 7$

10. For a given two-digit integer, the tens digit is 5 greater than the units digit. The sum of the digits is 11. Find the integer.

11. If the ratio of $2x$ to $5y$ is 3 to 4, what is the ratio of x to y ?

12. Kathleen's weekly salary was increased 8 percent to $237.60. What was her weekly salary before the increase?

13. A theater sells children's tickets for half the adult ticket price. If 5 adult tickets and 8 children's tickets cost a total of $27, what is the cost of an adult ticket?

14. Pat invested a total of $3,000. Part of the money yields 10 percent interest per year, and the rest yields 8 percent interest per year. If the total yearly interest from this investment is $256, how much did Pat invest at 10 percent and how much at 8 percent?

15. Two cars started from the same point and traveled on a straight course in opposite directions for exactly 2 hours, at which time they were 208 miles apart. If one car averaged 8 miles per hour faster than the other car, what was the average speed for each car for the 2-hour trip?

16. A group can charter a particular aircraft at a fixed total cost. If 36 people charter the aircraft rather than 40 people, the cost per person is greater by $12. What is the cost per person if 40 people charter the aircraft?

17. If 3 times Jane's age, in years, is equal to 8 times Beth's age, in years, and the difference between their ages is 15 years, how old are Jane and Beth?

ANSWERS TO ALGEBRA EXERCISES

1. (a) $37(5 - y^2)$, or $185 - 37y^2$

   (b) $\frac{(3x)^2}{7}$, or $\frac{9x^2}{7}$

   (c) $18 + (x+4)(y)$, or $18 + xy + 4y$

2. (a) $2x^2 + 6x + 5$

   (b) $14x + 1$

   (c) $x + 4$

   (d) $6x^2 + 13x - 5$

3. 49

4. $-\frac{31}{8}$

5. (a) n^2

   (b) $(st)^7$

   (c) r^8

   (d) $\frac{32a^5}{b^5}$

   (e) $\frac{1}{w^{15}}$

   (f) d^3

   (g) $\frac{x^{15}}{y^6}$

   (h) $9x^2y^3$

6. (a) 7

   (b) –3

   (c) $-\frac{9}{8}$

   (d) $-6, \frac{1}{2}$

   (e) –7, 2

   (f) $\frac{2}{3}, -4$

7. (a) $x = 21$

   $y = 3$

   (b) $x = 10$

   $y = 10$

   (c) $x = \frac{1}{2}$

   $y = -3$

8. (a) $x < -\frac{7}{4}$

   (b) $x \geq -\frac{3}{13}$

   (c) $x < 4$

9. $x < \frac{14}{9}$, $y < \frac{7}{9}$

10. 83

11. 15 to 8

12. $220

13. $3

14. $800 at 10%; $2,200 at 8%

15. 48 mph and 56 mph

16. $108

17. Beth is 9; Jane is 24.

GEOMETRY

3.1 Lines and Angles

In geometry, a basic building block is the *line*, which is understood to be a "straight" line. It is also understood that lines are *infinite* in length. In the figure below, A and B are points on

line ℓ. That part of line ℓ from A to B, including end points A and B, is called a *line segment,* which is *finite* in length. Sometimes the notation "AB" denotes line segment AB and sometimes it denotes the *length* of line segment AB. The exact meaning of the notation can be determined from the context.

Lines ℓ_1 and ℓ_2, shown below, intersect at point P. Whenever two lines intersect, they form four angles.

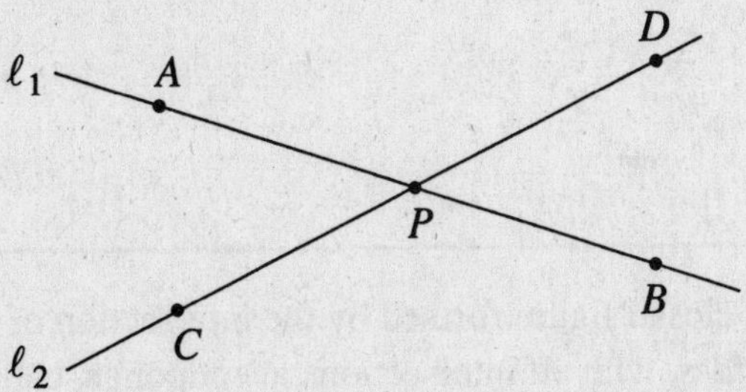

Opposite angles, called *vertical angles,* are the same size, i.e., have *equal measure*. Thus, $\angle APC$ and $\angle DPB$ have equal measure, and $\angle APD$ and $\angle CPB$ also have equal measure. The sum of the measures of the four angles is 360°.

If two lines intersect such that all four angles have equal measure (see figure below), we say that the lines are *perpendicular* or $\ell_1 \perp \ell_2$, and each of the four angles has a measure of 90°. An angle that measures 90° is called a *right angle.* Also, every line can be thought of as an "angle" with measure 180°.

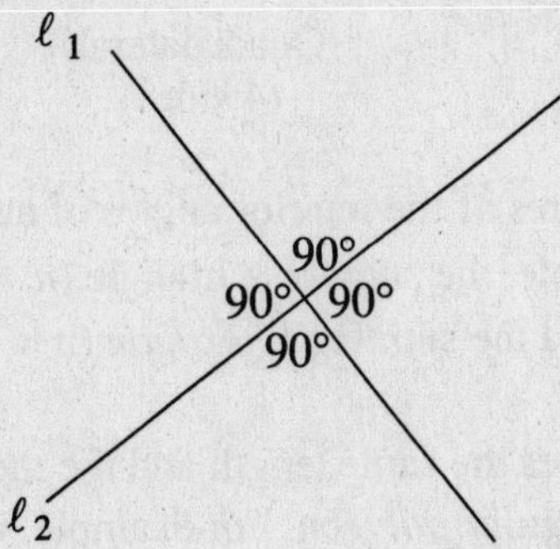

If two distinct lines in the same plane do not intersect, the lines are said to be *parallel*. The figure below shows two parallel lines, ℓ_1 *and* ℓ_2, which are intersected by a third line, ℓ_3, forming eight angles. Note that four of the angles have equal measure $(x°)$ and the remaining four have equal measure $(y°)$, such that $x + y = 180$.

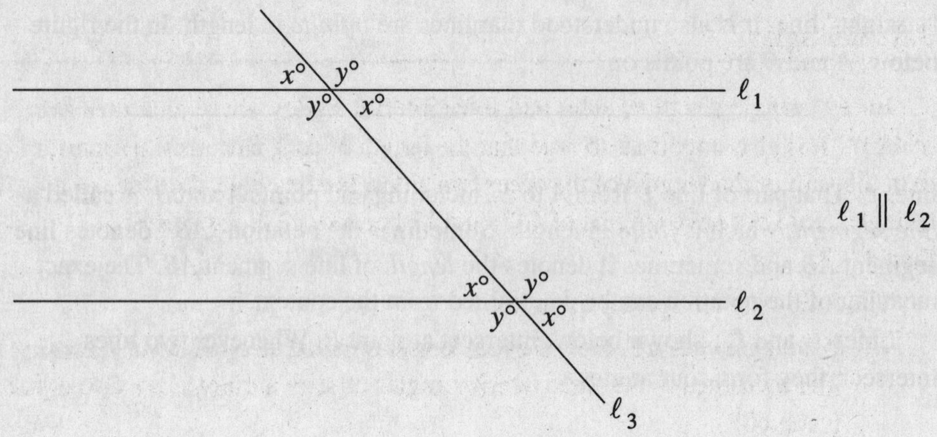

3.2 Polygons

A *polygon* is a closed figure formed by the intersection of three or more line segments, called *sides*, with all intersections at endpoints, called *vertices*. In this discussion, the term "polygon" will mean "convex polygon," that is, a polygon in which the measure of each interior angle is less than 180°. The figures below are examples of such polygons.

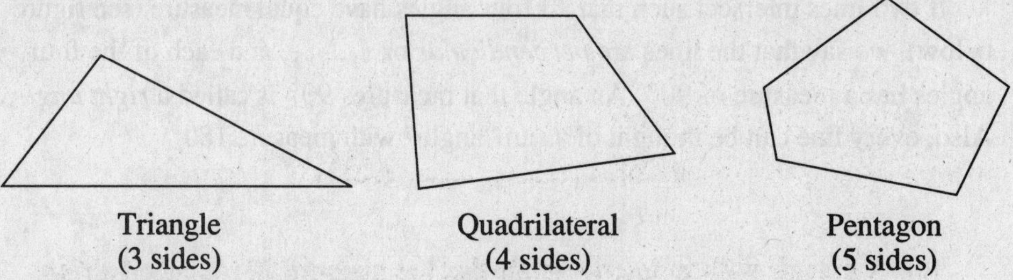

Triangle (3 sides) — Quadrilateral (4 sides) — Pentagon (5 sides)

The sum of the measures of the interior angles of an *n*-sided polygon is $(n-2)(180°)$. For example, the sum for a triangle ($n = 3$) is $(3-2)(180°) = 180°$, and the sum for a *hexagon* ($n = 6$) is $(6-2)(180°) = 720°$.

A polygon with all sides the same length and the measures of all interior angles equal is called a *regular polygon*. For example, in a *regular octagon* (8 sides of equal length), the sum of the measures of the interior angles is $(8-2)(180°) = 1{,}080°$. Therefore, the measure of each angle is $1{,}080° \div 8 = 135°$.

The *perimeter* of a polygon is defined as the sum of the lengths of its sides. The *area* of a polygon is the measure of the area of the region enclosed by the polygon. The methods for finding areas of certain polygons, and the definitions of various special polygons and their properties, are considered separately. We are concerned here primarily with triangles and quadrilaterals.

3.3 Triangles

Every triangle has three sides and three interior angles whose measures sum to 180°. It is also important to note that the length of each side must be shorter than the sum of the lengths of the other two sides. For example, the sides of a triangle could not have lengths of 4, 7, and 12 because 12 is not shorter than 4 + 7.

The following are special triangles.

(a) A triangle with all sides of equal length is called an *equilateral triangle*. The measures of the three interior angles of such a triangle are also equal (each 60°).

(b) A triangle with at least two sides of equal length is called an *isosceles triangle*. If a triangle has two sides of equal length, then the measures of the angles opposite the two sides are equal. The converse of the previous statement is also true. For example, in ΔABC below, since both $\angle ABC$ and $\angle BCA$ have measure 50°, it must be true that $BA = AC$. Also, since $50 + 50 + x = 180$, the measure of $\angle BAC$ must be 80°.

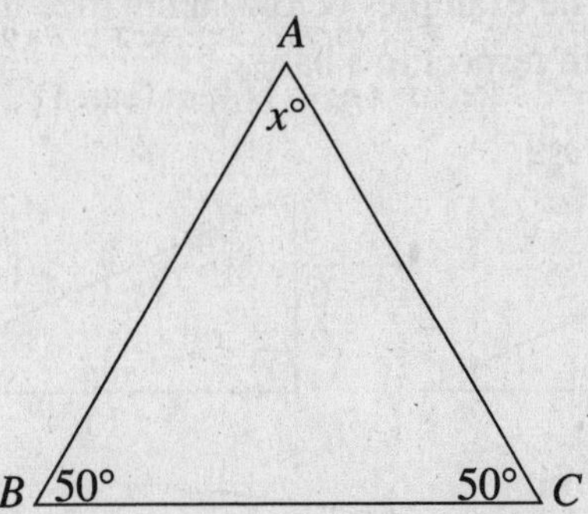

(c) A triangle with an interior angle that has measure 90° is called a *right triangle*. The two sides that form the 90° angle are called *legs* and the side opposite the 90° angle is called the *hypotenuse*.

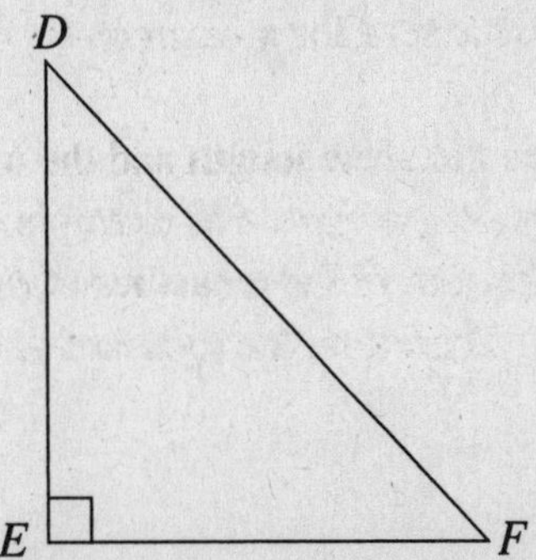

For right ΔDEF above, DE and EF are legs and DF is the hypotenuse. The *Pythagorean Theorem* states that for any right triangle, the square of the length of the hypotenuse equals the sum of the squares of the lengths of the legs. Thus, in right ΔDEF

$$(DF)^2 = (DE)^2 + (EF)^2$$

This relationship can be used to find the length of one side of a right triangle if the lengths of the other two sides are known. For example, if one leg of a right triangle has length 5 and the hypotenuse has length 8, then the length of the other side can be calculated as follows:

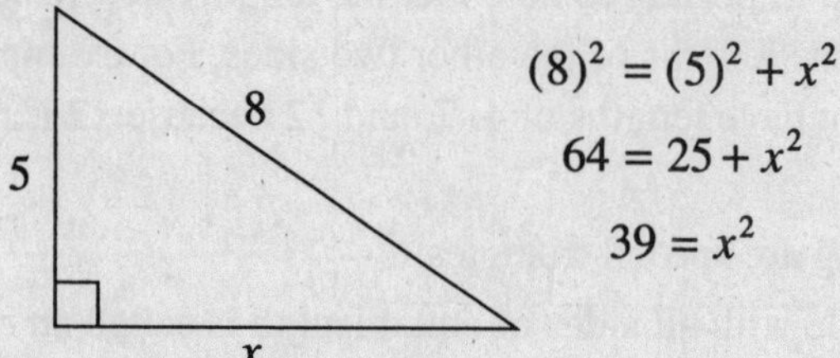

$$(8)^2 = (5)^2 + x^2$$
$$64 = 25 + x^2$$
$$39 = x^2$$

Since $x^2 = 39$ and x must be positive, $x = \sqrt{39}$, or approximately 6.2.

The *area* of a triangle is defined as half the length of a base (b) multiplied by the corresponding height (h), that is,

$$\text{Area} = \frac{bh}{2}$$

Any side of a triangle may be considered a base, and then the corresponding height is the perpendicular distance from the opposite vertex to the base (or an extension of the base). The examples below summarize three possible locations for measuring height with respect to a base.

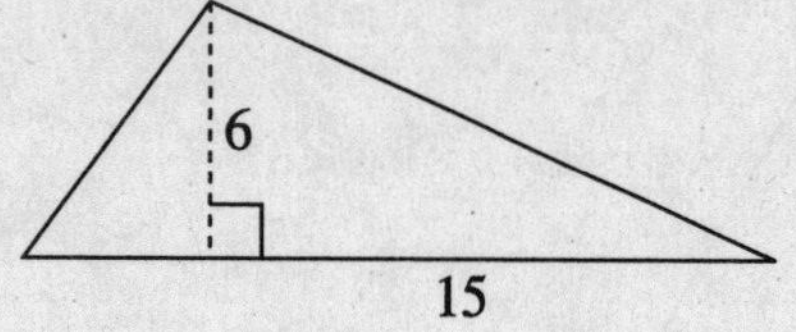

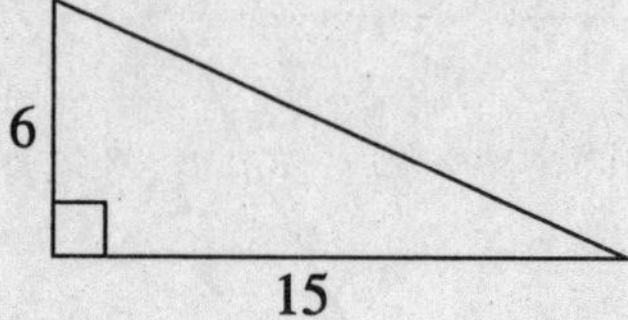

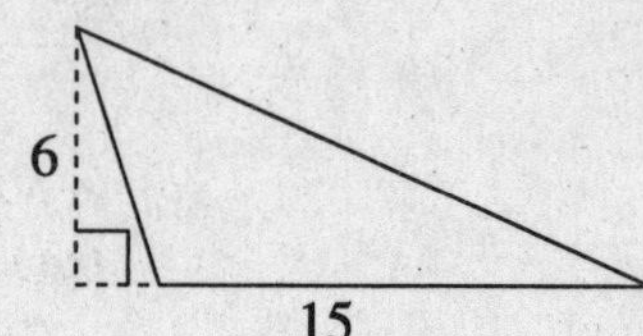

In all three triangles above, the area is $\frac{(15)(6)}{2}$, or 45.

3.4 Quadrilaterals

Every quadrilateral has four sides and four interior angles whose measures sum to $360°$. The following are special quadrilaterals.

(a) A quadrilateral with all interior angles of equal measure (each $90°$) is called a *rectangle*. Opposite sides are parallel and have equal length, and the two diagonals have equal length.

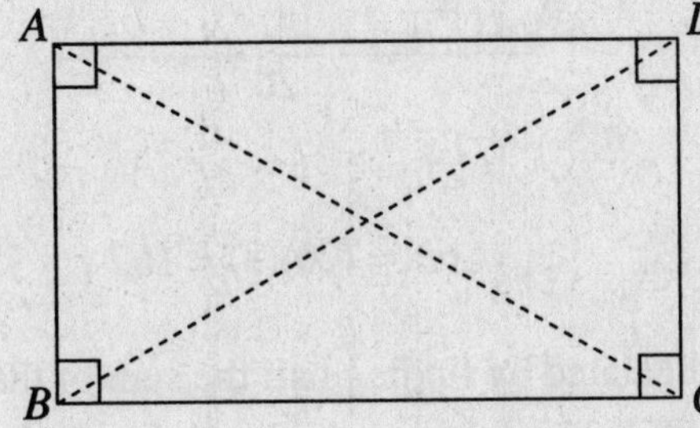

$AD \parallel BC,\ AB \parallel DC$

$AD = BC,\ AB = DC$

$AC = BD$

A rectangle with all sides of equal length is called a *square*.

(b) A quadrilateral with both pairs of opposite sides parallel is called a *parallelogram*. In a parallelogram, opposite sides have equal length, and opposite interior angles have equal measure.

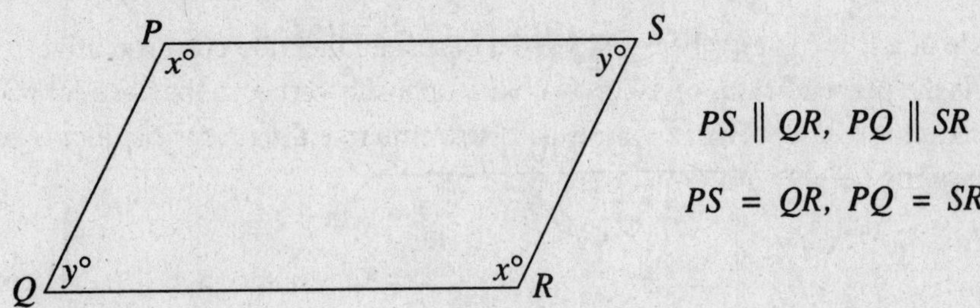

$PS \parallel QR,\ PQ \parallel SR$

$PS = QR,\ PQ = SR$

(c) A quadrilateral with one pair of opposite sides parallel is called a *trapezoid*.

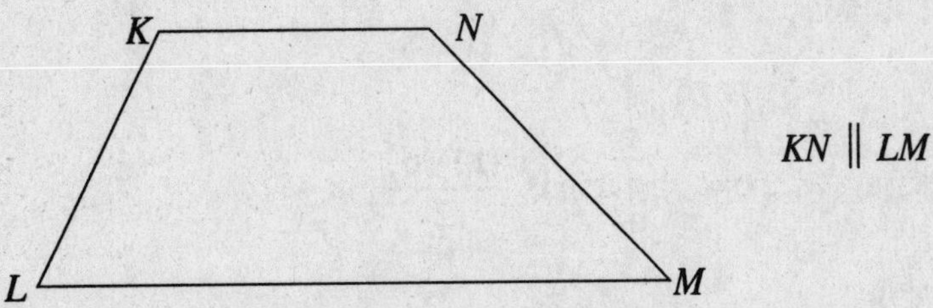

$KN \parallel LM$

For all rectangles and parallelograms the *area* is defined as the length of the base (b) multiplied by the height (h), that is

$$\text{Area} = bh$$

Any side may be considered a base, and then the height is either the length of an adjacent side (for a rectangle) or the length of a perpendicular line from the base to the opposite side (for a parallelogram). Examples of each are:

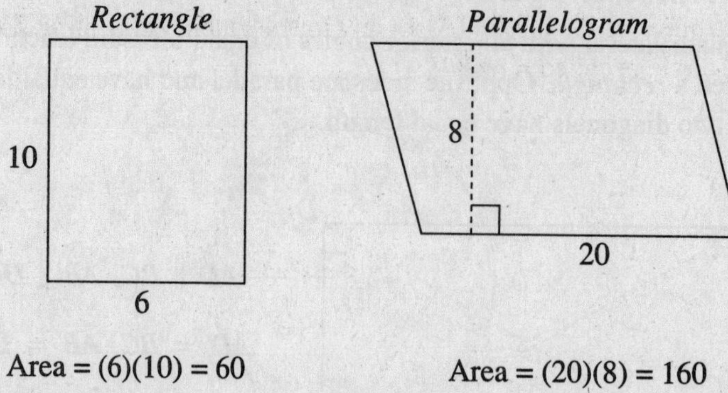

Area = (6)(10) = 60 Area = (20)(8) = 160

The area of a trapezoid may be calculated by finding half the sum of the lengths of the two parallel sides (b_1 and b_2) and then multiplying the result by the height (h), that is,

$$\text{Area} = \frac{1}{2}(b_1 + b_2)(h)$$

For example, for the trapezoid shown below with bases of lengths 10 and 18, and a height of 7.5,

$$\text{Area} = \frac{1}{2}(10 + 18)(7.5) = 105$$

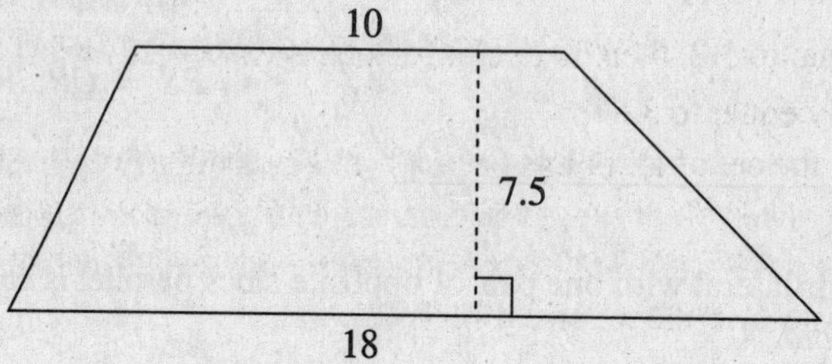

3.5 Circles

The set of all points in a plane that are a given distance r from a fixed point O is called a *circle*. The point O is called the *center* of the circle, and the distance r is called *the radius* of the circle. (Also, any line segment connecting point O to a point on the circle is called *a radius*.)

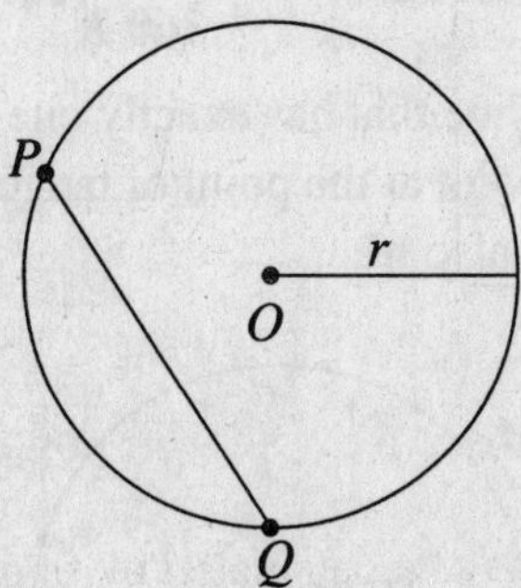

Any line segment that has its endpoints on a circle, such as PQ above, is called a *chord*. Any chord that passes through the center of a circle is called *a diameter*. The length of a diameter is called *the diameter* of a circle. Therefore, the diameter of a circle is always equal to twice its radius.

The distance around a circle is called its *circumference* (comparable to the perimeter of a polygon). The circumference, C, is defined by the equation

$$C = 2\pi r$$

The value of π (pi) is approximately equal to 3.14, or $\frac{22}{7}$. Therefore, if a circle has a radius equal to 5.2, then its circumference is $(2)(\pi)(5.2) = (10.4)(\pi)$, which is approximately equal to 32.7.

On a circle, the set of all points between and including two given points is called an *arc*. It is customary to refer to an arc with three points to avoid ambiguity. In the figure below, arc ABC is the short arc from A to C, but arc ADC is the long arc from A to C in the reverse direction.

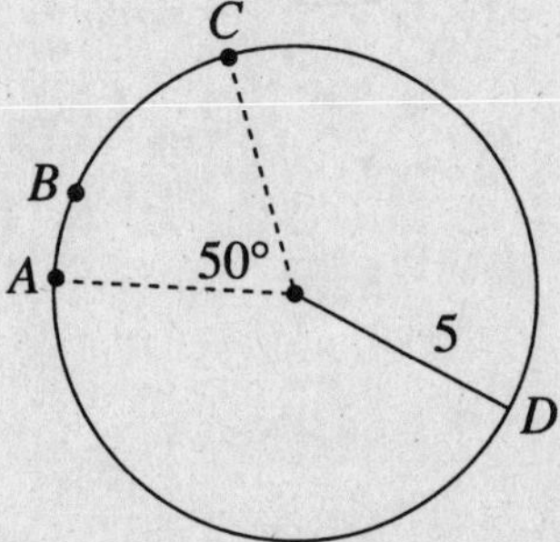

Arcs can be measured in degrees. The number of degrees of arc equals the number of degrees in the central angle formed by the two radii intersecting the arc's endpoints. The number of degrees of arc in the entire circle (one complete revolution) is 360. Thus, in the figure above, arc ABC is a 50° arc and arc ADC is a 310° arc.

To find the *length* of an arc it is important to know that the ratio of arc length to circumference is equal to the ratio of arc measure (in degrees) to 360. In the figure above, the circumference is 10π. Therefore,

$$\frac{\text{length of arc } ABC}{10\pi} = \frac{50}{360}, \text{ or}$$

$$\text{length of arc } ABC = \left(\frac{50}{360}\right)(10\pi) = \frac{25\pi}{18}$$

A *tangent* to a circle is a line that has exactly one point in common with the circle. A radius with its endpoint at the point of tangency is perpendicular to the tangent line. The converse is also true.

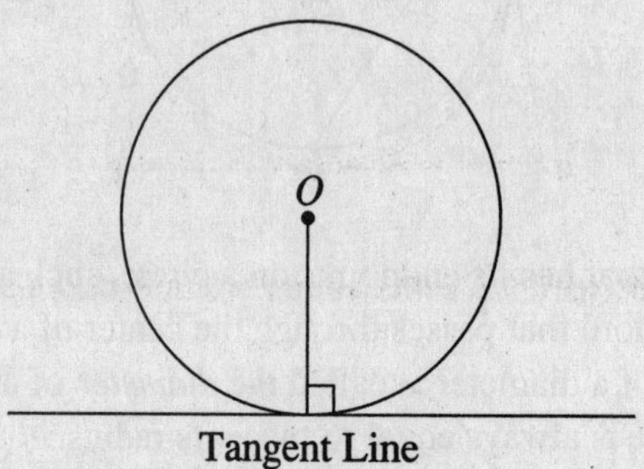

If each vertex of a polygon lies on a circle, then the polygon is *inscribed* in the circle, or equivalently, the circle is *circumscribed* about the polygon. Triangle *RST* below is inscribed in the circle with center *O*.

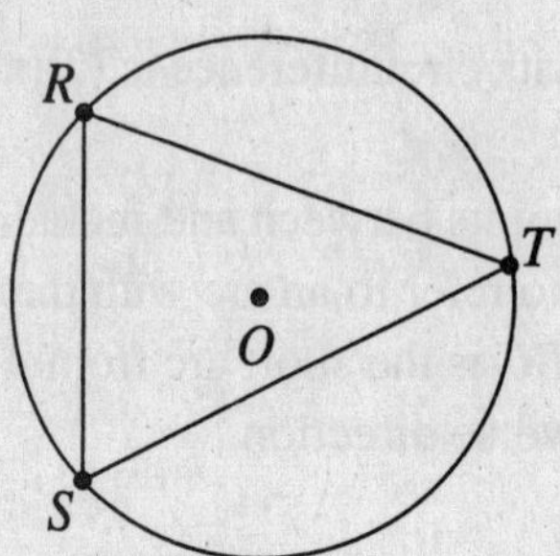

If each side of a polygon is tangent to a given circle, then the polygon is *circumscribed* about the circle, or equivalently, the circle is *inscribed* in the polygon. In the figure below, quadrilateral $ABCD$ is circumscribed about the circle with center O.

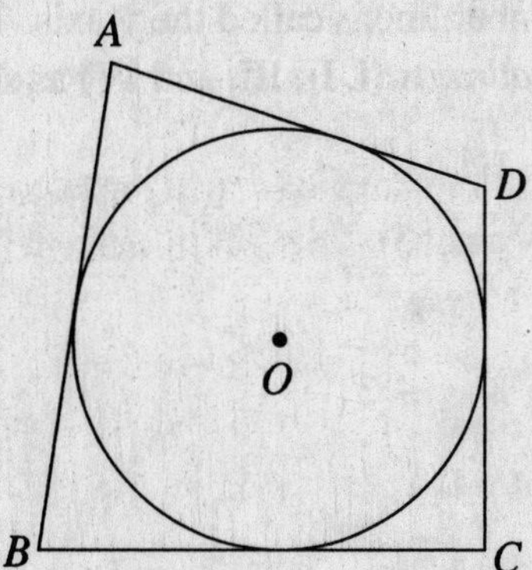

Two or more circles with the same center are called *concentric* circles.

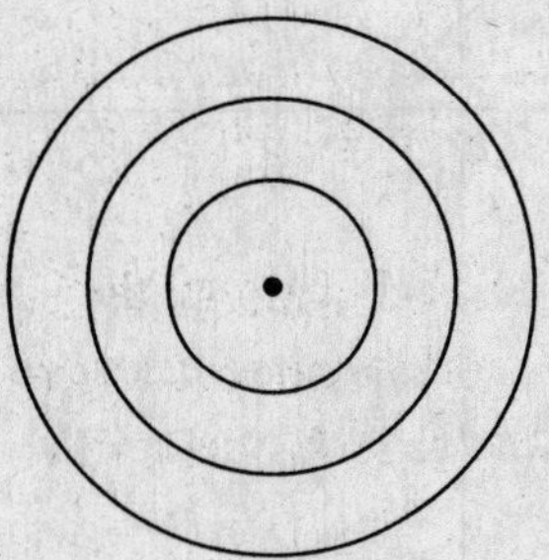

3.6 Coordinate Geometry

Two real number lines (as described in Section 1.5) intersecting at right angles through the zero point on each define a *rectangular coordinate system*, often called the *xy-coordinate system*. The horizontal number line is called the x-axis, and the vertical number line is called the y-axis. The lines divide the plane into four regions called *quadrants* (I, II, III, and IV) as shown below.

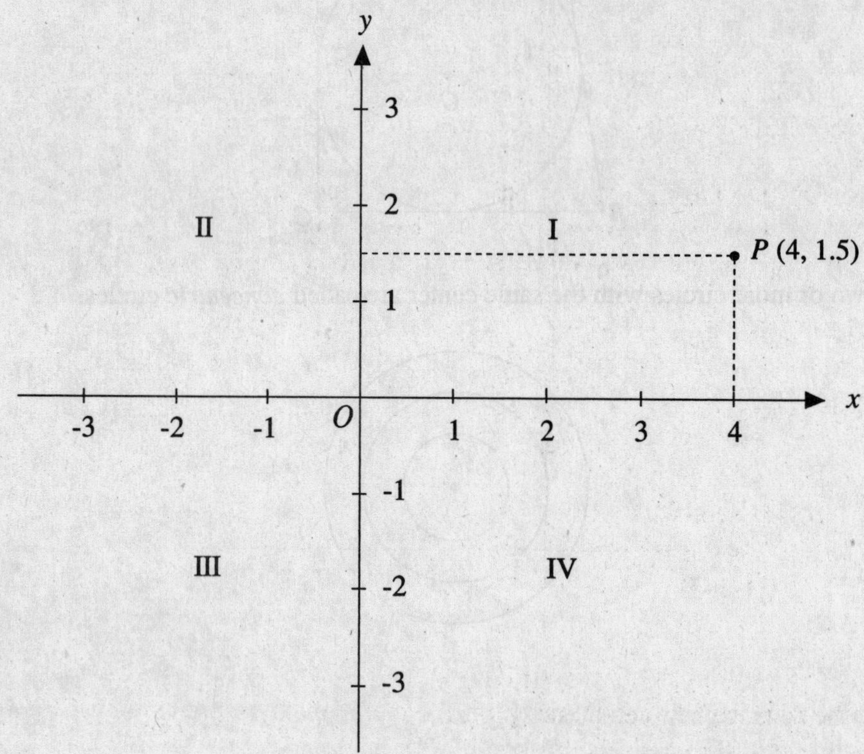

Each point in the system can be identified by an ordered pair of real numbers, (x,y), called *coordinates*. The x-coordinate expresses distance to the left (if negative) or right (if positive) of the y-axis, and the y-coordinate expresses distance below (if negative) or above (if positive) the x-axis. For example, since point P, shown above, is 4 units to the right of the y-axis and 1.5 units above the x-axis, it is identified by the ordered pair (4, 1.5). The *origin* O has coordinates (0, 0). Unless otherwise noted, the units used on the x-axis and the y-axis are the same.

To find the distance between two points, say $P(4, 1.5)$ and $Q(-2, -3)$, represented by the length of line segment PQ in the figure below, first construct a right triangle (see dotted lines) and then note that the legs of the triangle have lengths 6 and 4.5.

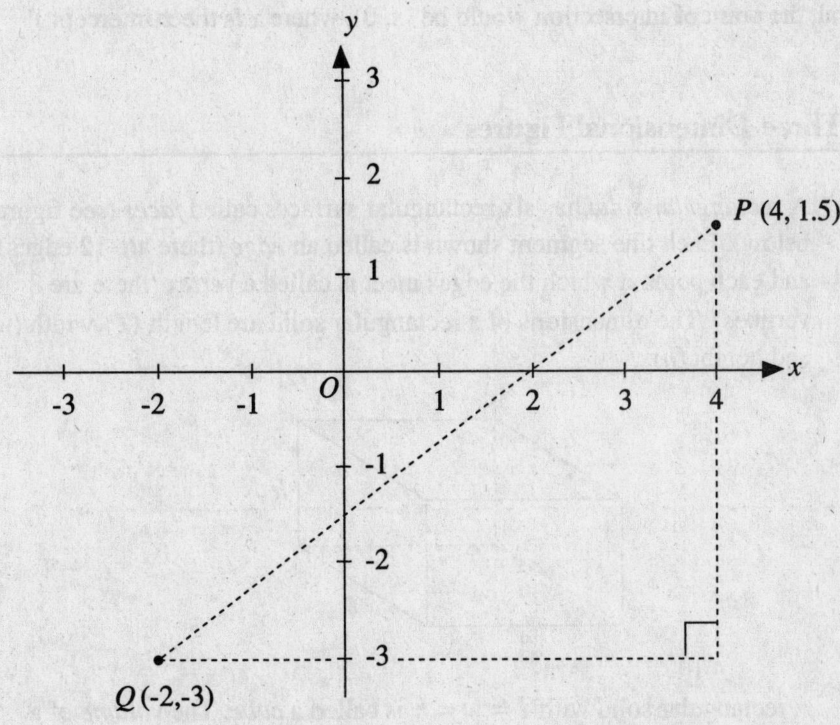

Since the distance between P and Q is the length of the hypotenuse, we can apply the Pythagorean Theorem, as follows:

$$PQ = \sqrt{(6)^2 + (4.5)^2} = \sqrt{56.25} = 7.5$$

A straight line in a coordinate system is a *graph* of a *linear equation* of the form $y = mx + b$, where m is called the *slope* of the line and b is called the *y-intercept*. The slope of a line passing through points $P(x_1, y_1)$ and $Q(x_2, y_2)$ is defined as

$$\text{slope} = \frac{y_1 - y_2}{x_1 - x_2} \quad (x_1 \neq x_2)$$

For example, in the coordinate system shown above, the slope of the line passing through points $P(4, 1.5)$ and $Q(-2, -3)$ is

$$\text{slope} = \frac{1.5 - (-3)}{4 - (-2)} = \frac{4.5}{6} = 0.75$$

The y-intercept is the distance from the origin to the point where the graph intersects the y-axis; it is positive if the point of intersection is above the origin and negative if the point of intersection is below the origin. Therefore, the y-intercept in the example above is -1.5 and the equation of the graph is $y = 0.75x - 1.5$. Note that the coordinates of the point of intersection are $(0, -1.5)$, and in general the coordinates of the point of intersection with the y-axis are $(0, y)$, where y is the y-intercept. (Similarly, the *x-intercept* is the distance from the origin to the point on the x-axis where the graph intersects, and therefore in general, the point of intersection would be $(x, 0)$, where x is the x-intercept.)

3.7 Three-Dimensional Figures

(a) A *rectangular solid* has six rectangular surfaces called *faces* (see figure below). Each line segment shown is called an *edge* (there are 12 edges), and each point at which the edges meet is called a *vertex* (there are 8 vertices). The dimensions of a rectangular solid are length (ℓ), width (w) and height (h).

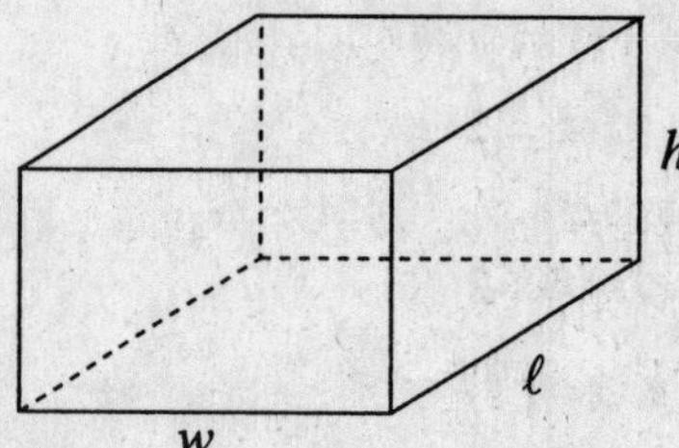

A rectangular solid with $\ell = w = h$ is called a *cube*. The *volume* of a rectangular solid is the product of the three dimensions,

$$V = \ell wh$$

The *surface area* of a rectangular solid is the sum of the areas of the six faces, or

$$A = 2(w\ell + \ell h + wh)$$

For example, if a rectangular solid has length 8.5, width 5, and height 10, then its volume is

$$V = (8.5)(5)(10) = 425,$$

and its surface area is

$$A = 2[(5)(8.5) + (8.5)(10) + (5)(10)] = 355$$

(b) A *right circular cylinder* is shown in the figure below. Its bases are circles with equal radii and centers P and Q, respectively, and its height PQ is perpendicular to both bases.

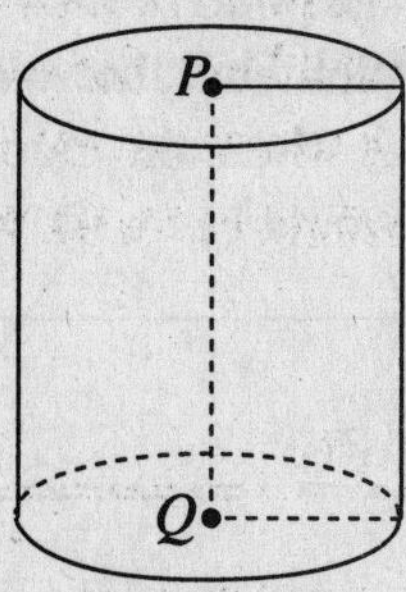

The *volume* of a right circular cylinder with a base radius r and height h is the area of the base multiplied by the height or

$$V = \pi r^2 h$$

The surface area of a right circular cylinder is the sum of the two base areas and the area of the curved surface, or

$$A = 2(\pi r^2) + 2\pi rh$$

For example, if a right circular cylinder has a base radius of 3 and a height of 6.5, then its volume is

$$V = \pi(3)^2(6.5) = 58.5\pi,$$

and its surface area is

$$A = (2)(\pi)(3)^2 + (2)(\pi)(3)(6.5) = 57\pi$$

(c) Other basic three-dimensional figures include *spheres, pyramids,* and *cones.*

GEOMETRY EXERCISES

(Answers on page 92)

1. Lines ℓ and m below are parallel. Find the values of x and y.

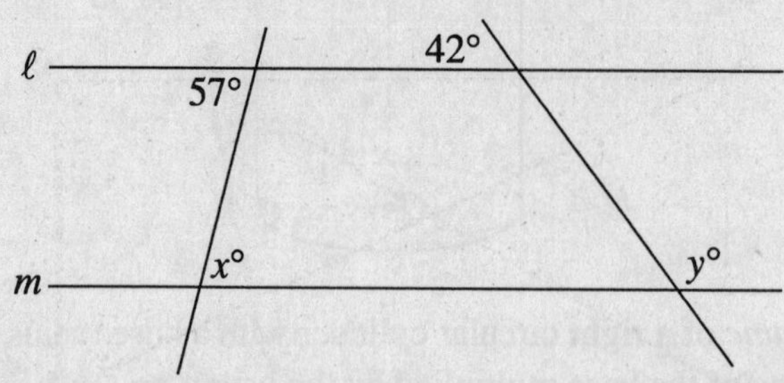

2. In the figure below, $AC = BC$. Find the values of x and y.

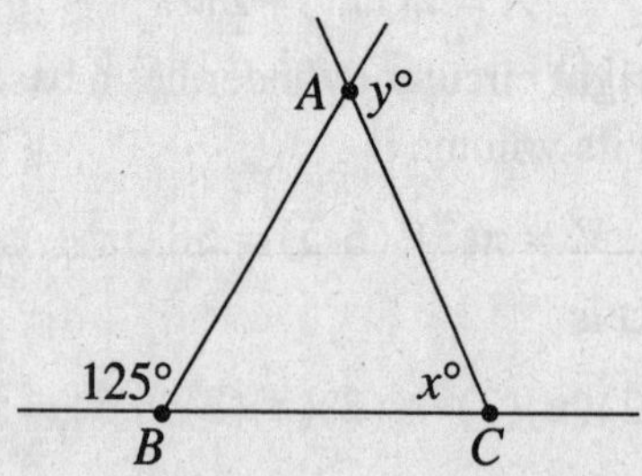

3. In the figure below, what relationship must hold among angle measures x, y, and z ?

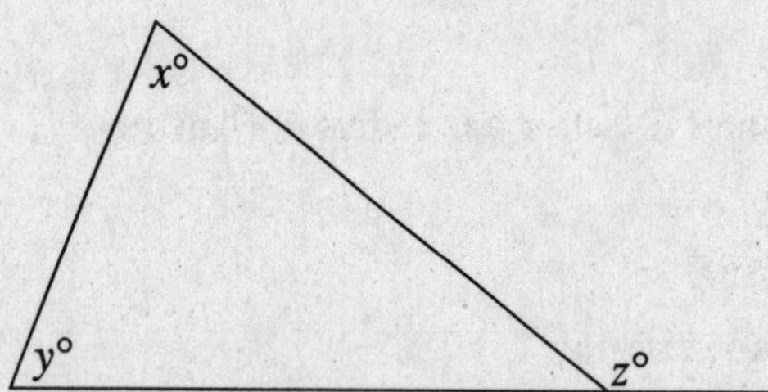

4. What is the sum of the measures of the interior angles of a decagon (10-sided polygon)?

5. If the polygon in #4 is regular, what is the measure of each interior angle?

6. The lengths of two sides of an isosceles triangle are 15 and 22, respectively. What are the possible values of the perimeter?

7. In rectangle $ABDE$ below, $AB = 5, BC = 7,$ and $CD = 3$. Find the
   (a) area of $ABDE$
   (b) area of triangle BCF
   (c) length of AD
   (d) perimeter of $ABDE$

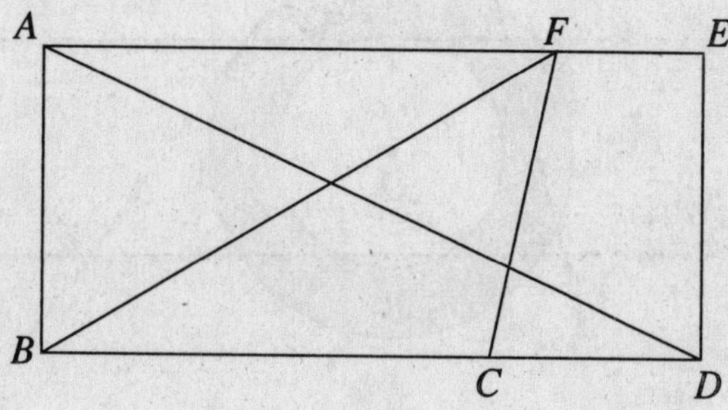

8. In parallelogram $ABCD$ below, find the
   (a) area
   (b) perimeter
   (c) length of diagonal AC

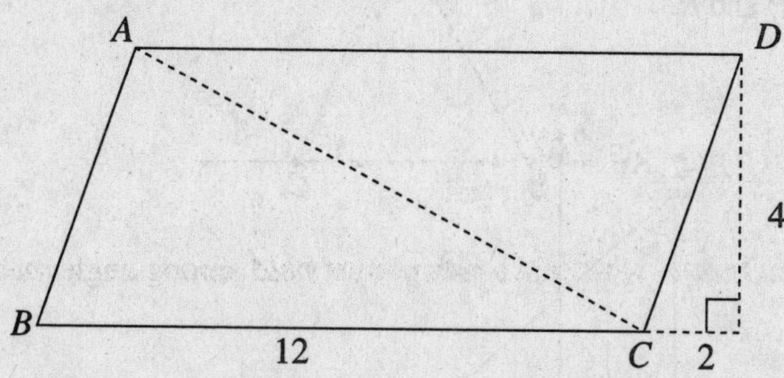

9. The circle with center O below has radius 4. Find the
   (a) circumference
   (b) length of arc ABC
   (c) area of the shaded region

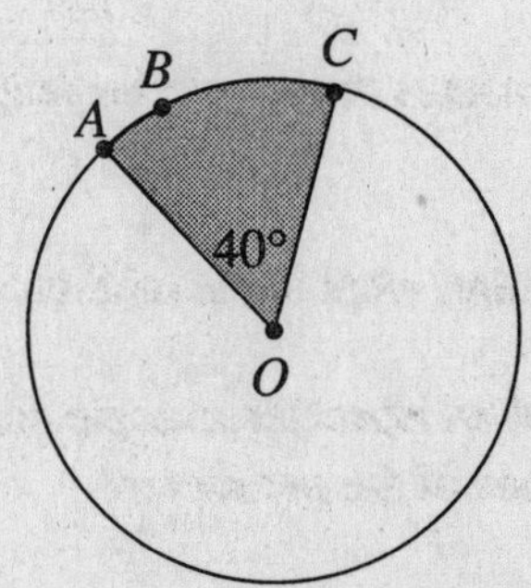

10. The figure below shows two concentric circles each with center O. If the larger circle has radius 12 and the smaller circle has radius 8, find the

(a) circumference of the larger circle

(b) area of the smaller circle

(c) area of the shaded region

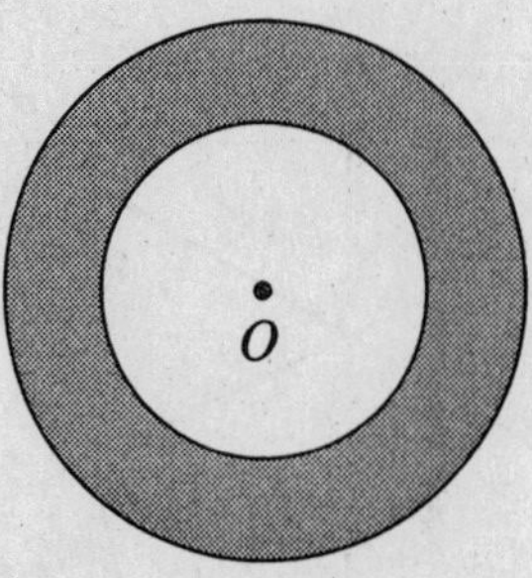

11. In the coordinate system below, find the

(a) coordinates of point Q

(b) perimeter of ΔPQR

(c) area of ΔPQR

(d) slope, y-intercept, and equation of the line passing through points P and R.

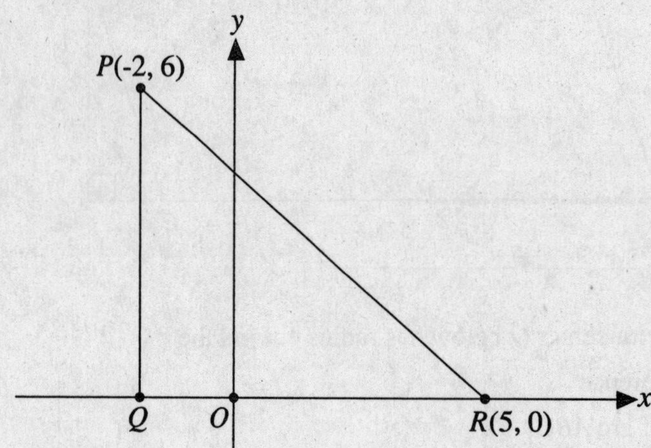

12. In the xy-coordinate system, find the

(a) slope and y-intercept of a graph with equation $2y + x = 6$.

(b) equation of the straight line passing through point (3, 2) with y-intercept 1.

(c) y-intercept of a straight line with slope 3 which passes through point (–2, 1).

(d) x-intercepts of the graphs in (a), (b), and (c).

13. For the rectangular solid below, find the

(a) surface area

(b) length of diagonal AB

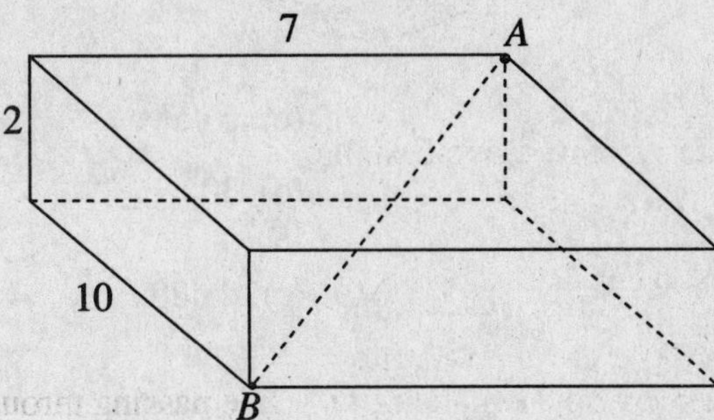

ANSWERS TO GEOMETRY EXERCISES

1. $x = 57,\ y = 138$

2. $x = 70,\ y = 125$

3. $z = x + y$

4. $1,440°$

5. $144°$

6. 52 or 59

7. (a) 50
   (b) 17.5
   (c) $5\sqrt{5}$
   (d) 30

8. (a) 48
   (b) $24 + 4\sqrt{5}$
   (c) $2\sqrt{29}$

9. (a) 8π
   (b) $\frac{8\pi}{9}$
   (c) $\frac{16\pi}{9}$

10. (a) 24π
    (b) 64π
    (c) 80π

11. (a) $(-2, 0)$
    (b) $13 + \sqrt{85}$
    (c) 21
    (d) slope = $\frac{-6}{7}$, y-intercept = $\frac{30}{7}$,
    $y = \frac{-6}{7}x + \frac{30}{7}$, or $7y + 6x = 30$

12. (a) slope = $-\frac{1}{2}$, y-intercept = 3
    (b) $y = \frac{x}{3} + 1$
    (c) 7
    (d) $6, -3, -\frac{7}{3}$

13. (a) 208
    (b) $3\sqrt{17}$

DATA ANALYSIS

4.1 Measures of Central Location

Two popular measures of central location, often called "average", for a discrete set of numerical values or measurements are the *arithmetic mean* and the *median*.

The *arithmetic mean* of n values is defined as the *sum of the n values divided by n*. For example, the arithmetic mean of the values 5, 8, 8, 14, 15, and 10 is $60 \div 6 = 10$.

If we order the n values from least to greatest, the *median* is defined as *the middle value if n is odd* and *the sum of the two middle values divided by 2 if n is even*. In the example above, $n = 6$, which is even. Ordered from least to greatest, the values are 5, 8, 8, 10, 14, and 15. Therefore, the median is

$$\frac{8 + 10}{2} = 9$$

Note that for the same set of values the arithmetic mean and the median need not be equal, although they could be. For example, the set of values 10, 20, 30, 40, and 50 has arithmetic mean = median = 30.

Another measure of central location is called the *mode*, which is defined as *the most frequently occurring value*. For the six measurements above, the mode is 8.

4.2 Measures of Dispersion

Measures of dispersion, or spread, for a discrete set of numerical values or measurements take many forms in data analyses. The simplest measure of dispersion is called the *range*, which is defined as the *greatest measurement minus the least measurement*. So, in the example in 4.1, the range for the six values is 15 minus 5, or 10.

Since the range is affected by only the two most extreme values in the set of measurements, other measures of dispersion have been developed which are affected by every measurement. The most commonly used of these other measures is called the *standard deviation*. The value of the standard deviation for a set of n measurements can be calculated by (1) first calculating the arithmetic mean, (2) finding the difference between that mean and each measurement, (3) squaring each of the differences, (4) summing the squared values, (5) dividing the sum by n, and finally (6) taking the positive square root of the quotient. The following demonstrates this calculation for the example used in 4.1.

x	$x–10$	$(x–10)^2$
5	–5	25
8	–2	4
8	–2	4
10	0	0
14	4	16
15	5	25
		74

$$\text{standard deviation} = \sqrt{\frac{74}{6}} = 3.5$$

The standard deviation can be roughly interpreted as the average distance from the arithmetic mean for the n measurements. The standard deviation cannot be negative, and when two sets of measurements are compared, the one with the larger dispersion will have the larger standard deviation.

4.3 Frequency Distributions

For some sets of measurements it is more convenient and informative to display the measurements in a *frequency distribution*. For example, the following values could represent the number of dependent children in each of 25 families living on a particular street:

1, 2, 0, 4, 1, 3, 3, 1, 2, 0, 4, 5, 2,
3, 2, 3, 2, 4, 1, 2, 3, 0, 2, 3, 1

These data can be grouped into a *frequency distribution* by listing each different value (x) and the frequency (f) of occurrence for each value.

Frequency Distribution

x	f
0	3
1	5
2	7
3	6
4	3
5	1
	25

The frequency distribution format not only provides a quick summary of the data, but it also simplifies the calculations of the central location and dispersion measures. For these data the x's can be summed by multiplying each x by its frequency and then adding the products. So, the arithmetic mean is

$$\frac{(0)(3) + (1)(5) + (2)(7) + (3)(6) + (4)(3) + 5(1)}{25} = 2.16$$

The median is the middle (13th) x value in order of size. The f values show that the 13th x value must be a 2. The range is 5 minus 0, or 5. The standard deviation can also be calculated more easily from a frequency distribution, although in practice it is likely that a programmable calculator would be used to calculate both the mean and the standard deviation directly from the 25 measurements.

4.4 Counting

Some definitions and principles basic to counting are:

(a) *If one task has* n *possible outcomes and a second task has* m *possible outcomes, then the joint occurrence of the two tasks has* (n)(m) *possible outcomes*. For example, if Town *A* and Town *B* are joined by 3 different roads, and Town *B* and Town *C* are joined by 4 different roads, then the number of different routes from Town *A* to Town *C* through *B* is (3)(4), or 12. Each time a coin is flipped, there are 2 possible outcomes: heads or tails. Therefore, if a coin is flipped 4 times, then the number of possible outcomes is (2)(2)(2)(2), or 16.

(b) *For any integer* n *greater than* 1, *the symbol* n!, *pronounced "*n *factorial", is defined as the product of all positive integers less than or equal to* n. *Also,* 0! = 1! = 1. Therefore,

$$0! = 1$$
$$1! = 1$$
$$2! = (2)(1) = 2$$
$$3! = (3)(2)(1) = 6$$
$$4! = (4)(3)(2)(1) = 24$$

and so on.

(c) *The number of ways that* n *objects can be ordered is* n!. For example, the number of ways that the letters *A*, *B*, and *C* can be ordered is 3!, or 6. The six orders are

ABC, *ACB*, *BAC*, *BCA*, *CAB*, and *CBA*

(d) *The number of different subsets of* r *objects that can be selected from* n *objects* ($r \leq n$)*, without regard to the order of selection, is*

$$\frac{n!}{(n-r)!\,r!}$$

For example, the number of different committees of 3 people that can be selected from 5 people is

$$\frac{5!}{(5-3)!\,3!} = \frac{5!}{2!\,3!} = \frac{120}{(2)(6)} = 10$$

These 10 subsets are called *combinations* of 5 objects selected 3 at a time.

4.5 Probability

Everyday there are occasions in which decisions must be made in the face of uncertainty. The decision-making process often involves the selection of a course of action based on an analysis of possible outcomes. For situations in which the possible outcomes are all equally likely, the *probability that an event E occurs*, represented by "P(E)", can be defined as

$$P(E) = \frac{\text{The number of outcomes involving the occurrence of E}}{\text{The total number of possible outcomes}}$$

For example, if a committee of 11 students consists of 2 seniors, 5 juniors, and 4 sophomores, and one student is to be selected at random to chair the committee, then the probability that the student selected will be a senior is $\frac{2}{11}$.

In general, "P(E)" can be thought of as a number assigned to an event E which expresses the likelihood that E occurs. If E cannot occur, then $P(E) = 0$, and if E must occur, then $P(E) = 1$. If the occurrence of E is uncertain, then $0 < P(E) < 1$. The probability that event E does NOT occur is $1 - P(E)$. For example, if the probability is 0.75 that it will rain tomorrow, then the probability that it will not rain tomorrow is $1 - 0.75$, or 0.25.

The probability that events E and F both occur can be represented by *P(E and F)**, and the probability that at least one of the two events occurs can be represented by *P(E or F)***. One of the fundamental relationships among probabilities is called the *Addition Law*:

$$P(E \text{ or } F) = P(E) + P(F) - P(E \text{ and } F)$$

* Many texts use $P(E \cap F)$.

** Many texts use $P(E \cup F)$.

For example, if a card is to be selected randomly from an ordinary deck of playing cards, E is the event that a heart is selected, and F is the event that a 9 is selected, then

$$P(E) = \frac{13}{52}, \quad P(F) = \frac{4}{52}, \quad \text{and } P(E \text{ and } F) = \frac{1}{52}$$

Therefore, $P(E \text{ or } F) = \frac{13}{52} + \frac{4}{52} - \frac{1}{52} = \frac{16}{52} = \frac{4}{13}$.

Two events are said to be *independent* if the occurrence or nonoccurrence of either one in no way affects the occurrence of the other. It follows that if events E and F are independent events, then P(E and F) = P(E) • P(F). Two events are said to be *mutually exclusive* if the occurrence of either one precludes the occurrence of the other. In other words, if events E and F are mutually exclusive, then P(E and F) = 0.

Example: If P(A) = 0.45 and P(B) = 0.20, and the two events are independent, what is P(A or B)?

According to the Addition Law:

$$\begin{aligned} P(A \text{ or } B) &= P(A) + P(B) - P(A \text{ and } B) \\ &= P(A) + P(B) - P(A) \cdot P(B) \\ &= 0.45 + 0.20 - (0.45)(0.20) \\ &= 0.56 \end{aligned}$$

If the two events in the example above had been mutually exclusive, then P(A or B) would have been found as follows:

$$\begin{aligned} P(A \text{ or } B) &= P(A) + P(B) - P(A \text{ and } B) \\ &= 0.45 + 0.20 - 0 \\ &= 0.65 \end{aligned}$$

4.6 Data Representation and Interpretation

Data can be summarized and represented in various forms, including tables, bar graphs, circle graphs, and linear graphs. The following are several examples of tables and graphs, each with questions that can be answered by selecting the appropriate information and applying mathematical techniques.

Example 1.

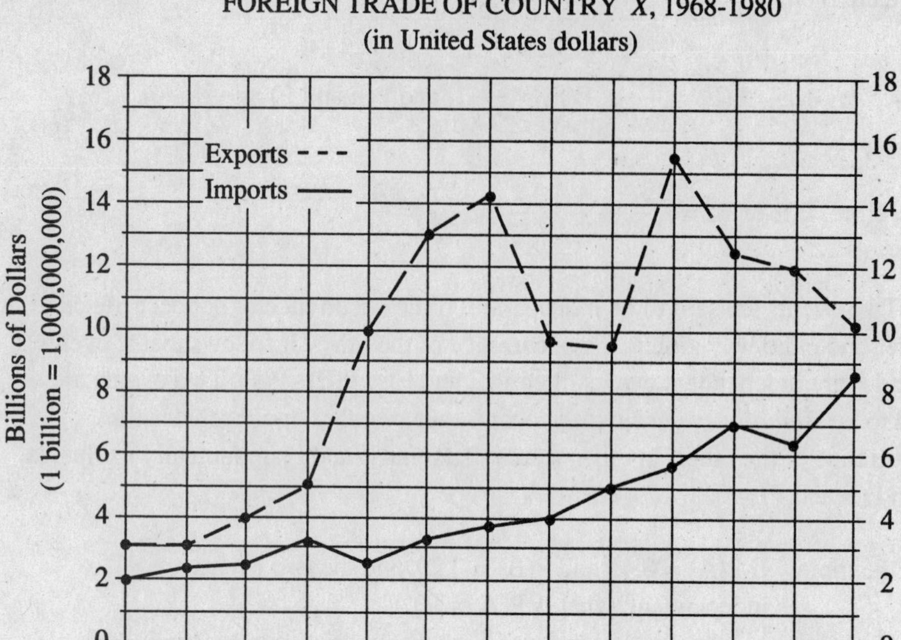

(a) For which year shown on the graph did exports exceed the previous year's exports by the greatest dollar amount?

(b) In 1973 the dollar value of imports was approximately what percent of the dollar value of exports?

(c) If it were discovered that the import dollar amount shown for 1978 was incorrect and should have been \$3.1 billion instead, then the average (arithmetic mean) import dollar amount per year for the 13 years would be how much less?

Solutions:

(a) The greatest increase in exports from one year to the next is represented by the dotted line segment with the steepest positive slope, which is found between 1976 and 1977. The increase was approximately \$6 billion. Thus, the answer is 1977.

(b) In 1973, the dollar value of imports was approximately \$3.3 billion, and the dollar value of exports was \$13 billion. Therefore, the answer is 3.3/13, or approximately 25%.

(c) If the import dollar amount in 1978 were \$3.1 billion, rather than the table amount, \$7 billion, then the sum of the import amounts for the 13 years would be reduced by \$3.9 billion. Therefore, the average per year would be reduced by \$3.9/13, which is \$0.3 billion, or \$300 million.

Example 2.

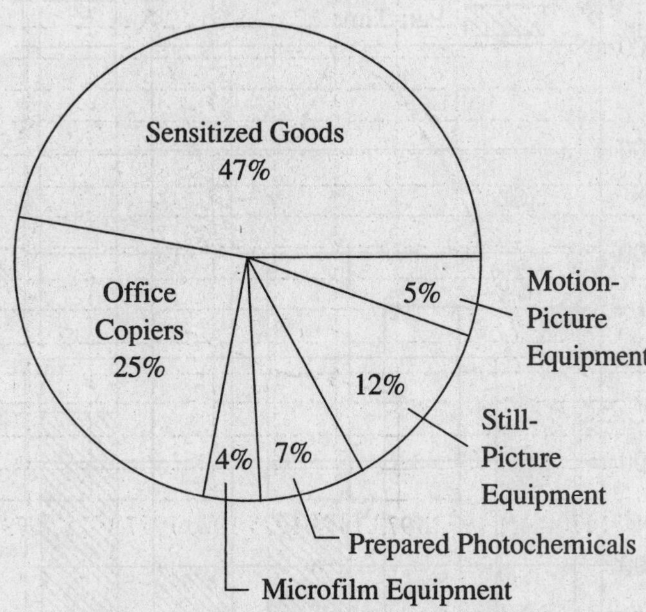

(a) In 1971 what was the ratio of the value of sensitized goods to the value of still-picture equipment produced in the United States?

(b) If the value of office copiers produced in 1971 was 30 percent higher than the corresponding value in 1970, what was the value of office copiers produced in 1970?

(c) If the areas of the sectors in the circle graph are drawn in proportion to the percents shown, what is the measure, in degrees, of the central angle of the sector representing the percent of prepared photochemicals produced?

Solutions:

(a) The ratio of the value of sensitized goods to the value of still-picture equipment is equal to the ratio of the corresponding percents shown. Therefore, the ratio is 47 to 12, or approximately 4 to 1.

(b) The value of office copiers produced in 1971 was (0.25)($3,980), or $995 million. Therefore, if the corresponding value in 1970 was x, then $x(1.30) = \$995$ million, or $x = \$765$ million.

(c) Since the sum of the central angles for the six sectors is 360°, the central angle for the sector representing prepared photochemicals is (0.07)(360)°, or 25.2°.

Example 3.

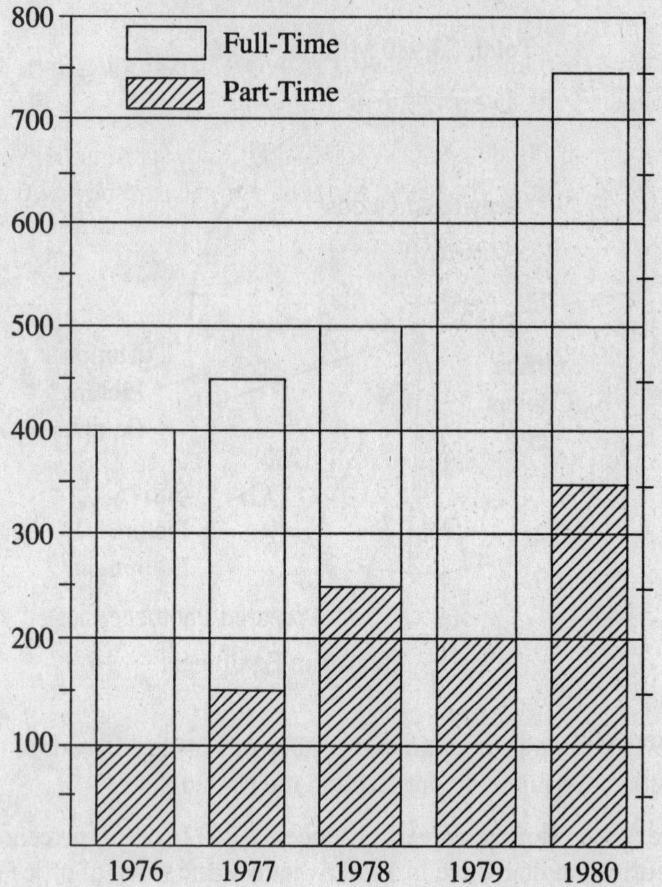

(a) For which year was the ratio of part-time enrollment to total enrollment the greatest?

(b) What was the full-time enrollment in 1977?

(c) What was the percent increase in total enrollment from 1976 to 1980?

Solutions:

(a) It is visually apparent that the height of the shaded bar compared to the total height of the bar is greatest in 1978 (about half the total height). No calculations are necessary.

(b) In 1977 the total enrollment was approximately 450 students, and the part-time enrollment was approximately 150 students. Thus, the full-time enrollment was 450 – 150, or 300 students.

(c) The total enrollments for 1976 and 1980 were approximately 400 and 750, respectively. Therefore, the percent increase from 1976 to 1980 was

$$\frac{750 - 400}{400} = \frac{350}{400} = 0.875 = 87.5\%$$

Example 4.

CONSUMER COMPLAINTS RECEIVED BY THE CIVIL AERONAUTICS BOARD

Category	1980 (percent)	1981 (percent)
Flight problems	20.0%	22.1%
Baggage	18.3	21.8
Customer service	13.1	11.3
Oversales of seats	10.5	11.8
Refund problems	10.1	8.1
Fares	6.4	6.0
Reservations and ticketing	5.8	5.6
Tours	3.3	2.3
Smoking	3.2	2.9
Advertising	1.2	1.1
Credit	1.0	0.8
Special passengers	0.9	0.9
Other	6.2	5.3
	100.0%	100.0%
Total Number of Complaints	22,998	13,278

(a) Approximately how many complaints concerning credit were received by the Civil Aeronautics Board in 1980?

(b) By approximately what percent did the total number of complaints decrease from 1980 to 1981?

(c) Which of the following statements can be inferred from the table?

I. In 1980 and in 1981, complaints about flight problems, baggage, and customer service together accounted for more than 50 percent of all consumer complaints received by the Civil Aeronautics Board.

II. The number of special passenger complaints was unchanged from 1980 to 1981.

III. From 1980 to 1981 the number of flight problem complaints increased by more than 2 percent.

Solutions:

(a) In 1980, 1 percent of the complaints concerned credit, so the number of complaints was approximately (0.01)(22,998), or 230.

(b) The decrease in total complaints from 1980 to 1981 was 22,998 – 13,278, or 9,720. Therefore, the percent decrease was 9,720 ÷ 22,998, or 42 percent.

(c) Since 20.0 + 18.3 + 13.1 and 22.1 + 21.8 + 11.3 are both greater than 50, statement I is true. The percent of special passenger complaints did remain the same from 1980 to 1981, but the *number* of special passenger complaints decreased because the total number of complaints decreased. Thus, statement II is false. The percents shown in the table for flight problems do in fact increase more than 2 percentage points. However, the *number* of flight problem complaints in 1980 was (0.2)(22,998), or 4,600, and the number in 1981 was (0.221)(13, 278), or 2,934. So, the number of flight problem complaints actually decreased from 1980 to 1981. Therefore, statement I is the only statement that can be inferred from the table.

DATA ANALYSIS EXERCISES

(Answers on page 111)

1. The daily temperatures, in degrees Fahrenheit, for 10 days in May were 61, 62, 65, 65, 65, 68, 74, 74, 75, and 77.

   (a) Find the mean, median, and mode for the temperatures.

   (b) If each day had been 7 degrees warmer, what would have been the mean, median, and mode for those 10 measurements?

2. The ages, in years, of the employees in a small company are 22, 33, 21, 28, 22, 31, 44, and 19.

   (a) Find the mean, median, and mode for the 8 ages.

   (b) Find the range and standard deviation for the 8 ages.

   (c) If each of the employees had been 10 years older, what would have been the range and standard deviation of their ages?

3. A group of 20 values has mean 85 and median 80. A different group of 30 values has mean 75 and median 72.

   (a) What is the mean of the 50 values?

   (b) What is the median of the 50 values?

4. Find the mean, median, mode, range, and standard deviation for x, given the frequency distribution below.

x	f
0	2
1	6
2	3
3	2
4	4

5. In the frequency distribution below, y represents age on last birthday for 40 people. Find the mean, median, mode, and range for y.

y	f
17	2
18	7
19	19
20	9
21	2
22	0
23	1

6. How many different ways can the letters in the word STUDY be ordered?

7. Martha invited 4 friends to go with her to the movies. There are 120 different ways in which they can sit together in a row. In how many of those ways is Martha sitting in the middle?

8. How many 3-digit numbers are odd and do not contain the digit "5"?

9. From a box of 10 light bulbs, 4 are to be removed. How many different sets of 4 bulbs could be removed?

10. A talent contest has 8 contestants. Judges must award prizes for first, second, and third places. If there are no ties, (a) how many different ways can the 3 prizes be awarded, and (b) how many different groups of 3 people can get prizes?

11. If the probability is 0.78 that Marshall will be late for work at least once next week, what is the probability that he will not be late for work next week?

12. If an integer is randomly selected from all positive 2-digit integers (i.e., the integers 10, 11, 12, . . . , 99), what is the probability that the integer chosen has

(a) a "4" in the tens place?

(b) at least one "4"?

(c) no "4s"?

13. In a box of 10 electrical parts, 2 are defective.

(a) If one part is chosen randomly from the box, what is the probability that it is not defective?

(b) If two parts are chosen randomly from the box, what is the probability that both are defective?

14. The table shows the distribution of a group of 40 college students by gender and class.

	Sophomores	Juniors	Seniors
Males	6	10	2
Females	10	9	3

If one student is randomly selected from this group, what is the probability that the student chosen is

(a) not a junior?

(b) a female or a sophomore?

(c) a male sophomore or a female senior?

15. $P(A \text{ or } B) = 0.60$ and $P(A) = 0.20$.

(a) Find $P(B)$ given that events A and B are mutually exclusive.

(b) Find $P(B)$ given that events A and B are independent.

16. Lin and Mark each attempt independently to decode a message. If the probability that Lin will decode the message is 0.8, and the probability that Mark will decode the message is 0.70, what is the probability that

(a) both will decode the message?

(b) at least one of them will decode the message?

(c) neither of them will decode the message?

17.

AVERAGE AND HIGH WIND SPEED FOR SELECTED STATIONS OVER A 10-YEAR PERIOD (1971-80) (miles per hour)		
Station	Average	High
Atlanta, GA	9.1	71
Boston, MA	12.6	65
Buffalo, NY	12.3	91
Chicago, IL	10.4	60
Cincinnati, OH	7.1	49
Denver, CO	9.0	56
Miami, FL	9.2	132
Montgomery, AL	6.7	72
New York, NY	9.4	70
Omaha, NE	10.8	109
Pittsburgh, PA	9.3	58
San Diego, CA	6.7	51
Washington, DC	9.3	78

SPEED AND OFFICIAL DESIGNATIONS OF WINDS	
Designation	Miles per Hour
Calm	Less than 1
Light air	1 to 3
Light breeze	4 to 7
Gentle breeze	8 to 12
Moderate breeze	13 to 18
Fresh breeze	19 to 24
Strong breeze	25 to 31
Near gale	32 to 38
Gale	39 to 46
Strong gale	47 to 54
Storm	55 to 63
Violent storm	64 to 73
Hurricane	74 and above

(a) Which station has a high wind speed which is the median of the high wind speeds for all the states listed?

(b) For those stations that have recorded hurricane winds at least once during the 10-year period, what is the arithmetic mean of their average wind speeds?

(c) For how many of the stations is the ratio of high wind speed to average wind speed greater than 10 to 1?

18.

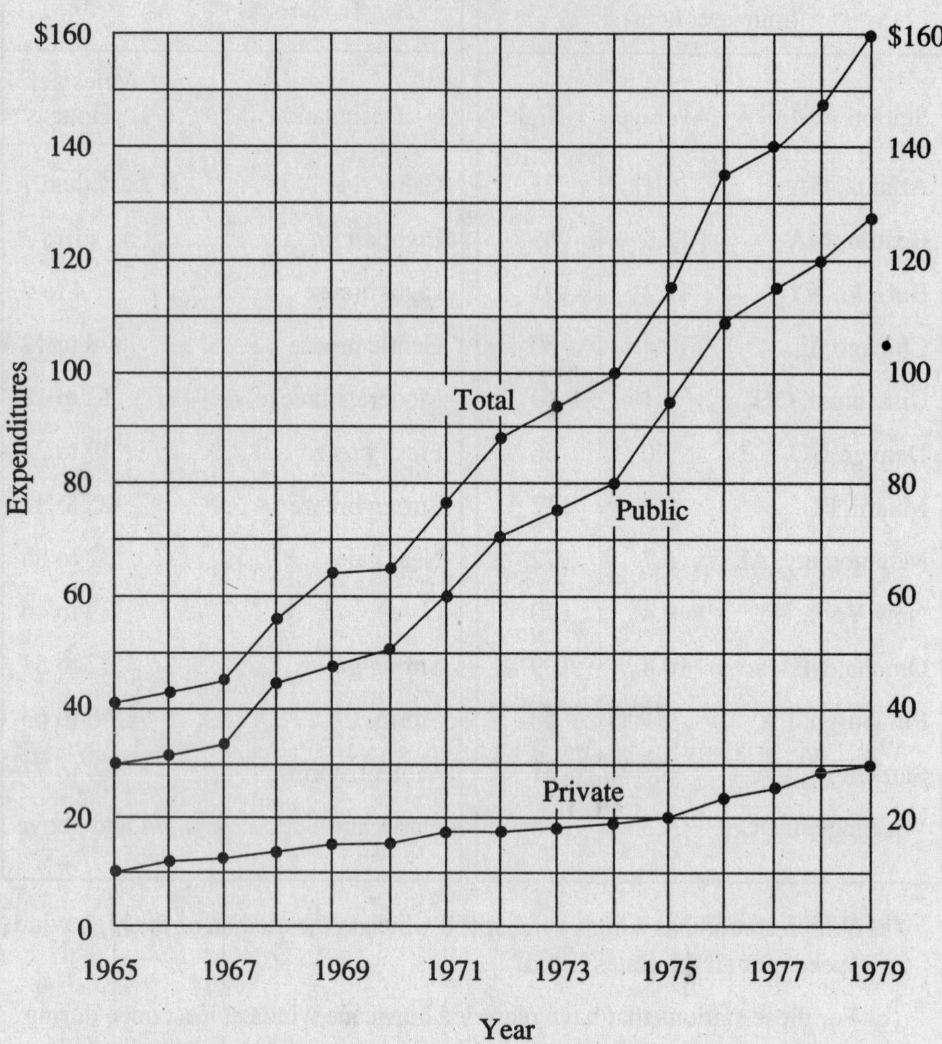

(a) In which year did total expenditures increase the most from the year before?

(b) In 1979 private school expenditures were approximately what percent of total expenditures?

19.

DISTRIBUTION OF WORK FORCE
BY OCCUPATIONAL CATEGORY FOR
COUNTRY *X* IN 1981 AND PROJECTED FOR 1995

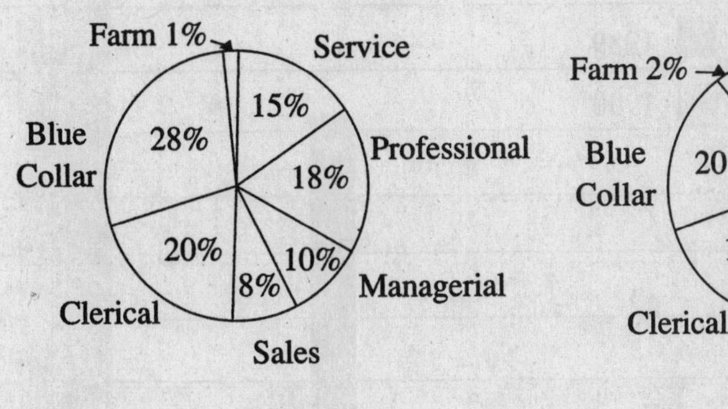

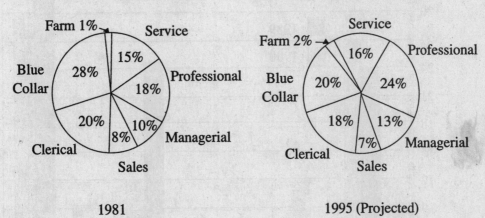

(a) In 1981, how many categories each comprised more than 25 million workers?

(b) What is the ratio of the number of workers in the Professional category in 1981 to the projected number of such workers in 1995?

(c) From 1981 to 1995, there is a projected increase in the number of workers in which of the following categories?

I. Sales

II. Service

III. Clerical

20.

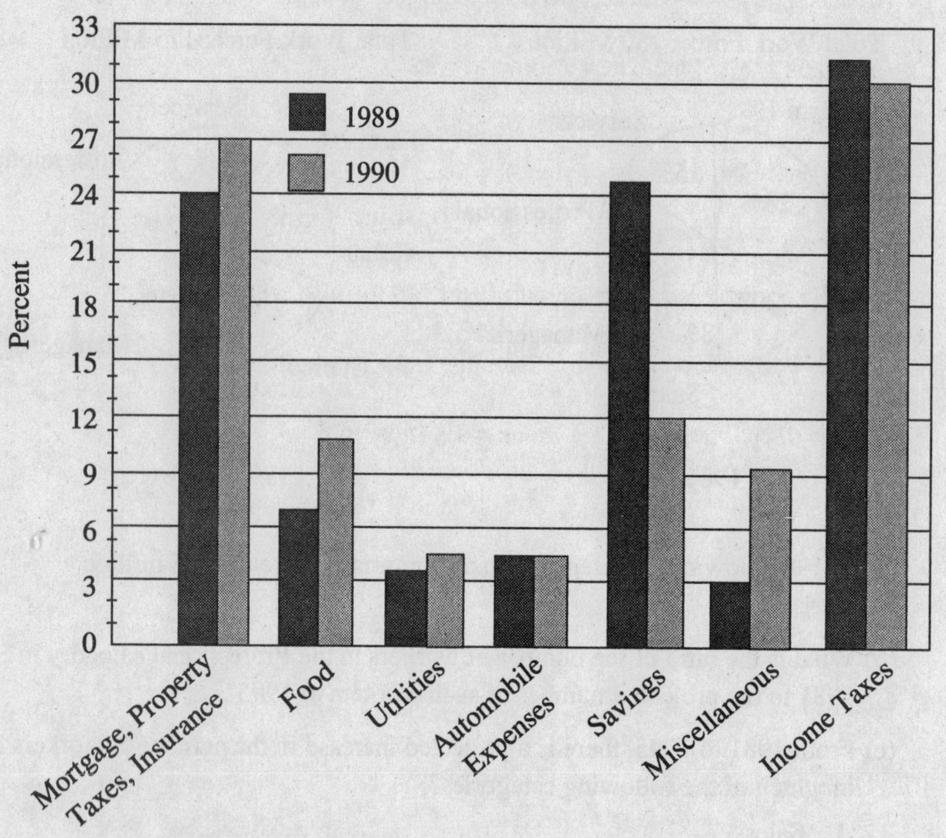

* In 1989, 100% = \$50,000
In 1990, 100% = \$45,000

(a) In 1989 Family *X* used a total of 49 percent of its gross annual income for two of the categories listed. What was the total amount of Family *X*'s income used for those same categories in 1990?

(b) Family *X*'s gross income is the sum of Mr. *X*'s income and Mrs. *X*'s income. In 1989 Mr. and Mrs. *X* each had an income of \$25,000. If Mr. *X*'s income increased by 10 percent from 1989 to 1990, by what percent did Mrs. *X*'s income decrease for the same period?

ANSWERS TO DATA ANALYSIS EXERCISES

1. (a) mean = 68.6, median = 66.5, mode = 65

   (b) Each measure would have been 7 degrees greater.

2. (a) mean = 27.5, median = 25, mode = 22

   (b) range = 25, standard deviation = 7.8

   (c) range = 25, standard deviation = 7.8

3. (a) mean = 79

   (b) The median cannot be determined from the information given.

4. mean = 2, median = 2, mode = 1, range = 4, standard deviation = 1.37

5. mean = 19.15, median = 19, mode = 19, range = 6

6. 120

7. 24

8. 288

9. 210

10. (a) 336 (b) 56

11. 0.22

12. (a) $\frac{1}{9}$ (b) $\frac{1}{5}$ (c) $\frac{4}{5}$

13. (a) $\frac{4}{5}$ (b) $\frac{1}{45}$

14. (a) $\frac{21}{40}$ (b) $\frac{7}{10}$ (c) $\frac{9}{40}$

15. (a) 0.40 (b) 0.50

16. (a) 0.56 (b) 0.94 (c) 0.06

17. (a) New York (b) 10.4 (c) 3

18. (a) 1976 (b) 19%

19. (a) 3 (b) 9 to 14, or 9/14 (c) I, II, and III

20. (a) $17,550 (b) 30%

FORM GRE 90-16

01

THE GRADUATE RECORD EXAMINATIONS®

General Test

Do not break the seal

until you are told to do so.

The contents of this test are confidential. Disclosure or reproduction of any portion of it is prohibited.

THIS TEST BOOK MUST NOT BE TAKEN FROM THE ROOM.

SECTION 1

Time—30 minutes

38 Questions

Directions: Each sentence below has one or two blanks, each blank indicating that something has been omitted. Beneath the sentence are five lettered words or sets of words. Choose the word or set of words for each blank that best fits the meaning of the sentence as a whole.

1. Agronomists are increasingly worried about "desertification," the phenomenon that is turning many of the world's ------- fields and pastures into ------- wastelands, unable to support the people living on them.

   (A) fertile. .barren
   (B) productive. .blooming
   (C) arid. .thriving
   (D) poorest. .marginal
   (E) largest. .saturated

2. Old beliefs die hard: even when jobs became -------, the long-standing fear that unemployment could return at a moment's notice -------.

   (A) vacant. .perished
   (B) easier. .changed
   (C) plentiful. .persisted
   (D) protected. .subsided
   (E) available. .receded

3. Intellectual ------- and flight from boredom have caused him to rush pell-mell into situations that less ------- spirits might hesitate to approach.

   (A) restlessness. .adventurous
   (B) agitation. .passive
   (C) resilience. .quiescent
   (D) tranquillity. .versatile
   (E) curiosity. .lethargic

4. Science advances in ------- spiral in that each new conceptual scheme ------- the phenomena explained by its predecessors and adds to those explanations.

   (A) a discontinuous . . . decries
   (B) a repetitive. .vitiates
   (C) a widening. .embraces
   (D) an anomalous. .captures
   (E) an explosive. .questions

5. Politeness is not a ------- attribute of human behavior, but rather a central virtue, one whose very existence is increasingly being ------- by the faddish requirement to "speak one's mind."

   (A) superficial. .threatened
   (B) pervasive. .undercut
   (C) worthless. .forestalled
   (D) precious. .repudiated
   (E) trivial. .affected

6. The painting was larger than it appeared to be, for, hanging in a darkened recess of the chapel, it was ------- by the perspective.

   (A) improved
   (B) aggrandized
   (C) embellished
   (D) jeopardized
   (E) diminished

7. Because folk art is neither completely rejected nor accepted as an art form by art historians, their final evaluations of it necessarily remain -------.

   (A) arbitrary
   (B) estimable
   (C) orthodox
   (D) unspoken
   (E) equivocal

GO ON TO THE NEXT PAGE.

Directions: In each of the following questions, a related pair of words or phrases is followed by five lettered pairs of words or phrases. Select the lettered pair that best expresses a relationship similar to that expressed in the original pair.

8. REFEREE : FIELD :: (A) scientist : results (B) mediator : deadlock (C) gladiator : contest (D) teacher : classroom (E) judge : courtroom

9. BLUSH : EMBARRASSMENT :: (A) scream : anger (B) smile : pleasure (C) laugh : outrage (D) love : sentimentality (E) whine : indecision

10. TANGO : DANCE ::
(A) arabesque : theme
(B) tonality : instrumentation
(C) rhyme : pattern
(D) stanza : line
(E) elegy : poem

11. CELL : MEMBRANE ::
(A) door : jamb
(B) yard : sidewalk
(C) seed : hull
(D) head : halo
(E) mountain : clouds

12. HYMN : PRAISE :: (A) waltz : joy (B) liturgy : rite (C) lullaby : child (D) dirge : grief (E) prayer : congregation

13. EMOLLIENT : SOOTHE ::
(A) dynamo : generate
(B) elevation : level
(C) precipitation : fall
(D) hurricane : track
(E) negative : expose

14. IMPLACABLE : COMPROMISE ::
(A) perfidious : conspire
(B) irascible : avenge
(C) honest : swindle
(D) amenable : deceive
(E) hasty : prevail

15. MISANTHROPE : PEOPLE ::
(A) patriot : country
(B) reactionary : government
(C) curmudgeon : children
(D) xenophobe : strangers
(E) miscreant : dogma

16. MILK : EXTRACT :: (A) squander : enjoy (B) exploit : utilize (C) research : investigate (D) hire : manage (E) wheedle : flatter

GO ON TO THE NEXT PAGE.

Directions: Each passage in this group is followed by questions based on its content. After reading a passage, choose the best answer to each question. Answer all questions following a passage on the basis of what is stated or implied in that passage.

Many critics of Emily Brontë's novel *Wuthering Heights* see its second part as a counterpoint that comments on, if it does not reverse, the first part, where a "romantic" reading receives more confirmation. Seeing the two parts as a whole is encouraged by the novel's sophisticated structure, revealed in its complex use of narrators and time shifts. Granted that the presence of these elements need not argue an authorial awareness of novelistic construction comparable to that of Henry James, their presence does encourage attempts to unify the novel's heterogeneous parts. However, any interpretation that seeks to unify all of the novel's diverse elements is bound to be somewhat unconvincing. This is not because such an interpretation necessarily stiffens into a thesis (although rigidity in any interpretation of this or of any novel is always a danger), but because *Wuthering Heights* has recalcitrant elements of undeniable power that, ultimately, resist inclusion in an all-encompassing interpretation. In this respect, *Wuthering Heights* shares a feature of *Hamlet*.

17. According to the passage, which of the following is a true statement about the first and second parts of *Wuthering Heights*?
    - (A) The second part has received more attention from critics.
    - (B) The second part has little relation to the first part.
    - (C) The second part annuls the force of the first part.
    - (D) The second part provides less substantiation for a "romantic" reading.
    - (E) The second part is better because it is more realistic.

18. Which of the following inferences about Henry James's awareness of novelistic construction is best supported by the passage?
    - (A) James, more than any other novelist, was aware of the difficulties of novelistic construction.
    - (B) James was very aware of the details of novelistic construction.
    - (C) James's awareness of novelistic construction derived from his reading of Brontë.
    - (D) James's awareness of novelistic construction has led most commentators to see unity in his individual novels.
    - (E) James's awareness of novelistic construction precluded him from violating the unity of his novels.

19. The author of the passage would be most likely to agree that an interpretation of a novel should
    - (A) not try to unite heterogeneous elements in the novel
    - (B) not be inflexible in its treatment of the elements in the novel
    - (C) not argue that the complex use of narrators or of time shifts indicates a sophisticated structure
    - (D) concentrate on those recalcitrant elements of the novel that are outside the novel's main structure
    - (E) primarily consider those elements of novelistic construction of which the author of the novel was aware

20. The author of the passage suggests which of the following about *Hamlet*?
    - I. *Hamlet* has usually attracted critical interpretations that tend to stiffen into theses.
    - II. *Hamlet* has elements that are not amenable to an all-encompassing critical interpretation.
    - III. *Hamlet* is less open to an all-encompassing critical interpretation than is *Wuthering Heights*.
    - IV. *Hamlet* has not received a critical interpretation that has been widely accepted by readers.

    - (A) I only
    - (B) II only
    - (C) I and IV only
    - (D) III and IV only
    - (E) I, II, and III only

GO ON TO THE NEXT PAGE.

The determination of the sources of copper ore used in the manufacture of copper and bronze artifacts of Bronze Age civilizations would add greatly to our knowledge of cultural contacts and trade in that era. Researchers have analyzed artifacts and ores for their concentrations of elements, but for a variety of reasons, these studies have generally failed to provide evidence of the sources of the copper used in the objects. Elemental composition can vary within the same copper-ore lode, usually because of varying admixtures of other elements, especially iron, lead, zinc, and arsenic. And high concentrations of cobalt or zinc, noticed in some artifacts, appear in a variety of copper-ore sources. Moreover, the processing of ores introduced poorly controlled changes in the concentrations of minor and trace elements in the resulting metal. Some elements evaporate during smelting and roasting; different temperatures and processes produce different degrees of loss. Finally, flux, which is sometimes added during smelting to remove waste material from the ore, could add quantities of elements to the final product.

An elemental property that is unchanged through these chemical processes is the isotopic composition of each metallic element in the ore. Isotopic composition, the percentages of the different isotopes of an element in a given sample of the element, is therefore particularly suitable as an indicator of the sources of the ore. Of course, for this purpose it is necessary to find an element whose isotopic composition is more or less constant throughout a given ore body, but varies from one copper ore body to another or, at least, from one geographic region to another.

The ideal choice, when isotopic composition is used to investigate the source of copper ore, would seem to be copper itself. It has been shown that small but measurable variations occur naturally in the isotopic composition of copper. However, the variations are large enough only in rare ores; between samples of the common ore minerals of copper, isotopic variations greater than the measurement error have not been found. An alternative choice is lead, which occurs in most copper and bronze artifacts of the Bronze Age in amounts consistent with the lead being derived from the copper ores and possibly from the fluxes. The isotopic composition of lead often varies from one source of common copper ore to another, with variations exceeding the measurement error; and preliminary studies indicate virtually uniform isotopic composition of the lead from a single copper-ore source. While some of the lead found in an artifact may have been introduced from flux or when other metals were added to the copper ore, lead so added in Bronze Age processing would usually have the same isotopic composition as the lead in the copper ore. Lead isotope studies may thus prove useful for interpreting the archaeological record of the Bronze Age.

21. The primary purpose of the passage is to
    (A) discuss the techniques of analyzing lead isotope composition
    (B) propose a way to determine the origin of the copper in certain artifacts
    (C) resolve a dispute concerning the analysis of copper ore
    (D) describe the deficiencies of a currently used method of chemical analysis of certain metals
    (E) offer an interpretation of the archaeological record of the Bronze Age

22. The author first mentions the addition of flux during smelting (lines 18-21) in order to
    (A) give a reason for the failure of elemental composition studies to determine ore sources
    (B) illustrate differences between various Bronze Age civilizations
    (C) show the need for using high smelting temperatures
    (D) illustrate the uniformity of lead isotope composition
    (E) explain the success of copper isotope composition analysis

23. The author suggests which of the following about a Bronze Age artifact containing high concentrations of cobalt or zinc?
    (A) It could not be reliably tested for its elemental composition.
    (B) It could not be reliably tested for its copper isotope composition.
    (C) It could not be reliably tested for its lead isotope composition.
    (D) It could have been manufactured from ore from any one of a variety of sources.
    (E) It could have been produced by the addition of other metals during the processing of the copper ore.

GO ON TO THE NEXT PAGE.

24. According to the passage, possible sources of the lead found in a copper or bronze artifact include which of the following?

I. The copper ore used to manufacture the artifact
II. Flux added during processing of the copper ore
III. Other metal added during processing of the copper ore

(A) I only
(B) II only
(C) III only
(D) II and III only
(E) I, II, and III

25. The author rejects copper as the "ideal choice" mentioned in line 33 because

(A) the concentration of copper in Bronze Age artifacts varies
(B) elements other than copper may be introduced during smelting
(C) the isotopic composition of copper changes during smelting
(D) among common copper ores, differences in copper isotope composition are too small
(E) within a single source of copper ore, copper isotope composition can vary substantially

26. The author makes which of the following statements about lead isotope composition?

(A) It often varies from one copper-ore source to another.
(B) It sometimes varies over short distances in a single copper-ore source.
(C) It can vary during the testing of artifacts, producing a measurement error.
(D) It frequently changes during smelting and roasting.
(E) It may change when artifacts are buried for thousands of years.

27. It can be inferred from the passage that the use of flux in processing copper ore can alter the lead isotope composition of the resulting metal EXCEPT when

(A) there is a smaller concentration of lead in the flux than in the copper ore
(B) the concentration of lead in the flux is equivalent to that of the lead in the ore
(C) some of the lead in the flux evaporates during processing
(D) any lead in the flux has the same isotopic composition as the lead in the ore
(E) other metals are added during processing

GO ON TO THE NEXT PAGE.

Directions: Each question below consists of a word printed in capital letters, followed by five lettered words or phrases. Choose the lettered word or phrase that is most nearly opposite in meaning to the word in capital letters.

Since some of the questions require you to distinguish fine shades of meaning, be sure to consider all the choices before deciding which one is best.

28. MUTTER: (A) please oneself (B) resolve conflict (C) speak distinctly (D) digress randomly (E) omit willingly

29. TRANSPARENT: (A) indelicate (B) neutral (C) opaque (D) somber (E) tangible

30. ENSEMBLE: (A) complement (B) cacophony (C) coordination (D) preface (E) solo

31. RETAIN: (A) allocate (B) distract (C) relegate (D) discard (E) misplace

32. RADIATE: (A) approach (B) cool (C) absorb (D) tarnish (E) vibrate

33. EPICURE:
(A) a person ignorant about art
(B) a person dedicated to a cause
(C) a person motivated by greed
(D) a person indifferent to food
(E) a person insensitive to emotions

34. PREVARICATION: (A) tact (B) consistency (C) veracity (D) silence (E) proof

35. AMORTIZE:
(A) loosen
(B) denounce
(C) suddenly increase one's indebtedness
(D) wisely cause to flourish
(E) grudgingly make provision for

36. EMACIATION: (A) invigoration (B) glorification (C) amelioration (D) inundation (E) magnification

37. UNALLOYED: (A) destabilized (B) unregulated (C) assimilated (D) adulterated (E) condensed

38. MINATORY: (A) reassuring (B) genuine (C) creative (D) obvious (E) awkward

STOP

IF YOU FINISH BEFORE TIME IS CALLED, YOU MAY CHECK YOUR WORK ON THIS SECTION ONLY. DO NOT TURN TO ANY OTHER SECTION IN THE TEST.

Section 2 starts on page 123.

NO TEST MATERIAL ON THIS PAGE

SECTION 2

Time—30 minutes

30 Questions

Numbers: All numbers used are real numbers.

Figures: Position of points, angles, regions, etc. can be assumed to be in the order shown; and angle measures can be assumed to be positive.

Lines shown as straight can be assumed to be straight.

Figures can be assumed to lie in a plane unless otherwise indicated.

Figures that accompany questions are intended to provide information useful in answering the questions. However, unless a note states that a figure is drawn to scale, you should solve these problems NOT by estimating sizes by sight or by measurement, but by using your knowledge of mathematics (see Example 2 below).

Directions: Each of the Questions 1-15 consists of two quantities, one in Column A and one in Column B. You are to compare the two quantities and choose

- A if the quantity in Column A is greater;
- B if the quantity in Column B is greater;
- C if the two quantities are equal;
- D if the relationship cannot be determined from the information given.

Note: Since there are only four choices, NEVER MARK (E).

Common Information: In a question, information concerning one or both of the quantities to be compared is centered above the two columns. A symbol that appears in both columns represents the same thing in Column A as it does in Column B.

	Column A	Column B	Sample Answers
Example 1:	2×6	$2 + 6$	● Ⓑ Ⓒ Ⓓ Ⓔ

Examples 2-4 refer to $\triangle PQR$.

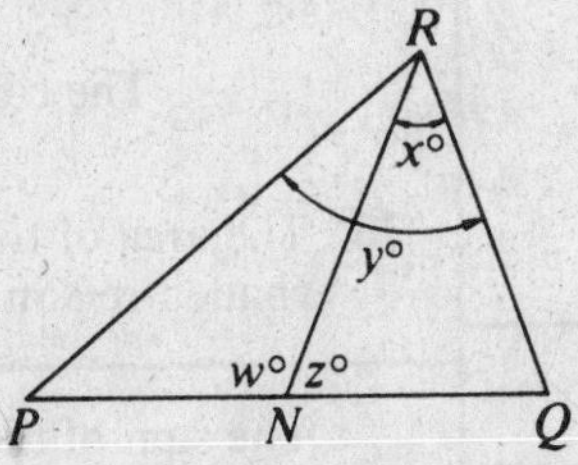

	Column A	Column B	Sample Answers
Example 2:	PN	NQ	Ⓐ Ⓑ Ⓒ ● Ⓔ (since equal measures cannot be assumed, even though PN and NQ appear equal)
Example 3:	x	y	Ⓐ ● Ⓒ Ⓓ Ⓔ (since N is between P and Q)
Example 4:	$w + z$	180	Ⓐ Ⓑ ● Ⓓ Ⓔ (since PQ is a straight line)

GO ON TO THE NEXT PAGE.

A if the quantity in Column A is greater;
B if the quantity in Column B is greater;
C if the two quantities are equal;
D if the relationship cannot be determined from the information given.

	Column A	Column B
1.	$5[(2 + 2) + 5]$	50

$j - k = 2$
$k - 6 = 4$

	Column A	Column B
2.	j	10

Richard's salary, which is greater than $10,000, is 75 percent of Sandra's salary. Ted's salary is 80 percent of Richard's salary.

	Column A	Column B
3.	Sandra's salary	Ted's salary
4.	$\frac{5}{3} \times 0.60$	1

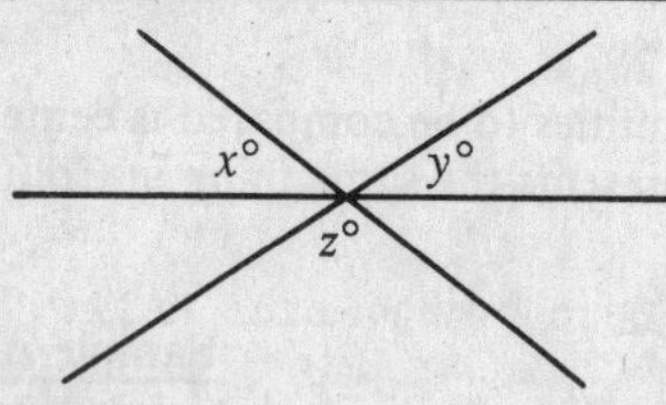

	Column A	Column B
5.	$x + y$	$180 - z$

On a trip, Marie drove 200 miles in 5 hours using gasoline that cost her $1.49 per gallon.

	Column A	Column B
6.	Marie's average speed for the trip in miles per hour	Marie's gas mileage for the trip in miles per gallon
7.	$\sqrt{100 + 36}$	16

The average (arithmetic mean) of 12 and 20 is equal to the average (arithmetic mean) of 15 and x.

	Column A	Column B
8.	x	16

The total surface area of cube C equals 150.

	Column A	Column B
9.	The length of one edge of cube C	4.5
10.	$x + 32y$	$32x + y$

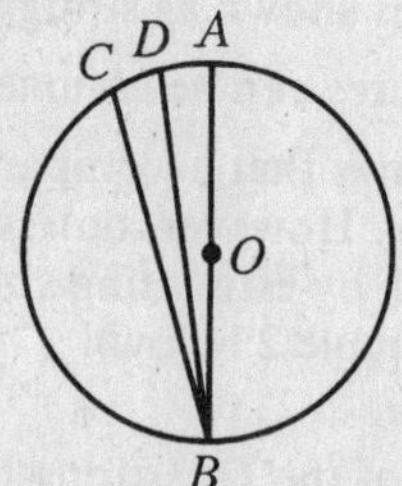

O is the center of the circle.

	Column A	Column B
11.	AB	The average (arithmetic mean) of CB and DB
12.	$(x - 1)(x + 1)$	x^2

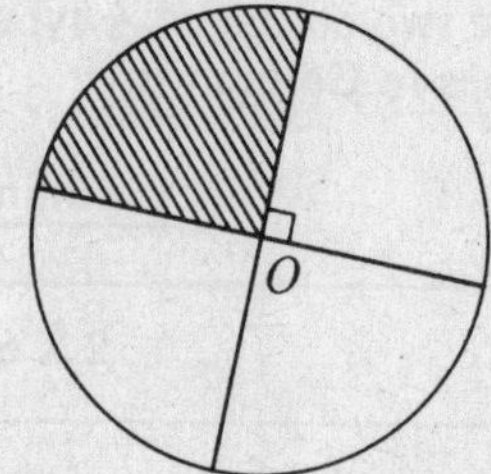

The circle has center O and radius 1.

	Column A	Column B
13.	The area of the shaded region	$\frac{\pi}{2}$

The sum of the lengths of two sides of isosceles triangle K is 7. K has a side of length 4.

	Column A	Column B
14.	The perimeter of K	11

S is the set of all fractions of the form $\frac{n}{n + 1}$, where n is a positive integer less than 20.

	Column A	Column B
15.	The product of all the fractions that are in S	$\frac{1}{20}$

GO ON TO THE NEXT PAGE.

Directions: Each of the Questions 16-30 has five answer choices. For each of these questions, select the best of the answer choices given.

---

16. 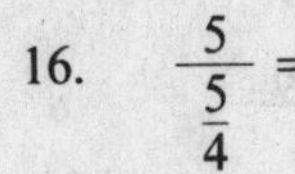
$\frac{5}{\frac{5}{4}} =$

(A) $\frac{1}{5}$

(B) $\frac{1}{4}$

(C) 4

(D) 5

(E) $\frac{25}{4}$

17. A 12-inch ruler is marked off in sixteenths of an inch. What is the distance, in inches, from the zero mark to the 111th mark after the zero mark?

(A) $6\frac{1}{4}$

(B) $6\frac{15}{16}$

(C) $7\frac{3}{4}$

(D) $9\frac{1}{4}$

(E) $11\frac{1}{16}$

18. If $(2x - 1)^2 = 0$, then $x =$

(A) $-\frac{1}{4}$

(B) $-\frac{1}{2}$

(C) 0

(D) $\frac{1}{2}$

(E) $\frac{1}{4}$

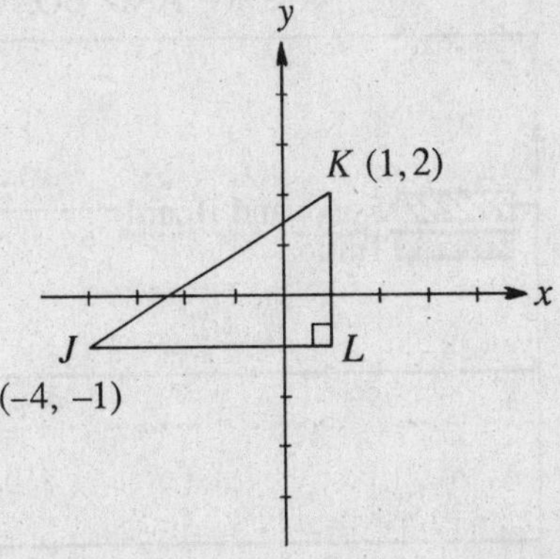

19. In the figure above, if JL and KL are parallel to the x and y axes, respectively, what is the area of $\triangle JKL$?

(A) 4.5
(B) 5
(C) 7.5
(D) 8
(E) 15

20. Which of the following is equal to 25,000,000 ?

(A) 25×10^7
(B) 2.5×10^{-7}
(C) $(2 \times 10^6) + (5 \times 10^5)$
(D) $(20 \times 10^{-7}) + (5 \times 10^{-6})$
(E) $(2 \times 10^7) + (5 \times 10^6)$

GO ON TO THE NEXT PAGE.

Questions 21-25 refer to the following graph. In these questions, all references to *charges* should be interpreted as the *average annual charges* shown on the graph.

AVERAGE ANNUAL TOTAL CHARGES* FOR UNDERGRADUATE TUITION, ROOM, AND BOARD AT AMERICAN COLLEGES, 1974 - 1984

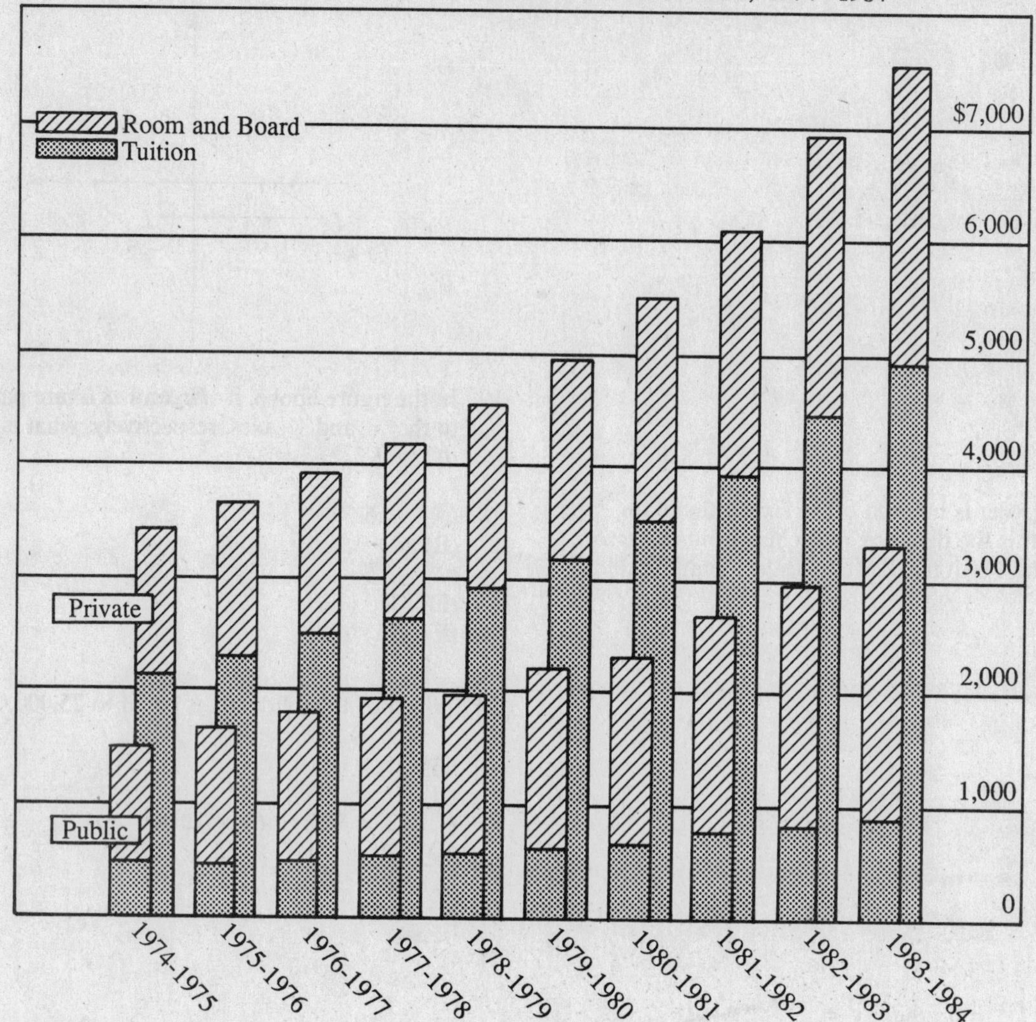

*The total charge consists of room, board, and tuition.

Note: Drawn to scale.

GO ON TO THE NEXT PAGE.

21. In which school year shown was the total charge for undergraduate tuition, room, and board at public colleges most nearly equal to \$3,000 ?

(A) 1983-1984
(B) 1982-1983
(C) 1981-1982
(D) 1980-1981
(E) 1979-1980

22. Which of the following charges increased by less than \$1,000 from the first to the last of the ten years represented on the graph?

(A) Tuition at public colleges
(B) Room and board at public colleges
(C) Total charge at public colleges
(D) Tuition at private colleges
(E) Total charge at private colleges

23. For how many of the school years shown was the total charge at private colleges at least \$3,000 more than the total charge at public colleges?

(A) Two
(B) Three
(C) Four
(D) Five
(E) Six

24. In the 1978-1979 school year, the ratio of the total charge at private colleges to the total charge at public colleges was closest to

(A) $\frac{5}{3}$

(B) $\frac{9}{5}$

(C) $\frac{2}{1}$

(D) $\frac{9}{4}$

(E) $\frac{3}{1}$

25. For the school year in which the charge for room and board at public colleges was most nearly equal to \$2,000, what was the approximate charge for tuition at private colleges?

(A) \$750
(B) \$3,500
(C) \$3,900
(D) \$4,500
(E) \$4,900

GO ON TO THE NEXT PAGE.

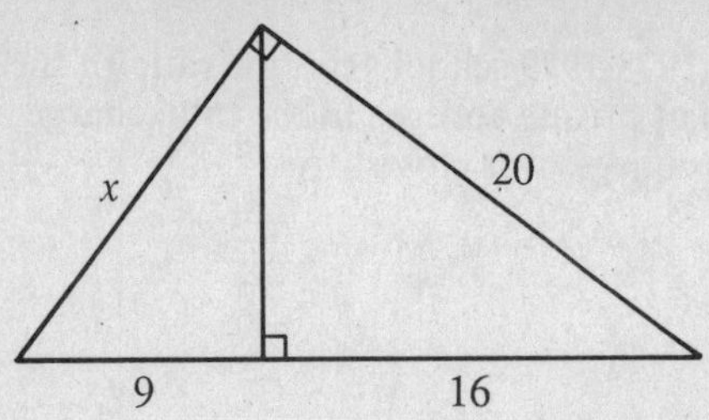

26. What is the value of x in the figure above?

(A) 12
(B) 12.5
(C) 15
(D) $9\sqrt{3}$
(E) 18

27. The number 10^{30} is divisible by all of the following EXCEPT

(A) 250
(B) 125
(C) 32
(D) 16
(E) 6

28. If $3x + 1$ represents an odd integer, which of the following represents the next larger odd integer?

(A) $3(x + 1)$
(B) $3(x + 2)$
(C) $3(x + 3)$
(D) $3x + 2$
(E) $3(x + 2) + 1$

29. In the sequence of numbers x_1, x_2, x_3, x_4, x_5, each number after the first is twice the preceding number. If $x_5 - x_1$ is 20, what is the value of x_1?

(A) $\frac{4}{3}$

(B) $\frac{5}{4}$

(C) 2

(D) $\frac{5}{2}$

(E) 4

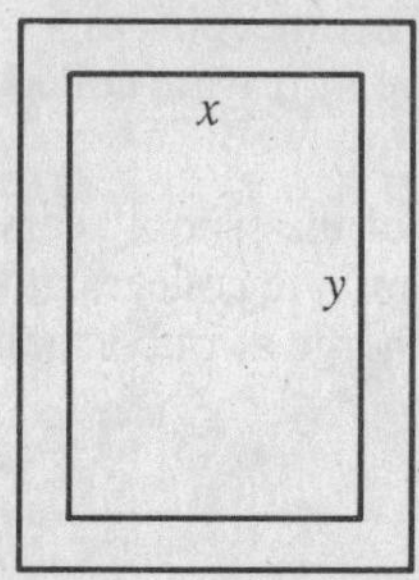

30. The rectangular garden represented in the figure above, with dimensions x feet by y feet, is surrounded by a walkway 2 feet wide. Which of the following represents the area of the walkway, in square feet?

(A) $2x + 2y + 4$
(B) $2x + 2y + 16$
(C) $4x + 4y + 8$
(D) $4x + 4y + 16$
(E) $4x + 4y + 32$

STOP

IF YOU FINISH BEFORE TIME IS CALLED, YOU MAY CHECK YOUR WORK ON THIS SECTION ONLY. DO NOT TURN TO ANY OTHER SECTION IN THE TEST.

Section 3 starts on page 130.

SECTION 3

Time—30 minutes

25 Questions

Directions: Each question or group of questions is based on a passage or set of conditions. In answering some of the questions, it may be useful to draw a rough diagram. For each question, select the best answer choice given.

Questions 1-7

At an art show, exactly five sculptures are to be displayed in a room with exactly five stands, arranged along a single wall and numbered consecutively 1 through 5. The sculptures are to be selected from a total of eight sculptures—M, N, P, Q, R, S, T, and U—and displayed, one sculpture on each stand, according to the following conditions:

Either M or U or both must be selected.
If M is selected, M must be on stand 1.
Either R or S must be on stand 3.
If T is selected, P must also be selected, and T and P must then be on stands that are immediately adjacent to one another.

1. Which of the following is an acceptable selection of sculptures to be displayed on stands 1 through 5 ?

	1	2	3	4	5
(A)	M	R	T	P	Q
(B)	N	T	S	U	Q
(C)	P	T	S	R	U
(D)	T	P	R	S	M
(E)	U	N	Q	P	T

2. If S is on stand 1, which of the following must be true?

(A) P is on stand 4.
(B) R is on stand 3.
(C) T is on stand 2.
(D) T is on stand 4.
(E) U is on stand 5.

3. If T is on stand 5, which of the following pairs of sculptures can be on stands that are immediately adjacent to each other?

(A) M and P
(B) Q and N
(C) Q and P
(D) R and T
(E) U and R

4. If U is on stand 4, any of the following can be on stand 5 EXCEPT

(A) N
(B) P
(C) Q
(D) R
(E) T

5. If T is on stand 2, which of the following sculptures must be selected?

(A) M
(B) N
(C) R
(D) S
(E) U

6. If P is not selected and R is on stand 1, which of the following lists, in alphabetical order, those sculptures that must also be selected?

(A) M, Q, T, and U
(B) N, Q, S, and T
(C) N, Q, S, and U
(D) N, S, T, and U
(E) Q, S, T, and U

7. If Q is displayed on a stand immediately adjacent to a stand on which R is displayed and immediately adjacent to a stand on which S is displayed, which of the following must be true?

(A) N is on either stand 4 or stand 5.
(B) Q is on either stand 2 or stand 4.
(C) R is on either stand 1 or stand 3.
(D) S is on either stand 3 or stand 5.
(E) U is on either stand 2 or stand 4.

GO ON TO THE NEXT PAGE.

8. For three years, while constructing a new elementary school, the Middletown school board has been sending large numbers of students from the town of Middletown to both Crestwood and Lynbrook elementary schools in the town of Edgewood. Therefore, when Middletown's new elementary school is completed next year, either Crestwood or Lynbrook will have to be closed and their student populations consolidated.

   The argument above presupposes that

   (A) withdrawal of the Middletown students from the Crestwood and Lynbrook schools will leave one or both of these schools seriously underpopulated
   (B) Middletown's new elementary school will be too small for the projected student population
   (C) the Middletown students represent only a small fraction of the total student populations at both Crestwood and Lynbrook schools
   (D) absorption of extra students from Middletown has placed a serious strain on the resources of both Crestwood and Lynbrook schools
   (E) students will not transfer between the Crestwood and Lynbrook schools in the next twelve months

9. During his three years in office, the governor of a state has frequently been accused of having sexist attitudes toward women. Yet he has filled five of the nineteen vacant high-level positions in his administration with women appointees, all of whom are still serving. This shows that the governor is not sexist.

   Which of the following statements, if true, would most seriously weaken the conclusion above?

   (A) One of the women appointed by the governor to a high-level position is planning to resign her post.
   (B) The platform of the governor's political party required him to appoint at least five women to high-level positions.
   (C) Forty-seven percent of the women who voted in the state gubernatorial election three years ago voted for the governor.
   (D) A governor of a neighboring state recently appointed seven women to high-level positions.
   (E) The governor appointed two Black Americans, two Hispanic Americans, and one Asian American to high-level positions in his administration.

10. Proportionally, more persons diagnosed as having the brain disorder schizophrenia were born in the winter months than at any other time of year. A recent study suggests that the cause may have been the nutrient-poor diets of some expectant mothers during the coldest months of the year, when it was hardest for people to get, or afford, a variety of fresh foods.

    Which of the following, if true, helps to support the conclusion presented above?

    (A) Over the years the number of cases of schizophrenia has not shown a correlation with degree of economic distress.
    (B) Most of the development of brain areas affected in schizophrenia occurs during the last month of the mother's pregnancy.
    (C) Suicide rates are significantly higher in winter than in any other season.
    (D) The nutrients in fresh foods have the same effects on the development of the brain as do the nutrients in preserved foods.
    (E) A sizable proportion of the patients involved in the study have a history of schizophrenia in the family.

GO ON TO THE NEXT PAGE.

Questions 11-15

From time to time, the managing director of a company appoints planning committees, each consisting of exactly three members. Eligible for appointment are three executives from Finance—F, G, and H—and three executives from Operations—K, L, and M. Any given committee is subject to the following restrictions on appointments:

At least one member must be from Finance, and at least one member must be from Operations.
If F is appointed, G cannot be appointed.
Neither H nor L can be appointed unless the other is appointed also.
If K is appointed, M must also be appointed.

11. Which of the following is an acceptable committee?

(A) F, H, and M
(B) G, L, and M
(C) H, K, and L
(D) H, L, and M
(E) K, L, and M

12. If appointees from Finance are in the majority on a committee, that committee must include

(A) F
(B) G
(C) K
(D) L
(E) M

13. If appointees from Operations are in the majority on a committee, that committee must include

(A) F
(B) G
(C) K
(D) L
(E) M

14. If F is appointed to the same committee as M, which of the following will be true of that committee?

(A) Appointees from Finance are in the majority.
(B) Appointees from Operations are in the majority.
(C) G is a committee member.
(D) L is a committee member.
(E) K is not a committee member.

15. If the restrictions on appointments apply also to a four-member committee appointed from the same group of executives, which of the following will be true?

(A) If F is appointed, M must also be appointed.
(B) If G is appointed, K must also be appointed.
(C) If H is appointed, F must also be appointed.
(D) If L is appointed, G must also be appointed.
(E) If M is appointed, K must also be appointed.

GO ON TO THE NEXT PAGE.

Questions 16-18

A psychologist has designed an experiment that involves running five mice—F, G, J, K, and M—through a maze that is connected to five compartments—1, 2, 3, 4, and 5. The psychologist places each mouse in one of the five compartments. When a bell is rung, each mouse leaves its compartment, runs through the maze, and enters or reenters one of the five compartments. At no point is there more than one mouse in any compartment.

When the bell is rung, any mouse placed in 4 always goes to 2, and any mouse placed in 2 always goes to 4.

When the bell is rung, any mouse placed in 5 always goes to 3, and any mouse placed in 3 always goes to 5.

The psychologist has designed the experiment such that, after the mice have run through the maze, the following outcomes always obtain:

M is neither in 3 nor in 4.
If J is in 1, K is in 2.
If M is in 2, K is in 5.

16. Which of the following is a possible distribution of the mice after they have run through the maze?

	1	2	3	4	5
(A)	J	K	M	F	G
(B)	G	M	K	J	F
(C)	F	J	G	M	K
(D)	J	M	F	K	G
(E)	M	K	G	F	J

17. If M is in 2 after the mice have run through the maze, K must have been in which of the following before running through the maze?

(A) 1
(B) 2
(C) 3
(D) 4
(E) 5

18. If F is in 5 after the mice have run through the maze, M must have been in which of the following before running through the maze?

(A) 1
(B) 2
(C) 3
(D) 4
(E) 5

GO ON TO THE NEXT PAGE.

Questions 19-22

A detective watching suspects Q, R, S, and T and their movements in and out of a downtown building has made the following observations:

Every day, each of the suspects enters, and later leaves, the building exactly once.
No suspect ever enters or leaves the building together with another suspect.
No suspect ever leaves the building in the same position—first, second, third, or fourth—in which he or she entered the building.
Both in entering the building and in leaving it, R is always earlier than S.

19. Which of the following could be the order, from first to last, in which the suspects leave the building on a day on which they enter it in the order T, Q, R, S?

(A) Q, R, S, T
(B) Q, R, T, S
(C) R, Q, S, T
(D) S, T, Q, R
(E) T, R, S, Q

20. If, on a certain day, Q and T enter the building second and third, respectively, and Q also leaves the building before T does, the order in which the suspects leave the building, from first to fourth, must be

(A) Q, R, S, T
(B) Q, R, T, S
(C) Q, T, R, S
(D) R, Q, S, T
(E) R, S, Q, T

21. On a day on which the two suspects who enter the building first are also the two suspects who leave it first, the last two suspects to enter the building could be

(A) Q and R
(B) Q and T
(C) R and S
(D) R and T
(E) S and T

22. On a day on which R enters the building second and T enters it third, which of the following must be true?

(A) Q leaves the building first.
(B) Q leaves the building third.
(C) R leaves the building first.
(D) S leaves the building third.
(E) T leaves the building second.

GO ON TO THE NEXT PAGE.

23. The primary schools in a city range from one to six stories in height. If a classroom in a primary school is above the second floor, it must have a fireproof door.

If the statements above are true, which of the following statements must also be true about primary-school rooms in the city?

(A) Some third-floor rooms in primary schools do not have fireproof doors.
(B) No second-floor classrooms in primary schools have fireproof doors.
(C) In primary schools, rooms above the second floor that are not classrooms do not have fireproof doors.
(D) Any fourth-floor classrooms in primary schools have fireproof doors.
(E) Primary schools with classrooms on the first floor only do not have any fireproof doors.

24. It is sometimes held that computer scientists would make better progress in developing sophisticated artificial-intelligence programs if only they knew more about how human beings think. This view is, however, open to the objection that not a single major step forward in airplane design has come from any insights into the nature of bird flight.

The objection above draws on an analogy that assumes that artificial-intelligence programs are similar to which of the following?

(A) Theories of human thought
(B) Blueprints for airplanes
(C) Hypotheses about how science achieves progress
(D) Computer simulations of birds in flight
(E) Research into the nature of bird flight

25. Two hundred corporations with net incomes of more than $122 million each accounted for 77 percent of total corporate gifts to United States higher education in 1985. That year, 26 percent of total corporate gifts to United States higher education came from 14 Japanese corporations, each of which received income from 27 or more countries.

If the statements above are true, which of the following must also be true?

(A) Most of the net income earned by the 14 Japanese corporations was earned outside of Japan.
(B) Individuals contributed 23 percent of total gifts to United States higher education in 1985.
(C) Gifts from corporations accounted for more than half of the total contributions to United States higher education in 1985.
(D) One or more of the 200 corporations with more than $122 million in net income received income from 27 or more countries.
(E) Most of the 14 Japanese corporations earned more than $122 million in net income in 1985.

STOP

IF YOU FINISH BEFORE TIME IS CALLED, YOU MAY CHECK YOUR WORK ON THIS SECTION ONLY. DO NOT TURN TO ANY OTHER SECTION IN THE TEST.

SECTION 4

Time—30 minutes

30 Questions

Numbers: All numbers used are real numbers.

Figures: Position of points, angles, regions, etc. can be assumed to be in the order shown; and angle measures can be assumed to be positive.

Lines shown as straight can be assumed to be straight.

Figures can be assumed to lie in a plane unless otherwise indicated.

Figures that accompany questions are intended to provide information useful in answering the questions. However, unless a note states that a figure is drawn to scale, you should solve these problems NOT by estimating sizes by sight or by measurement, but by using your knowledge of mathematics (see Example 2 below).

Directions: Each of the Questions 1-15 consists of two quantities, one in Column A and one in Column B. You are to compare the two quantities and choose

A if the quantity in Column A is greater;
B if the quantity in Column B is greater;
C if the two quantities are equal;
D if the relationship cannot be determined from the information given.

Note: Since there are only four choices, NEVER MARK (E).

Common Information: In a question, information concerning one or both of the quantities to be compared is centered above the two columns. A symbol that appears in both columns represents the same thing in Column A as it does in Column B.

	Column A	Column B	Sample Answers
Example 1:	2×6	$2 + 6$	● Ⓑ Ⓒ Ⓓ Ⓔ

Examples 2-4 refer to $\triangle PQR$.

R, x°, y°, w°, z°, P, N, Q

	Column A	Column B	Sample Answers
Example 2:	PN	NQ	Ⓐ Ⓑ Ⓒ ● Ⓔ (since equal measures cannot be assumed, even though PN and NQ appear equal)
Example 3:	x	y	Ⓐ ● Ⓒ Ⓓ Ⓔ (since N is between P and Q)
Example 4:	$w + z$	180	Ⓐ Ⓑ ● Ⓓ Ⓔ (since PQ is a straight line)

GO ON TO THE NEXT PAGE.

A if the quantity in Column A is greater;
B if the quantity in Column B is greater;
C if the two quantities are equal;
D if the relationship cannot be determined from the information given.

	Column A	Column B

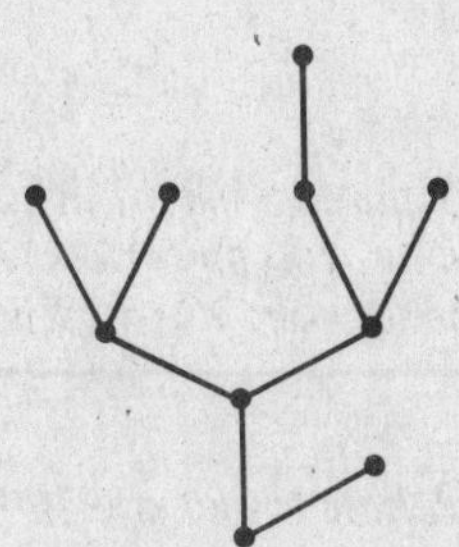

Each •——• represents a connection and each • represents a joint.

	Column A	Column B
1.	The total number of joints	The total number of connections

$y = \frac{3x}{4}$, $x = \frac{2z}{3}$, and $z = 20$.

	Column A	Column B
2.	y	11

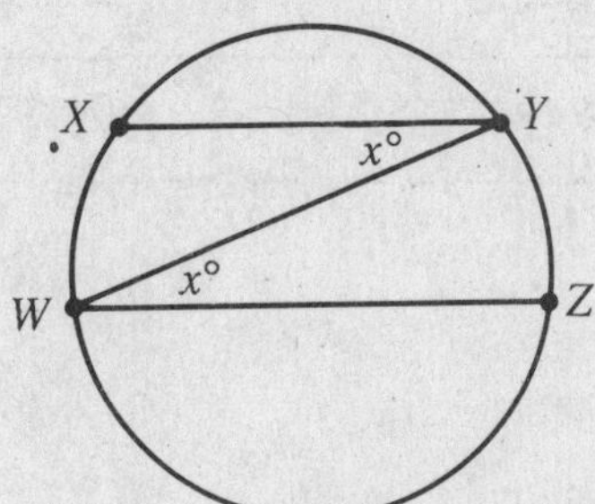

	Column A	Column B
3.	The length of minor arc WX of the circle	The length of minor arc YZ of the circle
4.	0.203×10^2	2.03×10
5.	40 percent of \$250	80 percent of \$125

	Column A	Column B

$x \neq 0$

	Column A	Column B
6.	$3x^2$	$(3x)^2$
7.	The greatest prime factor of 15	The greatest prime factor of 14
8.	The total savings on 20 gallons of gasoline purchased for \$1.169 per gallon instead of \$1.259 per gallon.	\$1.80

Three ships, X, Y, and Z, are near the equator. X is 8 miles due west of Z, and Y is 7 miles due north of Z.

	Column A	Column B
9.	The distance between X and Y	9 miles

B
30°
A
6
C

	Column A	Column B
10.	AB	BC

A retail business has determined that its net income, in terms of x, the number of items sold, is given by the expression $x^2 + x - 380$.

	Column A	Column B
11.	The number of items that must be sold for the net income to be zero	10

GO ON TO THE NEXT PAGE.

A if the quantity in Column A is greater;
B if the quantity in Column B is greater;
C if the two quantities are equal;
D if the relationship cannot be determined from the information given.

	Column A	Column B
	Rectangular region R has area 30.	
12.	The perimeter of R	25

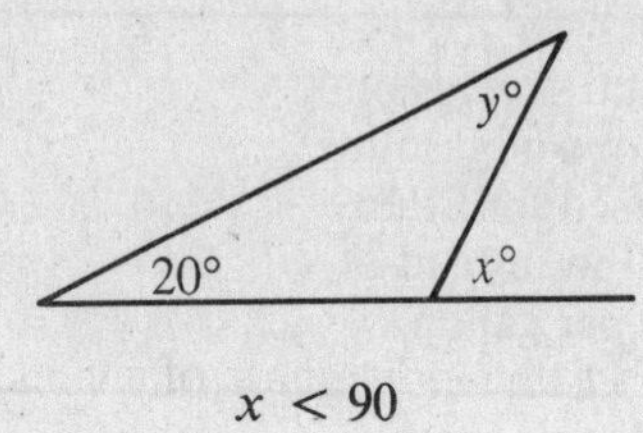

$x < 90$

	Column A	Column B
13.	y	70

	Column A	Column B
	$x^2 = 16$ $y^3 = 64$	
14.	x	y
15.	$\frac{2^{30} - 2^{29}}{2}$	2^{28}

GO ON TO THE NEXT PAGE.

Directions: Each of the Questions 16-30 has five answer choices. For each of these questions, select the best of the answer choices given.

16. A certain post office imposes a service charge of \$0.75 per order on any money order in the amount of \$25.00 or less, and \$1.00 per order on any money order in an amount from \$25.01 through \$700.00. If Dan purchases 3 money orders in the amounts of \$18.25, \$25.00, and \$127.50, what is the total service charge for his money orders?

(A) \$1.75
(B) \$2.25
(C) \$2.50
(D) \$2.75
(E) \$3.00

17. If $\frac{1}{4}(1 - x) = \frac{1}{16}$, then $x =$

(A) $\frac{15}{64}$

(B) $\frac{1}{4}$

(C) $\frac{3}{4}$

(D) $\frac{15}{16}$

(E) 4

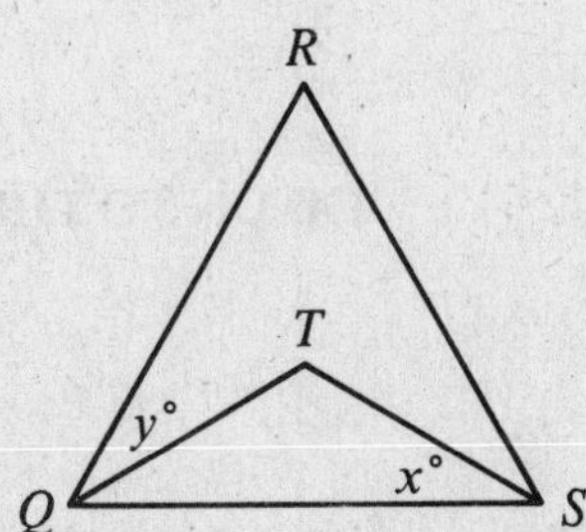

Note: Figure not drawn to scale.

18. In the figure above, QRS is an equilateral triangle and QTS is an isosceles triangle. If $x = 47$, what is the value of y?

(A) 13
(B) 23
(C) 30
(D) 47
(E) 53

19. $\frac{m + n}{4 + 5} =$

(A) $\frac{m + n}{4} + \frac{m + n}{5}$

(B) $\frac{m + n}{9} + \frac{m + n}{9}$

(C) $\frac{m}{5} + \frac{n}{4}$

(D) $\frac{m}{4} + \frac{n}{5}$

(E) $\frac{m}{9} + \frac{n}{9}$

20. What is the circumference of a circle with radius 8 ?

(A) $\frac{8}{\pi}$

(B) $\frac{16}{\pi}$

(C) 8π

(D) 16π

(E) 64π

GO ON TO THE NEXT PAGE.

Questions 21-25 refer to the following graph.

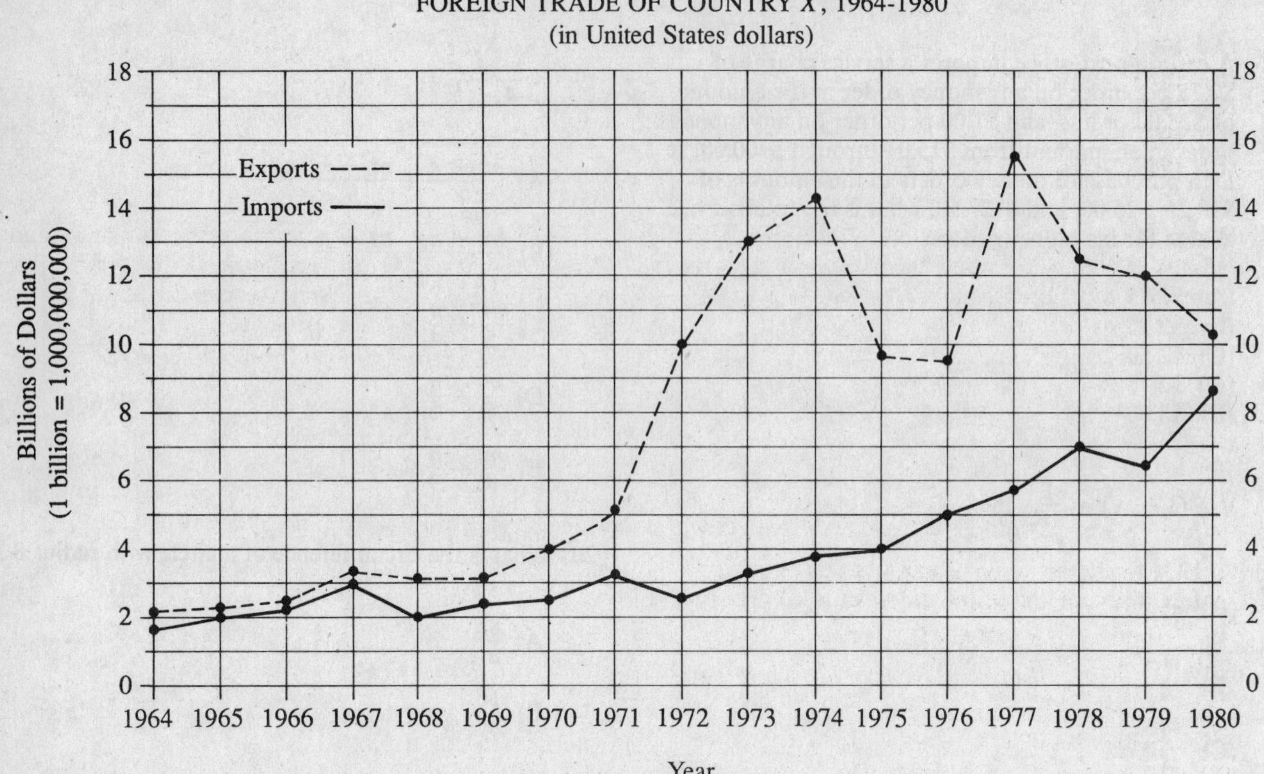

Note: Drawn to scale.

GO ON TO THE NEXT PAGE.

21. For which year shown on the graph did exports exceed the previous year's exports by the greatest dollar amount?

(A) 1972
(B) 1973
(C) 1975
(D) 1977
(E) 1980

22. Which of the following is closest to the amount, in billions of dollars, by which the increase in exports from 1971 to 1972 exceeds the increase in exports from 1972 to 1973 ?

(A) 1.9
(B) 3.9
(C) 5.0
(D) 6.1
(E) 8.0

23. In 1974 the dollar value of imports was approximately what percent of the dollar value of exports?

(A) 4%
(B) 17%
(C) 27%
(D) 79%
(E) 367%

24. For how many years shown on the graph did exports exceed imports by more than 5 billion dollars?

(A) Nine
(B) Seven
(C) Six
(D) Five
(E) Four

25. If it were discovered that the import dollar amount shown for 1978 was incorrect and should have been \$5.3 billion instead, then the average (arithmetic mean) import dollar amount per year for the 17 years would be how much less?

(A) \$100 million
(B) \$53 million
(C) \$47 million
(D) \$17 million
(E) \$7 million

GO ON TO THE NEXT PAGE.

26. On the number line, 1.4 is halfway between which of the following pairs of numbers?

(A) -1.4 and 2.4
(B) -1 and 2
(C) -0.3 and 3.1
(D) 0.15 and 1.55
(E) 0.4 and 1

27. If a and b are both positive even integers, which of the following must be even?

I. a^b
II. $(a + 1)^b$
III. $a^{(b + 1)}$

(A) I only
(B) II only
(C) I and II only
(D) I and III only
(E) I, II, and III

28. If t tablets cost c cents, then at this rate how many cents will 5 tablets cost?

(A) $5ct$
(B) $\frac{5c}{t}$
(C) $\frac{c}{5t}$
(D) $\frac{5t}{c}$
(E) $\frac{t}{5c}$

29. If a rectangular block that is 4 inches by 4 inches by 10 inches is placed inside a right circular cylinder of radius 3 inches and height 10 inches, the volume of the unoccupied portion of the cylinder is how many cubic inches?

(A) $6\pi - 16$
(B) $9\pi - 16$
(C) $160 - 30\pi$
(D) $60\pi - 160$
(E) $90\pi - 160$

$$x - y + z = 0$$
$$2x + y + 3z = 0$$

30. In the system of equations above, if $z \neq 0$, then the ratio of x to z is

(A) $-\frac{2}{1}$
(B) $-\frac{4}{3}$
(C) $-\frac{1}{2}$
(D) $\frac{3}{4}$
(E) $\frac{4}{3}$

STOP

IF YOU FINISH BEFORE TIME IS CALLED, YOU MAY CHECK YOUR WORK ON THIS SECTION ONLY. DO NOT TURN TO ANY OTHER SECTION IN THE TEST.

Section 5 starts on page 145.

NO TEST MATERIAL ON THIS PAGE

SECTION 5

Time—30 minutes

38 Questions

Directions: Each sentence below has one or two blanks, each blank indicating that something has been omitted. Beneath the sentence are five lettered words or sets of words. Choose the word or set of words for each blank that best fits the meaning of the sentence as a whole.

1. Because it is ------- to ------- all the business costs related to employee discontent, an accurate estimate of the magnitude of these costs is not easily calculated.

   (A) difficult. .measure
   (B) impossible. .justify
   (C) improper. .overlook
   (D) useless. .discover
   (E) necessary. .pinpoint

2. Consider the universal cannibalism of the sea, all of whose creatures ------- one another.

   (A) hide from
   (B) ferret out
   (C) prey on
   (D) glide among
   (E) compete against

3. How could words, confined as they individually are to certain ------- meanings specified in a dictionary, eventually come, when combined in groups, to create obscurity and actually to prevent thought from being -------?

   (A) indefinite. .articulated
   (B) conventional. .conceivable
   (C) unlikely. .classified
   (D) archaic. .expressed
   (E) precise. .communicable

4. Even though they tended to be ------- strangers, fifteenth-century Europeans did not automatically associate ------- and danger.

   (A) trusting of. .diversity
   (B) haughty with. .nonconformity
   (C) interested in. .enmity
   (D) antagonistic to. .rudeness
   (E) hostile to. .foreignness

5. The modern age is a permissive one in which things can be said explicitly, but the old tradition of ------- dies hard.

   (A) garrulousness
   (B) exaggeration
   (C) excoriation
   (D) bombast
   (E) euphemism

6. Although many findings of the Soviet and United States probes of Venus were complementary, the two sets of atmospheric results clearly could not be ------- without a major change of data or -------.

   (A) obtained. .experimentation
   (B) completed. .position
   (C) matched. .implementation
   (D) reconciled. .interpretation
   (E) produced. .falsification

7. While it is assumed that the mechanization of work has a ------- effect on the lives of workers, there is evidence available to suggest that, on the contrary, mechanization has served to ------- some of the traditional roles of women.

   (A) salutary. .improve
   (B) dramatic. .undermine
   (C) benign. .revise
   (D) debilitating. .weaken
   (E) revolutionary. .reinforce

GO ON TO THE NEXT PAGE.

Directions: In each of the following questions, a related pair of words or phrases is followed by five lettered pairs of words or phrases. Select the lettered pair that best expresses a relationship similar to that expressed in the original pair.

8. PILOT : SHIP :: (A) surveyor : landscape
(B) conductor : orchestra (C) guard : stockade
(D) actor : scene (E) philosopher : inspiration

9. TOPSOIL : ERODE :: (A) leather : tan
(B) veneer : varnish (C) roast : baste
(D) grain : mash (E) paint : peel

10. SCREEN : MOVIE :: (A) shelf : book
(B) frame : portrait (C) shadow : object
(D) stage : play (E) score : performance

11. VOLCANO : LAVA ::
(A) geyser : water
(B) fault : tremor
(C) glacier : fissure
(D) avalanche : snow
(E) cavern : limestone

12. COGENT : CONVINCE ::
(A) irrational : disturb
(B) repugnant : repel
(C) dangerous : avoid
(D) eloquent : refine
(E) generous : appreciate

13. CHARY : CAUTION ::
(A) circumspect : recklessness
(B) imperturbable : composure
(C) meticulous : resourcefulness
(D) exigent : stability
(E) fortuitous : pluck

14. USURY : INTEREST ::
(A) fraud : property
(B) gouging : price
(C) monopoly : production
(D) foreclosure : mortgage
(E) embezzlement : savings

15. EPITHET : DISPARAGE ::
(A) abbreviation : proliferate
(B) hieroglyphic : mythologize
(C) diminutive : respect
(D) code : simplify
(E) alias : mislead

16. OFFENSE : PECCADILLO ::
(A) envy : resentment
(B) quarrel : tiff
(C) affinity : wish
(D) depression : regret
(E) homesickness : nostalgia

GO ON TO THE NEXT PAGE.

Directions: Each passage in this group is followed by questions based on its content. After reading a passage, choose the best answer to each question. Answer all questions following a passage on the basis of what is stated or implied in that passage.

Since the Hawaiian Islands have never been connected to other land masses, the great variety of plants in Hawaii must be a result of the long-distance dispersal of seeds, a process that requires both a method of transport and an equivalence between the ecology of the source area and that of the recipient area.

There is some dispute about the method of transport involved. Some biologists argue that ocean and air currents are responsible for the transport of plant seeds to Hawaii. Yet the results of flotation experiments and the low temperatures of air currents cast doubt on these hypotheses. More probable is bird transport, either externally, by accidental attachment of the seeds to feathers, or internally, by the swallowing of fruit and subsequent excretion of the seeds. While it is likely that fewer varieties of plant seeds have reached Hawaii externally than internally, more varieties are known to be adapted to external than to internal transport.

17. The author of the passage is primarily concerned with

(A) discussing different approaches biologists have taken to testing theories about the distribution of plants in Hawaii
(B) discussing different theories about the transport of plant seeds to Hawaii
(C) discussing the extent to which air currents are responsible for the dispersal of plant seeds to Hawaii
(D) resolving a dispute about the adaptability of plant seeds to bird transport
(E) resolving a dispute about the ability of birds to carry plant seeds long distances

18. The author mentions the results of flotation experiments on plant seeds (lines 10-12) most probably in order to

(A) support the claim that the distribution of plants in Hawaii is the result of the long-distance dispersal of seeds
(B) lend credibility to the thesis that air currents provide a method of transport for plant seeds to Hawaii
(C) suggest that the long-distance dispersal of seeds is a process that requires long periods of time
(D) challenge the claim that ocean currents are responsible for the transport of plant seeds to Hawaii
(E) refute the claim that Hawaiian flora evolved independently from flora in other parts of the world

19. It can be inferred from information in the passage that the existence in alpine regions of Hawaii of a plant species that also grows in the southwestern United States would justify which of the following conclusions?

(A) The ecology of the southwestern United States is similar in important respects to the ecology of alpine regions of Hawaii.
(B) There are ocean currents that flow from the southwestern United States to Hawaii.
(C) The plant species discovered in Hawaii must have traveled from the southwestern United States only very recently.
(D) The plant species discovered in Hawaii reached there by attaching to the feathers of birds migrating from the southwestern United States.
(E) The plant species discovered in Hawaii is especially well adapted to transport over long distances.

20. The passage supplies information for answering which of the following questions?

(A) Why does successful long-distance dispersal of plant seeds require an equivalence between the ecology of the source area and that of the recipient area?
(B) Why are more varieties of plant seeds adapted to external rather than to internal bird transport?
(C) What varieties of plant seeds are birds that fly long distances most likely to swallow?
(D) What is a reason for accepting the long-distance dispersal of plant seeds as an explanation for the origin of Hawaiian flora?
(E) What evidence do biologists cite to argue that ocean and air currents are responsible for the transport of plant seeds to Hawaii?

GO ON TO THE NEXT PAGE.

A long-held view of the history of the English colonies that became the United States has been that England's policy toward these colonies before 1763 was dictated by commercial interests and that a change to a more imperial policy, dominated by expansionist militarist objectives, generated the tensions that ultimately led to the American Revolution. In a recent study, Stephen Saunders Webb has presented a formidable challenge to this view. According to Webb, England already had a military imperial policy for more than a century before the American Revolution. He sees Charles II, the English monarch between 1660 and 1685, as the proper successor of the Tudor monarchs of the sixteenth century and of Oliver Cromwell, all of whom were bent on extending centralized executive power over England's possessions through the use of what Webb calls "garrison government." Garrison government allowed the colonists a legislative assembly, but real authority, in Webb's view, belonged to the colonial governor, who was appointed by the king and supported by the "garrison," that is, by the local contingent of English troops under the colonial governor's command.

According to Webb, the purpose of garrison government was to provide military support for a royal policy designed to limit the power of the upper classes in the American colonies. Webb argues that the colonial legislative assemblies represented the interests not of the common people but of the colonial upper classes, a coalition of merchants and nobility who favored self-rule and sought to elevate legislative authority at the expense of the executive. It was, according to Webb, the colonial governors who favored the small farmer, opposed the plantation system, and tried through taxation to break up large holdings of land. Backed by the military presence of the garrison, these governors tried to prevent the gentry and merchants, allied in the colonial assemblies, from transforming colonial America into a capitalistic oligarchy.

Webb's study illuminates the political alignments that existed in the colonies in the century prior to the American Revolution, but his view of the crown's use of the military as an instrument of colonial policy is not entirely convincing. England during the seventeenth century was not noted for its military achievements. Cromwell did mount England's most ambitious overseas military expedition in more than a century, but it proved to be an utter failure. Under Charles II, the English army was too small to be a major instrument of government. Not until the war with France in 1697 did William III persuade Parliament to create a professional standing army, and Parliament's price for doing so was to keep the army under tight legislative control. While it may be true that the crown attempted to curtail the power of the colonial upper classes, it is hard to imagine how the English army during the seventeenth century could have provided significant military support for such a policy.

21. The passage can best be described as a

(A) survey of the inadequacies of a conventional viewpoint
(B) reconciliation of opposing points of view
(C) summary and evaluation of a recent study
(D) defense of a new thesis from anticipated objections
(E) review of the subtle distinctions between apparently similar views

22. The passage suggests that the view referred to in lines 1-7 argued that

(A) the colonial governors were sympathetic to the demands of the common people
(B) Charles II was a pivotal figure in the shift of English monarchs toward a more imperial policy in their governorship of the American colonies
(C) the American Revolution was generated largely out of a conflict between the colonial upper classes and an alliance of merchants and small farmers
(D) the military did not play a major role as an instrument of colonial policy until 1763
(E) the colonial legislative assemblies in the colonies had little influence over the colonial governors

23. It can be inferred from the passage that Webb would be most likely to agree with which of the following statements regarding garrison government?

(A) Garrison government gave legislative assemblies in the colonies relatively little authority, compared to the authority that it gave the colonial governors.
(B) Garrison government proved relatively ineffective until it was used by Charles II to curb the power of colonial legislatures.
(C) Garrison government became a less viable colonial policy as the English Parliament began to exert tighter legislative control over the English military.
(D) Oliver Cromwell was the first English ruler to make use of garrison government on a large scale.
(E) The creation of a professional standing army in England in 1697 actually weakened garrison government by diverting troops from the garrisons stationed in the American colonies.

GO ON TO THE NEXT PAGE.

24. According to the passage, Webb views Charles II as the "proper successor" (line 13) of the Tudor monarchs and Cromwell because Charles II

(A) used colonial tax revenues to fund overseas military expeditions
(B) used the military to extend executive power over the English colonies
(C) wished to transform the American colonies into capitalistic oligarchies
(D) resisted the English Parliament's efforts to exert control over the military
(E) allowed the American colonists to use legislative assemblies as a forum for resolving grievances against the crown

25. Which of the following, if true, would most seriously weaken the author's assertion in lines 54-58 ?

(A) Because they were poorly administered, Cromwell's overseas military expeditions were doomed to failure.
(B) Because it relied primarily on the symbolic presence of the military, garrison government could be effectively administered with a relatively small number of troops.
(C) Until early in the seventeenth century, no professional standing army in Europe had performed effectively in overseas military expeditions.
(D) Many of the colonial governors appointed by the crown were also commissioned army officers.
(E) Many of the English troops stationed in the American colonies were veterans of other overseas military expeditions.

26. According to Webb's view of colonial history, which of the following was (were) true of the merchants and nobility mentioned in line 30 ?

I. They were opposed to policies formulated by Charles II that would have transformed the colonies into capitalistic oligarchies.
II. They were opposed to attempts by the English crown to limit the power of the legislative assemblies.
III. They were united with small farmers in their opposition to the stationing of English troops in the colonies.

(A) I only
(B) II only
(C) I and II only
(D) II and III only
(E) I, II, and III

27. The author suggests that if William III had wanted to make use of the standing army mentioned in line 52 to administer garrison government in the American colonies, he would have had to

(A) make peace with France
(B) abolish the colonial legislative assemblies
(C) seek approval from the English Parliament
(D) appoint colonial governors who were more sympathetic to royal policy
(E) raise additional revenues by increasing taxation of large landholdings in the colonies

GO ON TO THE NEXT PAGE.

Directions: Each question below consists of a word printed in capital letters, followed by five lettered words or phrases. Choose the lettered word or phrase that is most nearly opposite in meaning to the word in capital letters.

Since some of the questions require you to distinguish fine shades of meaning, be sure to consider all the choices before deciding which one is best.

28. FLUCTUATE: (A) work for (B) flow over (C) follow from (D) remain steady (E) cling together

29. PRECARIOUS: (A) safe (B) covert (C) rescued (D) revived (E) pledged

30. FUMBLE: (A) organize neatly (B) say clearly (C) prepare carefully (D) handle adroitly (E) replace immediately

31. AUTHENTIC: (A) ordinary (B) criminal (C) unattractive (D) inexpensive (E) bogus

32. COWER: (A) swiftly disappear (B) brazenly confront (C) assuage (D) coast (E) invert

33. PRISTINE: (A) ruthless (B) seductive (C) coarse (D) commonplace (E) contaminated

34. LAMBASTE: (A) permit (B) prefer (C) extol (D) smooth completely (E) support openly

35. VISCID: (A) bent (B) prone (C) cool (D) slick (E) slight

36. TURPITUDE: (A) saintly behavior (B) clever conversation (C) lively imagination (D) agitation (E) lucidity

37. PHILISTINE: (A) perfectionist (B) aesthete (C) iconoclast (D) critic (E) cynic

38. ODIUM: (A) ease (B) fragrance (C) resignation (D) eccentricity (E) infatuation

STOP

IF YOU FINISH BEFORE TIME IS CALLED, YOU MAY CHECK YOUR WORK ON THIS SECTION ONLY. DO NOT TURN TO ANY OTHER SECTION IN THE TEST.

Section 7 starts on page 152.

SECTION 7

Time—30 minutes

25 Questions

Directions: Each question or group of questions is based on a passage or set of conditions. In answering some of the questions, it may be useful to draw a rough diagram. For each question, select the best answer choice given.

Questions 1-6

Seven airline flights—101, 102, 103, 104, 105, 106, and 107—are to be scheduled for departure, one at a time on the hour, from 9:00 a.m. until 3:00 p.m. The schedule must conform to the following requirements:

Flight 101 must depart at 9:00 a.m.
Flight 105 must depart later than Flight 103, and also later than Flight 102.
Flights 104, 106, and 107 must depart on consecutive hours in that order.

1. If Flight 107 is scheduled to depart at noon, Flight 105 must be scheduled to depart at

(A) 10:00 a.m.
(B) 11:00 a.m.
(C) 1:00 p.m.
(D) 2:00 p.m.
(E) 3:00 p.m.

2. If Flights 103 and 104 are scheduled to depart at 11:00 a.m. and 12 noon, respectively, Flight 102 must be scheduled to depart at

(A) 9:00 a.m.
(B) 10:00 a.m.
(C) 1:00 p.m.
(D) 2:00 p.m.
(E) 3:00 p.m.

3. Which of the following lists three flights in a sequence, from first to last, in which they could be scheduled to depart consecutively?

(A) 101, 104, 103
(B) 102, 103, 106
(C) 104, 105, 106
(D) 106, 107, 103
(E) 106, 107, 104

4. If Flight 106 is scheduled to depart at 2:00 p.m., Flight 105 must be scheduled to depart at

(A) 10:00 a.m.
(B) 11:00 a.m.
(C) 12 noon
(D) 1:00 p.m.
(E) 2:00 p.m.

5. Which of the following must be true about the scheduled order of the flights?

(A) Flight 103 is scheduled to depart later than Flight 102.
(B) Flight 104 is scheduled to depart later than Flight 103.
(C) Flight 105 is scheduled to depart later than Flight 104.
(D) Flight 106 is scheduled to depart later than Flight 105.
(E) Flight 107 is scheduled to depart later than Flight 106.

6. What is the latest hour at which Flight 102 can be scheduled to depart?

(A) 10:00 a.m.
(B) 11:00 a.m.
(C) 12 noon
(D) 1:00 p.m.
(E) 2:00 p.m.

GO ON TO THE NEXT PAGE.

7. In an experiment, two hundred mice of a strain that is normally free of leukemia were given equal doses of radiation. Half the mice were then allowed to eat their usual foods without restraint, while the other half were given adequate but limited amounts of the same foods. Of the first group, fifty-five developed leukemia; of the second, only three.

The experiment above best supports which of the following conclusions?

(A) Leukemia inexplicably strikes some individuals from strains of mice normally free of the disease.
(B) The incidence of leukemia in mice of this strain which have been exposed to the experimental doses of radiation can be kept down by limiting their intake of food.
(C) Experimental exposure to radiation has very little effect on the development of leukemia in any strain of mice.
(D) Given unlimited access to food, a mouse eventually settles on a diet that is optimum for its health.
(E) Allowing mice to eat their usual foods increases the likelihood that the mice will develop leukemia whether or not they have been exposed to radiation.

8. Children born blind or deaf and blind begin social smiling on roughly the same schedule as most children, by about three months of age.

The information above provides evidence to support which of the following hypotheses?

(A) For babies, the survival advantage of smiling consists in bonding the caregiver to the infant.
(B) Babies do not smile when no one else is present.
(C) The smiling response depends on an inborn trait determining a certain pattern of development.
(D) Smiling between persons basically signals a mutual lack of aggressive intent.
(E) When a baby begins smiling, its caregivers begin responding to it as they would to a person in conversation.

9. Restoration of the original paint colors in Colonial–era rooms has until now relied on the technique of scraping paint in a small area down to the chronological level that represents the paint layer of the Colonial period and then matching the color found at that level. This color was most often the color of putty.

Which of the following, if true, most seriously weakens the validity of the procedure described above?

(A) If the scraping is too deep, a scratch will be made in the surface of the original paint.
(B) In the Colonial period, it was customary to paint all the walls of a room the same solid color.
(C) It is possible to distinguish the paint used in stenciled border designs, such as those used in the Colonial period, from the underlying paint layer.
(D) The original colors were altered over the years by reactions with air, light, and dirt to become putty-colored.
(E) Contemporary paint materials include many that did not exist in Colonial times.

GO ON TO THE NEXT PAGE.

Questions 10-14

A farmer is deciding which crops to plant. Either three or four fields will be planted; in each field only one crop will be planted. Exactly the same fields that are planted the first year will be planted the second year, but no field will be planted to the same crop for two consecutive years. For each field, the farmer will choose from among five possible crops—corn, soybeans, alfalfa, rye, and barley—according to the following conditions:

In any year, at least one field will be planted to a cereal grain; the possible grains include corn, rye, and barley only.

The year after corn is planted in a field, either soybeans or alfalfa must be planted in that field.

10. In a year in which corn is not planted, which of the following is true?

(A) Either alfalfa or soybeans, but not both, must be planted.
(B) Either barley or rye, or both, must be planted.
(C) Both alfalfa and soybeans must be planted.
(D) Both alfalfa and rye must be planted.
(E) Either barley or soybeans must be the only crop planted.

11. If the farmer plants three fields, each of the following is a possible selection of crops for the first year EXCEPT

(A) barley, barley, barley
(B) barley, rye, soybeans
(C) corn, corn, corn
(D) corn, alfalfa, barley
(E) rye, rye, rye

12. If the farmer plants three fields to corn, corn, and soybeans, respectively, which of the following selections is possible for the same three fields the following year?

(A) Alfalfa, alfalfa, barley, respectively
(B) Alfalfa, soybeans, soybeans, respectively
(C) Rye, rye, soybeans, respectively
(D) Soybeans, corn, corn, respectively
(E) Soybeans, rye, rye, respectively

13. If the farmer plants four fields, with corn in two of the fields the first year, how many crops must there be that are not planted the first year in any field but have to be planted the next year in some field?

(A) 0
(B) 1
(C) 2
(D) 3
(E) 4

14. If the farmer plants four fields, the maximum number of the fields that can be planted to grains in both years is

(A) 0
(B) 1
(C) 2
(D) 3
(E) 4

GO ON TO THE NEXT PAGE.

Questions 15-17

A square, floating platform is supported at its corners by four hollow vessels that are labeled 1, 2, 3, and 4. 1 is diagonally across from 3, and 2 is diagonally across from 4. Three of the vessels are each filled with a different liquid—N, O, or P—and the remaining vessel is empty, except while there is a transfer of liquid in progress. The empty vessel can be filled to capacity by having all of the liquid from one of the other three vessels pumped into it as follows:

If 2 is empty, the liquid contained in 1 can be transferred to 2.
If 3 is empty, the liquid contained in 2 can be transferred to 3.
If 4 is empty, the liquid contained in 3 can be transferred to 4.
If 1 is empty, the liquid contained in 3 or the liquid contained in 4 can be transferred to 1.
No other transfers are possible.

O is the heaviest of the three liquids, and the platform is always tilted toward the vessel containing O; the platform is tilted maximally when, and only when, the vessel containing O is diagonally across from the empty vessel.

15. If 1, 3, and 4 contain N, O, and P, respectively, and if there is then exactly one transfer of liquid, that transfer must have which of the following results?

(A) N is in 2.
(B) O is in 1.
(C) O is in 2.
(D) O is in 4.
(E) P is in 1.

16. If P is in 4 and could be the next liquid to be transferred, which of the following must be true?

(A) The empty vessel is 1.
(B) The empty vessel is 2.
(C) The empty vessel is 3.
(D) N cannot be the next liquid to be transferred.
(E) O cannot be the next liquid to be transferred.

17. If 1, 2, and 4 contain O, N, and P, respectively, and if exactly three transfers are subsequently made, which of the following could be the resulting contents of the four vessels?

	1	2	3	4
(A)	Empty	O	P	N
(B)	N	P	O	Empty
(C)	O	Empty	N	P
(D)	P	N	Empty	O
(E)	P	O	N	Empty

GO ON TO THE NEXT PAGE.

Questions 18-22

Within an array there are four significant positions—positions 1 through 4. When the elements forming the array—R, S, T, and U—are stationary, there is one of them in each of the four positions. Periodically, there are reorderings of the elements in accordance with the following laws:

During each reordering, exactly one of the elements, the anchor, retains its position, and each of the other three elements moves to a new position.
Only R and U can be anchors.
U can be the anchor only when it is in position 3 or position 4.
Any reordering anchored by U must be followed by a reordering anchored by R.
R can be the anchor in up to two consecutive reorderings.
Any given array consists of the four elements in the order of their positions from 1 through 4.

18. If U R T S is an array and if exactly one reordering occurs, which of the following can be the array resulting from that reordering?

(A) R S T U
(B) S R T U
(C) S R U T
(D) T R U S
(E) U S R T

19. If R T S U is an array and if exactly one reordering occurs, with the result that S is in position 1, which of the following must also be a result of that reordering?

(A) R is in position 3.
(B) R is in position 4.
(C) T is in position 2.
(D) T is in position 3.
(E) U is in position 3.

20. If R moves from position 4 to position 1 in the course of a reordering, which of the following can also occur in the course of that reordering?

(A) S moves from position 1 to position 2.
(B) S moves from position 1 to position 3.
(C) S moves from position 1 to position 4.
(D) T moves from position 2 to position 3.
(E) T moves from position 3 to position 2.

21. If the array U S T R has resulted from a reordering, and if exactly two additional reorderings occur, with the result that S is again in position 2, which of the following must have been the array after the first of the two additional reorderings?

(A) S T U R
(B) T S U R
(C) T U S R
(D) U R S T
(E) U T R S

22. If S R U T is an array and if exactly two reorderings occur, the first anchored by R and the second anchored by U, which of the following must be true directly after the second of the two reorderings?

(A) R is in position 1.
(B) S is in position 1.
(C) R is in position 2.
(D) T is in position 3.
(E) U is in position 4.

GO ON TO THE NEXT PAGE.

23. Recent surveys show that many people who seek medical help are under a great deal of stress. Medical research also shows that stress can adversely affect an individual's immune system, which is responsible for combating many infections. Thus when a person is under stress, he or she is more likely to become ill.

Which of the following, if true, would most strengthen the conclusion above?

(A) Many businesses that provide health insurance for their employees also provide seminars on stress management.
(B) Many businesses report a significant decrease in absenteeism during periods when employees feel pressured by management.
(C) There is a marked decrease in the number of complaints presented at college infirmaries during vacation time.
(D) There is a marked increase in the number of illnesses treated at college infirmaries around the time of examinations.
(E) Most people report that being in a hospital or an infirmary is a stressful situation.

24. Although compact cars make up only 38 percent of the vehicles in traffic, 48 percent of the cars that are followed too closely ("tailgated") are compact. On the other hand, fewer than 27 percent of the cars tailgated are middle-sized, even though middle-sized cars make up 31 percent of the vehicles in traffic.

Which of the following, if true, most contributes to an explanation for the phenomenon described above?

(A) The shape of compact cars makes it easy for a tailgater to see far enough ahead around such cars to minimize the chances of a rear-end collision.
(B) Middle-sized cars, owned by families with children and pets, are likely to have bumper stickers that are so interesting to read that tailgaters stay behind such cars longer.
(C) Compact cars sometimes have superior engines that allow them to pass middle-sized cars on the highway easily.
(D) The percentage of cars on the highway that are middle-sized has been steadily decreasing over the last decade.
(E) Compact cars are often driven by fast drivers.

25. As part of a delicately balanced system, the human heart secretes a hormone, a substance that controls the amount of salt in the blood and the volume of blood circulating within the body. Only very small quantities of the hormone are required. This hormone is extremely important in regulating blood pressure and is found in large amounts in the blood of those suffering a heart attack.

If the statements above are true, then it must also be true that

(A) if there is a deficiency in the amount of heart hormone secreted, low blood pressure will result
(B) it is large quantities of the heart hormone that cause heart attacks to occur
(C) the effects of a small amount of the heart hormone will be long-lasting in the body
(D) if a device that is only a mechanical pump is used as an artificial heart, it will not perform all the functions of the human heart
(E) any drug that regulates blood pressure will have its effect by influencing the amount of the heart hormone secreted

STOP

IF YOU FINISH BEFORE TIME IS CALLED, YOU MAY CHECK YOUR WORK ON THIS SECTION ONLY. DO NOT TURN TO ANY OTHER SECTION IN THE TEST.

NO TEST MATERIAL ON THIS PAGE

NOTE: To ensure prompt processing of test results, it is important that you fill in the blanks exactly as directed.

GENERAL TEST

A. Print and sign your full name in this box:

PRINT: ____
(LAST) (FIRST) (MIDDLE)

SIGN: ____

Copy this code in box 6 on your answer sheet. Then fill in the corresponding ovals exactly as shown.

6. TITLE CODE

0	0	0	0	0
1	1	1	1	1
2	2	2	2	2
3	3	3	3	3
4	4	4	4	4
5	5	5	5	5
6	6	6	6	6
7	7	7	7	7
8	8	8	8	8
9	9	9	9	9

Copy the Test Name and Form Code in box 7 on your answer sheet.

TEST NAME General

FORM CODE GR90-16

GRADUATE RECORD EXAMINATIONS GENERAL TEST

B. You will have 3 hours and 30 minutes in which to work on this test, which consists of seven sections. During the time allowed for one section, you may work only on that section. The time allowed for each section is 30 minutes.

Each of your scores will be determined by the number of questions for which you select the best answer from the choices given. Questions for which you mark no answer or more than one answer are not counted in scoring. Nothing is subtracted from a score if you answer a question incorrectly. Therefore, to maximize your scores it is better for you to guess at an answer than not to respond at all.

You are advised to work as rapidly as you can without losing accuracy. Do not spend too much time on questions that are too difficult for you. Go on to the other questions and come back to the difficult ones later.

There are several different types of questions; you will find special directions for each type in the test itself. Be sure you understand the directions before attempting to answer any questions.

YOU MUST INDICATE ALL YOUR ANSWERS ON THE SEPARATE ANSWER SHEET. No credit will be given for anything written in this examination book, but you may write in the book as much as you wish to work out your answers. After you have decided on your response to a question, fill in the corresponding oval on the answer sheet. BE SURE THAT EACH MARK IS DARK AND COMPLETELY FILLS THE OVAL. Mark only one answer to each question. No credit will be given for multiple answers. Erase all stray marks. If you change an answer, be sure that all previous marks are erased completely. Incomplete erasures may be read as intended answers. Do not be concerned if your answer sheet provides spaces for more answers than there are questions in each section.

Example:

What city is the capital of France?

(A) Rome
(B) Paris
(C) London
(D) Cairo
(E) Oslo

Sample Answer

A ● C D E — BEST ANSWER PROPERLY MARKED

A B C D E
A B C D E
A B C D E
A B C D E
— IMPROPER MARKS

Some or all of the passages for this test have been adapted from published material to provide the examinee with significant problems for analysis and evaluation. To make the passages suitable for testing purposes, the style, content, or point of view of the original may have been altered in some cases. The ideas contained in the passages do not necessarily represent the opinions of the Graduate Record Examinations Board or Educational Testing Service.

DO NOT OPEN YOUR TEST BOOK UNTIL YOU ARE TOLD TO DO SO.

FOR GENERAL TEST, FORM GR90-16 ONLY
Answer Key and Percentages* of Examinees Answering Each Question Correctly

VERBAL ABILITY					
Section 1			Section 5		
Number	Answer	P+	Number	Answer	P+
1	A	94	1	A	90
2	C	91	2	C	94
3	A	77	3	E	69
4	C	66	4	E	71
5	A	61	5	E	51
6	E	53	6	D	58
7	E	27	7	E	36
8	E	82	8	B	86
9	B	83	9	E	91
10	E	65	10	D	80
11	C	81	11	A	79
12	D	53	12	B	42
13	A	47	13	B	37
14	C	45	14	B	30
15	D	33	15	E	27
16	B	28	16	B	45
17	D	49	17	B	86
18	B	47	18	D	82
19	B	37	19	A	47
20	B	68	20	D	61
21	B	60	21	C	58
22	A	72	22	D	37
23	D	37	23	A	68
24	E	58	24	B	69
25	D	46	25	B	49
26	A	61	26	B	40
27	D	39	27	C	55
28	C	93	28	D	94
29	C	81	29	A	78
30	E	79	30	D	80
31	D	80	31	E	81
32	C	79	32	B	84
33	D	33	33	E	44
34	C	31	34	C	36
35	C	34	35	D	37
36	A	22	36	A	38
37	D	29	37	B	30
38	A	17	38	E	22

QUANTITATIVE ABILITY					
Section 2			Section 4		
Number	Answer	P+	Number	Answer	P+
1	B	95	1	A	93
2	A	83	2	B	84
3	A	81	3	C	84
4	C	70	4	C	81
5	C	78	5	C	82
6	D	77	6	B	83
7	B	74	7	B	76
8	A	71	8	C	74
9	A	72	9	A	76
10	D	83	10	D	64
11	A	74	11	A	75
12	B	72	12	D	49
13	B	62	13	B	66
14	D	24	14	D	19
15	C	19	15	C	20
16	C	84	16	C	93
17	B	80	17	C	78
18	D	72	18	A	66
19	C	71	19	E	68
20	E	63	20	D	64
21	B	91	21	D	89
22	A	89	22	A	81
23	C	74	23	C	71
24	D	61	24	B	76
25	C	43	25	A	36
26	C	60	26	C	60
27	E	52	27	D	50
28	A	55	28	B	45
29	A	44	29	E	41
30	D	36	30	B	41

ANALYTICAL ABILITY					
Section 3			Section 7		
Number	Answer	P+	Number	Answer	P+
1	C	76	1	E	76
2	B	90	2	B	87
3	E	55	3	D	75
4	E	52	4	C	85
5	E	55	5	E	79
6	C	75	6	E	66
7	B	60	7	B	87
8	A	89	8	C	84
9	B	88	9	D	80
10	B	63	10	B	59
11	D	72	11	C	46
12	D	57	12	A	71
13	E	31	13	A	18
14	B	75	14	E	44
15	A	27	15	A	66
16	E	53	16	A	66
17	C	58	17	E	50
18	A	41	18	C	50
19	A	58	19	D	39
20	A	37	20	A	37
21	E	18	21	A	27
22	C	40	22	E	32
23	D	66	23	D	75
24	B	24	24	A	61
25	D	22	25	D	23

*Estimated P+ for the group of examinees who took the GRE General Test in a recent three-year period.

Score Conversions for GRE General Test GR90-16 Only and the Percents Below*

Raw Score	Verbal Scaled Score	Verbal % Below	Quantitative Scaled Score	Quantitative % Below	Analytical Scaled Score	Analytical % Below
73-76	800	99				
72	780	99				
71	770	99				
70	750	98				
69	740	98				
68	730	97				
67	720	96				
66	710	96				
65	700	95				
64	690	94				
63	670	92				
62	660	91				
61	650	89				
60	640	88	800	98		
59	630	86	800	98		
58	620	84	800	98		
57	610	83	780	95		
56	600	81	760	93		
55	590	79	740	89		
54	580	77	730	87		
53	570	75	710	83		
52	560	73	700	81		
51	550	70	680	77		
50	540	67	670	75	800	99
49	530	65	660	73	800	99
48	520	62	640	69	800	99
47	510	59	630	66	790	98
46	490	54	620	64	780	98
45	480	51	610	62	760	96
44	470	48	590	57	750	96
43	460	45	580	55	730	94
42	450	42	570	52	720	93
41	450	42	560	50	710	91
40	440	39	550	48	690	89
39	430	36	540	45	680	87
38	420	34	530	43	660	84
37	410	30	520	40	650	82
36	400	27	500	35	630	77
35	390	25	490	33	620	75
34	380	23	480	30	600	70
33	370	21	470	29	590	68
32	360	17	460	26	570	62
31	360	17	450	24	560	59
30	350	15	440	22	540	53
29	340	13	430	20	530	51
28	340	13	420	18	510	44
27	330	11	400	15	500	42
26	310	8	390	13	490	39
25	300	7	380	12	470	33
24	290	5	370	10	460	31
23	280	4	360	9	440	25
22	270	3	350	8	430	24
21	270	3	340	7	410	19
20	260	2	330	6	400	17
19	250	2	320	5	390	15
18	240	1	310	4	370	12
17	230	1	290	3	360	10
16	200	1	280	2	340	8
15	200	1	270	2	330	6
14	200	1	250	1	310	5
13	200	1	240	1	300	4
12	200	1	220	1	290	3
11	200	1	210	1	270	2
10	200	1	200	1	250	1
9	200	1	200	1	230	1
8	200	1	200	1	220	1
0-7	200	1	200	1	200	1

* Percent scoring below the scaled score is based on the performance of 876,691 examinees who took the General Test between October 1, 1985, and September 30, 1988. This percent below information is used for score reports during the 1989-90 testing year.

FORM GR86-2

01

THE GRADUATE RECORD EXAMINATIONS®

General Test
(with explanations)

SECTION 1

Time—30 minutes

38 Questions

Directions: Each sentence below has one or two blanks, each blank indicating that something has been omitted. Beneath the sentence are five lettered words or sets of words. Choose the word or set of words for each blank that best fits the meaning of the sentence as a whole.

1. Physicists rejected the innovative experimental technique because, although it ------- some problems, it also produced new -------.

   (A) clarified..data
   (B) eased..interpretations
   (C) resolved..complications
   (D) caused..hypotheses
   (E) revealed..inconsistencies

2. During a period of protracted illness, the sick can become infirm, ------- both the strength to work and many of the specific skills they once possessed.

   (A) regaining (B) denying (C) pursuing
   (D) insuring (E) losing

3. The pressure of population on available resources is the key to understanding history; consequently, any historical writing that takes no cognizance of ------- facts is ------- flawed.

   (A) demographic..intrinsically
   (B) ecological..marginally
   (C) cultural..substantively
   (D) psychological..philosophically
   (E) political..demonstratively

4. It is puzzling to observe that Jones's novel has recently been criticized for its ------- structure, since commentators have traditionally argued that its most obvious ------- is its relentlessly rigid, indeed schematic, framework.

   (A) attention to..preoccupation
   (B) speculation about..characteristic
   (C) parody of..disparity
   (D) violation of..contradiction
   (E) lack of..flaw

5. It comes as no surprise that societies have codes of behavior; the character of the codes, on the other hand, can often be -------.

   (A) predictable (B) unexpected
   (C) admirable (D) explicit (E) confusing

6. The characterization of historical analysis as a form of fiction is not likely to be received ------- by either historians or literary critics, who agree that history and fiction deal with ------- orders of experience.

   (A) quietly..significant
   (B) enthusiastically..shifting
   (C) passively..unusual
   (D) sympathetically..distinct
   (E) contentiously..realistic

7. For some time now, ------- has been presumed not to exist: the cynical conviction that everybody has an angle is considered wisdom.

   (A) rationality
   (B) flexibility
   (C) diffidence
   (D) disinterestedness
   (E) insincerity

GO ON TO THE NEXT PAGE.

Directions: In each of the following questions, a related pair of words or phrases is followed by five lettered pairs of words or phrases. Select the lettered pair that best expresses a relationship similar to that expressed in the original pair.

8. STUDY:LEARN :: (A) pervade:encompass (B) search:find (C) gather:win (D) agree:keep (E) accumulate:raise

9. CORRAL:HORSES :: (A) den:lions (B) meadow:sheep (C) herd:cattle (D) nest:birds (E) coop:chickens

10. LULLABY:SONG ::
(A) narrative:volume
(B) lecture:tutor
(C) paragraph:page
(D) diatribe:discourse
(E) invective:compliment

11. DIE:SHAPING :: (A) glue:attaching (B) anchor:sailing (C) drill:boring (D) pedal:propelling (E) ink:printing

12. MERCENARY:MONEY ::
(A) vindictive:revenge
(B) scholarly:library
(C) immaculate:cleanliness
(D) thirsty:water
(E) belligerent:invasion

13. AUTHORITATIVENESS:PUNDITS ::
(A) dedication:signatories
(B) sobriety:executors
(C) sensitivity:literati
(D) recklessness:warriors
(E) allegiance:partisans

14. STRUT:WING :: (A) lever:handle (B) axle:wheel (C) buttress:wall (D) beam:rivet (E) well:pipe

15. FAWN:IMPERIOUSNESS ::
(A) equivocate:directness
(B) elaborate:originality
(C) boggle:imagination
(D) manipulate:repression
(E) coddle:permissiveness

16. TROUBLED:DISTRAUGHT ::
(A) annoyed:disillusioned
(B) disturbed:interrupted
(C) covetous:rapacious
(D) outmoded:ostentatious
(E) tranquil:placid

GO ON TO THE NEXT PAGE.

Directions: Each passage in this group is followed by questions based on its content. After reading a passage, choose the best answer to each question. Answer all questions following a passage on the basis of what is stated or implied in that passage.

The evolution of intelligence among early large mammals of the grasslands was due in great measure to the interaction between two ecologically synchronized groups of these animals, the hunting carnivores and the herbivores that they hunted. The interaction resulting from the differences between predator and prey led to a general improvement in brain functions; however, certain components of intelligence were improved far more than others.

The kind of intelligence favored by the interplay of increasingly smarter catchers and increasingly keener escapers is defined by attention—that aspect of mind carrying consciousness forward from one moment to the next. It ranges from a passive, free-floating awareness to a highly focused, active fixation. The range through these states is mediated by the arousal system, a network of tracts converging from sensory systems to integrating centers in the brain stem. From the more relaxed to the more vigorous levels, sensitivity to novelty is increased. The organism is more awake, more vigilant; this increased vigilance results in the apprehension of ever more subtle signals as the organism becomes more sensitive to its surroundings. The processes of arousal and concentration give attention its direction. Arousal is at first general, with a flooding of impulses in the brain stem; then gradually the activation is channeled. Thus begins concentration, the holding of consistent images. One meaning of intelligence is the way in which these images and other alertly searched information are used in the context of previous experience. Consciousness links past attention to the present and permits the integration of details with perceived ends and purposes.

The elements of intelligence and consciousness come together marvelously to produce different styles in predator and prey. Herbivores and carnivores develop different kinds of attention related to escaping or chasing. Although in both kinds of animal, arousal stimulates the production of adrenaline and norepinephrine by the adrenal glands, the effect in herbivores is primarily fear, whereas in carnivores the effect is primarily aggression. For both, arousal attunes the animal to what is ahead. Perhaps it does not experience forethought as we know it, but the animal does experience something like it. The predator is searchingly aggressive, innerdirected, tuned by the nervous system and the adrenal hormones, but aware in a sense closer to human consciousness than, say, a hungry lizard's instinctive snap at a passing beetle. Using past events as a framework, the large mammal predator is working out a relationship between movement and food, sensitive to possibilities in cold trails and distant sounds—and yesterday's unforgotten lessons. The herbivore prey is of a different mind. Its mood of wariness rather than searching and its attitude of general expectancy instead of anticipating are silk-thin veils of tranquility over an explosive endocrine system.

17. The author is primarily concerned with

(A) disproving the view that herbivores are less intelligent than carnivores
(B) describing a relationship between animals' intelligence and their ecological roles
(C) establishing a direct link between early large mammals and their modern counterparts
(D) analyzing the ecological basis for the dominance of some carnivores over other carnivores
(E) demonstrating the importance of hormones in mental activity

18. The author refers to a hungry lizard (line 55) primarily in order to

(A) demonstrate the similarity between the hunting methods of mammals and those of nonmammals
(B) broaden the application of his argument by including an insectivore as an example
(C) make a distinction between higher and lower levels of consciousness
(D) provide an additional illustration of the brutality characteristic of predators
(E) offer an objection to suggestions that all animals lack consciousness

GO ON TO THE NEXT PAGE.

19. It can be inferred from the passage that in animals less intelligent than the mammals discussed in the passage

(A) past experience is less helpful in ensuring survival
(B) attention is more highly focused
(C) muscular coordination is less highly developed
(D) there is less need for competition among species
(E) environment is more important in establishing the proper ratio of prey to predator

20. The sensitivity described in lines 56-61 is most clearly an example of

(A) "free-floating awareness" (lines 16-17)
(B) "flooding of impulses in the brain stem" (lines 29-30)
(C) "the holding of consistent images" (lines 31-32)
(D) "integration of details with perceived ends and purposes" (lines 37-38)
(E) "silk-thin veils of tranquility" (line 64)

21. The author's attitude toward the mammals discussed in the passage is best described as

(A) superior and condescending
(B) lighthearted and jocular
(C) apologetic and conciliatory
(D) wistful and tender
(E) respectful and admiring

22. The author provides information that would answer which of the following questions?

I. Why is an aroused herbivore usually fearful?
II. What are some of the degrees of attention in large mammals?
III. What occurs when the stimulus that causes arousal of a mammal is removed?

(A) I only (B) III only (C) I and II only
(D) II and III only (E) I, II, and III

23. According to the passage, improvement in brain function among early large mammals resulted primarily from which of the following?

(A) Interplay of predator and prey
(B) Persistence of free-floating awareness in animals of the grasslands
(C) Gradual dominance of warm-blooded mammals over cold-blooded reptiles
(D) Interaction of early large mammals with less intelligent species
(E) Improvement of the capacity for memory among herbivores and carnivores

24. According to the passage, as the process of arousal in an organism continues, all of the following may occur EXCEPT

(A) the production of adrenaline
(B) the production of norepinephrine
(C) a heightening of sensitivity to stimuli
(D) an increase in selectivity with respect to stimuli
(E) an expansion of the range of states mediated by the brain stem

GO ON TO THE NEXT PAGE.

Tocqueville, apparently, was wrong. Jacksonian America was not a fluid, egalitarian society where individual wealth and poverty were ephemeral conditions. At least so argues E. Pessen in his iconoclastic study of the very rich in the United States between 1825 and 1850.

Pessen does present a quantity of examples, together with some refreshingly intelligible statistics, to establish the existence of an inordinately wealthy class. Though active in commerce or the professions, most of the wealthy were not self-made, but had inherited family fortunes. In no sense mercurial, these great fortunes survived the financial panics that destroyed lesser ones. Indeed, in several cities the wealthiest one percent constantly increased its share until by 1850 it owned half of the community's wealth. Although these observations are true, Pessen overestimates their importance by concluding from them that the undoubted progress toward inequality in the late eighteenth century continued in the Jacksonian period and that the United States was a class-ridden, plutocratic society even before industrialization.

25. According to the passage, Pessen indicates that all of the following were true of the very wealthy in the United States between 1825 and 1850 EXCEPT:

(A) They formed a distinct upper class.
(B) Many of them were able to increase their holdings.
(C) Some of them worked as professionals or in business.
(D) Most of them accumulated their own fortunes.
(E) Many of them retained their wealth in spite of financial upheavals.

26. The author's attitude toward Pessen's presentation of statistics can be best described as

(A) disapproving
(B) shocked
(C) suspicious
(D) amused
(E) laudatory

27. Which of the following best states the author's main point?

(A) Pessen's study has overturned the previously established view of the social and economic structure of early nineteenth-century America.
(B) Tocqueville's analysis of the United States in the Jacksonian era remains the definitive account of this period.
(C) Pessen's study is valuable primarily because it shows the continuity of the social system in the United States throughout the nineteenth century.
(D) The social patterns and political power of the extremely wealthy in the United States between 1825 and 1850 are well documented.
(E) Pessen challenges a view of the social and economic system in the United States from 1825 to 1850, but he draws conclusions that are incorrect.

GO ON TO THE NEXT PAGE.

Directions: Each question below consists of a word printed in capital letters, followed by five lettered words or phrases. Choose the lettered word or phrase that is most nearly opposite in meaning to the word in capital letters.

Since some of the questions require you to distinguish fine shades of meaning, be sure to consider all the choices before deciding which one is best.

28. BOISTEROUS: (A) grateful (B) angry (C) clever (D) frightened (E) quiet

29. EMIT: (A) absorb (B) demand (C) mistake (D) prevent (E) require

30. METAMORPHOSE: (A) move ahead (B) remain unaltered (C) descend slowly (D) examine in haste (E) prepare in advance

31. ALLY: (A) mediator (B) felon (C) adversary (D) inventor (E) conspirator

32. OFFHAND:
(A) accurate
(B) universal
(C) appropriate
(D) premeditated
(E) disputatious

33. BROACH: (A) keep track of (B) lay claim to (C) close off (D) soothe (E) simplify

34. GIST: (A) artificial manner (B) trivial point (C) informal procedure (D) eccentric method (E) singular event

35. DIVESTITURE: (A) acquisition (B) promotion (C) subsidization (D) consultation (E) monopolization

36. EXTANT: (A) extensive (B) extraneous (C) extricable (D) extinct (E) extra

37. TRACTABILITY: (A) infertility (B) implausibility (C) incorrigibility (D) impenetrability (E) indefatigability

38. NOISOME:
(A) attractively fragrant
(B) subtly flattering
(C) consistently patient
(D) softly glowing
(E) gradually diminishing

S T O P

IF YOU FINISH BEFORE TIME IS CALLED, YOU MAY CHECK YOUR WORK ON THIS SECTION ONLY. DO NOT WORK ON ANY OTHER SECTION IN THE TEST.

SECTION 2

Time—30 minutes

25 Questions

Directions: Each question or group of questions is based on a passage or set of conditions. In answering some of the questions, it may be useful to draw a rough diagram. For each question, select the best answer choice given.

Questions 1-7

A mail-order company sells packages of jam, each containing three jars of jam. The available flavors are: grape, orange, strawberry, peach, and quince. Each jar contains exactly one flavor of jam. Each package must conform to the following rules:

Each package must contain either two or three different flavors of jam.

A package containing any orange jam must also contain at least one jar of grape.

A package containing any grape jam must also contain at least one jar of orange.

Peach jam and quince jam cannot be packed in the same package.

A package containing any strawberry jam must also contain at least one jar of quince, but a package containing quince jam need not contain strawberry jam.

1. Which of the following is an acceptable package?

(A) One jar of peach, one jar of strawberry, and one jar of orange
(B) One jar of orange, one jar of strawberry, and one jar of grape
(C) Two jars of strawberry and one jar of quince
(D) Three jars of peach
(E) Three jars of orange

2. An acceptable package CANNOT contain which of the following combinations of jams?

(A) Grape and peach
(B) Peach and quince
(C) Orange and peach
(D) Orange and grape
(E) Strawberry and quince

3. Which of the following could be packed with a jar of strawberry to make an acceptable package?

(A) One jar of peach and one jar of orange
(B) One jar of grape and one jar of orange
(C) Two jars of quince
(D) Two jars of orange
(E) Two jars of grape

4. A jar of which of the following must be packed with a jar of orange and a jar of peach to make an acceptable package?

(A) Grape
(B) Orange
(C) Strawberry
(D) Peach
(E) Quince

5. Which of the following pairs of jars of jam could be packed with a jar of orange to make an acceptable package?

(A) One jar each of orange and strawberry
(B) One jar each of grape and strawberry
(C) Two jars of orange
(D) Two jars of grape
(E) Two jars of strawberry

6. Which of the following CANNOT be two of the three jars of jam in an acceptable package?

(A) One jar of strawberry and one jar of peach
(B) One jar of grape and one jar of orange
(C) Two jars of orange
(D) Two jars of grape
(E) Two jars of strawberry

7. An acceptable package CANNOT contain two jars of

(A) orange
(B) grape
(C) quince
(D) strawberry
(E) peach

GO ON TO THE NEXT PAGE.

8. A person who agrees to serve as mediator between two warring factions at the request of both abandons by so agreeing the right later to take sides. To take sides at a later point would be to suggest that the earlier presumptive impartiality was a sham.

The passage above emphasizes which of the following points about mediators?

(A) They should try to form no opinions of their own about any issue that is related to the dispute.
(B) They should not agree to serve unless they are committed to maintaining a stance of impartiality.
(C) They should not agree to serve unless they are equally acceptable to all parties to a dispute.
(D) They should feel free to take sides in the dispute right from the start, provided that they make their biases publicly known.
(E) They should reserve the right to abandon their impartiality so as not to be open to the charge of having been deceitful.

9. A study of attitudes toward prime-time television programs showed that programs with identical ratings in terms of number of people watching received highly divergent marks for quality from their viewers. This additional piece of information could prove valuable for advertisers, who might be well advised to spend their advertising dollars for programs that viewers feel are of high quality.

Which of the following, if true, supports the claim that information about viewers' perceptions of the quality of television programs could be valuable to advertisers?

(A) The number of programs judged to be of high quality constituted a high percentage of the total number of programs judged.
(B) Many of the programs judged to be of high quality were shown on noncommercial networks.
(C) Television viewers more frequently remember the sponsors of programs they admire than the sponsors of programs they judge mediocre.
(D) Television viewers tend to watch new programs only when those programs follow old, familiar programs.
(E) Television viewers report that the quality of a television advertisement has little effect on their buying habits.

10. Nineteenth-century art critics judged art by the realism of its method of representation. It was assumed that the realistic method developed from primitive beginnings to the perfection of formal realism. It is one of the permanent gains of the aesthetic revolution of the twentieth century that we are rid of this type of aesthetics.

It can be inferred from the passage above that the artistic revolution of the twentieth century had which of the following effects?

(A) It deemphasized realistic representation as an evaluative consideration for judging works of art.
(B) It permitted modern critics to appreciate the simplicity of primitive art.
(C) It repudiated the realistic representation found in the art of the past.
(D) It reinforced traditional ways of looking at and judging great art.
(E) It allowed art critics to understand the evolution and nature of art.

GO ON TO THE NEXT PAGE.

Questions 11-16

Three women—R, S, and T, two men—U and V, and four children—W, X, Y, and Z—are going to a game. They have a total of nine seats for the game, but the seats are in three different sections of the arena; they have a group of three adjacent seats in each section. For the game, the nine people must divide into groups of three according to the following restrictions:

No adults of the same sex can be together in any group.
W cannot be in R's group.
X must be in a group with S or U or both.

11. If R is the only adult in one group, the other members of her group must be
    (A) W and X
    (B) W and Y
    (C) X and Y
    (D) X and Z
    (E) Y and Z

12. If R and U are two of the three people in the first group, who can be in the second and third groups, respectively?
    (A) S, T, W ; V, Y, Z
    (B) S, W, Z ; T, V, X
    (C) S, X, Y ; T, W, Z
    (D) T, V, W; S, Y, Z
    (E) W, X, Y ; S, V, Z

13. Which of the following pairs of people can be in the same group as W ?
    (A) R and Y
    (B) S and U
    (C) S and V
    (D) U and V
    (E) X and Z

14. Which of the following must be true?
    (A) One of the women is in a group with two children.
    (B) One of the two men is in a group with W.
    (C) R is in a group with a man.
    (D) T's group includes exactly one child.
    (E) One of the groups includes no children.

15. Any of the following pairs of people could be in X's group EXCEPT
    (A) R and U
    (B) S and T
    (C) S and U
    (D) S and W
    (E) T and U

16. If T, Y, and Z are in one group, which of the following must be together in one of the other groups?
    (A) R, S, V
    (B) R, U, W
    (C) S, U, W
    (D) S, V, W
    (E) U, V, X

GO ON TO THE NEXT PAGE.

Questions 17-22

The manager of a repertory theater company is planning a schedule of productions for the company's five-week summer festival. Two different plays will be scheduled for each of the five weeks. The ten plays that will be scheduled are four plays by playwright R, two plays by playwright S, two plays by playwright T, one play by playwright U, and one play by playwright V. The scheduling is subject to the following restrictions:

No two plays by the same playwright will be scheduled for any of the five weeks, except for week 3, for which two plays by playwright R will be scheduled.

The play by playwright V will be scheduled for week 5.

No play by playwright S will be scheduled for the same week as any play by playwright R.

17. Which of the following could be the two plays scheduled for week 1 ?

(A) Two plays by playwright R
(B) Two plays by playwright S
(C) A play by playwright R and a play by playwright S
(D) A play by playwright R and the play by playwright U
(E) The play by playwright U and the play by playwright V

18. If the plays by playwright R will be scheduled for weeks 2, 3, and 4, which of the following must be true?

(A) A play by playwright S will be scheduled for week 2.
(B) A play by playwright S will be scheduled for week 5.
(C) A play by playwright T will be scheduled for week 2.
(D) A play by playwright T will be scheduled for week 4.
(E) The play by playwright U will be scheduled for week 1.

19. If the plays by playwright S will be scheduled for weeks 1 and 2, which of the following must be true?

(A) A play by playwright R will be scheduled for week 4.
(B) A play by playwright T will be scheduled for week 1.
(C) A play by playwright T will be scheduled for week 4.
(D) A play by playwright T will be scheduled for week 5.
(E) The play by playwright U will be scheduled for week 4.

20. Which of the following pairs of plays CANNOT be scheduled together for any week?

(A) A play by playwright R and a play by playwright T
(B) A play by playwright R and the play by playwright U
(C) A play by playwright S and a play by playwright T
(D) A play by playwright S and the play by playwright U
(E) A play by playwright T and the play by playwright U

21. If a play by playwright S and the play by playwright U will both be scheduled for the same week, which of the following must be true?

(A) A play by playwright R and a play by playwright T will both be scheduled for the same week.
(B) A play by playwright S and a play by playwright T will both be scheduled for the same week.
(C) The play by playwright U will be scheduled for week 2.
(D) A play by playwright S will be scheduled for week 4.
(E) A play by playwright T will be scheduled for week 5.

22. If the plays by playwright T will be scheduled for consecutive weeks, which of the following must be true?

(A) The plays by playwright S will be scheduled for weeks 1 and 2.
(B) The plays by playwright S will be scheduled for weeks 2 and 5.
(C) The plays by playwright S will be scheduled for weeks 4 and 5.
(D) The plays by playwright T will be scheduled for weeks 1 and 2.
(E) The plays by playwright T will be scheduled for weeks 4 and 5.

GO ON TO THE NEXT PAGE.

Questions 23-24

Why save endangered species? For the general public, endangered species appear to be little more than biological oddities. A very different perception is gained from considering the issue of extinction in a wider context. The important point is that many major social advances have been made on the basis of life forms whose worth would never have been perceived in advance. Consider the impact of rubber-producing plants on contemporary life and industry: approximately two-thirds of the world's rubber supply comes from rubber-producing plants and is made into objects as diverse as rubber washers and rubber boots.

23. The author's point is made chiefly by

(A) acknowledging the validity of two opposing points of view
(B) appealing to the emotions of the audience rather than to their intellects
(C) suggesting a useful perspective for viewing the question raised at the beginning of the passage
(D) trying to discredit the view of an opponent without presenting an alternative hypothesis
(E) generalizing from similar to dissimilar cases

24. All of the following facts could be used as illustrative examples in addition to the example of rubber-producing plants EXCEPT:

(A) The discovery of the vaccine for smallpox resulted from observing the effect of the cowpox virus on the hands of dairy workers.
(B) The major source of our pharmaceutical supplies is plants, some of them commonly thought of as weeds.
(C) Certain antibiotics were originally derived from mold growing on cantaloupe.
(D) Plastic is a unique product derived from petroleum and petroleum by-products.
(E) Hamsters and other rodents have played an important role in laboratory tests of medicine for use on humans.

25. In the United States between 1850 and 1880, the number of farmers continued to increase, but at a rate lower than that of the general population.

Which of the following statements directly contradicts the information presented above?

(A) The number of farmers in the general population increased slightly in the thirty years between 1850 and 1880.
(B) The rate of growth of the United States labor force and the rate of growth of the general population rose simultaneously in the thirty years between 1850 and 1880.
(C) The proportion of farmers in the United States labor force remained constant in the thirty years between 1850 and 1880.
(D) The proportion of farmers in the United States labor force decreased from 64 percent in 1850 to 49 percent in 1880.
(E) The proportion of farmers in the general population increased from 68 percent in 1850 to 72 percent in 1880.

S T O P

IF YOU FINISH BEFORE TIME IS CALLED, YOU MAY CHECK YOUR WORK ON THIS SECTION ONLY. DO NOT WORK ON ANY OTHER SECTION IN THE TEST.

Section 3 starts on page 176.

SECTION 3

Time—30 minutes

30 Questions

Numbers: All numbers used are real numbers.

Figures: Position of points, angles, regions, etc. can be assumed to be in the order shown; and angle measures can be assumed to be positive.

Lines shown as straight can be assumed to be straight.

Figures can be assumed to lie in a plane unless otherwise indicated.

Figures that accompany questions are intended to provide information useful in answering the questions. However, unless a note states that a figure is drawn to scale, you should solve these problems NOT by estimating sizes by sight or by measurement, but by using your knowledge of mathematics (see Example 2 below).

Directions: Each of the Questions 1-15 consists of two quantities, one in Column A and one in Column B. You are to compare the two quantities and choose

A if the quantity in Column A is greater;
B if the quantity in Column B is greater;
C if the two quantities are equal;
D if the relationship cannot be determined from the information given.

Note: Since there are only four choices, NEVER MARK (E).

Common Information: In a question, information concerning one or both of the quantities to be compared is centered above the two columns. A symbol that appears in both columns represents the same thing in Column A as it does in Column B.

	Column A	Column B	Sample Answers
Example 1:	2×6	$2 + 6$	● Ⓑ Ⓒ Ⓓ Ⓔ

Examples 2-4 refer to $\triangle PQR$.

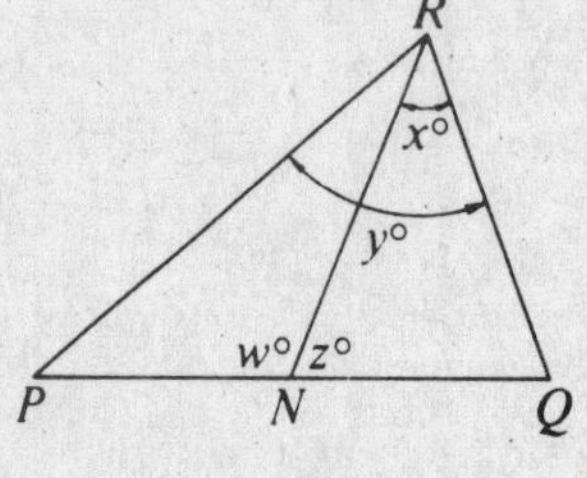

Example 2:	PN	NQ	Ⓐ Ⓑ Ⓒ ● Ⓔ (since equal measures cannot be assumed, even though PN and NQ appear equal)
Example 3:	x	y	Ⓐ ● Ⓒ Ⓓ Ⓔ (since N is between P and Q)
Example 4:	$w + z$	180	Ⓐ Ⓑ ● Ⓓ Ⓔ (since PQ is a straight line)

GO ON TO THE NEXT PAGE.

A if the quantity in Column A is greater;
B if the quantity in Column B is greater;
C if the two quantities are equal;
D if the relationship cannot be determined from the information given.

	Column A	Column B
1.	(40% of 50) + 60	(60% of 50) + 40
2.	$\frac{1}{12}$ of 17	$\frac{1}{17}$ of 12
	$x+y=-1$	
3.	x	y
4.	23(784)	24(783)
	$0<r<t$	
5.	$\frac{r}{t}$	$\frac{t}{r}$

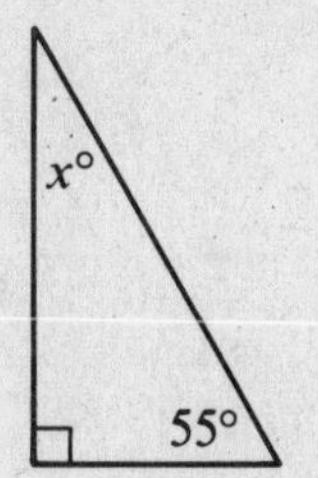

	Column A	Column B
6.	x	35

For each home in Town X, the amount of property tax is p percent of the value of the home. The property tax on a home whose value is $45,000 is $1,200.

	Column A	Column B
7.	The property tax on a home in Town X whose value is $54,000	$1,300

The area of square region S is 36.

	Column A	Column B
8.	The perimeter of S	24

A printer numbered consecutively the pages of a book, beginning with 1 on the first page. In numbering the pages, he printed a total of 189 digits.

	Column A	Column B
9.	The number of pages in the book	100

The average (arithmetic mean) of x, y, and 6 is 3.

	Column A	Column B
10.	$\frac{x+y}{2}$	$\frac{3}{2}$

GO ON TO THE NEXT PAGE.

A if the quantity in Column A is greater;
B if the quantity in Column B is greater;
C if the two quantities are equal;
D if the relationship cannot be determined from the information given.

	Column A	Column B

Triangular regions T_1 and T_2 have equal areas and have heights h_1 and h_2, respectively.

11. $\frac{\text{The area of } T_1}{h_1}$ $\qquad$ $\frac{\text{The area of } T_2}{h_2}$

12. $\frac{3\cdot 3\cdot 3}{6\cdot 6\cdot 6}$ $\qquad$ $\left(\frac{1}{2}\right)^3$

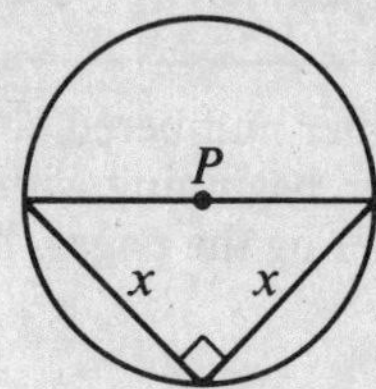

The area of the circular region with center P is 16π.

13. x $\qquad$ 4

	Column A	Column B

m, p, and x are positive integers and $mp = x$.

14. m $\qquad$ x

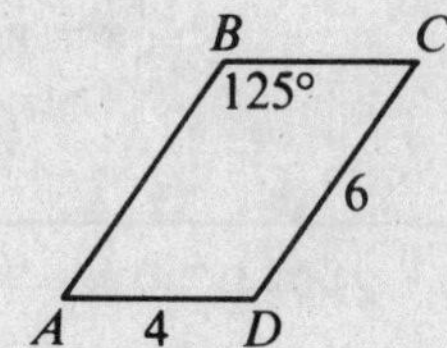

$ABCD$ is a parallelogram.

15. The area of region $ABCD$ $\qquad$ 24

GO ON TO THE NEXT PAGE.

Directions: Each of the Questions 16-30 has five answer choices. For each of these questions, select the best of the answer choices given.

---

16. When walking, a certain person takes 16 complete steps in 10 seconds. At this rate, how many complete steps does the person take in 72 seconds?

(A) 45
(B) 78
(C) 86
(D) 99
(E) 115

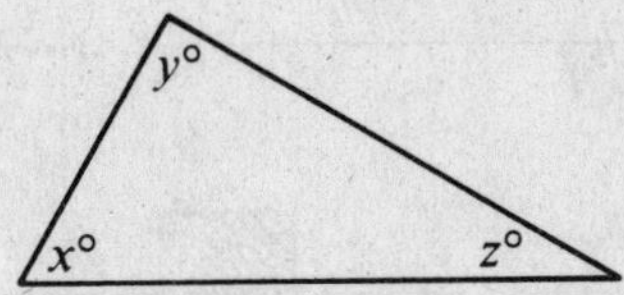

17. In the figure above, what is the value of $\frac{x+y+z}{45}$?

(A) 2 (B) 3 (C) 4 (D) 5 (E) 6

18. $52.68 \times \frac{1}{100} =$

(A) 0.05268 (B) 0.5268 (C) 5.268
(D) 526.8 (E) 52,680

19. If $b - c = 3$, and $a + c = 32$, then $a + b =$

(A) 30 (B) 35 (C) 40 (D) 42 (E) 50

20. A rectangular floor 18 feet by 10 feet is to be completely covered with carpeting that costs x dollars per square yard. In terms of x, how many dollars will the carpeting cost? (1 yard = 3 feet)

(A) $20x$
(B) $28x$
(C) $60x$
(D) $180x$
(E) $540x$

GO ON TO THE NEXT PAGE.

Questions 21-25 refer to the following graphs.

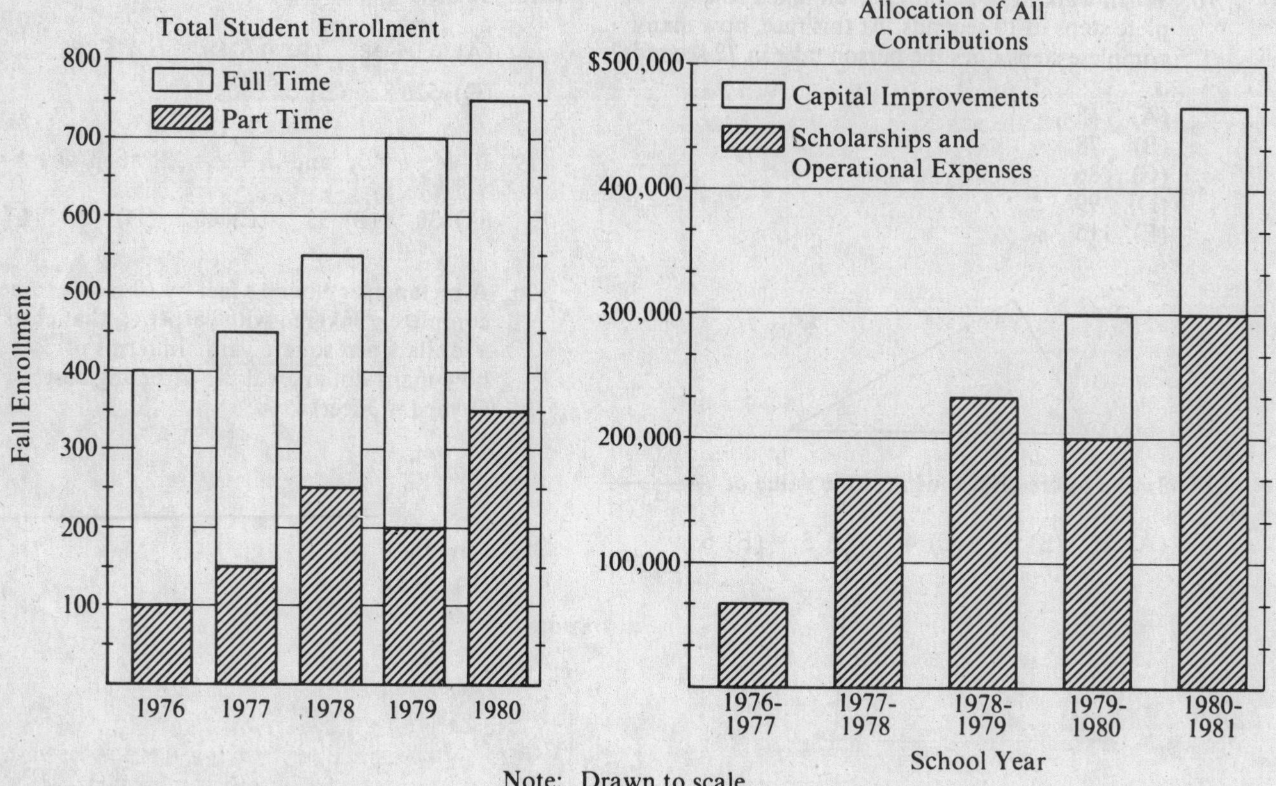

Note: Drawn to scale.

21. What was the total number of students enrolled at College R in the fall of 1979 ?

(A) 200
(B) 250
(C) 500
(D) 650
(E) 700

22. By what percent did the number of part-time students enrolled increase from the fall of 1979 to the fall of 1980 ?

(A) 7%
(B) 42%
(C) $66\frac{2}{3}\%$
(D) 75%
(E) 80%

GO ON TO THE NEXT PAGE.

23. What was the increase, if any, in the number of full-time students enrolled at College R from the fall of 1976 to the fall of 1977?

(A) 0 (B) 50 (C) 100
(D) 150 (E) 200

24. In the 1978-1979 school year, if 12 percent of the amount of contributions allocated to scholarships and operational expenses was allocated to heating costs, approximately how much was NOT allocated to heating costs?

(A) $2,000
(B) $25,000
(C) $176,000
(D) $205,000
(E) $250,000

25. Approximately what was the total amount of contributions to College R from the 1978-1979 school year through the 1980-1981 school year, inclusive?

(A) $967,000
(B) $1,000,000
(C) $9,000,000
(D) $9,667,000
(E) $10,000,000

---

26. If $x \neq 0$, then $\frac{x(x^2)^3}{x^2} =$

(A) x^2 (B) x^3 (C) x^4 (D) x^5 (E) x^6

27. Seven is equal to how many thirds of seven?

(A) $\frac{1}{3}$
(B) 1
(C) 3
(D) 7
(E) 21

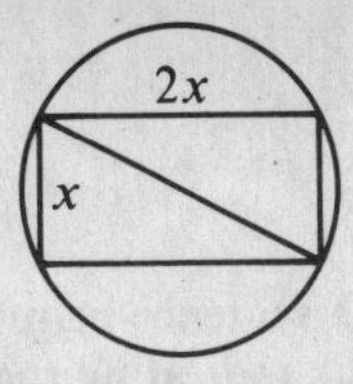

28. In the figure above, if the area of the inscribed rectangular region is 32, then the circumference of the circle is

(A) 20π (B) $4\pi\sqrt{5}$ (C) $4\pi\sqrt{3}$
(D) $2\pi\sqrt{5}$ (E) $2\pi\sqrt{3}$

29. Which of the following equals the reciprocal of $x - \frac{1}{y}$, where $x - \frac{1}{y} \neq 0$?

(A) $\frac{1}{x} - y$
(B) $-\frac{y}{x}$
(C) $\frac{y}{x-1}$
(D) $\frac{x}{xy-1}$
(E) $\frac{y}{xy-1}$

30. A certain integer n is a multiple of both 5 and 9. Which of the following must be true?

I. n is an odd integer.
II. n is equal to 45.
III. n is a multiple of 15.

(A) III only
(B) I and II only
(C) I and III only
(D) II and III only
(E) I, II, and III

S T O P

IF YOU FINISH BEFORE TIME IS CALLED, YOU MAY CHECK YOUR WORK ON THIS SECTION ONLY. DO NOT WORK ON ANY OTHER SECTION IN THE TEST.

SECTION 4

Time—30 minutes

38 Questions

Directions: Each sentence below has one or two blanks, each blank indicating that something has been omitted. Beneath the sentence are five lettered words or sets of words. Choose the word or set of words for each blank that best fits the meaning of the sentence as a whole.

1. The ------- of mass literacy coincided with the first industrial revolution; in turn, the new expansion in literacy, as well as cheaper printing, helped to nurture the ------- of popular literature.

(A) building..mistrust
(B) reappearance..display
(C) receipt..source
(D) selection..influence
(E) emergence..rise

2. Although ancient tools were ------- preserved, enough have survived to allow us to demonstrate an occasionally interrupted but generally ------- progress through prehistory.

(A) partially..noticeable
(B) superficially..necessary
(C) unwittingly..documented
(D) rarely..continual
(E) needlessly..incessant

3. In parts of the Arctic, the land grades into the landfast ice so ------- that you can walk off the coast and not know you are over the hidden sea.

(A) permanently (B) imperceptibly
(C) irregularly (D) precariously
(E) slightly

4. Kagan maintains that an infant's reactions to its first stressful experiences are part of a natural process of development, not harbingers of childhood unhappiness or ------- signs of adolescent anxiety.

(A) prophetic (B) normal
(C) monotonous (D) virtual
(E) typical

5. An investigation that is ------- can occasionally yield new facts, even notable ones, but typically the appearance of such facts is the result of a search in a definite direction.

(A) timely (B) unguided (C) consistent
(D) uncomplicated (E) subjective

6. Like many eighteenth-century scholars who lived by cultivating those in power, Winckelmann neglected to neutralize, by some ------- gesture of comradeship, the resentment his peers were bound to feel because of his ------- the high and mighty.

(A) quixotic..intrigue with
(B) enigmatic..familiarity with
(C) propitiatory..involvement with
(D) salutary..questioning of
(E) unfeigned..sympathy for

7. In a ------- society that worships efficiency, it is difficult for a sensitive and idealistic person to make the kinds of ------- decisions that alone spell success as it is defined by such a society.

(A) bureaucratic..edifying
(B) pragmatic..hardheaded
(C) rational..well-intentioned
(D) competitive..evenhanded
(E) modern..dysfunctional

GO ON TO THE NEXT PAGE.

Directions: In each of the following questions, a related pair of words or phrases is followed by five lettered pairs of words or phrases. Select the lettered pair that best expresses a relationship similar to that expressed in the original pair.

8. TABLECLOTH:TABLE :: (A) tent:ground (B) shirt:hanger (C) window:sill (D) sheet:mattress (E) cloud:earth

9. CANVAS:PAINTER :: (A) leather:shoe (B) brush:palette (C) chisel:wood (D) marble:sculptor (E) hammer:carpenter

10. MANSION:RESIDENCE ::
(A) limousine:automobile
(B) chandelier:candle
(C) tuxedo:wardrobe
(D) diamond:rhinestone
(E) yacht:harbor

11. DOOR:ROOM :: (A) rudder:anchor (B) boat:ship (C) patio:terrace (D) hatch:hold (E) basement:attic

12. CHOREOGRAPHY:DANCE ::
(A) ceremony:sermon
(B) agenda:advertisement
(C) poetry:recitation
(D) instrumentation:conductor
(E) plot:story

13. EVAPORATE:VAPOR ::
(A) petrify:stone (B) centrifuge:liquid (C) saturate:fluid (D) corrode:acid (E) incinerate:fire

14. ASSUAGE:SORROW ::
(A) retaliate:antipathy
(B) dampen:ardor
(C) entrust:reliability
(D) counsel:reluctance
(E) withhold:appreciation

15. NUMB:INSENSIBLE :: (A) reflect:luminous (B) burnish:lustrous (C) heckle:raucous (D) repulse:odious (E) braid:sinuous

16. AUDACIOUS:TREPIDATION ::
(A) refractory:intransigence
(B) laconic:volubility
(C) sordid:aspiration
(D) cursory:accumulation
(E) derisive:subordination

GO ON TO THE NEXT PAGE.

Directions: Each passage in this group is followed by questions based on its content. After reading a passage, choose the best answer to each question. Answer all questions following a passage on the basis of what is stated or implied in that passage.

"I want to criticize the social system, and to show it at work, at its most intense." Virginia Woolf's provocative statement about her intentions in writing *Mrs. Dalloway* has regularly been ignored by the critics, since it highlights an aspect of her literary interests very different from the traditional picture of the "poetic" novelist concerned with examining states of reverie and vision and with following the intricate pathways of individual consciousness. But Virginia Woolf was a realistic as well as a poetic novelist, a satirist and social critic as well as a visionary: literary critics' cavalier dismissal of Woolf's social vision will not withstand scrutiny.

In her novels, Woolf is deeply engaged by the questions of how individuals are shaped (or deformed) by their social environments, how historical forces impinge on people's lives, how class, wealth, and gender help to determine people's fates. Most of her novels are rooted in a realistically rendered social setting and in a precise historical time.

Woolf's focus on society has not been generally recognized because of her intense antipathy to propaganda in art. The pictures of reformers in her novels are usually satiric or sharply critical. Even when Woolf is fundamentally sympathetic to their causes, she portrays people anxious to reform their society and possessed of a message or program as arrogant or dishonest, unaware of how their political ideas serve their own psychological needs. (Her *Writer's Diary* notes: "the only honest people are the artists," whereas "these social reformers and philanthropists . . . harbor . . . discreditable desires under the disguise of loving their kind. . . .") Woolf detested what she called "preaching" in fiction, too, and criticized novelist D. H. Lawrence (among others) for working by this method.

Woolf's own social criticism is expressed in the language of observation rather than in direct commentary, since for her, fiction is a contemplative, not an active art. She describes phenomena and provides materials for a judgment about society and social issues; it is the reader's work to put the observations together and understand the coherent point of view behind them. As a moralist, Woolf works by indirection, subtly undermining officially accepted mores, mocking, suggesting, calling into question, rather than asserting, advocating, bearing witness: hers is the satirist's art.

Woolf's literary models were acute social observers like Chekhov and Chaucer. As she put it in *The Common Reader*, "It is safe to say that not a single law has been framed or one stone set upon another because of anything Chaucer said or wrote; and yet, as we read him, we are absorbing morality at every pore." Like Chaucer, Woolf chose to understand as well as to judge, to know her society root and branch—a decision crucial in order to produce art rather than polemic.

17. Which of the following would be the most appropriate title for the passage?
    - (A) Poetry and Satire as Influences on the Novels of Virginia Woolf
    - (B) Virginia Woolf: Critic and Commentator on the Twentieth-Century Novel
    - (C) Trends in Contemporary Reform Movements as a Key to Understanding Virginia Woolf's Novels
    - (D) Society as Allegory for the Individual in the Novels of Virginia Woolf
    - (E) Virginia Woolf's Novels: Critical Reflections on the Individual and on Society

18. In the first paragraph of the passage, the author's attitude toward the literary critics mentioned can best be described as
    - (A) disparaging
    - (B) ironic
    - (C) facetious
    - (D) skeptical but resigned
    - (E) disappointed but hopeful

19. It can be inferred from the passage that Woolf chose Chaucer as a literary model because she believed that
    - (A) Chaucer was the first English author to focus on society as a whole as well as on individual characters
    - (B) Chaucer was an honest and forthright author, whereas novelists like D. H. Lawrence did not sincerely wish to change society
    - (C) Chaucer was more concerned with understanding his society than with calling its accepted mores into question
    - (D) Chaucer's writing was greatly, if subtly, effective in influencing the moral attitudes of his readers
    - (E) her own novels would be more widely read if, like Chaucer, she did not overtly and vehemently criticize contemporary society

GO ON TO THE NEXT PAGE.

20. It can be inferred from the passage that the most probable reason Woolf realistically described the social setting in the majority of her novels was that she

(A) was aware that contemporary literary critics considered the novel to be the most realistic of literary genres
(B) was interested in the effect of a person's social milieu on his or her character and actions
(C) needed to be as attentive to detail as possible in her novels in order to support the arguments she advanced in them
(D) wanted to show that a painstaking fidelity in the representation of reality did not in any way hamper the artist
(E) wished to prevent critics from charging that her novels were written in an ambiguous and inexact style

21. Which of the following phrases best expresses the sense of the word "contemplative" as it is used in lines 43-44 of the passage?

(A) Gradually elucidating the rational structures underlying accepted mores
(B) Reflecting on issues in society without prejudice or emotional commitment
(C) Avoiding the aggressive assertion of the author's perspective to the exclusion of the reader's judgment
(D) Conveying a broad view of society as a whole rather than focusing on an isolated individual consciousness
(E) Appreciating the world as the artist sees it rather than judging it in moral terms

22. The author implies that a major element of the satirist's art is the satirist's

(A) consistent adherence to a position of lofty disdain when viewing the foibles of humanity
(B) insistence on the helplessness of individuals against the social forces that seek to determine an individual's fate
(C) cynical disbelief that visionaries can either enlighten or improve their societies
(D) fundamental assumption that some ambiguity must remain in a work of art in order for it to reflect society and social mores accurately
(E) refusal to indulge in polemic when presenting social mores to readers for their scrutiny

23. The passage supplies information for answering which of the following questions?

(A) Have literary critics ignored the social criticism inherent in the works of Chekhov and Chaucer?
(B) Does the author believe that Woolf is solely an introspective and visionary novelist?
(C) What are the social causes with which Woolf shows herself to be sympathetic in her writings?
(D) Was D. H. Lawrence as concerned as Woolf was with creating realistic settings for his novels?
(E) Does Woolf attribute more power to social environment or to historical forces as shapers of a person's life?

GO ON TO THE NEXT PAGE.

It is a popular misconception that nuclear fusion power is free of radioactivity; in fact, the deuterium-tritium reaction that nuclear scientists are currently exploring with such zeal produces both alpha particles and neutrons. (The neutrons are used to produce tritium from a lithium blanket surrounding the reactor.) Another common misconception is that nuclear fusion power is a virtually unlimited source of energy because of the enormous quantity of deuterium in the sea. Actually, its limits are set by the amount of available lithium, which is about as plentiful as uranium in the Earth's crust. Research should certainly continue on controlled nuclear fusion, but no energy program should be premised on its existence until it has proven practical. For the immediate future, we must continue to use hydroelectric power, nuclear fission, and fossil fuels to meet our energy needs. The energy sources already in major use are in major use for good reason.

24. The primary purpose of the passage is to

(A) criticize scientists who believe that the deuterium-tritium fusion reaction can be made feasible as an energy source
(B) admonish scientists who have failed to correctly calculate the amount of lithium available for use in nuclear fusion reactors
(C) defend the continued short-term use of fossil fuels as a major energy source
(D) caution against uncritical embrace of nuclear fusion power as a major energy source
(E) correct the misconception that nuclear fusion power is entirely free of radioactivity

25. It can be inferred from the passage that the author believes which of the following about the current state of public awareness concerning nuclear fusion power?

(A) The public has been deliberately misinformed about the advantages and disadvantages of nuclear fusion power.
(B) The public is unaware of the principal advantage of nuclear fusion over nuclear fission as an energy source.
(C) The public's awareness of the scientific facts concerning nuclear fusion power is somewhat distorted and incomplete.
(D) The public is not interested in increasing its awareness of the advantages and disadvantages of nuclear fusion power.
(E) The public is aware of the disadvantages of nuclear fusion power but not of its advantages.

26. The passage provides information that would answer which of the following questions?

(A) What is likely to be the principal source of deuterium for nuclear fusion power?
(B) How much incidental radiation is produced in the deuterium-tritium fusion reaction?
(C) Why are scientists exploring the deuterium-tritium fusion reaction with such zeal?
(D) Why must the tritium for nuclear fusion be synthesized from lithium?
(E) Why does the deuterium-tritium reaction yield both alpha particles and neutrons?

27. Which of the following statements concerning nuclear scientists is most directly suggested in the passage?

(A) Nuclear scientists are not themselves aware of all of the facts surrounding the deuterium-tritium fusion reaction.
(B) Nuclear scientists exploring the deuterium-tritium reaction have overlooked key facts in their eagerness to prove nuclear fusion practical.
(C) Nuclear scientists may have overestimated the amount of lithium actually available in the Earth's crust.
(D) Nuclear scientists have not been entirely dispassionate in their investigation of the deuterium-tritium reaction.
(E) Nuclear scientists have insufficiently investigated the lithium-to-tritium reaction in nuclear fusion.

GO ON TO THE NEXT PAGE.

Directions: Each question below consists of a word printed in capital letters, followed by five lettered words or phrases. Choose the lettered word or phrase that is most nearly opposite in meaning to the word in capital letters.

Since some of the questions require you to distinguish fine shades of meaning, be sure to consider all the choices before deciding which one is best.

28. PERSEVERE: (A) put into (B) send out (C) take away (D) give up (E) bring forward

29. WATERPROOF: (A) soggy (B) natural (C) unglazed (D) viscous (E) permeable

30. AMALGAMATE: (A) separate (B) fixate (C) terminate (D) calibrate (E) correlate

31. PUNGENCY: (A) boredom (B) redundancy (C) unresponsiveness (D) blandness (E) insignificance

32. ANARCHY: (A) courtesy (B) hope (C) order (D) neutrality (E) importance

33. INCURSION: (A) loss of respect (B) lack of resolve (C) reparation (D) relapse (E) retreat

34. ABROGATE: (A) uphold (B) defer (C) discuss secretly (D) admit willingly (E) read thoroughly

35. HAPLESS: (A) excited (B) elated (C) fortunate (D) completely self-reliant (E) assured of success

36. AVER: (A) collect (B) augment (C) placate (D) deny (E) encourage

37. SEDULOUS: (A) presumptuous (B) ponderous (C) treacherous (D) careless (E) useless

38. INSULARITY:
(A) overzealousness
(B) cosmopolitanism
(C) susceptibility
(D) willing hospitality
(E) knowledgeable consideration

S T O P

IF YOU FINISH BEFORE TIME IS CALLED, YOU MAY CHECK YOUR WORK ON THIS SECTION ONLY. DO NOT WORK ON ANY OTHER SECTION IN THE TEST.

SECTION 5

Time—30 minutes

25 Questions

Directions: Each question or group of questions is based on a passage or set of conditions. In answering some of the questions, it may be useful to draw a rough diagram. For each question, select the best answer choice given.

Questions 1-6

The consumer complaint department of a firm employs exactly six people who answer letters: G, H, I, J, K, and L. Every complaint letter received by the department is classified as either red or blue. The following procedures for answering the letters are used:

Red letters are given first to G or H.
Blue letters are given first to any one of the following: G, J, or I.

If a letter raises a problem that cannot be resolved by the person to whom it is given, it must be forwarded until it reaches someone who can resolve the problem and answer the letter. A letter must be forwarded as follows:

By G to I if the letter is red, but to J if the letter is blue;
By H to either G or I;
By I to J if the letter is red, but to K if the letter is blue;
By J to either I or K whether the letter is red or blue;
By K to L whether the letter is red or blue;
L answers every letter given to him.

1. Any of the following can be true EXCEPT:
   (A) G forwards a red letter to I.
   (B) H forwards a red letter to G.
   (C) H forwards a red letter to I.
   (D) I forwards a red letter to K.
   (E) J forwards a red letter to I.

2. A blue letter could reach L via which of the following sequences of people?
   (A) G to H to K
   (B) G to I to J
   (C) G to J to K
   (D) I to H to J
   (E) I to G to J to K

3. Any letter that reaches L must have been previously given to
   (A) G (B) H (C) I (D) J (E) K

4. Which of the following could be given to each of the six members of the consumer complaint department in turn?
   (A) A red letter that is first given to H
   (B) A red letter that is first given to G
   (C) A blue letter that is first given to G
   (D) A blue letter that is first given to I
   (E) A blue letter that is first given to J

5. Any letter that reaches L must have been given to a minimum of how many members of the consumer complaint department before reaching L?
   (A) 1 (B) 2 (C) 3 (D) 4 (E) 5

6. If a member of the consumer complaint department is given a letter that he or she had previously given to some other member of the department, the person who is given the letter a second time could be
   (A) G (B) H (C) J (D) K (E) L

GO ON TO THE NEXT PAGE.

7. Veteran screenwriters, aiming at creating a 120-page screenplay for a film, usually turn in a 135-page first draft. As one screenwriter put it, "That gives those in charge of the movie a chance to be creative when they get the script: at the very least, they can cut 15 pages."

The screenwriter's statement cited above conveys which of the following propositions?

(A) Screenwriters for a film are generally not involved in any aspects of filmmaking besides providing the script.
(B) Seasoned screenwriters are resigned to, and make allowance for, draft scripts being altered by those evaluating them.
(C) Truly creative screenwriters are too temperamental to adhere to page limits set for their work.
(D) It takes a special kind of creativity to recognize what is best left out of a film script.
(E) Even experienced screenwriters cannot be expected to write scripts of consistently high quality throughout.

8. During the day in Lake Constance, the zooplankton *D. hyalina* departs for the depths where food is scarce and the water cold. *D. galeata* remains near the warm surface where food is abundant. Even though *D. galeata* grows and reproduces much faster, its population is often outnumbered by *D. hyalina*.

Which of the following, if true, would help resolve the apparent paradox presented above?

(A) The number of species of zooplankton living at the bottom of the lake is twice that of species living at the surface.
(B) Predators of zooplankton, such as whitefish and perch, live and feed near the surface of the lake during the day.
(C) In order to make the most of scarce food resources, *D. hyalina* matures more slowly than *D. galeata*.
(D) *D. galeata* clusters under vegetation during the hottest part of the day to avoid the sun's rays.
(E) *D. galeata* produces twice as many offspring per individual in any given period of time as does *D. hyalina*.

9. Each year, fires in the United States cause $12 billion in property losses, insurance costs, fire-fighting expenses, and loss of worker productivity. These fire losses are seven times those of Japan on a per capita basis.

Which of the following, if true, would be LEAST likely to be a factor contributing to the difference between fire losses in Japan and those in the United States?

(A) The walls of Japanese homes are made mostly of wood and bamboo and are more combustible than the walls in most American homes.
(B) The rate of arson, a major contributor to fire statistics in the United States, is almost negligible in Japan.
(C) Most Japanese homes, unlike those in the United States, are equipped with specially designed and effective fire-extinguishing equipment.
(D) Foam-based and plastic furniture, less popular in Japan than in the United States, ignites readily and releases twice the heat energy of equivalent weights of natural fibers.
(E) Japanese fire departments devote proportionately more personnel time to inspection, training, and public education than do United States fire departments.

GO ON TO THE NEXT PAGE.

Questions 10-13

At a cooking school, the following six classes—F, G, H, J, K, and L—are to be scheduled to meet for one demonstration each during an all-day seminar. Each demonstration is 45 minutes long, and the only possible starting times for the class meetings are 9 a.m., 10 a.m., 11 a.m., 2 p.m., and 4 p.m. The schedule of class meetings is to be established in accordance with the following conditions:

F cannot meet at the same time that G meets.
H must meet earlier in the day than F.
J must meet in the afternoon.
None of the other classes can meet at the time that K meets.
L can meet in the morning or in the afternoon.

10. Any of the following could meet at 4 p.m. EXCEPT

(A) F (B) G (C) H (D) J (E) K

11. If J meets some time before K meets, which of the following could be true?

(A) F meets some time after J meets.
(B) G meets at 4 p.m.
(C) K meets at 2 p.m.
(D) L meets at 2 p.m.
(E) L meets some time after K meets.

12. If F meets at 10 a.m. and none of the classes meets at 4 p.m., which of the following must be true?

(A) H meets some time before L meets.
(B) H meets some time before K meets.
(C) K meets some time before G meets.
(D) L meets at the same time that G meets.
(E) L meets at the same time that J meets.

13. If H meets at 2 p.m., which of the following must be true?

(A) F meets later in the day than L.
(B) G meets at 2 p.m.
(C) G meets in the morning.
(D) J meets at 2 p.m.
(E) K meets in the morning.

GO ON TO THE NEXT PAGE.

Questions 14-18

Exactly seven persons—P, Q, R, S, T, U, and V—participate in and finish all of a series of swimming races. There are no ties for any position at the finish of any of the races.

V always finishes somewhere ahead of P.
P always finishes somewhere ahead of Q.
Either R finishes first and T finishes last, or S finishes first and U or Q finishes last.

14. If in a race V finishes fifth, which of the following must be true?
(A) S finishes first.
(B) R finishes second.
(C) T finishes third.
(D) Q finishes fourth.
(E) U finishes last.

15. If in a race R finishes first, V can finish no lower than
(A) second
(B) third
(C) fourth
(D) fifth
(E) sixth

16. If in a race S finishes second, which of the following can be true?
(A) P finishes before R.
(B) V finishes before S.
(C) P finishes before V.
(D) T finishes before Q.
(E) U finishes before V.

17. If in a race S finishes sixth and Q finishes fifth, which of the following can be true?
(A) V finishes first or fourth.
(B) R finishes second or third.
(C) P finishes second or fifth.
(D) U finishes third or fourth.
(E) T finishes fourth or fifth.

18. If in a race R finishes second and Q finishes fifth, which of the following must be true?
(A) S finishes third.
(B) P finishes third.
(C) V finishes fourth.
(D) T finishes sixth.
(E) U finishes sixth.

GO ON TO THE NEXT PAGE.

Questions 19-22

The membership of two committees, designated X and Y, must be drawn exclusively from a group of seven people: Frederick, Georgia, Helen, Irene, Jorge, Karin, and Lamont.

Each of the seven people must serve on X or Y.
No one can serve on both X and Y.
Frederick cannot serve on a committee with Georgia or with Jorge.
Helen cannot serve on a committee with Irene.

19. If Helen serves on X, which of the following must be true?

(A) Frederick serves on X.
(B) Georgia serves on Y.
(C) Irene serves on Y.
(D) Karin serves on X.
(E) Lamont serves on Y.

20. If exactly two people serve on X, which of the following can be one of the two?

(A) Georgia
(B) Helen
(C) Jorge
(D) Karin
(E) Lamont

21. If Lamont does not serve with Karin or Irene, which of the following CANNOT be true?

(A) Frederick serves with Irene.
(B) Georgia serves with Helen.
(C) Helen serves with Karin.
(D) Irene serves with Karin.
(E) Jorge serves with Lamont.

22. There would be only one possible distribution of people on the committees if which of the following restrictions were added to the original set of conditions?

(A) Frederick and Lamont must serve on X, and Helen must serve on Y.
(B) Jorge must serve on X, and Karin and Lamont must serve on Y.
(C) Georgia and Lamont must serve on X.
(D) Helen and four other people must serve on X.
(E) Irene and three other people must serve on Y.

GO ON TO THE NEXT PAGE.

23. Many researchers believe that the presence of RNA in brain cells is the biochemical basis of memory; that is, the presence of RNA enables us to remember. Because certain chemicals are known to inhibit the synthesis of RNA in the body, we can test this hypothesis. Animals that have learned particular responses can be injected with an RNA inhibitor and then tested for memory of the learned responses.

Which of the following test results would most seriously weaken the case for RNA as the basis of memory?

(A) After an injection of RNA inhibitor, a wide range of behaviors in addition to the learned responses were affected.
(B) After an injection of RNA inhibitor, animals that had not consistently been giving the learned responses were able to give them consistently.
(C) After injections of RNA inhibitor, some animals lost memory of the learned responses totally but others lost it only partially.
(D) After a small injection of RNA inhibitor, animals responded well, but as the size of the injection increased, they gave fewer of the learned responses.
(E) After an injection of RNA inhibitor, animals could not learn a new response.

24. The greatest chance for the existence of extraterrestrial life is on a planet beyond our solar system. The Milky Way galaxy alone contains 100 billion other suns, many of which could be accompanied by planets similar enough to Earth to make them suitable abodes of life.

The statement above assumes which of the following?

(A) Living creatures on another planet would probably have the same appearance as those on Earth.
(B) Life cannot exist on other planets in our solar system.
(C) If the appropriate physical conditions exist, life is an inevitable consequence.
(D) More than one of the suns in the galaxy is accompanied by an Earth-like planet.
(E) It is likely that life on another planet would require conditions similar to those on Earth.

25. A ten-year comparison between the United States and the Soviet Union in terms of crop yields per acre revealed that when only planted acreage is compared, Soviet yields are equal to 68 percent of United States yields. When total agricultural acreage (planted acreage plus fallow acreage) is compared, however, Soviet yield is 114 percent of United States yield.

From the information above, which of the following can be most reliably inferred about United States and Soviet agriculture during the ten-year period?

(A) A higher percentage of total agricultural acreage was fallow in the United States than in the Soviet Union.
(B) The United States had more fallow acreage than planted acreage.
(C) Fewer total acres of available agricultural land were fallow in the Soviet Union than in the United States.
(D) The Soviet Union had more planted acreage than fallow acreage.
(E) The Soviet Union produced a greater volume of crops than the United States produced.

S T O P

IF YOU FINISH BEFORE TIME IS CALLED, YOU MAY CHECK YOUR WORK ON THIS SECTION ONLY. DO NOT WORK ON ANY OTHER SECTION IN THE TEST.

SECTION 6

Time—30 minutes

30 Questions

Numbers: All numbers used are real numbers.

Figures: Position of points, angles, regions, etc. can be assumed to be in the order shown; and angle measures can be assumed to be positive.

Lines shown as straight can be assumed to be straight.

Figures can be assumed to lie in a plane unless otherwise indicated.

Figures that accompany questions are intended to provide information useful in answering the questions. However, unless a note states that a figure is drawn to scale, you should solve these problems NOT by estimating sizes by sight or by measurement, but by using your knowledge of mathematics (see Example 2 below).

Directions: Each of the Questions 1-15 consists of two quantities, one in Column A and one in Column B. You are to compare the two quantities and choose

A if the quantity in Column A is greater;
B if the quantity in Column B is greater;
C if the two quantities are equal;
D if the relationship cannot be determined from the information given.

Note: Since there are only four choices, NEVER MARK (E).

Common Information: In a question, information concerning one or both of the quantities to be compared is centered above the two columns. A symbol that appears in both columns represents the same thing in Column A as it does in Column B.

	Column A	Column B	Sample Answers
Example 1:	2×6	$2 + 6$	● Ⓑ Ⓒ Ⓓ Ⓔ

Examples 2-4 refer to $\triangle PQR$.

R, P, N, Q, $x°$, $y°$, $w°$, $z°$

	Column A	Column B	Sample Answers
Example 2:	PN	NQ	Ⓐ Ⓑ Ⓒ ● Ⓔ (since equal measures cannot be assumed, even though PN and NQ appear equal)
Example 3:	x	y	Ⓐ ● Ⓒ Ⓓ Ⓔ (since N is between P and Q)
Example 4:	$w + z$	180	Ⓐ Ⓑ ● Ⓓ Ⓔ (since PQ is a straight line)

GO ON TO THE NEXT PAGE

A if the quantity in Column A is greater;
B if the quantity in Column B is greater;
C if the two quantities are equal;
D if the relationship cannot be determined from the information given.

	Column A	Column B
	$k + n = 13$ $n + 3 = 8$	
1.	k	n

Betty spent $75 for a bicycle and she also spent $27 repairing it. She then sold it for $120.

	Column A	Column B
2.	The money Betty received in excess of the total amount she spent	$20

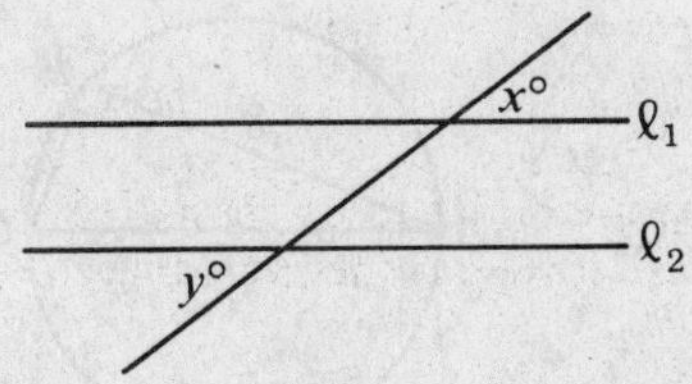

$\ell_1 \parallel \ell_2$

	Column A	Column B
3.	x	y
4.	$-2(-3)(-4)$	$0(4)(8)$

	Column A	Column B
5.	10	$11 + x$
6.	$\frac{1}{2} + \frac{3}{5}$	$\frac{1+3}{2+5}$

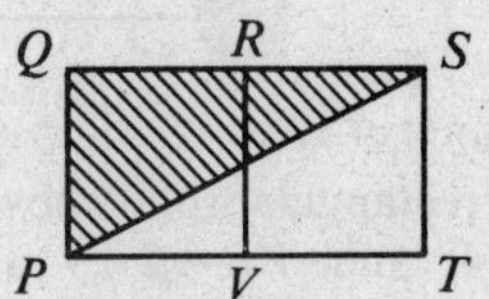

Squares $PQRV$ and $VRST$ have sides of length 6.

	Column A	Column B
7.	The area of shaded region PQS	36

R, S, and T are 3 consecutive odd integers and $R < S < T$.

	Column A	Column B
8.	$R + S + 1$	$S + T - 1$

GO ON TO THE NEXT PAGE.

A if the quantity in Column A is greater;
B if the quantity in Column B is greater;
C if the two quantities are equal;
D if the relationship cannot be determined from the information given.

	Column A	Column B

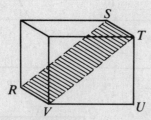

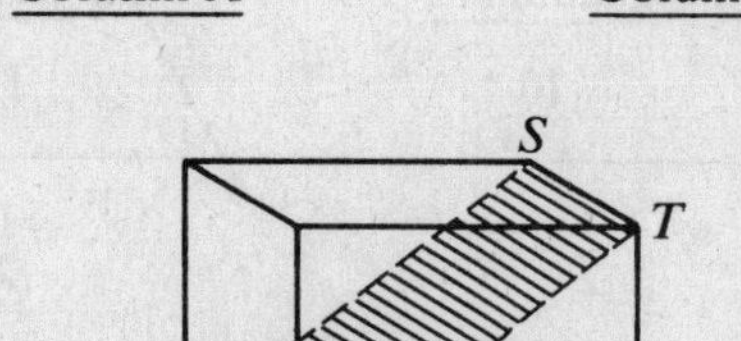

In the rectangular solid shown, $TU = 3$, $UV = 4$, and $VR = 2$.

	Column A	Column B
9.	The area of the shaded rectangular region	9

$x^2y > 0$
$xy^2 < 0$

	Column A	Column B
10.	x	y

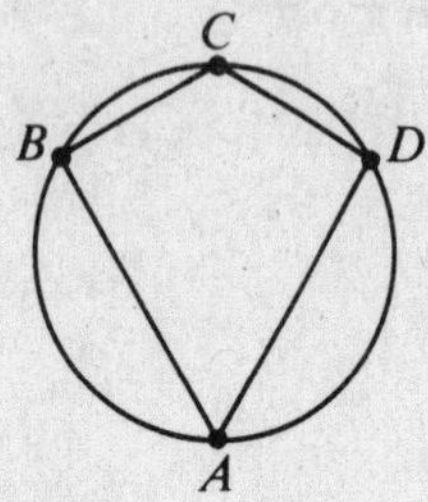

The diameter of the circle is 10.

	Column A	Column B
11.	The area of the region enclosed by quadrilateral $ABCD$	40

	Column A	Column B
12.	$2\frac{1}{2}$ percent of 1,120	$2^2 \cdot 7$

Working at constant rates, machine R completely presses x records in 0.5 hour and machine S completely presses x records in 0.75 hour $(x > 0)$.

	Column A	Column B
13.	The number of records completely pressed by R in 3 hours	The number of records completely pressed by S in 4 hours

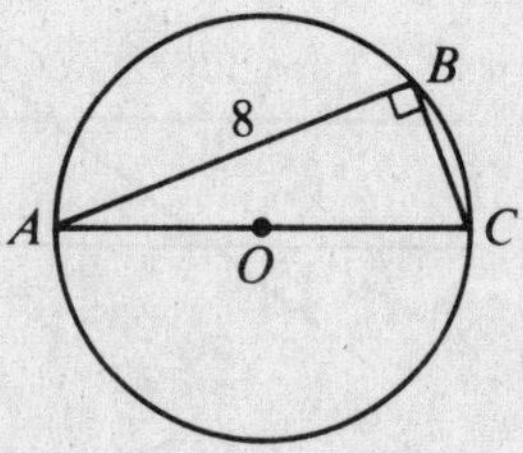

The circle with center O has a radius of 5.

	Column A	Column B
14.	The perimeter of ΔABC	24

x, y, and z are negative integers.

	Column A	Column B
15.	The product of x, y, and z	The sum of x, y, and z

GO ON TO THE NEXT PAGE.

Directions: Each of the Questions 16-30 has five answer choices. For each of these questions, select the best of the answer choices given.

---

16. $\sqrt{(42-6)(25+11)}$

(A) 6 (B) 18 (C) 36
(D) 120 (E) 1,296

17. The price per pair of brand X socks is \$2 and the price per pair of brand Y socks is \$3. If there is no sales tax and a customer chooses only from among these two brands, what is the greatest number of pairs of socks that he can buy with exactly \$25 ?

(A) 9
(B) 10
(C) 11
(D) 12
(E) 20

18. What is the remainder when 6^3 is divided by 8 ?

(A) 5
(B) 3
(C) 2
(D) 1
(E) 0

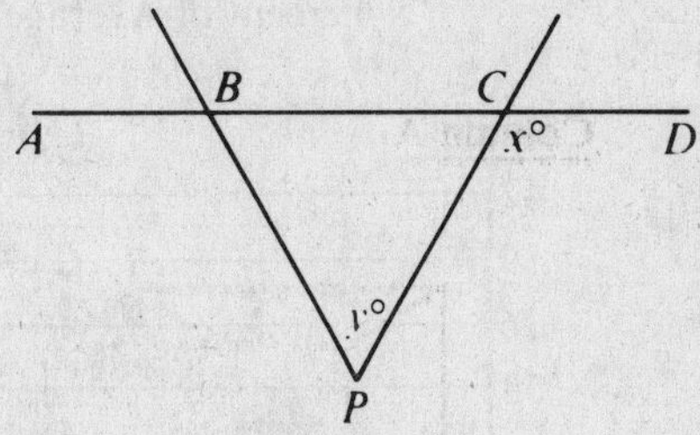

19. In the figure above, $BP = CP$. IF $x = 120$, then $y =$

(A) 30 (B) 60 (C) 75 (D) 90 (E) 120

20. If $y = 3x$ and $z = 2y$, then in terms of x, $x + y + z =$

(A) $10x$ (B) $9x$ (C) $8x$
(D) $6x$ (E) $5x$

GO ON TO THE NEXT PAGE.

Questions 21-25 refer to the following data.

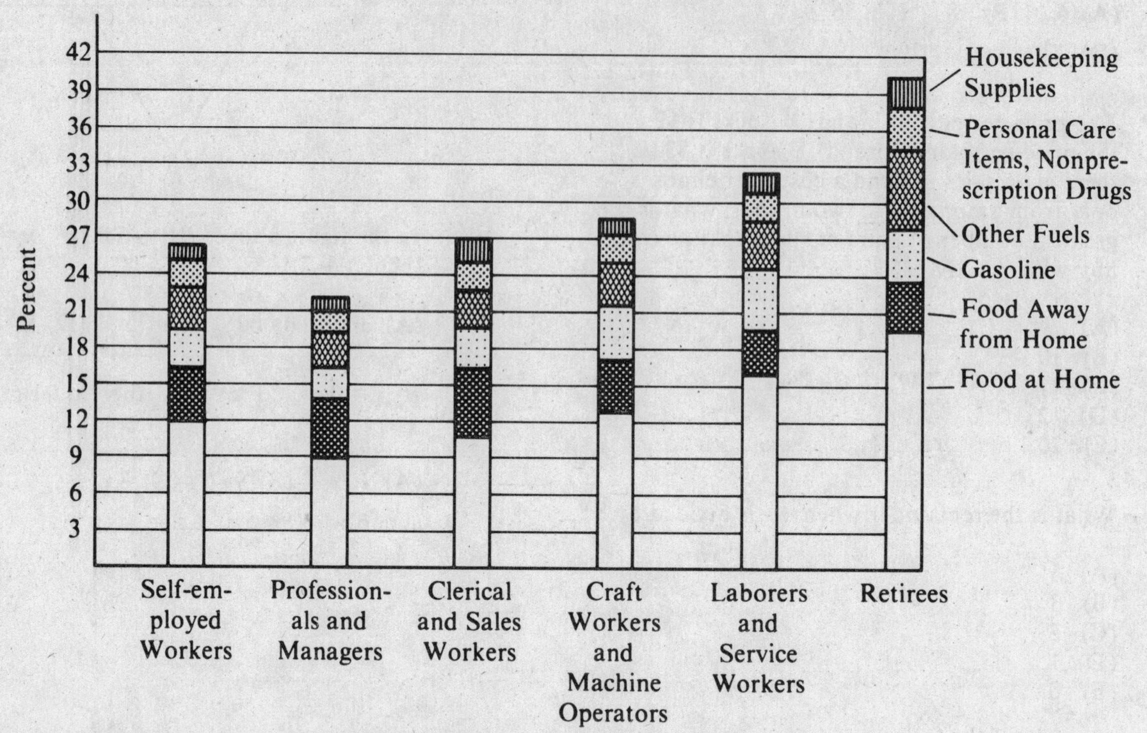

Note: Drawn to scale.

GO ON TO THE NEXT PAGE.

Average Weekly Food and Household Expenditures

Occupational Category of Family Head	Percent of Food and Household Expenditures						Average Weekly Food and Household Expenditures
	Food at Home						
	Meats, Poultry, Seafood	Cereals, Bakery and Dairy Products, Fruits and Vegetables	Other Food at Home	Food Away from Home	Personal Care Items, Nonprescription Drugs	House-keeping Supplies	
Self-employed Workers	22	25	14	22	10	7	$35.88
Professionals and Managers	19	23	11	29	11	7	$38.77
Clerical and Sales Workers	21	22	11	28	11	7	$32.07
Craft Workers and Machine Operators	23	25	15	21	9	7	$35.44
Laborers and Service Workers	24	27	14	19	9	7	$28.86
Retirees	23	29	14	16	11	7	$19.83

21. For which of the following categories was the percent of the average annual income (before taxes) spent on food at home the least?

    (A) Self-employed workers
    (B) Professionals and managers
    (C) Clerical and sales workers
    (D) Craft workers and machine operators
    (E) Laborers and service workers

22. Approximately what average amount per week did the families of professionals and managers spend on food away from home?

    (A) $2
    (B) $8
    (C) $11
    (D) $29
    (E) $38

23. Approximately what percent of the average weekly food and household expenditures of clerical and sales workers was spent on fruits and vegetables?

    (A) 4% (B) 7% (C) 22% (D) 25%
    (E) It cannot be determined from the information given.

24. Approximately what percent of the total average annual income (before taxes) of retirees was spent on meats, poultry, and seafood (consumed at home)?

    (A) 7% (B) 10% (C) 20%
    (D) 23% (E) 31%

25. Which of the following statements can be inferred from the information given?

    I. Of the categories shown, retirees had the greatest average annual incomes (before taxes).
    II. For all the categories shown, the average amount spent per week on housekeeping supplies was the same.
    III. Of the categories shown, the average amount spent per week on meats, poultry, and seafood (consumed at home) was greatest for craft workers and machine operators.

    (A) I only (B) II only (C) III only
    (D) I and II (E) II and III

GO ON TO THE NEXT PAGE.

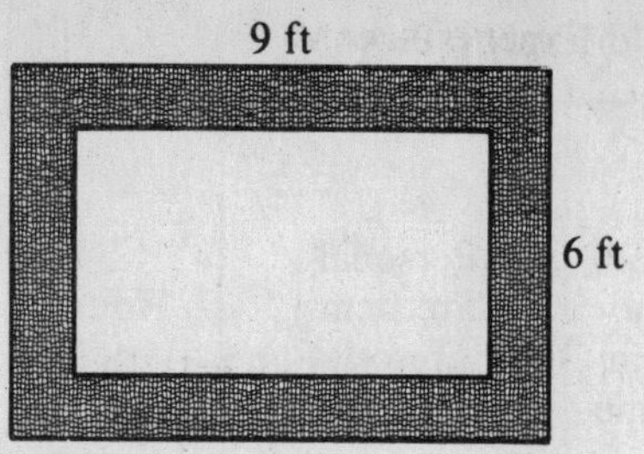

26. The rectangular rug shown in the figure above has a floral border 1 foot wide on all sides. What is the area, in square feet, of that portion of the rug that excludes the border?

(A) 28
(B) 40
(C) 45
(D) 48
(E) 53

27. If $\frac{d-3n}{7n-d} = 1$, which of the following must be true about the relationship between d and n?

(A) n is 4 more than d.

(B) d is 4 more than n.

(C) n is $\frac{7}{3}$ of d.

(D) d is 5 times n.

(E) d is 2 times n.

28. How many positive whole numbers less than 81 are NOT equal to squares of whole numbers?

(A) 9 (B) 70 (C) 71 (D) 72 (E) 73

29. Of the following, which could be the graph of $2 - 5x \leq \frac{6x-5}{-3}$?

(A) 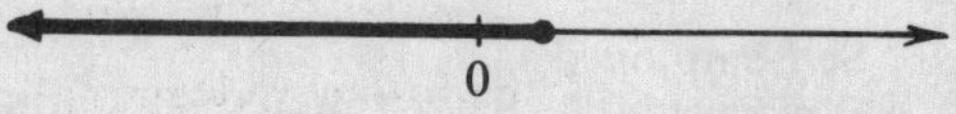

(B) 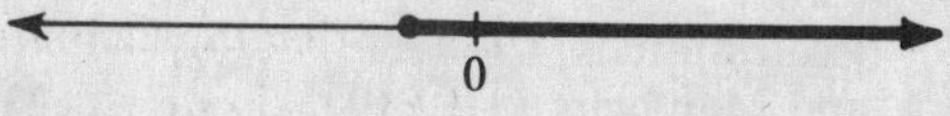

(C) 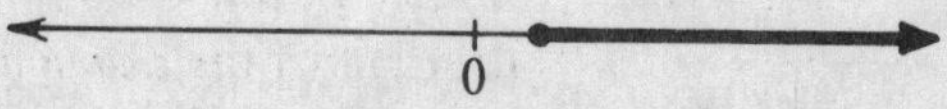

(D) 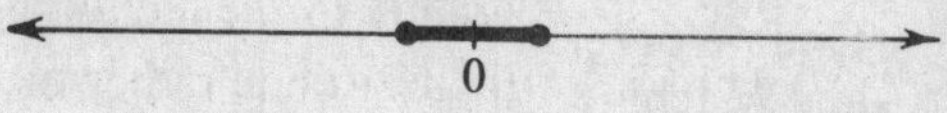

(E) 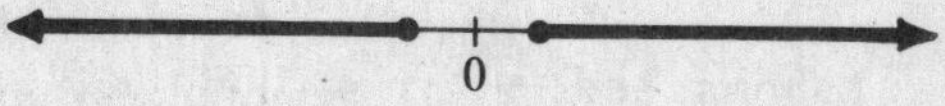

$$A = \frac{\pi d^2}{x}$$

30. If the formula above gives the area A of a circular region in terms of its diameter d, then $x =$

(A) $\frac{1}{4}$ (B) $\frac{1}{2}$ (C) 1 (D) 2 (E) 4

S T O P

IF YOU FINISH BEFORE TIME IS CALLED, YOU MAY CHECK YOUR WORK ON THIS SECTION ONLY. DO NOT WORK ON ANY OTHER SECTION IN THE TEST.

EXPLANATIONS OF ANSWERS TO QUESTIONS IN GRE GENERAL TEST GR86-2

SECTION 1

1. The word "because" indicates that the second part of the sentence, where the missing words appear, explains why an innovative experimental technique was rejected by physicists. The word "although" indicates that the technique had some redeeming feature; the first missing word is something positive that can be done to problems. The second missing word is some undesirable feature that the technique produced.

(A) is not the answer. To have "clarified" problems would be a redeeming feature of the technique. However, producing new "data" is also probably desirable, rather than undesirable.

(B) is not the answer. To have "eased" problems would be a redeeming feature of the technique. But producing new "interpretations" is also likely to be desirable, rather than undesirable.

(C) is the answer. Although a technique "resolved" some problems, it might still be rejected because it produced new "complications."

(D) is not the answer. To have "caused" problems is not a redeeming feature of a technique, and to produce new "hypotheses" is not an undesirable feature.

(E) is not the answer. To have "revealed" some problems may or may not be a redeeming feature of a technique. Producing "inconsistencies" may in some circumstances be undesirable. However, there is not enough information in the sentence to allow you to determine whether producing "inconsistencies" and revealing problems are desirable or undesirable.

2. The last part of the sentence explains what happens when the sick become infirm. To become infirm means to experience diminished vigor.

(A) is not the answer. Becoming infirm does not mean "regaining" strength and skills; it means the opposite.

(B) is not the answer. A person who has become infirm may be said to be denied strength and skills, rather than to be "denying" them.

(C) is not the answer. A person who has become infirm may at the same time be "pursuing" strength and skills, but the condition of infirmity is not defined in this way.

(D) is not the answer. To become infirm does not imply "insuring" strength and skills.

(E) is the answer. To experience diminished vigor implies "losing" strength and skills.

3. The first part of the sentence emphasizes that, in order to understand history, it is important to take into account the great importance of the pressure of population on available resources. The word "consequently" indicates that the second part of the sentence describes a conclusion that follows from the statement made in the first part. In this case, what follows is a judgment about any historical writing that does not show recognition of the correctness of the statement. The first missing word will provide a one-word description of the type of fact suggested by the first part of the sentence. The second missing word describes in what way writing that fails to take this type of fact into account is flawed.

(A) is the answer. "Demographic" facts are derived from the study of human populations. The "pressure of population" mentioned in the first clause is a "demographic" consideration. Because the sentence indicates that these facts are very important, you can conclude that the author believes that writing that fails to take them into account is "intrinsically" (essentially) flawed.

(B) is not the answer. The statement made in the first part of the sentence could be described as a statement about "ecological" facts (loosely, facts about the relationship of organisms to their environment). However, in view of the great importance ascribed to the information in the statement, it would be inappropriate to call work that ignores facts relating to the statement "marginally" flawed.

(C) is not the answer. The pressure of population on resources is not primarily a "cultural" fact. There is no information in the passage that suggests a relationship between culture, or a particular culture, and the pressure of population on resources.

(D) is not the answer. The pressure of population on resources is not primarily a "psychological" fact. There is no information in the sentence that suggests a relationship between psychology and the pressure of population on resources.

(E) is not the answer. The word "political" does not adequately describe the type of fact suggested by the information in the first part of the sentence.

4. The word "since" indicates that the second part of the sentence explains why recent criticism of the structure of Jones' novel is puzzling. The first missing word helps to explain why the novel has been recently criticized. The second part of the sentence gives the characteristic of the novel that has traditionally been criticized, and the second missing word is a general name for such a characteristic.

(A) is not the answer. If critics have traditionally argued that the novel's "preoccupation" is with structure, then it is not puzzling that it has been recently criticized for its "attention to" structure.

(B) is not the answer. Having a rigid framework as an obvious "characteristic" does not make "speculation about" structure puzzling.

(C) is not the answer. A "disparity" implies a difference among two or more elements, rather than a characteristic of a single entity.

(D) is not the answer. There is no information in the sentence that would lead one to regard a rigid framework as a "contradiction."

(E) is the answer. One might well be puzzled that a novel is criticized for "lack of" structure, when its rigid framework is often seen as an obvious "flaw."

5. The words "on the other hand" indicate that people's reactions to the character of societies' codes of behavior are not like their reactions to the fact of the codes' existence. Reaction to the existence of codes is likely to be the opposite of reaction to the character of codes.

(A) is not the answer. To be "predictable" means to come as no surprise.

(B) is the answer. To be "unexpected" means to be surprising.

(C) is not the answer. Being "admirable" is not the opposite of being unsurprising.

(D) is not the answer. To be "explicit" is not the opposite of being unsurprising.

(E) is not the answer. To be thought "confusing" is not the opposite of being thought unsurprising.

6. The first missing word describes a way in which historians and literary critics are not likely to react to the suggestion that historical analysis is a form of fiction. The second missing word will depend on how the first missing word characterizes this way of reacting.

(A) is not the answer. The agreement that history and fiction deal with "significant" orders of experience does not explain why neither historians nor literary critics will react "quietly."

(B) is not the answer. The agreement that history and fiction deal with "shifting" orders of experience does not explain why neither historians nor literary critics will react "enthusiastically."

(C) is not the answer. The agreement that history and fiction deal with "unusual" orders of experience does not explain why neither historians nor literary critics will react "passively."

(D) is the answer. If historians and literary critics agree that history and fiction are "distinct" orders of experience, then they are unlikely to react "sympathetically" to the idea that historical analysis is a form of fiction.

(E) is not the answer. The agreement that history and fiction deal with "realistic" orders of experience does not explain why neither historians nor literary critics will react "contentiously."

7. The colon (:) indicates that the second part of the sentence will explain the first part. The missing word will describe the opposite of the cynical conviction that "everybody has an angle," that is, that each person is concerned primarily with his or her own interests.

(A) is not the answer. "Rationality," or reasonableness, is not the opposite of self-interest.

(B) is not the answer. "Flexibility," which can mean a tendency to yield to influence or ability to respond to change, is not the opposite of self-interest.

(C) is not the answer. "Diffidence" (reserve, timidity, or lack of confidence) is not the opposite of self-interest.

(D) is the answer. "Disinterestedness" means lack of self-interest.

(E) is not the answer. "Insincerity," or lack of honesty, is not the opposite of self-interest.

8. People "study" in order to "learn." Therefore, a rationale for this analogy could be "People X (study) in order to Y (learn)," or "One way to Y (learn) is to X (study)."

(A) is not the answer. To "pervade" (spread through every part of something) is not a way to "encompass" (surround the outside of something).

(B) is the answer. People "search" in order to "find"; one way to "find" something is to "search" for it.

(C) is not the answer. There is no necessary connection between "gather" and "win"; winning is not implied in the definition of gathering.

(D) is not the answer. There is no necessary connection between "agree" and "keep"; keeping is not implied in the definition of agreeing.

(E) is not the answer. Without more specific information, one cannot conclude that people "accumulate" in order to "raise."

9. "Horses" are kept in a "corral." A rationale for this analogy could be "X is an enclosure where people keep Y."

(A) is not the answer. "Lions" may live in a "den," but a "den" is not an enclosure where they are kept by people.

(B) is not the answer. "Sheep" may live in a "meadow," but a "meadow" is not an enclosure.

(C) is not the answer. A "herd" is a group of "cattle," not an enclosure.

(D) is not the answer. "Birds" may live in a "nest," but a "nest" is not an enclosure where they are kept by people.

(E) is the answer. A "coop" is an enclosure where people keep "chickens."

10. A "lullaby" is a "song" sung to put children to sleep. Therefore, a rationale for this analogy could be "X is a particular kind of Y."

(A) is not the answer. A "narrative" is a story, which could appear in a "volume," or the telling of a story, which might have "volume" (loudness). A "narrative" is not a kind of "volume."

(B) is not the answer. A "lecture" may be given by a "tutor"; it is not a kind of "tutor."

(C) is not the answer. A "paragraph" may appear on a "page" and thus be part of a "page," but is is not a kind of "page."

(D) is the answer. A "diatribe" is a bitter or abusive kind of "discourse" (an extended expression of thought).

(E) is not the answer. "Invective" is verbal abuse, and not a kind of "compliment."

11. "Die" has several meanings, but its use with "shaping" suggests that here it should be taken to mean a tool used to form an object. This definition suggests that a rationale for this analogy could be "X is a tool used for Y, where Y is done to something else."

(A) is not the answer. "Glue" can be used for "attaching" things, but "glue" is a substance rather than a tool.

(B) is not the answer. An "anchor" is used in "sailing," but "sailing" is not done by the "anchor."

(C) is the answer. A "drill" is a tool used for "boring" (making holes by piercing).

(D) is not the answer. A "pedal," e.g., the gas pedal in an automobile, may be a part of a mechanism that propels something. However, a "pedal" cannot propel alone, but only as part of a more complex mechanism.

(E) is not the answer. "Ink" is used in "printing," but it is a substance rather than a tool.

12. "Mercenary" means having a strong desire for "money" or serving as a soldier for pay rather than for a cause. You can tell that "mercenary" is used as an adjective, not as a noun, because "vindictive," the first word in choice (A), can be used only as an adjective, and not as a noun. A rationale for this analogy could be "X is an attribute of human character that means to seek or desire Y."

(A) is the answer. "Vindictive" means disposed to seek "revenge"; to be "vindictive" means to desire "revenge."

(B) is not the answer. A "library" may be desired by one who is "scholarly," but this desire is not a part of the definition of scholarliness.

(C) is not the answer. One who is "immaculate" may desire "cleanliness," but "immaculate," which means being clean, is not necessarily a human attribute, as is "mercenary." In addition, to be "immaculate" is not usually thought of as an undesirable quality, as is being "mercenary."

(D) is not the answer. One who is "thirsty" may desire "water," but to be "thirsty" is not usually thought of as an undesirable quality, as is being "mercenary." Thirst is not an attribute of human character.

(E) is not the answer. One who is "belligerent" (combative) may wish to invade another's territory, but "invasion" is only one of many ways to show belligerence, and is not implied in the definition of belligerence.

13. "Pundits" are persons who are learned, or who are or act authoritative. Therefore, a rationale for this analogy could be "X is by definition a personal characteristic of persons called Y."

(A) is not the answer. "Signatories" are people who sign. In various situations, they may have many characteristics, including "dedication," but this specific characteristic is not necessarily implied in the word "signatories."

(B) is not the answer. One hopes that "executors" (for instance, people who execute wills) will be characterized by "sobriety," but "sobriety" is not necessarily a characteristic of "executors."

(C) is not the answer. "Literati" (people who are educated or intellectual) are not necessarily characterized by "sensitivity."

(D) is not the answer. "Recklessness" is not necessarily a characteristic of "warriors."

(E) is the answer. "Partisans" are people who support a particular person or cause and are therefore characterized by "allegiance."

14. A stationary structural element that is designed to support an airplane's "wing" is called a "strut." Therefore, a rationale for this analogy could be "X is a stationary structural element that can support a Y."

(A) is not the answer. A "lever" may have a "handle" or it may be a "handle," but a "lever" does not provide strengthening support for a "handle."

(B) is not the answer. An "axle" is a shaft on which a "wheel" revolves, and might be said to provide some support to the "wheel." However, a "wing" does not turn about a "strut" as a "wheel" turns about an "axle."

(C) is the answer. A "buttress" is a stationary structure whose primary purpose is to support a "wall."

(D) is not the answer. A "beam" may be fastened to something else by a "rivet," but the "rivet" does not support the "beam."

(E) is not the answer. A "pipe" might be considered part of a "well," or it might bring water from a "well," but a "pipe" is not designed to support a "well."

15. To "fawn" means to court favor in a cringing or flattering manner. One who fawns is not characterized by "imperiousness" (arrogance, or a commanding presence). A rationale for this analogy could be "To X is to show a lack of Y."

(A) is the answer. To "equivocate" means to lie or deceive, and shows a lack of "directness."

(B) is not the answer. To "elaborate" means to provide more detail; it does not imply anything about "originality."

(C) is not the answer. To "boggle" means to hesitate or to be startled; it does not indicate a lack of "imagination."

(D) is not the answer. To "manipulate" can mean to operate or to use deceitfully for one's own ends. To "manipulate" does not necessarily show a lack of "repression."

(E) is not the answer. To "coddle" means to pamper; it implies "permissiveness" rather than a lack of it.

16. To be "distraught" means to be greatly "troubled" or to show that one is "troubled." Therefore, a rationale for this analogy could be "To be Y is to be very X."

(A) is not the answer. To be "disillusioned" (shown an unpleasant truth) could cause one to become "annoyed," but "disillusioned" does not mean to be very "annoyed" or to show annoyance.

(B) is not the answer. To be "interrupted" means to be "disturbed" by a particular occurrence rather than to be "disturbed" to an extreme degree.

(C) is the answer. To be "covetous" means to desire the possessions of others. To be "rapacious" means to be excessively "covetous," or to be insatiable in desiring things.

(D) is not the answer. To be "ostentatious" means to make an excessive display of oneself or one's possessions. To be "outmoded" means to be unfashionable. The two cannot be directly related to one another without more information.

(E) is not the answer. "Tranquil" and "placid" both mean calm; neither implies an intensification of the other.

17. This question asks you to identify the author's primary concern. The author makes a number of different points, but all of them are focused on a single main concern.

(A) is not the answer. The author makes the point that herbivores and carnivores are both intelligent groups of animals but does not compare their intelligence.

(B) is the answer. The primary concern of the passage is introduced in the first paragraph, and the rest of the passage presents additional information about the relationship described in that paragraph.

(C) is not the answer. No direct comparison is made in the passage between early animals and their later counterparts. The author's emphasis is on gradual evolution of certain traits.

(D) is not the answer. There is no indication in the passage that some carnivores dominate others.

(E) is not the answer. Hormones are mentioned in the last paragraph as an important element in animal awareness, but to demonstrate their importance is not the author's primary concern.

18. This question refers you to a specific element in the passage. You are to identify the role this element plays in the passage, specifically its role in furthering the author's argument.

(A) is not the answer. The example of the hungry lizard provides a contrast to the hunting behavior of the large mammal predators discussed in the passage; it does not demonstrate a similarity.

(B) is not the answer. The example of the hungry lizard presents a contrast to the hunting behavior of large animal predators, rather than an extension of the author's argument.

(C) is the answer. The "hungry lizard's instinctive snap" is contrasted with the mammal's awareness. The purpose of the contrast is to make a distinction between higher and lower levels of consciousness.

(D) is not the answer. The lizard's behavior illustrates a particular form of consciousness, not a form of brutality. Brutality is not mentioned as a characteristic of predators.

(E) is not the answer. The hungry lizard is presented as an animal that lacks higher consciousness, not as an "objection" to the suggestion that all animals lack consciousness.

19. This question asks you to draw a conclusion from the information in the passage about animals, not discussed in the passage, that are less intelligent than the animals that are discussed.

(A) is the answer. In lines 32-35, the author defines intelligence in terms of an animal's use of past experience. In the context of the entire passage, it can be inferred that more intelligent animals, such as the grassland mammals discussed, are better able to use past experience to help them survive than are less intelligent animals.

(B) is not the answer. The second paragraph of the passage indicates that attention is more highly focused in animals of greater, rather than less, intelligence.

(C) is not the answer. The author does not discuss muscular coordination as an element in intelligence.

(D) is not the answer. The passage discusses the role played by competition in the development of intelligence in certain species but gives no indication that in less intelligent species there is less need for competition.

(E) is not the answer. There is no discussion in the passage of how a proper ratio of prey to predator is established.

20. To answer this question, you must determine the meaning of the words quoted from the passage in each option, and then determine which quotation is most clearly illustrated by the words quoted in lines 56-61.

(A) is not the answer. The "free-floating awareness" mentioned in lines 16-17 is described as passive, whereas the sensitivity described in lines 56-61 implies activity on the part of the predator.

(B) is not the answer. Lines 29-30 describe the general arousal that precedes the focusing of an animal's attention, whereas the sensitivity described in lines 56-61 illustrates more focused activity.

(C) is not the answer. Lines 56-61 describe an animal's use of consistent images not just its ability to hold these images.

(D) is the answer. In lines 56-61, the animal's sensitivity connects "details" such as cold trails and distant sounds with food, the perceived end.

(E) is not the answer. Line 64 is part of a description of prey. Lines 56-61 describe the sensitivity of predators.

21. This question asks you to use information in the passage to judge the author's attitude toward the main subject, intelligent mammals.

(A) is not the answer. Even though the author suggests in lines 49-56 that human consciousness is higher than that of other animals, the way in which this superiority is described does not indicate contempt, as "condescending" suggests.

(B) is not the answer. The author discusses mammals in terms of scientific theory, and not in a spirit of fun.

(C) is not the answer. There is no reason to believe that the author considers the mammals' feelings as he discusses them. There is no suggestion of apology or conciliation.

(D) is not the answer. There is no indication in the passage that the author wishes that the mammals or their situation were different, as "wistful" suggests, or that the author feels tenderness for them.

(E) is the answer. The author's description of the animals' intelligence and ability to focus attention, as well as the statement that these elements come together "marvelously" (line 40), suggests that the author respects and admires at least some of their characteristics.

22. To answer this question, you must first determine which of the three questions (I, II, and III) can be answered using the information in the passage. Then you must determine which of the given answer choices includes the Roman numerals of those questions.

I. can be answered. An aroused herbivore is fearful because it must be ready for what is ahead, including escaping from a predator.
II. can be answered. Lines 16-17 describe two degrees of attention in large mammals, the highest degree and the lowest.
III. cannot be answered. The author discusses only animals' reactions to the presence of stimuli, not their reaction to the removal of a stimulus.

(A) is not the answer. I can be answered using information provided in the passage, but II can also be answered.

(B) is not the answer. III cannot be answered using information provided in the passage.

(C) is the answer. Both I and II can be answered using information provided in the passage.

(D) is not the answer. II can be answered using information provided in the passage, but III cannot be answered.

(E) is not the answer. I and II can be answered using information provided in the passage, but III cannot be answered.

23. This question asks you to identify a reason given in the passage for improved brain function among early large mammals.

(A) is the answer. It directly paraphrases the statement in lines 6-8, which describes the author's view of the development of improved brain function in early mammals.

(B) is not the answer. It is likely that the persistence of "free-floating awareness" played a part in the animals' survival, but there is no indication in the passage that brain function improved because of it.

(C) is not the answer. The passage does not discuss the relationship between mammals and reptiles in general.

(D) is not the answer. There is no discussion in the passage of the interaction between large mammals and less intelligent species.

(E) is not the answer. Improved capacity for memory is an improvement in brain function, rather than a reason for improved brain function.

24. This question asks you what does NOT occur during arousal. To answer the question, you must first determine what does occur.

(A) is not the answer. According to lines 43-46, arousal does stimulate the production of adrenaline.

(B) is not the answer. According to lines 43-46, arousal does stimulate the production of norepinephrine.

(C) is not the answer. Lines 22-27 indicate that as arousal increases, sensitivity to stimuli increases.

(D) is not the answer. Lines 27-32 suggest that the animal becomes increasingly focused on certain stimuli as arousal increases.

(E) is the answer. There is no indication in the passage that the range of states mediated by the brain stem expands during arousal.

25. The author of the passage discusses the work of another author, Pessen. This question asks what statements the author of the passage attributes to Pessen concerning the very wealthy in the United States between 1825 and 1850. You are to identify the one statement that CANNOT be correctly attributed to Pessen. Therefore, you must first determine which of the statements given can be attributed to Pessen.

(A) is not the answer. According to the passage, Pessen presents examples to show the existence of a wealthy, or upper, class in Jacksonian America. Therefore, the statement in (A) can be attributed to Pessen.

(B) is not the answer. In the second paragraph, the author indicates that, according to Pessen, the wealthiest one percent in several cities "constantly increased its share." Therefore, the statement in (B) can be attributed to Pessen.

(C) is not the answer. In the second paragraph, the author indicates that, according to Pessen, some of the wealthy were "active in commerce (business) or the professions." Therefore, the statement in (C) can be attributed to Pessen.

(D) is the answer. According to the second paragraph, "most of the wealthy were not self-made, but had inherited family fortunes." Therefore, they did NOT accumulate their own fortunes.

(E) is not the answer. According to the passage, the fortunes of the most wealthy survived financial crises that destroyed lesser fortunes. Therefore, the statement in (E) can be attributed to Pessen.

26. To answer this question, you must determine the attitude of the author of the passage toward Pessen's presentation of statistics. The author of the passage discusses Pessen's statistics near the beginning of the second paragraph. He calls Pessen's statistics "refreshingly intelligible."

(A) is not the answer. At the end of the second paragraph, the author of the passage indicates disapproval of the conclusions Pessen draws from statistics. However, he is not "disapproving" of Pessen's presentation of those statistics.

(B) is not the answer. The author of the passage does not indicate that he is surprised or repulsed by Pessen's presentation of statistics.

(C) is not the answer. Though the author of the passage does not agree with the conclusions that Pessen draws from his statistics, he does not indicate that he is "suspicious" of Pessen's presentation of statistics.

(D) is not the answer. Though the author of the passage does not agree with the conclusions that Pessen draws from his statistics, he does not indicate that he is "amused" by Pessen's presentation of statistics.

(E) is the answer. The words "refreshingly intelligible" can be taken as praise, so "laudatory" describes the author's attitude toward Pessen's presentation of statistics.

27. This question asks you to identify the main point that the author of the passage makes. To do this, you must separate the author's description of Pessen's work and views from the author's evaluation of Pessen's work.

(A) is not the answer. According to the first paragraph, Pessen's argument, if it were true, would overturn a previously established view. However, in the rest of the passage, the author argues that Pessen has not succeeded in making a convincing case for the new view.

(B) is not the answer. The author seems to accept the idea that Pessen's views, which contrast with Toqueville's, have some merit, even though Pessen's conclusions are not entirely correct. The passage does not indicate that Toqueville's analysis is definitive.

(C) is not the answer. The author does not mention a primary reason why Pessen's study is valuable; in addition, only the first half of the nineteenth century is discussed.

(D) is not the answer. Pessen's study contributed to the documentation about the extremely wealthy, but the passage is about Pessen's study rather than about general documentation. In addition, the passage does not discuss explicitly the political power of the extremely wealthy.

(E) is the answer. According to the first paragraph, Pessen challenges Tocqueville's view. According to the second paragraph, Pessen's conclusions are incorrect.

28. "Boisterous" means noisy and high-spirited. It implies activity as well as noise.

(A) is not the answer. To be "grateful" means to appreciate something. The means of expressing appreciation is not necessarily associated with particular levels of noise or activity.

(B) is not the answer. One who is "angry" might be, but is not necessarily, quiet.

(C) is not the answer. To be "clever" means to be quick-witted or resourceful. It does not imply a level of activity or of feeling.

(D) is not the answer. A "frightened" person might not behave boisterously, but there is not, by definition, a connection between the two.

(E) is the answer. "Quiet" can imply low levels of both noise and activity.

29. To "emit" means to give out or send out.

(A) is the answer. To "absorb" means to take in.

(B) is not the answer. To "demand" means to ask for. It may imply a desire to take in, but it is not the opposite of sending out.

(C) is not the answer. To "mistake" means to make an error of an unspecified kind.

(D) is not the answer. To "prevent" means to keep from occurring. Emission might be prevented, but the preventing itself is not the opposite of emitting.

(E) is not the answer. To "require" means to have a compelling need. To need something does not mean the same thing as to receive it, so "require" is not the opposite of "emit."

30. To "metamorphose" means to change or be transformed into something else.

(A) is not the answer. Metamorphosis might be part of a process of moving ahead, but to "metamorphose" is not the opposite of moving ahead.

(B) is the answer. To "remain unaltered" is the opposite of changing or being transformed into something else.

(C) is not the answer. To "descend slowly" means to come down without speed. Coming down is not the opposite of transformation.

(D) is not the answer. Examining in haste has no clear relationship to metamorphosis.

(E) is not the answer. Preparing in advance is a preliminary step, not the opposite of transforming.

31. An "ally" is a helper or supporter. To be an "ally" has to do with a person's relationships with others, rather than with a particular quality a person has.

(A) is not the answer. A "mediator" is one who reconciles differences among other parties without taking sides.

(B) is the not answer. A "felon" is one who has committed a crime.

(C) is the answer. An "adversary" is an enemy, one who operates against another rather than helping or supporting.

(D) is not the answer. An "inventor" is one who comes up with new ideas. Inventiveness does not imply anything about a person's relationships with others.

(E) is not the answer. A "conspirator" is one who plots with others as an "ally." A conspiracy may involve a plot against another person, but to be a "conspirator" is not necessarily to be an enemy.

32. "Offhand" means done without preparation or much prior thought. It refers to a person's actions or statements.

(A) is not the answer. To be "accurate" means to be correct or free from error. An "offhand" statement is not necessarily an inaccurate one.

(B) is not the answer. To be "universal" means to be applicable everywhere. It does not imply anything about prior thought or preparation.

(C) is not the answer. Something "offhand" is not by definition the opposite of "appropriate."

(D) is the answer. "Premeditated" means thought about or prepared for ahead of time.

(E) is not the answer. To be "disputatious" means to be likely to argue. This quality does not imply anthing about either preparation or lack of preparation.

33. To "broach" means to open up. It can mean opening or breaking into an actual thing, such as a container or building, or it can refer to opening a topic for discussion.

(A) is not the answer. To "keep track of" means to follow the progress of something. It does not necessarily suggest opening or closing.

(B) is not the answer. To "lay claim to" means to call one's own. It raises questions of ownership but it is not the opposite of opening up or introducing.

(C) is the answer. To "close off" is to end discussion, or to end access to something.

(D) is not the answer. To "soothe" means to comfort or placate. In some situations, broaching could cause the opposite of comforting or placating, but "soothe" is not the opposite of "broach."

(E) is not the answer. To "simplify" means to lessen complication. To "broach" is not necessarily to complicate.

34. The "gist" (of an argument, for instance,) is the main, or most important, point.

(A) is not the answer. An "artificial manner" is an affected or unnatural way of behaving, rather than a part of an argument or discussion.

(B) is the answer. A "trivial point" is an unimportant one.

(C) is not the answer. An "informal procedure" is a method of operation that is not rigidly specified. There is no reason to suppose that it is unrelated to the main point.

(D) is not the answer. An "eccentric method" is a way of operating that is peculiar to a person or group. There is no reason to suppose that it is unrelated to the main point.

(E) is not the answer. A "singular event" is an occurrence that is individual or unusual. There is no reason to suppose that it is unrelated to the main point.

35. "Divestiture" is a taking away of something, presumably desirable, that was formerly possessed or owned. One can divest oneself, or one can be divested of something during "divestiture."

(A) is the answer. "Acquisition" means coming into possession of something desired.

(B) is not the answer. "Promotion" means the act of advancing or raising to a new, better position. One could be divested of a new position, but the idea of a position is not included in the definition of "divestiture" as it is in the definition of "promotion."

(C) is not the answer. "Subsidization" means the act of giving money or aid in any of several possible situations. "Subsidization" refers to a continuing process of being granted something rather than to the point at which something is attained.

(D) is not the answer. "Consultation" means a conferring among people. It does not have to do with giving or taking.

(E) is not the answer. "Monopolization" implies having all of something, whereas "divestiture" does not imply amount or degree of investing.

36. "Extant" means still existing. It may refer to living things, or to documents or other inanimate objects.

(A) is not the answer. To be "extensive" means to cover a large area. Something that is "extensive" must still exist.

(B) is not the answer. "Extraneous" means inessential, but it does not imply nonexistence.

(C) is not the answer. Something "extricable" can be removed or disentangled. Such a thing is not nonexistent.

(D) is the answer. "Extinct" means, in the case of an animal or kind of animal, no longer existing or living.

(E) is not the answer. "Extra" means additional. It may imply unimportance, but it does not imply nonexistence.

37. "Tractability" can be a characteristic of either persons or materials. When applied to materials, it suggests that something is easily changed or molded. When "tractability" refers to a person, it implies obedience or a tendency to be easily influenced by others.

(A) is not the answer. "Infertility" means inability to produce or reproduce. It does not imply anything about character when it is used to describe persons.

(B) is not the answer. "Implausibility" means unbelievability.

(C) is the answer. One who is incorrigible cannot be changed. "Incorrigibility" implies an unwillingness to be influenced by others.

(D) is not the answer. "Impenetrability" may, in some circumstances, suggest unwillingness to be influenced by others, but it goes further in that it implies an obliviousness to efforts to influence. An impenetrable person is unaware that influence is being exerted.

(E) is not the answer. "Indefatigability" means tirelessness. It does not, by itself, imply resistance to influence.

38. "Noisome" means bad-smelling. It suggests not only unpleasant smell, but also harmful nature or unwholesomeness.

(A) is the answer. To be "attractively fragrant" means to have a pleasant smell.

(B) is not the answer. To be "subtly flattering" means to pay a possibly undeserved compliment without seeming to do so. It does not necessarily suggest anything about smell or wholesomeness.

(C) is not the answer. To be "consistently patient" means to constantly carry on without complaint. It does not necessarily suggest anything about smell or wholesomeness.

(D) is not the answer. "Softly glowing" means giving off a non-glaring light. It does not imply anything about smell.

(E) is not the answer. "Gradually diminishing" means slowly becoming smaller. It does not necessarily suggest anything about how something smells or about its wholesomeness.

SECTION 2

1. (A) can be eliminated because it specifies orange jam but no grape jam. (B) can be eliminated because it specifies strawberry jam but no quince jam. (D) and (E) are not acceptable because they do not specify two or three flavors of jam. (C) is the only package that conforms to all the rules.

2. (B) is the correct answer because the fourth rule says that peach jam and quince jam cannot be packed together.

(A) is incorrect. Since one jar each of grape, peach, and orange makes an acceptable package, it is true that an acceptable package can contain the combination grape and peach.

(C) is incorrect. Since one jar each of orange, peach, and grape makes an acceptable package, it is true that an acceptable package can contain the combination orange and peach.

(D) is incorrect. Since one jar each of orange, grape, and peach makes an acceptable package, it is true that an acceptable package can contain the combination orange and grape.

(E) is incorrect. Two jars of either strawberry or quince, along with one jar of the other, form an acceptable package. Thus, the two flavors together can be contained in an acceptable package.

3. The last rule states that a package containing strawberry jam must also contain quince jam. Only (C) specifies quince jam. Thus, (C) is the only possible answer.

4. Orange jam must be packaged with grape, thereby eliminating all answer choices except (A), grape. Orange, grape, and peach can constitute an acceptable package. Thus, (A) is the correct answer.

5. If orange jam is put in a package, grape jam must also be put in the package. Only (B) and (D) specify any grape jam; (A), (C), and (E) can thus be eliminated. (B) must be eliminated because it specifies strawberry but no quince. (D) is the correct answer.

6. Strawberry and peach cannot be packed together since the strawberry would require the inclusion of quince and the peach simultaneously requires the exclusion of quince. (A) is therefore the correct answer.

(B) is incorrect. A jar of grape and a jar of orange, along with a third jar of grape, a third jar of orange, or a third jar of quince would make an acceptable package.

(C) is incorrect. Two jars of orange along with a third jar of grape would make an acceptable package.

(D) is incorrect. Two jars of grape along with a third jar of orange would make an acceptable package.

(E) is incorrect. Two jars of strawberry along with a third jar of quince would make an acceptable package.

7. Each package must contain at least two kinds of jam, so the package must contain a third jar of some flavor other than the one indicated. Since only three jars make up a package, there must be only one jar of jam in addition to the first two. Two jars of (E), peach, cannot be included in a package which meets these two requirements because strawberry, grape, or orange cannot be included in the package without another flavor, other than peach, in addition to themselves. Quince cannot be packaged with peach. Thus, (E) is the correct answer.

(A) is incorrect. Two jars of orange, along with one of grape, would make an acceptable package.

(B) is incorrect. Two jars of grape, along with one of orange, would make an acceptable package.

(C) is incorrect. Two jars of quince, along with one of strawberry, would make an acceptable package.

(D) is incorrect. Two jars of strawberry, along with one of quince, would make an acceptable package.

8. (B) is the correct answer because the passage asserts that a later absence of partiality calls into question an earlier seemingly impartial attitude. Thus, the passage stresses the importance of impartiality of mediators at all times, a point also emphasized in statement (B).

(A) is incorrect. (A) goes further than anything asserted in the passage. The passage does not rule out the possibility that one can have an opinion about issues related to a dispute without taking sides in the actual dispute.

(C) is incorrect since it is a presupposition on which the passage is based rather than the point of the passage; that is, the fact that the mediator is acceptable to both parties is a given, since they both ask the mediator to serve.

(D) is incorrect. (D) contradicts the assumption behind the second sentence of the passage, that mediators start out impartial.

(E) is incorrect. (E) contradicts the main point of the passage, the importance of impartiality at all times.

9. (C) is the correct answer, because advertisers are interested in having their products remembered favorably. By linking viewer perception of program quality with this goal, (C) gives advertisers a reason to care about the quality of programs they sponsor.

(A) is incorrect. That a large portion of programs are judged to be of high quality does not bolster the conclusion that information about viewer perception of program quality will be useful to advertisers. Rather, if a large portion of programs are judged to be of high quality, an advertiser may feel relatively safe in looking only at the ratings.

(B) is incorrect. Programs on noncommercial networks cannot contain ads. Information as to their quality will not help advertisers place ads with programs judged to be of high quality.

(D) is incorrect. This option makes no mention of either program quality or viewer buying habits and thus neither strengthens nor weakens the connection between the two. The idea expressed in the option thus has nothing to do with the importance of program quality to advertisers.

(E) is incorrect. This option connects the perception of the quality of advertisements to buying habits. It does not determine a connection between perception of the quality of programs and buying habits and thus is irrelevant to any interest advertisers may have in program quality.

10. The first two sentences of the passage focus on realism as the standard used in past art criticism. The final sentence says that the twentieth century artistic revolution got rid of aesthetics of the kind that was defined by this standard. Thus, (A) is the correct answer because it states this inference.

(B) is incorrect. The passage does not imply that primitive art was simple and hence could not imply anything about critics' attitudes toward such simplicity.

(C) is incorrect. The passage says that realism was rejected as the standard by which all art should be judged, not as a form of artistic representation.

(D) is incorrect. If it could be assumed that the nineteenth-century standards include the traditional standards in their entirety, the passage would imply that the tradition is challenged rather than, as (D) states, reinforced. If, on the other hand, the traditional standards are not merely those of the nineteenth century, the passage neither states nor implies anything about twentieth century agreement with those standards.

(E) is incorrect. The passage does not imply that twentieth century critics understand the evolution or nature of art, only that they are free of a previous misconception.

11. R cannot be in a group with W, so (A) and (B) can be eliminated. X can only be in a group with S or U or both. Since R is the only adult, neither S nor U can be in the group. Therefore, since (C) and (D) both contain X, they can be eliminated. (E) is the correct answer because the only two children remaining to fill out the group with R are Y and Z.

12. Since X must be in a group with S or U, or both, (B) and (E) can be eliminated. (A) lists two women, S and T, in the second group, while according to (C), the first group would contain U and V, both men; thus, both (A) and (C) can be eliminated. Option (D), consisting of groups R, U, X; T, V, W; and S, Y, Z, meets all of the restrictions and is the correct answer.

13. S, V, and W could form a group if the other two groups were R, Y, Z, and T, U, X or R, U, X and T, Y, Z. Thus, (C) is the correct answer.

(A) is incorrect. W cannot be in R's group.

(B) is incorrect. If S and U are in the same section, X must fill the remaining seat. But his option shows that seat to be taken by W. Therefore, it is not an acceptable solution.

(D) is incorrect. U and V are both men and cannot be in the same group.

(E) is incorrect. X must be in a group with either S or U or both, but there is room for neither in the group W, X, Z.

14. (A) is correct. Since no group may have two adults of the same sex, and there are three women, each of the three groups must contain a woman. Since there are more children than groups, some group must contain two children. That group will include a woman along with the two children.

(B) is incorrect. S, W, X; R, U, Y; and T, V, Z is one of several possible sets of seating groups in which W is not in the same group as one of the two men.

(C) is incorrect. R, Y, Z; S, U, X; and T, V, W is one of several possible sets of seating groups that includes R, Y, Z, a group that includes R but neither of the two men.

(D) is incorrect. T, W, Z; R, U, X; and S, V, Y is one of several possible sets of seating groups in which T's group includes more than one child.

(E) is incorrect. Every group must include one child, because a group of three with no children would have to include two adults of the same sex, thereby violating the rules.

15. S and T are both women and cannot be in the same group. Therefore, the correct answer is (B).

(A) is incorrect. R, U, X; S, V, W; and T, Y, Z is one of several possible sets of seating groups in which R and U are in X's group.

(C) is incorrect. S, U, X; R, Z, Y; and T, V, W is one of several possible sets of seating groups in which S and U are in X's group.

(D) is incorrect. S, W, X; R, V, Y; and T, U, Z is one of several possible sets of seating groups in which S and W are in X's group.

(E) is incorrect. T, U, X; R, V, Z; and S, Y, W is one of several possible sets of seating groups in which T and U are in X's group.

16. If T, Y, and Z form one group, the remaining two groups must be chosen from among R, S, U, V, W, and X. R and S must be in different groups since they are both women. W must be in the group with S because W cannot be in the group with R. X must thus be in the group with R, because both U and V are men and cannot both be in R's group. Since X must be in a group with U or S, and S is already in another group, the remaining slot with R and X must be taken by U. This leaves V to fill the remaining slot in S's group. Thus, (D) is the correct answer.

(A) is incorrect. R and S are both women and cannot be in the same group.

(B) is incorrect. R and W cannot be in the same group.

(C) is incorrect. X is not in the same group with either S or U or both, as required.

(E) is incorrect. U and V are both men and cannot be in the same group.

17. (A) and (B) can be eliminated because two plays by the same playwright cannot be scheduled in the first week. (C) can be eliminated because no play by R can be scheduled in the same week as any play by S. (E) can be eliminated because the play by playwright V is already scheduled for week 5 and is not available for the first week. (D) violates none of the requirements and is thus the correct answer.

18. Since plays by playwright S cannot be scheduled on weeks with plays by playwright R, only weeks 1 and 5 are open for plays by playwright S. Since playwright S's two plays cannot be scheduled for the same week, there must be a play by S both weeks, including week 5. Therefore, (B) is the right answer.

(A) is incorrect. A play by playwright S cannot be scheduled for the same week as one by R.

(C) is incorrect. Plays by playwright T can be scheduled for weeks 1 and 4 without violating the restrictions. Thus, a play by playwright T need not be scheduled for week 2.

(D) is incorrect. Plays by playwright T can be scheduled for weeks 1 and 2 without violating the restrictions. Thus, a play by playwright T need not be scheduled for week 4.

(E) is incorrect. The play by playwright U can be scheduled for either of weeks 2 or 4 without violating the restrictions. Thus, a play by playwright U need not be scheduled for week 1.

19. Since plays by playwright R cannot be scheduled for the same weeks as plays by playwright S, only weeks 3, 4, and 5 remain open for plays by playwright R. Since two will be scheduled for week 3, two are left to be scheduled for weeks 4 and 5. Since two cannot be scheduled for the same week, one must be scheduled for each of these weeks. Therefore, (A) is correct.

(B) is incorrect. The plays by playwright T can be scheduled for weeks 2 and 4 without violating the restrictions.

(C) is incorrect. The plays by playwright T can be scheduled for weeks 1 and 2 without violating the restrictions.

(D) is incorrect. If plays by playwright S are scheduled for the first two weeks, each of the later weeks must have at least one play by playwright R. The play by playwright V is scheduled for week 5; thus, week 5 will have plays by R and V, and there will be no room to schedule a play by playwright T.

(E) is incorrect. The play by playwright U can be scheduled for weeks 1 or 2 without violating the restrictions.

20. Since only Week 3 can have two plays by the same playwright and this playwright is R, both plays by playwright S must be scheduled during two different weeks. For the same reason, the four plays by playwright R must be scheduled during three different weeks. Since plays by playwrights R and S cannot be scheduled together, there must be a play by one or the other each week. And, since there will be only two plays a week, every play by any other playwright will be scheduled only with a play by either playwright R or playwright S, and with none by any other playwright. Therefore, a play by playwright T cannot be scheduled with a play by playwright U, and, thus, (E) is the correct answer.

(A) is incorrect. The following schedule is one of several that allow plays by playwrights R and T to be scheduled together:

Week 1: A play by playwright R and a play by playwright T
Week 2: A play by playwright R and a play by playwright T
Week 3: Two plays by playwright R
Week 4: A play by playwright S and a play by playwright U
Week 5: A play by playwright S and a play by playwright V

(B) is incorrect. The following schedule is one of several that allow plays by playwrights R and U to be scheduled together:

Week 1: A play by playwright S and a play by playwright T
Week 2: A play by playwright S and a play by playwright T
Week 3: Two plays by playwright R
Week 4: A play by playwright R and a play by playwright U
Week 5: A play by playwright R and a play by playwright V

(C) is incorrect. The following schedule is one of several that allow plays by playwrights S and T to be scheduled together:

Week 1: A play by playwright S and a play by playwright T
Week 2: A play by playwright S and a play by playwright T
Week 3: Two plays by playwright R
Week 4: A play by playwright R and a play by playwright U
Week 5: A play by playwright R and a play by playwright V

(D) is incorrect. The following schedule is one of several that allow plays by playwrights S and U to be scheduled together:

Week 1: A play by playwright S and a play by playwright U
Week 2: A play by playwright S and a play by playwright T
Week 3: Two plays by playwright R
Week 4: A play by playwright R and a play by playwright T
Week 5: A play by playwright R and a play by playwright V

21. Since plays by playwrights R and S cannot be scheduled for the same week, and only during the third week can two plays by the same playwright, playwright R, be scheduled, each week will have either a play by playwright R or a play by playwright S. There are only two plays by playwright S, and one of these is scheduled with one by playwright U; at most, one of these can be scheduled with one by playwright T. Therefore, at least one of the plays by playwright T will be scheduled for the same week as one of the plays by playwright R. Therefore, the right answer is (A).

(B) is incorrect. The play by playwright S that is not scheduled for the same time as the one by playwright U may be scheduled for the same week as the play by playwright V, so that no plays by playwright S will be available to schedule with a play by playwright T.

(C) is incorrect. The play by playwright U may be scheduled for either of weeks 1 or 4.

(D) is incorrect. If plays by playwright S are scheduled for weeks 1 and 2, 1 and 5, or 2 and 5, no play by S will be scheduled for week 4.

(E) is incorrect. A play by playwright T cannot be scheduled for week 5, because one of the two available slots for that week will be filled with the play by playwright V and the other will be filled by a play by either playwright S or playwright R.

22. Since plays by playwrights R and S cannot be scheduled for the same week, and only during the third week can two plays by the same playwright, playwright R, be scheduled, each week will have either a play by R or a play by S. Further, since the play by playwright V must be scheduled for week 5, two plays are already scheduled for the fifth week and a play by playwright T cannot be scheduled then. Similarly, since two plays by playwright R are scheduled for week 3, no play by playwright T may be scheduled for that week. Of the weeks left, only 1 and 2 are consecutive, so (D) is the correct answer.

(A) is incorrect. Plays by playwright S may be scheduled for any week except week 3.

(B) is incorrect. Plays by playwright S may be scheduled for any week except week 3.

(C) is incorrect. Plays by playwright S may be scheduled for any week except week 3.

(E) is incorrect. Since plays by playwright R and S cannot be scheduled for the same week, and only during the third week can two plays by the same playwright, playwright R, be scheduled, each week will have either a play by R or a play by S. Further, since the play by playwright V must be scheduled for week 5, two plays are already scheduled for the fifth week and a play by playwright T cannot be scheduled then.

23. The passage suggests that considering the possibility of extinction with an eye toward the possible utility of a previously unvalued species will lead to a different answer to the question than considering the possibility of extinction from a more general perspective. (C) describes the author's procedure of suggesting a new perspective and is thus the correct answer.

(A) is incorrect. The author argues that it is important to preserve endangered species without endorsing any opposing point of view. The view attributed to the general public is not accepted; rather, an argument is given to show what that view misses.

(B) is incorrect. The author uses an approach that is primarily factual, and does not seek to arouse the emotions of its audience.

(D) is incorrect. The author tries to undermine an opposing position by presenting an alternative to it.

(E) is incorrect. The generalization about the potential value of life forms whose value was not perceived in advance is supported by an example of a similar case, namely that of rubber plants.

24. Examples that would serve the same function as rubber-producing plants must involve a situation in which an organism previously thought to be useless is seen to be extremely beneficial for some human endeavor. Responses (A), (B), (C), and (E) are such examples. Petroleum is not an organism and is useful itself and thus is not such an example. Thus, (D) is the correct answer.

25. The passage indicates that the proportion of farmers in the general population decreased from 1850 to 1880. (E) says exactly the opposite — that this proportion increased; therefore, it contradicts the passage and is the correct response.

(A) is incorrect. The passage also indicates that the number of farmers increased between 1850 and 1880, and thus agrees with (A).

(B) is incorrect. The passages does not tell us about the rate of growth of the labor force. It can be inferred from the passage that the general population grew, but (B) agrees with, rather than contradicts, this conclusion.

(C) is incorrect. We cannot draw any conclusions about the proportion of farmers in the labor force from the passage alone.

(D) is incorrect. We cannot draw any conclusions about the proportion of farmers in the labor force from the passage alone.

SECTION 3

1. One way to compare these quantities is to note that

$$40\% \text{ is } \frac{40}{100} \text{ or } \frac{4}{10} \text{ or } \frac{2}{5} \text{ or } 0.4$$

and that

$$60\% \text{ is } \frac{60}{100} \text{ or } \frac{6}{10} \text{ or } \frac{3}{5} \text{ or } 0.6.$$

The following may be easiest:

(40% of 50) + 60
= (2/5 × 50) + 60 = 20 + 60
= 80

(60% of 50) + 40
= (3/5 × 50) + 40 = 30 + 40
= 70

Answer is A

2. $\frac{1}{12}$ of 17 is $\frac{17}{12}$ whereas

$\frac{1}{17}$ of 12 is $\frac{12}{17}$.

Since $\frac{17}{12} > 1$ and $1 > \frac{12}{17}$,

then $\frac{17}{12} > \frac{12}{17}$.

Answer is A

3. There are infinitely many pairs of values for x and y that will make the sentence true. Here are three examples:

$$\left(-\frac{1}{2}\right) + \left(-\frac{1}{2}\right) = -1$$

$$2 + (-3) = -1$$

$$-3 + 2 = -1$$

In the first example, $x = y$; in the second, $x > y$; and in the third, $x < y$. Therefore, the relationship between x and y cannot be determined.

Answer is D

4. You could multiply the given numbers to determine which (if either) is larger. However, you can avoid this by rewriting each product as follows:

(A) $23(784)$
$= 23(783 + 1)$
$= \underline{(23)(783)} + (23)(1)$

(B) $24(783)$
$= (23 + 1)(783)$
$= \underline{(23)(783)} + (1)(783)$

The underlined parts are equal, and $23 < 783$, so (B) is greater.

Answer is B

5. You are given that $0 < r < t$. This means that both t and r are positive numbers, and r is the smaller of the two. Since both numbers are positive, $\frac{r}{t}$ must be less than 1 whereas $\frac{t}{r}$ is greater than 1. (For example, $0 < 2 < 5$ and $\frac{2}{5}$ is less than 1 but $\frac{5}{2}$ is greater than 1.)

Answer is B

6. The sum of the measures of the three angles of any triangle is 180°. In the figure, one angle is designated as a right angle, or 90°. Therefore, $x + 55$ must also equal 90, so $x = 35$.

Answer is C

7. There are a number of ways to solve the problem posed here. One of the simplest is to notice that the home valued at \$54,000 has $1\frac{1}{5}$ the value of the \$45,000 home. Since the one valued at \$45,000 is taxed at \$1,200, the tax on the \$54,000 home should be $1\frac{1}{5} \times \$1{,}200$, or $\$1{,}200 + \frac{1}{5}(\$1{,}200)$, which is $\$1{,}200 + \$240 = \$1{,}440$.

Answer is A

For another solution, see the next page.

Since the tax rate is the same for each home in city X, you can set up a proportion as follows, comparing amount of tax to the value of the house:

$$\frac{x}{54{,}000} = \frac{1{,}200}{45{,}000}. \text{ Then}$$

$$45{,}000x = (54{,}000)(1{,}200)$$

$$\text{or} \quad 45x = (54)(1{,}200)$$

$$\text{so} \quad x = \frac{(54)(1{,}200)}{45}$$

$$= 1{,}440$$

Answer is A

8. You are given information about the area of a square region, and asked about its perimeter. If the area of the region is 36, then each side of the square must be 6, so the perimeter is $4 \times 6 = 24$.

Answer is C

9. If 99 pages each had a 2-digit page number (as, for example, p.10 and p.45), then the printer would print 99×2, or 198 digits. However, the first 9 pages (pp. 1-9) have only 1-digit page numbers, so in 99 pages, the printer would print $198 - 9$, or 189 digits. This means that there were 99 pages in the book.

Answer is B

10. You are given that the average of 3 numbers is 3. This means that their sum must be 9. That is,

$$\frac{x+y+6}{3} = 3,$$

$$\text{so } x+y+6 = 9.$$

$$\text{This means that } x + y = 3,$$

$$\text{so} \quad \frac{x+y}{2} = \frac{3}{2}.$$

Answer is C

11. You are given that the areas of the two regions are equal. It may help to let K stand for this number. You are therefore to compare

$$\frac{K}{h_1} \text{ with } \frac{K}{h_2}.$$

You do not know whether $h_1 = h_2$, $h_1 > h_2$, or $h_1 < h_2$. Therefore, $\frac{K}{h_1}$ may be equal to, less than, or greater than, $\frac{K}{h_2}$.

For example (trying some numbers and letting the areas be 24 in each case):

$$\frac{24}{4} = \frac{24}{4}, \text{ but } \frac{24}{6} < \frac{24}{4} \text{ and } \frac{24}{3} > \frac{24}{8}.$$
$$(h_1 = h_2) \qquad (h_1 > h_2) \qquad (h_1 < h_2)$$

Answer is D

12. You can think of

$$\frac{3 \cdot 3 \cdot 3}{6 \cdot 6 \cdot 6} \text{ as } \frac{3}{6} \cdot \frac{3}{6} \cdot \frac{3}{6}$$
$$= \frac{1}{2} \cdot \frac{1}{2} \cdot \frac{1}{2}$$
$$= \left(\frac{1}{2}\right)^3$$

Answer is C

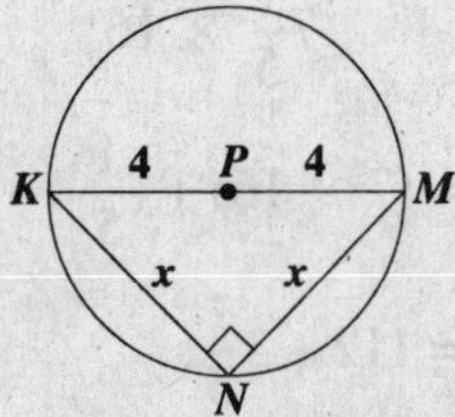

13. The area of a circular region is computed by the formula $A = \pi r^2$, where r is the length of the radius. In this case, since the area is given as 16π, r^2 must equal 16, and $r = 4$. Because KMN is a triangle, $x + x$, or $2x$, must be greater than the length of KM. That is, $2x > 8$, and $x > 4$. (Actually, by the Pythagorean Theorem, $x^2 + x^2 = 8^2$, which means that $2x^2 = 64$, or $x^2 = 32$. Since $x^2 = 32$, x must be between 5 and 6.)

Answer is A

14. You are given that m, p, and x are positive integers, which means they belong to the set $\{1, 2, 3, 4, \ldots\}$. You are also given that $mp = x$ and asked to compare the values of m and x. If you try some numbers, you can see that if $p = 1$, then $m = x$, but if $p > 1$, then $m < x$:

$$\begin{aligned} & 5(1) = 5 \\ \text{but } & 5(2) = 10 \\ & 5(3) = 15 \\ & 5(4) = 20 \\ & \text{and so forth.} \end{aligned}$$

Therefore, m may be equal to, or it may be less than, x.

Answer is D

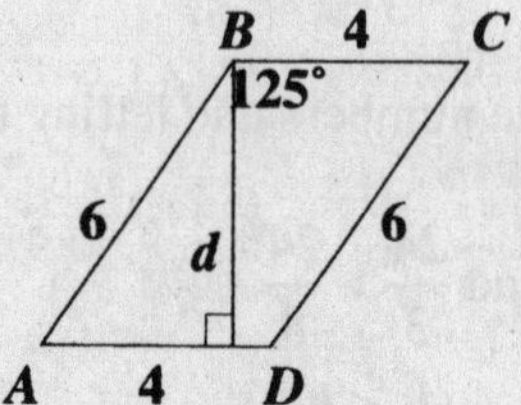

15. The area of the region enclosed by a parallelogram is computed by multiplying the lengths of the base and height. You are given that $\angle ABC$ measures 125°, so $ABCD$ is not a rectangle, and its height, as shown, is less than 6. Therefore, the area is less than 4×6.

Answer is B

16. 72 seconds represents 7 ten-second intervals plus $\frac{1}{5}$ of such an interval.

Therefore, the person who takes 16 steps in 10 seconds will take $7\frac{1}{5} \times 16$ steps in 72 seconds.

$$7\frac{1}{5} \times 16$$

$$= (7 \times 16) + (\frac{1}{5} \times 16)$$

$$= 112 + 3\frac{1}{5}.$$

Since $\frac{1}{5}$ of a step is not a complete step, the answer is 115.

Answer is E

You can also solve this problem by setting up a proportion as follows, comparing steps to time:

$$\frac{16}{10} = \frac{x}{72}.$$

Therefore, $10x = (16)(72)$

or $10x = 1{,}152$

and $x = 115.2$.

Answer is E

17. The sum of the measures of the angles of a triangle is 180°. In the figure, therefore, $x + y + z = 180$, so

$$\frac{x+y+z}{45} = \frac{180}{45} = 4.$$

Answer is C

18. $52.68 \times \frac{1}{100}$ is the same as

$52.68 \div 100$, or 0.5268.

Answer is B

19. You are given the value of $b - c$ and $a + c$. If you note that

$(b - c) + (a + c) = b + a = a + b$,

this value must be

$(3) + (32) = 35$.

Answer is B

20. The dimensions of the floor are given in feet and the cost of carpeting in square yards. A way to compute the area of the floor in square yards is as follows:

$$\frac{18}{3} \times \frac{10}{3} = \frac{180}{9} = 20.$$

Therefore, the cost of the carpeting is $20x$.

Answer is A

Questions 21-25

These questions are based on two graphs, and it is a good idea to scan both of these before attempting the questions. The left-hand graph shows the number of students enrolled in the fall at College *R* for the five years, 1976-1980. The right-hand graph shows the allocation (in dollars) of contributions during the five academic years, 1976-1981.

21. This question asks about the number of students, and can be read directly from the graph. The total number of students who enrolled in the fall of 1979 was 700.

Answer is E

22. This question asks about the percent increase in enrollment, and cannot be read directly from the graph.

In the fall of 1979, 200 part-time students enrolled; in the fall of 1980, 350 part-time students enrolled. This was an increase of 150 over the 1979 enrollment.

Since a percent is needed, it can be calculated as

$$\frac{150}{200} = \frac{75}{100}, \text{ which is } 75\%.$$

Answer is D

23. This question asks about the increase in the number of full-time students from 1976 to 1977.

In the fall of 1976, 300 full-time students enrolled (400 – 100); in the fall of 1977, there were also 300 full-time students (450 – 150).

Therefore, there was no increase.

Answer is A

24. This question refers to the allocation of contributions, so the right-hand graph is the source of information.

If 12% of the amount of contributions was allocated to heating costs, then 88% was not. The amount of contributions for the 1978-1979 school year was about $233,000, and 88% of $233,000 is slightly more than $205,000.

Answer is D

25. This question also refers to contributions, but asks for the total amount. You can read off the amount for each year and then add, but there is a somewhat easier way to determine the total. Notice that for the year 1979-1980, the contributions amounted to approximately \$300,000. Looking at the year 1978-1979 and the year 1980-81, the contributions for those two years would total \$700,000. That is, the contributions for 1978-79 are

\$200,000 + $(\frac{1}{3})$ (\$100,000), while the contributions for 1980-81 are

\$400,000 + $(\frac{2}{3})$ (\$100,000). Together, these total

\$600,000 + \$100,000 or \$700,000. The sum for the three years is therefore about \$300,000 + \$700,000.

Answer is B

26. To simplify $\frac{x(x^2)^3}{x^2}$, it can be helpful to think of the expression as written this way:

$$\frac{x(x^2)(x^2)(x^2)}{x^2}$$

Since both numerator and denominator can be divided by x^2, the expression can also be written as $x(x^2)(x^2)$, or x^5.

Answer is D

27. One-third of seven is $\frac{7}{3}$, and the question asks how many thirds of 7 are in 7. As an equation, this is

$$7 = N \cdot \frac{7}{3}.$$

Clearly, $N = 3$.

Answer is C

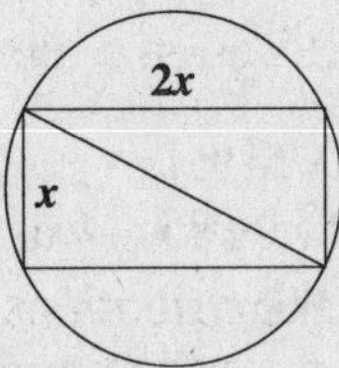

28. You are to find the circumference of the circle, which is equal to the diameter times π. Therefore, you need to determine the length of the diameter, which is not given in the problem. You are, however, given a rectangle inscribed in the circle. Since each angle of a rectangle is a right angle, $\angle KLM$ is inscribed in a semicircle. Therefore, a diagonal of the rectangle must be a diameter of the circle.

The diagonal of the inscribed rectangle is also the hypotenuse of one of the right triangles such as *KLM*. The legs of *KLM* have lengths x and $2x$ so if their lengths are known, the length of the diagonal *KM* can be calculated. The area of rectangular region *KLMN* is given as 32, so $(x)(2x) = 2x^2 = 32$, or $x^2 = 16$, which means that $x = 4$ and $2x = 8$. By the Pythagorean Theorem,

$$(KM)^2 = (LM)^2 + (KL)^2$$
$$= 4^2 + 8^2 = 16 + 64 = 80.$$

Therefore, $KM = \sqrt{80} = \sqrt{16 \cdot 5} = 4\sqrt{5}$, and this is the diameter of the circle. The circumference of the circle is therefore $(4\sqrt{5})(\pi)$, or $4\pi\sqrt{5}$.

Answer is B

29. The reciprocal of a nonzero number N is that number which, when multiplied by N, gives 1. For example, the reciprocal of 4 is $\frac{1}{4}$ and the reciprocal of $\frac{1}{4}$ is 4.
The given number is

$$x - \frac{1}{y} = \frac{xy}{y} - \frac{1}{y} = \frac{xy - 1}{y}.$$

The number that multipled by $\frac{xy-1}{y}$ gives 1 is $\frac{y}{xy-1}$.

Answer is E

30. You need to determine whether each of the sentences I, II, and III is true or false.

n is a multiple of 5, so it must end in a 5 or a 0. n is also a multiple of 9. Some multiples of both 5 and 9 are 90, 180, 270, and so forth. Since all of these are even, I is false.

The same examples show that n may be greater than 45, so II is false.

III is true since in order that n be a multiple of both 5 and 9, there must be an integer w such that

$$n = 5 \times 9 \times w = 5 \times (3 \times 3) \times w$$
$$= (5 \times 3) \times (3 \times w)$$
$$= 15 \times (3 \times w).$$

Answer is A

SECTION 4

1. The sentence describes a chain of occurrences. The first missing word suggests what happened to mass literacy during the industrial revolution. The words "in turn, the new expansion of literacy" are a strong clue for the first missing word. The second missing word suggests what happened to popular literature as a result of the expansion of literacy and the advent of cheaper printing.

(A) is not the answer. "Building" is an unlikely term to describe an expansion of literacy. It is also unlikely that cheaper printing would increase "mistrust" of popular literature. In addition, one would not be likely to nurture "mistrust."

(B) is not the answer. The new expansion of mass literacy could be a "reappearance," but there is nothing in the sentence to suggest this. It is unlikely that mass literacy nurtured the "display" of popular literature; in fact, a "display" is not something that can be nurtured.

(C) is not the answer. Mass literacy is not something that can be received, so "receipt" cannot be the first missing word. Printing does not directly affect the "source" of popular literature.

(D) is not the answer. Mass literacy is not something that is ordinarily thought of as being selected, so "selection" cannot be the first missing word.

(E) is the answer. The "emergence" of mass literacy corresponds to the "new expansion of literacy." It is reasonable to assume that increased literacy and cheaper printing are likely to have contributed to the "rise" of popular literature.

2. The first missing word describes how ancient tools were preserved. The phrase "enough have survived" indicates that not all survived, and the word "Although" indicates that the tools were preserved in a way that would not lead you to expect enough to survive. The second missing word describes a progress through prehistory. The word "but" suggests that the word that fills the second blank must contrast with the idea of occasional interruption.

(A) is not the answer. In this context, "partially" must describe the incomplete preservation of particular tools, rather than of a number of tools, as "enough have survived" suggests. "Noticeable" does not present a direct contrast with "interrupted."

(B) is not the answer. Superficial preservation would not permit tools to survive. There is no information in the sentence to suggest that a progress through prehistory is "necessary."

(C) is not the answer. The ancient tools could have been "unwittingly" (inadvertently) preserved, but "documented" does not contrast with "occasionally interrupted."

(D) is the answer. It is logical to say that enough tools have survived in spite of their being "rarely" preserved. A "continual" progress contrasts with one that is occasionally interrupted.

(E) is not the answer. "Needlessly" suggests that there was no good reason to preserve the tools, but "enough have survived" suggests that their preservation was important. Since "needlessly" is not in keeping with the sense of the rest of the sentence, it cannot be the missing word. "Incessant" suggests that the progress through prehistory never ceased.

3. The missing word describes how land grades (levels off gradually and smoothly) into ice. It explains why you can walk off the coast without realizing that you have done so.

(A) is not the answer. The fact that land grades "permanently" into ice does not explain why you cannot detect the grading.

(B) is the answer. "Imperceptibly" means undetectably. The fact that you cannot detect the grading explains why you can walk off the coast without realizing it.

(C) is not the answer. It is likely that grading that occurs "irregularly" is detectable. In any case, it is unlikely that irregularity alone could explain your inability to detect grading.

(D) is not the answer. "Precariously" suggests abrupt change leading to danger, so it is likely that grading described as precarious is detectable.

(E) is not the answer. A slight grade might be undetectable, but in this question another answer choice indicates even more clearly why you can walk off the coast without realizing it.

4. The sentence contrasts the infant's reactions, part of a normal developmental process, with future unhappiness and anxiety. The missing word describes signs of adolescent anxiety as they relate to the infant.

(A) is the answer. "Prophetic" signs, like harbingers, foretell future occurrences. For the infant, adolescent anxiety is a future occurrence.

(B) is not the answer. "Normal" signs of adolescent anxiety cannot occur in an infant.

(C) is not the answer. Signs of adolescent anxiety could be "monotonous," but these signs could not occur as such in an infant.

(D) is not the answer. An infant's reactions are unlikely to be mistaken for signs of adolescent anxiety, as "virtual" suggests.

(E) is not the answer. "Typical" signs of adolescent anxiety are unlikely to occur in an infant.

5. The missing word describes an investigation that contrasts with a "search in a definite direction."

(A) is not the answer. "Timely" does not contrast with the idea of definite direction.

(B) is the answer. An "unguided" investigation contrasts with a search in a definite direction.

(C) is not the answer. A "consistent" investigation does not contrast with a search in a definite direction.

(D) is not the answer. An "uncomplicated" investigation does not contrast with a search in a definite direction.

(E) is not the answer. A "subjective" investigation does not contrast with a search in a definite direction.

6. The first missing word describes a gesture of comradeship of a kind that would neutralize the resentment of Winkelmann's peers. The second missing word explains Winkelmann's relationship with the high and mighty.

(A) is not the answer. A "quixotic" gesture is idealistic or romantic. There is no reason to suppose that such a gesture would neutralize resentment, or that Winkelmann indulged in "intrigue with" the high and mighty.

(B) is not the answer. It is unlikely that an "enigmatic" gesture, one that is puzzling or obscure, would neutralize resentment.

(C) is the answer. A "propitiatory" gesture is one intended to divert anger. Winkelmann's "involvement with" the high and mighty is indicated by the fact that he cultivated those in power.

(D) is not the answer. A "salutary" gesture, one that has a beneficial effect, could have helped Winkelmann. However, there is no indication that Winkelmann engaged in "questioning of" the high and mighty.

(E) is not the answer. An "unfeigned" gesture might have helped Winkelmann, but there is no information in the sentence to suggest that unfeignedness was a needed characteristic of the gesture. In addition, the sentence provides no suggestion that Winkelmann felt "sympathy for" those he cultivated.

7. The first missing word describes a society that worships efficiency. The second missing word describes the kinds of decisions that such a society requires, and contrasts with the words "sensitive" and "idealistic" that characterize a person trying with difficulty to make such decisions.

(A) is not the answer. A "bureaucratic" society might worship efficiency. However, "edifying" cannot be the second missing word because, if the decisions required were truly "edifying," a sensitive and idealistic person would not find them so difficult to make.

(B) is the answer. A "pragmatic" society is one that is more concerned with practical matters than with idealism. Such a society might well require "hardheaded" decisions rather than the idealistic ones preferred by a sensitive and idealistic person.

(C) is not the answer. A "rational" society might worship efficiency, but a sensitive and idealistic person would not have difficulty making decisions that are "well-intentioned."

(D) is not the answer. Worship of efficiency is not implicit in the definition of a "competitive" society. There is no way of knowing whether a sensitive and idealistic person would have difficulty making "evenhanded" decisions.

(E) is not the answer. A "modern" society might or might not worship efficiency, and there is no reason to suppose that such a society would require "dysfunctional" decisions.

8. A "tablecloth" is used to cover a "table," either to decorate it or to protect it. A rationale for this analogy could be "The purpose of X (a tablecloth) is to cover Y (a table)."

(A) is not the answer. A "tent" may cover "ground," but this is not a tent's purpose.

(B) is not the answer. A "shirt" may cover a "hanger," but this is not the shirt's purpose.

(C) is not the answer. A "sill" is part of a "window"; a window's purpose is not to cover a "sill."

(D) is the answer. A "sheet" is used to cover a "mattress."

(E) is not the answer. Clouds may cover portions of the Earth, but it is not the purpose of a "cloud" to cover "earth."

9. A "painter" often paints on "canvas." A rationale for this analogy could be "X is a material commonly used in the work of person Y."

(A) is not the answer. A "shoe" may be made of "leather," but a "shoe" is not a person, and cannot use "leather."

(B) is not the answer. A "brush" and a "palette" are commonly used at the same time, but a "palette" is not a person, and cannot use a "brush."

(C) is not the answer. A "chisel" may be used by a person working on "wood," but "wood" is not a person, and cannot use a "chisel."

(D) is the answer. "Marble" is a material commonly used by a "sculptor." As a "painter" uses "canvas" in creating a work of art, so a "sculptor" uses "marble."

(E) is not the answer. A "carpenter" uses a "hammer," but the "hammer" is not a material that the carpenter uses in his or her work.

10. A "mansion" is a large and usually expensive "residence." A rationale for this analogy could be "X is a large, expensive member of class Y."

(A) is the answer. A "limousine" is a special kind of "automobile," specifically, a large and expensive one.

(B) is not the answer. A "chandelier" is a larger and usually more expensive source of light than a "candle," but "candle" is not a class to which "chandelier" belongs.

(C) is not the answer. A "tuxedo" is often associated with wealth, and it may be a part of a "wardrobe," but it is not a kind of "wardrobe."

(D) is not the answer. A "diamond" is a more valuable kind of stone than a "rhinestone," but it is not a kind of "rhinestone."

(E) is not the answer. A "yacht" may be kept in a "harbor," but it is not a kind of "harbor."

11. A "door" is a barrier that can be used to close off (access to) a "room." A rationale for this analogy could be "X is a barrier that can be used to close off (prevent entry into) Y."

(A) is not the answer. A "rudder" and an "anchor" are both parts of a ship, but a "rudder" does not close off an "anchor."

(B) is not the answer. "Boat" and "ship" are names for vessels that are similar in some ways, but a "boat" does not close off a "ship."

(C) is not the answer. A "patio" does not close off a "terrace."

(D) is the answer. A "hatch" is a barrier that is used to close off a "hold" (a place where cargo is kept).

(E) is not the answer. A "basement" and an "attic" are both parts of a house, but a "basement" does not close off an "attic."

12. "Choreography" (the art of composing dances) provides a structure that determines what will happen during a "dance." A rationale for this analogy could be "X provides the organizing structure for creation Y."

(A) is not the answer. A "sermon" may be part of a "ceremony," but a "ceremony" does not usually provide structure for the "sermon."

(B) is not the answer. An "agenda" is a plan of things to be discussed or done. It provides an appropriate structure for a meeting, but not for an "advertisement."

(C) is not the answer. "Poetry" may be recited, but it does not provide structure for a "recitation."

(D) is not the answer. "Instrumentation" provides structure for music rather than for a "conductor."

(E) is the answer. The "plot" provides structure for a "story," a creative endeavor.

13. To "evaporate" means to change or be changed into a "vapor." A rationale for this analogy could be "To X means to change into Y."

(A) is the answer. To "petrify" means to turn into "stone."

(B) is not the answer. To "centrifuge" means to subject to the action of centrifugal force, a process that may sometimes separate out a "liquid." But to "centrifuge" something does not necessarily mean to change it into a "liquid."

(C) is not the answer. One meaning of "saturate" is to add "fluid" to something until it cannot hold more, but to "saturate" does not mean to turn into a "fluid."

(D) is not the answer. "Acid" can "corrode," but to "corrode" does not mean to turn into "acid."

(E) is not the answer. To "incinerate" means to consume by "fire," rather than to turn into "fire."

14. To "assuage" means to lessen the intensity of, or to relieve, something like pain or "sorrow." A rationale for this analogy could be "To X means to lessen the intensity of an emotion such as Y."

(A) is not the answer. To "retaliate" means to get back at or to get revenge. Retaliation is a result of "antipathy," rather than a lessening of its intensity.

(B) is the answer. To "dampen" can mean to diminish the intensity of an emotion such as "ardor."

(C) is not the answer. To "entrust" to someone is to depend on his or her "reliability" rather than to lessen it.

(D) is not the answer. In some circumstances, one might "counsel" in order to lessen "reluctance," but lessening the intensity of an emotion is not part of the definition of counseling.

(E) is not the answer. To "withhold" does not necessarily imply a lessening of intensity.

15. One way to make something "insensible" is to "numb" it. You can tell that "numb" is used as a verb, not as an adjective, because "reflect" in choice (A) is used only as a verb, not as an adjective. A rationale for this analogy could be "To X something means to render it Y."

(A) is not the answer. Something "luminous" may be reflected, but to "reflect" does not mean to make it "luminous."

(B) is the answer. To "burnish" means to polish something so that it is shiny, or "lustrous."

(C) is not the answer. One may "heckle" in a "raucous" way, but to "heckle" someone does not mean to make him or her "raucous."

(D) is not the answer. One may wish to "repulse" the "odious," or undesirable, but to "repulse" does not mean to render "odious."

(E) is not the answer. To "braid" means to put things together, but to "braid" something does not necessarily mean to make it "sinuous" (winding or complicated).

16. An "audacious" person acts boldly and fearlessly, that is, without "trepidation" (nervousness or fear). A rationale for this analogy could be "A person properly described as X is not characterized by Y."

(A) is not the answer. A "refractory" (stubborn) person is by definition characterized by "intransigence" (stubbornness).

(B) is the answer. "Laconic" means not characterized by "volubility" (talkativeness).

(C) is not the answer. One who is "sordid" (grasping, dirty, or generally awful) is not necessarily lacking in "aspiration"; to aspire does not necessarily imply reaching toward worthy or acceptable goals.

(D) is not the answer. Neither cursoriness nor "accumulation" is a word used to characterize people; to be "cursory" (to treat something superficially) does not mean to lack "accumulation."

(E) is not the answer. To be "derisive" (contemptuous or ridiculing) does not necessarily indicate a lack of "subordination." "Subordination" is not a personal quality like "trepidation."

17. This question asks you to identify the most appropriate title for the passage. You should consider the passage as a self-contained unit, not as part of a larger work.

(A) is not the answer. The passage is concerned not with influences on Woolf's work, but with its content and her approach to it.

(B) is not the answer. The passage is not about Woolf as a critic of the novel, but as a novelist.

(C) is not the answer. Though much of Woolf's work is, according to the passage, concerned with criticism of society, specific trends in contemporary reform movements are not mentioned in the passage.

(D) is not the answer. There is no discussion in the passage of any use of allegory in Woolf's work.

(E) is the answer. The topic of the passage is Woolf's novels, and the author emphasizes that the novels contain observations concerning "how individuals are shaped (or deformed) by their social environments" (lines 16-17).

18. The literary critics discussed in the first paragraph ignored Woolf's intention to criticize society and saw her as a "poetic" novelist unconcerned with the real world. This question asks you to identify the tone of the remarks made by the author of the passage concerning this assessment of Woolf's work.

(A) is the answer. The author's characterization of the critics' assessment as "cavalier" (line 13) can be described as "disparaging."

(B) is not the answer. There is no indication in the passage that the author is expressing an incongruity between actual and expected results or events, as "ironic" suggests.

(C) is not the answer. The author's attitude toward the critics is not "facetious." Rather, he takes the criticisms seriously, explaining why they cannot be correct.

(D) is not the answer. The author is "skeptical" of the critics' assessment, but that he is not "resigned" is shown in the pains he takes to prove that the claims are incorrect.

(E) is not the answer. The author is "disappointed" in the critics' assessment to the extent that he does not agree with it; but there is no indication that he expected better of them, nor does he expect them to change their assessment, as "hopeful" suggests.

19. The author discusses Woolf's literary models, emphasizing Chaucer, in the last paragraph. The reason why Woolf chose Chaucer as her model is not directly stated in the passage but must be inferred from the information there.

(A) is not the answer. The passage states that Chaucer understood his society, but there is no indication that he was the first to fucus on society as a whole.

(B) is not the answer. Though Woolf criticized D. H. Lawrence's methods, there is no indication in the passage that she thought that Lawrence did not sincerely wish to change society.

(C) is not the answer. Though the last paragraph states that Chaucer was concerned with understanding his society, there is no information in the passage about his questioning of mores.

(D) is the answer. Line 49 indicates that Woolf's work as a moralist is subtle and done "by indirection." Woolf's statement that readers absorb morality at every pore despite the fact that no laws were changed because of Chaucer indicates that she believed Chaucer's influence to be subtle. Therefore, it is likely that it was Chaucer's subtle effectiveness that led Woolf to choose him as a model.

(E) is not the answer. There is no discussion in the passage of Woolf's beliefs concerning the acceptability of her own novels.

20. In lines 20-22, the author states that Woolf's novels presented social settings realistically. This question asks why Woolf did so.

(A) is not the answer. There is no indication in the passage either that critics considered the novel to be the most realistic genre or that Woolf believed that they thought so.

(B) is the answer. In lines 15-20, Woolf's interest in the effect of social environment on the individual is described. The juxtaposition of these lines with the statement in lines 20-22 strongly suggests that Woolf realistically described social settings because she was interested in their effect on character.

(C) is not the answer. Though it is conceivable that attention to detail could help Woolf advance her arguments, there is no information in the passage that suggests this.

(D) is not the answer. The passage indicates that Woolf's realistic rendering of society resulted from her interest in it, and not from a desire to prove that such a rendering was not a hindrance.

(E) is not the answer. The passage indicates that Woolf's realistic rendering of society resulted from her interest in it, and not from a desire to avoid criticism.

21. This question refers you to lines 43-44 of the passage so that you can evaluate the context in which the author uses the word "contemplative." You are to choose the definition of "contemplative" that is closest in meaning to the use of the word in that context.

(A) is not the answer. Since Woolf satirized society, it can be concluded that she did not find the structure of its mores to be rational.

(B) is not the answer. Though Woolf described rather than directly criticized society, the author's characterization of her as a satirist indicates that her work reflected emotional commitment.

(C) is the answer. Lines 41-44 suggest that a contemplative art is expressed indirectly, rather than by "aggressive assertion." Lines 44-48 point out that Woolf, as a contemplative novelist, encourages readers to make their own judgments.

(D) is not the answer. The author indicates that Woolf wished to criticize society rather than to focus on individual consciousness. However, the word "contemplative" in the context of lines 41-44 describes how she presented her criticism. (D) describes the objects of criticism rather than a method of criticism.

(E) is not the answer. The author indicates that Woolf believed the artist's view of the world to be an honest one. However, the passage does not imply that Woolf did not judge society in moral terms.

22. This question asks you to identify an element that the author thinks is important in the satirist's art. The colon in line 52 indicates that the information in lines 48-52 describing Woolf's work leads to the statement, "hers is the satirist's art." This statement indicates that conclusions about Woolf's work as a satirist can lead you to conclusions about the art of satirists in general.

(A) is not the answer. Though the author suggests that a satirist "works by indirection," there is no indication that "lofty disdain" underlies this method.

(B) is not the answer. The author discusses Woolf's interest in the influence of society on the individual, but there is no suggestion in the passage that Woolf as a satirist thought the individual helpless.

(C) is not the answer. The fact that Woolf was herself a "visionary" (line 12) suggests that she did not indulge in "cynical disbelief" concerning the influence of visionaries.

(D) is not the answer. There is no indication in the passage that satirists believe that a work of art must be ambiguous in order to be accurate.

(E) is the answer. Lines 48-52 describe Woolf's satirical art as providing the materials for judgments about mores in an indirect, subtle, and non-assertive way, that is, in a nonpolemical way.

23. This question asks you to determine which of the questions given can be answered using the information in the passage. To make this determination, you must first attempt to answer each question using only the information presented by the author.

(A) is not the answer. The author mentions Chekhov and Chaucer in the last paragraph as acute social observers who were models for Woolf. There is no mention of critics' treatment of their social criticism.

(B) is the answer. The answer to the question is "No." In lines 10-12, the author characterizes Woolf as realistic and satirical as well as introspective and visionary.

(C) is not the answer. Though the author characterizes Woolf as a social critic, he does not mention specific causes in which she is interested.

(D) is not the answer. The author mentions that Woolf criticized Lawrence's tendency to "preach," but there is no discussion of Lawrence's concern with realistic settings for his novels.

(E) is not the answer. Lines 15-20 suggest that Woolf believed social environment to be a force in shaping people's lives, but there is no comparison of her belief about the effect of this force with her belief about the effect of the force of history on people's lives.

24. This question asks you to determine the primary purpose of the passage. In order to do this, you must take into account all of the information in the passage.

(A) is not the answer. The author does not criticize scientists because they believe that the reaction may be a feasible energy source.

(B) is not the answer. The author states that miscalculation of the amount of lithium available is a problem, but he does not say who has miscalculated.

(C) is not the answer. The author does defend the continued short-term use of fossil fuels, but he mentions fossil fuels as one of several possible sources of energy.

(D) is the answer. The author mentions several reasons why nuclear fusion should not be accepted as a major source of energy at this time and recommends continued critical evaluation of its potential.

(E) is not the answer. The author does correct the misconception that nuclear fusion power is not radioactive, but to do so is not his primary purpose.

25. This question asks you to use the specific statements made in the passage to determine what the author believes about public awareness of nuclear fusion power.

(A) is not the answer. There is no information in the passage to indicate that the public has been misinformed deliberately, though several instances of misinformation are mentioned.

(B) is not the answer. No mention is made in the passage of the advantages of nuclear fusion as compared with those of nuclear fission.

(C) is the answer. The author specifically mentions two misconceptions about nuclear fusion that he believes are generally held, indicating that he believes that people's knowledge of the scientific facts is incomplete.

(D) is not the answer. The public's interest in increasing its awareness is not discussed.

(E) is not the answer. The author indicates, on the contrary, that the public is not aware of some of the limitations of nuclear fusion power.

26. This question asks you to determine which of the questions given can be answered using the information in the passage. To make this determination, you must first attempt to answer each question using only the information presented by the author.

(A) is the answer. The answer to the question posed in (A) is "the sea." The passage states that it is commonly believed that there is an enormous quantity of deuterium in the sea; the author does not deny this.

(B) is not the answer. The author states that radiation is produced by the deuterium-tritium reaction, but no amount is mentioned.

(C) is not the answer. The author mentions that scientists are studying the reaction with zeal, but no reason for their zeal is given.

(D) is not the answer. The author does not provide a rationale for the use of lithium to produce tritium.

(E) is not the answer. The author mentions that the deuterium-tritium reaction produces alpha particles and neutrons, but he does not explain why these are produced by the reaction.

27. The author mentions nuclear scientists only once, near the beginning of the passage. This question asks you to determine what the passage most directly suggests about them.

(A) is not the answer. It is probably true that scientists do not know all the facts, but the question asks what is suggested in the passage. Though the passage suggests that the public does not know all the facts, there is no information about how much scientists know.

(B) is not the answer. The author attributes zeal to nuclear scientists, but not particular misconceptions or errors. Thus, he does not associate misconceptions or errors with their zeal.

(C) is not the answer. The author does not say that the amount of lithium has been overestimated. He discusses only evaluations of the amount of deuterium available.

(D) is the answer. The author's statement that scientists are studying the deuterium-tritium reaction with "zeal" suggests that he believes that they are not dispassionate.

(E) is not the answer. The author cautions that scientists should continue to study nuclear fusion, but he does not single out the lithium-to-tritium reaction as one needing further study.

28. To "persevere" means to continue in an enterprise in spite of opposition or other difficulties.

(A) is not the answer. To "put into" could mean to invest, as energy, or, more generally, to insert.

(B) is not the answer. To "send out" means to emit.

(C) is not the answer. To "take away" means to subtract, to relieve someone of something, or to remove.

(D) is the answer. To "give up" can mean to cease to try to accomplish something.

(E) is not the answer. To "bring forward" can mean to move up or to carry over. It does not suggest a lack of perseverance.

29. Something that is "waterproof" cannot be penetrated by water.

(A) is not the answer. Something "soggy" has already been penetrated by a liquid. Something "soggy" is not "waterproof," but "soggy" implies more than being penetrable by water. It means having already absorbed a great deal of liquid.

(B) is not the answer. "Natural" does not indicate either resistance to water or lack of resistance.

(C) is not the answer. It is likely that an "unglazed" substance such as pottery is less "waterproof" than the same substance covered with a glaze. However, "unglazed" does not by definition mean lacking resistance to water.

(D) is not the answer. "Viscous" means gluey; it refers to the consistency of a material rather than to its resistance to water.

(E) is the answer. "Permeable" means capable of being penetrated, by water or other liquids.

30. To "amalgamate" means to mix together or unite.

(A) is the answer. To "separate" means to disunite.

(B) is not the answer. To "fixate" means to gaze steadily at something.

(C) is not the answer. To "terminate" means to put an end to or to come to an end. It does not necessarily imply dissolution.

(D) is not the answer. To "calibrate" means to adjust, as the markings on an instrument.

(E) is not the answer. To "correlate" means to show a relationship to something else.

31. In some contexts, "pungency" is a quality that is directly perceived. It implies sharpness, a stinging quality, and frequently applies to smells or tastes.

(A) is not the answer. Something that is the opposite of pungent might cause "boredom," but "boredom" is a feeling rather than a quality.

(B) is not the answer. "Redundancy" refers to that which is extra, unnecessary, or repetitive.

(C) is not the answer. "Pungency" is a quality that might provoke a response, but "unresponsiveness" is a characteristic of the perceiver, not of the thing perceived.

(D) is the answer. "Blandness" means lacking flavor, not irritating, stimulating, sharp, or stinging. It is frequently used to describe tastes.

(E) is not the answer. "Insignificance" is a quality, but it does not necessarily imply a lack of sharpness. It is not a common quality of tastes or smells.

32. "Anarchy" means absence of order.

(A) is not the answer. A lack of "courtesy" might well accompany a state of "anarchy," but this lack is not implied in the definition of "anarchy."

(B) is not the answer. "Hope" is an emotion, and not a state. It may or may not accompany "anarchy," but it is not the opposite of "anarchy."

(C) is the answer. "Order" is the opposite of a lack of order.

(D) is not the answer. "Neutrality," like "anarchy," can be a political state, but it does not necessarily imply orderliness.

(E) is not the answer. "Importance" is a quality that does not directly or necessarily have to do with order or the lack of it.

33. An "incursion" is an intrusion into another's territory. It suggests aggression, and is often used in a military context.

(A) is not the answer. To make an "incursion" does not necessarily inspire respect in those whose territory is invaded, so a "loss of respect" is not the opposite of "incursion."

(B) is not the answer. It is likely that "incursion" is preceded by a certain amount of resolve, but a "lack of resolve" is not the opposite of an intrusion.

(C) is not the answer. "Reparation" (repaying wartime damages, or making amends) may be required as a result of an "incursion," but repayment is not the opposite of an intrusion.

(D) is not the answer. A "relapse" is a return to a previous, undesirable state. It is not the opposite of an intrusion.

(E) is the answer. "Retreat" is often used in a military context to describe an end to formal aggression, a backing off from a former position. Though "retreat" is more general than "incursion" in that it does not necessarily refer to a position in another's territory, it is still the option most nearly opposite to "incursion."

34. To "abrogate" means to do away with, usually in a legal context, as when something official is done away with or when something is done away with by law.

(A) is the answer. To "uphold" means to support something. In a legal context, it is likely to mean to keep something (like a rule or law) in existence rather than to do away with it.

(B) is not the answer. In a legal context, to "defer" is most likely to mean to put off, or to delay.

(C) is not the answer. To "discuss secretly" is not necessarily to keep something in existence.

(D) is not the answer. To "admit willingly" does not necessarily mean to keep something in existence.

(E) is not the answer. To "read thoroughly" does not mean to keep something in existence.

35. "Hapless" means unlucky or unable to achieve success because of bad luck.

(A) is not the answer. "Excited" means stimulated, or showing strong feeling.

(B) is not the answer. One might feel "elated" if one were not "hapless," but elation is an emotional state rather than the state that causes emotion.

(C) is the answer. One who is "fortunate" is lucky.

(D) is not the answer. To be "completely self-reliant" means to be able to depend entirely on one's own abilities, and does not imply luck or lack of it.

(E) is not the answer. If one is "assured of success," one is not "hapless." However, luck or the lack of it is not a necessary element in the idea of being guaranteed success.

36. To "aver" means to state that something is certainly true, or to prove something positively to be true.

(A) is not the answer. To "collect" means to gather, and could refer to evidence in support of a position, but it does not refer to a statement or to proof.

(B) is not the answer. To "augment" means to make greater.

(C) is not the answer. To "placate" means to soothe. The ability of a statement to placate is not necessarily related to the certainty or truth of its content.

(D) is the answer. To "deny" is to state that something is false.

(E) is not the answer. To "encourage" is to inspire or to help along. Encouragement is not concerned with truth or the lack of it.

37. "Sedulous" means applying oneself faithfully to a task. It suggests continuing effort and attention to what is to be done.

(A) is not the answer. "Presumptuous" means showing arrogance by overstepping one's authority. Presumptuousness does not necessarily have to do with performance of a task.

(B) is not the answer. "Ponderous" means being hard to manage because of great weight or size. It does not suggest a lack of attention or application.

(C) is not the answer. "Treacherous" means likely to betray. It does not describe an approach to a task.

(D) is the answer. "Careless" can mean failing to apply due attention to performance of a task.

(E) is not the answer. Work might be made "useless" if effort and attention were not applied to it, but "useless" does not describe the worker's approach to the work.

38. "Insularity" means the state of being isolated or confined to a limited area. It often applies to nations or to peoples.

(A) is not the answer. "Overzealousness" is excessive concern over an issue. It might result from isolation or the lack of it, but it does not imply a lack of isolation.

(B) is the answer. "Cosmopolitanism" implies worldwide scope.

(C) is not the answer. "Insularity" might make a nation susceptible, but "susceptibility" means inability to resist some outside influence, and does not have to do directly with isolation.

(D) is not the answer. It is unlikely that an insular people would be characterized by "willing hospitality," but "willing hospitality" is not implied in the idea of a lack of isolation.

(E) is not the answer. "Insularity" might result from a lack of "knowledgeable consideration," but "knowledgeable consideration" is not itself a state like "insularity."

SECTION 5

1. A check of the procedures for letter forwarding shows that (A), (B), (C), and (E) can all happen. However, (D) cannot happen; I forwards red letters to J only. Therefore, (D) is the correct answer.

2. G may not forward a blue letter to either H or I; therefore, (A) and (B) are ruled out. I may not forward a blue letter to either H or G; therefore, (D) and (E) are ruled out. The sequence in (C) conforms fully with the procedures; therefore, (C) is the correct answer.

3. A letter may reach L via the sequence J to K to L without being seen by G, H, or I; thus, (A), (B), and (C) are ruled out. Another allowable sequence is I to K to L; thus, (D) is ruled out. Since no letters are given first to L and only K forwards letters to L, every letter that reaches L must have been previously given to K. Therefore, (E) is the correct answer.

4. Since no one forwards letters to H, any letter not given first to H will not be received by H. Thus, (B), (C), (D), and (E) are ruled out. A red letter first given to H could be given to each member of the department in the sequence H to G to I to J to K to L. Therefore, (A) is the correct answer.

5. L is not given letters initially, but when L is given letters they come from K only. K, who also is not given letters initially, receives them from either I or J, either of whom may be given letters initially. Thus, a minimum of two members of the department (I and K or J and K) must have received a letter before it reaches L, and (B) is the correct answer.

6. Since no one forwards letters to H, and only H forwards letters to G, neither G nor H could be given a letter for a second time. Thus, (A) and (B) are ruled out. Since K forwards letters to L only, and L answers every letter given to him, neither K nor L could be given a letter for a second time. Thus, (D) and (E) are ruled out. A red letter may be given to J a second time via the sequence H to I to J to I to J. Therefore, (C) is the correct answer.

7. The screenwriter's statement implies an acknowledgment that those evaluating screenplays will want to alter them, and it implies that screenwriters adjust the length of a first draft in order to allow evaluators to make alterations. Proposition (B) restates these implications and is the correct answer.

   (A) is incorrect. The statement says nothing about whether screenwriters do more than provide a script.

   (C) is incorrect. The statement says nothing about the temperament of screenwriters, and it gives a reason other than temperament for the length of first drafts.

(D) is incorrect. The statement does not imply that the cuts made by evaluators are always the best cuts that could have been made.

(E) is incorrect. The statement does not imply that the first drafts are of uneven quality.

8. The presence of predators of zooplankton, feeding near the surface during the day, would suggest that D. galeata is consumed at a higher rate than D. hyalina. Therefore, if (B) were true it would help resolve the apparent paradox that D. galeata grows and reproduces faster than D. hyalina, yet D. hyalina has the greater population.

(A) is incorrect. Nothing is said in the paragraph to show the relevance of the presence of other species of zooplankton to the relative population size of the two species.

(C) is incorrect. This information explains the slower growth and reproduction of D. hyalina, which is one aspect of the paradox; but it does nothing to show how D. hyalina can grow and reproduce more slowly and yet have the greater population.

(D) is incorrect. Nothing is said in the paragraph to show the relevance to the paradox of D. galeata's clustering under vegetation.

(E) is incorrect. More information on the faster reproduction of D. galeata does not show how, despite faster growth and reproduction, D. galeata has the lesser population.

9. The fact that the walls of Japanese homes are more combustible than the walls in most American homes would be a factor likely to contribute to greater fire loss in Japan than in the United States. Therefore, this factor would be very unlikely to contribute to lesser fire loss in Japan, and (A) is the correct answer.

(B) is incorrect. A greater incidence of arson in the United States would be likely to contribute to greater fire loss in the United States.

(C) is incorrect. More effective fire extinguishing equipment in more Japanese homes would be likely to contribute to lesser fire loss in Japan.

(D) is incorrect. The greater popularity of foam-based and plastic furniture in the United States would be likely to be a factor contributing to greater fire loss in the United States, since such furniture is a greater fire hazard than furniture of natural fibers.

(E) is incorrect. Greater attention to prevention and training by Japanese fire departments would be likely to contribute to lesser fire loss in Japan.

10. Four p.m. is the latest possible meeting time. Since H must meet earlier in the day than F, H cannot meet at 4 p.m. Each of the classes F, G, J, or K could meet at 4 p.m. Therefore, (C) is the correct answer.

11. If J meets sometime before K meets, then, since J must meet in the afternoon, J must meet at 2 p.m. and K must meet at 4 p.m. Thus, (C) is ruled out. Since no class meets when K meets, and 4 p.m. is the latest possible meeting time, (A), (B), and (E) are ruled out. L can meet at 2 p.m., when J meets; therefore, (D) is the correct answer.

12. Since H must meet earlier in the day than F, H must meet at 9 a.m. if F meets at 10 a.m. Since J must meet in the afternoon, J must meet at 2 p.m. if no class meets at 4 p.m. Since no other class can meet when K meets, and other classes are meeting at 9 a.m., 10 a.m., and 2 p.m., K must meet at 11 a.m. Thus, H must meet before K meets, and (B) is the correct answer.

(A) is incorrect. Both H and L can meet at 9 a.m. without violating any of the conditions.

(C) is incorrect. G can meet at 9 a.m. and K can meet at 11 a.m. without violating any of the conditions.

(D) is incorrect. L can meet at 2 p.m. and G can meet at 9 a.m. without violating any of the conditions.

(E) is incorrect. L can meet at 9 a.m. and J can meet at 2 p.m. without violating any of the conditions.

13. Since H must meet earlier than F, F must meet at 4 p.m. if H meets at 2 p.m. Then, since no other class can meet when K meets, K cannot meet later than 11 a.m. Therefore, (E) is the correct answer.

(A) is incorrect. F and L can both meet at 4 p.m. without violating any of the conditions.

(B) is incorrect. Besides 2 p.m., G can meet at 9 a.m., 10 a.m., or 11 a.m. without violating any of the conditions.

(C) is incorrect. Besides the morning, G can meet at 2 p.m. without violating any of the conditions.

(D) is incorrect. Besides 2 p.m., J can meet at 4 p.m. without violating any of the conditions.

14. Since V always finishes somewhere ahead of P and P always finishes somewhere ahead of Q, if V finishes fifth then P finishes sixth and Q finishes seventh (last). Whenever Q finishes last, S finishes first. Therefore, (A) is the correct answer.

(B) is incorrect. Besides second, R can finish third or fourth without violating any of the conditions.

(C) is incorrect. Besides third, T can finish second or fourth without violating any of the conditions.

(D) is incorrect. If V finishes fifth, Q cannot finish fourth since V always finishes somewhere ahead of P and P always finishes somewhere ahead of Q.

(E) is incorrect. Since Q finishes last and there are no ties, U cannot finish last.

15. If R finishes first, T finishes last (seventh). Since V always finishes somewhere ahead of P and P always finishes somewhere ahead of Q, V cannot finish fifth or sixth. Thus, (D) and (E) are ruled out. If P finishes fifth and Q finishes sixth, V can finish fourth. Thus, (A) and (B) are ruled out, and (C) is the correct answer.

16. If S finishes second, then R finishes first (since only R or S ever finish first) and T finishes last. Thus, (A), (B), and (D) are ruled out. Since V always finishes somewhere ahead of P, (C) is ruled out. It is possible that U finishes ahead of V; therefore, (E) is the correct answer.

17. If S finishes sixth, then, since only R or S ever finish first, R finishes first and T finishes last. Thus, (B) and (E) are ruled out. Since V always finishes somewhere ahead of P and first, fifth, sixth, and seventh places are taken by others, V finishes second or third, and P finishes third or fourth. Thus, (A) and (C) are ruled out. U can finish either third (if V finishes second and P finishes fourth) or fourth (if V and P finish second and third, respectively). Therefore, (D) is the correct answer.

18. If R finishes second and Q finishes fifth, then, since only R or S ever finish first, S finishes first and U finishes last. Since V always finishes somewhere ahead of P and P always finishes somewhere ahead of Q, V and P finish third and fourth, respectively. That leaves only sixth place in which T can finish; therefore, (D) is the correct answer.

19. Since Helen cannot serve on a committee with Irene and each person must serve on X or Y, if Helen serves on X, Irene must serve on Y. Therefore, (C) is the correct answer.

20. If either Georgia, Jorge, Karin, or Lamont serve on X with exactly one other person, then, since each person must serve on X or Y, either Frederick would serve on a committee with Georgia or with Jorge, or Helen would serve on a committee with Irene. None of these combinations is allowed; thus, (A), (C), (D), and (E) are ruled out. Helen can serve on X with Frederick without violating any of the membership rules; therefore, (B) is the correct answer.

21. Georgia, Jorge, and Lamont can serve on X while Frederick, Irene, and Karin serve on Y without violating any of the membership rules. Thus, the combinations described in (A), (B), (D), and (E) are possible. Since each person must serve on X or Y, Karin and Irene must serve on the same committee if neither serves with Lamont. Since Helen cannot serve on a committee with Irene, Helen cannot serve with Karin. Therefore, (C) is the correct answer.

22. If (D) is added, then since Helen cannot serve with Irene and Frederick cannot serve with Georgia or Jorge, Irene and Frederick must serve on Y and the other five people must serve on X (each person must serve on X or Y, and no one can serve on both X and Y). Therefore, (D) is the correct answer.

(A) is incorrect. Two distributions are possible without violating any of the membership rules: Frederick, Irene, Karin, and Lamont can serve on X while Georgia, Helen, and Jorge serve on Y; and Frederick, Irene, and Lamont can serve on X while Georgia, Helen, Karin, and Jorge serve on Y.

(B) is incorrect. Two distributions are possible without violating any of the membership rules: Georgia, Helen, and Jorge can serve on X while Frederick, Irene, Karin, and Lamont serve on Y; and Georgia, Irene, and Jorge can serve on X while Frederick, Helen, Karin, and Lamont serve on Y.

(C) is incorrect. Several distributions are possible without violating any of the membership rules. Two examples are: Georgia, Helen, Jorge, and Lamont can serve on X while Frederick, Irene, and Karin serve on Y; and Georgia, Irene, Jorge, and Lamont can serve on X while Frederick, Helen, and Karin serve on Y.

(E) is incorrect. Several distributions are possible without violating any of the membership rules. Two examples are: Frederick, Helen, and Lamont can serve on X while Georgia, Irene, Jorge, and Karin serve on Y; and Frederick, Helen, and Karin can serve on X while Georgia, Irene, Jorge, and Lamont serve on Y.

23. The researchers believe that the presence of RNA enables us to remember. However, if, after an injection of RNA inhibitor, animals gave learned responses more consistently than before, it would appear that the absence of RNA facilitates memory. Therefore, (B) is the correct answer.

(A) is incorrect. These results would suggest that RNA is the basis of other abilities in addition to that of memory, but there is nothing in them that would weaken the case for RNA as the basis of memory.

(C) is incorrect. These results support the case that RNA is the basis of memory, although they suggest that the degree of effectiveness of either RNA or RNA inhibitor may vary.

(D) is incorrect. These results would suggest that RNA must be strongly inhibited in order to impair memory, but still would support the case for RNA as the basis of memory.

(E) is incorrect. These results would suggest that RNA is necessary for new learning, and as the learning would require memory, the results would support the case for RNA as the basis of memory.

24. In stating that planets may exist that are similar enough to Earth to make them suitable for supporting life, the author implicitly rules out planets dissimilar to Earth as likely to support life. The assumption underlying the statement is that life on another planet is likely to require conditions similar to those on Earth. Therefore, (E) is the correct answer.

(A) is incorrect. The statement assumes nothing about the appearance of extraterrestrial life.

(B) is incorrect. The statement implies that it is relatively unlikely that life exists on other planets in our solar system, but it makes no assumption absolutely ruling out the possibility that such life exists.

(C) is incorrect. Although the statement suggests that there is the greatest chance for life when physical conditions are appropriate, it leaves open the possibility that no life will exist even with appropriate conditions.

(D) is incorrect. The statement says that it is possible that more than one of the suns in the galaxy is accompanied by an Earth-like planet, but it does not assume that there are actually any such suns.

25. If crop yield per planted acre was less in the Soviet Union than it was in the United States, yet crop yield per total (planted plus fallow) agricultural acreage was greater in the Soviet Union than it was in the United States, there must have been a lower percentage of the total acreage that was left fallow in the Soviet Union than there was in the United States. Therefore, (A) is the correct answer.

(B) is incorrect. From the information in the passage, it is impossible to tell whether the United States had more or less fallow acreage than planted acreage.

(C) is incorrect. Since the comparisons made in the passage are based on crop yields per acre, it is impossible to tell whether there was more or less fallow acreage in the Soviet Union than in the United States.

(D) is incorrect. From the information in the passage, it is impossible to tell whether the Soviet Union had more or less planted acreage than fallow acreage.

(E) is incorrect. Since the comparisons made in the passage are based on crop yields per acre, it is impossible to tell whether the Soviet Union produced a greater volume of crops than the United States produced.

SECTION 6

1. Since $n + 3 = 8$, n must be 5.
Since $k + n = k + 5 = 13$, k must be 8.

Answer is A

2. Betty spent \$102 on her bicycle (\$75 + \$27). Therefore, in selling the bicycle for \$120, she got \$18 in excess of what she spent.

Answer is B

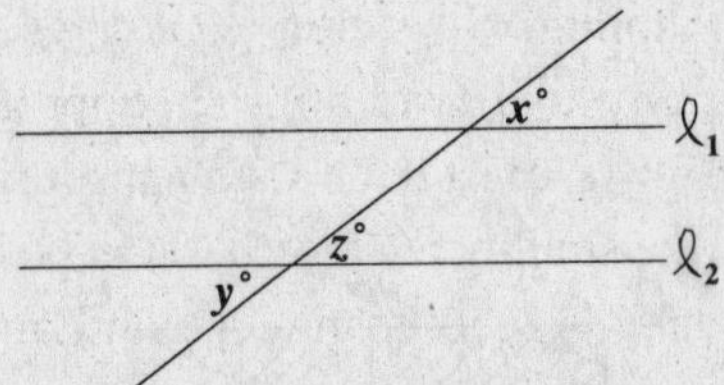

3. In the figure, $y = z$ because they are measures of a pair of vertical angles. Also, since $\ell_1 \parallel \ell_2$, $z = x$ because they are measures of a pair of corresponding angles. Therefore, $y = x$.

Answer is C

4. $-2(-3)(-4) < 0$. You can determine this by calculating the product or by realizing that the product of an odd number of negative factors must be negative. On the other hand, $0(4)(8) = 0$ since the product of 0 and any number is 0.

Answer is B

5. The value of $11 + x$ depends on the value of x. If $x \geq 0$, then $11 + x \geq 11$, but if $x < 0$, then $11 + x < 11$. For example,

if $x = 0$, then $11 + x = 11$;
if $x = -1$, then $11 + x = 10$;
and if $x = -2$, then $11 + x = 9$.

Therefore, $11 + x$ may be greater than, equal to, or less than 10.

Answer is D

6. $\frac{1}{2}+\frac{3}{5}>1$. You can determine this by computation or by noting that $\frac{3}{5}$ is greater than $\frac{1}{2}$, so that

$$\frac{1}{2}+\frac{3}{5}>\frac{1}{2}+\frac{1}{2}=1.$$

On the other hand,

$$\frac{1+3}{2+5}=\frac{4}{7}<1.$$

Answer is A

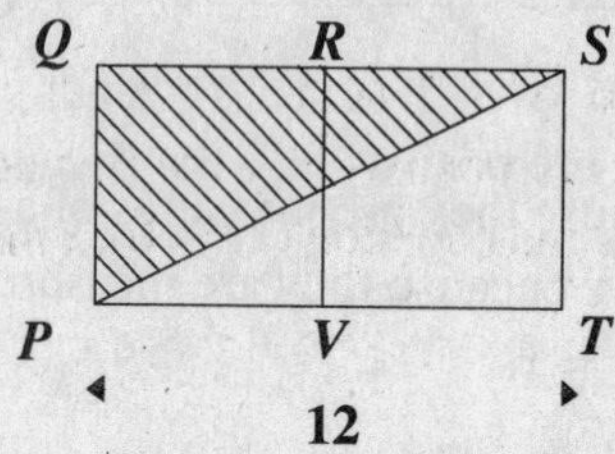

7. In the figure, the two squares have a common side, RV, so that $PQST$ is a 12 by 6 rectangle. Its area is therefore 72. You are asked to compare the area of region PQS with 36. Since diagonal PS splits region $PQST$ in half, the area of region PQS is $\frac{1}{2}$ of 72, or 36.

Answer is C

8. It is given that R, S, and T are consecutive **odd** integers, with $R < S < T$. This means that S is 2 more than R, and T is 2 more than S. (Examples of consecutive odd integers are 1, 3, and 5; and 19, 21, and 23.) You can use this to rewrite each of the expressions to be compared as follows:

$R + S + 1 = R + (R + 2) + 1 = \mathbf{2R + 3}$

$S + T - 1 = (R + 2) + (R + 4) - 1 = \mathbf{2R + 5}$

Since $5 > 3$, then $2R + 5 > 2R + 3$. You might also notice that both expressions to be compared contain S: $S + (R + 1)$ and $S + (T - 1)$.

Therefore, the real difference in the two expressions depends on the difference in value of $R + 1$ and $T - 1$. Since T is 4 more than R, $T - 1 > R + 1$.

Answer is B

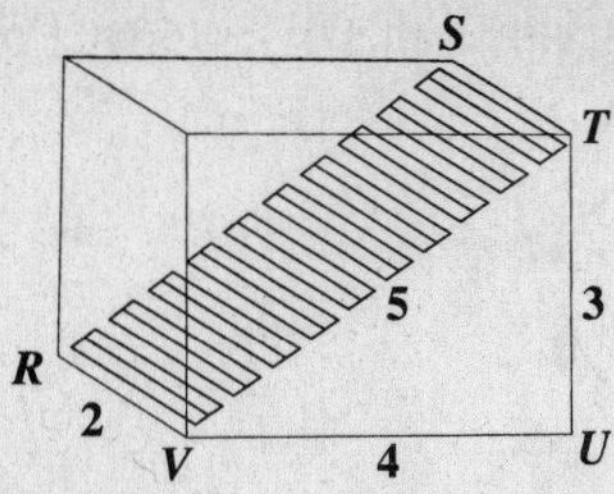

9. You need to determine the area of the shaded rectangular region. It is given that $VR = 2$, but the length of VT is not given. However, $UV = 4$ and $TU = 3$, and VTU is a right triangle, so by the Pythagorean theorem, $VT = 5$. Thus, the area of $RVTS$ (the shaded region) is 5×2, or 10, which is greater than 9.

Answer is A

10. It is given that $x^2y > 0$ and $xy^2 < 0$, so neither x nor y can be 0. If neither x nor y is 0, then both x^2 and y^2 are positive. By the first equation ($x^2y > 0$), y must also be positive; by the second equation ($xy^2 < 0$), x must be negative. That is, $x < 0 < y$.

Answer is B

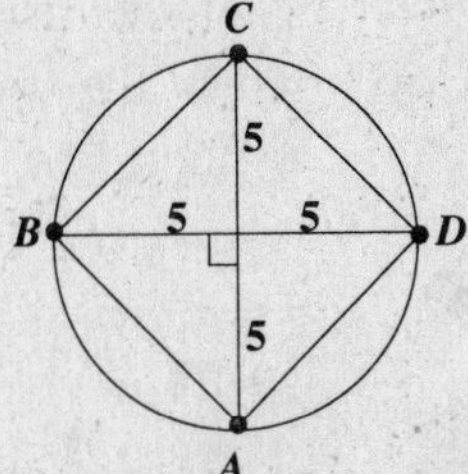

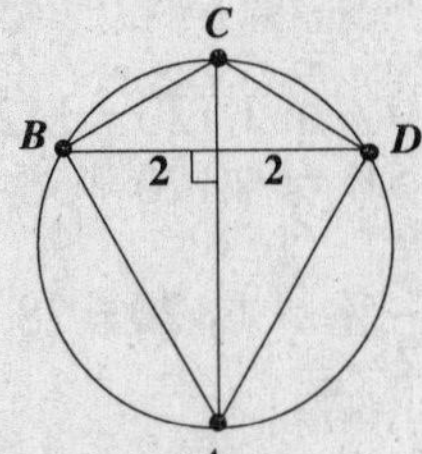

Figure 1 **Figure 2**

11. You are given no information about the location of points A, B, C, and D except that they are on a circle of diameter 10. In Figure 1 above, if AC and BD are perpendicular diameters, then:

$$\text{Area } \Delta\, ABC = \text{Area } \Delta\, ADC = \frac{10 \cdot 5}{2} = 25,$$

so the area of $ABCD$ is $2 \times 25 = 50$.

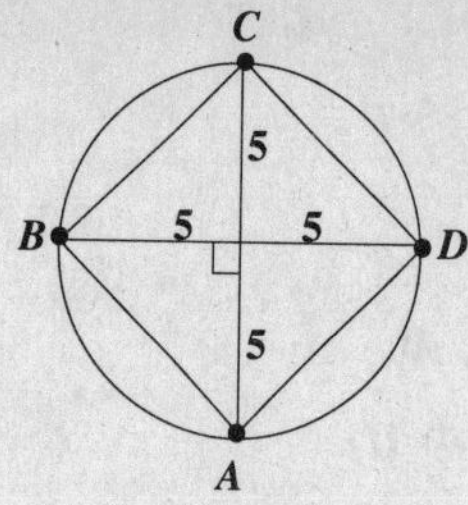

Figure 1

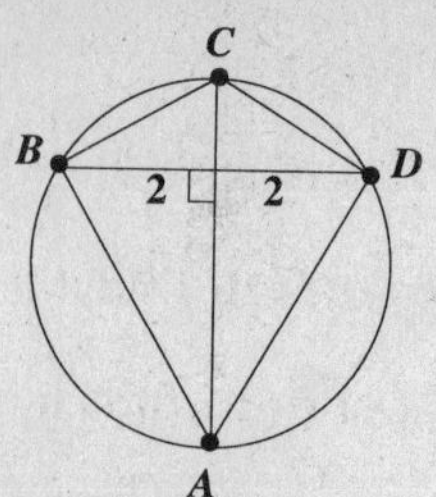

Figure 2

On the other hand, in Figure 2, although the bases of *ABC* and *ADC* are still 10, the altitude of each could be 2. In this case,

Area Δ *ABC* = Area Δ *ADC* = $(10 \cdot 2)/2 = 10$, so the area of *ABCD* is $2 \times 10 = 20$. These examples show that the area of *ABCD* may be greater or less than 40.

Answer is D

12. If you made an error in computation, you might think of the problem this way, noting that

5 is $\frac{1}{2}$ of 10, and $2\frac{1}{2}$ is $\frac{1}{2}$ of 5:

$$10\% \text{ of } 1{,}120 = 112,$$
$$\text{so } 5\% \text{ of } 1{,}120 = 56,$$
$$\text{and } 2\frac{1}{2}\% \text{ of } 1{,}120 = 28$$
$$= 4 \times 7 = 2^2 \cdot 7.$$

Answer is C

13. The number of records pressed by machine *R* in 3 hours is $6x$ — that is, $(3 \div 0.5)$ times x. The number of records pressed by machine *S* in 4 hours is $\left(5\frac{1}{3}\right)x$ — that is, $(4 \div 0.75)$ times x.

Answer is A

Alternate solution:

Machine R: x records in $\frac{1}{2}$ hour means

$2x$ records in 1 hour and

$3 \cdot 2x$ or $6x$ records in 3 hours.

Machine S: x records in $\frac{3}{4}$ hour means

$\frac{4}{3}x$ records in 1 hour and $4 \cdot \frac{4}{3}x$, or

$\left(5\frac{1}{3}\right)x$, records in 4 hours.

And $6x > \left(5\frac{1}{3}\right)x$.

Answer is A

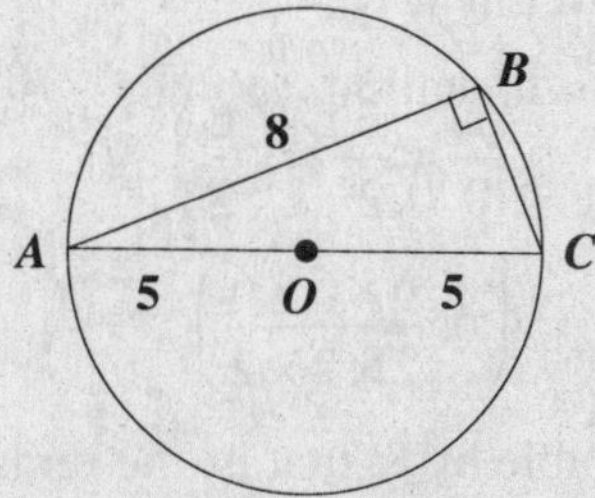

14. In the figure, since O is the center of the circle, AO and OC are radii, and $AO = OC = 5$. Triangle ABC is a right triangle in which diameter AC is the hypotenuse of the triangle. So by the Pythagorean theorem, $BC^2 = 10^2 - 8^2 = 100 - 64 = 36$. Thus $BC = 6$, so the perimeter is $6 + 8 + 10 = 24$.

Answer is C

15. If the three negative integers happen to be –1, –2, and –3, then

$$(-1)(-2)(-3) = (-1) + (-2) + (-3) = -6;$$

that is, the product is equal to the sum. However, if the integers are –2, –3, and –4, then

$(-2)(-3)(-4) < (-2) + (-3) + (-4)$ because $-24 < -9$.

In this case, the product is less than the sum. These examples show that the relative values of the sum and product can vary according to the numbers chosen.

Answer is D

16. $\sqrt{(42-6)(25+11)} =$

$\sqrt{(36)(36)} =$

$\sqrt{36} \times \sqrt{36} = 6 \times 6 = 36$

Answer is C

17. Since there are two brands of socks with different prices, the greatest number of pairs of socks that could be purchased for a given amount of money would be the cheaper brand — brand X. Since these are \$2 per pair, at most 12 pairs could be bought for \$25 if, as stated in the problem, there is no sales tax. Note that the customer could also buy 11 pairs at \$2 each and 1 pair at \$3 to use the entire \$25, but this would still be 12 pairs of socks.

Answer is D

18. You can solve this problem by calculation, but you might notice that $8 = 2^3$, so if you think of writing it this way,

$$\frac{6^3}{8} = \frac{6^3}{2^3} = \left(\frac{6}{2}\right)^3$$

$$\left(\text{or } \frac{6 \times 6 \times 6}{2 \times 2 \times 2}\right)$$

you can see that 6^3 is divisible by 8; that is, the remainder is 0.

Answer is E

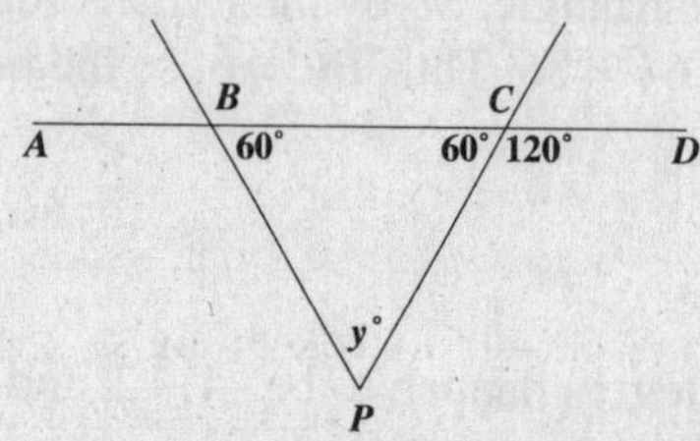

19. You are given that $x = 120$, so the measure of $\angle PCB$ must be 60°. You are also given that $BP = CP$, so $\angle PBC$ has the same measure as $\angle PCB$. Since the sum of the measures of the angles of ΔBPC is 180°, y must also be 60.

Answer is B

20.

$$\begin{aligned} \text{Since } z &= 2y \text{ and } y = 3x, \text{ then} \\ z &= 2(3x) = 6x. \text{ Thus,} \\ x + y + z &= x + (3x) + (6x) \\ &= (1 + 3 + 6)x = 10x. \end{aligned}$$

Answer is A

Questions 21-25 refer to a graph and a chart. Since there are 5 questions based on these sources, it is wise to scan both of them first to get an overview. In this case, the graph shows the percent of annual income spent on six categories of some food and nonfood items. The chart, on the other hand, shows the percent of expenditures for food and household items spent on six subcategories of these item.

21. This question asks about percent of annual income, so the necessary information is given in the graph. "Food at Home" is indicated by the unshaded portion of each of the bars, and the lowest percent (shortest portion) was spent by professionals and managers.

Answer is B

22. This question asks about expenditures, so all the needed information is given in the chart. For professionals and managers, an average of 29% of weekly expenditures ($38.77) was for food away home. To estimate this amount, you could think of this as a bit less than 30% of $39. Since 30% of $39 is $11.70, the best of the answer choices given is $11.

Answer is C

23. This question also asks about expenditures; this time about expenditures for fruits and vegetables. This category is included with others (cereals, and bakery and dairy products), so it is not possible to estimate the percent spent only on fruits and vegetables.

Answer is E

24. For this question, you must use both the chart (meats, poultry, and seafood) and the graph (annual income). According to the chart, retirees spend about 23% of food and household expenditures on meats, poultry, and seafood. However, "household expenditures" includes food at home, food away from home, personal care items, and housekeeping supplies. According to the graph, retirees spend about 29% of their annual income on these four categories (about 23% for food and 6% for the other two categories). Therefore, they spend about 23% of 29% for meats, poultry, and seafood. $.23 \times .29 = .0667$, which is approximately 7%.

Answer is A

Alternate solution: According to the graph, retirees spent about 19.5% of their annual income on Food at Home. According to the table, they spent 23% of the 66% of their average weekly Food at Home budget on meats, poultry, and seafood. Therefore, they spent about $\frac{23}{66}$ (19.5), or $\frac{1}{3}$ (19.5) of their annual income, on these foods. Since $\frac{1}{3}$ (19.5) = 6.5, and (19.5) > $\frac{1}{3}$ (19.5), this is about 7%.

Answer is A

25. You are to determine which of three given statements can be inferred from the data. Statement I cannot properly be inferred since the graph shows percents of annual incomes. (Although the bar for retirees is tallest, this does not mean that their actual income was greater: rather, it means that they spend a greater percent of their annual incomes on these categories than the other occupations listed.) Statement II cannot be inferred either — although each group spends about the same percent of their income on housekeeping supplies, the expenditures differed. For example, 7% of $35.88 is less than 7% of $38.77. Thus, III is the only possible correct inference. This can be verified by actual calculation (23% of $35.44 is greater than any of the other combinations).

Answer is C

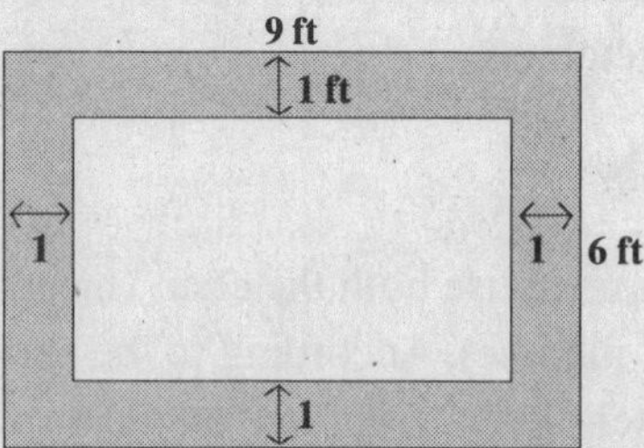

26. The rug is 9 feet by 6 feet. The border is 1 foot wide. This means that the portion of the rug that excludes the border is 7 feet by 4 feet. Its area is therefore 7 × 4.

Answer is A

27.

$$\frac{d-3n}{7n-d} = 1 \text{ means that}$$

$$d - 3n = 7n - d.$$

$$d - 3n = 7n - d$$

$$\text{means that } d = 10n - d$$

$$\text{or } 2d = 10n$$

$$\text{or } d = 5n.$$

Answer is D

28. There are 80 positive whole numbers that are less than 81. They include the squares of only the whole numbers 1 through 8 ($81 = 9^2$, and we're concerned with numbers less than 81). That is, there are 8 positive whole numbers less than 81 that are squares of whole numbers, and $80 - 8 = 72$ that are NOT squares of whole numbers.

Answer is D

29. If $2 - 5x \le \dfrac{6x-5}{-3}$, you should notice that $(-3)(2 - 5x) \ge 6x - 5$ because multipying an inequality by a negative number reverses the direction of the inequality.

Therefore, $-6 + 15x \ge 6x - 5,$
or $15x \ge 6x + 1$
or $9x \ge 1.$

That is, $x \ge \dfrac{1}{9}.$

Answer is C

30. The area of a circular region is usually given as $A = \pi r^2$, where r is the length of the radius.
Since

$$r = \frac{d}{2},$$

the formula, in terms of d,

is $A = \pi\left(\dfrac{d}{2}\right)^2 = \pi\dfrac{d^2}{4} = \dfrac{\pi d^2}{4}.$

Answer is E

I

NOTE: To ensure prompt processing of test results, it is important that you fill in the blanks exactly as directed.

GENERAL TEST

A. Print and sign your full name in this box:

PRINT: ______________________________
(LAST) (FIRST) (MIDDLE)

SIGN: ______________________________

Copy this code in box 6 on your answer sheet. Then fill in the corresponding ovals exactly as shown.

6. TITLE CODE

0	0	0	0	0
1	1	1	1	1
2	2	2	2	2
3	3	3	3	3
4	4	4	4	4
5	5	5	5	5
6	6	6	6	6
7	7	7	7	7
8	8	8	8	8
9	9	9	9	9

Copy the Test Name and Form Code in box 7 on your answer sheet.

TEST NAME General

FORM CODE GR86-2

GRADUATE RECORD EXAMINATIONS GENERAL TEST

B. You will have 3 hours and 30 minutes in which to work on this test, which consists of seven sections. During the time allowed for one section, you may work only on that section. The time allowed for each section is 30 minutes.

Each of your scores will be determined by the number of questions for which you select the best answer from the choices given. Questions for which you mark no answer or more than one answer are not counted in scoring. Nothing is subtracted from a score if you answer a question incorrectly. Therefore, to maximize your scores it is better for you to guess at an answer than not to respond at all.

You are advised to work as rapidly as you can without losing accuracy. Do not spend too much time on questions that are too difficult for you. Go on to the other questions and come back to the difficult ones later.

There are several different types of questions; you will find special directions for each type in the test itself. Be sure you understand the directions before attempting to answer any questions.

YOU MUST INDICATE ALL YOUR ANSWERS ON THE SEPARATE ANSWER SHEET. No credit will be given for anything written in this examination book, but you may write in the book as much as you wish to work out your answers. After you have decided on your response to a question, fill in the corresponding oval on the answer sheet. BE SURE THAT EACH MARK IS DARK AND COMPLETELY FILLS THE OVAL. Mark only one answer to each question. No credit will be given for multiple answers. Erase all stray marks. If you change an answer, be sure that all previous marks are erased completely. Incomplete erasures may be read as intended answers. Do not be concerned if your answer sheet provides spaces for more answers than there are questions in each section.

Example:

What city is the capital of France?

(A) Rome
(B) Paris
(C) London
(D) Cairo
(E) Oslo

Sample Answer

A ● C D E — BEST ANSWER PROPERLY MARKED

A B C D E
A B C D E
A B C D E
A B C D E
— IMPROPER MARKS

Some or all of the passages for this test have been adapted from published material to provide the examinee with significant problems for analysis and evaluation. To make the passages suitable for testing purposes, the style, content, or point of view of the original may have been altered in some cases. The ideas contained in the passages do not necessarily represent the opinions of the Graduate Record Examinations Board or Educational Testing Service.

DO NOT OPEN YOUR TEST BOOK UNTIL YOU ARE TOLD TO DO SO.

GENERAL TEST GR86-2

Answer Key and Percentages* of Examinees Answering Each Question Correctly

VERBAL ABILITY					
Section I			Section IV		
Number	Answer	P+	Number	Answer	P+
1	C	87	1	E	88
2	E	86	2	D	80
3	A	66	3	B	79
4	E	61	4	A	69
5	B	52	5	B	69
6	D	44	6	C	51
7	D	18	7	B	41
8	B	91	8	D	94
9	E	76	9	D	87
10	D	50	10	A	81
11	C	51	11	D	70
12	A	38	12	E	59
13	E	41	13	A	42
14	C	38	14	B	37
15	A	27	15	B	22
16	C	14	16	B	30
17	B	83	17	E	66
18	C	79	18	A	50
19	A	54	19	D	54
20	D	55	20	B	71
21	E	78	21	C	40
22	C	60	22	E	38
23	A	75	23	B	42
24	E	52	24	D	70
25	D	76	25	C	84
26	E	29	26	A	51
27	E	60	27	D	19
28	E	86	28	D	86
29	A	78	29	E	84
30	B	81	30	A	80
31	C	77	31	D	71
32	D	66	32	C	67
33	C	51	33	E	44
34	B	55	34	A	39
35	A	42	35	C	38
36	D	34	36	D	29
37	C	26	37	D	28
38	A	24	38	B	20

QUANTITATIVE ABILITY					
Section III			Section VI		
Number	Answer	P+	Number	Answer	P+
1	A	87	1	A	91
2	A	87	2	B	94
3	D	82	3	C	93
4	B	83	4	B	87
5	B	84	5	D	86
6	C	82	6	A	85
7	A	72	7	C	75
8	C	74	8	B	70
9	B	59	9	A	77
10	C	44	10	B	51
11	D	59	11	D	53
12	C	64	12	C	59
13	A	47	13	A	61
14	D	42	14	C	55
15	B	27	15	D	41
16	E	89	16	C	87
17	C	84	17	D	81
18	B	87	18	E	86
19	B	79	19	B	86
20	A	42	20	A	71
21	E	93	21	B	85
22	D	62	22	C	56
23	A	60	23	E	59
24	D	58	24	A	21
25	B	46	25	C	26
26	D	50	26	A	62
27	C	40	27	D	45
28	B	39	28	D	32
29	E	33	29	C	32
30	A	27	30	E	34

ANALYTICAL ABILITY					
Section II			Section V		
Number	Answer	P+	Number	Answer	P+
1	C	81	1	D	85
2	B	93	2	C	79
3	C	89	3	E	84
4	A	96	4	A	60
5	D	89	5	B	43
6	A	82	6	C	51
7	E	48	7	B	77
8	B	76	8	B	67
9	C	71	9	A	63
10	A	58	10	C	72
11	E	89	11	D	45
12	D	39	12	B	45
13	C	65	13	E	35
14	A	58	14	A	63
15	B	71	15	C	53
16	D	60	16	E	45
17	D	72	17	D	48
18	B	56	18	D	43
19	A	52	19	C	76
20	E	24	20	B	52
21	A	32	21	C	42
22	D	27	22	D	24
23	C	67	23	B	50
24	D	39	24	E	47
25	E	21	25	A	22

*Estimated P+ for the group of examinees who took the GRE General Test in a recent three-year period.

SCORE CONVERSIONS AND PERCENTS BELOW* for GRE GENERAL TEST, GR86-2

Raw Score	Scaled Scores and Percents Below					
	Verbal	%	Quantitative	%	Analytical	%
74-76	800	99				
73	790	99				
72	780	99				
71	770	99				
70	750	98				
69	740	98				
68	730	97				
67	720	96				
66	700	95				
65	690	94				
64	680	93				
63	670	92				
62	660	91				
61	650	89				
60	640	88	800	99		
59	620	85	800	99		
58	610	83	790	99		
57	600	81	780	98		
56	590	80	770	97		
55	580	78	750	94		
54	570	76	740	92		
53	560	73	730	91		
52	550	71	710	87		
51	540	68	700	85		
50	530	65	690	83	800	99
49	520	63	680	81	800	99
48	510	60	660	77	790	99
47	500	57	650	74	780	98
46	490	55	640	73	760	97
45	480	52	620	67	750	97
44	470	49	610	65	730	95
43	460	46	600	64	720	94
42	450	43	590	61	700	92
41	450	43	570	55	690	91
40	440	40	560	53	670	88
39	430	37	550	51	660	86
38	420	35	530	45	640	83
37	410	32	520	43	630	81
36	400	29	510	41	610	78

Raw Score	Scaled Scores and Percents Below					
	Verbal	%	Quantitative	%	Analytical	%
35	400	29	500	38	600	76
34	390	27	480	32	580	70
33	380	25	470	31	570	68
32	370	22	460	28	550	62
31	360	20	440	24	540	60
30	360	20	430	22	520	54
29	350	18	420	20	510	51
28	340	16	400	17	490	46
27	330	14	390	15	480	43
26	320	12	380	13	460	37
25	310	11	370	12	450	34
24	300	10	350	9	430	29
23	290	8	340	8	420	26
22	280	7	330	7	400	21
21	280	7	310	5	390	19
20	270	5	300	5	370	15
19	260	4	290	4	360	13
18	250	4	280	3	340	9
17	240	3	260	2	330	8
16	230	2	250	2	310	6
15	220	1	240	1	300	4
14	210	1	220	1	280	3
13	200	0	210	1	270	2
12	200		200	0	250	1
11	200		200		240	1
10	200		200		220	0
9	200		200		210	0
0-8	200		200		200	0

*Percent scoring below the given scaled score, based on the performance of the 785,276 examinees who took the General Test between October 1, 1981, and September 30, 1984.

GR 91-17

01

GRE®

THE GRADUATE RECORD EXAMINATIONS®

General Test

Do not break the seal

until you are told to do so.

The contents of this test are confidential. Disclosure or reproduction of any portion of it is prohibited.

THIS TEST BOOK MUST NOT BE TAKEN FROM THE ROOM.

SECTION 1

Time—30 minutes

25 Questions

Directions: Each question or group of questions is based on a passage or set of conditions. In answering some of the questions, it may be useful to draw a rough diagram. For each question, select the best answer choice given.

Questions 1-3

Samples of a yellow feed grain must be tested for contamination by one or more of the toxins R, S, and T. A sample retains the color it acquires from a test unless another test changes the color of the sample.

Test X turns a sample green if the sample contains R or S, or both, and orange if it contains neither R nor S.

Test Z turns a sample purple if the sample contains T; if not, the sample retains the color it had prior to test Z.

1. A sample that contains R and S but not T will yield which of the following sequences of colors, the first after test X is used and the second after test Z is used?

(A) Green, green
(B) Green, purple
(C) Orange, yellow
(D) Orange, orange
(E) Orange, purple

2. A sample that remains yellow when subjected to test Z and turns green when subjected to test X could be a sample containing

(A) R, S, and T
(B) S and T, but not containing R
(C) T, but containing neither R nor S
(D) S, but containing neither R nor T
(E) neither R nor S nor T

3. The two tests will NOT distinguish between two samples containing which of the following?

	Sample 1	Sample 2
(A)	R, S, and T	R and S, but not T
(B)	R and S, but not T	S and T, but not R
(C)	R and T, but not S	S and T, but not R
(D)	R, but neither S nor T	Neither R nor S nor T
(E)	S, but neither R nor T	Neither R nor S nor T

GO ON TO THE NEXT PAGE.

4. The burden of taxation on the back of a people is not unlike the burden of a weight on the back of a horse. Just as a small burden badly placed may distress a horse that could carry with ease a much larger burden properly adjusted, so a people may be impoverished and their power of producing wealth destroyed by taxation that, if levied another way, could be borne with ease.

   The author's point is made by

   (A) pointing out an ambiguity
   (B) using an analogy
   (C) refuting a supposed counterexample
   (D) appealing to an authority
   (E) generalizing from a particular case

5. Artificial seaweed made of plastic has been placed on a section of coast in order to reverse beach erosion. The inventor of the seaweed has concluded that the recent buildup of sand on that section of coast proves that the artificial seaweed reverses beach erosion.

   Which of the following, if true, would most seriously weaken the inventor's conclusion?

   (A) The amount of recent sand buildup on that section of coast was less than had been predicted on the basis of the results obtained in controlled experiments.
   (B) Because artificial seaweed would be buried eventually by additional sand deposits on the coast, more artificial seaweed would need to be put in place every four years.
   (C) Artificial seaweed of another material which had been previously developed by the inventor failed to add sand to coastline in past trials.
   (D) The amount of recent sand buildup on that section of coast is the same as the amount of recent sand buildup on otherwise very similar sections of coast without artificial seaweed.
   (E) The amount of recent sand buildup on that section of coast, although considerable, is not yet enough to replace the amount lost during storms on that section of coast in the last twenty years.

6. Metropolis' regulation limiting to four days the period during which milk can be sold to consumers after pasteurization is unreasonable. Under optimal conditions, pasteurized milk kept at 40 degrees Fahrenheit remains unspoiled for at least 14 days. If Metropolis' current limitation were changed to eight days, milk prices would drop, but product quality would be unaffected.

   Which of the following, if true, would most seriously weaken the conclusion drawn above?

   (A) Most consumers keep milk no more than three days after purchase.
   (B) A recent survey showed that 20 percent of Metropolis consumers favored extending the current limitation on the sale of milk to 8 days.
   (C) Metropolis' grocery-store owners would prefer small, frequent deliveries of milk to larger, infrequent deliveries.
   (D) Milk kept longer than 14 days after pasteurization generally presents no medical dangers if consumed.
   (E) In Metropolis, conditions for handling and storing milk after pasteurization are seldom close to optimum.

GO ON TO THE NEXT PAGE.

Questions 7-10

A commercial grower raises flowers in each of three different growing seasons every year—spring, summer, and fall-winter, with the year beginning in spring. Exactly seven different kinds of flowers—Q, R, S, T, W, X, and Z—are grown every year. Each kind of flower is grown at least once a year. The flowers are grown according to the following rules:

No more than three different kinds of flowers are grown in any one growing season.
No kind of flower can be grown for two growing seasons in a row.
Q can be grown neither in the fall-winter season nor in the same growing season as W or X.
S and T are always grown in the same growing season as each other.
R can be grown in a growing season only if Q was grown in the preceding growing season.

7. Which of the following is an acceptable schedule for the three growing seasons?

	Spring	Summer	Fall-Winter
(A)	Q	S, T, R	Q, X, Z
(B)	S, X	Q, T, Z	R, W
(C)	W, X	Q	Z, S, T, R
(D)	Q, S, T	R, W, X	Z
(E)	S, T, W	Q, Z	Q, X, R

8. If Z and R alone are grown in the fall-winter season, which of the following must be grown in the preceding spring?

(A) Q
(B) R
(C) S
(D) T
(E) W

9. If Z is grown in the spring and W in the summer of one year, which of the following can also be grown in the summer?

(A) Q
(B) S
(C) T
(D) X
(E) Z

10. If there is exactly one of the kinds of flowers that is grown one year during both of two growing seasons, that kind could be

(A) Q
(B) R
(C) S
(D) T
(E) W

GO ON TO THE NEXT PAGE.

Questions 11-13

An operating-room schedule is being set up for Monday and Tuesday of a certain week. On each of the days, either one long and two short operations or else four short operations must be scheduled. For each operation, a surgeon— Chakravarty, Silvers, or Tyson—will be scheduled. Patients to be scheduled will be selected from among patients 1, 2, 3, 4, 5, 6, 7, 8, and 9. The following conditions will be met:

A surgeon cannot be scheduled to perform two consecutive operations on one day.
If a surgeon is scheduled for a long operation, he or she cannot be scheduled for any other operation on the same day.
If a long operation is performed, it must be the first operation scheduled for the day it is performed.
The operations for patients 1 and 3 will be long, and the operations for the other patients will be short.
Patient 1 must be operated on by Dr. Tyson, patients 2 and 4 by Dr. Silvers, and patients 7 and 8 by Dr. Chakravarty.

11. Which of the following could be the schedule of patients from the first to the last patient to be operated on during the two days?

	Monday	Tuesday
(A)	9, 8, 7, 6	1, 2, 5
(B)	1, 9, 5	7, 6
(C)	5, 3, 7	2, 4, 6, 9
(D)	3, 2, 8	4, 6, 9, 7
(E)	1, 8, 7	3, 6, 4

12. If patient 1 is scheduled for the first operation on Monday, the surgeons' schedule for the other operations on Monday, in order of time, could be

(A) Chakravarty, Silvers
(B) Chakravarty, Tyson
(C) Silvers, Tyson
(D) Tyson, Chakravarty
(E) Tyson, Silvers

13. If patients 1 and 2 are among those whose operations are scheduled for Monday, which of the following patients is among those whose operations must be scheduled for Tuesday or not scheduled at all for the two days?

(A) 4
(B) 5
(C) 6
(D) 8
(E) 9

GO ON TO THE NEXT PAGE.

Questions 14-16

Six paintings—F, G, H, J, K, and L—are to be sold at a three-day auction. The paintings are to be divided into three groups—group 1, group 2, and group 3—and each group is to be sold on one of the days of the auction. The paintings to be included in each group are to be selected according to the following conditions:

Group 2 must contain at least as many paintings as group 1, and group 3 must contain at least as many paintings as group 2.
H and K, paintings by the same artist, must be in the same group as each other.
F and L, paintings of similar subjects, must be in different groups from each other.
G and H, estimated to be the two most valuable paintings, must be in different groups from each other.
If J is in group 3, K must also be in group 3 because of a request from the auctioneer for the third day.

14. If H is in group 1, which of the following must be true?

(A) F is in group 2.
(B) G is in group 2.
(C) J is in group 2.
(D) L is in group 2.
(E) L is in group 3.

15. If J is in group 3, which of the following could be in group 2 ?

(A) F and G
(B) F and L
(C) G and H
(D) H and K
(E) H and L

16. If G is in group 3, which of the following could be true?

(A) F is the only painting in group 1.
(B) J is the only painting in group 1.
(C) J is in group 3.
(D) H and J are in group 2.
(E) J and L are in group 2.

GO ON TO THE NEXT PAGE.

Questions 17-22

Exactly nine books must be arranged from first (leftmost) to ninth (rightmost) on a shelf.

Of the nine books, four are leather-bound books, three are clothbound books, and the remaining two are paperback books.

The four leather-bound books must be next to each other, and the two paperback books must be next to each other.

The three clothbound books do not have to be placed next to each other.

17. If the sixth book is a leather-bound book and the eighth book is a clothbound book, which of the following must be a paperback book?
    (A) The first
    (B) The second
    (C) The third
    (D) The fourth
    (E) The ninth

18. The clothbound books must be next to each other if a paperback book is in which of the following positions?
    (A) The first
    (B) The third
    (C) The fifth
    (D) The seventh
    (E) The ninth

19. If the second book is a clothbound book and the third book is a paperback book, which of the following can be a clothbound book?
    (A) The fourth
    (B) The sixth
    (C) The seventh
    (D) The eighth
    (E) The ninth

20. If no clothbound book is next to another clothbound book, any of the following could be paperback books EXCEPT the
    (A) second
    (B) third
    (C) fifth
    (D) seventh
    (E) eighth

21. If the first and seventh books have the same kind of binding, which of the following must be a leather-bound book?
    (A) The first
    (B) The second
    (C) The fourth
    (D) The sixth
    (E) The eighth

22. If a clothbound book is in the fifth position and a leather-bound book is in the ninth position, which of the following pairs of books must have different kinds of binding?
    (A) The first and the second
    (B) The second and the third
    (C) The second and the fourth
    (D) The third and the fourth
    (E) The third and the fifth

GO ON TO THE NEXT PAGE.

23. Company X recently bought Company Y. Since the two companies had previously been the only companies manufacturing cardboard containers, Company X now has a monopoly in this particular branch of industry and therefore will probably raise the price of its cardboard containers.

Which of the following statements, if true, would most seriously weaken the claim made above?

(A) An increase in the price of cardboard containers would not necessarily increase the retail price of items packed in these containers.
(B) The cost of lumber is a major determinant of the cost of cardboard containers.
(C) There has been a recent increase in demand for cardboard containers.
(D) Manufacturers of cardboard containers face increasingly stiff competition from manufacturers of plastic containers.
(E) Before Company X bought Company Y, Company X had consistently set the prices of its cardboard containers below the prices set by Company Y.

24. Chlorofluorocarbons (CFC's) pose known dangers to public health. Only when the United States government imposes a specific ban on the industrial use of CFC's will industry scientists make the alternatives to CFC's cost-effective, and thus reduce public health hazards.

Which of the following is an assumption on which the assertion made above is based?

(A) The alternatives to CFC's currently available are not widely used because they are not familiar to a sufficient number of industry scientists.
(B) The alternatives to CFC's are less hazardous to public health than are CFC's.
(C) Private industry has a responsibility to take voluntary measures to safeguard public health and absorb the costs of such measures.
(D) The use of CFC's can result in employee time lost because of illness.
(E) CFC's are currently the most serious public health hazard engendered by industry in the United States.

25. Lobsters usually develop one smaller, cutter claw and one larger, crusher claw. To show that exercise determines which claw becomes the crusher, researchers placed young lobsters in tanks and repeatedly prompted them to grab a probe with one claw—in each case always the same, randomly selected claw. In most of the lobsters the grabbing claw became the crusher. But in a second, similar experiment, when lobsters were prompted to use both claws equally for grabbing, most matured with two cutter claws, even though each claw was exercised as much as the grabbing claws had been in the first experiment.

Which of the following is best supported by the information above?

(A) Young lobsters usually exercise one claw more than the other.
(B) Most lobsters raised in captivity will not develop a crusher claw.
(C) Exercise is not a determining factor in the development of crusher claws in lobsters.
(D) Cutter claws are more effective for grabbing than are crusher claws.
(E) Young lobsters that do not exercise either claw will nevertheless usually develop one crusher and one cutter claw.

STOP

IF YOU FINISH BEFORE TIME IS CALLED, YOU MAY CHECK YOUR WORK ON THIS SECTION ONLY. DO NOT TURN TO ANY OTHER SECTION IN THE TEST.

Section 2 starts on page 274.

SECTION 2

Time—30 minutes

30 Questions

Numbers: All numbers used are real numbers.

Figures: Position of points, angles, regions, etc. can be assumed to be in the order shown; and angle measures can be assumed to be positive.

Lines shown as straight can be assumed to be straight.

Figures can be assumed to lie in a plane unless otherwise indicated.

Figures that accompany questions are intended to provide information useful in answering the questions. However, unless a note states that a figure is drawn to scale, you should solve these problems NOT by estimating sizes by sight or by measurement, but by using your knowledge of mathematics (see Example 2 below).

Directions: Each of the Questions 1-15 consists of two quantities, one in Column A and one in Column B. You are to compare the two quantities and choose

A if the quantity in Column A is greater;
B if the quantity in Column B is greater;
C if the two quantities are equal;
D if the relationship cannot be determined from the information given.

Note: Since there are only four choices, NEVER MARK (E).

Common Information: In a question, information concerning one or both of the quantities to be compared is centered above the two columns. A symbol that appears in both columns represents the same thing in Column A as it does in Column B.

	Column A	Column B	Sample Answers
Example 1:	2×6	$2 + 6$	● Ⓑ Ⓒ Ⓓ Ⓔ

Examples 2-4 refer to $\triangle PQR$.

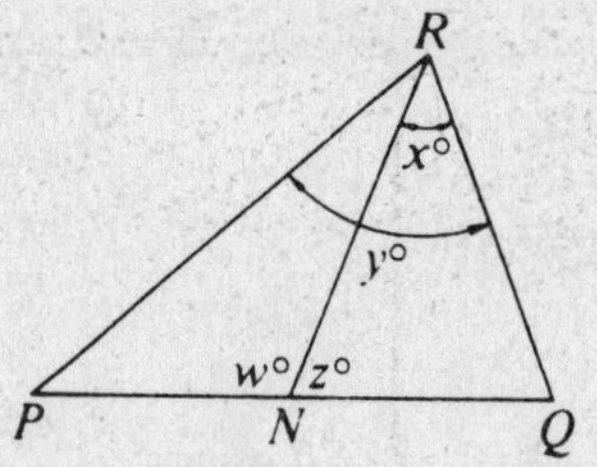

R, $x°$, $y°$, $w°$, $z°$, P, N, Q

	Column A	Column B	Sample Answers
Example 2:	PN	NQ	Ⓐ Ⓑ Ⓒ ● Ⓔ (since equal measures cannot be assumed, even though PN and NQ appear equal)
Example 3:	x	y	Ⓐ ● Ⓒ Ⓓ Ⓔ (since N is between P and Q)
Example 4:	$w + z$	180	Ⓐ Ⓑ ● Ⓓ Ⓔ (since PQ is a straight line)

GO ON TO THE NEXT PAGE.

A if the quantity in Column A is greater;
B if the quantity in Column B is greater;
C if the two quantities are equal;
D if the relationship cannot be determined from the information given.

	Column A	Column B
	m is equal to 8 or -2.	
1.	$(m - 3)^2$	25

	Column A	Column B
	x and y are each greater than 1.	
2.	$2xy$	$(2x)(2y)$

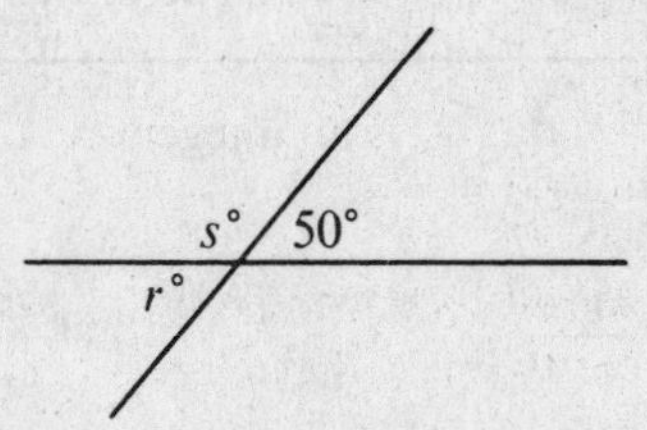

	Column A	Column B
3.	$3r$	s
4.	$(-2)^8$	$-(2^8)$

A decrease in the number of sales personnel in Company K to 85 percent of the original sales force resulted in a decrease of 500 in the number of monthly sales.

	Column A	Column B
5.	The percent decrease in the number of Company K's monthly sales	The percent decrease in the number of Company K's sales personnel

	Column A	Column B
6.	$1 - \frac{1}{7}$	$1 - \frac{1}{8}$

Jim is 3 years older than Jonathon.
Myra is 5 years older than Melissa.
Jonathon is 2 years older than Melissa.

	Column A	Column B
7.	Jim's age	Myra's age

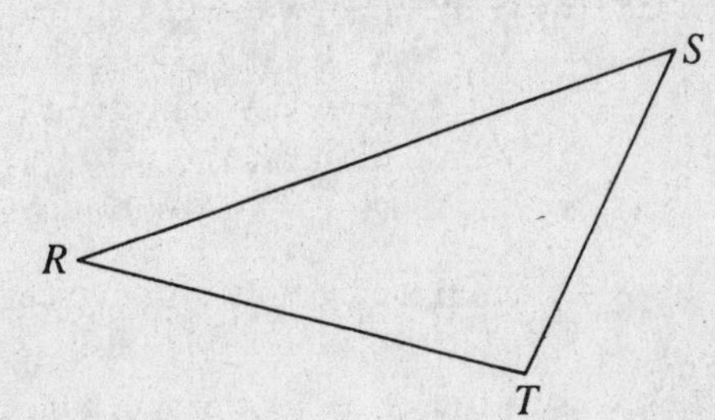

	Column A	Column B
8.	$ST + TR$	RS

$750 < n < 1{,}500$

	Column A	Column B
9.	$1{,}500 - n$	$n - 750$

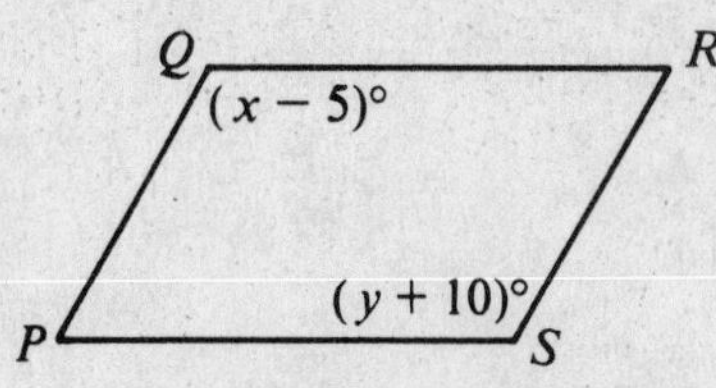

$PQRS$ is a parallelogram.

	Column A	Column B
10.	x	y

GO ON TO THE NEXT PAGE.

A if the quantity in Column A is greater;
B if the quantity in Column B is greater;
C if the two quantities are equal;
D if the relationship cannot be determined from the information given.

	Column A	Column B
	$\frac{x + 2y + z}{2} = y$	
11.	x	$-z$
	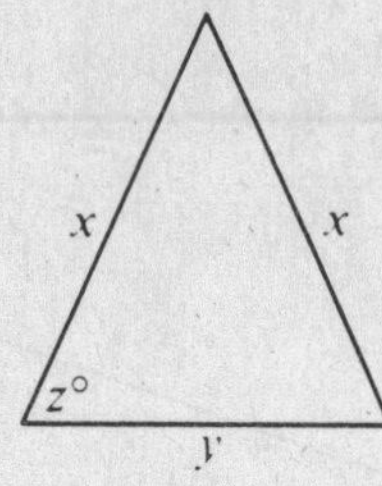 $x > y$	
12.	z	60
13.	$(x + 3)(x + 3)$	$x^2 + 9$

	Column A	Column B
	Three tennis balls of identical size are stacked one on top of the other so that they fit exactly inside a closed right cylindrical can, as shown.	
14.	The height of the stack of 3 balls	The circumference of one of the balls
	t is an integer.	
15.	$\frac{1}{1 + 2^t}$	$\frac{1}{1 + 3^t}$

GO ON TO THE NEXT PAGE.

Directions: Each of the Questions 16-30 has five answer choices. For each of these questions, select the best of the answer choices given.

16. If $\frac{1}{6}n = \frac{1}{5}$, then $n =$

(A) $\frac{1}{30}$

(B) $\frac{5}{6}$

(C) $\frac{6}{5}$

(D) 6

(E) 30

17. If membership in the Elks Club increases from 120 to 150, what is the percent increase?

(A) 15%
(B) 25%
(C) 30%
(D) 40%
(E) 80%

18. The value of $\left(1 - \frac{5}{7}\right)\left(1 + \frac{3}{4}\right)$ is

(A) $\frac{1}{28}$

(B) $\frac{3}{14}$

(C) $\frac{9}{28}$

(D) $\frac{13}{28}$

(E) $\frac{1}{2}$

19. If the circumference of a circle is less than 10π, which of the following could be the area of the circle?

(A) 20π
(B) 25π
(C) 36π
(D) 81π
(E) 100π

20. If a, b, and c are consecutive positive integers and $a < b < c$, which of the following must be an odd integer?

(A) abc

(B) $a + b + c$

(C) $a + bc$

(D) $a(b + c)$

(E) $(a + b)(b + c)$

GO ON TO THE NEXT PAGE.

Questions 21-25 refer to the following graphs.

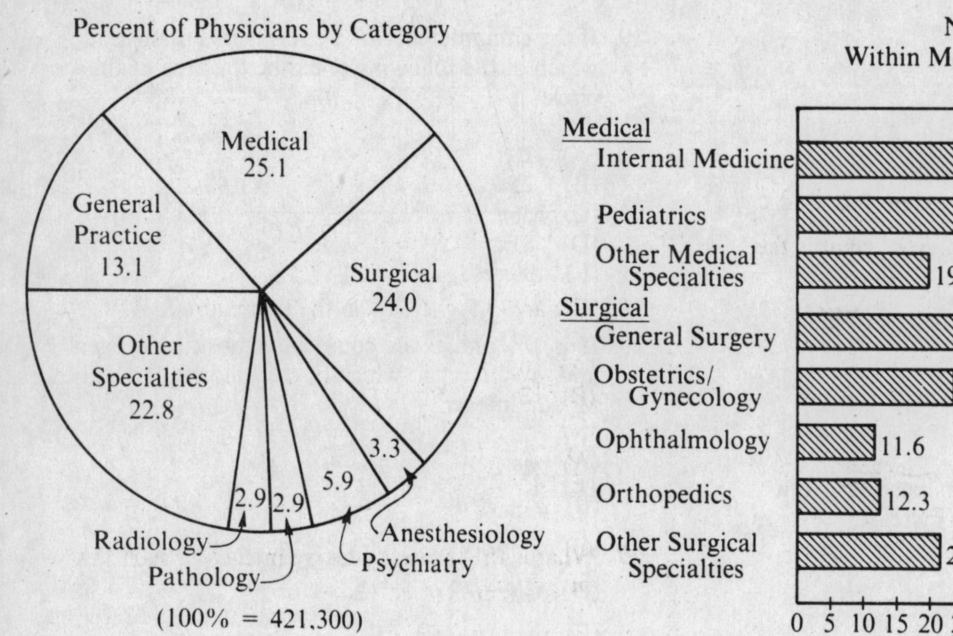

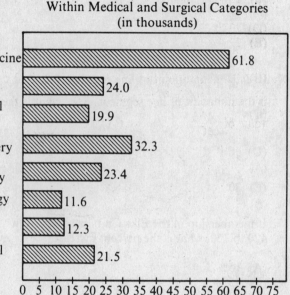

21. Approximately what was the ratio of physicians in the surgical category to physicians in pathology?

    (A) 10 to 1
    (B) 8 to 1
    (C) 7 to 1
    (D) 5 to 6
    (E) 4 to 5

22. Approximately how many more physicians were in psychiatry than in radiology?

    (A) 3,000
    (B) 6,300
    (C) 12,600
    (D) 24,800
    (E) 37,000

23. Approximately how many of the physicians in the medical category were not in pediatrics?

    (A) 61,800
    (B) 76,000
    (C) 81,700
    (D) 92,600
    (E) 101,100

24. If there was a total of 334,000 physicians in 1970, what was the approximate percent increase in the number of physicians from 1970 to 1977 ?

    (A) 10%
    (B) 12%
    (C) 16%
    (D) 20%
    (E) 26%

25. In 1977, if twice as many anesthesiologists as orthopedists were sued for malpractice and 10 percent of the orthopedists were sued, approximately what percent of the anesthesiologists were sued?

    (A) 5%
    (B) 9%
    (C) 18%
    (D) 22%
    (E) 25%

GO ON TO THE NEXT PAGE.

26. If x can have only the values -3, 0, and 2, and y can have only the values -4, 2, and 3, what is the greatest possible value for $2x + y^2$?

(A) 13
(B) 15
(C) 16
(D) 20
(E) 22

27. If B is the midpoint of line segment AD and C is the midpoint of line segment BD, what is the value of $\frac{AB}{AC}$?

(A) $\frac{3}{4}$

(B) $\frac{2}{3}$

(C) $\frac{1}{2}$

(D) $\frac{1}{3}$

(E) $\frac{1}{4}$

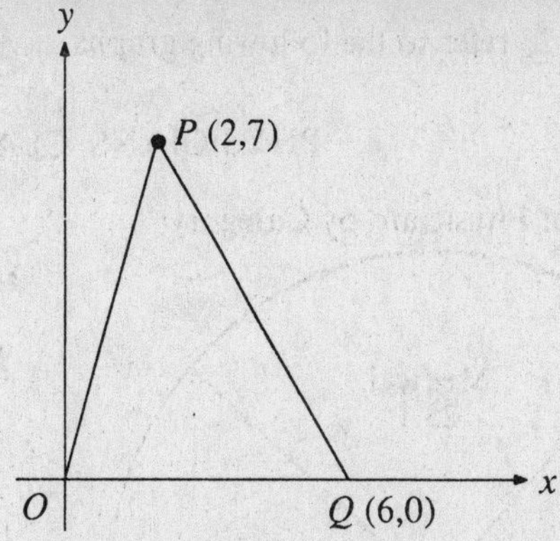

28. The area of $\triangle OPQ$ in the figure above is

(A) 6
(B) 12
(C) 14
(D) 21
(E) 42

29. What is the greatest positive integer n such that 2^n is a factor of 12^{10}?

(A) 10
(B) 12
(C) 16
(D) 20
(E) 60

30. For each of n people, Margie bought a hamburger and a soda at a restaurant. For each of n people, Paul bought 3 hamburgers and a soda at the same restaurant. If Margie spent a total of \$5.40 and Paul spent a total of \$12.60, how much did Paul spend just for hamburgers? (Assume that all hamburgers cost the same and all sodas cost the same.)

(A) \$10.80
(B) \$9.60
(C) \$7.20
(D) \$3.60
(E) \$2.40

STOP

IF YOU FINISH BEFORE TIME IS CALLED, YOU MAY CHECK YOUR WORK ON THIS SECTION ONLY. DO NOT TURN TO ANY OTHER SECTION IN THE TEST.

NO TEST MATERIAL ON THIS PAGE

SECTION 3

Time—30 minutes

38 Questions

Directions: Each sentence below has one or two blanks, each blank indicating that something has been omitted. Beneath the sentence are five lettered words or sets of words. Choose the word or set of words for each blank that best fits the meaning of the sentence as a whole.

1. Although economists have traditionally considered the district to be solely an agricultural one, the ------- of the inhabitants' occupations makes such a classification obsolete.

   (A) productivity (B) diversity (C) predictability (D) profitability (E) stability

2. The author of this book ------- overlooks or minimizes some of the problems and shortcomings in otherwise highly successful foreign industries in order to ------- the points on which they excel and on which we might try to emulate them.

   (A) accidentally. .exaggerate
   (B) purposely. .emphasize
   (C) occasionally. .counterbalance
   (D) intentionally. .confuse
   (E) cleverly. .compound

3. Crosby's colleagues have never learned, at least not in time to avoid embarrassing themselves, that her occasional ------- air of befuddlement ------- a display of her formidable intelligence.

   (A) genuine. .dominates (B) alert. .contradicts (C) acute. .precludes (D) bogus. .presages (E) painstaking. .succeeds

4. To ensure the development and exploitation of a new technology, there must be a constant ------- of several nevertheless distinct activities.

   (A) interplay (B) implementation (C) comprehending (D) improvement (E) exploration

5. Some customs travel well; often, however, behavior that is considered the epitome of ------- at home is perceived as impossibly rude or, at the least, harmlessly bizarre abroad.

   (A) novelty (B) eccentricity (C) urbanity (D) coarseness (E) tolerance

6. The ------- of the early Greek philosophers' attempts to explain the operations of the cosmos led certain later thinkers to inquire into the ------- of human reason.

   (A) difficulty. .origin
   (B) meaning. .supremacy
   (C) complexity. .reality
   (D) equivocations. .subtlety
   (E) failures. .efficacy

7. Ever prey to vagrant impulses that impelled him to ------- his talents on a host of unworthy projects, his very -------- nonetheless enhanced his reputation, for the sheer energy of his extravagance dazzled observers.

   (A) undermine. .enthusiasm
   (B) isolate. .selectiveness
   (C) display. .affability
   (D) squander. .dissipation
   (E) implicate. .genius

GO ON TO THE NEXT PAGE.

Directions: In each of the following questions, a related pair of words or phrases is followed by five lettered pairs of words or phrases. Select the lettered pair that best expresses a relationship similar to that expressed in the original pair.

8. MULTIPLY : DIVIDE ::
(A) enumerate : count
(B) speak : communicate
(C) enter : leave
(D) drive : ride
(E) compute : estimate

9. RECLUSE : WITHDRAWN ::
(A) isolationist : unreserved
(B) pacifist : aggressive
(C) miser : liberal
(D) bigot : biased
(E) procrastinator : unmanageable

10. CURATOR : ART ::
(A) functionary : administration
(B) archivist : documents
(C) referee : laws
(D) physician : research
(E) raconteur : stories

11. ABACUS : CALCULATE ::
(A) organ : worship
(B) patent : invent
(C) calipers : regulate
(D) manuscript : edit
(E) sextant : navigate

12. STRAY : GROUP ::
(A) miscalculate : solution
(B) improvise : suggestion
(C) slur : pronunciation
(D) delete : change
(E) digress : subject

13. ESCAPE : CAPTURE ::
(A) warn : danger
(B) immerse : dampness
(C) feint : thrust
(D) dodge : blow
(E) invest : bankruptcy

14. LEVEE : RIVER ::
(A) seam : fabric
(B) corona : sun
(C) cordon : crowd
(D) petal : flower
(E) moat : castle

15. MERCURIAL : MOOD ::
(A) energetic : delirium
(B) jovial : conviviality
(C) fickle : affection
(D) martial : anarchy
(E) paranoid : suspicion

16. ENUNCIATE : WORDS ::
(A) limn : lines
(B) parse : sentences
(C) hear : sounds
(D) run : steps
(E) stint : savings

GO ON TO THE NEXT PAGE.

Directions: Each passage in this group is followed by questions based on its content. After reading a passage, choose the best answer to each question. Answer all questions following a passage on the basis of what is stated or implied in that passage.

A serious critic has to comprehend the particular content, unique structure, and special meaning of a work of art. And here she faces a dilemma. The critic must recognize the artistic element of uniqueness that requires subjective reaction; yet she must not be unduly prejudiced by such reactions. Her likes and dislikes are less important than what the work itself communicates, and her preferences may blind her to certain qualities of the work and thereby prevent an adequate understanding of it. Hence, it is necessary that a critic develop a sensibility informed by familiarity with the history of art and aesthetic theory. On the other hand, it is insufficient to treat the artwork solely historically, in relation to a fixed set of ideas or values. The critic's knowledge and training are, rather, a preparation of the cognitive and emotional abilities needed for an adequate personal response to an artwork's own particular qualities.

17. According to the author, a serious art critic may avoid being prejudiced by her subjective reactions if she

(A) treats an artwork in relation to a fixed set of ideas and values
(B) brings to her observation a knowledge of art history and aesthetic theory
(C) allows more time for the observation of each artwork
(D) takes into account the preferences of other art critics
(E) limits herself to that art with which she has adequate familiarity

18. The author implies that it is insufficient to treat a work of art solely historically because

(A) doing so would lead the critic into a dilemma
(B) doing so can blind the critic to some of the artwork's unique qualities
(C) doing so can insulate the critic from personally held beliefs
(D) subjective reactions can produce a biased response
(E) critics are not sufficiently familiar with art history

19. The passage suggests that the author would be most likely to agree with which of the following statements?

(A) Art speaks to the passions as well as to the intellect.
(B) Most works of art express unconscious wishes or desires.
(C) The best art is accessible to the greatest number of people.
(D) The art produced in the last few decades is of inferior quality.
(E) The meaning of art is a function of the social conditions in which it was produced.

20. The author's argument is developed primarily by the use of

(A) an attack on sentimentality
(B) an example of successful art criticism
(C) a critique of artists' training
(D) a warning against extremes in art criticism
(E) an analogy between art criticism and art production

GO ON TO THE NEXT PAGE.

Viruses, infectious particles consisting of nucleic acid packaged in a protein coat (the capsid), are difficult to resist. Unable to reproduce outside a living cell, viruses reproduce only by subverting the genetic mechanisms of a host cell. In one kind of viral life cycle, the virus first binds to the cell's surface, then penetrates the cell and sheds its capsid. The exposed viral nucleic acid produces new viruses from the contents of the cell. Finally, the cell releases the viral progeny, and a new cell cycle of infection begins. The human body responds to a viral infection by producing antibodies: complex, highly specific proteins that selectively bind to foreign molecules such as viruses. An antibody can either interfere with a virus' ability to bind to a cell, or can prevent it from releasing its nucleic acid.

Unfortunately, the common cold, produced most often by rhinoviruses, is intractable to antiviral defense. Humans have difficulty resisting colds because rhinoviruses are so diverse, including at least 100 strains. The strains differ most in the molecular structure of the proteins in their capsids. Since disease-fighting antibodies bind to the capsid, an antibody developed to protect against one rhinovirus strain is useless against other strains. Different antibodies must be produced for each strain.

A defense against rhinoviruses might nonetheless succeed by exploiting hidden similarities among the rhinovirus strains. For example, most rhinovirus strains bind to the same kind of molecule (delta-receptors) on a cell's surface when they attack human cells. Colonno, taking advantage of these common receptors, devised a strategy for blocking the attachment of rhinoviruses to their appropriate receptors. Rather than fruitlessly searching for an antibody that would bind to all rhinoviruses, Colonno realized that an antibody binding to the common receptors of a human cell would prevent rhinoviruses from initiating an infection. Because human cells normally do not develop antibodies to components of their own cells, Colonno injected human cells into mice, which did produce an antibody to the common receptor. In isolated human cells, this antibody proved to be extraordinarily effective at thwarting the rhinovirus. Moreover, when the antibody was given to chimpanzees, it inhibited rhinoviral growth, and in humans it lessened both the severity and duration of cold symptoms.

Another possible defense against rhinoviruses was proposed by Rossman, who described rhinoviruses' detailed molecular structure. Rossman showed that protein sequences common to all rhinovirus strains lie at the base of a deep "canyon" scoring each face of the capsid. The narrow opening of this canyon possibly prevents the relatively large antibody molecules from binding to the common sequence, but smaller molecules might reach it. Among these smaller, nonantibody molecules, some might bind to the common sequence, lock the nucleic acid in its coat, and thereby prevent the virus from reproducing.

21. The primary purpose of the passage is to

(A) discuss viral mechanisms and possible ways of circumventing certain kinds of those mechanisms
(B) challenge recent research on how rhinoviruses bind to receptors on the surfaces of cells
(C) suggest future research on rhinoviral growth in chimpanzees
(D) defend a controversial research program whose purpose is to discover the molecular structure of rhinovirus capsids
(E) evaluate a dispute between advocates of two theories about the rhinovirus life cycle

22. It can be inferred from the passage that the protein sequences of the capsid that vary most among strains of rhinovirus are those

(A) at the base of the "canyon"
(B) outside of the "canyon"
(C) responsible for producing nucleic acid
(D) responsible for preventing the formation of delta-receptors
(E) preventing the capsid from releasing its nucleic acid

23. It can be inferred from the passage that a cell lacking delta-receptors will be

(A) unable to prevent the rhinoviral nucleic acid from shedding its capsid
(B) defenseless against most strains of rhinovirus
(C) unable to release the viral progeny it develops after infection
(D) protected from new infections by antibodies to the rhinovirus
(E) resistant to infection by most strains of rhinovirus

24. Which of the following research strategies for developing a defense against the common cold would the author be likely to find most promising?

(A) Continuing to look for a general antirhinoviral antibody
(B) Searching for common cell-surface receptors in humans and mice
(C) Continuing to look for similarities among the various strains of rhinovirus
(D) Discovering how the human body produces antibodies in response to a rhinoviral infection
(E) Determining the detailed molecular structure of the nucleic acid of a rhinovirus

GO ON TO THE NEXT PAGE.

25. It can be inferred from the passage that the purpose of Colonno's experiments was to determine whether

(A) chimpanzees and humans can both be infected by rhinoviruses
(B) chimpanzees can produce antibodies to human cell-surface receptors
(C) a rhinovirus' nucleic acid might be locked in its protein coat
(D) binding antibodies to common receptors could produce a possible defense against rhinoviruses
(E) rhinoviruses are vulnerable to human antibodies

26. According to the passage, Rossman's research suggests that

(A) a defense against rhinoviruses might exploit structural similarities among the strains of rhinovirus
(B) human cells normally do not develop antibodies to components of their own cells
(C) the various strains of rhinovirus differ in their ability to bind to the surface of a host cell
(D) rhinovirus versatility can work to the benefit of researchers trying to find a useful antibody
(E) Colonno's research findings are probably invalid

27. According to the passage, in order for a given antibody to bind to a given rhinoviral capsid, which of the following must be true?

(A) The capsid must have a deep "canyon" on each of its faces.
(B) The antibody must be specific to the molecular structure of the particular capsid.
(C) The capsid must separate from its nucleic acid before binding to an antibody.
(D) The antibody must bind to a particular cell-surface receptor before it can bind to a rhinovirus.
(E) The antibody must first enter a cell containing the particular rhinovirus.

GO ON TO THE NEXT PAGE.

Directions: Each question below consists of a word printed in capital letters, followed by five lettered words or phrases. Choose the lettered word or phrase that is most nearly opposite in meaning to the word in capital letters.

Since some of the questions require you to distinguish fine shades of meaning, be sure to consider all the choices before deciding which one is best.

28. DOMINANT: (A) defective (B) multiple (C) inferred (D) shifting (E) recessive

29. DISPUTE: (A) accept (B) simplify (C) frustrate (D) silence (E) understand

30. PERJURY:
(A) truthful deposition
(B) vivid recollection
(C) voluntary testimony
(D) inadvertent disclosure
(E) inexplicable fabrication

31. DORMANCY: (A) momentum (B) hysteria (C) availability (D) activity (E) cultivation

32. PLETHORA: (A) deterioration (B) embellishment (C) scarcity (D) vacillation (E) affirmation

33. STOCK: (A) unique (B) unfounded (C) desirable (D) unhealthy (E) trustworthy

34. BURGEON: (A) retreat (B) evolve (C) wither (D) sever (E) minimize

35. OCCULT: (A) foresee (B) bare (C) assert (D) transform (E) presume

36. NASCENT: (A) widely displaced (B) completely clear (C) totally natural (D) strongly contrary (E) fully established

37. AMPLIFY: (A) condemn (B) disburse (C) decipher (D) garble (E) abridge

38. EXTENUATING: (A) opposing (B) severe (C) intractable (D) aggravating (E) internal

STOP

IF YOU FINISH BEFORE TIME IS CALLED, YOU MAY CHECK YOUR WORK ON THIS SECTION ONLY. DO NOT TURN TO ANY OTHER SECTION IN THE TEST.

Section 5 starts on page 288.

SECTION 5

Time—30 minutes

30 Questions

Numbers: All numbers used are real numbers.

Figures: Position of points, angles, regions, etc. can be assumed to be in the order shown; and angle measures can be assumed to be positive.

Lines shown as straight can be assumed to be straight.

Figures can be assumed to lie in a plane unless otherwise indicated.

Figures that accompany questions are intended to provide information useful in answering the questions. However, unless a note states that a figure is drawn to scale, you should solve these problems NOT by estimating sizes by sight or by measurement, but by using your knowledge of mathematics (see Example 2 below).

Directions: Each of the Questions 1-15 consists of two quantities, one in Column A and one in Column B. You are to compare the two quantities and choose

A if the quantity in Column A is greater;
B if the quantity in Column B is greater;
C if the two quantities are equal;
D if the relationship cannot be determined from the information given.

Note: Since there are only four choices, NEVER MARK (E).

Common Information: In a question, information concerning one or both of the quantities to be compared is centered above the two columns. A symbol that appears in both columns represents the same thing in Column A as it does in Column B.

	Column A	Column B	Sample Answers
Example 1:	2×6	$2 + 6$	● Ⓑ Ⓒ Ⓓ Ⓔ

Examples 2-4 refer to $\triangle PQR$.

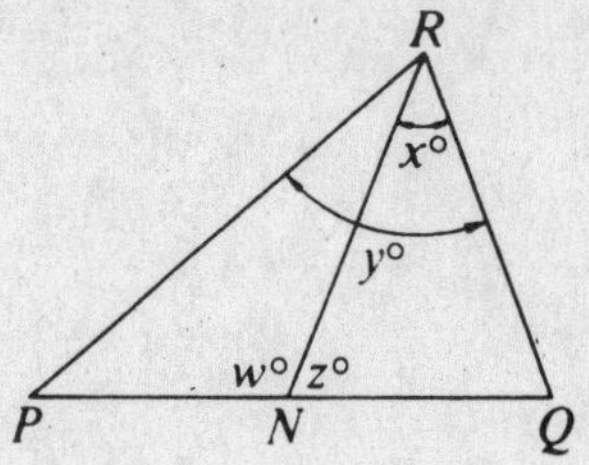

	Column A	Column B	Sample Answers
Example 2:	*PN*	*NQ*	Ⓐ Ⓑ Ⓒ ● Ⓔ (since equal measures cannot be assumed, even though *PN* and *NQ* appear equal)
Example 3:	x	y	Ⓐ ● Ⓒ Ⓓ Ⓔ (since *N* is between *P* and *Q*)
Example 4:	$w + z$	180	Ⓐ Ⓑ ● Ⓓ Ⓔ (since *PQ* is a straight line)

A if the quantity in Column A is greater;
B if the quantity in Column B is greater;
C if the two quantities are equal;
D if the relationship cannot be determined from the information given.

	Column A	Column B
1.	$\frac{4}{5} + \frac{2}{11}$	1
2.	$(1.9)^3$	$(1.999)^2$

The numbers that correspond to points X and Y on the number line are $-\frac{3}{4}$ and $\frac{5}{4}$, respectively.

	Column A	Column B
3.	The number that corresponds to the point halfway between X and Y	$\frac{1}{3}$

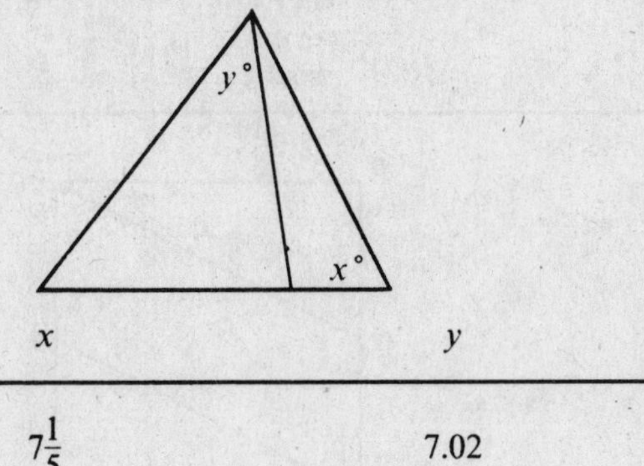

	Column A	Column B
4.	x	y
5.	$7\frac{1}{5}$	7.02

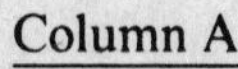

	Column A	Column B
6.	$\frac{y}{2}$	$\frac{x + y}{2}$

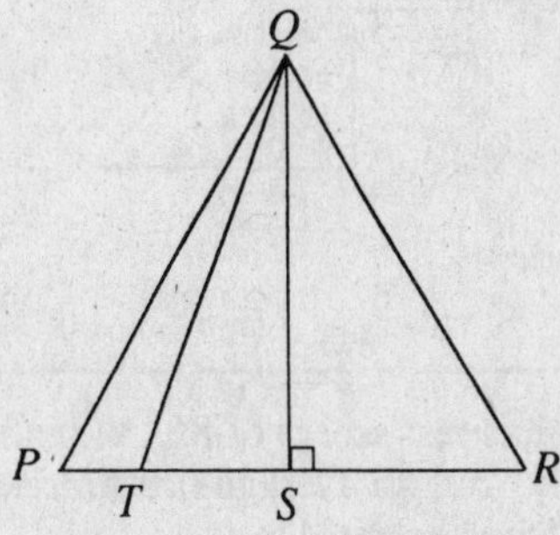

S is the midpoint of segment PR.

	Column A	Column B
7.	The length of segment QT	The length of segment QR

A merchant made a profit of $2.75 on the sale price of a sweater that cost the merchant $12.25.

	Column A	Column B
8.	The profit expressed as a percent of the cost to the merchant	The profit expressed as a percent of the sale price

GO ON TO THE NEXT PAGE.

A if the quantity in Column A is greater;
B if the quantity in Column B is greater;
C if the two quantities are equal;
D if the relationship cannot be determined from the information given.

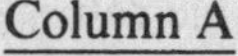

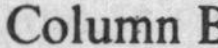

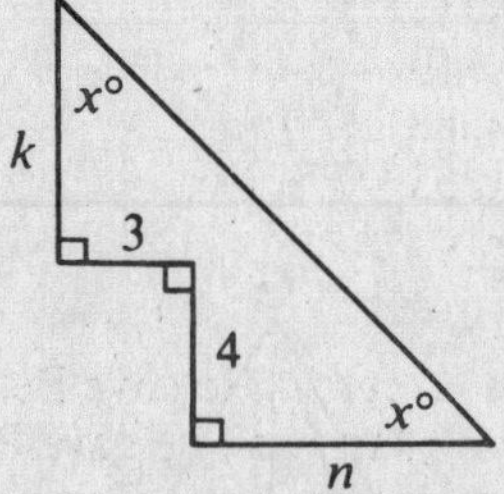

9. k | n

A student has test scores of 85, x, and y, respectively, and an average (arithmetic mean) score of 95 on the three tests.

10. The average (arithmetic mean) of x and y | 100

$$y^2 + 4y - 12 = 0$$

11. y^2 | 30

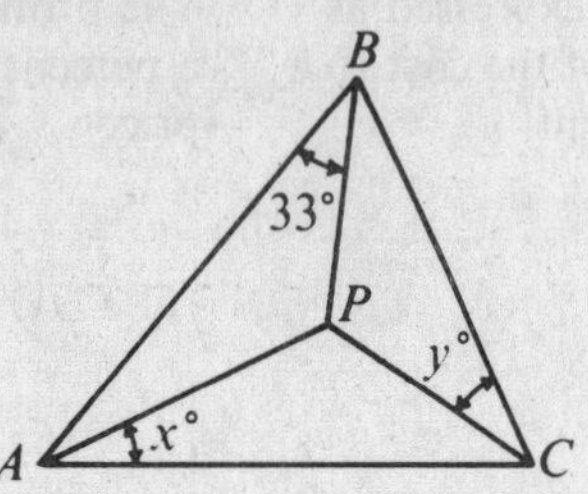

Segments PA, PB, and PC are the angle bisectors of $\triangle ABC$.

12. $x + y$ | 57

Column A | Column B

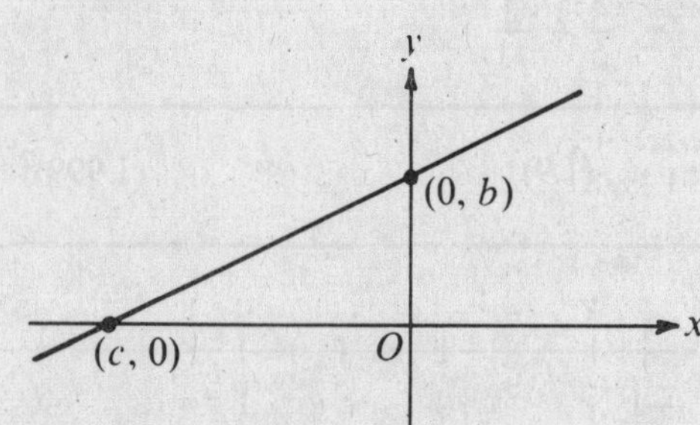

The line $y = ax + b$ is graphed on the rectangular coordinate axes.

13. a | $\frac{b}{-c}$

For all numbers n, $n^* = 32 - n$.

14. $(n^*)^*$ | n

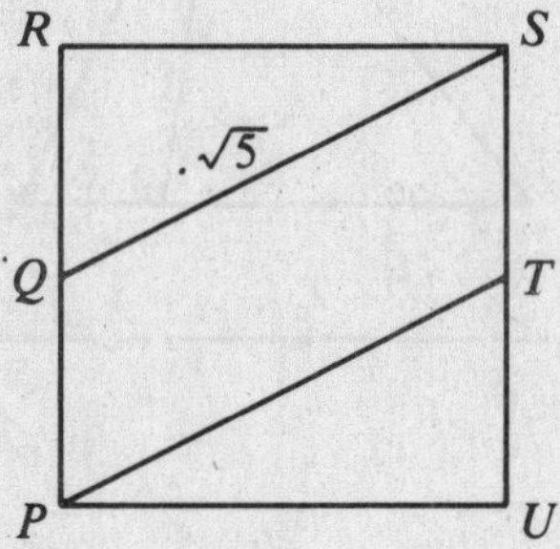

Q and T are the midpoints of opposite sides of square $PRSU$.

15. The area of region $PQST$ | $\frac{3}{2}$

GO ON TO THE NEXT PAGE.

Directions: Each of the Questions 16-30 has five answer choices. For each of these questions, select the best of the answer choices given.

16. If a certain company purchased its computer terminals for a total of \$540,400 and each of the terminals was purchased for \$350, how many terminals did the company purchase?

(A) 1,624
(B) 1,544
(C) 1,434
(D) 1,384
(E) 1,264

17. $\dfrac{\frac{2}{3} \times 9 \times \frac{2}{5} \times 15}{\frac{1}{3} \times 18 \times \frac{1}{5} \times 30} =$

(A) 2

(B) 1

(C) $\frac{1}{2}$

(D) $\frac{1}{3}$

(E) $\frac{1}{4}$

18. If $2x = -10$, then $4x^2 - 6x - 5 =$

(A) 65
(B) 75
(C) 125
(D) 130
(E) 135

19. If $3 < x < 8$ and $5 < y < 11$, which of the following represents all the possible values of xy?

(A) $3 < xy < 11$
(B) $8 < xy < 19$
(C) $15 < xy < 88$
(D) $24 < xy < 55$
(E) $33 < xy < 40$

20. Chris gave Jane x cards. He gave Betty one card more than he gave Jane and he gave Paul two cards fewer than he gave Betty. In terms of x, how many cards did Chris give Betty, Jane, and Paul altogether?

(A) $3x + 1$

(B) $3x$

(C) $3x - 1$

(D) $x - 1$

(E) $\frac{x}{3}$

GO ON TO THE NEXT PAGE.

Questions 21-25 refer to the following floor plan.

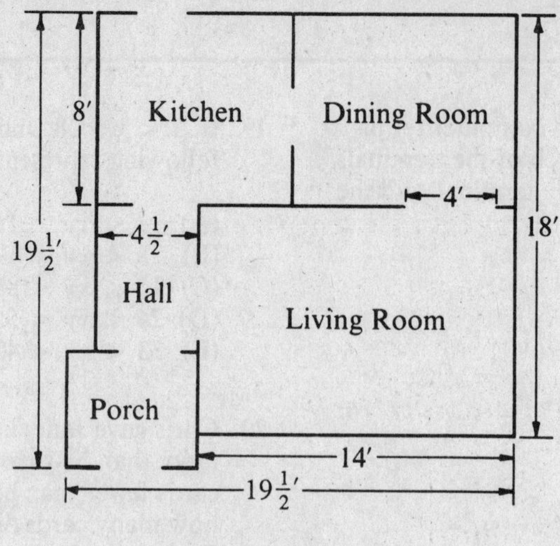

Note: Figure drawn to scale.

The figure above shows the plan for the ground floor of a house. The thickness of the walls should be ignored in answering the questions. The dimensions are in feet, and each region is rectangular.

21. What is the area, in square feet, of the living room?

(A) 161
(B) 140
(C) 133
(D) 126
(E) 115

22. If the ceilings and walls of the living room, dining room, kitchen, and hall are to be painted, how many square feet must be painted?

(A) $231\frac{1}{4}$
(B) 324
(C) 333
(D) $380\frac{1}{4}$
(E) It cannot be determined from the information given.

23. If the hall is $6\frac{1}{2}$ feet long, what is the perimeter, in feet, of the porch area?

(A) 18
(B) 19
(C) 20
(D) 21
(E) 22

24. How many more feet does the porch extend in front of the house than it does beyond the side of the house?

(A) $\frac{1}{2}$
(B) 1
(C) $1\frac{1}{2}$
(D) 2
(E) It cannot be determined from the information given.

25. If the kitchen is square, what is the ratio of the area of the kitchen to the area of the dining room?

(A) $\frac{16}{37}$
(B) $\frac{3}{7}$
(C) $\frac{4}{7}$
(D) $\frac{8}{11}$
(E) $\frac{16}{21}$

GO ON TO THE NEXT PAGE.

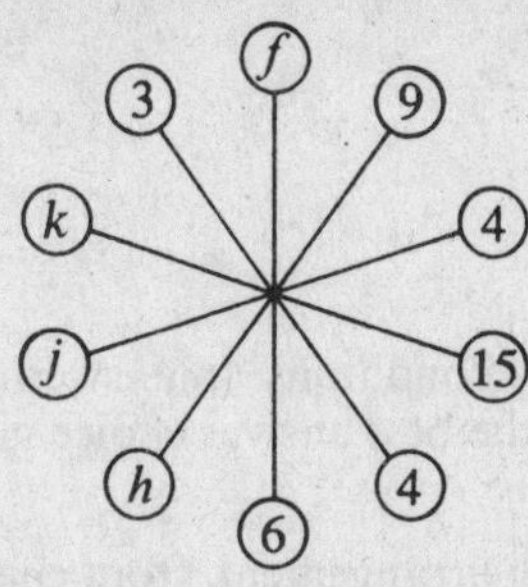

26. In the figure above, the product of any two numbers in adjacent circles is equal to the product of the two numbers that are opposite those circles. For example, $3 \cdot f = 4 \cdot 6$. What is the value of j?

(A) 3
(B) 4
(C) 6
(D) 12
(E) 20

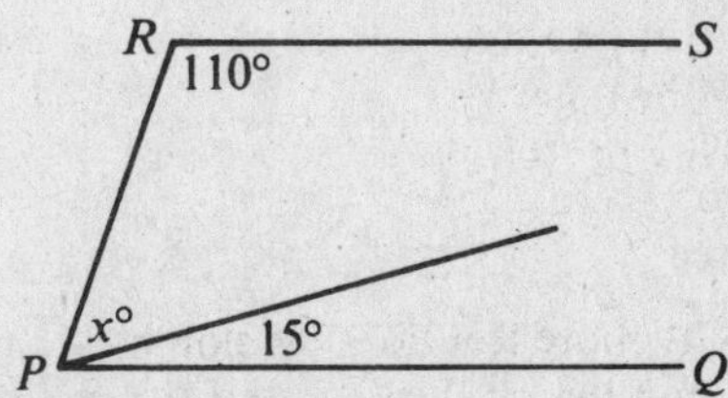

27. In the figure above, if $PQ \parallel RS$, then $x =$

(A) 95
(B) 85
(C) 75
(D) 65
(E) 55

28. If $x \neq 0$, then $\frac{x+7}{7x} - \frac{1}{x} =$

(A) $\frac{x+6}{6x}$

(B) $\frac{x+6}{7x}$

(C) $\frac{-6x+7}{7x}$

(D) $\frac{1}{7}$

(E) $-\frac{1}{7}$

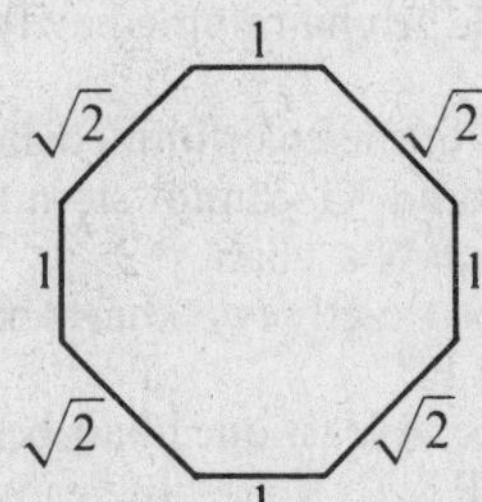

29. The figure above shows the lengths of the sides of an equiangular polygon. What is the area of the polygon?

(A) 7

(B) 8

(C) 9

(D) $14\sqrt{2}$

(E) It cannot be determined from the information given.

30. A certain recipe makes enough batter for exactly 8 circular pancakes that are each 10 inches in diameter. How many circular pancakes, each 5 inches in diameter and of the same thickness as the 10-inch pancakes, should the recipe make?

(A) 4
(B) 16
(C) 24
(D) 32
(E) 40

STOP

IF YOU FINISH BEFORE TIME IS CALLED, YOU MAY CHECK YOUR WORK ON THIS SECTION ONLY. DO NOT TURN TO ANY OTHER SECTION IN THE TEST.

SECTION 6

Time—30 minutes

25 Questions

Directions: Each question or group of questions is based on a passage or set of conditions. In answering some of the questions, it may be useful to draw a rough diagram. For each question, select the best answer choice given.

Questions 1-5

Seven dignitaries—F, G, H, I, N, O, and P—are to be seated together at a diplomatic ceremony. They will be seated in a row of seven chairs, numbered from 1 to 7, from front to back. Any seating is acceptable as long as all seven dignitaries are seated, one in each chair, and the seating conforms to the following rules:

F must sit in the chair immediately behind O's chair.
G cannot sit in the chair immediately in front of N's chair, and G cannot sit in the chair immediately behind N's chair.
There must be exactly two chairs between the chairs of H and P.
There must be at least one chair between the chairs of I and P.
N must sit in chair 3.

1. Which of the following seating arrangements, from chair 1 through chair 7, conforms to the rules?

(A) F, I, N, P, G, O, H
(B) G, P, N, I, H, O, F
(C) I, G, N, P, O, F, H
(D) I, H, N, P, O, F, G
(E) O, F, H, N, I, P, G

2. If F sits in chair 6 and H sits in chair 7, which of the following dignitaries must sit in chair 2?

(A) G
(B) I
(C) N
(D) O
(E) P

3. If the seating arrangement, from chair 1 through chair 7, is G, I, N, H, O, F, P, which of the following pairs of dignitaries can exchange seats without violating the rules?

(A) F and G
(B) G and H
(C) G and I
(D) H and P
(E) I and P

4. If O sits in chair 1 and H sits in chair 7, then the number of chairs between F's chair and I's chair must be

(A) zero
(B) one
(C) two
(D) three
(E) four

5. If H sits in chair 4 and F sits in chair 6, then the dignitaries in chairs 1 and 7, respectively, must be

(A) G and O
(B) G and P
(C) I and P
(D) O and I
(E) P and O

GO ON TO THE NEXT PAGE.

6. A judicial order of a few years ago was intended to foster competition in the telephone industry; it was thought that competition would lead to savings for consumers. Long-distance calls made during the day are now cheaper than they were before the order, but the average residential user's charges for long-distance calls have risen by 25 percent.

Which of the following, if true, would most directly explain the higher long-distance charges incurred by residential users?

(A) More long-distance calls are made by businesses than by residential users.
(B) Telephone companies are expanding their services in the areas of computing and data processing.
(C) Rates for calls made during the evening, the time when most residential users make long-distance calls, have increased.
(D) Increased competition has led telephone companies to expand their budgets for the development of new technology.
(E) Telephone companies must receive approval from regulatory agencies before putting rate changes into effect.

7. A program of steady, moderate aerobic exercise coupled with a diet low in saturated fats and cholesterol has been associated with reduced risk of heart attacks and strokes. Therefore, no one who exercises regularly and eats only foods that are low in saturated fats and cholesterol will have a heart attack or stroke.

Of the following, the best criticism of the argument above is that the argument does not

(A) take into account the possibility of heart attacks and strokes that occur regardless of diet and level of exercise
(B) take into account all of the possible physiological effects of saturated fats and cholesterol
(C) specify whether foods high in saturated fats also contain cholesterol
(D) indicate whether an increased risk of heart attacks and strokes is due more to poor diet or more to lack of exercise
(E) differentiate between the causes of heart attacks and the causes of strokes

8. The number of boats sold in 1973 was greater than the number of boats sold in 1987. However, more money was spent buying boats in 1987 than was spent buying boats in 1973.

Which of the following statements can be properly inferred from the statements above?

(A) In 1973 the demand for boats exceeded the supply, while in 1987 the supply of boats exceeded the demand.
(B) People were willing to invest a greater proportion of their income in boats in 1987 than they were in 1973.
(C) Between 1973 and 1987, there was a gradual increase in the proportion of large and luxuriously equipped boats sold.
(D) The average (mean) price of boats sold in 1973 was less than that of boats sold in 1987.
(E) Between 1973 and 1987, the number of new boats being made increased.

GO ON TO THE NEXT PAGE.

Questions 9-12

The following are the nine options that are available for the Sleuth, a certain make of automobile: air conditioning, power brakes, power steering, power windows, a heavy-duty engine, heavy-duty shock absorbers, a hatchback, a sunroof, a tinted windshield. Because of certain manufacturing and safety considerations, the purchase of these options must conform to the following conditions:

If air conditioning is chosen, a heavy-duty engine, heavy-duty shock absorbers, and a tinted windshield are also required.
If any of the power-assisted options (power brakes, power steering, power windows) are chosen, a heavy-duty engine is also required.
If a heavy-duty engine is chosen, power brakes are also required.
If a hatchback is chosen, a sunroof cannot be chosen.
A tinted windshield can be chosen only for an automobile for which either a sunroof or air conditioning or both are chosen.

9. Of the following, which could be a completed selection of optional equipment that conforms to the conditions?

(A) Power steering, a sunroof
(B) A hatchback, a sunroof, a tinted windshield
(C) Power brakes, power steering, a heavy-duty engine, heavy-duty shock absorbers, a hatchback
(D) Air conditioning, power brakes, a heavy-duty engine, a hatchback, a tinted windshield
(E) Air conditioning, power brakes, a heavy-duty engine, heavy-duty shock absorbers, a hatchback

10. Which of the following must be true?

(A) A Sleuth equipped with air conditioning must also be equipped with power brakes.
(B) A Sleuth equipped with a tinted windshield must also be equipped with a heavy-duty engine.
(C) A Sleuth equipped with power brakes must also be equipped with power steering.
(D) A Sleuth equipped with air conditioning must also be equipped with a sunroof.
(E) A Sleuth equipped with a sunroof must also be equipped with a tinted windshield.

11. Which of the following options can be chosen without the purchase of additional options?

(A) Heavy-duty shock absorbers
(B) Power windows
(C) Power brakes
(D) A heavy-duty engine
(E) A tinted windshield

12. A buyer who does not want air conditioning but otherwise wants the maximum number of options for a Sleuth CANNOT purchase

(A) power steering
(B) power brakes
(C) power windows
(D) a tinted windshield
(E) a hatchback

GO ON TO THE NEXT PAGE.

Questions 13-18

The art director of an advertising company is preparing a sales brochure for a boat-manufacturing company. To represent her client's line of products, she wants a separate full-page color advertisement in the brochure for each of the following five types of boats: kayak, motorboat, pedal boat, raft, and sailboat. Thus, there will be exactly five printed pages, numbered consecutively one through five, in the brochure. Because she also wants to show the range of colors that the manufacturer uses, one of the boats pictured must be green, one must be orange, one must be tan, one must be white, and one must be yellow. In designing the brochure, she has made the following decisions:

The motorboat will be advertised on a lower-numbered page than the pedal boat.
The sailboat will be advertised on a lower-numbered page than the kayak.
The white boat will be advertised on a lower-numbered page than the yellow boat.
The orange boat will be advertised on page three.
The pedal boat advertised will be tan.

13. Which of the following could be the colors of the boats advertised on pages 1 through 5, respectively?

(A) White, tan, orange, green, yellow
(B) Green, orange, white, yellow, tan
(C) Green, tan, orange, yellow, white
(D) Orange, yellow, white, tan, green
(E) Tan, yellow, orange, green, white

14. Any of the boats could be advertised on page 3 EXCEPT the

(A) kayak
(B) motorboat
(C) pedal boat
(D) raft
(E) sailboat

15. If the kayak is advertised on a lower-numbered page than the orange boat, which of the following must be true?

(A) The kayak is advertised on page 1.
(B) The motorboat is advertised on page 2.
(C) The pedal boat is advertised on page 5.
(D) The raft is advertised on page 3.
(E) The sailboat is advertised on page 1.

16. If the kayak is green, the boat advertised on page 1 must be

(A) green
(B) orange
(C) tan
(D) white
(E) yellow

17. If the motorboat is green and is advertised on page 4, which of the following must be true?

(A) The kayak is advertised on page 2.
(B) The raft is advertised on page 3.
(C) The sailboat is advertised on page 1.
(D) The white boat is advertised on page 1.
(E) The tan boat is advertised on page 2.

18. If the sailboat is advertised on page 2 and the green boat is advertised on page 5, the sailboat must be

(A) green
(B) orange
(C) tan
(D) white
(E) yellow

GO ON TO THE NEXT PAGE.

Questions 19-22

On each weekday evening, Monday through Friday, for one week, a financial consulting firm is offering a class on investments. A pair of exactly two instructors—one experienced and one inexperienced—will be chosen to teach each evening. The available experienced instructors are Salazar, Tang, and Uhl. The available inexperienced instructors are Vine, Wolfe, Xavier, Yamashita, and Ziegler. Instructors will be assigned to teach classes according to the following conditions:

No instructor can be assigned to teach classes on two consecutive evenings.
Salazar and Xavier, if either is assigned to teach, must always be assigned as a pair.
Vine must be assigned to teach Wednesday's class.
Yamashita cannot be assigned to teach a class on an evening immediately preceding or following an evening when Ziegler is assigned to teach.

19. Which of the following can be the pair of instructors assigned to teach Tuesday's class?

(A) Salazar and Ziegler
(B) Tang and Uhl
(C) Tang and Yamashita
(D) Uhl and Xavier
(E) Wolfe and Yamashita

20. If Tang and Ziegler are assigned to teach Monday's class, which of the following pairs of instructors can be assigned to teach Tuesday's class?

(A) Salazar and Wolfe
(B) Salazar and Xavier
(C) Tang and Wolfe
(D) Uhl and Vine
(E) Uhl and Yamashita

21. If exactly two of the inexperienced instructors are assigned to teach classes during the week, which of the following must be true?

(A) Salazar is assigned to teach exactly two classes.
(B) Tang is assigned to teach exactly two classes.
(C) Uhl is assigned to teach exactly three classes.
(D) Vine is assigned to teach exactly three classes.
(E) Xavier is assigned to teach exactly one class.

22. If Uhl is assigned to teach exactly one class, which is on Tuesday, which of the following is one of the instructors who must be assigned to teach Thursday's class?

(A) Salazar
(B) Tang
(C) Wolfe
(D) Yamashita
(E) Ziegler

GO ON TO THE NEXT PAGE.

23. In the 1950's sixty percent of treated cancer patients lived at least five years after detection of the disease. Now, sixty percent live at least seven years after detection. This fact demonstrates that, because of improved methods of treatment, cancer patients now live longer after they contract the disease than cancer patients did in the 1950's.

The conclusion of the argument above depends on which of the following assumptions?

(A) In the 1950's only sixty percent of cancer patients received treatment, whereas now a substantially higher percentage does.
(B) Free medical treatment is more likely to be available now to people who have no health insurance than it was in the 1950's.
(C) Detection of cancer does not now take place, on average, significantly earlier in the progression of the disease than it did in the 1950's.
(D) Physicians now usually predict a longer life for cancer patients after detection of the disease than did physicians in the 1950's.
(E) The number of cancer patients now is approximately the same as it was in the 1950's.

24. The large amounts of carbon dioxide now being released into the atmosphere by the burning of fossil fuels will not, in fact, result in a greenhouse effect—an increase in average global temperatures. Since plants use carbon dioxide in larger quantities if the supply is increased, they are able to grow larger and multiply more vigorously, and atmospheric carbon dioxide concentrations will eventually become stable.

Which of the following, if true, would most seriously weaken the conclusion that a greenhouse effect will not result from the current release of large amounts of carbon dioxide into the atmosphere?

(A) The expected rise in average global temperatures has not yet been observed.
(B) Ocean waters absorb carbon dioxide at a greater rate when the atmospheric concentration of carbon dioxide is higher.
(C) Since the beginning of the Industrial Revolution, increased atmospheric concentrations of carbon dioxide have resulted in improved agricultural productivity.
(D) When plants decay, they produce methane, another gas that can have a marked greenhouse effect.
(E) The fact that carbon dioxide levels have risen and fallen many times in the Earth's history suggests that there is some biological process that can reverse the greenhouse effect.

25. The number of people 85 or older in the United States started increasing dramatically during the last ten years. The good health care that these people enjoyed in the United States during their vulnerable childhood years is primarily responsible for this trend.

Which of the following, if true, most seriously weakens the explanation above?

(A) Seventy-five percent of the people in the United States who are 85 or older are the children of people who themselves lived less than 65 years.
(B) The people in the United States who are now 85 represent an age group that was smaller in numbers at birth than the immediately preceeding and succeeding age groups.
(C) Thirty-five percent of the people in the United States who are 85 or older require some form of twenty-four-hour nursing care.
(D) Many of the people in the United States who are 85 or older immigrated to the United States when they were 20 years old or older.
(E) Because of decreased federal funding for medical care for pregnant mothers and for children, the life expectancy of United States citizens is likely to decrease.

STOP

IF YOU FINISH BEFORE TIME IS CALLED, YOU MAY CHECK YOUR WORK ON THIS SECTION ONLY.
DO NOT TURN TO ANY OTHER SECTION IN THE TEST.

NO TEST MATERIAL ON THIS PAGE

SECTION 7

Time—30 minutes

38 Questions

Directions: Each sentence below has one or two blanks, each blank indicating that something has been omitted. Beneath the sentence are five lettered words or sets of words. Choose the word or set of words for each blank that best fits the meaning of the sentence as a whole.

1. Given the existence of so many factions in the field, it was unrealistic of Anna Freud to expect any ------- of opinion.

   (A) freedom (B) reassessment (C) uniformity (D) expression (E) formation

2. Although specific concerns may determine the intent of a research project, its results are often -------.

   (A) unanticipated (B) beneficial (C) expensive (D) spectacular (E) specialized

3. To list Reilly's achievements in a fragmentary way is -------, for it distracts our attention from the ------- themes of her work.

   (A) unproductive. .disparate
   (B) misleading. .integrating
   (C) pragmatic. .comprehensive
   (D) logical. .important
   (E) inevitable. .unsettling

4. People frequently denigrate books about recent catastrophes as morally ------- attempts to profit from misfortune, but in my view our desire for such books, together with the venerable tradition to which they belong, ------- them.

   (A) inopportune. .encourages
   (B) fortuitous. .fosters
   (C) treacherous. .safeguards
   (D) despicable. .legitimizes
   (E) corrupt. .generates

5. That many of the important laws of science were discovered during experiments designed to ------- other phenomena suggests that experimental results are the ------- of inevitable natural forces rather than of planning.

   (A) analyze. .foundations
   (B) disprove. .predecessors
   (C) alter. .adjuncts
   (D) illuminate. .consequence
   (E) verify. .essence

6. Although in eighteenth-century England an active cultural life accompanied the beginnings of middle-class consumerism, the ------- of literacy was ------- with the rise of such consumerism in the different areas of the country.

   (A) repudiation. .reconciled
   (B) renewal. .inconsistent
   (C) promotion. .combined
   (D) spread. .compatible
   (E) degree. .uncorrelated

7. The trainees were given copies of a finished manual to see whether they could themselves begin to ------- the inflexible, though tacit, rules for composing more of such instructional materials.

   (A) design (B) revise (C) disrupt (D) standardize (E) derive

GO ON TO THE NEXT PAGE.

Directions: In each of the following questions, a related pair of words or phrases is followed by five lettered pairs of words or phrases. Select the lettered pair that best expresses a relationship similar to that expressed in the original pair.

8. BUTTER : MARGARINE ::
(A) sugar : saccharin
(B) porcelain : tile
(C) photograph : painting
(D) music : tape
(E) signal : whistle

9. MUTED : COLOR ::
(A) archaic : diction
(B) pastoral : composition
(C) muffled : sound
(D) haunting : tune
(E) unconcerned : interest

10. MUFFLER : NECK ::
(A) sandal : foot
(B) collar : blouse
(C) earring : ear
(D) mitten : hand
(E) suspenders : trousers

11. PLANT : SOIL ::
(A) germ : bacteria
(B) organism : medium
(C) sample : growth
(D) nutrient : liquid
(E) tree : root

12. POTTERY : SHARD ::
(A) symphony : musician
(B) bread : crumb
(C) wall : brick
(D) shoe : heel
(E) building : architect

13. PURIFICATION : DROSS ::
(A) distillation : vinegar
(B) assay : gold
(C) desalinization : salt
(D) condensation : vapor
(E) reaction : catalyst

14. DISGUISE : RECOGNITION ::
(A) prevarication : statement
(B) infidelity : marriage
(C) camouflage : infiltration
(D) espionage : diplomacy
(E) padding : damage

15. GUST : WIND ::
(A) rapids : river
(B) blizzard : snowstorm
(C) cloudburst : rainfall
(D) mist : fog
(E) surf : sea

16. DISABUSE : ERROR ::
(A) rehabilitate : addiction
(B) persevere : dereliction
(C) belittle : imperfection
(D) discredit : reputation
(E) discern : discrimination

GO ON TO THE NEXT PAGE.

Directions: Each passage in this group is followed by questions based on its content. After reading a passage, choose the best answer to each question. Answer all questions following a passage on the basis of what is stated or implied in that passage.

Diamonds, an occasional component of rare igneous rocks called lamproites and kimberlites, have never been dated satisfactorily. However, some diamonds contain minute inclusions of silicate minerals, commonly olivine, pyroxene, and garnet. These minerals can be dated by radioactive decay techniques because of the very small quantities of radioactive trace elements they, in turn, contain. Usually, it is possible to conclude that the inclusions are older than their diamond hosts, but with little indication of the time interval involved. Sometimes, however, the crystal form of the silicate inclusions is observed to resemble more closely the internal structure of diamond than that of other silicate minerals. It is not known how rare this resemblance is, or whether it is most often seen in inclusions of silicates such as garnet, whose crystallography is generally somewhat similar to that of diamond; but when present, the resemblance is regarded as compelling evidence that the diamonds and inclusions are truly cogenetic.

17. The author implies that silicate inclusions were most often formed

(A) with small diamonds inside of them
(B) with trace elements derived from their host minerals
(C) by the radioactive decay of rare igneous rocks
(D) at an earlier period than were their host minerals
(E) from the crystallization of rare igneous material

18. According to the passage, the age of silicate minerals included in diamonds can be determined due to a feature of the

(A) trace elements in the diamond hosts
(B) trace elements in the rock surrounding the diamonds
(C) trace elements in the silicate minerals
(D) silicate minerals' crystal structure
(E) host diamonds' crystal structure

19. The author states that which of the following generally has a crystal structure similar to that of diamond?

(A) Lamproite (B) Kimberlite (C) Olivine (D) Pyroxene (E) Garnet

20. The main purpose of the passage is to

(A) explain why it has not been possible to determine the age of diamonds
(B) explain how it might be possible to date some diamonds
(C) compare two alternative approaches to determining the age of diamonds
(D) compare a method of dating diamonds with a method used to date certain silicate minerals
(E) compare the age of diamonds with that of certain silicate minerals contained within them

GO ON TO THE NEXT PAGE.

Discussion of the assimilation of Puerto Ricans in the United States has focused on two factors: social standing and the loss of national culture. In general, excessive stress is placed on one factor or the other, depending on whether the commentator is North American or Puerto Rican. Many North American social scientists, such as Oscar Handlin, Joseph Fitzpatrick, and Oscar Lewis, consider Puerto Ricans as the most recent in a long line of ethnic entrants to occupy the lowest rung on the social ladder. Such a "sociodemographic" approach tends to regard assimilation as a benign process, taking for granted increased economic advantage and inevitable cultural integration, in a supposedly egalitarian context. However, this approach fails to take into account the colonial nature of the Puerto Rican case, with this group, unlike their European predecessors, coming from a nation politically subordinated to the United States. Even the "radical" critiques of this mainstream research model, such as the critique developed in *Divided Society*, attach the issue of ethnic assimilation too mechanically to factors of economic and social mobility and are thus unable to illuminate the cultural subordination of Puerto Ricans as a colonial minority.

In contrast, the "colonialist" approach of island-based writers such as Eduardo Seda-Bonilla, Manuel Maldonado-Denis, and Luis Nieves-Falcón tends to view assimilation as the forced loss of national culture in an unequal contest with imposed foreign values. There is, of course, a strong tradition of cultural accommodation among other Puerto Rican thinkers. The writings of Eugenio Fernández Méndez clearly exemplify this tradition, and many supporters of Puerto Rico's commonwealth status share the same universalizing orientation. But the Puerto Rican intellectuals who have written most about the assimilation process in the United States all advance cultural nationalist views, advocating the preservation of minority cultural distinctions and rejecting what they see as the subjugation of colonial nationalities.

This cultural and political emphasis is appropriate, but the colonialist thinkers misdirect it, overlooking the class relations at work in both Puerto Rican and North American history. They pose the clash of national cultures as an absolute polarity, with each culture understood as static and undifferentiated. Yet both the Puerto Rican and North American traditions have been subject to constant challenge from cultural forces within their own societies, forces that may move toward each other in ways that cannot be written off as mere "assimilation." Consider, for example, the indigenous and Afro-Caribbean traditions in Puerto Rican culture and how they influence and are influenced by other Caribbean cultures and Black cultures in the United States. The elements of coercion and inequality, so central to cultural contact according to the colonialist framework, play no role in this kind of convergence of racially and ethnically different elements of the same social class.

21. The author's main purpose is to
    (A) criticize the emphasis on social standing in discussions of the assimilation of Puerto Ricans in the United States
    (B) support the thesis that assimilation has not been a benign process for Puerto Ricans
    (C) defend a view of the assimilation of Puerto Ricans that emphasizes the preservation of national culture
    (D) indicate deficiencies in two schools of thought on the assimilation of Puerto Ricans in the United States
    (E) reject the attempt to formulate a general framework for discussion of the assimilation of Puerto Ricans in the United States

22. According to the passage, cultural accommodation is promoted by
    (A) Eduardo Seda-Bonilla
    (B) Manuel Maldonado-Denis
    (C) the author of *Divided Society*
    (D) the majority of social scientists writing on immigration
    (E) many supporters of Puerto Rico's commonwealth status

23. It can be inferred from the passage that a writer such as Eugenio Fernández Méndez would most likely agree with which of the following statements concerning members of minority ethnic groups?
    (A) It is necessary for the members of such groups to adapt to the culture of the majority.
    (B) The members of such groups generally encounter a culture that is static and undifferentiated.
    (C) Social mobility is the most important feature of the experience of members of such groups.
    (D) Social scientists should emphasize the cultural and political aspects of the experience of members of such groups.
    (E) The assimilation of members of such groups requires the forced abandonment of their authentic national roots.

GO ON TO THE NEXT PAGE.

24. The author implies that the Puerto Rican writers who have written most about assimilation do NOT do which of the following?

(A) Regard assimilation as benign.
(B) Resist cultural integration.
(C) Describe in detail the process of assimilation.
(D) Take into account the colonial nature of the Puerto Rican case.
(E) Criticize supporters of Puerto Rico's commonwealth status.

25. It can be inferred from the passage that the "colonialist" approach is so called because its practitioners

(A) support Puerto Rico's commonwealth status
(B) have a strong tradition of cultural accommodation
(C) emphasize the class relations at work in both Puerto Rican and North American history
(D) pose the clash of national cultures as an absolute polarity in which each culture is understood as static and undifferentiated
(E) regard the political relation of Puerto Rico to the United States as a significant factor in the experience of Puerto Ricans

26. The author regards the emphasis by island-based writers on the cultural and political dimensions of assimilation as

(A) ironic
(B) dangerous
(C) fitting but misdirected
(D) illuminating but easily misunderstood
(E) peculiar but benign

27. The example discussed in lines 51-54 is intended by the author to illustrate a

(A) strength of the sociodemographic approach
(B) strength of the "colonialist" approach
(C) weakness of the sociodemographic approach
(D) weakness of the "colonialist" approach
(E) weakness of the cultural-accommodationist approach

GO ON TO THE NEXT PAGE.

Directions: Each question below consists of a word printed in capital letters, followed by five lettered words or phrases. Choose the lettered word or phrase that is most nearly opposite in meaning to the word in capital letters.

Since some of the questions require you to distinguish fine shades of meaning, be sure to consider all the choices before deciding which one is best.

28. OVERREACH:
(A) disparage another's work
(B) aim below one's potential
(C) seek to buy at a lower price
(D) say less than one intends
(E) tend to overstate

29. BULGE: (A) depressed region (B) tilted plane (C) steep slope (D) rippled surface (E) short line

30. FACILITATE: (A) evict (B) thwart (C) define (D) make excuses for (E) call attention to

31. EULOGY: (A) defamation (B) fluctuation (C) characterization (D) hallucination (E) deprivation

32. FRACAS:
(A) functional compromise
(B) reasonable judgment
(C) peaceable discussion
(D) plausible exception
(E) theoretical approach

33. HARROW: (A) assuage (B) levy (C) suffice (D) repel (E) invert

34. BOOR: (A) forthright individual (B) brave fighter (C) deceitful ally (D) civil person (E) steadfast friend

35. HACKNEYED: (A) fresh (B) illicit (C) careful (D) unpopular (E) dissenting

36. SODDEN: (A) barren (B) desiccated (C) temperate (D) expedient (E) artificial

37. GAINSAY: (A) hesitate (B) intercede (C) perceive (D) concur (E) praise

38. NICE: (A) indirect (B) indecisive (C) imperceptible (D) imprecise (E) imperturbable

STOP

IF YOU FINISH BEFORE TIME IS CALLED, YOU MAY CHECK YOUR WORK ON THIS SECTION ONLY. DO NOT TURN TO ANY OTHER SECTION IN THE TEST.

NO TEST MATERIAL ON THIS PAGE

NO TEST MATERIAL ON THIS PAGE

NOTE: To ensure prompt processing of test results, it is important that you fill in the blanks exactly as directed.

GENERAL TEST

A. Print and sign your full name in this box:

PRINT: ____
(LAST) (FIRST) (MIDDLE)

SIGN: ____

Copy this code in box 6 on your answer sheet. Then fill in the corresponding ovals exactly as shown.

6. TITLE CODE

0	0	0	0	0
1	1	1	1	1
2	2	2	2	2
3	3	3	3	3
4	4	4	4	4
5	5	5	5	5
6	6	6	6	6
7	7	7	7	7
8	8	8	8	8
9	9	9	9	9

Copy the Test Name and Form Code in box 7 on your answer sheet.

TEST NAME General

FORM CODE GR91-17

GRADUATE RECORD EXAMINATIONS GENERAL TEST

B. You will have 3 hours and 30 minutes in which to work on this test, which consists of seven sections. During the time allowed for one section, you may work only on that section. The time allowed for each section is 30 minutes.

Each of your scores will be determined by the number of questions for which you select the best answer from the choices given. Questions for which you mark no answer or more than one answer are not counted in scoring. Nothing is subtracted from a score if you answer a question incorrectly. Therefore, to maximize your scores it is better for you to guess at an answer than not to respond at all.

You are advised to work as rapidly as you can without losing accuracy. Do not spend too much time on questions that are too difficult for you. Go on to the other questions and come back to the difficult ones later.

There are several different types of questions; you will find special directions for each type in the test itself. Be sure you understand the directions before attempting to answer any questions.

YOU MUST INDICATE ALL YOUR ANSWERS ON THE SEPARATE ANSWER SHEET. No credit will be given for anything written in this examination book, but you may write in the book as much as you wish to work out your answers. After you have decided on your response to a question, fill in the corresponding oval on the answer sheet. BE SURE THAT EACH MARK IS DARK AND COMPLETELY FILLS THE OVAL. Mark only one answer to each question. No credit will be given for multiple answers. Erase all stray marks. If you change an answer, be sure that all previous marks are erased completely. Incomplete erasures may be read as intended answers. Do not be concerned if your answer sheet provides spaces for more answers than there are questions in each section.

Example:

What city is the capital of France?

(A) Rome
(B) Paris
(C) London
(D) Cairo
(E) Oslo

Sample Answer

Ⓐ ● Ⓒ Ⓓ Ⓔ BEST ANSWER PROPERLY MARKED

Ⓐ ⊗ Ⓒ Ⓓ Ⓔ
Ⓐ ✓ Ⓒ Ⓓ Ⓔ
Ⓐ ◉ Ⓒ Ⓓ Ⓔ
Ⓐ ◐ Ⓒ Ⓓ Ⓔ
IMPROPER MARKS

Some or all of the passages for this test have been adapted from published material to provide the examinee with significant problems for analysis and evaluation. To make the passages suitable for testing purposes, the style, content, or point of view of the original may have been altered in some cases. The ideas contained in the passages do not necessarily represent the opinions of the Graduate Record Examinations Board or Educational Testing Service.

DO NOT OPEN YOUR TEST BOOK UNTIL YOU ARE TOLD TO DO SO.

FOR GENERAL TEST, FORM GR91-17 ONLY
Answer Key and Percentages* of Examinees Answering Each Question Correctly

VERBAL ABILITY					
Section 3			Section 7		
Number	Answer	P +	Number	Answer	P +
1	B	89	1	C	85
2	B	88	2	A	84
3	D	51	3	B	80
4	A	48	4	D	59
5	C	49	5	D	55
6	E	44	6	E	48
7	D	30	7	E	34
8	C	76	8	A	92
9	D	83	9	C	86
10	B	77	10	D	77
11	E	67	11	B	58
12	E	61	12	B	57
13	D	54	13	C	43
14	C	34	14	E	35
15	C	35	15	C	33
16	A	14	16	A	33
17	B	88	17	D	63
18	B	74	18	C	70
19	A	79	19	E	90
20	D	54	20	B	48
21	A	81	21	D	59
22	B	26	22	E	64
23	E	52	23	A	30
24	C	42	24	A	38
25	D	76	25	E	26
26	A	50	26	C	63
27	B	44	27	D	44
28	E	92	28	B	86
29	A	90	29	A	91
30	A	86	30	B	75
31	D	83	31	A	85
32	C	75	32	C	74
33	A	43	33	A	42
34	C	39	34	D	45
35	B	34	35	A	38
36	E	29	36	B	30
37	E	26	37	D	25
38	D	7	38	D	20

QUANTITATIVE ABILITY					
Section 2			Section 5		
Number	Answer	P +	Number	Answer	P +
1	C	87	1	B	85
2	B	85	2	A	86
3	A	87	3	B	81
4	A	88	4	D	74
5	D	77	5	A	83
6	B	74	6	D	78
7	C	70	7	B	76
8	A	61	8	A	61
9	D	57	9	B	50
10	A	56	10	C	61
11	C	40	11	D	41
12	A	43	12	C	35
13	D	31	13	C	32
14	B	45	14	C	23
15	D	29	15	A	47
16	C	81	16	B	83
17	B	69	17	B	77
18	E	79	18	C	74
19	A	53	19	C	65
20	E	42	20	B	68
21	B	84	21	B	79
22	C	66	22	E	76
23	C	69	23	D	56
24	E	47	24	A	51
25	C	36	25	E	37
26	D	65	26	A	49
27	B	64	27	E	51
28	D	65	28	D	56
29	D	25	29	A	29
30	A	30	30	D	25

ANALYTICAL ABILITY					
Section 1			Section 6		
Number	Answer	P +	Number	Answer	P +
1	A	81	1	B	79
2	D	62	2	B	77
3	C	53	3	D	75
4	B	94	4	D	59
5	D	82	5	B	66
6	E	63	6	C	79
7	D	80	7	A	89
8	E	40	8	D	77
9	D	74	9	C	62
10	E	57	10	A	43
11	D	40	11	A	70
12	A	69	12	E	44
13	A	54	13	A	70
14	C	29	14	C	71
15	A	56	15	E	55
16	E	16	16	D	57
17	B	48	17	D	36
18	C	35	18	E	36
19	E	48	19	C	58
20	C	44	20	B	65
21	C	48	21	D	27
22	C	36	22	A	24
23	D	48	23	C	42
24	B	53	24	D	48
25	A	28	25	D	51

*Estimated P+ for the group of examinees who took the GRE General Test in a recent three-year period.

Score Conversions for GRE General Test GR91-17 Only and the Percents Below*

Raw Score	Verbal Scaled Score	Verbal % Below	Quantitative Scaled Score	Quantitative % Below	Analytical Scaled Score	Analytical % Below	Raw Score	Verbal Scaled Score	Verbal % Below	Quantitative Scaled Score	Quantitative % Below	Analytical Scaled Score	Analytical % Below
73-76	800	99					39	440	38	590	57	700	90
72	790	99					38	430	36	580	54	690	88
71	780	99					37	420	33	570	51	680	87
70	760	99					36	410	30	560	49	660	83
							35	400	26	550	48	650	81
69	750	98					34	400	26	540	45	630	76
68	730	97					33	390	24	530	42	620	74
67	720	96					32	380	22	520	40	600	69
66	710	95					31	370	20	500	35	590	67
65	700	95					30	360	16	490	32	570	61
64	690	94											
63	680	93					29	350	14	480	30	550	55
62	670	92					28	350	14	470	28	540	52
61	660	90					27	340	12	460	26	520	46
60	650	89	800	97			26	330	10	450	24	500	40
							25	320	9	430	20	490	38
59	630	85	800	97			24	310	7	420	18	470	32
58	620	84	800	97			23	300	6	410	16	460	31
57	610	82	790	96			22	300	6	400	14	440	24
56	600	80	780	94			21	290	5	380	12	420	20
55	590	78	760	92			20	280	4	370	10	400	17
54	580	76	750	89									
53	570	74	740	88			19	270	3	350	7	390	15
52	560	72	730	86			18	260	2	340	6	370	12
51	550	69	730	86			17	250	1	330	5	360	10
50	540	67	720	84	800	99	16	240	1	310	4	340	7
							15	230	1	290	2	320	6
49	530	64	700	80	800	99	14	220	1	280	2	310	4
48	520	61	690	78	800	99	13	210	1	260	1	290	3
47	510	59	680	77	800	99	12	200	1	250	1	280	2
46	500	56	670	74	800	99	11	200	1	230	1	270	2
45	490	54	660	72	790	98	10	200	1	220	1	250	1
44	480	51	650	70	770	97							
43	470	48	640	68	760	96	9	200	1	200	1	240	1
42	460	44	620	63	750	96	8	200	1	200	1	230	1
41	450	41	610	61	730	94	7	200	1	200	1	210	1
40	450	41	600	59	720	92	0-6	200	1	200	1	200	1

*Percent scoring below the scaled score is based on the performance of 923,359 examinees who took the General Test between October 1, 1986, and September 30, 1989. This percent below information is used for score reports during the 1990-91 testing year.

GR91-18

01

THE GRADUATE RECORD EXAMINATIONS®

GRE®

General Test

Do not break the seal until you are told to do so.

The contents of this test are confidential. Disclosure or reproduction of any portion of it is prohibited.

THIS TEST BOOK MUST NOT BE TAKEN FROM THE ROOM.

SECTION 1

Time—30 minutes

38 Questions

Directions: Each sentence that follows has one or two blanks, each blank indicating that something has been omitted. Following the sentence are five lettered words or sets of words. Choose the word or set of words for each blank that best fits the meaning of the sentence as a whole.

1. The availability of oxygen is an essential ------- for animal life, while carbon dioxide is equally ------- for plant life.

   (A) choice. .optional
   (B) duplication. .selective
   (C) conversion. .exchangeable
   (D) condition. .necessary
   (E) luxury. .harmful

2. Prudery actually draws attention to the vice it is supposed to -------; the very act that forbids speech or prohibits sight ------- what is hidden.

   (A) condemn. .distorts
   (B) monitor. .signals
   (C) repress. .dramatizes
   (D) obviate. .fosters
   (E) divulge. .conceals

3. After thirty years of television, people have become "speed watchers"; consequently, if the camera lingers, the interest of the audience -------.

   (A) broadens (B) begins (C) varies (D) flags (E) clears

4. Compared mathematically to smoking and driving, almost everything else seems relatively risk-free, ------- almost nothing seems worth regulating.

   (A) yet (B) since (C) so (D) even though (E) as long as

5. Ironically, Carver's precision in sketching lives on the edge of despair ensures that his stories will sometimes be read too narrowly, much as Dickens' social-reformer role once caused his broader concerns to be -------.

   (A) ignored (B) reinforced (C) contradicted (D) diminished (E) diversified

6. The demise of the rigorous academic curriculum in high school resulted, in part, from the progressive rhetoric that ------- the study of subjects previously thought ------- as part of school learning.

   (A) advocated. .necessary
   (B) enhanced. .indispensable
   (C) restricted. .impractical
   (D) undermined. .popular
   (E) sanctioned. .inappropriate

7. While some see in practical jokes a wish for mastery in miniature over a world that seems very -------, others believe that the jokes' purpose is to disrupt, by reducing all transactions to -------.

   (A) dubious. .confusion
   (B) disorderly. .symmetry
   (C) harmonious. .dissonance
   (D) unruly. .chaos
   (E) turbulent. .uniformity

GO ON TO THE NEXT PAGE.

Directions: In each of the following questions, a related pair of words or phrases is followed by five lettered pairs of words or phrases. Select the lettered pair that best expresses a relationship similar to that expressed in the original pair.

8. ATHLETE : TROPHY :: (A) detective : badge (B) presenter : award (C) soldier : medal (D) bettor : stake (E) musician : instrument

9. ARTICULATE : UNCLEAR ::
(A) assign : unencumbered
(B) elaborate : sketchy
(C) explain : lucid
(D) grieve : somber
(E) march : planned

10. INVENTORY : STOCK :: (A) calculation : ledger (B) poll : balloting (C) survey : territory (D) census : population (E) petition : names

11. LOGIC : REASONING ::
(A) sensitivity : morality
(B) arrogance : leadership
(C) ethics : behavior
(D) creativity : enthusiasm
(E) bravery : charisma

12. MIMICRY : CAMOUFLAGE ::
(A) photosynthesis : pollination
(B) territoriality : migration
(C) hibernation : generation
(D) mutation : variation
(E) digestion : rumination

13. APPREHENSION : TERROR ::
(A) interest : conspiracy
(B) affection : adoration
(C) indifference : animosity
(D) reluctance : termination
(E) anxiety : faith

14. LUMBER : GRACE :: (A) dissemble : pretense (B) relent : energy (C) castigate : justice (D) waver : resolution (E) insinuate : subtlety

15. CAUSTIC : EAT AWAY ::
(A) hormone : inhibit
(B) reagent : bind
(C) explosive : destroy
(D) synthetic : substitute
(E) desiccant : dry

16. MALINGERER : DUTY :: (A) scholar : pedantry (B) recluse : humanity (C) rebel : responsibility (D) miser : wealth (E) patron : criticism

GO ON TO THE NEXT PAGE.

Directions: Each passage in this group is followed by questions based on its content. After reading a passage, choose the best answer to each question. Answer all questions following a passage on the basis of what is stated or implied in that passage.

Classical physics defines the vacuum as a state of absence: a vacuum is said to exist in a region of space if there is nothing in it. In the quantum field theories that describe the physics of elementary particles, the vacuum becomes somewhat more complicated. Even in empty space, particles can appear spontaneously as a result of fluctuations of the vacuum. For example, an electron and a positron, or antielectron, can be created out of the void. Particles created in this way have only a fleeting existence; they are annihilated almost as soon as they appear, and their presence can never be detected directly. They are called virtual particles in order to distinguish them from real particles, whose lifetimes are not constrained in the same way, and which can be detected. Thus it is still possible to define the vacuum as a space that has no real particles in it.

One might expect that the vacuum would always be the state of lowest possible energy for a given region of space. If an area is initially empty and a real particle is put into it, the total energy, it seems, should be raised by at least the energy equivalent of the mass of the added particle. A surprising result of some recent theoretical investigations is that this assumption is not invariably true. There are conditions under which the introduction of a real particle of finite mass into an empty region of space can reduce the total energy. If the reduction in energy is great enough, an electron and a positron will be spontaneously created. Under these conditions the electron and positron are not a result of vacuum fluctuations but are real particles, which exist indefinitely and can be detected. In other words, under these conditions the vacuum is an unstable state and can decay into a state of lower energy; i.e., one in which real particles are created.

The essential condition for the decay of the vacuum is the presence of an intense electric field. As a result of the decay of the vacuum, the space permeated by such a field can be said to acquire an electric charge, and it can be called a charged vacuum. The particles that materialize in the space make the charge manifest. An electric field of sufficient intensity to create a charged vacuum is likely to be found in only one place: in the immediate vicinity of a superheavy atomic nucleus, one with about twice as many protons as the heaviest natural nuclei known. A nucleus that large cannot be stable, but it might be possible to assemble one next to a vacuum for long enough to observe the decay of the vacuum. Experiments attempting to achieve this are now under way.

17. Which of the following titles best describes the passage as a whole?

(A) The Vacuum: Its Fluctuations and Decay
(B) The Vacuum: Its Creation and Instability
(C) The Vacuum: A State of Absence
(D) Particles That Materialize in the Vacuum
(E) Classical Physics and the Vacuum

18. According to the passage, the assumption that the introduction of a real particle into a vacuum raises the total energy of that region of space has been cast into doubt by which of the following?

(A) Findings from laboratory experiments
(B) Findings from observational field experiments
(C) Accidental observations made during other experiments
(D) Discovery of several erroneous propositions in accepted theories
(E) Predictions based on theoretical work

19. It can be inferred from the passage that scientists are currently making efforts to observe which of the following events?

(A) The decay of a vacuum in the presence of virtual particles
(B) The decay of a vacuum next to a superheavy atomic nucleus
(C) The creation of a superheavy atomic nucleus next to an intense electric field
(D) The creation of a virtual electron and a virtual positron as a result of fluctuations of a vacuum
(E) The creation of a charged vacuum in which only real electrons can be created in the vacuum's region of space

GO ON TO THE NEXT PAGE.

20. Physicists' recent investigations of the decay of the vacuum, as described in the passage, most closely resemble which of the following hypothetical events in other disciplines?

(A) On the basis of data gathered in a carefully controlled laboratory experiment, a chemist predicts and then demonstrates the physical properties of a newly synthesized polymer.
(B) On the basis of manipulations of macroeconomic theory, an economist predicts that, contrary to accepted economic theory, inflation and unemployment will both decline under conditions of rapid economic growth.
(C) On the basis of a rereading of the texts of Jane Austen's novels, a literary critic suggests that, contrary to accepted literary interpretations, Austen's plots were actually metaphors for political events in early nineteenth-century England.
(D) On the basis of data gathered in carefully planned observations of several species of birds, a biologist proposes a modification in the accepted theory of interspecies competition.
(E) On the basis of a study of observations incidentally recorded in ethnographers' descriptions of non-Western societies, an anthropologist proposes a new theory of kinship relations.

21. According to the passage, the author considers the reduction of energy in an empty region of space to which a real particle has been added to be

(A) a well-known process
(B) a frequent occurrence
(C) a fleeting aberration
(D) an unimportant event
(E) an unexpected outcome

22. According to the passage, virtual particles differ from real particles in which of the following ways?

I. Virtual particles have extremely short lifetimes.
II. Virtual particles are created in an intense electric field.
III. Virtual particles cannot be detected directly.

(A) I only
(B) II only
(C) III only
(D) I and II only
(E) I and III only

23. The author's assertions concerning the conditions that lead to the decay of the vacuum would be most weakened if which of the following occurred?

(A) Scientists created an electric field next to a vacuum, but found that the electric field was not intense enough to create a charged vacuum.
(B) Scientists assembled a superheavy atomic nucleus next to a vacuum, but found that no virtual particles were created in the vacuum's region of space.
(C) Scientists assembled a superheavy atomic nucleus next to a vacuum, but found that they could not then detect any real particles in the vacuum's region of space.
(D) Scientists introduced a virtual electron and a virtual positron into a vacuum's region of space, but found that the vacuum did not then fluctuate.
(E) Scientists introduced a real electron and a real positron into a vacuum's region of space, but found that the total energy of the space increased by the energy equivalent of the mass of the particles.

GO ON TO THE NEXT PAGE.

Simone de Beauvoir's work greatly influenced Betty Friedan's—indeed, made it possible. Why, then, was it Friedan who became the prophet of women's emancipation in the United States? Political conditions, as well as a certain anti-intellectual bias, prepared Americans and the American media to better receive Friedan's deradicalized and highly pragmatic *The Feminine Mystique*, published in 1963, than Beauvoir's theoretical reading of women's situation in *The Second Sex*. In 1953 when *The Second Sex* first appeared in translation in the United States, the country had entered the silent, fearful fortress of the anticommunist McCarthy years (1950-1954), and Beauvoir was suspected of Marxist sympathies. Even *The Nation*, a generally liberal magazine, warned its readers against "certain political leanings" of the author. Open acknowledgement of the existence of women's oppression was too radical for the United States in the fifties, and Beauvoir's conclusion, that change in women's economic condition, though insufficient by itself, "remains the basic factor" in improving women's situation, was particularly unacceptable.

24. According to the passage, one difference between *The Feminine Mystique* and *The Second Sex* is that Friedan's book

(A) rejects the idea that women are oppressed
(B) provides a primarily theoretical analysis of women's lives
(C) does not reflect the political beliefs of its author
(D) suggests that women's economic condition has no impact on their status
(E) concentrates on the practical aspects of the question of women's emancipation

25. The author quotes from *The Nation* most probably in order to

(A) modify an earlier assertion
(B) point out a possible exception to her argument
(C) illustrate her central point
(D) clarify the meaning of a term
(E) cite an expert opinion

26. It can be inferred from the passage that which of the following is not a factor in the explanation of why *The Feminine Mystique* was received more positively in the United States than was *The Second Sex*?

(A) By 1963 political conditions in the United States had changed.
(B) Friedan's book was less intellectual and abstract than Beauvoir's.
(C) Readers did not recognize the powerful influence of Beauvoir's book on Friedan's ideas.
(D) Friedan's approach to the issue of women's emancipation was less radical than Beauvoir's.
(E) American readers were more willing to consider the problem of the oppression of women in the sixties than they had been in the fifties.

27. According to the passage, Beauvoir's book asserted that the status of women

(A) is the outcome of political oppression
(B) is inherently tied to their economic condition
(C) can be best improved under a communist government
(D) is a theoretical, rather than a pragmatic, issue
(E) is a critical area of discussion in Marxist economic theory

GO ON TO THE NEXT PAGE.

Directions: Each question below consists of a word printed in capital letters, followed by five lettered words or phrases. Choose the lettered word or phrase that is most nearly opposite in meaning to the word in capital letters.

Since some of the questions require you to distinguish fine shades of meaning, be sure to consider all the choices before deciding which one is best.

28. STERILIZE: (A) uncover (B) irritate (C) contaminate (D) operate (E) agitate

29. INADVERTENT: (A) well known (B) quite similar (C) fortunate (D) normal (E) intentional

30. SUBLIMINAL: (A) adroit (B) gentle (C) downcast (D) able to be manipulated (E) at a perceptible level

31. PLACATE: (A) avert (B) antagonize (C) procure (D) subside (E) revolt

32. INUNDATE: (A) drain (B) erupt (C) exit (D) decelerate (E) disturb

33. FLOURISH:
(A) lack of consistency
(B) lack of embellishment
(C) lack of sense
(D) lack of spontaneity
(E) lack of substance

34. SUMMARILY:
(A) after long deliberation
(B) with benevolent intent
(C) in general disagreement
(D) under close scrutiny
(E) from questionable premises

35. STOLID: (A) excitable (B) friendly (C) slender (D) brittle (E) weak

36. IDYLL:
(A) negative appraisal
(B) pedestrian argument
(C) object created for a purpose
(D) experience fraught with tension
(E) action motivated by greed

37. ASPERITY:
(A) failure of imagination
(B) brevity of speech
(C) sureness of judgment
(D) mildness of temper
(E) lack of beauty

38. DESULTORY:
(A) highly inimical
(B) cheerfully accepted
(C) strongly highlighted
(D) lightly considered
(E) strictly methodical

STOP

IF YOU FINISH BEFORE TIME IS CALLED, YOU MAY CHECK YOUR WORK ON THIS SECTION ONLY. DO NOT TURN TO ANY OTHER SECTION IN THE TEST.

SECTION 2

Time—30 minutes

30 Questions

Numbers: All numbers used are real numbers.

Figures: Position of points, angles, regions, etc. can be assumed to be in the order shown; and angle measures can be assumed to be positive.

Lines shown as straight can be assumed to be straight.

Figures can be assumed to lie in a plane unless otherwise indicated.

Figures that accompany questions are intended to provide information useful in answering the questions. However, unless a note states that a figure is drawn to scale, you should solve these problems NOT by estimating sizes by sight or by measurement, but by using your knowledge of mathematics (see Example 2 below).

Directions: Each of the Questions 1-15 consists of two quantities, one in Column A and one in Column B. You are to compare the two quantities and choose

A if the quantity in Column A is greater;
B if the quantity in Column B is greater;
C if the two quantities are equal;
D if the relationship cannot be determined from the information given.

Note: Since there are only four choices, NEVER MARK (E).

Common Information: In a question, information concerning one or both of the quantities to be compared is centered above the two columns. A symbol that appears in both columns represents the same thing in Column A as it does in Column B.

	Column A	Column B	Sample Answers
Example 1:	2×6	$2 + 6$	● Ⓑ Ⓒ Ⓓ Ⓔ

Examples 2-4 refer to $\triangle PQR$.

R, x°, y°, w°, z°, P, N, Q

	Column A	Column B	Sample Answers
Example 2:	PN	NQ	Ⓐ Ⓑ Ⓒ ● Ⓔ (since equal measures cannot be assumed, even though PN and NQ appear equal)
Example 3:	x	y	Ⓐ ● Ⓒ Ⓓ Ⓔ (since N is between P and Q)
Example 4:	$w + z$	180	Ⓐ Ⓑ ● Ⓓ Ⓔ (since PQ is a straight line)

GO ON TO THE NEXT PAGE.

A if the quantity in Column A is greater;
B if the quantity in Column B is greater;
C if the two quantities are equal;
D if the relationship cannot be determined from the information given.

	Column A	Column B
1.	$3{,}960 \div 65$	60

Team X scored 10 points in the first half of a certain game. In the second half of the game, team Y scored 15 points more than team X.

	Column A	Column B
2.	The number of points scored by team X in the first half of the game	The number of points scored by team Y in the first half of the game
3.	$\frac{5}{8}$	$\frac{7}{11}$

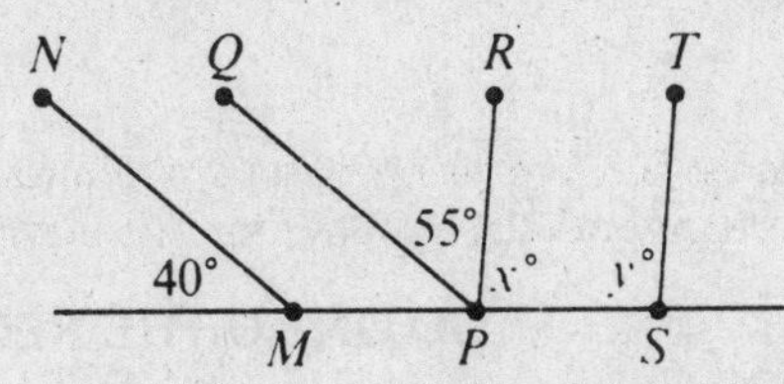

$MN \parallel PQ$ and $PR \parallel ST$

	Column A	Column B
4.	$y - x$	15

$\frac{3}{4}y - 5 = 7$

	Column A	Column B
5.	y	15
6.	90 percent of 30	13.5 percent of 200

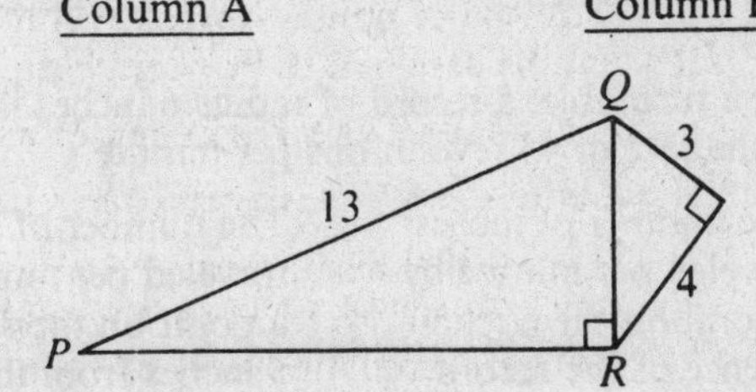

	Column A	Column B
7.	The perimeter of triangle PQR	36

$x > y > w > 0$

	Column A	Column B
8.	$\frac{xy}{w}$	$\frac{yw}{x}$
9.	$4 + 2\sqrt{2}$	$2 + 4\sqrt{2}$
10.	$x + y$	$p + q$

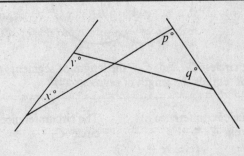

GO ON TO THE NEXT PAGE.

A if the quantity in Column A is greater;
B if the quantity in Column B is greater;
C if the two quantities are equal;
D if the relationship cannot be determined from the information given.

	Column A	Column B

On a turntable, a record of radius 6 inches is rotating at the rate of 45 revolutions per minute.

	Column A	Column B
11.	The number of inches traveled per minute by a point on the circumference of the record	The number of inches traveled per minute by a point on the record 5 inches from the center of the record
12.	The greatest even factor of 180 that is less than 90	The greatest odd factor of 180

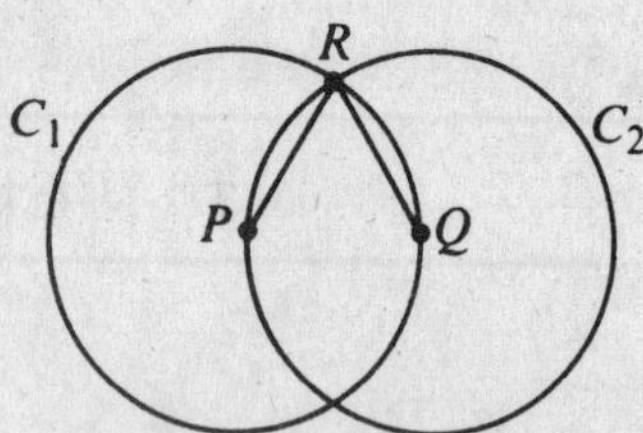

In circles C_1 and C_2, the length of segment PR equals the length of segment QR.

	Column A	Column B
13.	The circumference of circle C_1	The circumference of circle C_2

In a history class that consisted of 30 students, the number of seniors was 3 more than twice the number of juniors, and $\frac{3}{10}$ of the students were neither juniors nor seniors.

	Column A	Column B
14.	The number of juniors in the class	6
15.	$4x^2 + 4y^2$	$(2x + 2y)^2$

GO ON TO THE NEXT PAGE.

Directions: Each of the Questions 16-30 has five answer choices. For each of these questions, select the best of the answer choices given.

16. If 25 percent of a certain number is 1,600, what is 10 percent of the number?

(A) 40
(B) 400
(C) 640
(D) 1,440
(E) 4,000

17. The ratio of 1.8 to 2 is equal to the ratio of

(A) 9 to 1
(B) 9 to 10
(C) 9 to 20
(D) 18 to 100
(E) 18 to 200

18. If $2x + 7 = 12$, then $4x - 7 =$

(A) 2 (B) 2.5 (C) 3 (D) 10 (E) 13

19. If $x + y = n$, then $x^2 + 2xy + y^2 =$

(A) $2n$
(B) n^2
(C) $n(x-y)$
(D) $n^2 + 2y(n-y)$
(E) $n^2 + xn - x^2$

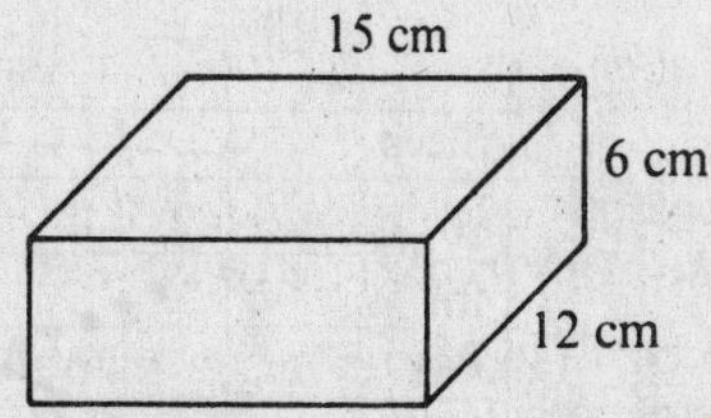

20. What is the maximum number of cubes, each 3 centimeters on an edge, that can be packed into a rectangular box with inside dimensions as shown above?

(A) 360 (B) 120 (C) 90 (D) 40 (E) 20

GO ON TO THE NEXT PAGE.

Questions 21-25 refer to the following graphs.

AVERAGE NUMBER OF HOURS PER WEEK SPENT IN MAJOR TYPES OF ACTIVITIES BY EMPLOYED PERSONS

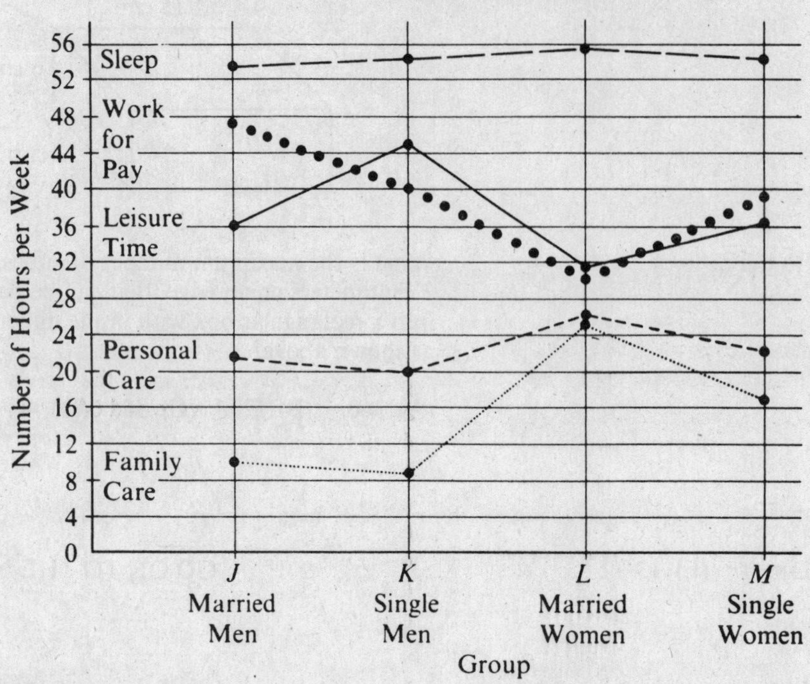

AVERAGE NUMBER OF HOURS PER WEEK SPENT IN LEISURE-TIME ACTIVITIES BY EMPLOYED PERSONS

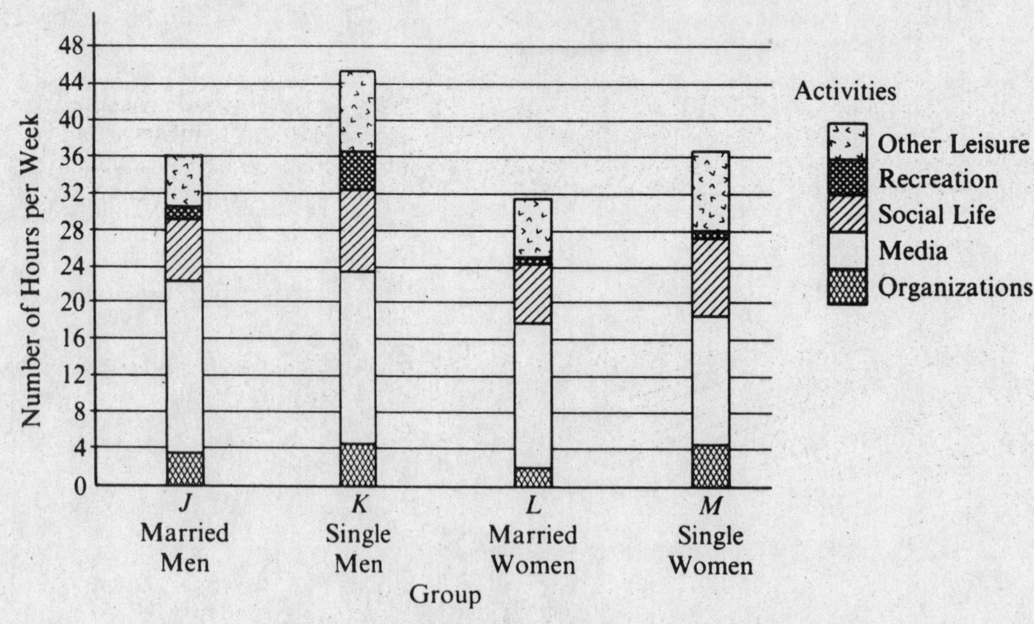

Note: Graphs drawn to scale.

GO ON TO THE NEXT PAGE.

21. In which major type of activity is the average number of hours spent per week most nearly the same for all four groups?

(A) Sleep
(B) Work for pay
(C) Leisure time
(D) Personal care
(E) Family care

22. Approximately what is the average number of hours per week that employed single women spend in leisure-time activities?

(A) 47 (B) 39 (C) 37 (D) 30 (E) 17

23. Approximately what is the average number of hours per week that employed married men spend on media activities?

(A) 12
(B) 16
(C) 19
(D) 22
(E) 25

24. Which of the following lists the four groups from least to greatest with respect to the average number of hours per week that each spends working for pay?

(A) J, K, M, L
(B) J, L, M, K
(C) L, J, M, K
(D) L, K, M, J
(E) L, M, K, J

25. Approximately what percent of the average number of hours per week spent in leisure-time activities by employed single men is spent on social-life activities?

(A) 5% (B) 9% (C) 15%
(D) 20% (E) 27%

26. If x is an integer and $y = 9x + 13$, what is the greatest value of x for which y is less than 100 ?

(A) 12 (B) 11 (C) 10 (D) 9 (E) 8

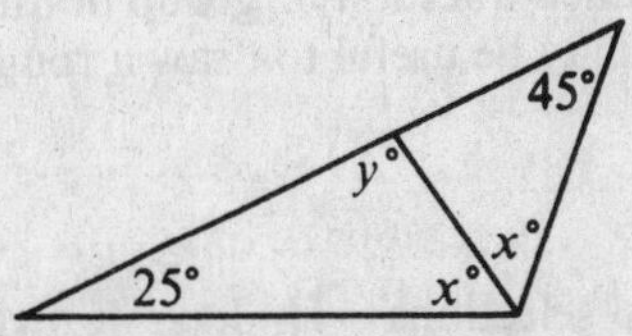

27. What is the value of y in the figure above?

(A) 70 (B) 80 (C) 90
(D) 100 (E) 110

28. What is the perimeter, in meters, of a rectangular playground 24 meters wide that has the same area as a rectangular playground 64 meters long and 48 meters wide?

(A) 112
(B) 152
(C) 224
(D) 256
(E) 304

29. Saplings are to be planted 30 feet apart along one side of a straight lane 455 feet long. If the first sapling is to be planted at one end of the lane, how many saplings are needed?

(A) 18 (B) 16 (C) $15\frac{1}{6}$ (D) 15 (E) 14

30. The average (arithmetic mean) of five numbers is 25. After one of the numbers is removed, the average (arithmetic mean) of the remaining numbers is 31. What number has been removed?

(A) 1
(B) 6
(C) 11
(D) 24
(E) It cannot be determined from the information given.

STOP

IF YOU FINISH BEFORE TIME IS CALLED, YOU MAY CHECK YOUR WORK ON THIS SECTION ONLY. DO NOT TURN TO ANY OTHER SECTION IN THE TEST.

SECTION 3

Time—30 minutes

25 Questions

Directions: Each question or group of questions is based on a passage or set of conditions. In answering some of the questions, it may be useful to draw a rough diagram. For each question, select the best answer choice given.

Questions 1-7

Seven musical selections—H, I, J, K, M, O, and P—must appear on a single two-sided long-playing record. For a given side, any choice of selections and any sequence of selections will be acceptable so long as the following conditions are met:

P must be first or last on a side.
H must be placed on the same side as M, either immediately before M or immediately after M.
I cannot be placed on the same side as K.
O can be placed on the same side as H, but neither immediately before nor immediately after H.
Side 1 cannot begin with K.
Each side must have at least two selections.
Each selection must appear on the record exactly one time.

1. If side 2 begins with K, which of the following selections must appear on side 1 ?

(A) H
(B) I
(C) J
(D) M
(E) O

2. If side 1 has exactly three selections and the first is O, which of the following could be the other two selections on side 1 ?

(A) H followed by I
(B) I followed by K
(C) J followed by H
(D) K followed by P
(E) P followed by J

3. Which of the following is a possible arrangement, in order, of the seven musical selections?

	Side 1	Side 2
(A)	H, M, K, P	I, O, J
(B)	P, O, H, M	K, I, J
(C)	I, O, J	M, H, P, K
(D)	J, O, M	H, I, P, K
(E)	K, H, P	O, M, I, J

4. If I and J are the only selections on side 1, which of the following is a possible order of the selections for side 2 ?

(A) H, M, O, P, K
(B) K, H, O, M, P
(C) M, H, O, K, P
(D) P, H, M, O, K
(E) P, M, O, K, H

5. If side 2 contains exactly four selections, beginning with M and ending with K, which of the following must be true?

(A) H appears on side 1.
(B) I appears on side 2.
(C) J appears on side 2.
(D) O is the first selection on side 1.
(E) P is the last selection on side 1.

6. If O, H, and P are among the selections on side 1, which of the following must be true?

(A) I appears on side 1.
(B) K appears on side 2.
(C) J is the first selection on side 2.
(D) Side 2 has exactly three selections.
(E) Side 1 has exactly five selections.

7. If I, J, and P are all of the selections that appear on side 1, and side 2 begins with M, which of the following must be true?

(A) The second selection on side 2 is K.
(B) The third selection on side 2 is H.
(C) The third selection on side 2 is O.
(D) The last selection on side 2 is H.
(E) The last selection on side 2 is O.

GO ON TO THE NEXT PAGE.

8. Many farmers in the United States are turning away from synthetic fertilizers and pesticides, whose costs are rising rapidly, and choosing systems of organic farming designed to replenish nutrients in the soil. Studies indicate that although in some instances crop yields are lower in the years immediately after a farmer converts from a chemical to an organic system, the farmer's net income in each of those years is nevertheless likely to be higher.

   Which of the following, if true, would help explain why the farmer's annual net income is likely to be higher following conversion to an organic system?

   (A) The most successful systems of organic farming are intended to ensure the continued productivity of farmland.
   (B) The amount of money the farmer loses by reducing crop yield is generally less than the amount the farmer saves in production costs by switching from chemical farming to an organic system.
   (C) Farmers for whom environmental concerns are paramount are willing to take financial losses to avoid synthetic fertilizers and pesticides.
   (D) By growing nitrogen-fixing plants alongside a cash crop over a period of years, a farmer can usually increase crop yield dramatically.
   (E) Many farmers who have purchased equipment used in chemical farming feel that they have irrevocably committed themselves to using synthetic fertilizers and pesticides.

9. For some years health authorities have believed that people with high blood pressure (hypertension) should restrict their salt intake. Recently scientists found in a large, well-designed study that those with chronic hypertension consume less salt than do their counterparts with normal blood pressure.

   If it is true that a diet relatively high in salt is causally linked to the onset of hypertension, which of the following, if true, most plausibly accounts for the new findings?

   (A) Only a minority of those with hypertension have been properly diagnosed.
   (B) Chronic hypertension is not a serious problem in the population studied.
   (C) Most people with chronic hypertension have intentionally restricted their salt intake.
   (D) Hypertension occurs most frequently in those who have a family history of hypertension.
   (E) Excess salt intake is inherently dangerous to health.

10. A successful defense against attack by ballistic missiles would have to be controlled by a large-scale computer system.

    A defense against attack by ballistic missiles, to be successful, would have to work on first use, and a full preliminary test would be impossible.

    Despite careful planning, every large-scale computer system has on use proved to have flaws that in some situations would cause serious failure.

    If the statements above are true, which of the following conclusions is best supported by them?

    (A) If care is taken in planning the computer system to be used for defense against attack by ballistic missiles, there is a high probability that the defense system will be successful if and when it is needed.
    (B) Methods for reducing errors in constructing large-scale computer systems will not be found.
    (C) A defense against ballistic missile attack will not work successfully when it is first called on.
    (D) Some means for control other than a large-scale computer system will have to be found for a system for defense against ballistic missiles.
    (E) A defense against attack by ballistic missiles cannot be assured of success the first time it is used.

GO ON TO THE NEXT PAGE.

Questions 11-16

A builder is planning the colors to be used for painting the rooms and hallways of a group of new houses. The builder will use only one color for each room or hallway and will select from the following colors: warm colors—rose and peach; neutral colors—ivory and gold; cool colors—aqua, blue, and lavender.

Two colors are adjacent if two rooms, two hallways, or a room and a hallway that are painted in the colors are connected by a door. The builder will observe the following restrictions:

No two different warm colors can be adjacent.
No two different cool colors can be adjacent.
Aqua cannot be adjacent to peach or rose.
Lavender cannot be adjacent to ivory.

There are no further restrictions.

11. Which of the following colors can be used for painting a hallway that is connected by doors to only two rooms, which will be painted aqua and blue?

(A) Rose
(B) Peach
(C) Ivory
(D) Aqua
(E) Lavender

12. The builder can use which of the following color schemes where the only doors in two adjacent rooms are doors that connect the rooms to each other and connect each of the rooms to a common hallway, itself not connected to any other rooms?

	First Room	Second Room	Hallway
(A)	Rose	Peach	Ivory
(B)	Aqua	Gold	Ivory
(C)	Aqua	Ivory	Blue
(D)	Ivory	Blue	Lavender
(E)	Rose	Gold	Aqua

13. Which of the following color schemes can the builder use for three rooms and a hallway if there are doors between room 1 and room 2 and between room 2 and room 3, and if room 1 and room 3 are both connected by doors to a common hallway?

	Room 1	Room 2	Room 3	Hallway
(A)	Blue	Ivory	Rose	Lavender
(B)	Aqua	Rose	Ivory	Lavender
(C)	Blue	Ivory	Rose	Ivory
(D)	Lavender	Blue	Lavender	Rose
(E)	Ivory	Blue	Aqua	Rose

14. Which of the following colors can be used for a hallway that is connected by doors to each of seven rooms, when each of the rooms will be painted a different color?

(A) Rose
(B) Peach
(C) Ivory
(D) Gold
(E) Aqua

15. Which of the following colors can be used for a room that is connected by doors to each of three rooms that are painted lavender, blue, and peach, respectively?

(A) Ivory
(B) Rose
(C) Peach
(D) Blue
(E) Aqua

16. The builder can use all of the colors in which of the following sets of colors to paint the rooms and hallways on an entire floor, no matter how the doors are arranged among the rooms and hallways?

(A) Ivory, gold
(B) Aqua, lavender
(C) Aqua, ivory, blue
(D) Rose, peach, ivory
(E) Rose, ivory, aqua

GO ON TO THE NEXT PAGE.

Questions 17-22

In a certain emergency medical practice, seven physicians—N, O, P, R, S, T, and U—are assigned to accompany three mobile trauma vans during a single 12-hour shift. Each physician must be assigned to just one of the vans according to the following rules:

At least two physicians must be assigned to van 1.
At least three physicians, one of whom must be S, must be assigned to van 3.
If N is assigned to van 1, R must also be assigned to van 1.
O must be assigned to van 2.
U cannot be assigned to van 3.

17. Which of the following is a possible assignment of the seven physicians to the three vans?

	Van 1	Van 2	Van 3
(A)	N	O, P, R	S, T, U
(B)	N, R	O, S	P, T, U
(C)	N, O	R, U	P, S, T
(D)	R, U	O, N	P, S, T
(E)	R, O	P, U	N, S, T

18. If R is assigned to van 2, which of the following must be true?

(A) N is assigned to van 1.
(B) T is assigned to van 3.
(C) P is assigned to van 1.
(D) P is assigned to van 3.
(E) U is assigned to van 1.

19. If N and U are assigned to van 1, all of the following must be true EXCEPT:

(A) P is assigned to van 2.
(B) T is assigned to van 3.
(C) Exactly one physician is assigned to van 2.
(D) Exactly three physicians are assigned to van 1.
(E) Exactly three physicians are assigned to van 3.

20. If R and U are the only physicians assigned to van 1, which of the following is the largest group of physicians that could possibly be assigned to van 3 ?

(A) O, P
(B) P, T
(C) N, S, T
(D) N, P, S, T
(E) O, P, S, T

21. If exactly three physicians are assigned to van 1, which of the following must be true?

(A) N is assigned to van 3.
(B) R is assigned to van 1.
(C) T is assigned to van 1.
(D) N is assigned to the same van as R.
(E) O alone is assigned to van 2.

22. If R is the only physician not yet assigned, and if, at this point, R could be assigned to any one of the three vans, which of the following must be true?

(A) N is assigned to van 1.
(B) P is assigned to van 1.
(C) P is assigned to van 3.
(D) T is assigned to van 3.
(E) U is assigned to van 1.

---

23. For acrylic, a clear rigid plastic, to be cast, fairly complex molecules must be induced to link up, in a process called polymerization. Polymerization is exothermic; i.e., its net effect is that each time molecules link, a small quantity of heat is generated. In addition, the rate of linking speeds up as temperature increases.

Which of the following can be inferred from the passage above?

(A) The method used to trigger the process of polymerization is a sharp increase in the temperature of the surrounding air.
(B) Unless the heat that results from the linking of molecules is drawn off promptly, there will be a heat buildup at an accelerating rate as acrylic is cast.
(C) In the casting of thin sheets of acrylic, which lose heat quickly to the surrounding air, polymerization proceeds much faster than it does in the casting of thick pieces.
(D) If air temperatures are kept steady when acrylic is cast, the rate at which the molecules link remains constant.
(E) Once the process of polymerization has been induced, it cannot be slowed before all possible links among molecules have been formed.

GO ON TO THE NEXT PAGE.

24. A steady decline in annual movie-ticket sales is about to begin. More than half of the tickets sold last year were sold to the age group under twenty-five years of age, representing twenty-seven percent of the population. However, the number of individuals under twenty-five will steadily decline during the next decade.

Which of the following, if true, casts most doubt on the prediction above regarding future movie-ticket sales?

(A) Medical advances have lowered the mortality rates for those who are forty to sixty years of age.
(B) Many people gradually lose interest in going to the movies after they reach twenty-five years of age.
(C) The number of movie theaters has been increasing, and this trend is expected to continue during the next ten years.
(D) Movie-ticket sales tend to increase as the size of the work force increases, and the size of the work force will increase annually during the next decade.
(E) Experts agree that people under twenty-five years of age will continue to account for more than half of the total number of tickets sold in each of the next ten years.

25. Any lender about to make a loan wishes to know the real rate of interest; i.e., the contractual rate of interest less the rate of inflation. But what rate of inflation to use, past or expected? Past inflation is the better choice, because we have specific firm figures for it so that the real rate of interest will also emerge as a specific figure.

Which of the following, if true, is the strongest point that an opponent of the position above might make in arguing that the rate of expected inflation is the proper figure to use?

(A) Since the contractual interest is future income to a prospective lender, it is more appropriate to adjust that income in terms of inflation expected for the future.
(B) Since estimating the rate of expected inflation presupposes careful economic analysis, lenders might derive coincidental benefits from doing such an estimate.
(C) The rate of expected inflation will differ little from the rate of past inflation when inflation is steady.
(D) No official rate of past inflation is computed for any period shorter than a month.
(E) The official rate of past inflation is a figure that depends on what commodities, in what proportions, determine the official price index.

STOP

IF YOU FINISH BEFORE TIME IS CALLED, YOU MAY CHECK YOUR WORK ON THIS SECTION ONLY. DO NOT TURN TO ANY OTHER SECTION IN THE TEST.

Section 4 starts on page 333.

NO TEST MATERIAL ON THIS PAGE

SECTION 4

Time—30 minutes
38 Questions

Directions: Each sentence below has one or two blanks, each blank indicating that something has been omitted. Beneath the sentence are five lettered words or sets of words. Choose the word or set of words for each blank that best fits the meaning of the sentence as a whole.

1. Aspartame, a new artificial sugar substitute, is only ------- replacement for saccharin because, unlike saccharin, it breaks down and loses its sweetening characteristics at high temperatures, making it ------- for baking.

(A) an interim. .ideal
(B) an apparent. .excellent
(C) a potential. .versatile
(D) a significant. .problematic
(E) a partial. .unsuitable

2. Trapped thousands of years ago in Antarctic ice, recently discovered air bubbles are ------- time capsules filled with information for scientists who chart the history of the atmosphere.

(A) inconsequential (B) broken (C) veritable (D) resplendent (E) impenetrable

3. In the days before the mass marketing of books, censorship was ------- source of -------, which helped the sale of the book and inspired Ralph Waldo Emerson to remark: "Every burned book enlightens the world."

(A) a respected. .opinion
(B) a constant. .guidance
(C) a prime. .publicity
(D) an unnoticed. .opposition
(E) an unpromising. .criticism

4. It was not only the ------- of geologists that ------- earlier development of the revolutionary idea that the Earth's continents were moving plates; classical physicists, who could not then explain the mechanism, had declared continental movement impossible.

(A) indecisiveness. .challenged
(B) radicalism. .deterred
(C) conservatism. .hindered
(D) assumptions. .hastened
(E) resistance. .mandated

5. Although often extremely critical of the medical profession as a whole, people are rarely willing to treat their personal doctors with equal -------.

(A) impetuosity (B) sarcasm (C) mockery (D) contempt (E) condescension

6. Aalto, like other modernists, believed that form follows function; consequently, his furniture designs asserted the ------- of human needs, and the furniture's form was ------- human use.

(A) universality. .refined by
(B) importance. .relegated to
(C) rationale. .emphasized by
(D) primacy. .determined by
(E) variability. .reflected in

7. A ------- acceptance of contemporary forms of social behavior has misled a few into believing that values in conflict with the present age are for all practical purposes -------.

(A) casual. .reliable
(B) superficial. .trenchant
(C) complacent. .superseded
(D) cautious. .redemptive
(E) plaintive. .redundant

GO ON TO THE NEXT PAGE.

Directions: In each of the following questions, a related pair of words or phrases is followed by five lettered pairs of words or phrases. Select the lettered pair that best expresses a relationship similar to that expressed in the original pair.

8. TEACHER : CERTIFICATION ::
(A) driver : license (B) officer : handcuffs
(C) librarian : book (D) mechanic : tool
(E) architect : blueprint

9. FOOD : NOURISH :: (A) organ : secrete
(B) fluids : circulate (C) cells : degenerate
(D) antibodies : protect (E) fats : saturate

10. HACK : CARVE :: (A) grind : polish
(B) snip : mince (C) hew : fell
(D) whet : blunt (E) gouge : engrave

11. DETOXIFY : POISON :: (A) determine : certainty
(B) destabilize : deviance (C) disguise : costume
(D) dissolve : liquid (E) dehydrate : water

12. SUPERIMPOSE : ABOVE ::
(A) permeate : beside (B) focus : around
(C) insert : between (D) splice : below
(E) fuse : behind

13. TAMPER : ADJUST ::
(A) misrepresent : communicate
(B) warp : deform
(C) confess : tell
(D) mar : deface
(E) undermine : stop

14. METAPHOR : LITERAL ::
(A) biography : accurate
(B) melody : spoken
(C) poem : rhythmic
(D) anthem : patriotic
(E) ballet : intricate

15. COURAGE : RASHNESS ::
(A) generosity : prodigality
(B) temperance : modesty
(C) mettle : spirit
(D) honor : humility
(E) compassion : contempt

16. PRESCIENCE : FUTURE ::
(A) irrationality : sanity
(B) predictability : past
(C) irascibility : emotions
(D) erudition : esoterica
(E) talkativeness : loquacity

GO ON TO THE NEXT PAGE.

Directions: Each passage in this group is followed by questions based on its content. After reading a passage, choose the best answer to each question. Answer all questions following a passage on the basis of what is stated or implied in that passage.

One of the questions of interest in the study of the evolution of spiders is whether the weaving of orb webs evolved only once or several times. About half the 35,000 known kinds of spiders make webs; a third of the web weavers make orb webs. Since most orb weavers belong either to the Araneidae or the Uloboridae families, the origin of the orb web can be determined only by ascertaining whether the families are related.

Recent taxonomic analysis of individuals from both families indicates that the families evolved from different ancestors, thereby contradicting Wiehle's theory. This theory postulates that the families must be related, based on the assumption that complex behavior, such as web building, could evolve only once. According to Kullman, web structure is the only characteristic that suggests a relationship between families. The families differ in appearance, structure of body hair, and arrangement of eyes. Only Uloborids lack venom glands. Further identification and study of characteristic features will undoubtedly answer the question of the evolution of the orb web.

17. The primary purpose of the passage is to

(A) settle the question of whether orb webs evolved once or more than once
(B) describe scientific speculation concerning an issue related to the evolution of orb webs
(C) analyze the differences between the characteristic features of spiders in the Araneidae and Uloboridae families
(D) question the methods used by earlier investigators of the habits of spiders
(E) demonstrate that Araneidae spiders are not related to Uloboridae spiders

18. It can be inferred from the passage that all orb-weaving spiders belong to types of spiders that

(A) lack venom glands
(B) are included either in the Uloboridae or Araneidae families
(C) share few characteristic features with other spider types
(D) comprise less than a third of all known types of spiders
(E) are more recently evolved than other types of spiders

19. According to the passage, members of the Araneidae family can be distinguished from members of the Uloboridae family by all of the following EXCEPT

(A) the presence of venom glands
(B) the type of web they spin
(C) the structure of their body hair
(D) the arrangement of their eyes
(E) their appearance

20. Which of the following statements, if true, most weakens Wiehle's theory that complex behavior could evolve only once?

(A) Horses, introduced to the New World by the Spaniards, thrived under diverse climatic conditions.
(B) Plants of the Palmaceae family, descendants of a common ancestor, evolved unique seed forms even though the plants occupy similar habitats throughout the world.
(C) All mammals are descended from a small, rodentlike animal whose physical characteristics in some form are found in all its descendants.
(D) Plants in the Cactaceae and Euphorbiaceae families, although they often look alike and have developed similar mechanisms to meet the rigors of the desert, evolved independently.
(E) The Cuban anole, which was recently introduced in the Florida wilds, is quickly replacing the native Florida chameleon because the anole has no competitors.

GO ON TO THE NEXT PAGE.

"Popular art" has a number of meanings, impossible to define with any precision, which range from folklore to junk. The poles are clear enough, but the middle tends to blur. The Hollywood Western of the 1930's, for example, has elements of folklore, but is closer to junk than to high art or folk art. There can be great trash, just as there is bad high art. The musicals of George Gershwin are great popular art, never aspiring to high art. Schubert and Brahms, however, used elements of popular music—folk themes—in works clearly intended as high art. The case of Verdi is a different one: he took a popular genre—bourgeois melodrama set to music (an accurate definition of nineteenth-century opera)—and, without altering its fundamental nature, transmuted it into high art. This remains one of the greatest achievements in music, and one that cannot be fully appreciated without recognizing the essential trashiness of the genre.

As an example of such a transmutation, consider what Verdi made of the typical political elements of nineteenth-century opera. Generally in the plots of these operas, a hero or heroine—usually portrayed only as an individual, unfettered by class—is caught between the immoral corruption of the aristocracy and the doctrinaire rigidity or secret greed of the leaders of the proletariat. Verdi transforms this naïve and unlikely formulation with music of extraordinary energy and rhythmic vitality, music more subtle than it seems at first hearing. There are scenes and arias that still sound like calls to arms and were clearly understood as such when they were first performed. Such pieces lend an immediacy to the otherwise veiled political message of these operas and call up feelings beyond those of the opera itself.

Or consider Verdi's treatment of character. Before Verdi, there were rarely any characters at all in musical drama, only a series of situations which allowed the singers to express a series of emotional states. Any attempt to find coherent psychological portrayal in these operas is misplaced ingenuity. The only coherence was the singer's vocal technique: when the cast changed, new arias were almost always substituted, generally adapted from other operas. Verdi's characters, on the other hand, have genuine consistency and integrity, even if, in many cases, the consistency is that of pasteboard melodrama. The integrity of the character is achieved through the music: once he had become established, Verdi did not rewrite his music for different singers or countenance alterations or substitutions of somebody else's arias in one of his operas, as every eighteenth-century composer had done. When he revised an opera, it was only for dramatic economy and effectiveness.

21. The author refers to Schubert and Brahms in order to suggest

(A) that their achievements are no less substantial than those of Verdi
(B) that their works are examples of great trash
(C) the extent to which Schubert and Brahms influenced the later compositions of Verdi
(D) a contrast between the conventions of nineteenth-century opera and those of other musical forms
(E) that popular music could be employed in compositions intended as high art

22. According to the passage, the immediacy of the political message in Verdi's operas stems from the

(A) vitality and subtlety of the music
(B) audience's familiarity with earlier operas
(C) portrayal of heightened emotional states
(D) individual talents of the singers
(E) verisimilitude of the characters

23. According to the passage, all of the following characterize musical drama before Verdi EXCEPT

(A) arias tailored to a particular singer's ability
(B) adaptation of music from other operas
(C) psychological inconsistency in the portrayal of characters
(D) expression of emotional states in a series of dramatic situations
(E) music used for the purpose of defining a character

GO ON TO THE NEXT PAGE.

24. It can be inferred that the author regards Verdi's revisions to his operas with

(A) regret that the original music and texts were altered
(B) concern that many of the revisions altered the plots of the original work
(C) approval for the intentions that motivated the revisions
(D) puzzlement, since the revisions seem largely insignificant
(E) enthusiasm, since the revisions were aimed at reducing the conventionality of the operas' plots

25. According to the passage, one of Verdi's achievements within the framework of nineteenth-century opera and its conventions was to

(A) limit the extent to which singers influenced the musical composition and performance of his operas
(B) use his operas primarily as forums to protest both the moral corruption and dogmatic rigidity of the political leaders of his time
(C) portray psychologically complex characters shaped by the political environment surrounding them
(D) incorporate elements of folklore into both the music and plots of his operas
(E) introduce political elements into an art form that had traditionally avoided political content

26. Which of the following best describes the relationship of the first paragraph of the passage to the passage as a whole?

(A) It provides a group of specific examples from which generalizations are drawn later in the passage.
(B) It leads to an assertion that is supported by examples later in the passage.
(C) It defines terms and relationships that are challenged in an argument later in the passage.
(D) It briefly compares and contrasts several achievements that are examined in detail later in the passage.
(E) It explains a method of judging a work of art, a method that is used later in the passage.

27. It can be inferred that the author regards the independence from social class of the heroes and heroines of nineteenth-century opera as

(A) an idealized but fundamentally accurate portrayal of bourgeois life
(B) a plot convention with no real connection to political reality
(C) a plot refinement unique to Verdi
(D) a symbolic representation of the position of the bourgeoisie relative to the aristocracy and the proletariat
(E) a convention largely seen as irrelevant by audiences

GO ON TO THE NEXT PAGE.

Directions: Each question below consists of a word printed in capital letters, followed by five lettered words or phrases. Choose the lettered word or phrase that is most nearly opposite in meaning to the word in capital letters.

Since some of the questions require you to distinguish fine shades of meaning, be sure to consider all the choices before deciding which one is best.

28. PERISH: (A) move on (B) survive (C) come after (D) transgress (E) strive

29. UNPREDICTABLE: (A) sensitive (B) compliant (C) dependable (D) mature (E) laudable

30. TRIBUTE: (A) denunciation (B) torment (C) betrayal (D) menace (E) penalty

31. FINESSE: (A) indecision (B) heavy-handedness (C) extroversion (D) extravagance (E) competitiveness

32. SAP: (A) reinstate (B) condone (C) bolster (D) satiate (E) facilitate

33. CONVOLUTED: (A) symmetrical (B) separate (C) straightforward (D) completely flexible (E) consistently calm

34. MITIGATE: (A) exacerbate (B) preponderate (C) accelerate (D) elevate (E) extrapolate

35. TORPOR: (A) rigidity (B) randomness (C) agility (D) obscurity (E) vigor

36. ZENITH: (A) decline (B) anticlimax (C) foundation (D) nadir (E) abyss

37. VENAL: (A) pleasant (B) clever (C) healthy (D) unstinting (E) incorruptible

38. PERIPATETIC: (A) stationary (B) enclosed (C) discrete (D) essential (E) careful

STOP

IF YOU FINISH BEFORE TIME IS CALLED, YOU MAY CHECK YOUR WORK ON THIS SECTION ONLY.
DO NOT TURN TO ANY OTHER SECTION IN THE TEST.

Section 5 starts on page 340.

SECTION 5

Time—30 minutes

30 Questions

Numbers: All numbers used are real numbers.

Figures: Position of points, angles, regions, etc. can be assumed to be in the order shown; and angle measures can be assumed to be positive.

Lines shown as straight can be assumed to be straight.

Figures can be assumed to lie in a plane unless otherwise indicated.

Figures that accompany questions are intended to provide information useful in answering the questions. However, unless a note states that a figure is drawn to scale, you should solve these problems NOT by estimating sizes by sight or by measurement, but by using your knowledge of mathematics (see Example 2 below).

Directions: Each of the Questions 1-15 consists of two quantities, one in Column A and one in Column B. You are to compare the two quantities and choose

A if the quantity in Column A is greater;
B if the quantity in Column B is greater;
C if the two quantities are equal;
D if the relationship cannot be determined from the information given.

Note: Since there are only four choices, NEVER MARK (E).

Common Information: In a question, information concerning one or both of the quantities to be compared is centered above the two columns. A symbol that appears in both columns represents the same thing in Column A as it does in Column B.

	Column A	Column B	Sample Answers
Example 1:	2×6	$2 + 6$	● Ⓑ Ⓒ Ⓓ Ⓔ

Examples 2-4 refer to $\triangle PQR$.

R, x°, y°, w°, z°, P, N, Q

	Column A	Column B	Sample Answers
Example 2:	PN	NQ	Ⓐ Ⓑ Ⓒ ● Ⓔ (since equal measures cannot be assumed, even though PN and NQ appear equal)
Example 3:	x	y	Ⓐ ● Ⓒ Ⓓ Ⓔ (since N is between P and Q)
Example 4:	$w + z$	180	Ⓐ Ⓑ ● Ⓓ Ⓔ (since PQ is a straight line)

GO ON TO THE NEXT PAGE.

A if the quantity in Column A is greater;
B if the quantity in Column B is greater;
C if the two quantities are equal;
D if the relationship cannot be determined from the information given.

	Column A	Column B
1.	$\frac{2}{3}\left(1-\frac{1}{3}\right)$	$\frac{2}{9}$
	$n = \frac{1}{2} + \frac{1}{4} + \frac{1}{8} + \frac{1}{16}$	
2.	$1 - n$	$\frac{1}{16}$
3.	5^3	3^5
	R and S are distinct points on a circle of radius 1.	
4.	The length of line segment RS	2
	$x < 5$ and $y > 12$.	
5.	$y - x$	7
	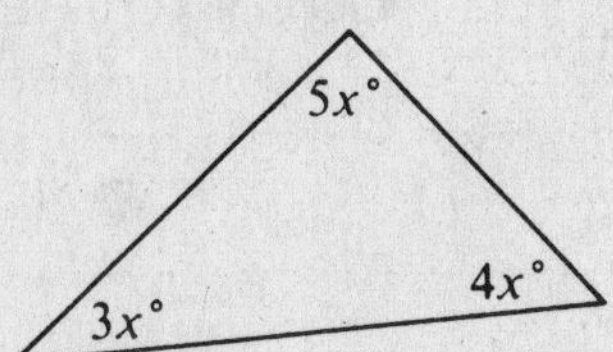	
6.	x	20
7.	$\frac{\sqrt{8}}{\sqrt{2}}$	$\frac{\sqrt{12}}{\sqrt{3}}$

	Column A	Column B
	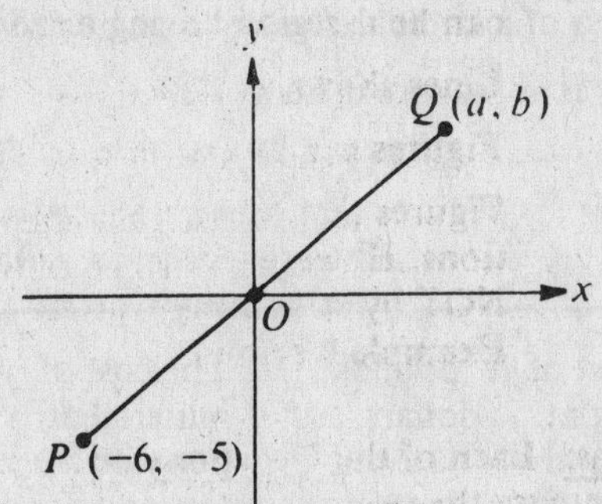	
8.	a	b
	$3x = 4y$ $xy \neq 0$	
9.	The ratio of x to y	The ratio of y to x
	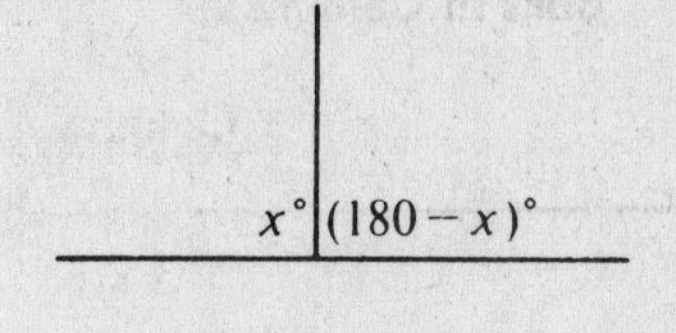	
10.	x	$180 - x$

GO ON TO THE NEXT PAGE.

A if the quantity in Column A is greater;
B if the quantity in Column B is greater;
C if the two quantities are equal;
D if the relationship cannot be determined from the information given.

	Column A	Column B
	The area of a circular region having a radius of $\frac{1}{4}$ meter is x square meters.	
11.	x	$\frac{1}{4}$
12.	The cost of x pounds of meat at y dollars per pound	The cost of y yards of material at x dollars per yard
	$(a + 5)(a - 5) = 0$ $(b + 5)(b - 5) = 0$	
13.	$a + 5$	$b + 5$

	Column A	Column B
	Average (arithmetic mean) of Test Scores in Class R	
	Average score for the boys 90 Average score for the girls 81 Average score for the class 84	
14.	The number of boys in the class who took the test	The number of girls in the class who took the test
	$x > 1$ $y > 1$	
15.	$\dfrac{1}{\frac{1}{x} + \frac{1}{y}}$	$\frac{1}{x} + \frac{1}{y}$

GO ON TO THE NEXT PAGE.

Directions: Each of the Questions 16-30 has five answer choices. For each of these questions, select the best of the answer choices given.

16. If $\frac{1}{7}$ of a certain number is 4, then $\frac{1}{4}$ of the number is

(A) $\frac{7}{16}$

(B) 2

(C) $\frac{16}{7}$

(D) 7

(E) 28

17. At College C there are from 2 to 4 introductory philosophy classes each semester, and each of these classes has from 20 to 30 students enrolled. If one semester 10 percent of the students enrolled in introductory philosophy failed, what is the greatest possible number who failed?

(A) 12
(B) 10
(C) 8
(D) 6
(E) 3

18. The lengths of the sides of triangle T are $x + 1$, $2x$, and $3x$. The sum of the degree measures of the three interior angles of T is

(A) $6x$
(B) $60x$
(C) 90
(D) 180
(E) not determinable from the information given

19. Today is Jack's 12th birthday and his father's 40th birthday. How many years from today will Jack's father be twice as old as Jack is at that time?

(A) 12
(B) 14
(C) 16
(D) 18
(E) 20

20. If $a + b = 10$, then $\left(a + \frac{b}{2}\right) + \left(b + \frac{a}{2}\right) =$

(A) 5
(B) 10
(C) 15
(D) 20
(E) 25

GO ON TO THE NEXT PAGE.

Questions 21-25 refer to the following graphs.

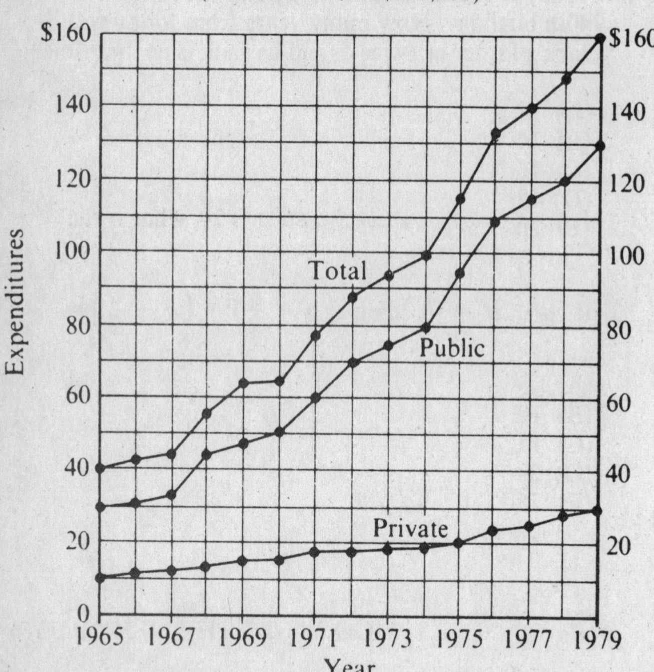

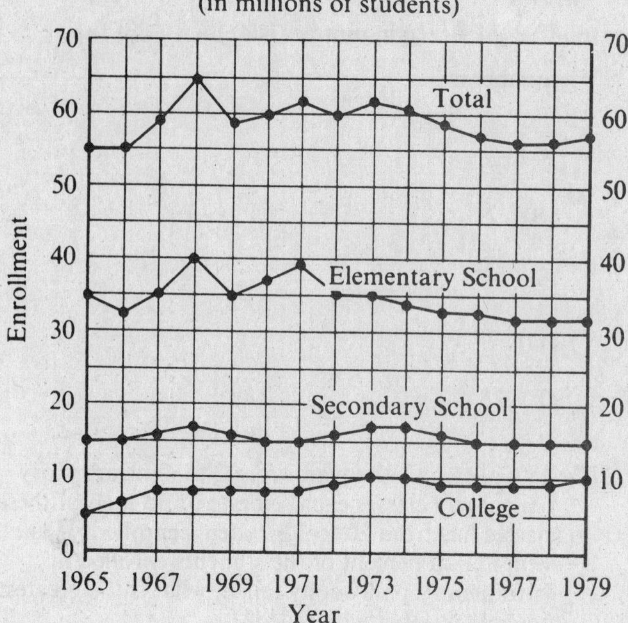

21. Of the following years, which showed the <u>least</u> difference between public school expenditures and private school expenditures?

(A) 1965
(B) 1970
(C) 1974
(D) 1978
(E) 1979

22. For each year from 1965 to 1979, the total enrollment in college, secondary school, and elementary school was in which of the following ranges?

(A) 50 to 60 million
(B) 55 to 60 million
(C) 55 to 65 million
(D) 60 to 65 million
(E) 60 to 70 million

23. In 1970, approximately how many billion dollars were spent on public elementary schools?

(A) 37
(B) 50
(C) 60
(D) 87
(E) It cannot be determined from the information given.

24. Which of the following periods showed a continual increase in the total school enrollment?

(A) 1967-1969
(B) 1969-1971
(C) 1971-1973
(D) 1973-1975
(E) 1975-1977

25. In 1972, public school expenditures were approximately what percent of the total school expenditures for that year?

(A) 20%
(B) 60%
(C) 70%
(D) 80%
(E) 90%

GO ON TO THE NEXT PAGE.

26. If the sum of the first n positive integers is equal to $\frac{n(n+1)}{2}$, then the sum of the first 25 positive integers is

(A) 51
(B) 52
(C) 313
(D) 325
(E) 326

27. If $\frac{2x-1}{3} = \frac{12}{9}$, then $x =$

(A) $\frac{3}{2}$

(B) $\frac{5}{2}$

(C) 4

(D) $\frac{13}{2}$

(E) 7

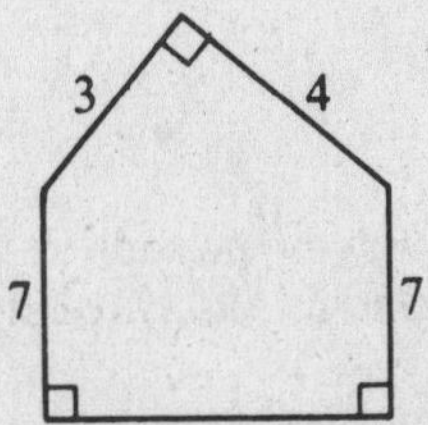

28. What is the perimeter of the pentagon above?

(A) 21
(B) 26
(C) 28
(D) 31
(E) 41

29. If x is positive and y is 1 less than the square of x, which of the following expresses x in terms of y?

(A) $x = y^2 - 1$

(B) $x = y^2 + 1$

(C) $x = \sqrt{y} + 1$

(D) $x = \sqrt{1 - y}$

(E) $x = \sqrt{y + 1}$

30. If the total surface area of a cube is 24, what is the volume of the cube?

(A) 8

(B) 24

(C) 64

(D) $48\sqrt{6}$

(E) 216

STOP

IF YOU FINISH BEFORE TIME IS CALLED, YOU MAY CHECK YOUR WORK ON THIS SECTION ONLY. DO NOT TURN TO ANY OTHER SECTION IN THE TEST.

SECTION 6

Time—30 minutes

25 Questions

Directions: Each question or group of questions is based on a passage or set of conditions. In answering some of the questions, it may be useful to draw a rough diagram. For each question, select the best answer choice given.

Questions 1- 4

A gardener will plant eight fruit trees in eight evenly spaced holes dug along a fence line. He has learned the following:

The types of fruit tree that do well in his area are apple, apricot, cherry, peach, pear, and plum. He will make his selection from that group.

Apple, apricot, peach, and pear trees require cross-pollination to bear fruit and must therefore be grown in pairs of a kind, immediately next to each other in the row.

If both plums and peaches are to be planted, each kind will produce more fruit if separated from the other kind by at least three other trees.

The gardener will plant no more than two trees of any one type. He must prepare a plan for planting that will maximize the probability that all of the trees he plants will bear as much fruit as possible.

1. In a plan that meets his requirements, the gardener could plant exactly one of which of the following types of trees?

(A) Apple
(B) Apricot
(C) Peach
(D) Pear
(E) Plum

2. If an apple tree is planted in the first hole in the row along the fence, the tree planted in the second hole must be

(A) an apple tree
(B) an apricot tree
(C) a cherry tree
(D) a plum tree
(E) a pear tree

3. Which of the following is an acceptable order of trees in the row along the fence?

(A) Apple, apple, pear, peach, plum, pear, peach, plum
(B) Apple, apple, pear, pear, apricot, apricot, peach, peach
(C) Peach, apple, apple, pear, pear, cherry, plum, peach
(D) Peach, apple, apple, pear, pear, cherry, plum, plum
(E) Plum, peach, peach, cherry, apple, apple, apple, cherry

4. If the gardener plants a peach tree in the fourth hole in the row along the fence, he could plant a plum tree in which of the following holes?

(A) The first
(B) The second
(C) The third
(D) The sixth
(E) The eighth

GO ON TO THE NEXT PAGE.

5. In a recent study on the connection between brain abnormalities and violent behavior, the researcher examined more than three hundred people who had engaged in unusually violent behavior toward friends and family members. In most of the people studied, the researcher found clues of brain abnormalities, including evidence of past brain injury and physical abnormality. The researcher concluded that evidence of brain abnormalities could be used to predict violent behavior.

   Which of the following, if true, would most seriously weaken the researcher's conclusion?

   (A) The incidence of brain abnormalities in the general population is as high as that in the group examined.
   (B) The brain abnormalities discovered in those studied are of two distinct kinds.
   (C) A wide variety of violent actions were exhibited by those studied.
   (D) Those studied in the experiment acted violently toward strangers as well as toward people they knew.
   (E) The study drew its subjects from a large geographical area.

6. Why can human beings outlast many faster four-legged animals when running long distances? Perhaps because early humans evolved as hunters on the hot African savannas. Humans developed the ability to release heat by sweating, but most mammals must pant, a function hard to regulate while running. Also, four-legged animals must adopt a pace that lets them breathe once in mid-stride; otherwise, the impact of the front legs hitting the ground will prevent deep inhalation. Humans can vary the number of breaths per stride, set a pace unsuited to the prey, and so eventually exhaust it.

   The author's explanation of why human beings have evolved as superior distance runners would be most weakened if it were shown that

   (A) early humans typically hunted animals that were less well adapted than humans for long-distance running
   (B) early humans were only one of a number of species that hunted prey on the African savannas
   (C) early humans hunted mainly in groups by sneaking up on prey and trapping it within a circle
   (D) hunting was just as essential for later humans in colder climates as it was for early humans on the African savannas
   (E) human beings of today have retained the ability to run long distances but no longer hunt by chasing prey

7. The government officials of a nation share its citizens' understandings regarding the rules that governments are obligated to honor in their actions. Thus, when a nation deliberately ignores international law, the attitudes of even its government officials will become less favorable toward their government.

   The argument above assumes which of the following?

   (A) People's understandings of governmental obligations change from time to time.
   (B) The citizens of a nation will respond favorably to the nation's attempts to extend its international power by legal means.
   (C) Some officials of totalitarian governments are insensitive to the rules embodied in international law.
   (D) Each nation's citizens believe that international laws are among the rules by which governments ought to operate.
   (E) Elected government officials are more likely to doubt the wisdom of their own government's actions than are appointed government officials.

GO ON TO THE NEXT PAGE.

Questions 8-12

A communications system has exactly four message exchanges, which are called nodes: W, X, Y, and Z. Messages travel from one node directly to another node only as follows:

From W to X, but not vice versa
From W to Y, but not vice versa
From W to Z, and vice versa
From X to Y, and vice versa
From X to Z, but not vice versa
From Z to Y, but not vice versa

A single direct path going in one direction from one node to another is called a leg.

8. If a message is to travel from Y to X over as few legs as possible, it must travel in which of the following ways?

(A) Directly from Y to X
(B) Via W but no other node
(C) Via Z but no other node
(D) Via W and Z, in that order
(E) Via Z and W, in that order

9. Which of the following is a complete and accurate list of nodes to which a message can be sent along exactly one leg from Z?

(A) W
(B) Y
(C) W, Y
(D) X, Y
(E) W, X, Y

10. Which of the following sequences of legs is a path over which a message could travel from X back to X?

(A) From X to W, from W to X
(B) From X to Y, from Y to W, from W to Z, from Z to X
(C) From X to Y, from Y to Z, from Z to W, from W to X
(D) From X to Z, from Z to W, from W to Y, from Y to X
(E) From X to Z, from Z to Y, from Y to W, from W to X

11. If all of the legs in the system are equal in length, and if messages always travel along the shortest possible path, then the longest path any message travels in the system is the path from

(A) X to W
(B) Y to W
(C) Y to Z
(D) Z to W
(E) Z to X

12. If certain restricted messages cannot travel any further than one leg, and if an addition of one leg is to be made to the system so that such restricted messages can be sent from each node to at least two others and also be received by each node from at least two others, then that addition must be from

(A) X to W
(B) Y to W
(C) Y to Z
(D) Z to W
(E) Z to X

GO ON TO THE NEXT PAGE.

Questions 13-18

A conductor is distributing musical pieces I, K, L, M, O, and P between two musical ensembles, the Camerata and the Waites. I and K are the most difficult pieces and O and P are the easiest pieces. There will be a single concert in which each ensemble will perform exactly three pieces and no piece will be performed more than once. The ensembles will take turns performing their pieces. The conductor will reward the ensembles for the preparation of the difficult pieces in the following way:

An ensemble that performs I in a concert in which the other performs O is excused from one rehearsal during the week after the concert.

An ensemble that performs K in a concert in which the other performs P is excused from one rehearsal during the week after the concert.

No other excuses from rehearsals will be given.

13. If the Waites performed O, I, and K, which of the following must be true?

(A) The Waites are not excused from any rehearsals.
(B) The Waites are excused from exactly one rehearsal.
(C) The Waites are excused from exactly two rehearsals.
(D) The Camerata are excused from exactly one rehearsal.
(E) The Camerata are excused from exactly two rehearsals.

14. If P and L are among the pieces the Camerata perform, each of the following is possible EXCEPT:

(A) The Waites are not excused from any rehearsals.
(B) The Waites are excused from exactly one rehearsal.
(C) The Waites are excused from exactly two rehearsals.
(D) The Camerata are excused from exactly one rehearsal.
(E) The Camerata are excused from exactly two rehearsals.

15. If each ensemble is excused from exactly one rehearsal, neither ensemble could have performed both

(A) I and P
(B) K and O
(C) L and M
(D) L and P
(E) M and O

16. If, after each ensemble has performed exactly one piece, one ensemble is already assured of being excused from one rehearsal, which of the following could be the four pieces that have not yet been performed?

(A) I, K, L, P
(B) I, L, M, O
(C) I, L, M, P
(D) I, M, O, P
(E) K, L, M, O

17. If I and P are among the pieces the Camerata perform, which of the following must be true?

(A) At least one of the ensembles will be excused from exactly one rehearsal.
(B) At least one of the ensembles will be excused from exactly two rehearsals.
(C) Exactly one ensemble will not be excused from any rehearsals.
(D) Neither ensemble will be excused from any rehearsals.
(E) Neither ensemble will be excused from exactly one rehearsal.

18. If neither ensemble is excused from any rehearsals, which of the following pieces could have been performed by one of the ensembles?

(A) I, K, and P
(B) I, L, and M
(C) I, O, and P
(D) K, M, and O
(E) K, M, and P

GO ON TO THE NEXT PAGE.

Questions 19-22

After an accidental soaking has destroyed the labels on five identical bottles—bottles 1, 2, 3, 4, and 5—containing similar white powders, a pharmacist must determine which of the bottles contain powder P. She knows that exactly two of the bottles contain powder P, but she does not know what any of the remaining three bottles contain. No bottle contains more than one kind of powder. The pharmacist can use only the following tests on samples of the powders:

Test X: Put a sample of powder into solvent S. If powder P is put into solvent S, it will dissolve. Powder P is not the only kind of powder that will dissolve in solvent S.

Test Y: Mix two samples of powder and put the mixture into water. If powder P is mixed with powder Q and then put into water, the water will turn a distinctive shade of blue. The mixture of powders P and Q is the only means of producing this result in water.

The pharmacist has a supply of powder Q, but it is expensive to use in tests.

19. If the pharmacist mixes a sample of powder Q with a sample from bottle 5 and uses test Y on the mixture, the results will show definitely

(A) whether bottle 5 contains powder Q
(B) whether the powder in bottle 5 dissolves in solvent S
(C) that bottle 5 is one of the bottles containing powder P
(D) whether bottle 5 contains powder P
(E) which kind of powder is contained in bottle 5

20. If the pharmacist puts samples from bottles 1 and 2 into solvent S separately and finds that both samples fail to dissolve, she can properly infer that

(A) she has established which two bottles contain powder P
(B) she will establish which two bottles contain powder P if she uses test X on a sample from exactly one more bottle
(C) the results of using test X on a sample from one more bottle might or might not establish which two bottles contain powder P
(D) it is necessary to test samples from exactly two more bottles with test X to establish which two bottles contain powder P
(E) test X must be used on samples from all the bottles in order to establish which two bottles contain powder P

21. If the pharmacist puts a mixture of samples from bottles 3 and 4 into water and gets the shade of blue required in test Y, and then she finds that a sample from bottle 4 does not dissolve in solvent S, she can properly infer that

(A) bottle 3 contains powder P
(B) bottle 3 contains powder Q
(C) bottle 4 contains powder P
(D) neither bottle 3 nor bottle 4 contains powder P
(E) a sample from bottle 3 will not dissolve in solvent S

22. If a mixture of samples from bottles 2 and 3, put into water, fails to produce the shade of blue required in test Y, which of the following is true?

(A) Bottles 2 and 3 could be the ones containing powder P.
(B) It is possible that bottle 3 contains powder P and bottle 2 contains powder Q.
(C) It is impossible to succeed in finding the bottles containing powder P by using test Y alone.
(D) It is impossible to succeed in finding the bottles containing powder P by using test X alone.
(E) Test X alone must be used to find the bottles containing powder P.

---

23. The teacher of yoga said that he knows how good the yoga exercises feel and how beneficial they are to his mental and spiritual health. After all, he said, there must be something sound to any human practice that endures more than three thousand years of history.

Which of the following, if true, is the strongest relevant objection to the argument the teacher makes on the basis of the time yoga has endured?

(A) The teacher benefits by the teaching of yoga and so, as a beneficiary, is not a disinterested witness.
(B) The practice of yoga has changed somewhat over three thousand years.
(C) The teacher cites the experience of only one person, whose well-being might be due to other causes.
(D) War, which cannot on balance be called sound, has lasted the length of human history.
(E) Three thousand years is an underestimate of the time period.

GO ON TO THE NEXT PAGE.

24. Researchers compared 42 average-weight and 47 obese infants, aged 7 to 9 months, with respect to current daily nutrient intake, ratio of formula or breast milk to solids in the diet, and maternal reliance on external feeding cues, such as time of day. Mothers completed a three-day food record at home before answering questions on current feeding practices. The researchers concluded from all of these data that, contrary to popular belief, the feeding practices of mothers of obese babies do not contribute significantly to their babies' obesity.

Which of the following could be an assumption on which the researchers relied in drawing their conclusion?

(A) Babies over 9 months are less likely to be obese than are babies under 9 months because babies over 9 months eat less frequently than do babies under 9 months.
(B) In the months before the study, the feeding practices of the mothers in the study did not differ significantly from their feeding practices at the time of the study.
(C) Babies gain weight at a slower rate between the ages of 7 and 9 months than they do between the ages of 4 and 6 months.
(D) Obesity is genetically rather than environmentally determined.
(E) Breast-fed babies are more likely to be obese than are formula-fed babies.

25. Ironically, people who use aspartame as a sweetener to reduce their caloric intake could wind up defeating their purpose, since studies show that high levels of aspartame may trigger a craving for carbohydrates by depleting the brain of a chemical that registers carbohydrate satiety.

Which of the following conclusions can most properly be drawn if the statements above are true?

(A) Aspartame can be more hazardous than carbohydrates to people's health.
(B) People who do not use aspartame are not likely to develop a craving for carbohydrates.
(C) The caloric content of foods that are high in carbohydrates is significant.
(D) People tend to prefer sweet foods to those high in carbohydrates.
(E) Food products that contain aspartame are typically low in carbohydrates.

STOP

IF YOU FINISH BEFORE TIME IS CALLED, YOU MAY CHECK YOUR WORK ON THIS SECTION ONLY. DO NOT TURN TO ANY OTHER SECTION IN THE TEST.

NO TEST MATERIAL ON THIS PAGE

NOTE: To ensure prompt processing of test results, it is important that you fill in the blanks exactly as directed.

GENERAL TEST

A. Print and sign your full name in this box:

PRINT: ______________________________
(LAST) (FIRST) (MIDDLE)

SIGN: ______________________________

Copy this code in box 6 on your answer sheet. Then fill in the corresponding ovals exactly as shown.

6. TITLE CODE				
⓪	⓪	⓪	⓪	⓪
①	①	①	①	①
②	②	②	②	②
③	③	③	③	③
④	④	④	④	④
⑤	⑤	⑤	⑤	⑤
⑥	⑥	⑥	⑥	⑥
⑦	⑦	⑦	⑦	⑦
⑧	⑧	⑧	⑧	⑧
⑨	⑨	⑨	⑨	⑨

Copy the Test Name and Form Code in box 7 on your answer sheet.

TEST NAME General

FORM CODE GR91-18

GRADUATE RECORD EXAMINATIONS GENERAL TEST

B. You will have 3 hours and 30 minutes in which to work on this test, which consists of seven sections. During the time allowed for one section, you may work only on that section. The time allowed for each section is 30 minutes.

Each of your scores will be determined by the number of questions for which you select the best answer from the choices given. Questions for which you mark no answer or more than one answer are not counted in scoring. Nothing is subtracted from a score if you answer a question incorrectly. Therefore, to maximize your scores it is better for you to guess at an answer than not to respond at all.

You are advised to work as rapidly as you can without losing accuracy. Do not spend too much time on questions that are too difficult for you. Go on to the other questions and come back to the difficult ones later.

There are several different types of questions; you will find special directions for each type in the test itself. Be sure you understand the directions before attempting to answer any questions.

YOU MUST INDICATE ALL YOUR ANSWERS ON THE SEPARATE ANSWER SHEET. No credit will be given for anything written in this examination book, but you may write in the book as much as you wish to work out your answers. After you have decided on your response to a question, fill in the corresponding oval on the answer sheet. BE SURE THAT EACH MARK IS DARK AND COMPLETELY FILLS THE OVAL. Mark only one answer to each question. No credit will be given for multiple answers. Erase all stray marks. If you change an answer, be sure that all previous marks are erased completely. Incomplete erasures may be read as intended answers. Do not be concerned if your answer sheet provides spaces for more answers than there are questions in each section.

Example:

What city is the capital of France?

(A) Rome
(B) Paris
(C) London
(D) Cairo
(E) Oslo

Sample Answer

Ⓐ ● Ⓒ Ⓓ Ⓔ — BEST ANSWER PROPERLY MARKED

Ⓐ ⊗ Ⓒ Ⓓ Ⓔ
Ⓐ ✓ Ⓒ Ⓓ Ⓔ
Ⓐ ● Ⓒ Ⓓ Ⓔ
Ⓐ ◐ Ⓒ Ⓓ Ⓔ
— IMPROPER MARKS

Some or all of the passages for this test have been adapted from published material to provide the examinee with significant problems for analysis and evaluation. To make the passages suitable for testing purposes, the style, content, or point of view of the original may have been altered in some cases. The ideas contained in the passages do not necessarily represent the opinions of the Graduate Record Examinations Board or Educational Testing Service.

DO NOT OPEN YOUR TEST BOOK UNTIL YOU ARE TOLD TO DO SO.

FOR GENERAL TEST, FORM GR91-18 ONLY
Answer Key and Percentages* of Examinees Answering Each Question Correctly

VERBAL ABILITY					
Section 1			Section 4		
Number	Answer	P+	Number	Answer	P+
1	D	97	1	E	91
2	C	62	2	C	74
3	D	63	3	C	80
4	C	60	4	C	61
5	A	47	5	D	55
6	E	47	6	D	50
7	D	45	7	C	41
8	C	95	8	A	98
9	B	85	9	D	92
10	D	76	10	E	84
11	C	71	11	E	79
12	D	58	12	C	73
13	B	65	13	A	37
14	D	48	14	B	47
15	E	34	15	A	36
16	B	18	16	D	29
17	A	53	17	B	67
18	E	73	18	D	29
19	B	59	19	B	79
20	B	51	20	D	65
21	E	63	21	E	76
22	E	62	22	A	59
23	C	37	23	E	55
24	E	50	24	C	64
25	C	63	25	A	23
26	C	35	26	B	40
27	B	69	27	B	29
28	C	95	28	B	91
29	E	84	29	C	88
30	E	86	30	A	83
31	B	68	31	B	80
32	A	51	32	C	53
33	B	46	33	C	63
34	A	38	34	A	44
35	A	36	35	E	34
36	D	33	36	D	25
37	D	24	37	E	28
38	E	13	38	A	25

QUANTITATIVE ABILITY					
Section 2			Section 5		
Number	Answer	P+	Number	Answer	P+
1	A	82	1	A	87
2	D	82	2	C	80
3	B	80	3	B	90
4	B	76	4	D	78
5	A	74	5	A	77
6	C	72	6	B	76
7	B	76	7	C	74
8	A	74	8	A	44
9	B	60	9	A	56
10	C	48	10	D	48
11	A	63	11	B	45
12	A	70	12	C	37
13	D	39	13	D	33
14	C	43	14	B	38
15	D	28	15	D	21
16	C	86	16	D	90
17	B	79	17	A	87
18	C	85	18	D	76
19	B	66	19	C	81
20	D	63	20	C	65
21	A	89	21	A	97
22	C	88	22	C	85
23	C	70	23	E	57
24	E	61	24	B	80
25	D	49	25	D	63
26	D	71	26	D	69
27	D	48	27	B	73
28	E	38	28	B	63
29	B	33	29	E	54
30	A	29	30	A	47

ANALYTICAL ABILITY					
Section 3			Section 6		
Number	Answer	P+	Number	Answer	P+
1	B	85	1	E	81
2	D	59	2	A	87
3	A	85	3	B	82
4	D	83	4	E	73
5	C	51	5	A	70
6	E	43	6	C	58
7	E	64	7	D	72
8	B	80	8	A	90
9	C	73	9	C	53
10	E	64	10	D	80
11	C	83	11	B	53
12	B	60	12	B	37
13	C	61	13	B	62
14	D	66	14	E	36
15	C	38	15	C	56
16	A	55	16	B	47
17	D	71	17	A	49
18	E	38	18	E	30
19	A	21	19	D	50
20	D	48	20	C	46
21	E	34	21	A	49
22	E	19	22	A	26
23	B	37	23	D	45
24	D	35	24	B	52
25	A	42	25	C	40

*Estimated P+ for the group of examinees who took the GRE General Test in a recent three-year period.

Score Conversions for GRE General Test GR91-18 Only and the Percents Below*

Raw Score	Verbal Scaled Score	Verbal % Below	Quantitative Scaled Score	Quantitative % Below	Analytical Scaled Score	Analytical % Below
74-76	800	99				
73	790	99				
72	780	99				
71	770	99				
70	750	98				
69	740	98				
68	730	97				
67	720	96				
66	710	95				
65	690	94				
64	680	93				
63	670	92				
62	660	90				
61	650	89				
60	640	87	800	97		
59	630	85	790	96		
58	620	84	780	94		
57	610	82	760	92		
56	590	78	750	89		
55	580	76	740	88		
54	570	74	730	86		
53	560	72	720	84		
52	550	69	710	82		
51	540	67	690	78		
50	530	64	680	77	800	99
49	520	61	670	74	800	99
48	520	61	660	72	800	99
47	510	59	650	70	790	98
46	500	56	640	68	770	97
45	490	54	620	63	760	96
44	480	51	610	61	750	96
43	470	48	600	59	730	94
42	460	44	590	57	720	92
41	450	41	580	54	710	91
40	440	38	570	51	700	90

Raw Score	Verbal Scaled Score	Verbal % Below	Quantitative Scaled Score	Quantitative % Below	Analytical Scaled Score	Analytical % Below
39	430	36	550	48	680	87
38	420	33	540	45	670	85
37	420	33	530	42	660	83
36	410	30	520	40	650	81
35	400	26	510	37	630	76
34	390	24	500	35	620	74
33	380	22	480	30	610	72
32	370	20	470	28	590	67
31	370	20	460	26	580	64
30	360	16	450	24	570	61
29	350	14	440	22	550	55
28	340	12	430	20	540	52
27	340	12	410	16	520	46
26	330	10	400	14	500	40
25	320	9	390	13	490	38
24	310	7	380	12	470	32
23	300	6	370	10	450	27
22	290	5	360	9	440	24
21	280	4	340	6	420	20
20	270	3	330	5	410	18
19	260	2	320	5	390	15
18	250	1	310	4	370	12
17	240	1	300	3	360	10
16	230	1	290	2	340	7
15	220	1	270	2	330	6
14	210	1	260	1	310	4
13	200	1	250	1	290	3
12	200	1	240	1	270	2
11	200	1	230	1	260	1
10	200	1	220	1	240	1
9	200	1	200	1	230	1
8	200	1	200	1	220	1
7	200	1	200	1	210	1
0-6	200	1	200	1	200	1

*Percent scoring below the scaled score is based on the performance of 923,359 examinees who took the General Test between October 1, 1986, and September 30, 1989. This percent below information is used for score reports during the 1990-91 testing year.

GR 91-19

01

GRE®

THE GRADUATE RECORD EXAMINATIONS®

General Test

Do not break the seal

until you are told to do so:

The contents of this test are confidential. Disclosure or reproduction of any portion of it is prohibited.

THIS TEST BOOK MUST NOT BE TAKEN FROM THE ROOM.

SECTION 1

Time—30 minutes

30 Questions

Numbers: All numbers used are real numbers.

Figures: Position of points, angles, regions, etc. can be assumed to be in the order shown; and angle measures can be assumed to be positive.

Lines shown as straight can be assumed to be straight.

Figures can be assumed to lie in a plane unless otherwise indicated.

Figures that accompany questions are intended to provide information useful in answering the questions. However, unless a note states that a figure is drawn to scale, you should solve these problems NOT by estimating sizes by sight or by measurement, but by using your knowledge of mathematics (see Example 2 below).

Directions: Each of the Questions 1-15 consists of two quantities, one in Column A and one in Column B. You are to compare the two quantities and choose

A if the quantity in Column A is greater;
B if the quantity in Column B is greater;
C if the two quantities are equal;
D if the relationship cannot be determined from the information given.

Note: Since there are only four choices, NEVER MARK (E).

Common Information: In a question, information concerning one or both of the quantities to be compared is centered above the two columns. A symbol that appears in both columns represents the same thing in Column A as it does in Column B.

	Column A	Column B	Sample Answers
Example 1:	2×6	$2 + 6$	● Ⓑ Ⓒ Ⓓ Ⓔ

Examples 2-4 refer to $\triangle PQR$.

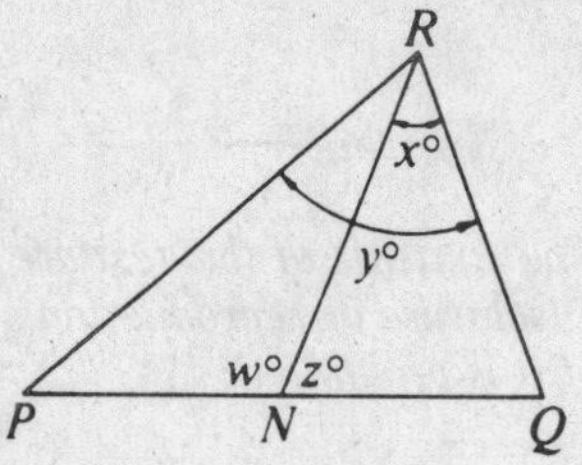

R, x°, y°, w°, z°, P, N, Q

	Column A	Column B	Sample Answers
Example 2:	PN	NQ	Ⓐ Ⓑ Ⓒ ● Ⓔ (since equal measures cannot be assumed, even though PN and NQ appear equal)
Example 3:	x	y	Ⓐ ● Ⓒ Ⓓ Ⓔ (since N is between P and Q)
Example 4:	$w + z$	180	Ⓐ Ⓑ ● Ⓓ Ⓔ (since PQ is a straight line)

GO ON TO THE NEXT PAGE.

A if the quantity in Column A is greater;
B if the quantity in Column B is greater;
C if the two quantities are equal;
D if the relationship cannot be determined from the information given.

	Column A	Column B

$n > 1$

1. $\frac{n}{n+1} + 1$ — $1 - \frac{1}{n+1}$

Maria purchased 3 pounds of candy X for \$7.98 and 5 pounds of candy Y for \$10.95.

2. The price Maria paid per pound for candy X — The price Maria paid per pound for candy Y

x is an integer greater than 1.

3. $2x + 5$ — $5x + 2$

4. $3(2^5)$ — $5(3^2)$

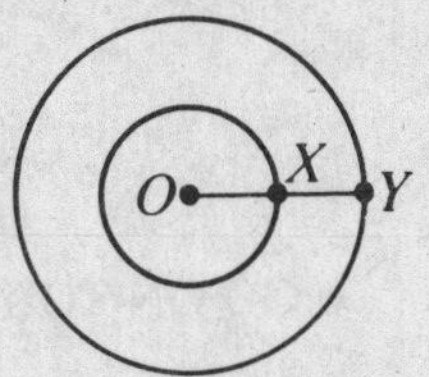

O is the center of the two circles and $OX = XY = 1$.

5. Half the circumference of the larger circle — The circumference of the smaller circle

$tq = 0$
$rq = 1$

6. t — 0

7. 0.9×0.9 — $0.9 \times 0.9 \times 0.9$

A student can purchase a research report for \$5.00, or reproduce the x pages of the report at a cost of \$0.15 per page.

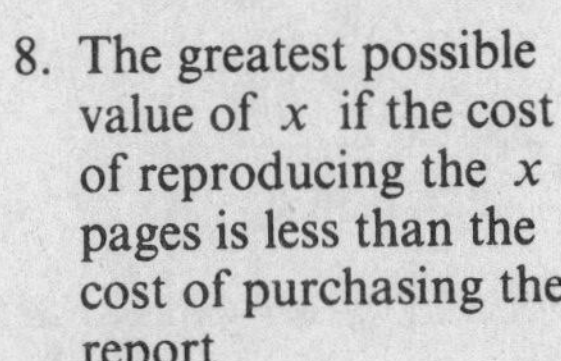

8. The greatest possible value of x if the cost of reproducing the x pages is less than the cost of purchasing the report — 34

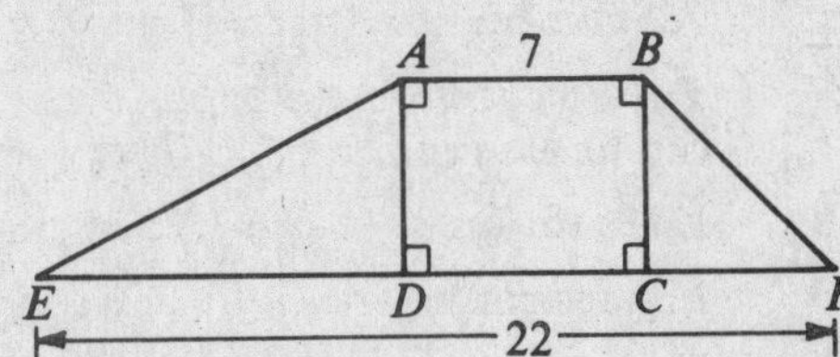

9. The area of rectangular region $ABCD$ — The area of triangular region ADE

$x < y < 0$

10. $x + y$ — xy

In $\triangle ABC$, $AB = BC$.

11. The measure of $\angle B$ — $60°$

Questions 12-13 refer to the following number line.

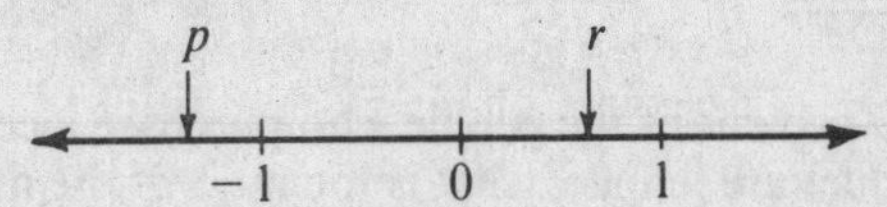

12. $-p$ — r

13. $p + r$ — $r - p$

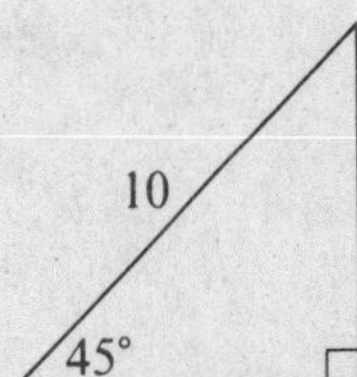

14. The area of the triangular region — 25

The length of a rectangular garden is increased by p percent and its width is decreased by p percent.

15. The area of the new garden if $p = 10$ — The area of the new garden if $p = 20$

GO ON TO THE NEXT PAGE.

Directions: Each of the Questions 16-30 has five answer choices. For each of these questions, select the best of the answer choices given.

16. Which of the following is NOT a divisor of 264 ?

(A) 4
(B) 8
(C) 9
(D) 11
(E) 12

17. If $3(x + 1) = 4x - 1$, then $x =$

(A) $\frac{4}{7}$

(B) $\frac{3}{4}$

(C) 2

(D) 3

(E) 4

18. If 55 percent of the people who purchase a certain product are female, what is the ratio of the number of females who purchase the product to the number of males who purchase the product?

(A) $\frac{11}{9}$

(B) $\frac{10}{9}$

(C) $\frac{9}{10}$

(D) $\frac{9}{11}$

(E) $\frac{5}{9}$

19. C is a circle, L is a line, and P is a point on line L. If C, L, and P are in the same plane and P is inside C, how many points do C and L have in common?

(A) 0
(B) 1
(C) 2
(D) 3
(E) 4

20. If one number exceeds another number by 13 and the larger number is $\frac{3}{2}$ times the smaller number, then the smaller number is

(A) 13
(B) 26
(C) 31
(D) 39
(E) 65

GO ON TO THE NEXT PAGE.

Questions 21-25 refer to the following graph.

COUNTRY *X*'S TOTAL WHEAT IMPORTS COMPARED TO ITS WHEAT IMPORTS FROM THE UNITED STATES, 1973-1983

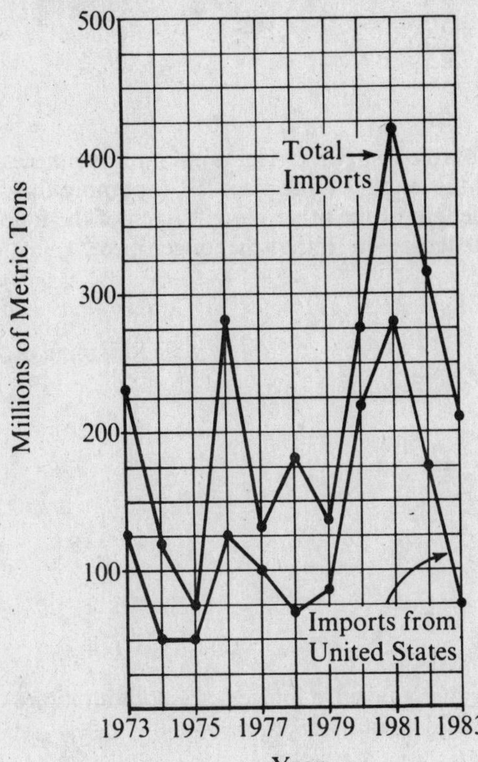

Note: Drawn to scale.

21. From 1973 to 1977, inclusive, how many million metric tons of wheat did Country *X* import from the United States?

    (A) 450
    (B) 400
    (C) 350
    (D) 320
    (E) 250

22. For how many of the years shown did Country *X* import more than 200 million metric tons of wheat?

    (A) Two
    (B) Five
    (C) Six
    (D) Seven
    (E) Eight

23. The amount of wheat Country *X* imported from countries other than the United States was greatest in which of the following years?

    (A) 1974
    (B) 1976
    (C) 1978
    (D) 1981
    (E) 1983

24. For the year in which total wheat imports and wheat imports from the United States were most nearly equal, how many million metric tons of wheat did Country *X* import?

    (A) 150
    (B) 125
    (C) 90
    (D) 75
    (E) 50

25. For the year in which the amount of Country *X*'s total wheat imports was greatest, approximately what percent of that total was imported from the United States?

    (A) 35%
    (B) 40%
    (C) 50%
    (D) 65%
    (E) 75%

GO ON TO THE NEXT PAGE.

26. $\left(2+\frac{3}{4}\right)^2-\left(2-\frac{1}{4}\right)^2=$

(A) $\frac{37}{8}$

(B) $\frac{9}{2}$

(C) 3

(D) 1

(E) $\frac{1}{2}$

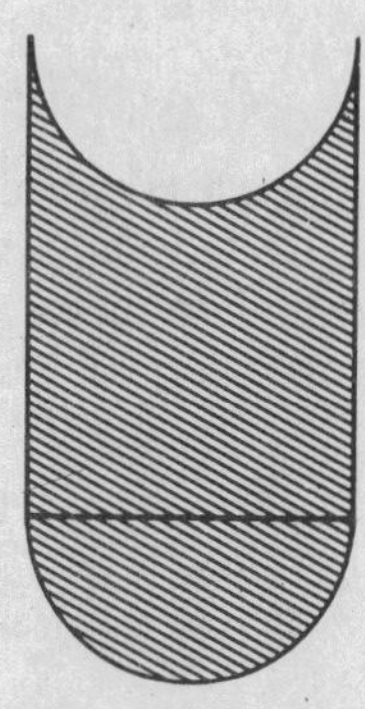

27. If each curved side in the figure above is a semicircle with radius 20, and the two parallel sides each have length 100, what is the area of the shaded region?

(A) 2,000
(B) 4,000
(C) $2{,}000 - 200\pi$
(D) $4{,}000 - 200\pi$
(E) $4{,}000 - 400\pi$

28. If the degree measures of the angles of a triangle are in the ratio 3 : 4 : 5, what is the degree measure of the smallest angle?

(A) 15°
(B) 30°
(C) 45°
(D) 60°
(E) 75°

29. A board of length L feet is cut into two pieces such that the length of one piece is 1 foot more than twice the length of the other piece. Which of the following is the length, in feet, of the longer piece?

(A) $\frac{L+2}{2}$

(B) $\frac{2L+1}{2}$

(C) $\frac{L-1}{3}$

(D) $\frac{2L+3}{3}$

(E) $\frac{2L+1}{3}$

30. How many positive integers are both multiples of 4 and divisors of 64 ?

(A) Two
(B) Three
(C) Four
(D) Five
(E) Six

STOP

IF YOU FINISH BEFORE TIME IS CALLED, YOU MAY CHECK YOUR WORK ON THIS SECTION ONLY. DO NOT TURN TO ANY OTHER SECTION IN THE TEST.

Section 2 starts on page 364.

SECTION 2

Time—30 minutes

25 Questions

Directions: Each question or group of questions is based on a passage or set of conditions. In answering some of the questions, it may be useful to draw a rough diagram. For each question, select the best answer choice given.

Questions 1-4

A group of three objects must be selected from six objects—K, O, S, T, V, and W—according to the following conditions:

Either K or S, or both, must be selected.
Either O or V must be selected, but neither V nor S can be selected with O.

1. Which of the following is an acceptable selection of objects?

(A) K, O, and S
(B) K, S, and T
(C) K, S, and V
(D) O, S, and V
(E) O, T, and V

2. Which of the following pairs of objects CANNOT both be among the objects selected?

(A) K and O
(B) K and T
(C) O and W
(D) T and W
(E) V and W

3. If S is selected, which of the following must also be among the objects selected?

(A) K
(B) O
(C) T
(D) V
(E) W

4. If V is not selected, which pair of objects must be among those selected?

(A) K and O
(B) K and T
(C) K and W
(D) O and T
(E) O and W

GO ON TO THE NEXT PAGE.

5. Research has proved that eating lots of fish greatly decreases the risk of developing heart disease. The key factor providing protection has been identified as omega-3 fatty acids, a family of fatty acids found in fish oils. Therefore, if people take dietary supplements of omega-3's in capsule form, they will decrease their risk of developing heart disease.

   Which of the following, if true, would most seriously weaken the conclusion drawn above?

   (A) Some dietary supplements have been shown to have harmful side effects.
   (B) Omega-3's occur in extremely low quantities in some kinds of fish.
   (C) Omega-3's are effective only because they interact with other substances found mainly in fish.
   (D) The majority of people who eat fish say that they do so because they like the taste of fish.
   (E) Researchers have found evidence that fish oil supplements would also reduce the effects of asthma and arthritis for some persons.

6. It is no wonder that some domestic car companies have to attract potential buyers with rebates and low interest rates. Why do not those companies produce cars that are more fuel-efficient? If all domestic manufacturers built cars that were as fuel-efficient as imported cars, rebates and low interest rates would not be needed.

   The argument above would be most strengthened if which of the following were true?

   (A) The offer of rebates has always signified that an industry is in decline.
   (B) For a majority of buyers of new cars, high fuel efficiency is the most important criterion in choosing a car.
   (C) Some cars built by domestic manufacturers are more fuel-efficient than many of the popular imported cars.
   (D) Many car buyers prefer to purchase midsize and larger cars.
   (E) Many car buyers rate operating costs as less important than initial purchase price when choosing a car.

7. Ergot is a fungus that can infest the seed heads of any grain crop but is common only on rye. Ergot contains chemicals poisonous to humans.

   Rye was introduced in Europe in the Middle Ages as a crop for land too poor and damp for wheat to grow well. Thus, rye tended to be the staple of the poorer peasants.

   Which of the following hypotheses is best supported by the information above?

   (A) Ergot did not occur in Europe prior to the Middle Ages.
   (B) People in the Middle Ages were well aware of the toxicity of ergot.
   (C) Before the introduction of rye, no attempts had been made to cultivate the poor and damp land in Europe.
   (D) In Europe during the Middle Ages, prosperous people were less at risk from ergot poisoning than poor people were.
   (E) Prior to the Middle Ages, Europe was as densely populated as dependence on a single grain crop permitted.

GO ON TO THE NEXT PAGE.

Questions 8-12

A map representing countries R, S, W, X, Y, and Z is to be drawn. Adjacent countries cannot be the same color on the map.

The only countries adjacent to each other are as follows:

R, S, X, and Y are each adjacent to W.
X is adjacent to Y.
R and S are each adjacent to Z.

8. Which of the following is a pair of countries that must be different in color from each other?

(A) R and X
(B) S and X
(C) S and Z
(D) X and Z
(E) Y and Z

9. If X is the same color as Z, then it must be true that

(A) R is the same color as Y
(B) S is the same color as X
(C) X is the same color as Y
(D) S is a different color from any other country
(E) W is a different color from any other country

10. Which of the following is a pair of countries that can be the same color as each other?

(A) R and S
(B) S and W
(C) W and X
(D) W and Y
(E) X and Y

11. Which of the following countries can be the same color as W ?

(A) R
(B) S
(C) X
(D) Y
(E) Z

12. If the fewest possible colors are used and one of the countries is the only one of a certain color, that country could be

(A) W, but not any of the other countries
(B) Z, but not any of the other countries
(C) R or S, but not any of the other countries
(D) W or X or Y, but not any of the other countries
(E) W or Y or Z, but not any of the other countries

GO ON TO THE NEXT PAGE.

Questions 13-18

Three sizes of hats—small, medium, and large—are stored in four sealed boxes.
For each of the three sizes of hats, there are exactly three boxes that contain that size.
Four labels accurately reflecting the contents of the boxes were prepared.
However, only two of the labels were placed on the correct boxes, and the other two labels were placed on the wrong boxes.
As a result, the boxes are labeled as follows:

Box 1—Small and medium
Box 2—Small and large
Box 3—Medium and large
Box 4—Small, medium, and large

13. If box 3 actually contains no small hats, which of the following must be true?

(A) Box 1 is correctly labeled.
(B) Box 2 is correctly labeled.
(C) Box 3 is correctly labeled.
(D) Box 1 contains no small hats.
(E) Box 2 contains no medium-sized hats.

14. If box 4 actually contains no small hats, which of the following must be true?

(A) Box 3 is correctly labeled.
(B) Box 4 is correctly labeled.
(C) Box 1 is incorrectly labeled.
(D) Box 2 is incorrectly labeled.
(E) Box 3 is incorrectly labeled.

15. If box 1 is correctly labeled, which of the following must be true?

(A) Box 2 contains no small hats.
(B) Box 2 contains no medium-sized hats.
(C) Box 2 contains no large hats.
(D) Box 4 contains some small hats.
(E) Box 4 contains some large hats.

16. If box 1 and box 4 are the mislabeled boxes, which of the following must be true?

(A) Box 1 contains some hats of all three sizes.
(B) Box 2 contains some hats of all three sizes.
(C) Box 3 contains some hats of all three sizes.
(D) Box 3 contains no medium-sized hats.
(E) Box 3 contains no large hats.

17. If box 1 and box 4 are the correctly labeled boxes, which of the following must be true?

(A) Both box 1 and box 2 contain small hats.
(B) Both box 1 and box 2 contain medium-sized hats.
(C) Both box 1 and box 3 contain medium-sized hats.
(D) Both box 2 and box 3 contain small hats.
(E) Both box 3 and box 4 contain medium-sized hats.

18. If at least small and medium-sized hats are known to be in box 4, which of the following must be true?

(A) If box 1 contains at least small and medium-sized hats, box 2 contains large hats.
(B) If box 1 contains only small and medium-sized hats, box 2 contains small hats.
(C) If box 2 contains only small and medium-sized hats, box 1 does not contain small hats.
(D) If box 2 contains at least medium-sized and large hats, box 4 does not contain large hats.
(E) If box 3 contains at least small and large hats, box 2 does not contain large hats.

GO ON TO THE NEXT PAGE.

Questions 19-22

A snowplow driver must clear all six shipping terminals—F, G, H, J, N, R—of snow one at a time. The sequence in which the clearing is done must conform to the following specific rules:

Terminal R must be cleared sometime before terminal F and also sometime before terminal N.

Terminal G must be cleared sometime after terminal F and also sometime after terminal J.

Terminal H cannot be cleared immediately before or immediately after terminal J.

A terminal that is about to receive shipments must, when it is consistent with the rules above, be cleared before a terminal that is not.

19. If H and N alone are about to receive shipments, the terminals can be cleared in which of the following sequences?

(A) R, N, F, H, G, J
(B) H, N, R, J, F, G
(C) R, H, F, N, J, G
(D) H, R, N, J, F, G
(E) R, N, F, J, G, H

20. If J alone is about to receive shipments, the terminals can be cleared in which of the following sequences?

(A) J, F, H, G, R, N
(B) J, H, G, R, F, N
(C) J, R, N, F, H, G
(D) R, F, N, J, H, G
(E) R, J, G, F, N, H

21. If G and N alone are about to receive shipments, which of the following must be true?

(A) N is cleared first.
(B) R is cleared second.
(C) J is cleared third.
(D) F is cleared fourth.
(E) H is cleared sixth.

22. If G and J alone are about to receive shipments, then the terminals can be cleared in which of the following sequences?

(A) R, J, F, G, H, N
(B) R, J, G, N, F, H
(C) J, G, R, H, F, N
(D) J, R, F, N, G, H
(E) J, R, F, G, N, H

GO ON TO THE NEXT PAGE.

23. During the last twenty years, eleven percent of those people who received certification to practice in a particular profession were women, and all those people who received certification during those years obtained full-time positions. Nevertheless, only five percent of the full-time positions in this profession are currently held by women.

Which of the following, if true, could explain the difference in the percentages mentioned in the passage above?

(A) It was easier to obtain certification twenty years ago than it is currently.
(B) The majority of those currently in the profession were hired more than twenty years ago, when virtually everyone in the profession was male.
(C) The women certified in the last twenty years have tended to choose different specialties within the profession than the men have tended to choose.
(D) Male and female members of the profession have been paid according to equal pay scales for all of the past twenty years.
(E) Although women currently hold five percent of the full-time positions in the profession, they hold only two percent of the supervisory positions.

24. To be mentally healthy, people must have self-respect. People can maintain self-respect only by continually earning the respect of others they esteem. They can earn this respect only by treating these others morally.

Which of the following conclusions can be properly drawn from the statements above?

(A) People who are mentally healthy will be treated morally by others.
(B) People who are mentally healthy will have treated morally those they esteem.
(C) People who are mentally healthy must have self-respect in order to be treated morally by others.
(D) People can expect to be treated morally by others only if they esteem these others.
(E) People who have self-respect seldom treat morally those they esteem.

25. People often recall having felt chilled before the onset of a cold. This supports the hypothesis that colds are, at least sometimes, caused by becoming chilled; it is the chill that allows a rhinovirus, if present, to infect a person.

Which of the following, if true, most seriously weakens the force of the evidence cited above?

(A) Being chilled is a form of stress, and stress lowers the defenses of a person's immune system, which guards against infection.
(B) After a rhinovirus has incubated in a person for several days, the first symptom it causes is a feeling of chilliness.
(C) People who are tired and then become chilled are more likely to catch severe colds than are people who are chilled without being tired.
(D) Some people who catch colds are not sure what it was that allowed them to catch cold.
(E) Rhinoviruses are not always present in the environment, and so a person could become chilled without catching a cold.

STOP

IF YOU FINISH BEFORE TIME IS CALLED, YOU MAY CHECK YOUR WORK ON THIS SECTION ONLY. DO NOT TURN TO ANY OTHER SECTION IN THE TEST.

NO TEST MATERIAL ON THIS PAGE

SECTION 3

Time—30 minutes

38 Questions

Directions: Each sentence below has one or two blanks, each blank indicating that something has been omitted. Beneath the sentence are five lettered words or sets of words. Choose the word or set of words for each blank that best fits the meaning of the sentence as a whole.

1. With its maverick approach to the subject, Shere Hite's book has been more widely debated than most; the media throughout the country have brought the author's ------- opinions to the public's attention.

   (A) controversial
   (B) authoritative
   (C) popular
   (D) conclusive
   (E) articulate

2. Though many medieval women possessed devotional books that had belonged to their mothers, formal written evidence of women bequeathing books to their daughters is scarce, which suggests that such bequests were ------- and required no -------.

   (A) unselfish. .rationalization
   (B) tangential. .approval
   (C) customary. .documentation
   (D) covert. .discretion
   (E) spurious. .record

3. Although their initial anger had ------- somewhat, they continued to ------- the careless worker who had broken the machine.

   (A) blazed. .assail
   (B) diminished. .appease
   (C) abated. .berate
   (D) subsided. .condone
   (E) intensified. .torment

4. Borrowing a copyrighted book from a library amounts to a form of theft ------- by entrenched custom: the copyright owner's property, the book, is used repeatedly without ------- for such use.

   (A) engendered. .application
   (B) anticipated. .acknowledgment
   (C) sanctioned. .compensation
   (D) provoked. .adjustment
   (E) perpetrated. .permission

5. The notion that a parasite can alter the behavior of a host organism is not mere fiction; indeed, the phenomenon is not even -------.

   (A) observable (B) real (C) comprehended (D) rare (E) imaginable

6. Although Shakespeare received little formal education, scholarship has in recent years ------- the view that he was ------- the work of classical authors.

   (A) substantiated. .unimpressed by
   (B) eroded. .obsessed by
   (C) supported. .oblivious to
   (D) questioned. .influenced by
   (E) undermined. .unfamiliar with

7. Darwin's method did not really ------- the idea of race as an important conceptual category; even the much more central idea of species was little more than a theoretical -------.

   (A) require. .convenience
   (B) apply. .measurement
   (C) exclude. .practice
   (D) subsume. .validation
   (E) reject. .fact

GO ON TO THE NEXT PAGE.

Directions: In each of the following questions, a related pair of words or phrases is followed by five lettered pairs of words or phrases. Select the lettered pair that best expresses a relationship similar to that expressed in the original pair.

8. DENTURE : TEETH :: (A) scarf : head
(B) toupee : hair (C) fingernail : hand
(D) eyebrow : eye (E) bandage : wound

9. PROFESSIONAL : ROOKIE :: (A) player : fan
(B) ranger : cowhand (C) prisoner : thief
(D) soldier : recruit (E) conductor : musician

10. SCRIPT : PLAY :: (A) refrain : song
(B) assignment : course (C) score : symphony
(D) collection : story (E) debate : candidate

11. BUOYANT : SINK :: (A) frozen : melt
(B) liquid : evaporate (C) brittle : cleave
(D) insoluble : dissolve (E) gaseous : expand

12. CRAWL : PROCEED :: (A) plummet : descend
(B) nurture : grow (C) inundate : flood
(D) rampage : destroy (E) dwindle : decrease

13. ELEGY : SORROW ::
(A) paean : distress
(B) encomium : criticism
(C) requiem : euphoria
(D) tirade : joy
(E) eulogy : admiration

14. FRIEZE : ORNAMENT :: (A) arch : divide
(B) relief : form (C) arabesque : accentuate
(D) nave : border (E) pillar : support

15. DECELERATE : SPEED ::
(A) desiccate : dryness
(B) extinguish : oxygen
(C) interpolate : interval
(D) decontaminate : sterility
(E) enervate : vitality

16. DESPOTIC : TYRANNY ::
(A) authoritarian : superiority
(B) skillful : celebrity
(C) generous : liberality
(D) suspect : illegality
(E) peaceful : benevolence

GO ON TO THE NEXT PAGE.

Directions: Each passage in this group is followed by questions based on its content. After reading a passage, choose the best answer to each question. Answer all questions following a passage on the basis of what is stated or implied in that passage.

(The article from which the passage was taken appeared in 1982.)

Theorists are divided concerning the origin of the Moon. Some hypothesize that the Moon was formed in the same way as were the planets in the inner solar system (Mercury, Venus, Mars, and Earth)—from planet-forming materials in the presolar nebula. But, unlike the cores of the inner planets, the Moon's core contains little or no iron, while the typical planet-forming materials were quite rich in iron. Other theorists propose that the Moon was ripped out of the Earth's rocky mantle by the Earth's collison with another large celestial body after much of the Earth's iron fell to its core. One problem with the collision hypothesis is the question of how a satellite formed in this way could have settled into the nearly circular orbit that the Moon has today. Fortunately, the collision hypothesis is testable. If it is true, the mantlerocks of the Moon and the Earth should be the same geochemically.

17. The primary purpose of the passage is to

(A) present two hypotheses concerning the origin of the Moon
(B) discuss the strengths and weaknesses of the collision hypothesis concerning the origin of the Moon
(C) propose that hypotheses concerning the Moon's origin be tested
(D) argue that the Moon could not have been formed out of the typical planet-forming materials of the presolar nebula
(E) describe one reason why the Moon's geochemical makeup should resemble that of the Earth

18. According to the passage, Mars and the Earth are similar in which of the following ways?

I. Their satellites were formed by collisions with other celestial bodies.
II. Their cores contain iron.
III. They were formed from the presolar nebula.

(A) III only
(B) I and II only
(C) I and III only
(D) II and III only
(E) I, II, and III

19. The author implies that a nearly circular orbit is unlikely for a satellite that

(A) circles one of the inner planets
(B) is deficient in iron
(C) is different from its planet geochemically
(D) was formed by a collision between two celestial bodies
(E) was formed out of the planet-forming materials in the presolar nebula

20. Which of the following, if true, would be most likely to make it difficult to verify the collision hypothesis in the manner suggested by the author?

(A) The Moon's core and mantlerock are almost inactive geologically.
(B) The mantlerock of the Earth has changed in composition since the formation of the Moon, while the mantlerock of the Moon has remained chemically inert.
(C) Much of the Earth's iron fell to the Earth's core long before the formation of the Moon, after which the Earth's mantlerock remained unchanged.
(D) Certain of the Earth's elements, such as platinum, gold, and iridium, followed iron to the Earth's core.
(E) The mantlerock of the Moon contains elements such as platinum, gold, and iridium.

GO ON TO THE NEXT PAGE.

Surprisingly enough, modern historians have rarely interested themselves in the history of the American South in the period before the South began to become self-consciously and distinctively "Southern"—the decades after 1815. Consequently, the cultural history of Britain's North American empire in the seventeenth and eighteenth centuries has been written almost as if the Southern colonies had never existed. The American culture that emerged during the Colonial and Revolutionary eras has been depicted as having been simply an extension of New England Puritan culture. However, Professor Davis has recently argued that the South stood apart from the rest of American society during this early period, following its own unique pattern of cultural development. The case for Southern distinctiveness rests upon two related premises: first, that the cultural similarities among the five Southern colonies were far more impressive than the differences, and second, that what made those colonies alike also made them different from the other colonies. The first, for which Davis offers an enormous amount of evidence, can be accepted without major reservations; the second is far more problematic.

What makes the second premise problematic is the use of the Puritan colonies as a basis for comparison. Quite properly, Davis decries the excessive influence ascribed by historians to the Puritans in the formation of American culture. Yet Davis inadvertently adds weight to such ascriptions by using the Puritans as the standard against which to assess the achievements and contributions of Southern colonials. Throughout, Davis focuses on the important, and undeniable, differences between the Southern and Puritan colonies in motives for and patterns of early settlement, in attitudes toward nature and Native Americans, and in the degree of receptivity to metropolitan cultural influences.

However, recent scholarship has strongly suggested that those aspects of early New England culture that seem to have been most distinctly Puritan, such as the strong religious orientation and the communal impulse, were not even typical of New England as a whole, but were largely confined to the two colonies of Massachusetts and Connecticut. Thus, what in contrast to the Puritan colonies appears to Davis to be peculiarly Southern—acquisitiveness, a strong interest in politics and the law, and a tendency to cultivate metropolitan cultural models—was not only more typically English than the cultural patterns exhibited by Puritan Massachusetts and Connecticut, but also almost certainly characteristic of most other early modern British colonies from Barbados north to Rhode Island and New Hampshire. Within the larger framework of American colonial life, then, not the Southern but the Puritan colonies appear to have been distinctive, and even they seem to have been rapidly assimilating to the dominant cultural patterns by the late Colonial period.

21. The author is primarily concerned with

(A) refuting a claim about the influence of Puritan culture on the early American South
(B) refuting a thesis about the distinctiveness of the culture of the early American South
(C) refuting the two premises that underlie Davis' discussion of the culture of the American South in the period before 1815
(D) challenging the hypothesis that early American culture was homogeneous in nature
(E) challenging the contention that the American South made greater contributions to early American culture than Puritan New England did

22. The passage implies that the attitudes toward Native Americans that prevailed in the Southern colonies

(A) were in conflict with the cosmopolitan outlook of the South
(B) derived from Southerners' strong interest in the law
(C) were modeled after those that prevailed in the North
(D) differed from those that prevailed in the Puritan colonies
(E) developed as a response to attitudes that prevailed in Massachusetts and Connecticut

23. According to the author, the depiction of American culture during the Colonial and Revolutionary eras as an extension of New England Puritan culture reflects the

(A) fact that historians have overestimated the importance of the Puritans in the development of American culture
(B) fact that early American culture was deeply influenced by the strong religious orientation of the colonists
(C) failure to recognize important and undeniable cultural differences between New Hampshire and Rhode Island on the one hand and the Southern colonies on the other
(D) extent to which Massachusetts and Connecticut served as cultural models for the other American colonies
(E) extent to which colonial America resisted assimilating cultural patterns that were typically English

GO ON TO THE NEXT PAGE.

24. The author of the passage is in agreement with which of the following elements of Davis' book?

    I. Davis' claim that acquisitiveness was a characteristic unique to the South during the Colonial period
    II. Davis' argument that there were significant differences between Puritan and Southern culture during the Colonial period
    III. Davis' thesis that the Southern colonies shared a common culture

    (A) I only
    (B) II only
    (C) III only
    (D) I and II only
    (E) II and III only

25. It can be inferred from the passage that the author would find Davis' second premise (lines 18-20) more plausible if it were true that

    (A) Puritan culture had displayed the tendency characteristic of the South to cultivate metropolitan cultural models
    (B) Puritan culture had been dominant in all the non-Southern colonies during the seventeenth and eighteenth centuries
    (C) the communal impulse and a strong religious orientation had been more prevalent in the South
    (D) the various cultural patterns of the Southern colonies had more closely resembled each other
    (E) the cultural patterns characteristic of most early modern British colonies had also been characteristic of the Puritan colonies

26. The passage suggests that by the late Colonial period the tendency to cultivate metropolitan cultural models was a cultural pattern that was

    (A) dying out as Puritan influence began to grow
    (B) self-consciously and distinctively Southern
    (C) spreading to Massachusetts and Connecticut
    (D) more characteristic of the Southern colonies than of England
    (E) beginning to spread to Rhode Island and New Hampshire

27. Which of the following statements could most logically follow the last sentence of the passage?

    (A) Thus, had more attention been paid to the evidence, Davis would not have been tempted to argue that the culture of the South diverged greatly from Puritan culture in the seventeenth century.
    (B) Thus, convergence, not divergence, seems to have characterized the cultural development of the American colonies in the eighteenth century.
    (C) Thus, without the cultural diversity represented by the American South, the culture of colonial America would certainly have been homogeneous in nature.
    (D) Thus, the contribution of Southern colonials to American culture was certainly overshadowed by that of the Puritans.
    (E) Thus, the culture of America during the Colonial period was far more sensitive to outside influences than historians are accustomed to acknowledge.

GO ON TO THE NEXT PAGE.

Directions: Each question below consists of a word printed in capital letters, followed by five lettered words or phrases. Choose the lettered word or phrase that is most nearly opposite in meaning to the word in capital letters.

Since some of the questions require you to distinguish fine shades of meaning, be sure to consider all the choices before deciding which one is best.

28. HARMONY: (A) dishonesty (B) indignity (C) insecurity (D) discord (E) irritation

29. SLACK: (A) twisted (B) taut (C) compact (D) durable (E) shattered

30. JOCULAR: (A) active (B) serious (C) unknown (D) equable (E) destructive

31. IMPEDE: (A) assist (B) entreat (C) dislodge (D) ascribe (E) avow

32. SAP: (A) fortify (B) alleviate (C) lend credence (D) hold fast (E) draw out

33. CONTROL:
(A) minor variable
(B) weak assumption
(C) improper simulation
(D) group experimented on
(E) expression substituted for

34. RECONDITE: (A) intended (B) defeated (C) widely understood (D) freely dispensed (E) recently discovered

35. INIMITABLE: (A) inclined to disagree (B) unwilling to compete (C) eager to advise (D) intelligible (E) ordinary

36. DISINTER: (A) restrain (B) confiscate (C) resist (D) bury (E) fund

37. DIATRIBE:
(A) laudatory piece of writing
(B) formal speech by one person
(C) written agreement
(D) farewell address
(E) witty poem

38. HOODWINK: (A) explain (B) shock (C) lead (D) disregard (E) disabuse

STOP

IF YOU FINISH BEFORE TIME IS CALLED, YOU MAY CHECK YOUR WORK ON THIS SECTION ONLY. DO NOT TURN TO ANY OTHER SECTION IN THE TEST.

Section 4 starts on page 378.

SECTION 4

Time—30 minutes

25 Questions

Directions: Each question or group of questions is based on a passage or set of conditions. In answering some of the questions, it may be useful to draw a rough diagram. For each question, select the best answer choice given.

Questions 1-5

A college president wishes to select four members of a faculty-student committee as representatives to meet with the college's board of trustees. The faculty-student committee consists of exactly four faculty members—F, G, H, and I—and four students—R, S, T, and U. The president can select any of the committee members as representatives as long as she observes the following restrictions:

The group of four representatives must consist of exactly two faculty members and two students.
Either F or G must be one of the representatives, but F and G cannot both be representatives.
If R is a representative, H must also be a representative.
If T is a representative, G cannot be a representative.

1. If R is a representative, which of the following CANNOT also be a representative?

(A) H
(B) I
(C) S
(D) T
(E) U

2. If neither S nor U is a representative, which of the following is the pair of faculty members who must be representatives?

(A) F and G
(B) F and H
(C) F and I
(D) G and H
(E) G and I

3. If G is a representative, which of the following can be the other three representatives?

(A) F, S, U
(B) H, I, R
(C) H, R, S
(D) H, S, T
(E) I, R, U

4. If G, I, and S are representatives, which of the following must also be a representative?

(A) F
(B) H
(C) R
(D) T
(E) U

5. If T is a representative and H is not a representative, the group of representatives would be completely determined if it were also true that

(A) F is a representative
(B) I is a representative
(C) G is not a representative
(D) R is not a representative
(E) U is not a representative

GO ON TO THE NEXT PAGE.

6. Injections of small quantities of a drug, the active ingredient of which is a human hormone, have been shown to reverse very high blood pressure rapidly and without causing undesirable side effects. However, high blood pressure is a condition that must be treated for a patient's entire lifetime, and because the frequency of injections that would be necessary renders the drug unsatisfactory for such long-term treatment, doctors continue to treat patients with injections of other medications.

   Which of the following can be properly concluded from the statements above?

   (A) The beneficial effects of the drug in the doses in which it is administered are short-lived compared to the effects of some other injected medications.
   (B) Less-frequent injections of the drug in larger doses would provide a satisfactory treatment for very high blood pressure.
   (C) The human body can be stimulated to produce the hormone whenever blood pressure reaches dangerously high levels.
   (D) When the drug is administered orally rather than by injection, it reverses very high blood pressure but also causes undesirable side effects.
   (E) Drugs that are administered orally can reverse very high blood pressure even more rapidly than can drugs taken by injection.

7. The neurons in the human brain have a unique property: they are cells that, in adults, do not divide. This property makes them immune from cancer. If the mechanism that keeps neurons from proliferating can be found and transferred to other types of cells, the complete prevention of the cancers afflicting those cells will be possible.

   Which of the following, if true, would provide a good reason for not trying to prevent cancer by the method indicated above?

   (A) The human brain contains cell types other than neurons.
   (B) The process of normal cell division has been studied extensively and is well understood.
   (C) Most human tissue depends on the periodic division of cells for its health.
   (D) The mechanism that keeps neurons from proliferating in adults has never been known to fail.
   (E) Some kinds of cancer whose causes are known can be prevented now, but there are few kinds for which it is practically feasible to eliminate the causes.

8. Twenty percent of all energy consumed in the United States is consumed by home appliances. If appliances that are twice as energy-efficient as those currently available are produced, this figure will eventually be reduced to about ten percent.

   The argument above requires which of the following assumptions?

   (A) Home-appliance usage would not increase along with the energy efficiency of the appliances.
   (B) It would not be expensive to produce home appliances that are energy-efficient.
   (C) Home-appliance manufacturers now have the technology to produce appliances that are twice as energy-efficient as those currently available.
   (D) The cost of energy to the consumer would rise with increases in the energy efficiency of home appliances.
   (E) The percentage of energy consumed by home appliances will increase if existing appliances are not replaced by more energy-efficient models.

GO ON TO THE NEXT PAGE.

Questions 9 -14

A selection from six colored lights—M, O, P, R, T, and Y—is projected onto a wall, one light at a time, in a continuous sequence that lasts exactly 30 seconds. A single projection of a light lasts exactly six seconds. A single projection of a light can be followed immediately by another projection of the same light. A color cannot be projected any more than three times in any thirty-second sequence. Any sequence is organized according to the following conditions:

No time elapses between the end of one six-second projection and the beginning of another.
R cannot be projected in any sequence more than once.
If R is the first color projected in a sequence, Y cannot be projected in that sequence.
If P is projected at least once after T in a sequence, P is projected exactly twice in that sequence.
M is projected for the last six seconds in every sequence.

9. Which of the following is an acceptable sequence?

(A) M, O, R, R, M
(B) R, O, P, T, M
(C) R, O, T, P, M
(D) T, M, M, M, M
(E) Y, R, O, R, P

10. Which of the following must be true of any thirty-second sequence that is made up of exactly two colors?

(A) R is not projected.
(B) Y is not projected.
(C) O is projected.
(D) P is projected.
(E) T is projected.

11. P can occupy 18 seconds of a sequence if the sequence begins with any of the following colors EXCEPT

(A) M
(B) O
(C) R
(D) T
(E) Y

12. If R is the first color projected and O is the second color projected in a sequence that contains the maximum number of colors, the third and fourth colors projected must be

(A) M and then Y
(B) T and then Y
(C) T and then P
(D) P and then T
(E) P and then M

13. If a sequence begins with 12 seconds of Y, any of the following could be projected in the next 12 seconds EXCEPT

(A) 12 seconds of M
(B) 6 seconds of O, followed by 6 seconds of R
(C) 6 seconds of R, followed by 6 seconds of M
(D) 6 seconds of T, followed by 6 seconds of P
(E) 6 seconds of Y, followed by 6 seconds of P

14. If the first three lights projected in a sequence are O, R, and T, in that order, which of the following must be true of that sequence?

(A) P is not projected.
(B) Y is not projected.
(C) M is projected exactly once.
(D) Exactly four different colors make up the sequence.
(E) Exactly five different colors make up the sequence.

GO ON TO THE NEXT PAGE.

Questions 15-18

A large office complex has exactly seven buildings—R, S, T, U, V, W, and X. A delivery service with four vans—van 1, van 2, van 3, and van 4—carries packages by van from building to building at the complex. Each van has a unique route, which it repeats throughout the day:

Van 1 travels only from R to S, from S to T, from T to U, from U to V, and from V to R.
Van 2 travels only from S to W and back to S.
Van 3 travels only from T to V and back to T.
Van 4 travels only from U to X and back to U.

Vans stop at each building to which they travel, and packages can be picked up or delivered at any stop. Any van can also leave a package for any other van to pick up at any building where both vans stop.

15. A package sent by van can be delivered with no intermediate stops if it is sent from

(A) R to W
(B) S to R
(C) T to R
(D) U to T
(E) V to T

16. On its way to any building in the complex, a package sent by van from W must travel to

(A) R
(B) S
(C) T
(D) U
(E) V

17. What is the minimum number of intermediate stops for a package sent by van from R to V?

(A) One
(B) Two
(C) Three
(D) Four
(E) Six

18. Which of the following lists all of the vans, in the order of use, that would be needed to send a package by van from X to T with the minimum number of intermediate stops?

(A) Van 3, van 1
(B) Van 4, van 1
(C) Van 1, van 2, van 3
(D) Van 2, van 1, van 4
(E) Van 4, van 1, van 3

GO ON TO THE NEXT PAGE.

Questions 19-22

A house inspection company must inspect each of seven houses—F, G, H, J, K, L, and M. The company will use two inspectors, each of whom will be assigned a group of houses to inspect. The houses will be divided into group 1 and group 2 according to the following conditions:

Each group must include at least three houses.
No house can be in both groups.
F must be in the same group as M.
If H is in group 1, L must be in group 1.
If J is in group 2, G must be in group 1.

19. Which of the following is an acceptable assignment of houses to groups?

	Group 1	Group 2
(A)	F, H, J, L	G, K, M
(B)	F, H, L, M	G, J, K
(C)	G, H, K, L	F, J, M
(D)	G, K, L, M	F, H, J
(E)	H, K, L	F, G, J, M

20. If G and L are in group 2, which of the following must be together in one of the groups?

(A) F and H
(B) F and K
(C) H and J
(D) H and K
(E) J and M

21. Any of the following could be true EXCEPT:

(A) F and H are in group 2.
(B) G and J are in group 1.
(C) L and M are in group 1.
(D) F, K, and L are in group 1.
(E) J, K, and H are in group 2.

22. If F is in group 2 with only two other houses, which of the following must be in group 1 ?

(A) G
(B) H
(C) J
(D) K
(E) L

GO ON TO THE NEXT PAGE.

23. When a large bird, the dodo, still inhabited the island of Mauritius, one of its favorite foods was the fruit of a particular species of tree. After the dodo became extinct, new fruit trees of that species ceased to sprout on the island.

Which of the following, if true, would most help to account for the phenomenon described above?

(A) The dodo ate a variety of other fruits as well; trees producing these other fruits continued to flourish after the dodo's extinction.
(B) Although other birds also ate the tree's fruit, the dodo was the largest and thus required the greatest quantities of fruit.
(C) When the fruit of the tree was not eaten, it gradually decayed, and the seeds within the fruit were deposited in soil.
(D) The dodo's digestive processes softened the seeds of the tree's fruit before the dodo excreted the seeds; the seeds germinated only after being thus softened.
(E) The dodo tended to live where the tree's fruit was plentiful; it was in these areas that new fruit trees of that species sprouted before the dodo's extinction.

Questions 24-25

Mercury, one of the deadliest toxins, makes up approximately fifty percent of the amalgam used by dentists in silver fillings. The effects of acute mercury poisoning are well known—kidney failure, muscle tremors, memory loss, and even death. It is clear that responsible dentists should remove all of their patients' silver fillings and replace them with fillings of plastic composites.

24. Which of the following, if true, most seriously weakens the author's argument?

(A) Plastic composite fillings are more expensive than silver fillings.
(B) Most patients are satisfied with the durability of their silver fillings.
(C) A patient's exposure to mercury from multiple silver fillings is at a harmless level.
(D) Most dental insurance plans do not consider the replacing of silver fillings to be necessary.
(E) Mercury is also present in certain seafoods, alcoholic beverages, and medications.

25. Which of the following, if true, most strengthens the author's argument?

(A) Silver fillings gradually corrode and small amounts of mercury leak from the amalgam.
(B) It is difficult to measure the amount of mercury in a person's body.
(C) Some patients have more than one filling per tooth.
(D) Mercury poisoning produces a range of subtle but distinctive symptoms.
(E) The materials for plastic composite fillings are readily available to dentists.

STOP

IF YOU FINISH BEFORE TIME IS CALLED, YOU MAY CHECK YOUR WORK ON THIS SECTION ONLY. DO NOT TURN TO ANY OTHER SECTION IN THE TEST.

NO TEST MATERIAL ON THIS PAGE

SECTION 5

Time—30 minutes

30 Questions

Numbers: All numbers used are real numbers.

Figures: Position of points, angles, regions, etc. can be assumed to be in the order shown; and angle measures can be assumed to be positive.

Lines shown as straight can be assumed to be straight.

Figures can be assumed to lie in a plane unless otherwise indicated.

Figures that accompany questions are intended to provide information useful in answering the questions. However, unless a note states that a figure is drawn to scale, you should solve these problems NOT by estimating sizes by sight or by measurement, but by using your knowledge of mathematics (see Example 2 below).

Directions: Each of the Questions 1-15 consists of two quantities, one in Column A and one in Column B. You are to compare the two quantities and choose

A if the quantity in Column A is greater;
B if the quantity in Column B is greater;
C if the two quantities are equal;
D if the relationship cannot be determined from the information given.

Note: Since there are only four choices, NEVER MARK (E).

Common Information: In a question, information concerning one or both of the quantities to be compared is centered above the two columns. A symbol that appears in both columns represents the same thing in Column A as it does in Column B.

	Column A	Column B	Sample Answers
Example 1:	2×6	$2 + 6$	● Ⓑ Ⓒ Ⓓ Ⓔ

Examples 2-4 refer to ΔPQR.

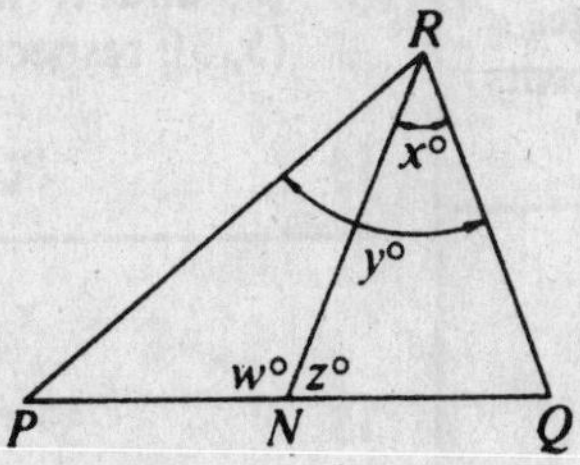

R, x°, y°, w°, z°, P, N, Q

	Column A	Column B	Sample Answers
Example 2:	PN	NQ	Ⓐ Ⓑ Ⓒ ● Ⓔ (since equal measures cannot be assumed, even though PN and NQ appear equal)
Example 3:	x	y	Ⓐ ● Ⓒ Ⓓ Ⓔ (since N is between P and Q)
Example 4:	$w + z$	180	Ⓐ Ⓑ ● Ⓓ Ⓔ (since PQ is a straight line)

GO ON TO THE NEXT PAGE.

A if the quantity in Column A is greater;
B if the quantity in Column B is greater;
C if the two quantities are equal;
D if the relationship cannot be determined from the information given.

	Column A	Column B
1.	The number of seconds in an hour	The number of days in 10 years
2.	The average (arithmetic mean) of 13, 31, and 81	The average (arithmetic mean) of 13, 30, and 81

$x = 4$

	Column A	Column B
3.	$3x^2$	144

$x°$, $44°$, $44°$

	Column A	Column B
4.	x	88
5.	$(598.95)^2$	360,000
6.	$3.4(5.5)$	$3(5.5) + 0.4(5.5)$
7.	The cost of x apples at a cost of $y + 2$ cents apiece	The cost of y oranges at a cost of $x + 2$ cents apiece
8.	$\sqrt{5^2}$	$5\sqrt{5}$

A rectangular box is 2 feet wide and 3 feet long and has a volume of 15 cubic feet.

	Column A	Column B
9.	The height of the box	3 feet
10.	24 percent of 75	75 percent of 24

The height of right circular cylinder C is 3 times the diameter of its base.

	Column A	Column B
11.	The circumference of the base of C	The height of C
12.	The area of a square region with perimeter 24	The area of a rectangular region with perimeter 28

$2x + 3y = 10$
$x + 2y = 8$

	Column A	Column B
13.	$x + y$	2

In the rectangular coordinate plane, points P, Q, and R have coordinates (2, 3), (5, 6), and (5, 3), respectively.

	Column A	Column B
14.	PQ	QR

x is an integer greater than 1.

	Column A	Column B
15.	3^{x+1}	4^x

GO ON TO THE NEXT PAGE.

Directions: Each of the Questions 16-30 has five answer choices. For each of these questions, select the best of the answer choices given.

16. If $n + n = k + k + k$ and $n + k = 5$, then $n =$

(A) 2
(B) 3
(C) 5
(D) 6
(E) 9

17. What is the length of a rectangle that has width 10 and perimeter 60 ?

(A) 15
(B) 20
(C) 25
(D) 30
(E) 40

18. A watch gains 7 minutes and 6 seconds every 6 days. If the rate of gain is constant, how much does the watch gain in one day?

(A) 1 min 1 sec
(B) 1 min 6 sec
(C) 1 min 11 sec
(D) 1 min 16 sec
(E) 1 min 21 sec

19. If $2x = 7$ and $3y = 2$, then $9xy =$

(A) 14
(B) 18
(C) 21
(D) 28
(E) 63

20. If $\sqrt{x} = 16$, then $x =$

(A) 4
(B) 8
(C) 16
(D) 32
(E) 256

GO ON TO THE NEXT PAGE.

Questions 21-25 refer to the following graph.

PERCENT OF TOTAL MALE FACULTY AND PERCENT OF TOTAL FEMALE FACULTY AT UNIVERSITY *X* BY FIELD

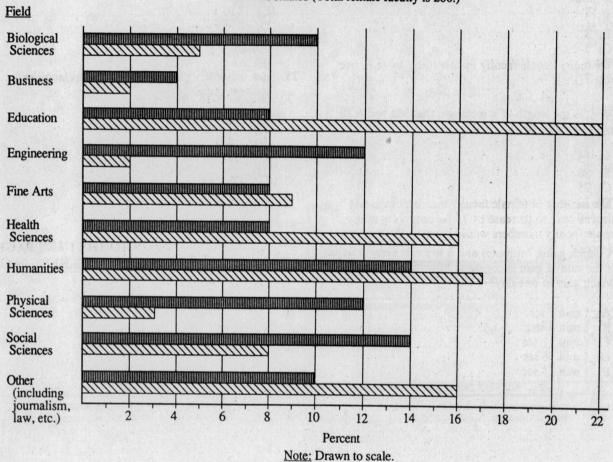

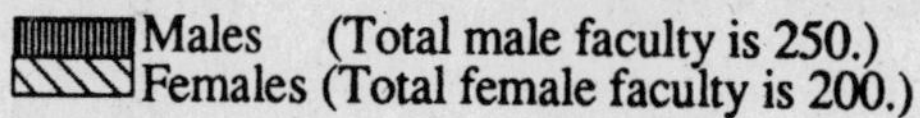

Field

Biological Sciences

Business

Education

Engineering

Fine Arts

Health Sciences

Humanities

Physical Sciences

Social Sciences

Other (including journalism, law, etc.)

2 4 6 8 10 12 14 16 18 20 22

Percent

Note: Drawn to scale.

GO ON TO THE NEXT PAGE.

21. For how many of the fields is the percent of total male faculty at University *X* greater than 11 percent?

(A) Two
(B) Three
(C) Four
(D) Five
(E) Six

22. How many female faculty members are there in fine arts?

(A) 14
(B) 16
(C) 17
(D) 18
(E) 20

23. If the number of female faculty members in social sciences were to increase by 75 percent, how many female faculty members would there be in social sciences?

(A) 12
(B) 14
(C) 21
(D) 28
(E) 30

24. If there are 275 students in engineering at University *X*, what is the approximate ratio of the number of engineering students to the number of engineering faculty?

(A) 8 to 1
(B) 12 to 1
(C) 14 to 1
(D) 18 to 1
(E) 20 to 1

25. Approximately what percent of the humanities faculty is male?

(A) 35%
(B) 38%
(C) 41%
(D) 45%
(E) 51%

GO ON TO THE NEXT PAGE.

26. If $2r - s = 3s - 2r$, what is s in terms of r?

(A) $\frac{r}{3}$

(B) $\frac{r}{2}$

(C) r

(D) $2r$

(E) $3r$

27. If $n \neq 0$, which of the following must be greater than n?

I. $2n$
II. n^3
III. $4 - n$

(A) None
(B) I only
(C) II only
(D) I and II
(E) I and III

28. The distance from point X to point Y is 20 miles, and the distance from point X to point Z is 12 miles. If d is the distance, in miles, between points Y and Z, then the range of possible values for d is indicated by

(A) $8 \leqq d \leqq 20$
(B) $8 \leqq d \leqq 32$
(C) $12 \leqq d \leqq 20$
(D) $12 \leqq d \leqq 32$
(E) $20 \leqq d \leqq 32$

29. What is the least integer value of n such that $\frac{1}{2^n} < 0.01$?

(A) 7
(B) 11
(C) 50
(D) 51
(E) There is no such least value.

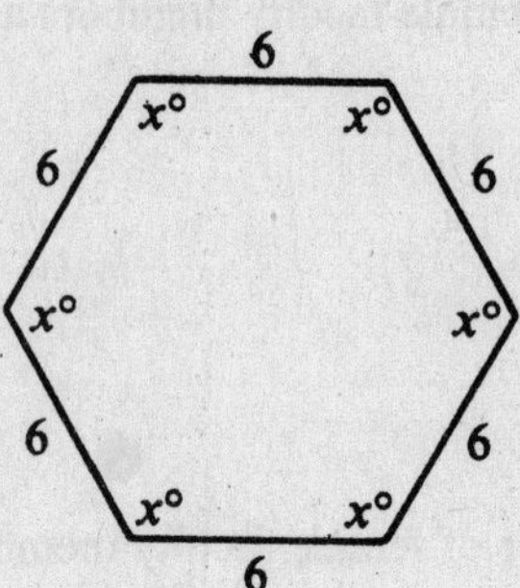

30. What is the area of the hexagonal region shown in the figure above?

(A) $54\sqrt{3}$

(B) 108

(C) $108\sqrt{3}$

(D) 216

(E) It cannot be determined from the information given.

STOP

IF YOU FINISH BEFORE TIME IS CALLED, YOU MAY CHECK YOUR WORK ON THIS SECTION ONLY. DO NOT TURN TO ANY OTHER SECTION IN THE TEST.

Section 6 starts on page 392.

SECTION 6

Time—30 minutes

38 Questions

Directions: Each sentence below has one or two blanks, each blank indicating that something has been omitted. Beneath the sentence are five lettered words or sets of words. Choose the word or set of words for each blank that best fits the meaning of the sentence as a whole.

1. The functions of the hands, eyes, and brain are so ------- that using the hands during early childhood helps to promote the child's entire ------- development.

   (A) intertwined. .perceptual
   (B) unalterable. .intellectual
   (C) enigmatic. .psychological
   (D) regulated. .adolescent
   (E) individualized. .social

2. Before 1500 North America was inhabited by more than 300 cultural groups, each with different customs, social structures, world views, and languages; such diversity -------- the existence of a single Native American culture.

   (A) complements (B) implies (C) reiterates (D) argues against (E) explains away

3. That dealers ------- enough to nurture a young modern painter's career rather than plunder it exist is not impossible, but the public's ------- appetite for modern art makes such dealers less and less likely.

   (A) chivalrous. .discriminating
   (B) magnanimous. .quirky
   (C) patient. .insatiable
   (D) cynical. .finicky
   (E) reckless. .zealous

4. In the absence of any ------- caused by danger, hardship, or even cultural difference, most utopian communities deteriorate into ------- but enervating backwaters.

   (A) turmoil. .frantic
   (B) mistrust. .naïve
   (C) amelioration. .ignorant
   (D) decimation. .intrusive
   (E) stimulation. .placid

5. As Juanita argued, this new code of conduct is laughable; its principles are either -------, offering no wisdom but the obvious, or are so devoid of specific advice as to make almost any action -------.

   (A) irresolute. .unlikely
   (B) corroborative. .redundant
   (C) platitudinous. .justifiable
   (D) homogeneous. .impartial
   (E) labyrinthine. .unacceptable

6. Histocompatibility antigens that attack foreign tissue in the body cannot have been ------- through evolution expressly to ------- organ transplantation; on the contrary, they have been found to facilitate many essential biological functions.

   (A) designed. .retain
   (B) produced. .aid
   (C) developed. .enhance
   (D) selected. .promote
   (E) conserved. .foil

7. Their air of cheerful self-sacrifice and endless complaisance won them undeserved praise, for their seeming gallantry was wholly motivated by a ------- wish to avoid conflict of any sort.

   (A) poignant
   (B) sincere
   (C) plaintive
   (D) laudable
   (E) craven

GO ON TO THE NEXT PAGE.

Directions: In each of the following questions, a related pair of words or phrases is followed by five lettered pairs of words or phrases. Select the lettered pair that best expresses a relationship similar to that expressed in the original pair.

8. RUST : CORROSION ::
(A) vapor : flammability
(B) dew : condensation
(C) crystal : purification
(D) solution : precipitation
(E) mold : disinfection

9. CLAIM : LEGITIMATED ::
(A) hypothesis : confirmed
(B) verdict : appealed
(C) counterargument : doubted
(D) proposition : repeated
(E) speculation : disbelieved

10. ENCLOSE : PARENTHESES ::
(A) abbreviate : brackets
(B) emphasize : hyphen
(C) separate : comma
(D) join : period
(E) omit : colon

11. ANTENNA : SIGNAL :: (A) bread : grain
(B) story : reporter (C) stem : flower
(D) net : fish (E) telegram : sender

12. WAG : HUMOROUS ::
(A) ruffian : frightened
(B) spendthrift : inattentive
(C) dolt : stupid
(D) pirate : merciless
(E) sinner : repentant

13. FIRM : IRONCLAD :: (A) bruised : broken
(B) polished : shining (C) smart : brilliant
(D) hard : stiff (E) jovial : merry

14. FOIL : METAL :: (A) pebble : concrete
(B) suede : leather (C) glaze : pottery
(D) veneer : wood (E) paper : cardboard

15. LEAVE : ABSCOND :: (A) take : steal
(B) evacuate : flee (C) interest : astound
(D) build : renovate (E) evaluate : downgrade

16. QUAFF : SIP :: (A) bolt : run (B) punch : hit
(C) gnaw : nibble (D) trudge : plod
(E) stride : mince

GO ON TO THE NEXT PAGE.

Directions: Each passage in this group is followed by questions based on its content. After reading a passage, choose the best answer to each question. Answer all questions following a passage on the basis of what is stated or implied in that passage.

For some time scientists have believed that cholesterol plays a major role in heart disease because people with familial hypercholesterolemia, a genetic defect, have six to eight times the normal level of cholesterol in their blood and they invariably develop heart disease. These people lack cell-surface receptors for low-density lipoproteins (LDL's), which are the fundamental carriers of blood cholesterol to the body cells that use cholesterol. Without an adequate number of cell-surface receptors to remove LDL's from the blood, the cholesterol-carrying LDL's remain in the blood, increasing blood cholesterol levels. Scientists also noticed that people with familial hypercholesterolemia appear to produce more LDL's than normal individuals. How, scientists wondered, could a genetic mutation that causes a slowdown in the removal of LDL's from the blood also result in an increase in the synthesis of this cholesterol-carrying protein?

Since scientists could not experiment on human body tissue, their knowledge of familial hypercholesterolemia was severely limited. However, a breakthrough came in the laboratories of Yoshio Watanabe of Kobe University in Japan in 1980. Watanabe noticed that a male rabbit in his colony had ten times the normal concentration of cholesterol in its blood. By appropriate breeding, Watanabe obtained a strain of rabbits that had very high cholesterol levels. These rabbits spontaneously developed heart disease. To his surprise, Watanabe further found that the rabbits, like humans with familial hypercholesterolemia, lacked LDL receptors. Thus, scientists could study these Watanabe rabbits to gain a better understanding of familial hypercholesterolemia in humans.

Prior to the breakthrough at Kobe University, it was known that LDL's are secreted from the liver in the form of a precursor, called very low-density lipoproteins (VLDL's), which carry triglycerides as well as relatively small amounts of cholesterol. The triglycerides are removed from the VLDL's by fatty and other tissues. What remains is a remnant particle that must be removed from the blood. What scientists learned by studying the Watanabe rabbits is that the removal of the VLDL remnant requires the LDL receptor. Normally, the majority of the VLDL remnants go to the liver where they bind to LDL receptors and are degraded. In the Watanabe rabbit, due to a lack of LDL receptors on liver cells, the VLDL remnants remain in the blood and are eventually converted to LDL's. The LDL receptors thus have a dual effect in controlling LDL levels. They are necessary to prevent oversynthesis of LDL's from VLDL remnants and they are necessary for the normal removal of LDL's from the blood. With this knowledge, scientists are now well on the way toward developing drugs that dramatically lower cholesterol levels in people afflicted with certain forms of familial hypercholesterolemia.

17. In the passage, the author is primarily concerned with

(A) presenting a hypothesis and describing compelling evidence in support of it
(B) raising a question and describing an important discovery that led to an answer
(C) showing that a certain genetically caused disease can be treated effectively with drugs
(D) explaining what causes the genetic mutation that leads to heart disease
(E) discussing the importance of research on animals for the study of human disease

18. Which of the following drugs, if developed, would most likely be an example of the kind of drug mentioned in line 53 ?

(A) A drug that stimulates the production of VLDL remnants
(B) A drug that stimulates the production of LDL receptors on the liver
(C) A drug that stimulates the production of an enzyme needed for cholesterol production
(D) A drug that suppresses the production of body cells that use cholesterol
(E) A drug that prevents triglycerides from attaching to VLDL's

19. The passage supplies information to answer which of the following questions?

(A) Which body cells are the primary users of cholesterol?
(B) How did scientists discover that LDL's are secreted from the liver in the form of a precursor?
(C) Where in the body are VLDL remnants degraded?
(D) Which body tissues produce triglycerides?
(E) What techniques are used to determine the presence or absence of cell-surface receptors?

GO ON TO THE NEXT PAGE.

20. According to the passage, by studying the Watanabe rabbits scientists learned that

    (A) VLDL remnants are removed from the blood by LDL receptors in the liver
    (B) LDL's are secreted from the liver in the form of precursors called VLDL's
    (C) VLDL remnant particles contain small amounts of cholesterol
    (D) triglycerides are removed from VLDL's by fatty tissues
    (E) LDL receptors remove LDL's from the blood

21. The development of drug treatments for some forms of familial hypercholesterolemia is regarded by the author as

    (A) possible, but not very important
    (B) interesting, but too costly to be practical
    (C) promising, but many years off
    (D) extremely unlikely
    (E) highly probable

22. The passage implies that if the Watanabe rabbits had had as many LDL receptors on their livers as do normal rabbits, the Watanabe rabbits would have been

    (A) less likely than normal rabbits to develop heart disease
    (B) less likely than normal rabbits to develop high concentrations of cholesterol in their blood
    (C) less useful than they actually were to scientists in the study of familial hypercholesterolemia in humans
    (D) unable to secrete VLDL's from their livers
    (E) immune to drugs that lower cholesterol levels in people with certain forms of familial hypercholesterolemia

23. The passage implies that Watanabe rabbits differ from normal rabbits in which of the following ways?

    (A) Watanabe rabbits have more LDL receptors than do normal rabbits.
    (B) The blood of Watanabe rabbits contains more VLDL remnants than does the blood of normal rabbits.
    (C) Watanabe rabbits have fewer fatty tissues than do normal rabbits.
    (D) Watanabe rabbits secrete lower levels of VLDL's than do normal rabbits.
    (E) The blood of Watanabe rabbits contains fewer LDL's than does the blood of normal rabbits.

GO ON TO THE NEXT PAGE.

(The article from which this passage was taken appeared in 1981.)

When speaking of Romare Bearden, one is tempted to say, "A great Black American artist." The subject matter of Bearden's collages is certainly Black. Portrayals of the folk of Mecklenburg County, North Carolina, whom he remembers from early childhood, of the jazz musicians and tenement roofs of his Harlem days, of Pittsburgh steelworkers, and his reconstruction of classical Greek myths in the guise of the ancient Black kingdom of Benin, attest to this. In natural harmony with this choice of subject matter are the social sensibilities of the artist, who remains active today with the Cinque Gallery in Manhattan, which he helped found and which is devoted to showing the work of minority artists.

Then why not call Bearden a Black American artist? Because ultimately this categorization is too narrow. "What stands up in the end is structure," Bearden says. "What I try to do is amplify. If I were just creating a picture of a farm woman from back home, it would have meaning to her and people there. But art amplifies itself to something universal."

24. According to the passage, all of the following are depicted in Bearden's collages EXCEPT

(A) workers in Pittsburgh's steel mills
(B) scenes set in the ancient kingdom of Benin
(C) people Bearden knew as a child
(D) traditional representations of the classical heroes of Greek mythology
(E) the jazz musicians of the Harlem Bearden used to know

25. The author suggests that Bearden should not be called a Black American artist because

(A) there are many collages by Bearden in which the subject matter is not Black
(B) Bearden's work reflects the Black American experience in a highly individual style
(C) through the structure of Bearden's art his Black subjects come to represent all of humankind
(D) Bearden's true significance lies not so much in his own work as in his efforts to help other minority artists
(E) much of Bearden's work uses the ancient Black kingdom of Benin for its setting

26. Bearden's social sensibilities and the subject matter of his collages are mentioned by the author in order to explain

(A) why one might be tempted to call Bearden a Black American artist
(B) why Bearden cannot be readily categorized
(C) why Bearden's appeal is thought by many to be ultimately universal
(D) how deeply an artist's artistic creations are influenced by the artist's social conscience
(E) what makes Bearden unique among contemporary Black American artists

27. The author of the passage is chiefly concerned with

(A) discussing Bearden's philosophy of art
(B) assessing the significance of the ethnic element in Bearden's work
(C) acknowledging Bearden's success in giving artistic expression to the Black American experience
(D) pointing out Bearden's helpfulness to other minority artists
(E) tracing Bearden's progress toward artistic maturity

GO ON TO THE NEXT PAGE.

Directions: Each question below consists of a word printed in capital letters, followed by five lettered words or phrases. Choose the lettered word or phrase that is most nearly opposite in meaning to the word in capital letters.

Since some of the questions require you to distinguish fine shades of meaning, be sure to consider all the choices before deciding which one is best.

28. INSERT: (A) remove (B) improve (C) revise (D) lessen (E) copy

29. BANKRUPTCY: (A) hypocrisy (B) solvency (C) advocacy (D) comparability (E) adversity

30. RELEVANT: (A) immaterial (B) random (C) hidden (D) false (E) inopportune

31. IMPLOSION:
(A) high-frequency pitch
(B) violent chemical reaction
(C) rapid outward movement
(D) complete change in composition
(E) uncontrolled variation in temperature

32. SLAB: (A) nib (B) streak (C) husk (D) sliver (E) shield

33. RAREFY: (A) contract suddenly (B) converge slowly (C) blend thoroughly (D) make denser (E) cool quickly

34. IMPETUOUS: (A) appropriate (B) respectful (C) uninteresting (D) voracious (E) deliberate

35. VITUPERATIVE: (A) suggestive (B) complimentary (C) genuine (D) undirected (E) pessimistic

36. FOMENT: (A) squelch (B) sweeten (C) dilute (D) liberate (E) clear

37. INCHOATE: (A) explicit (B) dependable (C) pragmatic (D) therapeutic (E) enduring

38. TYRO: (A) underling (B) expert (C) eccentric (D) truthful person (E) beneficent ruler

STOP

IF YOU FINISH BEFORE TIME IS CALLED, YOU MAY CHECK YOUR WORK ON THIS SECTION ONLY. DO NOT TURN TO ANY OTHER SECTION IN THE TEST.

NO TEST MATERIAL ON THIS PAGE

NOTE: To ensure prompt processing of test results, it is important that you fill in the blanks exactly as directed.

GENERAL TEST

A. Print and sign your full name in this box:

PRINT: ____
(LAST) (FIRST) (MIDDLE)

SIGN: ____

Copy this code in box 6 on your answer sheet. Then fill in the corresponding ovals exactly as shown.

6. TITLE CODE				
0	0	0	0	0
1	1	1	1	1
2	2	2	2	2
3	3	3	3	3
4	4	4	4	4
5	5	5	5	5
6	6	6	6	6
7	7	7	7	7
8	8	8	8	8
9	9	9	9	9

Copy the Test Name and Form Code in box 7 on your answer sheet.

TEST NAME General

FORM CODE GR91-19

GRADUATE RECORD EXAMINATIONS GENERAL TEST

B. You will have 3 hours and 30 minutes in which to work on this test, which consists of seven sections. During the time allowed for one section, you may work only on that section. The time allowed for each section is 30 minutes.

Each of your scores will be determined by the number of questions for which you select the best answer from the choices given. Questions for which you mark no answer or more than one answer are not counted in scoring. Nothing is subtracted from a score if you answer a question incorrectly. Therefore, to maximize your scores it is better for you to guess at an answer than not to respond at all.

You are advised to work as rapidly as you can without losing accuracy. Do not spend too much time on questions that are too difficult for you. Go on to the other questions and come back to the difficult ones later.

There are several different types of questions; you will find special directions for each type in the test itself. Be sure you understand the directions before attempting to answer any questions.

YOU MUST INDICATE ALL YOUR ANSWERS ON THE SEPARATE ANSWER SHEET. No credit will be given for anything written in this examination book, but you may write in the book as much as you wish to work out your answers. After you have decided on your response to a question, fill in the corresponding oval on the answer sheet. BE SURE THAT EACH MARK IS DARK AND COMPLETELY FILLS THE OVAL. Mark only one answer to each question. No credit will be given for multiple answers. Erase all stray marks. If you change an answer, be sure that all previous marks are erased completely. Incomplete erasures may be read as intended answers. Do not be concerned if your answer sheet provides spaces for more answers than there are questions in each section.

Example:

What city is the capital of France?

(A) Rome
(B) Paris
(C) London
(D) Cairo
(E) Oslo

Sample Answer

A ● C D E — BEST ANSWER PROPERLY MARKED

A B C D E
A B C D E
A B C D E
A B C D E
— IMPROPER MARKS

Some or all of the passages for this test have been adapted from published material to provide the examinee with significant problems for analysis and evaluation. To make the passages suitable for testing purposes, the style, content, or point of view of the original may have been altered in some cases. The ideas contained in the passages do not necessarily represent the opinions of the Graduate Record Examinations Board or Educational Testing Service.

DO NOT OPEN YOUR TEST BOOK UNTIL YOU ARE TOLD TO DO SO.

FOR GENERAL TEST, FORM GR91-19 ONLY
Answer Key and Percentages* of Examinees Answering Each Question Correctly

VERBAL ABILITY

Section 3 Number	Section 3 Answer	Section 3 P+	Section 6 Number	Section 6 Answer	Section 6 P+
1	A	96	1	A	89
2	C	74	2	D	75
3	C	71	3	C	59
4	C	55	4	E	50
5	D	59	5	C	57
6	E	43	6	E	39
7	A	28	7	E	24
8	B	94	8	B	81
9	D	83	9	A	86
10	C	75	10	C	84
11	D	63	11	D	57
12	E	49	12	C	51
13	E	39	13	C	43
14	E	37	14	D	30
15	E	32	15	A	32
16	C	27	16	E	14
17	A	75	17	B	54
18	D	71	18	B	74
19	D	80	19	C	52
20	B	68	20	A	57
21	B	42	21	E	83
22	D	69	22	C	53
23	A	47	23	B	54
24	E	38	24	D	65
25	B	41	25	C	83
26	C	31	26	A	45
27	B	41	27	B	33
28	D	89	28	A	98
29	B	82	29	B	81
30	B	72	30	A	83
31	A	74	31	C	76
32	A	57	32	D	64
33	D	42	33	D	39
34	C	36	34	E	41
35	E	31	35	B	31
36	D	29	36	A	26
37	A	29	37	A	28
38	E	17	38	B	21

QUANTITATIVE ABILITY

Section 1 Number	Section 1 Answer	Section 1 P+	Section 5 Number	Section 5 Answer	Section 5 P+
1	A	90	1	B	88
2	A	83	2	A	85
3	B	88	3	B	85
4	A	83	4	A	81
5	C	84	5	B	80
6	C	68	6	C	77
7	A	83	7	D	77
8	B	71	8	B	77
9	D	70	9	B	67
10	B	76	10	C	64
11	D	52	11	A	48
12	A	64	12	D	41
13	B	74	13	C	46
14	C	33	14	A	60
15	A	32	15	D	20
16	C	86	16	B	77
17	E	76	17	B	84
18	A	78	18	C	72
19	C	63	19	C	74
20	B	62	20	E	80
21	A	76	21	C	90
22	C	68	22	D	83
23	B	59	23	D	65
24	D	64	24	A	68
25	D	64	25	E	44
26	B	53	26	C	64
27	B	45	27	A	54
28	C	37	28	B	47
29	E	20	29	A	37
30	D	19	30	A	21

ANALYTICAL ABILITY

Section 2 Number	Section 2 Answer	Section 2 P+	Section 4 Number	Section 4 Answer	Section 4 P+
1	C	75	1	B	56
2	D	54	2	B	78
3	D	59	3	C	78
4	A	82	4	E	86
5	C	71	5	E	41
6	B	76	6	A	79
7	D	73	7	C	78
8	C	80	8	A	68
9	E	54	9	B	76
10	A	72	10	A	57
11	E	86	11	D	66
12	D	10	12	D	47
13	C	62	13	D	42
14	E	60	14	A	37
15	E	28	15	E	67
16	A	51	16	B	89
17	B	42	17	B	29
18	A	27	18	E	51
19	D	33	19	C	73
20	C	62	20	E	32
21	E	22	21	D	25
22	E	21	22	E	10
23	B	56	23	D	69
24	B	61	24	C	75
25	B	46	25	A	66

*Estimated P+ for the group of examinees who took the GRE General Test in a recent three-year period.

Score Conversions for GRE General Test GR91-19 Only and the Percents Below*

Raw Score	Verbal Scaled Score	Verbal % Below	Quantitative Scaled Score	Quantitative % Below	Analytical Scaled Score	Analytical % Below
74-76	800	99				
73	800	99				
72	790	99				
71	780	99				
70	770	99				
69	750	98				
68	740	98				
67	730	97				
66	720	96				
65	710	95				
64	700	95				
63	690	94				
62	680	93				
61	670	92				
60	660	90	800	97		
59	650	89	800	97		
58	640	87	800	97		
57	630	85	800	97		
56	620	84	780	94		
55	610	82	760	92		
54	600	80	750	89		
53	590	78	730	86		
52	580	76	720	84		
51	570	74	700	80		
50	560	72	690	78	800	99
49	550	69	670	74	800	99
48	540	67	660	72	800	99
47	520	61	640	68	800	99
46	510	59	630	66	780	98
45	500	56	610	61	770	97
44	490	54	600	59	760	96
43	480	51	590	57	740	95
42	470	48	570	51	720	92
41	460	44	560	49	710	91
40	450	41	550	48	690	88

Raw Score	Verbal Scaled Score	Verbal % Below	Quantitative Scaled Score	Quantitative % Below	Analytical Scaled Score	Analytical % Below
39	450	41	540	45	680	87
38	440	38	530	42	670	85
37	430	36	520	40	650	81
36	420	33	510	37	630	76
35	410	30	500	35	620	74
34	400	26	490	32	610	72
33	390	24	470	28	590	67
32	390	24	460	26	580	64
31	380	22	450	24	560	58
30	370	20	440	22	550	55
29	360	16	430	20	530	49
28	360	16	420	18	520	46
27	350	14	410	16	500	40
26	340	12	400	14	490	38
25	330	10	390	13	480	35
24	320	9	370	10	460	31
23	310	7	360	9	450	27
22	300	6	350	7	430	23
21	290	5	340	6	420	20
20	280	4	330	5	400	17
19	270	3	320	5	390	15
18	260	2	310	4	370	12
17	250	1	300	3	360	10
16	230	1	290	2	340	7
15	220	1	270	2	330	6
14	200	1	250	1	310	4
13	200	1	240	1	290	3
12	200	1	230	1	280	2
11	200	1	210	1	260	1
10	200	1	200	1	240	1
9	200	1	200	1	230	1
8	200	1	200	1	210	1
7	200	1	200	1	200	1
0-6	200	1	200	1	200	1

*Percent scoring below the scaled score is based on the performance of 923,359 examinees who took the General Test between October 1, 1986, and September 30, 1989. This percent below information is used for score reports during the 1990-91 testing year.

GR 92-1

01

THE GRADUATE RECORD EXAMINATIONS®

GRE®

General Test

Do not break the seal

until you are told to do so.

The contents of this test are confidential. Disclosure or reproduction of any portion of it is prohibited.

THIS TEST BOOK MUST NOT BE TAKEN FROM THE ROOM.

SECTION 1

Time—30 minutes

25 Questions

Directions: Each question or group of questions is based on a passage or set of conditions. In answering some of the questions, it may be useful to draw a rough diagram. For each question, select the best answer choice given.

Questions 1-6

Two maps are being designed. One will show subway lines; the other will show bus routes. There are three subway lines and four bus routes, and each line or route must be represented on the maps by a color used to represent it only. The colors available to the designer of the maps are blue, green, orange, purple, red, tan, and yellow. Any assignment of colors to lines and routes is acceptable provided the following conditions are met:

Blue cannot be used on the same map as purple.
Orange cannot be used on the same map as red, nor on the same map as yellow.

1. If blue is used on the subway map, which of the following must be true?

(A) Orange is used on the subway map.
(B) Yellow is used on the subway map.
(C) Purple is used on the bus map.
(D) Green is used on the bus map.
(E) Red is used on the bus map.

2. If red is used on the bus map, which of the following colors must be used on the subway map?

(A) Blue
(B) Orange
(C) Purple
(D) Tan
(E) Yellow

3. If yellow and purple are used on the subway map, the third color used on that map must be

(A) blue
(B) green
(C) orange
(D) red
(E) tan

4. If red and blue are used on the bus map, which of the following could be the other two colors used on that map?

(A) Green and purple
(B) Green and tan
(C) Green and yellow
(D) Orange and tan
(E) Purple and yellow

5. If green is not used on the same map as blue, nor on the same map as yellow, which of the following must be true?

(A) Blue is used on the subway map.
(B) Blue is used on the bus map.
(C) Green is used on the same map as red.
(D) Purple is used on the same map as orange.
(E) Tan is used on the same map as red.

6. There will be only one acceptable assignment of colors to each of the two maps if which of the following conditions is added to the original ones?

(A) Purple and tan must be used on the subway map.
(B) Green and purple must be used on the bus map.
(C) Blue cannot be used on the same map as green.
(D) Green cannot be used on the same map as yellow.
(E) Purple cannot be used on the same map as red.

GO ON TO THE NEXT PAGE.

7. The claim that learning computer programming is a sure way to a bright future is analogous to the contention, popular a few years ago, that if one wanted a successful career, one should study law. Now, of course, there are more law students graduating than the market can absorb.

The point of the analogy above is that

(A) lawyers are making increasing use of computers in their work
(B) computer programmers will increasingly need the services of lawyers
(C) there will soon be more jobs for lawyers than there are now
(D) there will soon be more programming students graduating than there are jobs for them
(E) graduating law students and programming students will soon be competing with each other for the same jobs

8. Whenever Ned is outdoors and the sun is shining, Ned wears his sunglasses. Whenever Ned is outdoors and the sun is not shining, Ned carries his sunglasses in his pocket. Sometimes the sun is shining when Ned is not outdoors.

If the statements above are true and Ned is not wearing his sunglasses, which of the following statements must also be true?

(A) Ned is carrying his sunglasses in his pocket.
(B) Ned is not outdoors.
(C) Ned is not outdoors and the sun is not shining.
(D) Ned is not outdoors and/or the sun is not shining.
(E) Ned is outdoors and/or the sun is not shining.

9. Between 1950 and 1965, the federal government spent one-third more on research and development than industry did from its own funds. In 1980, for the first time, industry spent more on research and development than the federal government did. Representatives of industry claim that these statistics show an increased commitment on the part of industry to develop competitive products.

Which of the following, if true, would help to refute the claim of the representatives of industry?

(A) In 1980 the federal government spent half as much on research and development as it spent in 1965.
(B) Between 1965 and 1980, industry in the United States experienced increasing competition from industry in other countries.
(C) In 1979 the federal government shifted research allocations from pharmaceuticals to electronics.
(D) Since 1965, industry has developed major product innovations, such as the personal computer.
(E) Before 1985, money spent by industry on research and development was not taxed by the federal government.

GO ON TO THE NEXT PAGE.

<u>Questions 10-13</u>

Seven offices in an office building are to be painted. The offices, which are on one side of a hallway, are numbered consecutively, one to seven, from the front of the building to the back. Each office is to be painted one color only according to the following conditions:

Two offices must be painted white; two offices must be painted blue; two offices must be painted green; and one office must be painted yellow.
The two offices painted green must be next to each other.
The two offices painted blue cannot be next to each other.
The office painted yellow cannot be next to an office painted white.
Office 3 must be painted white.

10. If office 2 is painted green, which of the following offices must also be painted green?

(A) 1
(B) 3
(C) 4
(D) 5
(E) 6

11. If office 5 is painted white, which of the following could be true?

(A) Office 1 is painted blue.
(B) Office 2 is painted yellow.
(C) Office 4 is painted green.
(D) Office 4 is painted yellow.
(E) Office 6 is painted blue.

12. If office 4 is painted white and an office that is painted green is next to an office that is painted white, which of the following must be true?

(A) Office 1 is painted green.
(B) Office 1 is painted yellow.
(C) Office 5 is painted blue.
(D) Office 6 is painted yellow.
(E) Office 7 is painted blue.

13. Which of the following conditions, when combined with the original conditions, has the consequence of completely determining the color that each office is painted?

(A) Office 1 must be painted yellow.
(B) Office 1 must be painted green.
(C) Office 4 must be painted blue.
(D) Office 6 must be painted white.
(E) Office 6 must be painted blue.

GO ON TO THE NEXT PAGE.

Questions 14-17

A mail carrier must deliver mail by making a stop at each of six buildings: K, L, M, O, P, and S. Mail to be delivered is of two types, ordinary mail and priority mail. The delivery of both types of mail is subject to the following conditions:

Regardless of the type of mail to be delivered, mail to P and mail to S must be delivered before mail to M is delivered.

Regardless of the type of mail to be delivered, mail to L and mail to K must be delivered before mail to S is delivered.

Mail to buildings receiving some priority mail must be delivered, as far as the above conditions permit, before mail to buildings receiving only ordinary mail.

14. If K is the only building receiving priority mail, which of the following lists the buildings in an order, from first through sixth, in which they can receive their mail?

(A) L, K, P, S, O, M
(B) L, K, S, P, M, O
(C) K, L, P, M, S, O
(D) K, P, L, S, O, M
(E) O, K, L, P, S, M

15. If L, M, and S are each receiving priority mail, which of the following lists the buildings in an order, from first to sixth, in which they must receive their mail?

(A) K, L, P, S, O, M
(B) L, K, O, P, S, M
(C) L, K, S, P, M, O
(D) M, L, S, P, K, O
(E) S, L, M, P, K, O

16. If the sequence of buildings to which mail is delivered is O, P, L, K, S, M and if S is receiving priority mail, which of the following is a complete and accurate list of buildings that must also be receiving priority mail?

(A) O, L
(B) O, P
(C) P, L
(D) P, M
(E) O, P, L, K

17. If only one building is to receive priority mail, and, as a result, O can be no earlier than fourth in the order of buildings, which of the following must be the building receiving priority mail that day?

(A) K
(B) L
(C) M
(D) P
(E) S

GO ON TO THE NEXT PAGE.

Questions 18-22

Six musicians—Ann, Betsy, Gordon, Juan, Marian, and Ted—are planning to perform a program consisting entirely of three quartets. Each quartet requires two violins, one cello, and a piano.

Each person must play in at least one quartet, and each person can play, at most, one instrument in a quartet. No person can play the same type of instrument (violin, cello, or piano) in two successive quartets.

Ann plays violin only, and must play in the first quartet.
Betsy plays violin or piano.
Gordon plays violin or cello.
Juan plays cello only.
Marian plays violin or piano.
Ted plays piano only.

18. Any of the following musicians could play in the second quartet EXCEPT

(A) Ann
(B) Betsy
(C) Gordon
(D) Juan
(E) Ted

19. If Juan plays cello in the first quartet, which of the following must be true?

(A) Betsy plays piano in the first quartet.
(B) Gordon plays cello in the second quartet.
(C) Gordon plays cello in the third quartet.
(D) Juan plays cello in the second quartet.
(E) Ted plays piano in the first quartet.

20. If Ann, Betsy, Gordon, and Juan play in the first quartet, which of the following could be the group of musicians playing in the second quartet?

(A) Ann, Betsy, Gordon, and Marian
(B) Ann, Gordon, Marian, and Ted
(C) Betsy, Gordon, Juan, and Marian
(D) Betsy, Gordon, Marian, and Ted
(E) Betsy, Juan, Marian, and Ted

21. Which of the following groups of musicians includes all those, and only those, who CANNOT be scheduled to play in all three quartets, no matter what schedule is devised?

(A) Ann, Betsy, and Gordon
(B) Ann, Juan, and Ted
(C) Betsy, Gordon, and Marian
(D) Betsy, Juan, and Marian
(E) Gordon, Juan, and Ted

22. Unavailability of which of the following musicians would still permit scheduling the five remaining players so that the proposed program could be performed?

(A) Betsy
(B) Gordon
(C) Juan
(D) Marian
(E) Ted

GO ON TO THE NEXT PAGE.

23. It is impossible to believe scientific predictions that a long "nuclear winter" would envelop the Earth as a result of nuclear war. Atmospheric scientists and weather experts cannot reliably and accurately predict tomorrow's weather. Yet the effect of nuclear explosions on local and worldwide atmospheric conditions must follow the sàme laws that control everyday weather changes. If the weather cannot be predicted with present knowledge, neither can a nuclear-winter scenario.

Which of the following, if true, would most seriously weaken the argument made above that if scientists cannot reliably predict the daily weather, their predictions of a "nuclear winter" cannot be believed?

(A) The scientific theory of a nuclear winter uses data that is available to those who forecast the daily weather.
(B) Scientists' predictions about a nuclear winter are necessarily speculative, since they cannot be verified by harmless experimentation.
(C) Weather forecasters usually do not insist that their predictions are infallible.
(D) Scientific predictions of catastrophic natural events such as volcanic eruptions and earthquakes usually have less reliability than everyday weather predictions.
(E) The scientific theory of a nuclear winter is concerned with drastic climatic changes rather than day-to-day fluctuations in the weather.

24. Carla and Joel took five courses together but achieved the same grade in only one of the courses—history. Each course was graded on a scale ranging from 60 to 100.

Which of the following statements allows one to determine whether the average of the grades Carla achieved in the five courses was higher than the average of the grades Joel achieved in those courses?

(A) Carla's lowest grade was in history, but Joel's lowest grade was in math.
(B) Joel's highest grade was higher than Carla's highest grade.
(C) Carla achieved higher grades than Joel in three courses.
(D) Carla's lowest grade and Joel's highest grade were the same.
(E) Joel's lowest grade and Carla's highest grade were for the same course.

25. In the 1960's, long-term studies of primate behavior often used as subjects tamarins, small monkeys that were thought ideal because they require only small cages, breed frequently, and grow quickly. Field studies were not used because they were costly and difficult. Tamarins were kept caged in male-female pairs, because otherwise, serious fights erupted between unrelated females. On the basis of the fact that breeding occurred, tamarins were viewed as monogamous.

The view taken by the researchers concerning the monogamy of tamarins depended on a questionable assumption. Which of the following could have served as that assumption?

(A) The suppression of fighting between related females serves to protect their common genetic inheritance.
(B) Adult male tamarins contribute to the care of tamarin infants.
(C) The social system of tamarins requires monogamous pairing.
(D) Male tamarin monkeys do not display aggressive behavior in the wild.
(E) The way the tamarins were kept in cages did not affect their mating behavior.

STOP

IF YOU FINISH BEFORE TIME IS CALLED, YOU MAY CHECK YOUR WORK ON THIS SECTION ONLY. DO NOT TURN TO ANY OTHER SECTION IN THE TEST.

NO TEST MATERIAL ON THIS PAGE

SECTION 2

Time—30 minutes

38 Questions

Directions: Each sentence below has one or two blanks, each blank indicating that something has been omitted. Beneath the sentence are five lettered words or sets of words. Choose the word or set of words for each blank that best fits the meaning of the sentence as a whole.

1. Though some of the information the author reveals about Russian life might surprise Americans, her major themes are ------- enough.

(A) familiar (B) thorough (C) vital (D) original (E) interesting

2. In the early twentieth century, the discovery of radium ------- the popular imagination; not only was its discoverer, Marie Curie, idolized, but its market value ------- that of the rarest gemstone.

(A) stormed. .sank to
(B) horrified. .approached
(C) taxed. .was equal to
(D) enflamed. .exceeded
(E) escaped. .was comparable to

3. The president's secretary and his chief aide adored him, and both wrote obsessively ------- personal memoirs about him; unfortunately, however, ------- does not make for true intimacy.

(A) fatuous. .frankness
(B) devoted. .idolatry
(C) garrulous. .confidentiality
(D) candid. .discretion
(E) rancorous. .criticism

4. Despite claims that his philosophy can be traced to ------- source, the philosophy in fact draws liberally on several traditions and methodologies and so could justifiably be termed -------.

(A) a particular. .consistent
(B) a schematic. .multifaceted
(C) a dominant. .cogent
(D) an authoritative. .derivative
(E) a single. .eclectic

5. Du Bois' foreign trips were the highlight, not the -------, of his travels; he was habitually on the go across and around the United States.

(A) idiosyncrasy (B) result (C) precursor (D) culmination (E) totality

6. Business forecasts usually prove reasonably accurate when the assumption that the future will be much like the past is -------; in times of major ------- in the business environment, however, forecasts can be dangerously wrong.

(A) specified. .discontinuities
(B) questioned. .surges
(C) contradicted. .improvements
(D) entertained. .risks
(E) satisfied. .shifts

7. It is almost always desirable to increase the yield of a crop if ------- increases are not also necessary in energy, labor, and other inputs of crop production.

(A) predetermined (B) commensurate (C) compatible (D) measured (E) equivocal

GO ON TO THE NEXT PAGE.

Directions: In each of the following questions, a related pair of words or phrases is followed by five lettered pairs of words or phrases. Select the lettered pair that best expresses a relationship similar to that expressed in the original pair.

8. MISER : STINGY :: (A) porter : strong (B) rebel : idle (C) sage : docile (D) friend : snide (E) loner : solitary

9. AQUEDUCT : WATER :: (A) capillary : saliva (B) artery : blood (C) esophagus : breath (D) corridor : aircraft (E) tanker : fluids

10. ENZYME : CATALYST :: (A) vaccine : allergy (B) bacterium : microbe (C) gland : muscle (D) vein : organ (E) neuron : corpuscle

11. LIEN : CLAIM ::
(A) brief : investigation
(B) mortgage : interest
(C) foreclosure : pleading
(D) garnishment : presumption
(E) subpoena : command

12. VERBOSITY : WORDS ::
(A) harmoniousness : relationships
(B) floridness : embellishments
(C) interrogation : answers
(D) supposition : proposals
(E) condemnation : acts

13. QUIXOTIC : IDEALISTIC ::
(A) churlish : polite
(B) whimsical : steady
(C) disinterested : impartial
(D) touchy : sensitive
(E) central : random

14. PREEMPT : PRECEDENCE ::
(A) dissemble : diplomacy
(B) superintend : culpability
(C) preside : arbitration
(D) acquire : possession
(E) divest : implication

15. MALINGER : AIL :: (A) study : learn (B) qualify : achieve (C) sneer : respect (D) flatter : appreciate (E) clash : resolve

16. ARBOREAL : TREES :: (A) terrestrial : plains (B) amphibious : rivers (C) herbaceous : plants (D) subterranean : caves (E) sidereal : stars

GO ON TO THE NEXT PAGE.

Directions: Each passage in this group is followed by questions based on its content. After reading a passage, choose the best answer to each question. Answer all questions following a passage on the basis of what is stated or implied in that passage.

Zooplankton, tiny animals adapted to an existence in the ocean, have evolved clever mechanisms for obtaining their food, miniscule phytoplankton (plant plankton). A very specialized feeding adaptation in zooplankton is that of the tadpolelike appendicularian who lives in a walnut-sized (or smaller) balloon of mucus equipped with filters that capture and concentrate phytoplankton. The balloon, a transparent structure that varies in design according to the type of appendicularian inhabiting it, also protects the animal and helps to keep it afloat. Water containing phytoplankton is pumped by the appendicularian's muscular tail into the balloon's incurrent filters, passes through the feeding filter where the appendicularian sucks the food into its mouth, and then goes through an exit passage. Found in all the oceans of the world, including the Arctic Ocean, appendicularians tend to remain near the water's surface where the density of phytoplankton is greatest.

17. It can be inferred from the passage that which of the following is true of appendicularians?
    (A) They are exclusively carnivorous.
    (B) They have more than one method of obtaining food.
    (C) They can tolerate frigid water.
    (D) They can disguise themselves by secreting mucus.
    (E) They are more sensitive to light than are other zooplankton.

18. The author is primarily concerned with
    (A) explaining how appendicularians obtain food
    (B) examining the flotation methods of appendicularians
    (C) mapping the distribution of appendicularians around the world
    (D) describing how appendicularians differ from other zooplankton
    (E) comparing the various types of balloons formed by appendicularians

19. According to the passage, all of the following are descriptive of appendicularians EXCEPT
    (A) tailed (B) vegetarian (C) small-sized (D) single-celled (E) ocean-dwelling

20. The passage suggests that appendicularians tend to remain in surface waters because they
    (A) prefer the warmer water near the surface
    (B) are unable to secrete mucus at the lower levels of the ocean
    (C) use the contrast of light and shadow at the surface to hide from predators
    (D) live in balloons that cannot withstand the water pressure deeper in the ocean
    (E) eat food that grows more profusely near the surface

GO ON TO THE NEXT PAGE.

Students of United States history, seeking to identify the circumstances that encouraged the emergence of feminist movements, have thoroughly investigated the mid-nineteenth-century American economic and social conditions that affected the status of women. These historians, however, have analyzed less fully the development of specifically feminist ideas and activities during the same period. Furthermore, the ideological origins of feminism in the United States have been obscured because, even when historians did take into account those feminist ideas and activities occurring within the United States, they failed to recognize that feminism was then a truly international movement actually centered in Europe. American feminist activists who have been described as "solitary" and "individual theorists" were in reality connected to a movement—utopian socialism—which was already popularizing feminist ideas in Europe during the two decades that culminated in the first women's rights conference held at Seneca Falls, New York, in 1848. Thus, a complete understanding of the origins and development of nineteenth-century feminism in the United States requires that the geographical focus be widened to include Europe and that the detailed study already made of social conditions be expanded to include the ideological development of feminism.

The earliest and most popular of the utopian socialists were the Saint-Simonians. The specifically feminist part of Saint-Simonianism has, however, been less studied than the group's contribution to early socialism. This is regrettable on two counts. By 1832 feminism was the central concern of Saint-Simonianism and entirely absorbed its adherents' energy; hence, by ignoring its feminism, European historians have misunderstood Saint-Simonianism. Moreover, since many feminist ideas can be traced to Saint-Simonianism, European historians' appreciation of later feminism in France and the United States remained limited.

Saint-Simon's followers, many of whom were women, based their feminism on an interpretation of his project to reorganize the globe by replacing brute force with the rule of spiritual powers. The new world order would be ruled together by a male, to represent reflection, and a female, to represent sentiment. This complementarity reflects the fact that, while the Saint-Simonians did not reject the belief that there were innate differences between men and women, they nevertheless foresaw an equally important social and political role for both sexes in their utopia.

Only a few Saint-Simonians opposed a definition of sexual equality based on gender distinction. This minority believed that individuals of both sexes were born similar in capacity and character, and they ascribed male-female differences to socialization and education. The envisioned result of both currents of thought, however, was that women would enter public life in the new age and that sexual equality would reward men as well as women with an improved way of life.

21. It can be inferred that the author considers those historians who describe early feminists in the United States as "solitary" to be

(A) insufficiently familiar with the international origins of nineteenth-century American feminist thought
(B) overly concerned with the regional diversity of feminist ideas in the period before 1848
(C) not focused narrowly enough in their geographical scope
(D) insufficiently aware of the ideological consequences of the Seneca Falls conference
(E) insufficiently concerned with the social conditions out of which feminism developed

22. According to the passage, which of the following is true of the Seneca Falls conference on women's rights?

(A) It was primarily a product of nineteenth-century Saint-Simonian feminist thought.
(B) It was the work of American activists who were independent of feminists abroad.
(C) It was the culminating achievement of the utopian socialist movement.
(D) It was a manifestation of an international movement for social change and feminism.
(E) It was the final manifestation of the women's rights movement in the United States in the nineteenth century.

23. The author's attitude toward most European historians who have studied the Saint-Simonians is primarily one of

(A) approval of the specific focus of their research
(B) disapproval of their lack of attention to the issue that absorbed most of the Saint-Simonians' energy after 1832
(C) approval of their general focus on social conditions
(D) disapproval of their lack of attention to links between the Saint-Simonians and their American counterparts
(E) disagreement with their interpretation of the Saint-Simonian belief in sexual equality

GO ON TO THE NEXT PAGE.

24. The author mentions all of the following as characteristic of the Saint-Simonians EXCEPT:

(A) The group included many women among its members.
(B) The group believed in a world that would be characterized by sexual equality.
(C) The group was among the earliest European socialist groups.
(D) Most members believed that women should enter public life.
(E) Most members believed that women and men were inherently similar in ability and character.

25. It can be inferred from the passage that the Saint-Simonians envisioned a utopian society having which of the following characteristics?

(A) It would be worldwide.
(B) It would emphasize dogmatic religious principles.
(C) It would most influence the United States.
(D) It would have armies composed of women rather than of men.
(E) It would continue to develop new feminist ideas.

26. It can be inferred from the passage that the author believes that study of Saint-Simonianism is necessary for historians of American feminism because such study

(A) would clarify the ideological origins of those feminist ideas that influenced American feminism
(B) would increase understanding of a movement that deeply influenced the utopian socialism of early American feminists
(C) would focus attention on the most important aspect of Saint-Simonian thought before 1832
(D) promises to offer insight into a movement that was a direct outgrowth of the Seneca Falls conference of 1848
(E) could increase understanding of those ideals that absorbed most of the energy of the earliest American feminists

27. According to the passage, which of the following would be the most accurate description of the society envisioned by most Saint-Simonians?

(A) A society in which women were highly regarded for their extensive education
(B) A society in which the two genders played complementary roles and had equal status
(C) A society in which women did not enter public life
(D) A social order in which a body of men and women would rule together on the basis of their spiritual power
(E) A social order in which distinctions between male and female would not exist and all would share equally in political power

GO ON TO THE NEXT PAGE.

Directions: Each question below consists of a word printed in capital letters, followed by five lettered words or phrases. Choose the lettered word or phrase that is most nearly opposite in meaning to the word in capital letters.

Since some of the questions require you to distinguish fine shades of meaning, be sure to consider all the choices before deciding which one is best.

28. TOY: (A) think over seriously
(B) admire overtly (C) use sporadically
(D) praise unstintingly (E) covet irrationally

29. QUACK: (A) hard worker (B) true believer
(C) honest practitioner (D) careful employee
(E) experienced planner

30. FRINGE: (A) center (B) proximity
(C) breadth (D) outlet (E) continuity

31. FALLACIOUS: (A) safe (B) valid
(C) energetic (D) diverted (E) persuasive

32. CRYPTIC: (A) resonant (B) superficial
(C) unobjectionable (D) self-explanatory
(E) other-directed

33. RENT: (A) in abeyance (B) occupied
(C) undeserved (D) turned down
(E) made whole

34. CONSIDER: (A) activate (B) infer
(C) table (D) encourage (E) deter

35. TENUOUS: (A) finite (B) embedded
(C) convinced (D) substantial (E) proximate

36. MERCURIAL: (A) earthy (B) honest
(C) thoughtful (D) clumsy (E) constant

37. OPPROBRIUM: (A) good repute
(B) fair recompense (C) fidelity
(D) exposure (E) patience

38. VENERATION: (A) derision (B) blame
(C) avoidance (D) ostracism (E) defiance

STOP

IF YOU FINISH BEFORE TIME IS CALLED, YOU MAY CHECK YOUR WORK ON THIS SECTION ONLY. DO NOT TURN TO ANY OTHER SECTION IN THE TEST.

Section 3 starts on page 418.

SECTION 3

Time—30 minutes

30 Questions

Numbers: All numbers used are real numbers.

Figures: Position of points, angles, regions, etc. can be assumed to be in the order shown; and angle measures can be assumed to be positive.

Lines shown as straight can be assumed to be straight.

Figures can be assumed to lie in a plane unless otherwise indicated.

Figures that accompany questions are intended to provide information useful in answering the questions. However, unless a note states that a figure is drawn to scale, you should solve these problems NOT by estimating sizes by sight or by measurement, but by using your knowledge of mathematics (see Example 2 below).

Directions: Each of the Questions 1-15 consists of two quantities, one in Column A and one in Column B. You are to compare the two quantities and choose

A if the quantity in Column A is greater;
B if the quantity in Column B is greater;
C if the two quantities are equal;
D if the relationship cannot be determined from the information given.

Note: Since there are only four choices, NEVER MARK (E).

Common Information: In a question, information concerning one or both of the quantities to be compared is centered above the two columns. A symbol that appears in both columns represents the same thing in Column A as it does in Column B.

	Column A	Column B	Sample Answers
Example 1:	2×6	$2 + 6$	● Ⓑ Ⓒ Ⓓ Ⓔ

Examples 2-4 refer to $\triangle PQR$.

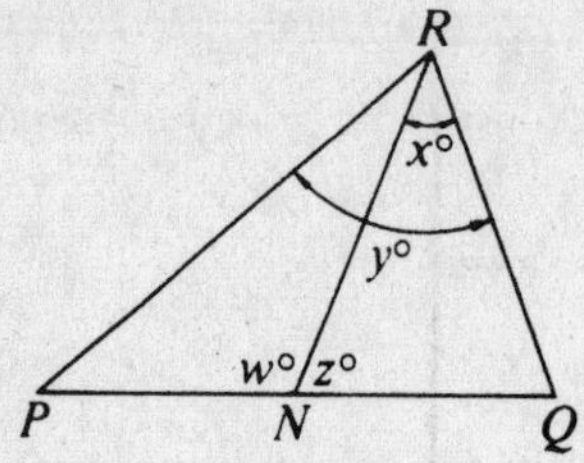

R, $x°$, $y°$, $w°$, $z°$, P, N, Q

	Column A	Column B	Sample Answers
Example 2:	PN	NQ	Ⓐ Ⓑ Ⓒ ● Ⓔ (since equal measures cannot be assumed, even though PN and NQ appear equal)
Example 3:	x	y	Ⓐ ● Ⓒ Ⓓ Ⓔ (since N is between P and Q)
Example 4:	$w + z$	180	Ⓐ Ⓑ ● Ⓓ Ⓔ (since PQ is a straight line)

GO ON TO THE NEXT PAGE.

A if the quantity in Column A is greater;
B if the quantity in Column B is greater;
C if the two quantities are equal;
D if the relationship cannot be determined from the information given.

	Column A	Column B
	A hardware store purchased identical snow shovels at a cost of $9 apiece and sold each of them for 20 percent above cost.	
1.	The price at which the hardware store sold each shovel	$10.80
	$n + \frac{2}{5} = 5 + \frac{7}{5}$	
2.	n	$6\frac{4}{5}$
	$x < 0$	
3.	$x - 1$	$1 - x$

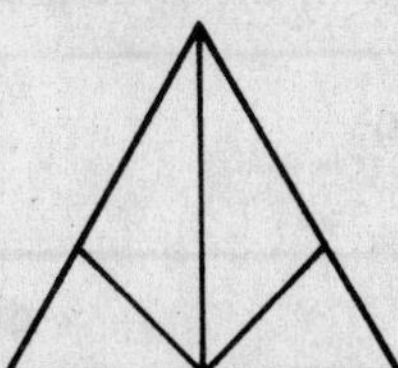

	Column A	Column B
4.	The total number of triangles shown above	6
5.	3^4	4^3
	$x + k = 8$ $x - k = 4$	
6.	x	k

	Column A	Column B
	Carol is c centimeters tall, and Diane is d centimeters shorter than Carol. $(d > 0)$	
7.	The sum of Carol's height and Diane's height	$2c$ centimeters

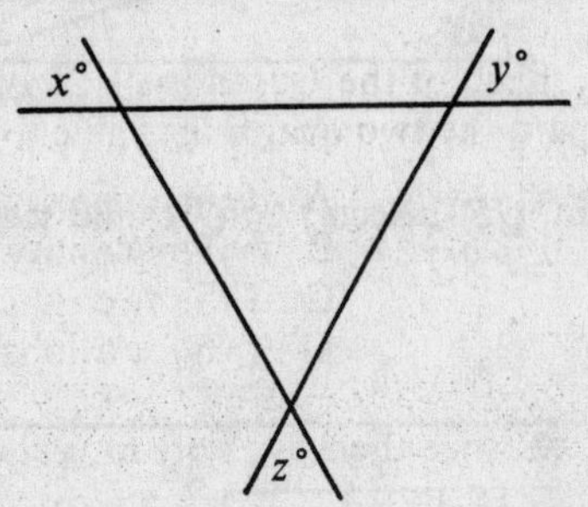

	Column A	Column B
8.	$x + y + z$	150
	$n = 105.873$	
9.	$\frac{n \times 10^3}{10^5}$	1

GO ON TO THE NEXT PAGE.

A if the quantity in Column A is greater;
B if the quantity in Column B is greater;
C if the two quantities are equal;
D if the relationship cannot be determined from the information given.

	Column A	Column B

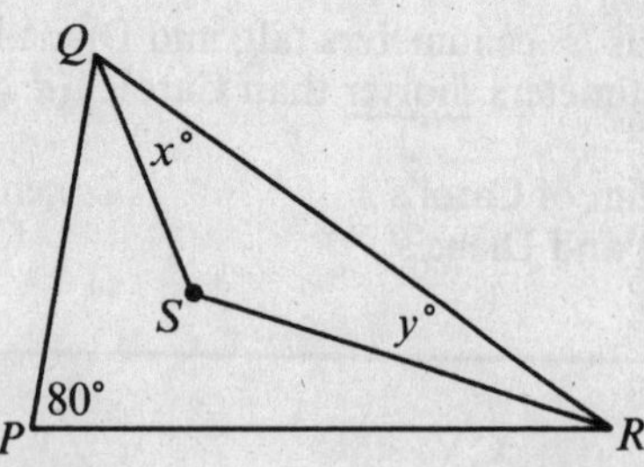

Segment QS bisects $\angle PQR$ and segment RS bisects $\angle PRQ$.

10.	x	y

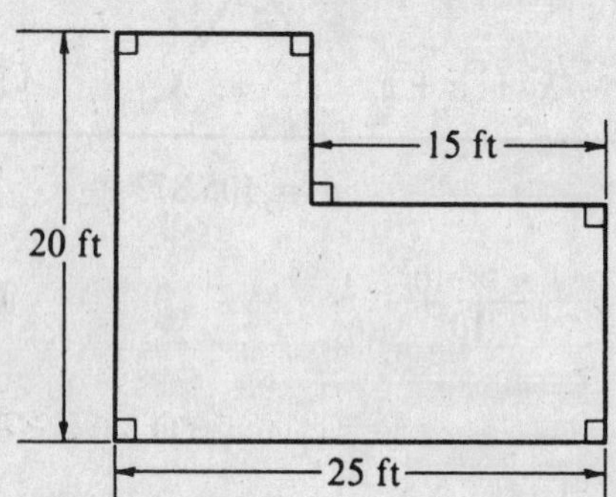

The figure represents the floor of a certain room.

11.	The area of the floor	350 square feet

	Column A	Column B

$$x^2 - 3x + 2 = 0$$

12.	Twice the sum of the roots of the equation	6

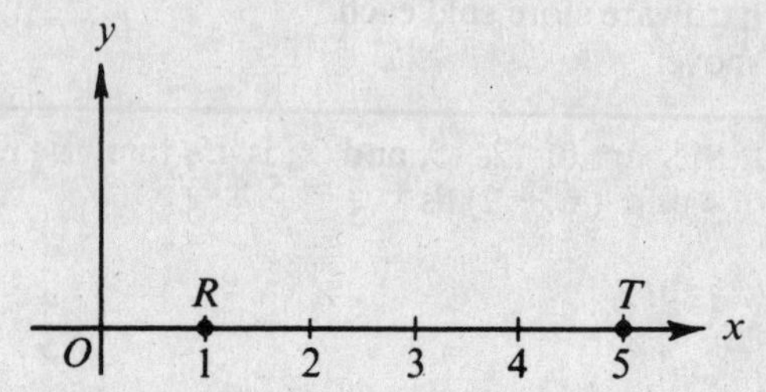

Point S (not shown) lies above the x-axis such that $\triangle RST$ has area equal to 6.

13.	The x-coordinate of point S	The y-coordinate of point S
14.	$\frac{10^5}{5^3}$	$2^5 \cdot 5^2$

$$rs \neq 0$$

15.	$(r + s)^2$	$r^2 + s^2$

GO ON TO THE NEXT PAGE.

Directions: Each of the Questions 16-30 has five answer choices. For each of these questions, select the best of the answer choices given.

16. If $9x - 3 = 15$, then $3x - 1 =$

(A) $\frac{5}{3}$

(B) 3

(C) 5

(D) 6

(E) 45

17. If the sum of 12, 15, and x is 45, then the product of 5 and $(x + 2)$ is

(A) 100
(B) 92
(C) 80
(D) 41
(E) 25

18. If the average (arithmetic mean) of two numbers is 20 and one of the numbers is x, what is the other number in terms of x?

(A) $40 - x$
(B) $40 - 2x$
(C) $20 + x$
(D) $20 - x$
(E) $20 - 2x$

19. $\frac{1}{\frac{1}{2}} + \frac{2}{\frac{2}{3}} + \frac{3}{\frac{3}{4}} =$

(A) $\frac{1}{9}$

(B) $\frac{13}{12}$

(C) $\frac{29}{12}$

(D) 8

(E) 9

20. What is the area of a circular region that has circumference 8π?

(A) 4π
(B) 8π
(C) 16π
(D) 32π
(E) 64π

GO ON TO THE NEXT PAGE.

Questions 21-25 refer to the following graphs.

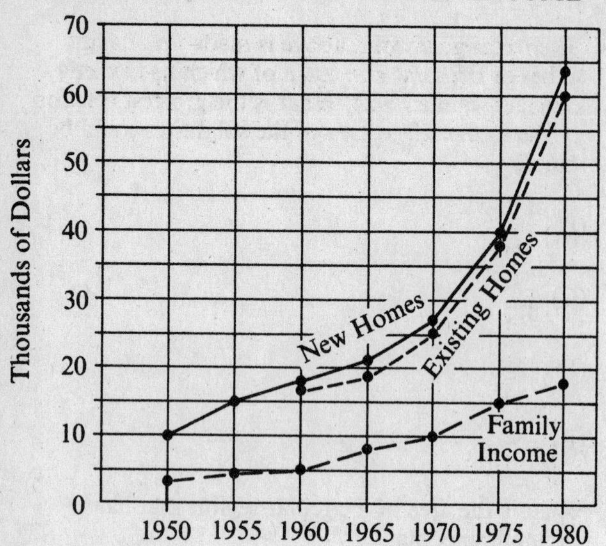

*median sale price and median family income

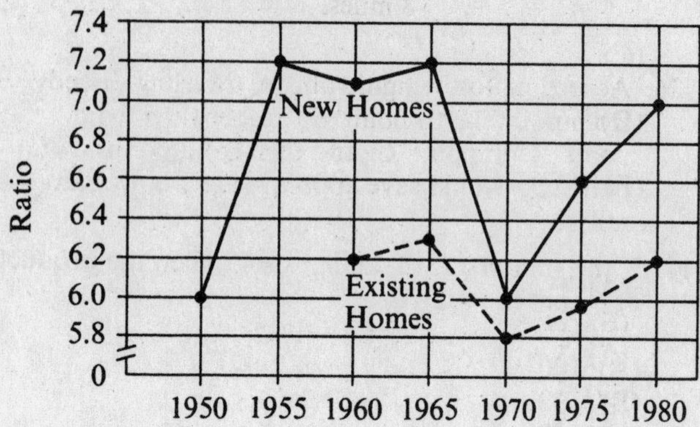

$$**\text{Ratio} = \frac{\text{Housing Price (median sale price)}}{\text{Per Capita Income}}$$

Note: Graphs drawn to scale.

21. Approximately what was the median sale price of an existing home in 1975 ?

(A) $15,000
(B) $35,000
(C) $36,000
(D) $38,000
(E) $40,000

22. In 1980, what was the approximate difference between the median sale price of an existing home and the median family income?

(A) $42,000
(B) $45,000
(C) $46,000
(D) $46,500
(E) $47,500

23. For which of the following years was the ratio of the median sale price of a new home minus the median sale price of an existing home to per capita income least?

(A) 1960
(B) 1965
(C) 1970
(D) 1975
(E) 1980

24. If in 1985 the per capita income was $7,200 and the ratio of the median sale price of an existing home to per capita income was the same as in 1980, what was the median sale price of an existing home in 1985 ?

(A) $50,040
(B) $44,640
(C) $11,600
(D) $5,040
(E) $1,160

25. By approximately what percent did the median sale price of a new home increase from 1955 to 1975 ?

(A) 26%

(B) $37\frac{1}{2}$%

(C) $62\frac{1}{2}$%

(D) 167%

(E) 267%

GO ON TO THE NEXT PAGE.

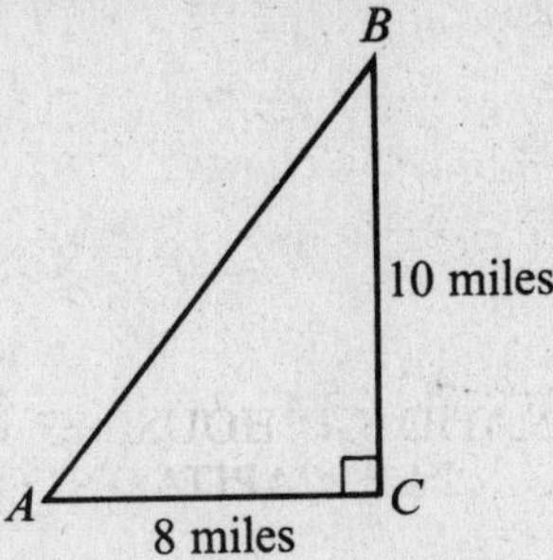

26. According to the figure above, traveling directly from point A to point B, rather than from point A to point C and then from point C to point B, would save approximately how many miles?

(A) 1
(B) 2
(C) 3
(D) 4
(E) 5

27. $0.50\% =$

(A) $\frac{1}{500}$

(B) $\frac{1}{200}$

(C) $\frac{1}{50}$

(D) $\frac{1}{20}$

(E) $\frac{1}{2}$

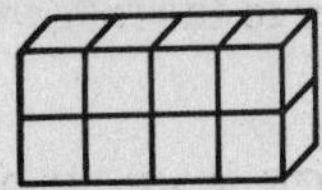

28. The rectangular solid above is made up of eight cubes of the same size, each of which has exactly one face painted blue. What is the greatest fraction of the total surface area of the solid that could be blue?

(A) $\frac{1}{6}$

(B) $\frac{3}{14}$

(C) $\frac{1}{4}$

(D) $\frac{2}{7}$

(E) $\frac{1}{3}$

29. If $a > 0$, $b > 0$, and $c > 0$, $a + \cfrac{1}{b + \cfrac{1}{c}} =$

(A) $\frac{a + b}{c}$

(B) $\frac{ac + bc + 1}{c}$

(C) $\frac{abc + b + c}{bc}$

(D) $\frac{a + b + c}{abc + 1}$

(E) $\frac{abc + a + c}{bc + 1}$

30. The buyer of a certain mechanical toy must choose 2 of 4 optional motions and 4 of 5 optional accessories. How many different combinations of motions and accessories are available to the buyer?

(A) 8
(B) 11
(C) 15
(D) 20
(E) 30

STOP

IF YOU FINISH BEFORE TIME IS CALLED, YOU MAY CHECK YOUR WORK ON THIS SECTION ONLY. DO NOT TURN TO ANY OTHER SECTION IN THE TEST.

NO TEST MATERIAL ON THIS PAGE

SECTION 4

Time—30 minutes

38 Questions

Directions: Each sentence below has one or two blanks, each blank indicating that something has been omitted. Beneath the sentence are five lettered words or sets of words. Choose the word or set of words for each blank that best fits the meaning of the sentence as a whole.

1. Job failure means being fired from a job, being asked to resign, or leaving ------- to protect yourself because you had very strong evidence that one of the first two was ------- .

   (A) voluntarily. .impending
   (B) abruptly. .significant
   (C) knowingly. .operative
   (D) understandably. .pertinent
   (E) eventually. .intentional

2. The tone of Jane Carlyle's letter is guarded, and her feelings are always ------- by the wit and pride that made ------- plea for sympathy impossible for her.

   (A) masked. .a direct
   (B) bolstered. .a needless
   (C) controlled. .a circumspect
   (D) enhanced. .an intentional
   (E) colored. .an untimely

3. French folktales almost always take place within the basic ------- that correspond to the ------- setting of peasant life: on the one hand, the household and village and on the other, the open road.

   (A) contexts. .hierarchical
   (B) structures. .personal
   (C) frameworks. .dual
   (D) chronologies. .generic
   (E) narratives. .ambivalent

4. Nurturing the Royal Ballet's artistic growth while preserving its institutional stability has been difficult, because the claims of the latter seem inescapably to ------- development; apparently, attaining artistic success is simpler than ------- it.

   (A) ensure. .promoting
   (B) inhibit. .perpetuating
   (C) undermine. .resurrecting
   (D) modify. .appreciating
   (E) supplement. .confining

5. Inspired interim responses to hitherto unknown problems, New Deal economic strategems became ------- as a result of bureaucratization, their flexibility and adaptibility destroyed by their transformation into rigid policies.

   (A) politicized
   (B) consolidated
   (C) ossified
   (D) ungovernable
   (E) streamlined

6. Biologists ------- isolated oceanic islands like the Galapagos, because, in such small, laboratory-like settings, the rich hurly-burly of continental plant and animal communities is reduced to a scientifically ------- complexity.

   (A) explore. .diverse
   (B) desert. .manageable
   (C) exploit. .intimidating
   (D) reject. .intricate
   (E) prize. .tractable

7. The startling finding that variations in the rate of the Earth's rotation depend to an ------- degree on the weather has necessitated a complete ------- of the world's time-keeping methods.

   (A) unexpected. .overhaul
   (B) anticipated. .recalibration
   (C) indeterminate. .rejection
   (D) unobservable. .review
   (E) estimated. .acceptance

GO ON TO THE NEXT PAGE.

4 4 4 4 4 4 4 4 4 4 4

Directions: In each of the following questions, a related pair of words or phrases is followed by five lettered pairs of words or phrases. Select the lettered pair that best expresses a relationship similar to that expressed in the original pair.

8. ORCHESTRA : INSTRUMENTAL ::
(A) choir : vocal (B) pianist : discordant
(C) trio : harmonic (D) singer : sacred
(E) band : martial

9. TROPHY : CONTESTANT :: (A) baton : runner
(B) pride : parent (C) book : bibliography
(D) loan : cashier (E) honors : student

10. LISTENER : EAVESDROPPER ::
(A) spectator : game (B) viewer : gazer
(C) observer : spy (D) speaker : chatterbox
(E) leader : demagogue

11. FIDGET : NERVOUSNESS :: (A) cringe : dread
(B) stall : frustration (C) regale : amusement
(D) doubt : consternation (E) nag : annoyance

12. DORMANT : INACTIVITY ::
(A) stark : ornateness (B) malleable : plasticity
(C) prone : uprightness (D) infuriating : tedium
(E) slack : excess

13. WAFT : PLUMMET :: (A) skim : glide
(B) dream : captivate (C) toss : catch
(D) flail : assault (E) meander : dash

14. PRUDISH : PROPRIETY ::
(A) fanatical : violence
(B) authoritative : evidence
(C) finicky : quality
(D) obstinate : accuracy
(E) fearful : comfort

15. POSEUR : SINCERITY :: (A) brat : insolence
(B) flirt : decency (C) grouch : patience
(D) recluse : gregariousness (E) rogue : empathy

16. MORALISTIC : PRINCIPLED ::
(A) simplistic : unsophisticated
(B) pedantic : learned
(C) positivistic : empirical
(D) dogmatic : prejudiced
(E) fantastic : imaginative

GO ON TO THE NEXT PAGE.

Directions: Each passage in this group is followed by questions based on its content. After reading a passage, choose the best answer to each question. Answer all questions following a passage on the basis of what is stated or implied in that passage.

Historically, a cornerstone of classical empiricism has been the notion that every true generalization must be confirmable by specific observations. In classical empiricism, the truth of "All balls are red," for example, is assessed by inspecting balls; any observation of a *non*red ball refutes unequivocally the proposed generalization.

For W.V.O. Quine, however, this constitutes an overly "narrow" conception of empiricism. "All balls are red," he maintains, forms one strand within an entire web of statements (our knowledge); individual observations can be referred only to this web as a whole. As new observations are collected, he explains, they must be integrated into the web. Problems occur only if a contradiction develops between a new observation, say, "That ball is blue," and the preexisting statements. In that case, he argues, *any* statement or combination of statements (not merely the "offending" generalization, as in classical empiricism) can be altered to achieve the fundamental requirement, a system free of contradictions, even if, in some cases, the alteration consists of labeling the new observation a "hallucination."

17. The author of the passage is primarily concerned with presenting
    (A) criticisms of Quine's views on the proper conceptualization of empiricism
    (B) evidence to support Quine's claims about the problems inherent in classical empiricism
    (C) an account of Quine's counterproposal to one of the traditional assumptions of classical empiricism
    (D) an overview of classical empiricism and its contributions to Quine's alternate understanding of empiricism
    (E) a history of classical empiricism and Quine's reservations about it

18. According to Quine's conception of empiricism, if a new observation were to contradict some statement already within our system of knowledge, which of the following would be true?
    (A) The new observation would be rejected as untrue.
    (B) Both the observation and the statement in our system that it contradicted would be discarded.
    (C) New observations would be added to our web of statements in order to expand our system of knowledge.
    (D) The observation or some part of our web of statements would need to be adjusted to resolve the contradiction.
    (E) An entirely new field of knowledge would be created.

19. As described in the passage, Quine's specific argument against classical empiricism would be most strengthened if he did which of the following?
    (A) Provided evidence that many observations are actually hallucinations.
    (B) Explained why new observations often invalidate preexisting generalizations.
    (C) Challenged the mechanism by which specific generalizations are derived from collections of particular observations.
    (D) Mentioned other critics of classical empiricism and the substance of their approaches.
    (E) Gave an example of a specific generalization that has not been invalidated despite a contrary observation.

20. It can be inferred from the passage that Quine considers classical empircism to be "overly 'narrow' " (lines 7-8) for which of the following reasons?

    I. Classical empiricism requires that our system of generalizations be free of contradictions.
    II. Classical empiricism demands that in the case of a contradiction between an individual observation and a generalization, the generalization must be abandoned.
    III. Classical empiricism asserts that every observation will either confirm an existing generalization or initiate a new generalization.

    (A) II only
    (B) I and II only
    (C) I and III only
    (D) II and III only
    (E) I, II, and III

GO ON TO THE NEXT PAGE.

Until recently astronomers have been puzzled by the fate of red giant and supergiant stars. When the core of a giant star whose mass surpasses 1.4 times the present mass of our Sun ($M_{\odot}$) exhausts its nuclear fuel, it is unable to support its own weight and collapses into a tiny neutron star. The gravitational energy released during this implosion of the core blows off the remainder of the star in a gigantic explosion, or a supernova. Since around 50 percent of all stars are believed to begin their lives with masses greater than 1.4 $M_{\odot}$, we might expect that one out of every two stars would die as a supernova. But in fact, only one star in thirty dies such a violent death. The rest expire much more peacefully as planetary nebulas. Apparently most massive stars manage to lose sufficient material that their masses drop below the critical value of 1.4 $M_{\odot}$ before they exhaust their nuclear fuel.

Evidence supporting this view comes from observations of IRC + 10216, a pulsating giant star located 700 light-years away from Earth. A huge rate of mass loss (1 $M_{\odot}$ every 10,000 years) has been deduced from infrared observations of ammonia (NH_3) molecules located in the circumstellar cloud around IRC + 10216. Recent microwave observations of carbon monoxide (CO) molecules indicate a similar rate of mass loss and demonstrate that the escaping material extends outward from the star for a distance of at least one light-year. Because we know the size of the cloud around IRC + 10216 and can use our observations of either NH_3 or CO to measure the outflow velocity, we can calculate an age for the circumstellar cloud. IRC + 10216 has apparently expelled, in the form of molecules and dust grains, a mass equal to that of our entire Sun within the past ten thousand years. This implies that some stars can shed huge amounts of matter very quickly and thus may never expire as supernovas. Theoretical models as well as statistics on supernovas and planetary nebulas suggest that stars that begin their lives with masses around 6 $M_{\odot}$ shed sufficient material to drop below the critical value of 1.4 $M_{\odot}$. IRC + 10216, for example, should do this in a mere 50,000 years from its birth, only an instant in the life of a star.

But what place does IRC + 10216 have in stellar evolution? Astronomers suggest that stars like IRC + 10216 are actually "protoplanetary nebulas"—old giant stars whose dense cores have almost but not quite rid themselves of the fluffy envelopes of gas around them. Once the star has lost the entire envelope, its exposed core becomes the central star of the planetary nebula and heats and ionizes the last vestiges of the envelope as it flows away into space. This configuration is a full-fledged planetary nebula, long familiar to optical astronomers.

21. The primary purpose of the passage is to
    - (A) offer a method of calculating the age of circumstellar clouds
    - (B) describe the conditions that result in a star's expiring as a supernova
    - (C) discuss new evidence concerning the composition of planetary nebulas
    - (D) explain why fewer stars than predicted expire as supernovas
    - (E) survey conflicting theories concerning the composition of circumstellar clouds

22. The passage implies that at the beginning of the life of IRC + 10216, its mass was approximately
    - (A) 7.0 $M_{\odot}$ (B) 6.0 $M_{\odot}$ (C) 5.0 $M_{\odot}$
    - (D) 1.4 $M_{\odot}$ (E) 1.0 $M_{\odot}$

23. The view to which line 18 refers serves to
    - (A) reconcile seemingly contradictory facts
    - (B) undermine a previously held theory
    - (C) take into account data previously held to be insignificant
    - (D) resolve a controversy
    - (E) question new methods of gathering data

24. It can be inferred from the passage that the author assumes which of the following in the discussion of the rate at which IRC + 10216 loses mass?
    - (A) The circumstellar cloud surrounding IRC + 10216 consists only of CO and NH_3 molecules.
    - (B) The circumstellar cloud surrounding IRC + 10216 consists of material expelled from that star.
    - (C) The age of a star is equal to that of its circumstellar cloud.
    - (D) The rate at which IRC + 10216 loses mass varies significantly from year to year.
    - (E) Stars with a mass greater than 6 $M_{\odot}$ lose mass at a rate faster than stars with a mass less than 6 $M_{\odot}$ do.

GO ON TO THE NEXT PAGE.

25. According to information provided by the passage, which of the following stars would astronomers most likely describe as a planetary nebula?

(A) A star that began its life with a mass of 5.5 $M_\odot$, has exhausted its nuclear fuel, and has a core that is visible to astronomers
(B) A star that began its life with a mass of 6 $M_\odot$, lost mass at a rate of 1 $M_\odot$ per 10,000 years, and exhausted its nuclear fuel in 40,000 years
(C) A star that has exhausted its nuclear fuel, has a mass of 1.2 $M_\odot$, and is surrounded by a circumstellar cloud that obscures its core from view
(D) A star that began its life with a mass greater than 6 $M_\odot$, has just recently exhausted its nuclear fuel, and is in the process of releasing massive amounts of gravitational energy
(E) A star that began its life with a mass of 5.5 $M_\odot$, has yet to exhaust its nuclear fuel, and exhibits a rate of mass loss similar to that of IRC + 10216

26. Which of the following statements would be most likely to follow the last sentence of the passage?

(A) Supernovas are not necessarily the most spectacular events that astronomers have occasion to observe.
(B) Apparently, stars that have a mass of greater than 6 $M_\odot$ are somewhat rare.
(C) Recent studies of CO and NH_3 in the circumstellar clouds of stars similar to IRC + 10216 have led astronomers to believe that the formation of planetary nebulas precedes the development of supernovas.
(D) It appears, then, that IRC + 10216 actually represents an intermediate step in the evolution of a giant star into a planetary nebula.
(E) Astronomers have yet to develop a consistently accurate method for measuring the rate at which a star exhausts its nuclear fuel.

27. Which of the following titles best summarizes the content of the passage?

(A) New Methods of Calculating the Age of Circumstellar Clouds
(B) New Evidence Concerning the Composition of Planetary Nebulas
(C) Protoplanetary Nebula: A Rarely Observed Phenomenon
(D) Planetary Nebulas: An Enigma to Astronomers
(E) The Diminution of a Star's Mass: A Crucial Factor in Stellar Evolution

GO ON TO THE NEXT PAGE.

Directions: Each question below consists of a word printed in capital letters, followed by five lettered words or phrases. Choose the lettered word or phrase that is most nearly opposite in meaning to the word in capital letters.

Since some of the questions require you to distinguish fine shades of meaning, be sure to consider all the choices before deciding which one is best.

28. SEND: (A) drop (B) lift (C) attempt (D) receive (E) locate

29. INTERLOCKING: (A) independent (B) internal (C) peripheral (D) sequential (E) variable

30. REFLECT: (A) diffuse (B) polarize (C) absorb (D) focus (E) propagate

31. LACKLUSTER: (A) necessary (B) descriptive (C) radiant (D) organized (E) mature

32. ZENITH: (A) shortest line (B) furthest edge (C) lowest point (D) roughest curve (E) smallest surface

33. ENGENDER: (A) enumerate (B) emulate (C) exculpate (D) eradicate (E) encapsulate

34. ANOMALOUS:
(A) veracious
(B) precise
(C) essential
(D) conforming to an established rule
(E) proceeding in a timely fashion

35. GRIEVOUS: (A) slight (B) stereotyped (C) solicitous (D) sophisticated (E) sparkling

36. PRECIPITATE: (A) desperate (B) determined (C) dissident (D) deliberate (E) divided

37. PROLIXITY: (A) intense devotion (B) vehement protest (C) serious offense (D) exact measurement (E) extreme brevity

38. DISABUSE: (A) afflict with pain (B) lead into error (C) force into exile (D) remove from grace (E) free from obligation

STOP

IF YOU FINISH BEFORE TIME IS CALLED, YOU MAY CHECK YOUR WORK ON THIS SECTION ONLY. DO NOT TURN TO ANY OTHER SECTION IN THE TEST.

Section 6 starts on page 432.

SECTION 6

Time—30 minutes

30 Questions

Numbers: All numbers used are real numbers.

Figures: Position of points, angles, regions, etc. can be assumed to be in the order shown; and angle measures can be assumed to be positive.

Lines shown as straight can be assumed to be straight.

Figures can be assumed to lie in a plane unless otherwise indicated.

Figures that accompany questions are intended to provide information useful in answering the questions. However, unless a note states that a figure is drawn to scale, you should solve these problems NOT by estimating sizes by sight or by measurement, but by using your knowledge of mathematics (see Example 2 below).

Directions: Each of the Questions 1-15 consists of two quantities, one in Column A and one in Column B. You are to compare the two quantities and choose

A if the quantity in Column A is greater;
B if the quantity in Column B is greater;
C if the two quantities are equal;
D if the relationship cannot be determined from the information given.

Note: Since there are only four choices, NEVER MARK (E).

Common Information: In a question, information concerning one or both of the quantities to be compared is centered above the two columns. A symbol that appears in both columns represents the same thing in Column A as it does in Column B.

	Column A	Column B	Sample Answers
Example 1:	2×6	$2 + 6$	● Ⓑ Ⓒ Ⓓ Ⓔ

Examples 2-4 refer to $\triangle PQR$.

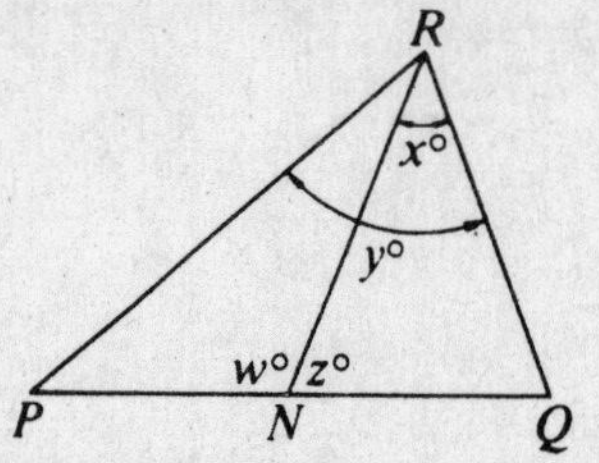

R, $x°$, $y°$, $w°$, $z°$, P, N, Q

	Column A	Column B	Sample Answers
Example 2:	PN	NQ	Ⓐ Ⓑ Ⓒ ● Ⓔ (since equal measures cannot be assumed, even though PN and NQ appear equal)
Example 3:	x	y	Ⓐ ● Ⓒ Ⓓ Ⓔ (since N is between P and Q)
Example 4:	$w + z$	180	Ⓐ Ⓑ ● Ⓓ Ⓔ (since PQ is a straight line)

GO ON TO THE NEXT PAGE.

A if the quantity in Column A is greater;
B if the quantity in Column B is greater;
C if the two quantities are equal;
D if the relationship cannot be determined from the information given.

	Column A	Column B
1.	6% of 9	8% of 7

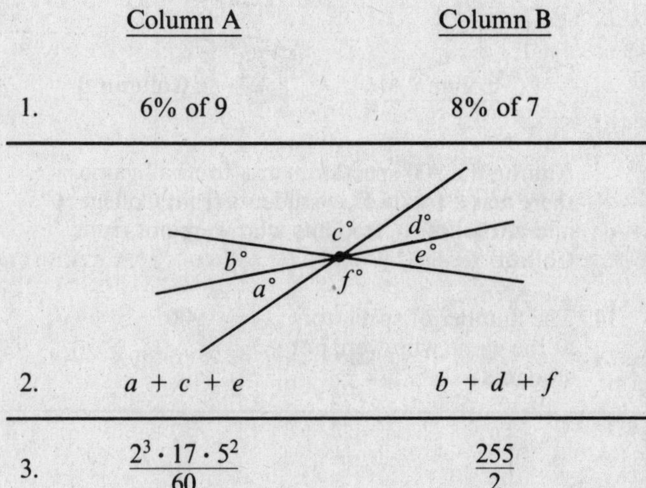

	Column A	Column B
2.	$a + c + e$	$b + d + f$
3.	$\frac{2^3 \cdot 17 \cdot 5^2}{60}$	$\frac{255}{2}$

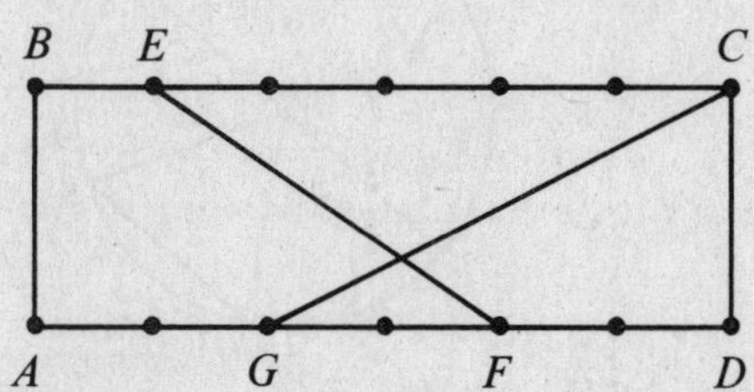

In rectangle $ABCD$, sides AD and BC have been divided into segments of equal length as shown.

	Column A	Column B
4.	The length of EF	The length of GC

AREAS OF THE FIVE LARGEST STATES

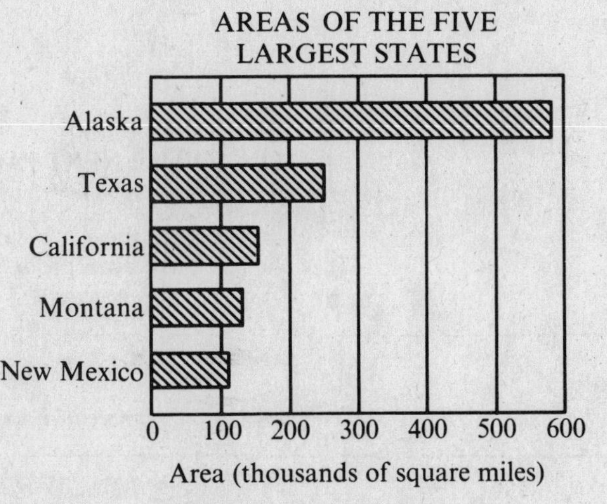

Note: Drawn to scale.

	Column A	Column B
5.	Sum of the areas of Texas, California, Montana, and New Mexico	Area of Alaska

$$x + 5 = 21$$
$$y - x = -8$$

	Column A	Column B
6.	y	6
7.	0.125	$\frac{1}{8}$

The price of a pen is $(10x + y)$ cents, the price of a notebook is $(10y + x)$ cents, and the sum of the two prices is $1.43.

	Column A	Column B
8.	x	y

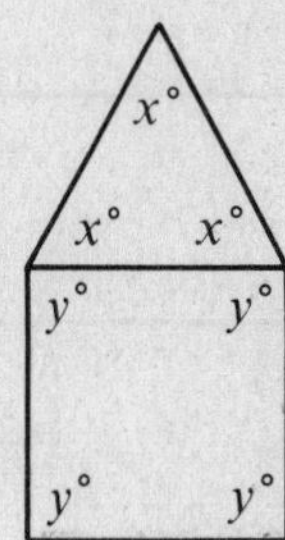

	Column A	Column B
9.	$x + y$	120
10.	$\cfrac{1}{4 + \cfrac{1}{3 + \cfrac{1}{2}}}$	$\cfrac{1}{2 + \cfrac{1}{3 + \cfrac{1}{4}}}$

GO ON TO THE NEXT PAGE.

A if the quantity in Column A is greater;
B if the quantity in Column B is greater;
C if the two quantities are equal;
D if the relationship cannot be determined from the information given.

	Column A	Column B
	x and y are positive integers. $x > 1$, $y < 2$	
11.	x	$2y$
	$\dfrac{\frac{1}{r}}{\frac{1}{t}} = \dfrac{3}{5}$	
12.	$\dfrac{r}{t}$	$\dfrac{t}{r}$

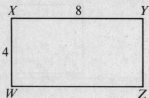

	Column A	Column B
13.	The area of a square region with a perimeter equal to the perimeter of rectangular region $WXYZ$	36

Among the 900 spectators at a football game, there was a total of x students from College C and a total of y students who were not from College C.

	Column A	Column B
14.	The number of spectators at the game who were not students	$900 - x - y$

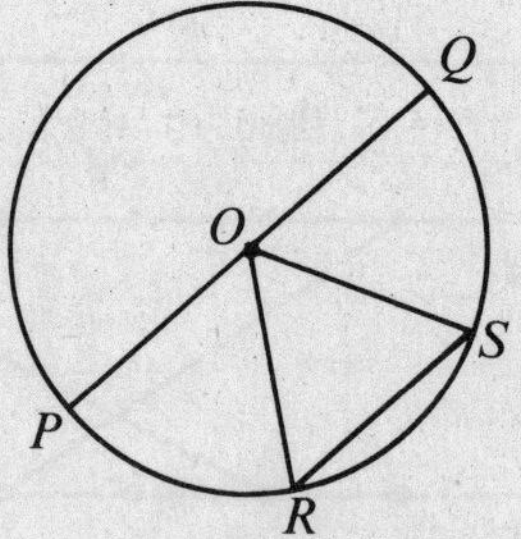

O is the center of the circle, and $\angle ROS$ is a right angle.

	Column A	Column B
15.	$\dfrac{PQ}{RS}$	$\dfrac{2}{1}$

GO ON TO THE NEXT PAGE.

Directions: Each of the Questions 16-30 has five answer choices. For each of these questions, select the best of the answer choices given.

16. If $\frac{x}{2} + 1 = 15$, then $x =$

(A) 5
(B) 7
(C) 13
(D) 28
(E) 29

17. If 15 pies cost a total of \$11.50, then at this rate, what is the cost of 9 pies?

(A) \$6.75
(B) \$6.90
(C) \$7.50
(D) \$8.50
(E) \$9.45

18. If $2(x + y) = 5$, then, in terms of x, $y =$

(A) $\frac{5}{2} - x$

(B) $\frac{5}{2} + x$

(C) $5 - 2x$

(D) $5 - \frac{x}{2}$

(E) $\frac{5}{2} + \frac{x}{2}$

19. If the average (arithmetic mean) of 16, 20, and n is between 18 and 21, inclusive, what is the greatest possible value of n?

(A) 18
(B) 21
(C) 27
(D) 54
(E) 63

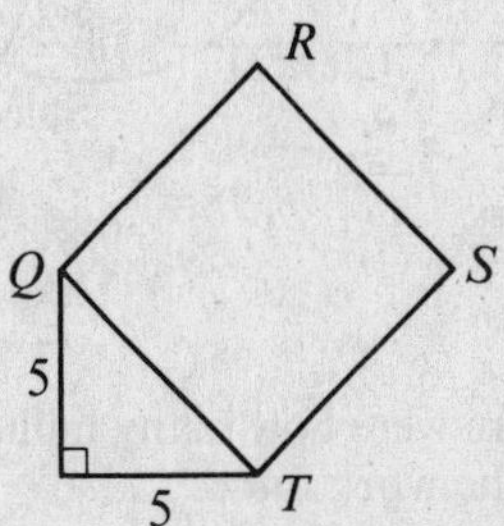

20. In the figure above, what is the area of square $QRST$?

(A) 25
(B) $20\sqrt{2}$
(C) $25\sqrt{2}$
(D) 50
(E) $50\sqrt{2}$

GO ON TO THE NEXT PAGE.

Questions 21-25 refer to the following graphs.

DISTRIBUTION OF WORK FORCE BY OCCUPATIONAL CATEGORY FOR COUNTRY *X* IN 1981 AND PROJECTED FOR 1995

Total Work Force: 150 Million

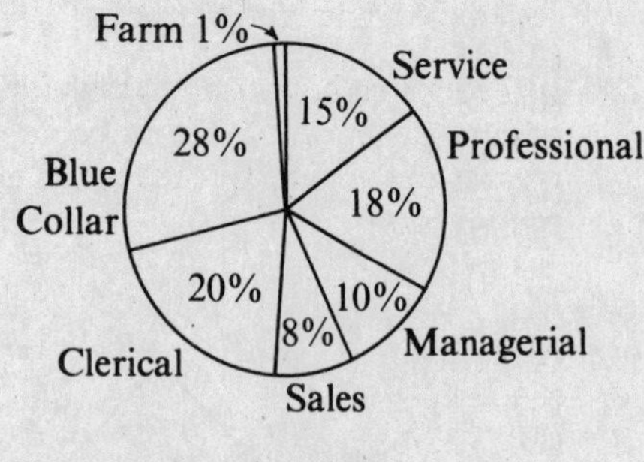

1981

Total Work Force: 175 Million

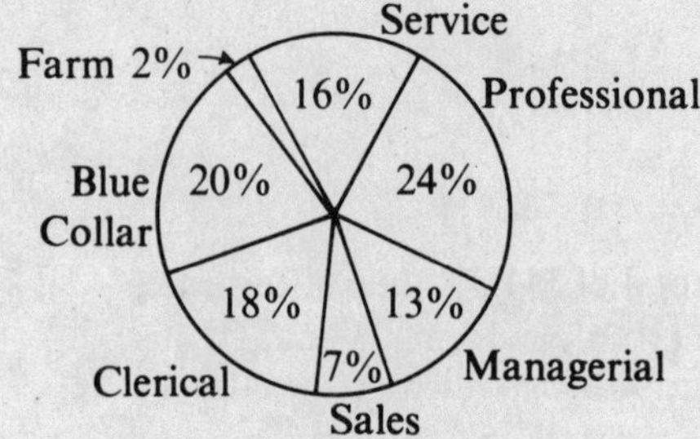

1995 (Projected)

21. In 1981, there were how many million Service workers in the work force?

(A) 15.0
(B) 20.5
(C) 22.5
(D) 28.0
(E) 175.0

22. In 1981, how many categories each comprised more than 25 million workers?

(A) One
(B) Two
(C) Three
(D) Four
(E) Five

23. What is the ratio of the number of workers in the Professional category in 1981 to the projected number of such workers in 1995?

(A) $\frac{4}{9}$

(B) $\frac{5}{14}$

(C) $\frac{9}{14}$

(D) $\frac{3}{4}$

(E) $\frac{14}{9}$

24. From 1981 to 1995, there is a projected increase in the number of workers in which of the following categories?

I. Sales
II. Service
III. Clerical

(A) None
(B) III only
(C) I and II only
(D) II and III only
(E) I, II, and III

25. Approximately what is the projected percent decrease in the number of Blue-Collar workers in the work force of Country *X* from 1981 to 1995?

(A) 42%
(B) 35%
(C) 20%
(D) 17%
(E) 7%

GO ON TO THE NEXT PAGE.

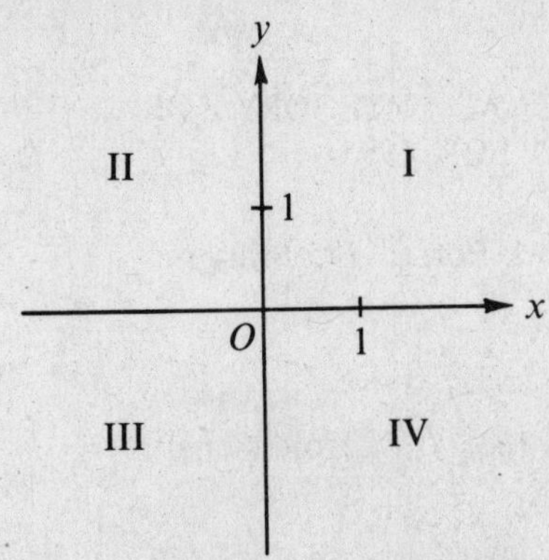

26. Points $(x, -3)$ and $(-2, y)$, not shown in the figure above, are in quadrants IV and II, respectively. If $xy \neq 0$, in which quadrant is point (x, y)?

(A) I
(B) II
(C) III
(D) IV
(E) It cannot be determined from the information given.

27. $(\sqrt{3} - \sqrt{2})^2 =$

(A) $1 - 2\sqrt{6}$
(B) $1 - \sqrt{6}$
(C) $5 - 2\sqrt{6}$
(D) $5 - 2\sqrt{3}$
(E) 1

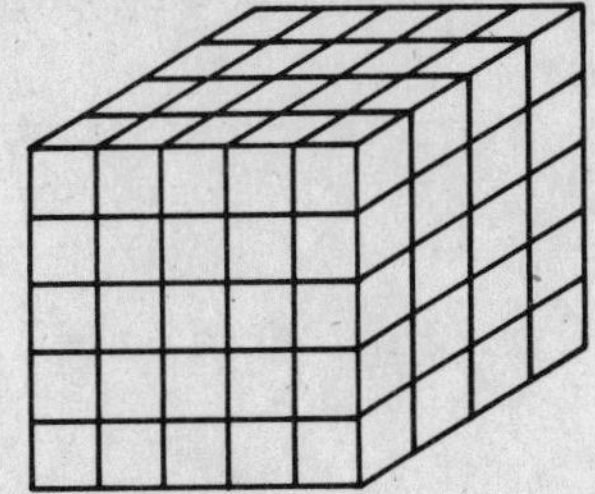

28. If the figure above is a rectangular solid composed of cubes, each with edge of length 4 centimeters, what is the volume of the rectangular solid in cubic centimeters?

(A) 100
(B) 256
(C) 400
(D) 5,120
(E) 6,400

29. If $L = (a - b) - c$ and $R = a - (b - c)$, then $L - R =$

(A) $2b$
(B) $2c$
(C) 0
(D) $-2b$
(E) $-2c$

30. At the rate of 3,000 revolutions per minute, how many revolutions will a wheel make in k seconds?

(A) $3{,}000k$
(B) $50k$
(C) $\frac{50}{k}$
(D) $\frac{3{,}000}{k}$
(E) $\frac{180{,}000}{k}$

STOP

IF YOU FINISH BEFORE TIME IS CALLED, YOU MAY CHECK YOUR WORK ON THIS SECTION ONLY. DO NOT TURN TO ANY OTHER SECTION IN THE TEST.

NO TEST MATERIAL ON THIS PAGE

SECTION 7

Time—30 minutes

25 Questions

Directions: Each question or group of questions is based on a passage or set of conditions. In answering some of the questions, it may be useful to draw a rough diagram. For each question, select the best answer choice given.

Questions 1-5

In order to gain full course credit for her tour of a foreign city, Sue must visit exactly seven famous points of interest—a factory, a garden, the harbor, a library, a museum, a palace, and a theater. Any tour plan that Sue devises will allow her to keep to her timetable and is thus acceptable, except that she must plan her tour to conform with the following conditions:

The factory must be one of the first three points visited.
The harbor must be visited immediately before the garden.
The library can be neither the first nor the last point visited.
The museum must be either the first or the last point visited.
The palace must be one of the last three points visited.

1. Which of the following is an acceptable order in which Sue may tour all seven points of interest?

(A) Factory, theater, harbor, library, palace, garden, and museum
(B) Harbor, garden, factory, library, theater, palace, and museum
(C) Library, theater, factory, harbor, garden, museum, and palace
(D) Museum, factory, palace, harbor, library, garden, and theater
(E) Museum, library, harbor, garden, factory, palace, and theater

2. If, on her tour, Sue visits the theater, the library, and the factory, one directly after the other in the order given, she must visit the garden

(A) second
(B) third
(C) fourth
(D) fifth
(E) sixth

3. If Sue begins her tour at the harbor, which of the following could be the fourth point of interest she visits on the tour?

(A) The factory
(B) The garden
(C) The library
(D) The museum
(E) The palace

4. If Sue is to visit the palace sixth, she could visit the harbor in any of the following positions on her tour EXCEPT

(A) first
(B) second
(C) third
(D) fourth
(E) fifth

5. If Sue visits exactly one point of interest between her visits to the factory and the palace, that point must be either the

(A) garden or the harbor
(B) garden or the theater
(C) harbor or the museum
(D) library or the museum
(E) library or the theater

GO ON TO THE NEXT PAGE.

6. Miko: Academic products developed at a university are properly considered the results of "work for hire" and really belong to the institution. Therefore, the university should own the copyright for any computer software developed by its faculty.

Kofi: But a copyright policy this restrictive can impede a university's primary mission of generating and disseminating knowledge.

Kofi's response has which of the following relationships to Miko's argument?

(A) Kofi contradicts Miko's evidence.
(B) Kofi points out a hidden assumption required by Miko's argument.
(C) Kofi points out a problematic consequence of accepting Miko's argument.
(D) Kofi shows that Miko's reasoning is circular.
(E) Kofi shows that Miko forms a generalization from an atypical case.

7. Within the last fifty years, the majority of the United States work force has moved from the manufacturing to the service sector of the economy. This shift has occurred, not because of a decline in the production of goods, but because, with applications of new technology, more production of goods can now be achieved with relatively fewer people, and more people are therefore available to satisfy the increased demand for services.

Which of the following, if true, provides evidence to support the claim made above that more production of goods can now be achieved with relatively fewer people?

(A) Many manufacturing industries in the United States have lost a significant share of their domestic and foreign markets to foreign producers.
(B) Services accounted for half of all jobs in the late 1940's but today account for seventy percent of all jobs.
(C) Manufacturing output was one-third higher in 1980 than in 1970, while manufacturing employment grew only five percent during that period.
(D) Manufacturing industries, on average, pay a higher per-hour wage and use fewer part-time employees than do service industries.
(E) Living standards in states that have shifted to manufacturing economies within the last fifty years are closer to the national average now than in 1940.

8. John: I have tried several different types of psychotherapy at various times in my life: three kinds of "talk" therapy (Freudian, Rogerian, and cognitive) and also behavior therapy. Since the periods when I was in therapy were the least happy times of my life, I have concluded that psychotherapy cannot work for me.

Which of the following statements, if true, would most weaken John's conclusion?

(A) Behavior therapy is designed to address different problems from those addressed by "talk" therapies.
(B) The techniques used in behavior therapy are quite different from those used in "talk" therapies.
(C) People who try several different types of psychotherapy tend to be happier than people who try only one type of psychotherapy.
(D) People who try several different types of psychotherapy are more likely to find one that works for them than are people who try only one type of psychotherapy.
(E) People undergoing psychotherapy that ultimately works are often unhappy while they are in therapy.

GO ON TO THE NEXT PAGE.

Questions 9-14

An elementary school librarian is assigning after-school library duty to parent volunteers for each school day, Monday through Friday, during a single week. Exactly five volunteers—J, K, L, M, and N—are available. The librarian must assign exactly two volunteers to work each day of that week according to the following conditions:

Each of the volunteers must work at least once.
None of the volunteers can work on three consecutive days.
K must work on Monday.
M must work on Thursday and on Friday.
J cannot work on any day on which K works.

9. Any of the following volunteers could be assigned to work on Wednesday EXCEPT
   (A) J
   (B) K
   (C) L
   (D) M
   (E) N

10. If J is assigned to work on exactly three days of the week, those days must include
   (A) Monday and Wednesday
   (B) Tuesday and Wednesday
   (C) Tuesday and Friday
   (D) Wednesday and Friday
   (E) Thursday and Friday

11. If K is assigned to work on exactly four days of the week, which of the following could be the pair of volunteers assigned to work on Wednesday?
   (A) J and L
   (B) J and M
   (C) K and L
   (D) K and N
   (E) M and N

12. If J is assigned to work whenever and only when M is assigned to work, which of the following could be true?
   (A) J is assigned to work on Monday.
   (B) J is assigned to work on Wednesday.
   (C) K is assigned to work on Friday.
   (D) L is assigned to work on Friday.
   (E) N is assigned to work on Tuesday.

13. If K is assigned to work on only one day and L is assigned to work on exactly four days, which of the following pairs of volunteers must be assigned to work on Wednesday?
   (A) J and L
   (B) J and N
   (C) K and L
   (D) L and M
   (E) L and N

14. If each volunteer is assigned to work exactly twice, which of the following must be true?
   (A) Either J or K is assigned to work on at least one of the days on which M is assigned to work.
   (B) K is assigned to work on both of the days on which L is assigned to work.
   (C) L is assigned to work on Tuesday.
   (D) L is assigned to work on one of the days on which K is assigned to work and on one of the days on which J is assigned to work.
   (E) N is assigned to work on two consecutive days.

GO ON TO THE NEXT PAGE.

Questions 15-19

The editors of a journal that publishes three issues a year will devote the upcoming winter, spring, and fall issues—in that order—exclusively to articles written by seven authors: J, K, L, M, N, O, and P. Each of the seven authors will have at least one article published, but some may have more than one article published. The following restrictions apply to the publication of their articles:

If an article by J appears in an issue, then an article by K must also appear in that issue.
If an article by M appears in an issue, then an article by O must appear in the immediately preceding issue.
An article by O cannot be published in an issue that contains an article by P.
No author may publish in each of two consecutively published issues or twice in the same issue.
Each of the issues being prepared must contain at least two articles.
The seven authors' articles can only appear in the upcoming winter, spring, and fall issues.

15. The winter issue of the journal can consist exclusively of articles by which of the following groups of authors?

(A) J and L
(B) M and O
(C) J, O, and P
(D) L, N, and O
(E) J, K, N, O, and P

16. If the winter issue consists exclusively of articles by J and K, then the spring issue can consist exclusively of articles by which of the following groups of authors?

(A) L and N
(B) L and O
(C) M and P
(D) J, K, and P
(E) L, O, and P

17. Which of the following authors CANNOT contribute to the winter issue of the journal?

(A) L
(B) M
(C) N
(D) O
(E) P

18. If the winter issue consists exclusively of articles by K, L, and P, then the fall issue must contain an article by which of the following authors?

(A) K
(B) L
(C) N
(D) O
(E) P

19. If the fall issue consists exclusively of articles by K, L, and M, then the spring issue must have consisted of articles by which of the following groups of authors?

(A) J and N
(B) J and P
(C) K and O
(D) N and O
(E) N and P

GO ON TO THE NEXT PAGE.

Questions 20-22

A pastry chef who is visiting a culinary school wishes to schedule three classes on pastry making—one at 10 a.m., one at 2 p.m., and one at 6 p.m. Eight student chefs—Q, R, S, T, W, X, Y, and Z—who have registered to attend class will each be assigned to one of the three classes. Each class will contain either two or three student chefs. The assignment of student chefs to each class must conform to the following restrictions:

Q must be assigned to a class to which only one other student is assigned.
R must be assigned to the same class as Y.
S must not be assigned to the same class as X.
T must be assigned to either the 10 a.m. class or the 6 p.m. class.
X must be assigned to a class that meets earlier in the day than the class to which W is assigned.

20. Which of the following is a possible assignment of students to the classes?

	10 a.m.	2 p.m.	6 p.m.
(A)	Q, X	R, T, Z	S, W, Y
(B)	Q, W	R, X, Y	S, T, Z
(C)	R, X, Y	S, W, Z	Q, T
(D)	R, X, Y	Q, S, W	T, Z
(E)	S, T, X	R, Y, Z	Q, W

21. If S and Q are assigned to the 6 p.m. class, which of the following must be the group of students assigned to the 10 a.m. class?

(A) R, T, Y
(B) R, X, Y
(C) R, Y, Z
(D) T, W, Z
(E) T, X, Z

22. If Q and Z are assigned to the 10 a.m. class, which of the following must be the group of students assigned to the 6 p.m. class?

(A) R, T, Y
(B) R, W, Y
(C) S, T, W
(D) S, T, X
(E) T, X, Z

23. Board member: As a longtime member of the college's board of trustees, I believe that the board has functioned well in the past because each of its members has had a broad range of experience and interests. Thus, if in the future any members are elected primarily to press for a particular policy, such as reducing tuition, the board will function less well.

In drawing the conclusion above, the board member must have been making which of the following assumptions?

(A) The college will suffer financially if the board reduces tuition.
(B) The college will not be able to operate if and when the board functions less well than it does currently.
(C) The board functions well because its members are primarily interested in particular academic policies rather than in financial policies such as the level of tuition.
(D) In order to be elected as a member of the board, one must have a broad range of experience and interests.
(E) Each of the people who would be elected to the board primarily to press for a particular policy lacks a broad range of experience or interests.

GO ON TO THE NEXT PAGE.

24. When school administrators translate educational research into a standardized teaching program and mandate its use by teachers, students learn less and learn less well than they did before, even though the teachers are the same. The translation by the administrators of theory into prescribed practice must therefore be flawed.

The argument above is based on which of the following assumptions?

(A) Teachers differ in their ability to teach in accordance with standardized programs.
(B) The educational research on which the standardized teaching programs are based is sound.
(C) Researchers should be the ones to translate their own research into teaching programs.
(D) The ways in which teachers choose to implement the programs are ineffective.
(E) The level of student learning will vary from state to state.

25. Figures issued by the government of a certain country show that in 1980 the public sector and the private sector each employed the same number of people. Between 1980 and 1984, according to the government, total employment decreased in the public sector more than it increased in the private sector.

If, according to governmental figures, the unemployment rate in this country was the same in both 1980 and 1984, which of the following statements must be true about this country?

(A) Fewer people were in the labor force, as counted by the government, in 1984 than in 1980.
(B) The competition for the available work increased between 1980 and 1984.
(C) The government's figures for total employment increased between 1980 and 1984.
(D) The number of people counted by the government as unemployed was the same in 1980 and 1984.
(E) In 1984 more people sought work in the private sector than in the public sector.

STOP

IF YOU FINISH BEFORE TIME IS CALLED, YOU MAY CHECK YOUR WORK ON THIS SECTION ONLY. DO NOT TURN TO ANY OTHER SECTION IN THE TEST.

NO TEST MATERIAL ON THIS PAGE

NO TEST MATERIAL ON THIS PAGE

NOTE: To ensure prompt processing of test results, it is important that you fill in the blanks exactly as directed.

GENERAL TEST

A. Print and sign your full name in this box:

PRINT: ______________________________
(LAST) (FIRST) (MIDDLE)

SIGN: ______________________________

Copy this code in box 6 on your answer sheet. Then fill in the corresponding ovals exactly as shown.

6. TITLE CODE				
0	0	0	0	0
1	1	1	1	1
2	2	2	2	2
3	3	3	3	3
4	4	4	4	4
5	5	5	5	5
6	6	6	6	6
7	7	7	7	7
8	8	8	8	8
9	9	9	9	9

Copy the Test Name and Form Code in box 7 on your answer sheet.

TEST NAME General

FORM CODE GR92-1

GRADUATE RECORD EXAMINATIONS GENERAL TEST

B. You will have 3 hours and 30 minutes in which to work on this test, which consists of seven sections. During the time allowed for one section, you may work only on that section. The time allowed for each section is 30 minutes.

Each of your scores will be determined by the number of questions for which you select the best answer from the choices given. Questions for which you mark no answer or more than one answer are not counted in scoring. Nothing is subtracted from a score if you answer a question incorrectly. Therefore, to maximize your scores it is better for you to guess at an answer than not to respond at all.

You are advised to work as rapidly as you can without losing accuracy. Do not spend too much time on questions that are too difficult for you. Go on to the other questions and come back to the difficult ones later.

There are several different types of questions; you will find special directions for each type in the test itself. Be sure you understand the directions before attempting to answer any questions.

YOU MUST INDICATE ALL YOUR ANSWERS ON THE SEPARATE ANSWER SHEET. No credit will be given for anything written in this examination book, but you may write in the book as much as you wish to work out your answers. After you have decided on your response to a question, fill in the corresponding oval on the answer sheet. BE SURE THAT EACH MARK IS DARK AND COMPLETELY FILLS THE OVAL. Mark only one answer to each question. No credit will be given for multiple answers. Erase all stray marks. If you change an answer, be sure that all previous marks are erased completely. Incomplete erasures may be read as intended answers. Do not be concerned if your answer sheet provides spaces for more answers than there are questions in each section.

Example:

What city is the capital of France?

(A) Rome
(B) Paris
(C) London
(D) Cairo
(E) Oslo

Sample Answer

A ● C D E — BEST ANSWER PROPERLY MARKED

A B C D E
A B C D E
A B C D E
A B C D E — IMPROPER MARKS

Some or all of the passages for this test have been adapted from published material to provide the examinee with significant problems for analysis and evaluation. To make the passages suitable for testing purposes, the style, content, or point of view of the original may have been altered in some cases. The ideas contained in the passages do not necessarily represent the opinions of the Graduate Record Examinations Board or Educational Testing Service.

DO NOT OPEN YOUR TEST BOOK UNTIL YOU ARE TOLD TO DO SO.

FOR GENERAL TEST, FORM GR92-1 ONLY
Answer Key and Percentages* of Examinees Answering Each Question Correctly

VERBAL ABILITY					
Section 2			Section 4		
Number	Answer	P +	Number	Answer	P +
1	A	85	1	A	95
2	D	71	2	A	79
3	B	74	3	C	79
4	E	59	4	B	64
5	E	51	5	C	45
6	E	40	6	E	58
7	B	37	7	A	50
8	E	83	8	A	90
9	B	87	9	E	88
10	B	54	10	C	83
11	E	58	11	A	59
12	B	42	12	B	54
13	D	35	13	E	57
14	D	44	14	C	48
15	D	28	15	D	36
16	E	11	16	B	31
17	C	64	17	C	63
18	A	84	18	D	61
19	D	79	19	E	45
20	E	90	20	A	14
21	A	74	21	D	61
22	D	38	22	B	65
23	B	53	23	A	40
24	E	47	24	B	49
25	A	57	25	A	22
26	A	49	26	D	61
27	B	67	27	E	47
28	A	77	28	D	94
29	C	78	29	A	88
30	A	79	30	C	76
31	B	73	31	C	79
32	D	56	32	C	75
33	E	38	33	D	51
34	C	33	34	D	44
35	D	35	35	A	32
36	E	34	36	D	26
37	A	22	37	E	33
38	A	29	38	B	15

QUANTITATIVE ABILITY					
Section 3			Section 6		
Number	Answer	P +	Number	Answer	P +
1	C	88	1	B	81
2	B	83	2	C	85
3	B	81	3	B	81
4	A	84	4	B	81
5	A	87	5	A	89
6	A	71	6	A	87
7	B	74	7	C	87
8	A	76	8	D	68
9	A	77	9	A	72
10	D	59	10	B	65
11	D	52	11	D	67
12	C	44	12	A	63
13	D	50	13	C	50
14	C	33	14	C	49
15	D	29	15	B	30
16	C	88	16	D	85
17	A	78	17	B	77
18	A	64	18	A	74
19	E	64	19	C	71
20	C	64	20	D	57
21	D	87	21	C	79
22	A	83	22	C	75
23	C	63	23	C	40
24	B	59	24	E	42
25	D	38	25	D	35
26	E	52	26	A	53
27	B	48	27	C	39
28	D	43	28	E	52
29	E	33	29	E	32
30	E	28	30	B	49

ANALYTICAL ABILITY					
Section 1			Section 7		
Number	Answer	P +	Number	Answer	P +
1	C	76	1	B	81
2	B	78	2	D	74
3	D	60	3	C	86
4	C	51	4	E	69
5	D	55	5	E	78
6	A	28	6	C	87
7	D	93	7	C	65
8	D	62	8	E	77
9	A	45	9	D	79
10	A	91	10	C	47
11	E	65	11	A	68
12	E	29	12	E	66
13	D	28	13	B	64
14	D	54	14	A	37
15	C	64	15	D	62
16	B	44	16	B	39
17	E	19	17	B	48
18	A	62	18	A	13
19	B	56	19	D	51
20	D	49	20	C	61
21	B	56	21	E	35
22	E	31	22	C	51
23	E	50	23	E	44
24	D	40	24	B	33
25	E	42	25	A	31

*Estimated P+ for the group of examinees who took the GRE General Test in a recent three-year period.

Score Conversions for GRE General Test GR92-1 Only and the Percents Below*

Raw Score	Verbal Scaled Score	Verbal % Below	Quantitative Scaled Score	Quantitative % Below	Analytical Scaled Score	Analytical % Below
72-76	800	99				
71	780	99				
70	770	99				
69	750	98				
68	740	98				
67	730	97				
66	720	96				
65	710	95				
64	690	94				
63	680	93				
62	670	91				
61	660	90				
60	650	88	800	96		
59	640	87	800	96		
58	630	85	800	96		
57	620	83	790	95		
56	610	82	780	93		
55	600	80	770	92		
54	590	78	750	88		
53	580	75	740	87		
52	570	73	730	85		
51	560	71	710	81		
50	550	69	700	79	800	99
49	540	66	690	77	800	99
48	530	63	680	75	800	99
47	520	60	660	71	800	99
46	510	58	650	69	800	99
45	500	55	640	67	780	97
44	490	52	630	65	770	97
43	480	50	620	62	760	96
42	470	47	600	58	750	95
41	460	43	590	56	730	93
40	460	43	580	53	720	92

Raw Score	Verbal Scaled Score	Verbal % Below	Quantitative Scaled Score	Quantitative % Below	Analytical Scaled Score	Analytical % Below
39	450	40	570	51	700	89
38	440	37	560	49	690	87
37	430	34	550	46	670	84
36	420	31	540	44	660	81
35	410	28	530	41	640	78
34	400	25	520	39	630	75
33	400	25	510	37	610	70
32	390	23	500	34	600	67
31	380	20	490	32	590	65
30	370	18	470	28	570	59
29	360	15	460	25	560	56
28	360	15	450	23	540	50
27	350	13	440	21	530	47
26	340	11	430	19	510	42
25	340	11	410	16	500	38
24	330	9	400	14	480	33
23	320	8	390	12	470	30
22	310	7	380	11	450	26
21	300	5	370	10	440	23
20	290	4	360	8	420	19
19	280	3	340	6	410	17
18	270	2	330	5	390	14
17	260	2	320	4	380	12
16	250	1	310	3	360	9
15	250	1	290	2	350	8
14	240	1	280	2	330	6
13	230	1	260	1	320	5
12	220	1	250	1	300	3
11	210	1	230	1	280	2
10	200	1	210	1	260	1
9	200	1	200	1	250	1
8	200	1	200	1	230	1
7	200	1	200	1	210	1
0-6	200	1	200	1	200	1

*Percent scoring below the scaled score is based on the performance of 954,995 examinees who took the General Test between October 1, 1987, and September 30, 1990. This percent below information is used for score reports during the 1991-92 testing year.

GR 92-2

01

GRE®

THE GRADUATE RECORD EXAMINATIONS®

General Test

Do not break the seal

until you are told to do so.

The contents of this test are confidential. Disclosure or reproduction of any portion of it is prohibited.

THIS TEST BOOK MUST NOT BE TAKEN FROM THE ROOM.

NO TEST MATERIAL ON THIS PAGE

SECTION 1

Time—30 minutes

38 Questions

Directions: Each sentence below has one or two blanks, each blank indicating that something has been omitted. Beneath the sentence are five lettered words or sets of words. Choose the word or set of words for each blank that best fits the meaning of the sentence as a whole.

1. In the British theater young people under thirty-five have not had much ------- getting recognition onstage, but offstage—in the ranks of playwrights, directors, designers, administrators—they have mostly been relegated to relative obscurity.

   (A) trouble (B) satisfaction (C) curiosity about (D) success at (E) fear of

2. An institution concerned about its reputation is at the mercy of the actions of its members, because the misdeeds of individuals are often used to ------- the institutions of which they are a part.

   (A) reform (B) coerce (C) honor (D) discredit (E) intimidate

3. Since many casual smokers develop lung cancer and many -------- smokers do not, scientists believe that individuals differ in their -------- the cancer-causing agents known to be present in cigarette smoke.

   (A) heavy. .susceptibility to
   (B) chronic. .concern about
   (C) habitual. .proximity to
   (D) devoted. .reliance upon
   (E) regular. .exposure to

4. We accepted the theory that as people become more independent of one another, they begin to feel so isolated and lonely that freedom becomes ------- condition that most will seek to -------.

   (A) a permanent. .postpone
   (B) a common. .enter
   (C) a negative. .escape
   (D) a political. .impose
   (E) an irreparable. .avoid

5. If animal parents were judged by human standards, the cuckoo would be one of nature's more ------- creatures, blithely laying its eggs in the nests of other birds, and leaving the incubating and nurturing to them.

   (A) mettlesome (B) industrious (C) domestic (D) lackluster (E) feckless

6. The current penchant for ------- a product by denigrating a rival, named in the advertisement by brand name, seems somewhat -------: suppose the consumer remembers only the rival's name?

   (A) criticizing. .inefficient
   (B) touting. .foolhardy
   (C) enhancing. .insipid
   (D) evaluating. .cumbersome
   (E) flaunting. .gullible

7. His imperturbability in the face of evidence indicating his deliberate fraud failed to reassure supporters of his essential ------- ; instead, it suggested a talent for ------- that they had never suspected.

   (A) culpability. .intrigue (B) wisdom. .reproof (C) remorse. .loquacity (D) probity. .guile (E) combativeness. .compromise

GO ON TO THE NEXT PAGE.

Directions: In each of the following questions, a related pair of words or phrases is followed by five lettered pairs of words or phrases. Select the lettered pair that best expresses a relationship similar to that expressed in the original pair.

8. JUDGE : GAVEL ::
(A) detective : uniform
(B) doctor : stethoscope
(C) referee : whistle
(D) soldier : insignia
(E) lecturer : podium

9. ORGAN : KIDNEY ::
(A) skeleton : kneecap
(B) bone : rib
(C) neuron : synapse
(D) abdomen : stomach
(E) blood : aorta

10. SOOT : COMBUSTION ::
(A) lint : brushing
(B) gravel : crushing
(C) gristle : tenderizing
(D) rubbish : housecleaning
(E) sawdust : woodcutting

11. PURIFY : IMPERFECTION ::
(A) align : adjustment
(B) weary : boredom
(C) disagree : controversy
(D) verify : doubtfulness
(E) hone : sharpness

12. CENTRIFUGE : SEPARATE ::
(A) thermometer : calibrate
(B) statue : chisel
(C) floodgate : overflow
(D) colander : drain
(E) television : transmit

13. MOCK : IMITATE
(A) satirize : charm
(B) condense : summarize
(C) placate : assuage
(D) adapt : duplicate
(E) taunt : challenge

14. MALADROIT : SKILL ::
(A) intemperate : anger
(B) unreasonable : intuition
(C) sluggish : fatigue
(D) glib : profundity
(E) morose : depression

15. EQUIVOCATION : AMBIGUOUS ::
(A) mitigation : severe
(B) contradiction : peremptory
(C) platitude : banal
(D) precept : obedient
(E) explanation : unintelligible

16. VOLATILE : TEMPER ::
(A) prominent : notoriety
(B) ready : wit
(C) catastrophic : disaster
(D) gentle : heart
(E) expressive : song

GO ON TO THE NEXT PAGE.

Directions: Each passage in this group is followed by questions based on its content. After reading a passage, choose the best answer to each question. Answer all questions following a passage on the basis of what is stated or implied in that passage.

(This passage is from an article published in 1973)

The recent change to all-volunteer armed forces in the United States will eventually produce a gradual increase in the proportion of women in the armed forces and in the variety of women's assignments, but probably not the dramatic gains for women that might have been expected. This is so even though the armed forces operate in an ethos of institutional change oriented toward occupational equality and under the federal sanction of equal pay for equal work. The difficulty is that women are unlikely to be trained for any direct combat operations. A significant portion of the larger society remains uncomfortable as yet with extending equality in this direction. Therefore, for women in the military, the search for equality will still be based on functional equivalence, not identity or even similarity of task. Opportunities seem certain to arise. The growing emphasis on deterrence is bound to offer increasing scope for women to become involved in novel types of noncombat military assignments.

17. The primary purpose of the passage is to

(A) present an overview of the different types of assignments available to women in the new United States all-volunteer armed forces
(B) present a reasoned prognosis of the status of women in the new United States all-volunteer armed forces
(C) present the new United States all-volunteer armed forces as a model case of equal employment policies in action
(D) analyze reforms in the new United States all-volunteer armed forces necessitated by the increasing number of women in the military
(E) analyze the use of functional equivalence as a substitute for occupational equality in the new United States all-volunteer armed forces

18. According to the passage, despite the United States armed forces' commitment to occupational equality for women in the military, certain other factors preclude women's

(A) receiving equal pay for equal work
(B) having access to positions of responsibility at most levels
(C) drawing assignments from a wider range of assignments than before
(D) benefiting from opportunities arising from new noncombat functions
(E) being assigned all of the military tasks that are assigned to men

19. The passage implies that which of the following is a factor conducive to a more equitable representation of women in the United States armed forces than has existed in the past?

(A) The all-volunteer character of the present armed forces
(B) The past service records of women who had assignments functionally equivalent to men's assignments
(C) The level of awareness on the part of the larger society of military issues
(D) A decline in the proportion of deterrence-oriented noncombat assignments
(E) Restrictive past policies governing the military assignments open to women

20. The "dramatic gains for women" (line 5) and the attitude, as described in lines 11-12, of a "significant portion of the larger society" are logically related to each other inasmuch as the author puts forward the latter as

(A) a public response to achievement of the former
(B) the major reason for absence of the former
(C) a precondition for any prospect of achieving the former
(D) a catalyst for a further extension of the former
(E) a reason for some of the former being lost again

GO ON TO THE NEXT PAGE.

Of the thousands of specimens of meteorites found on Earth and known to science, only about 100 are igneous; that is, they have undergone melting by volcanic action at some time since the planets were first formed. These igneous meteorites are known as achondrites because they lack chondrules— small stony spherules found in the thousands of meteorites (called "chondrites") composed primarily of unaltered minerals that condensed from dust and gas at the origin of the solar system. Achondrites are the only known samples of volcanic rocks originating outside the Earth-Moon system. Most are thought to have been dislodged by interbody impact from asteroids, with diameters of from 10 to 500 kilometers, in solar orbit between Mars and Jupiter.

Shergottites, the name given to three anomalous achondrites so far discovered on Earth, present scientists with a genuine enigma. Shergottites crystallized from molten rock less than 1.1 billion years ago (some 3.5 billion years later than typical achondrites) and were presumably ejected into space when an object impacted on a body similar in chemical composition to Earth.

While most meteorites appear to derive from comparatively small bodies, shergottites exhibit properties that indicate that their source was a large planet, conceivably Mars. In order to account for such an unlikely source, some unusual factor must be invoked, because the impact needed to accelerate a fragment of rock to escape the gravitational field of a body even as small as the Moon is so great that no meteorites of lunar origin have been discovered.

While some scientists speculate that shergottites derive from Io (a volcanically active moon of Jupiter), recent measurements suggest that since Io's surface is rich in sulfur and sodium, the chemical composition of its volcanic products would probably be unlike that of the shergottites. Moreover, any fragments dislodged from Io by interbody impact would be unlikely to escape the gravitational pull of Jupiter.

The only other logical source of shergottites is Mars. Space-probe photographs indicate the existence of giant volcanoes on the Martian surface. From the small number of impact craters that appear on Martian lava flows, one can estimate that the planet was volcanically active as recently as a half-billion years ago—and may be active today. The great objection to the Martian origin of shergottites is the absence of lunar meteorites on Earth. An impact capable of ejecting a fragment of the Martian surface into an Earth-intersecting orbit is even less probable than such an event on the Moon, in view of the Moon's smaller size and closer proximity to Earth. A recent study suggests, however, that permafrost ices below the surface of Mars may have altered the effects of impact on it. If the ices had been rapidly vaporized by an impacting object, the expanding gases might have helped the ejected fragments reach escape velocity. Finally, analyses performed by space probes show a remarkable chemical similarity between Martian soil and the shergottites.

21. The passage implies which of the following about shergottites?

    I. They are products of volcanic activity.
    II. They derive from a planet larger than Earth.
    III. They come from a planetary body with a chemical composition similar to that of Io.

    (A) I only
    (B) II only
    (C) I and II only
    (D) II and III only
    (E) I, II, and III

22. According to the passage, a meteorite discovered on Earth is unlikely to have come from a large planet for which of the following reasons?

    (A) There are fewer large planets in the solar system than there are asteroids.
    (B) Most large planets have been volcanically inactive for more than a billion years.
    (C) The gravitational pull of a large planet would probably prohibit fragments from escaping its orbit.
    (D) There are no chondrites occurring naturally on Earth and probably none on other large planets.
    (E) Interbody impact is much rarer on large than on small planets because of the density of the atmosphere on large planets.

23. The passage suggests that the age of shergottites is probably

    (A) still entirely undetermined
    (B) less than that of most other achondrites
    (C) about 3.5 billion years
    (D) the same as that of typical achondrites
    (E) greater than that of the Earth

GO ON TO THE NEXT PAGE.

24. According to the passage, the presence of chondrules in a meteorite indicates that the meteorite

(A) has probably come from Mars
(B) is older than the solar system itself
(C) has not been melted since the solar system formed
(D) is certainly less than 4 billion years old
(E) is a small fragment of an asteroid

25. The passage provides information to answer which of the following questions?

(A) What is the precise age of the solar system?
(B) How did shergottites get their name?
(C) What are the chemical properties shared by shergottites and Martian soils?
(D) How volcanically active is the planet Jupiter?
(E) What is a major feature of the Martian surface?

26. It can be inferred from the passage that each of the following is a consideration in determining whether a particular planet is a possible source of shergottites that have been discovered on Earth EXCEPT the

(A) planet's size
(B) planet's distance from Earth
(C) strength of the planet's field of gravity
(D) proximity of the planet to its moons
(E) chemical composition of the planet's surface

27. It can be inferred from the passage that most meteorites found on Earth contain which of the following?

(A) Crystals (B) Chondrules (C) Metals
(D) Sodium (E) Sulfur

GO ON TO THE NEXT PAGE.

<u>Directions:</u> Each question below consists of a word printed in capital letters, followed by five lettered words or phrases. Choose the lettered word or phrase that is most nearly <u>opposite</u> in meaning to the word in capital letters.

Since some of the questions require you to distinguish fine shades of meaning, be sure to consider all the choices before deciding which one is best.

28. LIMP: (A) true (B) firm (C) clear (D) stark (E) endless

29. GLOBAL: (A) local (B) unusual (C) unpredictable (D) hot-headed (E) single-minded

30. STABILITY: (A) disparity (B) inconstancy (C) opposition (D) carelessness (E) weariness

31. DILATE: (A) narrow (B) strengthen (C) bend (D) push (E) soften

32. CONSOLE: (A) pretend sympathy (B) reveal suffering (C) aggravate grief (D) betray (E) vilify

33. EXCULPATE: (A) attribute guilt (B) avoid responsibility (C) establish facts (D) control hostilities (E) show anxiety

34. ACCRETION:
(A) ingestion of a nutrient
(B) loss of the security on a loan
(C) discernment of subtle differences
(D) reduction in substance caused by erosion
(E) sudden repulsion from an entity

35. CADGE: (A) conceal (B) influence (C) reserve (D) earn (E) favor

36. ABJURE: (A) commingle (B) arbitrate (C) espouse (D) appease (E) pardon

37. SPECIOUS: (A) unfeigned (B) significant (C) valid (D) agreeable (E) restricted

38. QUOTIDIAN: (A) extraordinary (B) certain (C) wishful (D) secret (E) premature

STOP

IF YOU FINISH BEFORE TIME IS CALLED, YOU MAY CHECK YOUR WORK ON THIS SECTION ONLY.
DO NOT TURN TO ANY OTHER SECTION IN THE TEST.

Section 2 starts on page 460.

SECTION 2

Time—30 minutes

30 Questions

Numbers: All numbers used are real numbers.

Figures: Position of points, angles, regions, etc. can be assumed to be in the order shown; and angle measures can be assumed to be positive.

Lines shown as straight can be assumed to be straight.

Figures can be assumed to lie in a plane unless otherwise indicated.

Figures that accompany questions are intended to provide information useful in answering the questions. However, unless a note states that a figure is drawn to scale, you should solve these problems NOT by estimating sizes by sight or by measurement, but by using your knowledge of mathematics (see Example 2 below).

Directions: Each of the Questions 1-15 consists of two quantities, one in Column A and one in Column B. You are to compare the two quantities and choose

A if the quantity in Column A is greater;
B if the quantity in Column B is greater;
C if the two quantities are equal;
D if the relationship cannot be determined from the information given.

Note: Since there are only four choices, NEVER MARK (E).

Common Information: In a question, information concerning one or both of the quantities to be compared is centered above the two columns. A symbol that appears in both columns represents the same thing in Column A as it does in Column B.

	Column A	Column B	Sample Answers
Example 1:	2×6	$2 + 6$	● Ⓑ Ⓒ Ⓓ Ⓔ

Examples 2-4 refer to $\triangle PQR$.

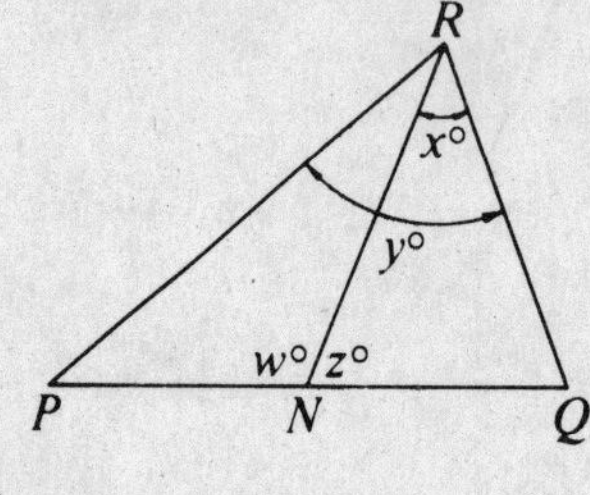

	Column A	Column B	Sample Answers
Example 2:	PN	NQ	Ⓐ Ⓑ Ⓒ ● Ⓔ (since equal measures cannot be assumed, even though PN and NQ appear equal)
Example 3:	x	y	Ⓐ ● Ⓒ Ⓓ Ⓔ (since N is between P and Q)
Example 4:	$w + z$	180	Ⓐ Ⓑ ● Ⓓ Ⓔ (since PQ is a straight line)

GO ON TO THE NEXT PAGE.

A if the quantity in Column A is greater;
B if the quantity in Column B is greater;
C if the two quantities are equal;
D if the relationship cannot be determined from the information given.

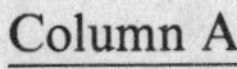

	Column A	Column B
1.	0.8	$\frac{1}{2} + \frac{1}{3}$

Pat is older than Lee, and Lee is younger than Maria.

	Column A	Column B
2.	Maria's age	Pat's age

A farmer has two large plots of land that are equal in area. The first is divided into 16 parcels with n acres in each and the second is divided into 20 parcels with m acres in each.

	Column A	Column B
3.	n	m

$x > 1$

	Column A	Column B
4.	$x - 4$	-2

Rectangular region R has width 8 and perimeter 40.

	Column A	Column B
5.	The area of R	256
6.	$4n^2$	$(2n + 1)(2n - 1)$

a and b are both greater than 0 and less than 1.

	Column A	Column B
7.	$a^2 + b^2$	$a + b$

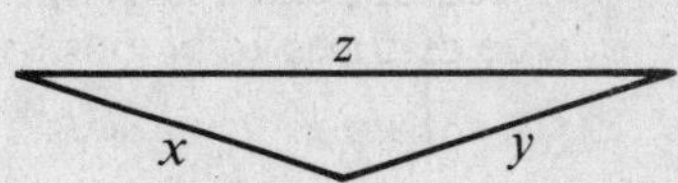

	Column A	Column B
8.	$x + y$	z
9.	3^x	4^x

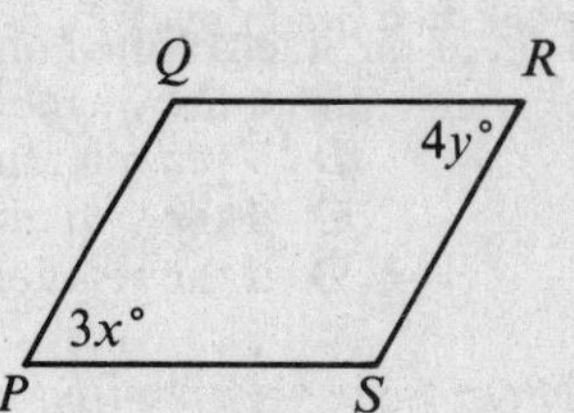

$PQRS$ is a parallelogram.

	Column A	Column B
10.	x	y
11.	The sum of all the integers from 19 to 59, inclusive	The sum of all the integers from 22 to 60, inclusive

GO ON TO THE NEXT PAGE.

A if the quantity in Column A is greater;
B if the quantity in Column B is greater;
C if the two quantities are equal;
D if the relationship cannot be determined from the information given.

Column A	Column B

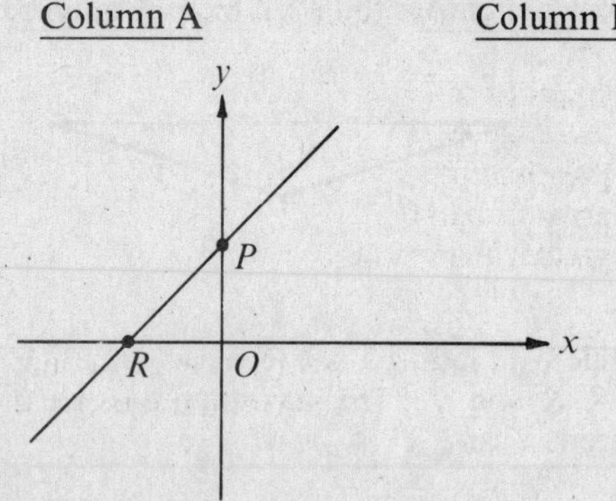

The equation of the line graphed on the rectangular coordinate system above is:

$$y = \frac{8x}{9} + 3$$

12. *PO* | *RO*

$0 > a > b$

13. ab | $(ab)^2$

Column A	Column B

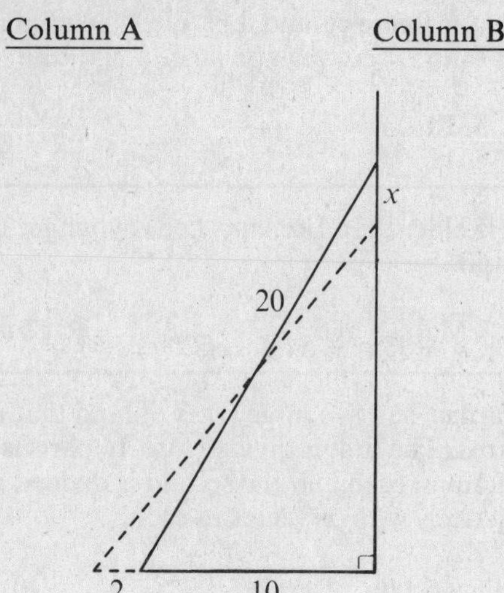

A 20-foot ladder leaning against a vertical wall with the base of the ladder 10 feet from the wall is pulled 2 feet farther out from the wall, causing the top of the ladder to drop x feet.

14. x | 2

15. $\frac{99^9}{9^{99}}$ | $\frac{11^9}{9^{90}}$

GO ON TO THE NEXT PAGE.

Directions: Each of the Questions 16-30 has five answer choices. For each of these questions, select the best of the answer choices given.

16. If the sales tax on an appliance priced at \$300 is between 5 percent and 8 percent, then the cost (price plus sales tax) of the appliance could be

(A) \$310
(B) \$312
(C) \$314
(D) \$318
(E) \$325

17. $2[2x + (3x + 5x)] - (3x + 5x) =$

(A) $4x$
(B) $8x$
(C) $10x$
(D) $12x$
(E) $22x$

18. Which of the following is the product of two positive integers whose sum is 3 ?

(A) 0
(B) 1
(C) 2
(D) 3
(E) 4

19. If an integer y is subtracted from an integer x and the result is greater than x, then y must be

(A) equal to x
(B) less than 0
(C) less than x
(D) greater than 0
(E) greater than x

20. A circle with radius 2 is intersected by a line at points R and T. The maximum possible distance between R and T is

(A) 1
(B) 2
(C) π
(D) 4
(E) 4π

GO ON TO THE NEXT PAGE.

Questions 21-25 refer to the following graphs.

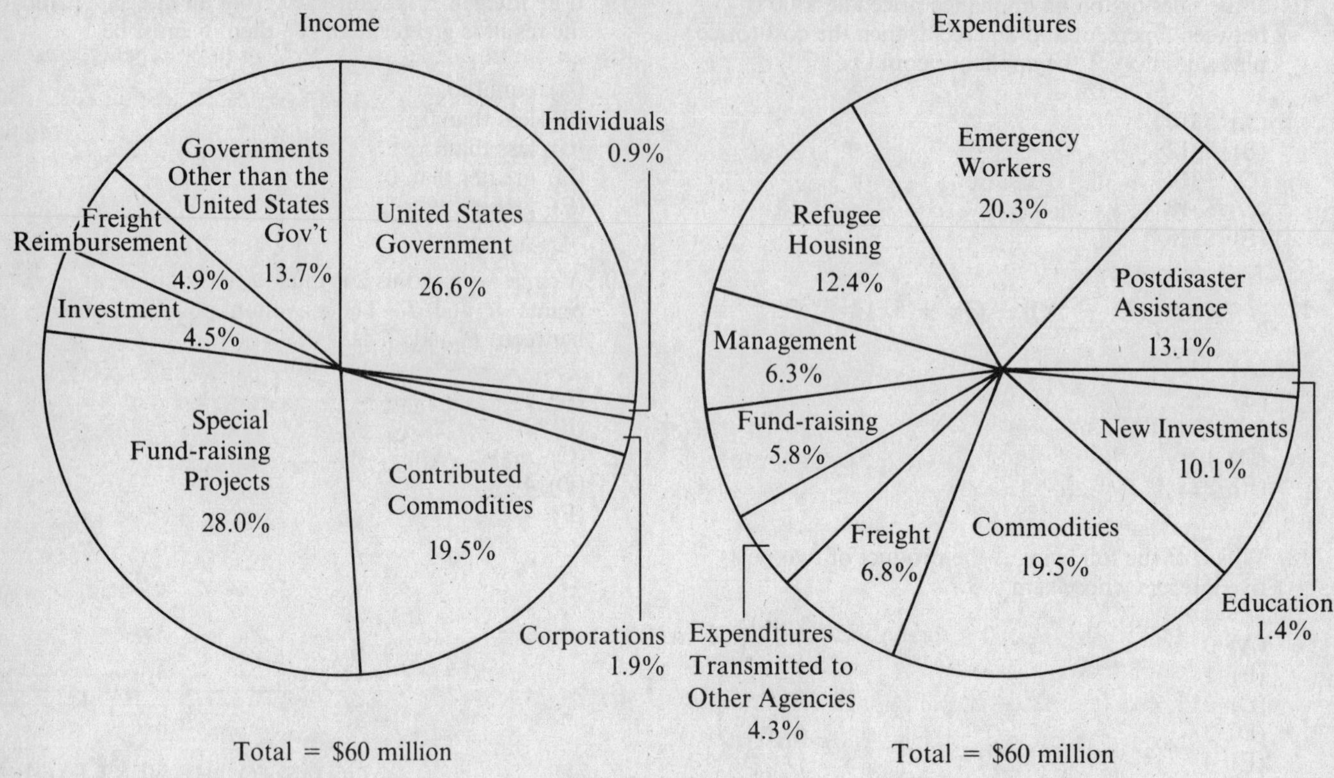

GO ON TO THE NEXT PAGE.

21. Approximately how much of the agency's income was provided by contributed commodities?

(A) \$12 million
(B) \$14 million
(C) \$15 million
(D) \$17 million
(E) \$19 million

22. Of the following, the category that had expenditures most nearly equal to the average (arithmetic mean) expenditures per category was

(A) refugee housing
(B) emergency workers
(C) postdisaster assistance
(D) new investments
(E) commodities

23. Income from which of the following sources was most nearly equal to \$2.9 million?

(A) United States government
(B) Freight reimbursement
(C) Investment
(D) Individuals
(E) Corporations

24. In year X, $\frac{1}{3}$ of the agency's refugee housing expenditures, $\frac{1}{5}$ of its emergency workers expenditures, $\frac{1}{4}$ of its commodities expenditures, and $\frac{2}{3}$ of its post-disaster assistance expenditures were directly related to one earthquake. The total of these expenditures was approximately how many millions of dollars?

(A) 5
(B) 7
(C) 9
(D) 11
(E) 13

25. Of the following, which is the closest appproximation to the percent of freight expenditures NOT covered by freight reimbursement income?

(A) 12%
(B) 28%
(C) 35%
(D) 39%
(E) 72%

GO ON TO THE NEXT PAGE.

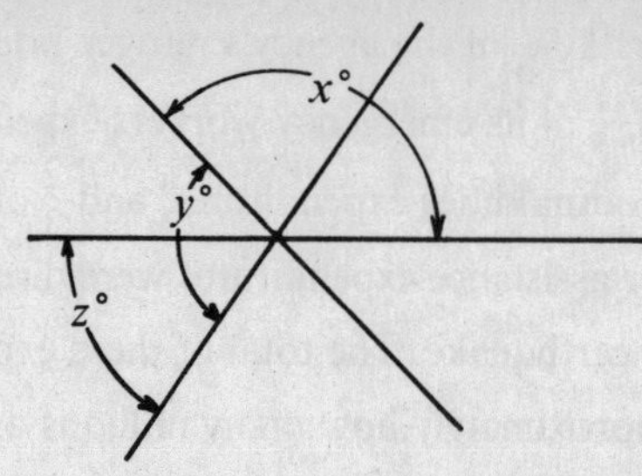

26. In the figure above, if $x = 110$ and $y = 120$, then $z =$

(A) 10
(B) 40
(C) 50
(D) 60
(E) 70

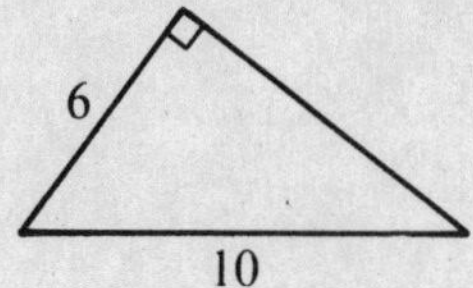

27. What is the area of the triangular region above?

(A) 24
(B) 30
(C) 40
(D) 48
(E) 60

28. A widow received $\frac{1}{3}$ of her husband's estate, and each of her three sons received $\frac{1}{3}$ of the balance. If the widow and one of her sons received a total of \$60,000 from the estate, what was the amount of the estate?

(A) \$90,000
(B) \$96,000
(C) \$108,000
(D) \$135,000
(E) \$180,000

29. If $\frac{x + 2}{y - 3} = 0$, which of the following must be true?

(A) $x = 2$ and $y = 3$
(B) $x = 2$ and $y \neq 3$
(C) $x = 0$ and $y = 0$
(D) $x = -2$ and $y = 3$
(E) $x = -2$ and $y \neq 3$

30. If $x = 0.888$, $y = \sqrt{0.888}$, and $z = (0.888)^2$, then which of the following is true?

(A) $x < y < z$
(B) $x < z < y$
(C) $y < x < z$
(D) $y < z < x$
(E) $z < x < y$

STOP

IF YOU FINISH BEFORE TIME IS CALLED, YOU MAY CHECK YOUR WORK ON THIS SECTION ONLY. DO NOT TURN TO ANY OTHER SECTION IN THE TEST.

Section 3 starts on page 468.

SECTION 3

Time—30 minutes

25 Questions

Directions: Each question or group of questions is based on a passage or set of conditions. In answering some of the questions, it may be useful to draw a rough diagram. For each question, select the best answer choice given.

Questions 1-6

A circus manager must divide eight circus acts—F, L, M, O, R, T, X, and Z—into two groups of four acts each, one group scheduled to perform, one act at a time, in ring 1 and the other group scheduled to perform, also one act at a time, in ring 2. All acts take equally long to perform, and every act that takes place in one of the rings must be scheduled for exactly the same time slot as an act that takes place in the other ring. The schedule must also conform to the following conditions:

Act F must take place in one of the rings at the same time that act M takes place in the other ring.
Act L must take place in one of the rings at the same time that act O takes place in the other ring.
Act R must take place in the same ring as act F.
Act T must take place in the same ring as act O.
Act X must be the second act that takes place in ring 2.

1. Which of the following, without regard to the order in which they will be performed, could be the group of acts to be scheduled for performance in ring 1?

(A) F, L, M, and T
(B) F, L, O, and R
(C) L, M, O, and T
(D) M, O, T, and Z
(E) O, R, T, and Z

2. If act T performs in ring 1, which of the following acts must perform in ring 2?

(A) F
(B) L
(C) M
(D) R
(E) Z

3. If act R must perform in one of the rings at the same time that act T performs in the other ring, which of the following must be the second act in ring 1?

(A) F
(B) L
(C) M
(D) O
(E) Z

4. If the order, from first to last, of circus acts in ring 2 is O, X, T, M, which of the following is an acceptable order of acts in ring 1, also from first to last?

(A) F, R, L, Z
(B) L, Z, F, R
(C) L, Z, R, F
(D) Z, L, F, R
(E) Z, R, L, F

5. If act F must perform between act X and act R in ring 2, which of the following must be the first act in ring 1?

(A) L
(B) M
(C) O
(D) T
(E) Z

6. If act T must take place in ring 1 immediately after act F and immediately before act R, which act must be the third act in ring 2?

(A) L
(B) M
(C) O
(D) T
(E) Z

GO ON TO THE NEXT PAGE.

7. The federal government expects hospitals to perform 10,000 organ transplants next year. But it is doubtful that this many donor organs will be available, since the number of fatalities resulting from car and motorcycle accidents has been dropping steadily over the past decade.

   The argument above makes which of the following assumptions?

   (A) A significant number of the organs used in transplants come from people who die in car and motorcycle accidents.
   (B) The number of car and motorcycle accidents will increase significantly during the next year.
   (C) No more than 10,000 people will be in need of organ transplants during the next year.
   (D) In the past the federal government's estimates of the number of organ transplants needed during a given year have been very unreliable.
   (E) For any given fatality resulting from a car or motorcycle accident, there is a hospital in the vicinity in need of an organ for a transplant.

8. Verbal patterns in four works known to be written by a certain author were compared to those in a work of uncertain authorship sometimes attributed to that author. Many patterns were studied, including frequency of specific words and recurrence of certain phrases. The questioned work displayed verbal patterns very similar to those in the other four works, establishing that the same author wrote all five.

   Which of the following, if true, most strengthens the conclusion above?

   (A) No two writers are likely to display similar verbal patterns in their works.
   (B) Writers from different historical periods sometimes use the same words and phrases, but the meanings of such words and phrases change over time.
   (C) Many writers consciously attempt to experiment with innovative verbal patterns in each new work.
   (D) A relatively small number of words in any language occur with great frequency, and those words make up the largest portion of all discourse.
   (E) Word choice is generally considered an insignificant component of an author's style.

9. Because incumbent members of Congress are given a great deal of attention by the news media and because they enjoy such perquisites as free mail privileges and generous travel allowances, incumbents enjoy an overwhelming advantage over their challengers in elections for the United States Congress.

   Which of the following, if true, best supports the claim above?

   (A) In the last congressional elections, incumbents met with a larger number of lobbyists than did challengers.
   (B) In the last congressional elections, 98 percent of the incumbents in the House of Representatives who were seeking reelection won.
   (C) Incumbent members of Congress are frequently critical of the amount of attention given to them by the news media.
   (D) The support that political action committees provide to challengers for congressional seats often compensates for the perquisites enjoyed by incumbent members of Congress.
   (E) Of all incumbent senators surveyed before the last congressional elections, 78 percent said that their challengers did not pose a serious threat to their chances for reelection.

GO ON TO THE NEXT PAGE.

Questions 10-14

In a display of products available from a paper manufacturer, exactly eight folders are to be displayed on eight stands that are lined up in a straight line and numbered consecutively 1 through 8 from left to right. There are three gray folders, two purple folders, two yellow folders, and one orange folder. The folders must be displayed according to the following conditions:

At least one of the purple folders must be next to a yellow folder.
The orange folder cannot be next to a yellow folder.
The three gray folders cannot be placed on three consecutive stands.
Stand 5 must hold a gray folder.
Either stand 1 or stand 8 or both must hold a yellow folder.

10. Which of the following is an acceptable ordering of colors of folders from left to right?

	Stand 1	Stand 2	Stand 3	Stand 4	Stand 5	Stand 6	Stand 7	Stand 8
(A)	Gray	Gray	Yellow	Orange	Gray	Purple	Purple	Yellow
(B)	Orange	Gray	Yellow	Gray	Purple	Purple	Gray	Yellow
(C)	Purple	Yellow	Gray	Gray	Gray	Orange	Purple	Yellow
(D)	Yellow	Gray	Purple	Yellow	Gray	Orange	Purple	Gray
(E)	Yellow	Gray	Yellow	Gray	Gray	Purple	Orange	Purple

11. If a gray folder is placed on stand 4, another gray folder could be placed on any of the following stands EXCEPT

(A) 1
(B) 3
(C) 5
(D) 7
(E) 8

12. If purple folders are on stands 1 and 2, which of the following must be true?

(A) A gray folder is on stand 3.
(B) The orange folder is on stand 4.
(C) A gray folder is on stand 4.
(D) A yellow folder is on stand 6.
(E) The orange folder is on stand 8.

13. If stand 2 holds an orange folder, which of the following must be true?

(A) Stand 1 holds a gray folder.
(B) Stand 3 holds a purple folder.
(C) Stand 6 holds a purple folder.
(D) Stand 7 holds a yellow folder.
(E) Stand 8 holds a yellow folder.

14. If stands 1 and 3 hold gray folders, any of the following could be true EXCEPT:

(A) Stand 2 holds a yellow folder.
(B) Stand 4 holds an orange folder.
(C) Stand 6 holds a purple folder.
(D) Stand 7 holds a yellow folder.
(E) Stand 7 holds an orange folder.

GO ON TO THE NEXT PAGE.

Questions 15-18

Five persons—J, K, L, M, and O—have gathered to play a game called "forest and trees." Four players play in each round, with one person sitting out. Rounds are played by two competing teams of two persons each. The players have agreed on the following rules of participation:

No two players can play as a team in two consecutive rounds of the game.

After a round is concluded, one person from the losing team in that round must sit out the next round of the game.

After a round is concluded, the person who has sat out that round and a person from the winning team in that round join to form the team that is known as "the forest" for the next round.

After a round is concluded, one person from the losing team in that round and one person from the winning team in that round join to form the team that is known as "the trees" for the next round.

No round of the game can end in a tie.

Because L and O are perceived as having the greatest individual strengths as players, L and O can never play on the same team.

15. If, in the first round of a game, J and O are the winning team and L sits out, which of the following must be a team in the second round of that game?

(A) J and L
(B) K and L
(C) K and M
(D) L and M
(E) M and O

16. If, in the first round of a game, K and L are the winning team and J sits out, which of the following could be a team in the second round of that game?

(A) J and M
(B) J and O
(C) K and L
(D) K and O
(E) M and O

17. If J and M are the winning team in the first round, each of the following could be a member of "the forest" during the second round EXCEPT

(A) J
(B) K
(C) L
(D) M
(E) O

18. If M sits out the first round, each of the following could be a team in the first round EXCEPT

(A) J and K
(B) J and L
(C) J and O
(D) K and L
(E) K and O

GO ON TO THE NEXT PAGE.

Questions 19-22

Seven persons—N, Q, R, S, T, U, and W—are all the persons present at a party. All of them join distinct conversational groups that form during the party and that consist of two, three, or four persons at a time. At any time during the party, each of the persons present is considered to be a member of exactly one of the conversational groups. During the party the following conditions are satisfied:

N can never be in the same conversational group as S.
T must be in a conversational group that includes either S or W, but T cannot be in a conversational group with both S and W.
W must be in a conversational group that consists of exactly three persons.

19. Which of the following lists three conversational groups that can exist at the same time during the party?

(A) N and S	Q, T, and W	R and U
(B) N and T	R and S	Q, U, and W
(C) N and U	R and S	Q, T, and W
(D) N and W	S and U	Q, R, and T
(E) N, U, and W	S and Q	R and T

20. If, at a certain point during the party, R, T, and W are members of three distinct conversational groups, S must at that point be in a conversational group that includes

(A) Q
(B) R
(C) T
(D) U
(E) W

21. If, at a certain point during the party, a group of three persons and a group of four persons have formed and W is in the same conversational group as U, which of the following must at that point be in the group with W and U?

(A) N
(B) Q
(C) R
(D) S
(E) T

22. If, at a certain point during the party, one of the conversational groups consists only of Q, R, and W, at that point N must be part of a group of exactly

(A) two persons, whose other member is T
(B) two persons, whose other member is U
(C) four persons, whose other members include S
(D) four persons, whose other members include T
(E) four persons, whose other members include U

GO ON TO THE NEXT PAGE.

23. Instead of relying on general tax revenue, as it now does, the government should rely more heavily on passenger fares to finance public bus and train service. In order for public transportation to be maintained without cutting service, users should pay all the operating costs even if these costs should increase. Such charges would be fair since only users benefit from public transportation.

Which of the following is a principle on which the position above could be based?

(A) The number of users of a public service should determine the amount of governmental financial support for the service.
(B) The amount of public transportation provided should be dependent on the operating cost of each transportation service.
(C) If necessary, general taxes should be raised to ensure that public transportation services are provided.
(D) The government should provide support from general tax revenue to any transportation industry that has passenger service available to the public.
(E) General tax revenues should not be used to finance public services that benefit a limited number of people.

24. When the manufacturer of Voltage, a major soft drink, changed its secret formula last year, the export earnings of an island in the Indian Ocean began to fall. This island's only export comprises more than half of the world's supply of vanilla beans. Analysts concluded that the original formula of Voltage contained vanilla from beans, but the new formula did not.

Which of the following, if true, would most strengthen the conclusion drawn by the analysts?

(A) The vanilla-bean plantings of a nearby island were beginning to produce crops.
(B) A new process for synthesizing vanilla was under development in a laboratory in the United States.
(C) The island's trade agreement, under which the vanilla beans were exported to the country that manufactures Voltage, had lapsed.
(D) Imports of vanilla beans dropped in countries where Voltage is made.
(E) There were decreases in sales of several widely sold products that were known to contain vanilla.

25. Carol is shorter than Juan, but she is taller than Ed. Sandra is shorter than Juan, and she is shorter than Ed. Wallie is taller than Sandra, but shorter than Juan.

If the statements above are true, one can validly conclude that Bill is shorter than Carol if it is true that

(A) Carol is equal in height to Wallie
(B) Wallie is equal in height to Bill
(C) Bill is taller than Sandra, but shorter than Wallie
(D) Bill is shorter than Juan, but taller than Ed
(E) Wallie is taller than Bill, but shorter than Ed

STOP

IF YOU FINISH BEFORE TIME IS CALLED, YOU MAY CHECK YOUR WORK ON THIS SECTION ONLY. DO NOT TURN TO ANY OTHER SECTION IN THE TEST.

NO TEST MATERIAL ON THIS PAGE

SECTION 4

Time—30 minutes

38 Questions

Directions: Each sentence below has one or two blanks, each blank indicating that something has been omitted. Beneath the sentence are five lettered words or sets of words. Choose the word or set of words for each blank that best fits the meaning of the sentence as a whole.

1. Although providing wild chimpanzees with food makes them less ------- and easier to study, it is also known to ------- their normal social patterns.

(A) interesting. .reinforce (B) manageable. .upset (C) shy. .disrupt (D) poised. .inhibit (E) accessible. .retard

2. There is something ------- about the way the building of monasteries proliferated in eighteenth-century Bavaria, while in the rest of the Western world religious ardor was ------- and church building was consequently declining.

(A) enigmatic. .coalescing
(B) destructive. .changing
(C) immutable. .dissipating
(D) incongruous. .diminishing
(E) momentous. .diversifying

3. Because they had various meanings in nineteenth-century biological thought, "mechanism" and "vitalism" ought not to be considered ------- terms; thus, I find the recent insistence that the terms had single definitions to be entirely ------- .

(A) univocal. .erroneous
(B) problematic. .anachronistic
(C) intractable. .obtuse
(D) congruent. .suspect
(E) multifaceted. .vapid

4. Many Americans believe that individual initiative epitomized the 1890's and see the entrepreneur as the ------- of that age.

(A) caricature (B) salvation (C) throwback (D) aberration (E) personification

5. Neither the ideas of philosophers nor the practices of ordinary people can, by themselves, ------- reality; what in fact changes reality and kindles revolution is the ------- of the two.

(A) constitute. .divergence
(B) affect. .aim
(C) transform. .interplay
(D) preserve. .conjunction
(E) alter. .intervention

6. There has been a tendency among art historians not so much to revise as to eliminate the concept of the Renaissance—to ------- not only its uniqueness, but its very existence.

(A) explain (B) extol (C) transmute (D) regret (E) contest

7. Employees had become so inured to the caprices of top management's personnel policies that they greeted the announcement of a company-wide dress code with-------.

(A) astonishment (B) impassivity (C) resentment (D) apprehension (E) confusion

GO ON TO THE NEXT PAGE.

Directions: In each of the following questions, a related pair of words or phrases is followed by five lettered pairs of words or phrases. Select the lettered pair that best expresses a relationship similar to that expressed in the original pair.

8. SURGEON : DEXTERITY ::
(A) engineer : clarity
(B) sailor : navigation
(C) magistrate : precedent
(D) industrialist : capital
(E) acrobat : agility

9. PRUNE : HEDGE ::
(A) shuck : corn
(B) trim : hair
(C) cut : bouquet
(D) reap : crop
(E) shave : mustache

10. PHOTOGRAPH : LIGHT ::
(A) script : scene
(B) film : negative
(C) recording : sound
(D) rehearsal : practice
(E) concert : song

11. ANTIBIOTIC : INFECTION ::
(A) hormone : modification
(B) enzyme : digestion
(C) narcotic : dependency
(D) coagulant : bleeding
(E) stimulant : relaxation

12. EULOGY : PRAISE ::
(A) comedy : laughter
(B) epic : contempt
(C) tirade : awe
(D) elegy : lament
(E) parody : respect

13. DAMP : VIBRATION ::
(A) drench : moisture
(B) concentrate : extraction
(C) boil : liquid
(D) seal : perforation
(E) stanch : flow

14. ABRADED : FRICTION ::
(A) refined : distillate
(B) anodized : metal
(C) diluted : gas
(D) strengthened : pressure
(E) vaporized : heat

15. QUARRY : STONE ::
(A) fell : timber
(B) dredge : canal
(C) assay : gold
(D) bale : hay
(E) mold : clay

16. CREDULOUS : DUPE ::
(A) wealthy : monarch
(B) insensitive : boor
(C) argumentative : lawyer
(D) spontaneous : extrovert
(E) extravagant : miser

GO ON TO THE NEXT PAGE.

Directions: Each passage in this group is followed by questions based on its content. After reading a passage, choose the best answer to each question. Answer all questions following a passage on the basis of what is stated or implied in that passage.

The transplantation of organs from one individual to another normally involves two major problems: (1) organ rejection is likely unless the transplantation antigens of both individuals are nearly identical, and (2) the introduction of any unmatched transplantation antigens induces the development by the recipient of donor-specific lymphocytes that will produce violent rejection of further transplantations from that donor. However, we have found that among many strains of rats these "normal" rules of transplantation are not obeyed by liver transplants. Not only are liver transplants never rejected, but they even induce a state of donor-specific unresponsiveness in which subsequent transplants of other organs, such as skin, from that donor are accepted permanently. Our hypothesis is that (1) many strains of rats simply cannot mount a sufficiently vigorous destructive immune-response (using lymphocytes) to outstrip the liver's relatively great capacity to protect itself from immune-response damage and that (2) the systemic unresponsiveness observed is due to concentration of the recipient's donor-specific lymphocytes at the site of the liver transplant.

17. The primary purpose of the passage is to treat the accepted generalizations about organ transplantation in which of the following ways?

(A) Explicate their main features
(B) Suggest an alternative to them
(C) Examine their virtues and limitations
(D) Criticize the major evidence used to support them
(E) Present findings that qualify them

18. It can be inferred from the passage that the author believes that an important difference among strains of rats is the

(A) size of their livers
(B) constitution of their skin
(C) strength of their immune-response reactions
(D) sensitivity of their antigens
(E) adaptability of their lymphocytes

19. According to the hypothesis of the author, after a successful liver transplant, the reason that rats do not reject further transplants of other organs from the same donor is that the

(A) transplantation antigens of the donor and the recipient become matched
(B) lymphocytes of the recipient are weakened by the activity of the transplanted liver
(C) subsequently transplanted organ is able to repair the damage caused by the recipient's immune-response reaction
(D) transplanted liver continues to be the primary locus for the recipient's immune-response reaction
(E) recipient is unable to manufacture the lymphocytes necessary for the immune-response reaction

20. Which of the following new findings about strains of rats that do not normally reject liver transplants, if true, would support the authors' hypothesis?

I. Stomach transplants are accepted by the recipients in all cases.
II. Increasing the strength of the recipient's immune-response reaction can induce liver-transplant rejection.
III. Organs from any other donor can be transplanted without rejection after liver transplantation.
IV. Preventing lymphocytes from being concentrated at the liver transplant produces acceptance of skin transplants.

(A) II only
(B) I and III only
(C) II and IV only
(D) I, II, and III only
(E) I, III, and IV only

GO ON TO THE NEXT PAGE.

Practically speaking, the artistic maturing of the cinema was the single-handed achievement of David W. Griffith (1875-1948). Before Griffith, photography in dramatic films consisted of little more than placing the actors before a stationary camera and showing them in full length as they would have appeared on stage. From the beginning of his career as a director, however, Griffith, because of his love of Victorian painting, employed composition. He conceived of the camera image as having a foreground and a rear ground, as well as the middle distance preferred by most directors. By 1910 he was using close-ups to reveal significant details of the scene or of the acting and extreme long shots to achieve a sense of spectacle and distance. His appreciation of the camera's possibilities produced novel dramatic effects. By splitting an event into fragments and recording each from the most suitable camera position, he could significantly vary the emphasis from camera shot to camera shot.

Griffith also achieved dramatic effects by means of creative editing. By juxtaposing images and varying the speed and rhythm of their presentation, he could control the dramatic intensity of the events as the story progressed. Despite the reluctance of his producers, who feared that the public would not be able to follow a plot that was made up of such juxtaposed images, Griffith persisted, and experimented as well with other elements of cinematic syntax that have become standard ever since. These included the flashback, permitting broad psychological and emotional exploration as well as narrative that was not chronological, and the crosscut between two parallel actions to heighten suspense and excitement. In thus exploiting fully the possibilities of editing, Griffith transposed devices of the Victorian novel to film and gave film mastery of time as well as space.

Besides developing the cinema's language, Griffith immensely broadened its range and treatment of subjects. His early output was remarkably eclectic: it included not only the standard comedies, melodramas, westerns, and thrillers, but also such novelties as adaptations from Browning and Tennyson, and treatments of social issues. As his successes mounted, his ambitions grew, and with them the whole of American cinema. When he remade *Enoch Arden* in 1911, he insisted that a subject of such importance could not be treated in the then conventional length of one reel. Griffith's introduction of the American-made multireel picture began an immense revolution. Two years later, *Judith of Bethulia,* an elaborate historicophilosophical spectacle, reached the unprecedented length of four reels, or one hour's running time. From our contemporary viewpoint, the pretensions of this film may seem a trifle ludicrous, but at the time it provoked endless debate and discussion and gave a new intellectual respectability to the cinema.

21. The primary purpose of the passage is to
    (A) discuss the importance of Griffith to the development of the cinema
    (B) describe the impact on cinema of the flashback and other editing innovations
    (C) deplore the state of American cinema before the advent of Griffith
    (D) analyze the changes in the cinema wrought by the introduction of the multireel film
    (E) document Griffith's impact on the choice of subject matter in American films

22. The author suggests that Griffith's film innovations had a direct effect on all of the following EXCEPT
    (A) film editing (B) camera work
    (C) scene composing (D) sound editing
    (E) directing

23. It can be inferred from the passage that before 1910 the normal running time of a film was
    (A) 15 minutes or less
    (B) between 15 and 30 minutes
    (C) between 30 and 45 minutes
    (D) between 45 minutes and 1 hour
    (E) 1 hour or more

24. The author asserts that Griffith introduced all of the following into American cinema EXCEPT
    (A) consideration of social issues
    (B) adaptations from Tennyson
    (C) the flashback and other editing techniques
    (D) photographic approaches inspired by Victorian painting
    (E) dramatic plots suggested by Victorian theater

GO ON TO THE NEXT PAGE.

25. The author suggests that Griffith's contributions to the cinema had which of the following results?

    I. Literary works, especially Victorian novels, became popular sources for film subjects.
    II. Audience appreciation of other film directors' experimentations with cinematic syntax was increased.
    III. Many of the artistic limitations thought to be inherent in filmmaking were shown to be really nonexistent.

    (A) II only
    (B) III only
    (C) I and II only
    (D) II and III only
    (E) I, II, and III

26. It can be inferred from the passage that Griffith would be most likely to agree with which of the following statements?

    (A) The good director will attempt to explore new ideas as quickly as possible.
    (B) The most important element contributing to a film's success is the ability of the actors.
    (C) The camera must be considered an integral and active element in the creation of a film.
    (D) The cinema should emphasize serious and sober examinations of fundamental human problems.
    (E) The proper composition of scenes in a film is more important than the details of their editing.

27. The author's attitude toward photography in the cinema before Griffith can best be described as

    (A) sympathetic (B) nostalgic (C) amused
    (D) condescending (E) hostile

GO ON TO THE NEXT PAGE.

Directions: Each question below consists of a word printed in capital letters, followed by five lettered words or phrases. Choose the lettered word or phrase that is most nearly opposite in meaning to the word in capital letters.

Since some of the questions require you to distinguish fine shades of meaning, be sure to consider all the choices before deciding which one is best.

28. ADHERE: (A) detach (B) cleanse (C) engulf (D) incise (E) contain

29. UNCONVENTIONALITY: (A) perceptibility (B) inscrutability (C) imperturbability (D) fidelity to custom (E) formality of discourse

30. PINCH: (A) important accomplishment (B) apt translation (C) abundant amount (D) opportune acquisition (E) unfamiliar period

31. OUTSET: (A) regression (B) series (C) exit (D) interruption (E) termination

32. RAREFY:
(A) make less humid
(B) make less opaque
(C) make more voluminous
(D) make more dense
(E) make more oily

33. EFFRONTERY: (A) charity (B) deference (C) simplicity (D) deceitfulness (E) stupidity

34. SCURVY: (A) completely centered (B) above reproach (C) imaginative (D) valiant (E) carefree

35. OBDURATE: (A) complaisant (B) similar (C) commensurate (D) uncommunicative (E) transitory

36. AVER:
(A) resign indignantly (B) condemn unjustly (C) refuse (D) deny (E) resent

37. PITH: (A) untimely action (B) insufficient attention (C) routine treatment (D) rigid formulation (E) superficial element

38. SUPINE: (A) vigilant (B) flustered (C) distorted (D) brittle (E) awkward

STOP

IF YOU FINISH BEFORE TIME IS CALLED, YOU MAY CHECK YOUR WORK ON THIS SECTION ONLY. DO NOT TURN TO ANY OTHER SECTION IN THE TEST.

Section 6 starts on page 482.

SECTION 6

Time—30 minutes

30 Questions

Numbers: All numbers used are real numbers.

Figures: Position of points, angles, regions, etc. can be assumed to be in the order shown; and angle measures can be assumed to be positive.

Lines shown as straight can be assumed to be straight.

Figures can be assumed to lie in a plane unless otherwise indicated.

Figures that accompany questions are intended to provide information useful in answering the questions. However, unless a note states that a figure is drawn to scale, you should solve these problems NOT by estimating sizes by sight or by measurement, but by using your knowledge of mathematics (see Example 2 below).

Directions: Each of the Questions 1-15 consists of two quantities, one in Column A and one in Column B. You are to compare the two quantities and choose

A if the quantity in Column A is greater;
B if the quantity in Column B is greater;
C if the two quantities are equal;
D if the relationship cannot be determined from the information given.

Note: Since there are only four choices, NEVER MARK (E).

Common Information: In a question, information concerning one or both of the quantities to be compared is centered above the two columns. A symbol that appears in both columns represents the same thing in Column A as it does in Column B.

	Column A	Column B	Sample Answers
Example 1:	2×6	$2 + 6$	● Ⓑ Ⓒ Ⓓ Ⓔ

Examples 2-4 refer to $\triangle PQR$.

R, x°, y°, w°, z°, P, N, Q

	Column A	Column B	Sample Answers
Example 2:	PN	NQ	Ⓐ Ⓑ Ⓒ ● Ⓔ (since equal measures cannot be assumed, even though PN and NQ appear equal)
Example 3:	x	y	Ⓐ ● Ⓒ Ⓓ Ⓔ (since N is between P and Q)
Example 4:	$w + z$	180	Ⓐ Ⓑ ● Ⓓ Ⓔ (since PQ is a straight line)

GO ON TO THE NEXT PAGE.

A if the quantity in Column A is greater;
B if the quantity in Column B is greater;
C if the two quantities are equal;
D if the relationship cannot be determined from the information given.

	Column A	Column B
1.	$\frac{4}{5} - \frac{4}{7}$	$\frac{4}{7} - \frac{2}{5}$
2.	The average (arithmetic mean) of 87, 95, and 130	The average (arithmetic mean) of 88, 95, and 129
3.	The time that it takes Jim to drive 300 miles at a speed of 52 miles per hour	The time that it takes Lila to drive 240 miles at a speed of 40 miles per hour
4.	$(-5)^6$	$(-6)^5$

Ms. Rogers bought an electric range on the installment plan. The cash price of the range was $400. The amount she paid was $120 down and 12 monthly payments of $28 each.

	Column A	Column B
5.	The amount she paid for the electric range in excess of the cash price	$56

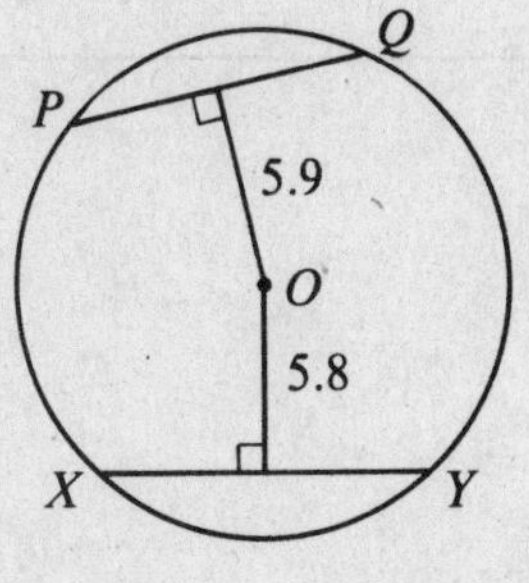

P, Q, 5.9, O, 5.8, X, Y

Circle with center O

	Column A	Column B
6.	The length of chord PQ	The length of chord XY

$\frac{n}{x} = 428$ and $\frac{n}{y} = 107.$

$n > 0$

	Column A	Column B
7.	x	y

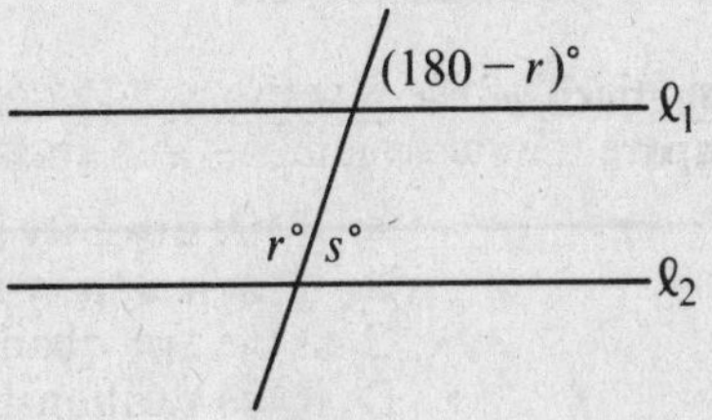

$(180-r)°$, ℓ_1, $r°$, $s°$, ℓ_2

$\ell_1 \parallel \ell_2$

	Column A	Column B
8.	s	60

6 is x percent of 24.
y is 25 percent of 96.

	Column A	Column B
9.	x	y

$2x + y < 3$
$x > 2$

	Column A	Column B
10.	y	0

GO ON TO THE NEXT PAGE.

A if the quantity in Column A is greater;
B if the quantity in Column B is greater;
C if the two quantities are equal;
D if the relationship cannot be determined from the information given.

Column A	Column B

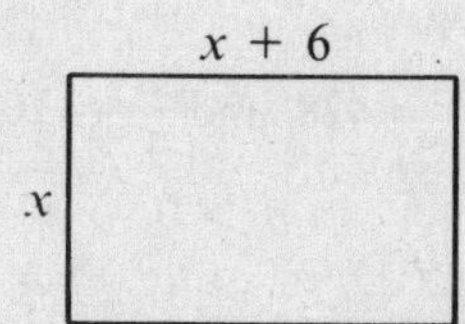

The perimeter of square S is equal to the perimeter of the rectangle above.

	Column A	Column B
11.	The length of a side of S	$x + 3$

$0 < a < b < c$

	Column A	Column B
12.	$\frac{b}{a}$	$\frac{c}{b}$

C is a circle with radius 3.

	Column A	Column B
13.	The ratio of the circumference of C to the diameter of C	3

Column A	Column B

$rt > 0$

	Column A	Column B
14.	$\frac{3}{r} + \frac{4}{t}$	$\frac{3t + 4r}{r + t}$

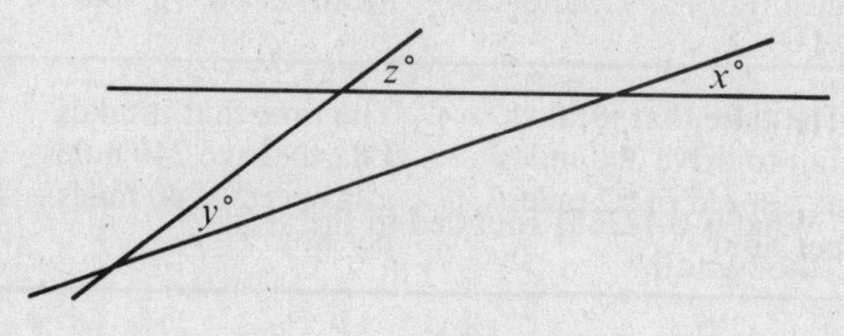

	Column A	Column B
15.	$z - x$	y

GO ON TO THE NEXT PAGE.

Directions: Each of the Questions 16-30 has five answer choices. For each of these questions, select the best of the answer choices given.

16. $\frac{9^2 - 6^2}{3} =$

(A) 1

(B) $\frac{15}{9}$

(C) 5

(D) 8

(E) 15

17. What is 0.423658 rounded to the nearest thousandth?

(A) 0.42
(B) 0.423
(C) 0.424
(D) 0.4236
(E) 0.4237

18. If $3(x + 2) = x - 4$, then $x =$

(A) -5
(B) -3
(C) 1
(D) 3
(E) 5

19. If $x^2 + 2xy + y^2 = 9$, then $(x + y)^4 =$

(A) 3
(B) 18
(C) 27
(D) 36
(E) 81

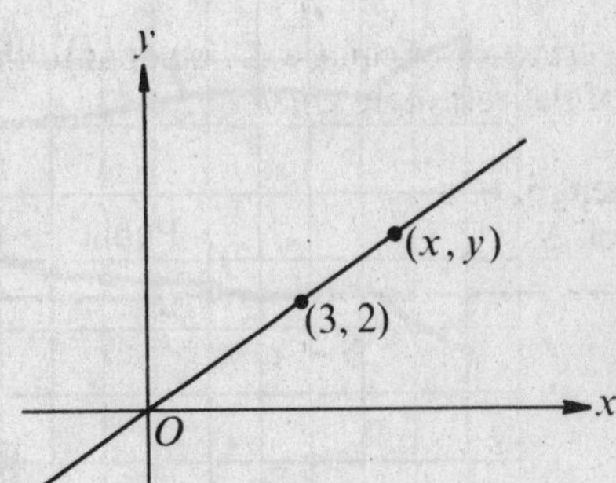

20. In the rectangular coordinate system above, if $x = 4.8$, then $y =$

(A) 3.0
(B) 3.2
(C) 3.4
(D) 3.6
(E) 3.8

GO ON TO THE NEXT PAGE.

Questions 21-25 refer to the following graphs.

NATIONAL HEALTH EXPENDITURES FOR COUNTRY *X*, 1975-1986
(1 billion = 1,000,000,000)

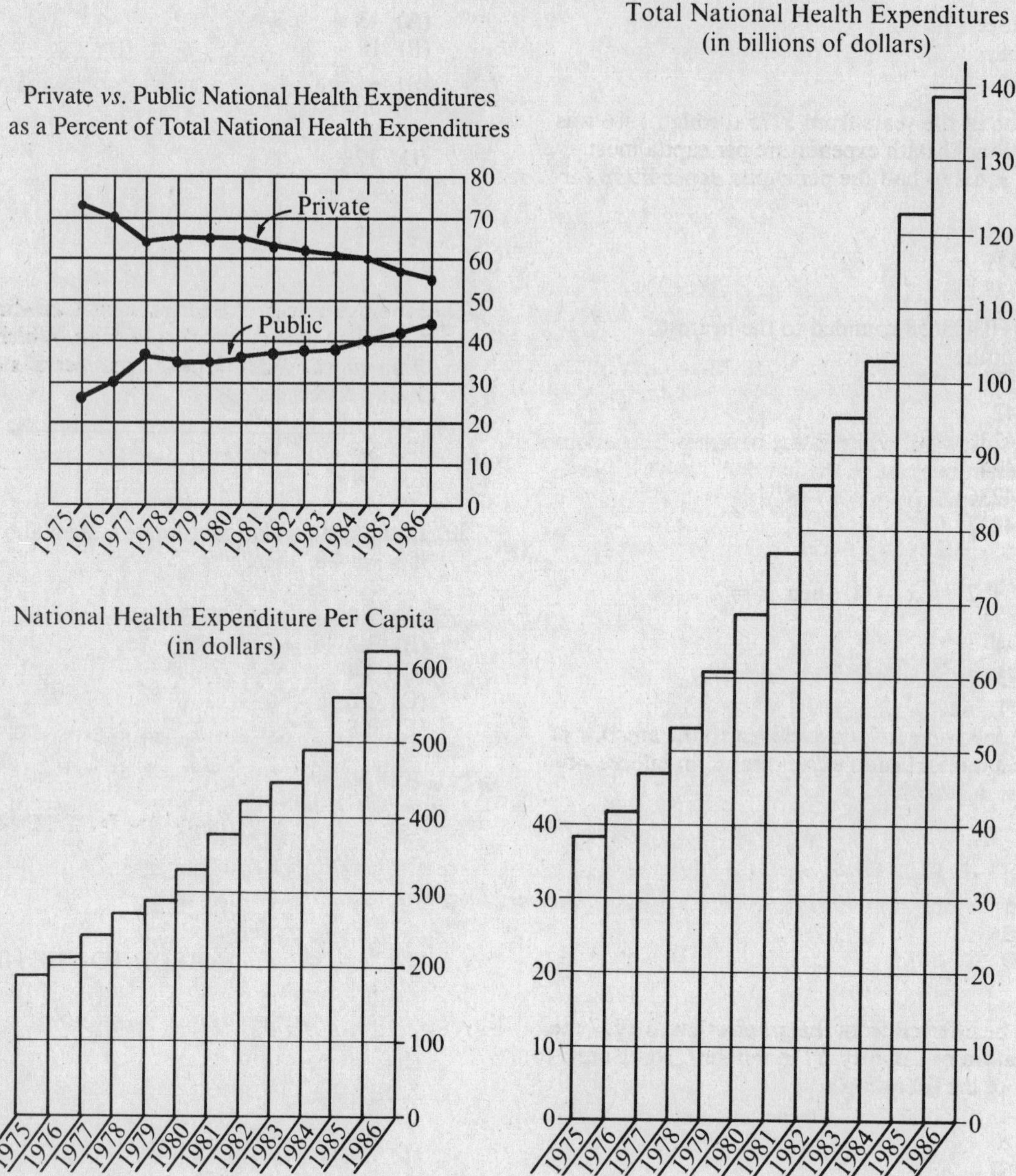

Note: Drawn to scale.

GO ON TO THE NEXT PAGE.

21. For how many of the years shown was the amount of private health expenditures at least double the amount of public health expenditures?

(A) None
(B) One
(C) Two
(D) Three
(E) Four

22. In which of the years from 1975 through 1986 was the national health expenditure per capita most nearly equal to half the per capita expenditure for 1984 ?

(A) 1975
(B) 1977
(C) 1979
(D) 1980
(E) 1982

23. Of the following, which is the best approximation of the percent increase in the national health expenditure per capita from 1981 to 1982 ?

(A) 35%
(B) 30%
(C) 20%
(D) 10%
(E) 5%

24. Of the following, which is closest to the amount of public national health expenditures, in billions of dollars, in 1980 ?

(A) 25
(B) 30
(C) 35
(D) 45
(E) 70

25. It can be inferred from the graphs that in 1977 the population of Country X, in millions, was closest to which of the following?

(A) 120
(B) 150
(C) 190
(D) 240
(E) 250

26. If x is the number on the number line between 5 and 15 that is twice as far from 5 as from 15, then x is

(A) $5\frac{2}{3}$

(B) 10

(C) $11\frac{2}{3}$

(D) $12\frac{1}{2}$

(E) $13\frac{1}{3}$

27. Jane has exactly 3 times as many Canadian as non-Canadian stamps in her collection. Which of the following CANNOT be the number of stamps in Jane's collection?

(A) 96
(B) 80
(C) 72
(D) 68
(E) 54

GO ON TO THE NEXT PAGE.

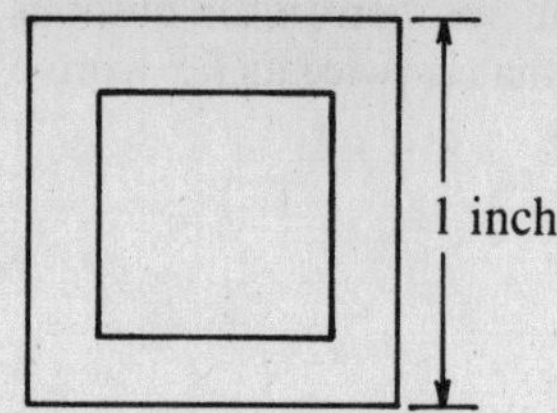

28. In the figure above, if the area of the smaller square region is $\frac{1}{2}$ the area of the larger square region, then the diagonal of the larger square is how many inches longer than the diagonal of the smaller square?

(A) $\sqrt{2} - 1$

(B) $\frac{1}{2}$

(C) $\frac{\sqrt{2}}{2}$

(D) $\frac{\sqrt{2} + 1}{2}$

(E) $\sqrt{2}$

29. A distillate flows into an empty 64-gallon drum at spout A and out of the drum at spout B. If the rate of flow through A is 2 gallons per hour, how many gallons per hour must flow out at spout B so that the drum is full in exactly 96 hours?

(A) $\frac{3}{8}$

(B) $\frac{1}{2}$

(C) $\frac{2}{3}$

(D) $\frac{4}{3}$

(E) $\frac{8}{3}$

30. A farmer has two rectangular fields. The larger field has twice the length and 4 times the width of the smaller field. If the smaller field has area K, then the area of the larger field is greater than the area of the smaller field by what amount?

(A) $2K$
(B) $6K$
(C) $7K$
(D) $8K$
(E) $12K$

STOP

IF YOU FINISH BEFORE TIME IS CALLED, YOU MAY CHECK YOUR WORK ON THIS SECTION ONLY. DO NOT TURN TO ANY OTHER SECTION IN THE TEST.

Section 7 starts on page 490.

SECTION 7

Time—30 minutes

25 Questions

Directions: Each question or group of questions is based on a passage or set of conditions. In answering some of the questions, it may be useful to draw a rough diagram. For each question, select the best answer choice given.

Questions 1-4

Three adults—Roberto, Sarah, and Vicky—will be traveling in a van with five children—Freddy, Hilary, Jonathan, Lupe, and Marta. The van has a driver's seat and one passenger seat in the front, and two benches behind the front seats, one bench behind the other. Each bench has room for exactly three people. Everyone must sit in a seat or on a bench, and seating is subject to the following restrictions:

An adult must sit on each bench.
Either Roberto or Sarah must sit in the driver's seat.
Jonathan must sit immediately beside Marta.

1. Which of the following can sit in the front passenger seat?

(A) Jonathan
(B) Lupe
(C) Roberto
(D) Sarah
(E) Vicky

2. Which of the following groups of three can sit together on a bench?

(A) Freddy, Jonathan, and Marta
(B) Freddy, Jonathan, and Vicky
(C) Freddy, Sarah, and Vicky
(D) Hilary, Lupe, and Sarah
(E) Lupe, Marta, and Roberto

3. If Freddy sits immediately beside Vicky, which of the following CANNOT be true?

(A) Jonathan sits immediately beside Sarah.
(B) Lupe sits immediately beside Vicky.
(C) Hilary sits in the front passenger seat.
(D) Freddy sits on the same bench as Hilary.
(E) Hilary sits on the same bench as Roberto.

4. If Sarah sits on a bench that is behind where Jonathan is sitting, which of the following must be true?

(A) Hilary sits in a seat or on a bench that is in front of where Marta is sitting.
(B) Lupe sits in a seat or on a bench that is in front of where Freddy is sitting.
(C) Freddy sits on the same bench as Hilary.
(D) Lupe sits on the same bench as Sarah.
(E) Marta sits on the same bench as Vicky.

GO ON TO THE NEXT PAGE.

5. Private ownership of services traditionally considered to be the responsibility of the government will typically improve those services. The turnpike system in the United States of the nineteenth century demonstrates the truth of this principle; the system, which had previously been controlled by the government, became a more reliable system when taken over by private organizations.

   Which of the following describes a significant flaw in the author's argument above?

   (A) The author defends the conclusion by appealing to a person of authority.
   (B) The author distorts an opposing view in trying to show its weaknesses.
   (C) The author defends what the author perceives as a wrong action by pointing out another perceived wrong action.
   (D) The author generalizes from a sample not representative enough to establish the conclusion.
   (E) The author attributes two very different meanings to the same word.

6. A recent state survey of human resources found that the age to which secretarial school graduates are expected to live is four years in excess of the age to which other graduates of high school are expected to live. One possible conclusion is that secretarial school attendance is beneficial to one's health.

   To evaluate the conclusion above, it would be most important to know the answer to which of the following questions?

   (A) Have the average age of new high school graduates and the average age of new secretarial school graduates recently increased?
   (B) Do some secretarial school graduates have college degrees?
   (C) Given that women have a greater life expectancy than men, what are the relative proportions of men and women among high school and secretarial school graduates?
   (D) Given that women have a greater life expectancy than men, what proportion of all women attend secretarial school?
   (E) Has the proportion of high school graduates who attend secretarial school increased in recent years?

7. Some insects are able to feed on the leaves of milkweed, a toxic plant, by first cutting and draining the vein that secretes the toxin. This method of detoxification guarantees that some insects will always be able to eat milkweed, because the plant could never evolve to produce a toxin that is lethal in the trace amounts left after the vein is cut.

   The conclusion drawn in the passage above depends on which of the following assumptions?

   (A) The insects that successfully detoxify milkweed are not able to undergo the evolutionary changes necessary to allow them to detoxify other plants.
   (B) Unlike milkweed, other kinds of toxic plants would be able to overcome their vulnerabilities to predators through evolutionary changes.
   (C) The toxin-carrying veins of the milkweed plant can never evolve in such a way that insects cannot cut through.
   (D) The method of detoxification used by insect predators of milkweed would not successfully detoxify other kinds of toxic plants.
   (E) There are insects that use means other than draining the toxin in order to feed on toxic plants.

GO ON TO THE NEXT PAGE.

Questions 8-12

Three desk drawers—I, II, and III—are being stocked with seven types of articles. Hand computers, ink pens, labels, markers, rulers, stationery, and tapes are to be placed in the drawers so that the articles belonging to any given type are all together in one drawer and no drawer contains more than three types of articles. The arrangement of the types of articles is subject to the following further constraints:

Hand computers and rulers must be in a drawer together.
Neither ink pens nor markers can be in the same drawer as labels.
Neither ink pens nor markers can be in the same drawer as stationery.
The stationery must be in either drawer I or drawer II.
Each type of article must be in some drawer or other.

8. Which of the following is an acceptable arrangement?

	Drawer I	Drawer II	Drawer III
(A)	Ink pens	Markers, stationery, tapes	Hand computers, labels, rulers
(B)	Ink pens, labels, stationery	Markers, tapes	Hand computers, rulers
(C)	Labels, stationery, tapes	Hand computers, ink pens, markers	Rulers
(D)	Labels, stationery, tapes	Ink pens, markers	Hand computers, rulers
(E)	Labels, tapes	Ink pens, markers	Hand computers, rulers, stationery

9. If labels are in I and stationery is in II, which of the following must be true?

(A) Hand computers are in I.
(B) Hand computers are in II.
(C) Hand computers are in III.
(D) Ink pens are in II.
(E) Ink pens are in III.

10. If labels are in II and stationery is in I, any of the following can be true EXCEPT:

(A) Hand computers are in II.
(B) Hand computers are in III.
(C) Rulers are in I.
(D) Rulers are in II.
(E) Tapes are in III.

11. If hand computers, rulers, and tapes are in I, which of the following must be true?

(A) Ink pens are in II.
(B) Labels are in I.
(C) Labels are in III.
(D) Markers are in II.
(E) Markers are in III.

12. If rulers are in II, which of the following is acceptable?

(A) Hand computers are in I and tapes are in II.
(B) Ink pens are in I and markers are in II.
(C) Ink pens are in I and markers are in III.
(D) Markers are in I and tapes are in II.
(E) Stationery is in I and labels are in II.

GO ON TO THE NEXT PAGE.

Questions 13-18

A flat wilderness area has four widely separated shelters—F, G, W, and X—that are connected by exactly four straight trails—Q, R, S, and T—that are equal to each other in length and connect the shelters in the following ways:

Q connects F and W only.
R connects G and W only.
S connects F and G only.
T connects G and X only.

The shelters are at the ends of the trails.

13. Which of the following is the order in which a hiker, starting at F, using only trails and using no trail more than once, must reach the other shelters?

(A) G, W, X
(B) W, G, X
(C) W, X, G
(D) X, G, W
(E) X, W, G

14. If a hiker is at X and wants to reach F by a sequence of trails no longer than necessary, there are how many trail sequences of minimal length from which to choose?

(A) One
(B) Two
(C) Three
(D) Four
(E) Five

15. If a hiker restricts herself to the trails, any of the following is a possible sequence in which full lengths of trails are hiked EXCEPT

(A) Q, S, R, T, S
(B) R, Q, S, R, Q
(C) S, T, T, R, Q
(D) T, R, R, T, T
(E) T, S, Q, R, T

16. If a hiker walks the full length of each trail exactly once, which of the following lists all those shelters and only those shelters at which the hiker must be exactly twice?

(A) G
(B) F and G
(C) G and W
(D) G and X
(E) G, W, and X

17. If, by taking shortcuts that stray from the trails, a hiker could travel from W to X over a shorter distance than the shortest distance between W and X by trail alone, which of the following must be true?

(A) The shortest distance by trail alone from F to X is less than the shortest distance by trail alone from W to X.
(B) The shortest sequence of trails between F and X is the shortest distance between F and X.
(C) The route composed of R and T is not a straight line.
(D) The route composed of S and T is not a straight line.
(E) R meets T at a right angle.

18. If the straight-line distance between F and X is the same as the straight-line distance between W and X, which of the following can result if new straight trails are added between F and X and between W and X?

(A) The shortest distance by trail between any shelter and any other shelter is the same.
(B) The number of trails required for the shortest possible hike by trail between any shelter and any other shelter is one.
(C) The shortest distance by trail between F and X is less than the shortest distance between W and X.
(D) A hiker must travel fewer trails to travel the shortest distance between F and X than to travel the shortest distance between F and G.
(E) A hiker must travel fewer trails to travel the shortest distance between W and G than to travel the shortest distance between W and F.

GO ON TO THE NEXT PAGE.

Questions 19-22

A contractor will build five houses in a certain town on a street that currently has no houses on it. The contractor will select from seven different models of houses—T, U, V, W, X, Y, and Z. The town's planning board has placed the following restrictions on the contractor:

No model can be selected for more than one house.
Either model W must be selected or model Z must be selected, but both cannot be selected.
If model Y is selected, then model V must also be selected.
If model U is selected, then model W cannot be selected.

19. If model U is one of the models selected for the street, then which of the following models must also be selected?

(A) T
(B) W
(C) X
(D) Y
(E) Z

20. If T, U, and X are three of the models selected for the street, then which of the following must be the other two models selected?

(A) V and W
(B) V and Y
(C) V and Z
(D) W and Y
(E) Y and Z

21. Which of the following is an acceptable combination of models that can be selected for the street?

(A) T, U, V, X, Y
(B) T, U, X, Y, Z
(C) T, V, X, Y, Z
(D) U, V, W, X, Y
(E) V, W, X, Y, Z

22. If model Z is one model not selected for the street, then the other model NOT selected must be which of the following?

(A) T
(B) U
(C) V
(D) W
(E) X

GO ON TO THE NEXT PAGE.

23. The greater the division of labor in an economy, the greater the need for coordination. This is because increased division of labor entails a larger number of specialized producers, which results in a greater burden on managers and, potentially, in a greater number of disruptions of supply and production.

There is always more division of labor in market economies than in planned economies.

If all of the statements above are true, then which of the following must also be true?

(A) Disruptions of supply and production are more frequent in planned economies than in market economies.
(B) There are more specialized producers in planned economies than in market economies.
(C) The need for coordination in market economies is greater than in planned economies.
(D) A manager's task is easier in a market economy than in a planned economy.
(E) Division of labor functions more effectively in market economies than in planned economies.

24. Clay absorbs radiation with time, releasing it only when heated. By heating a clay sculpture and measuring the radiation it releases, experts can determine to within a century when the sculpture was last heated. The original firing of the finished sculpture might be the occasion of that most recent heating.

Experts who obtain the year A.D. 1450 as an estimate for a given sculpture using the method described above would thereby most seriously undermine any claim that the sculpture was made in

(A) A.D. 1000
(B) A.D. 1400
(C) A.D. 1450
(D) A.D. 1500
(E) A.D. 1900

25. The overall operating costs borne by many small farmers are reduced when the farmers eliminate expensive commercial chemical fertilizers and pesticides in favor of crop rotation and the twice-yearly use of manure as fertilizer. Therefore, large farmers should adopt the same measures. They will then realize even greater total savings than do the small farmers.

The argument above assumes that

(A) it is more cost-effective for small farmers to eliminate the use of commercial fertilizers and pesticides than it is for large farmers to do so
(B) a sufficient amount of manure will be available for the fields of large farmers
(C) large farmers would not realize similar cost benefits by using treated sewage sludge instead of commercial chemical fertilizers
(D) large farmers generally look to small farmers for innovative ways of increasing crop yields or reducing operating costs
(E) the smaller the farm, the more control the farmer has over operating costs

STOP

IF YOU FINISH BEFORE TIME IS CALLED, YOU MAY CHECK YOUR WORK ON THIS SECTION ONLY. DO NOT TURN TO ANY OTHER SECTION IN THE TEST.

NO TEST MATERIAL ON THIS PAGE

NOTE: To ensure prompt processing of test results, it is important that you fill in the blanks exactly as directed.

GENERAL TEST

A. Print and sign your full name in this box:

PRINT: ____
(LAST) (FIRST) (MIDDLE)

SIGN: ____

Copy this code in box 6 on your answer sheet. Then fill in the corresponding ovals exactly as shown.

6. TITLE CODE

0	0	0	0	0
1	1	1	1	1
2	2	2	2	2
3	3	3	3	3
4	4	4	4	4
5	5	5	5	5
6	6	6	6	6
7	7	7	7	7
8	8	8	8	8
9	9	9	9	9

Copy the Test Name and Form Code in box 7 on your answer sheet.

TEST NAME General

FORM CODE GR 92-2

GRADUATE RECORD EXAMINATIONS GENERAL TEST

B. You will have 3 hours and 30 minutes in which to work on this test, which consists of seven sections. During the time allowed for one section, you may work only on that section. The time allowed for each section is 30 minutes.

Each of your scores will be determined by the number of questions for which you select the best answer from the choices given. Questions for which you mark no answer or more than one answer are not counted in scoring. Nothing is subtracted from a score if you answer a question incorrectly. Therefore, to maximize your scores it is better for you to guess at an answer than not to respond at all.

You are advised to work as rapidly as you can without losing accuracy. Do not spend too much time on questions that are too difficult for you. Go on to the other questions and come back to the difficult ones later.

There are several different types of questions; you will find special directions for each type in the test itself. Be sure you understand the directions before attempting to answer any questions.

YOU MUST INDICATE ALL YOUR ANSWERS ON THE SEPARATE ANSWER SHEET. No credit will be given for anything written in this examination book, but you may write in the book as much as you wish to work out your answers. After you have decided on your response to a question, fill in the corresponding oval on the answer sheet. BE SURE THAT EACH MARK IS DARK AND COMPLETELY FILLS THE OVAL. Mark only one answer to each question. No credit will be given for multiple answers. Erase all stray marks. If you change an answer, be sure that all previous marks are erased completely. Incomplete erasures may be read as intended answers. Do not be concerned if your answer sheet provides spaces for more answers than there are questions in each section.

Example:

What city is the capital of France?

(A) Rome
(B) Paris
(C) London
(D) Cairo
(E) Oslo

Sample Answer

A ● C D E — BEST ANSWER PROPERLY MARKED

A B C D E
A B C D E
A B C D E
A B C D E
— IMPROPER MARKS

Some or all of the passages for this test have been adapted from published material to provide the examinee with significant problems for analysis and evaluation. To make the passages suitable for testing purposes, the style, content, or point of view of the original may have been altered in some cases. The ideas contained in the passages do not necessarily represent the opinions of the Graduate Record Examinations Board or Educational Testing Service.

DO NOT OPEN YOUR TEST BOOK UNTIL YOU ARE TOLD TO DO SO.

FOR GENERAL TEST, FORM GR92-2 ONLY
Answer Key and Percentages* of Examinees Answering Each Question Correctly

VERBAL ABILITY

Section 1			Section 4		
Number	Answer	P+	Number	Answer	P+
1	A	79	1	C	76
2	D	95	2	D	70
3	A	88	3	A	57
4	C	75	4	E	72
5	E	56	5	C	63
6	B	57	6	E	55
7	D	42	7	B	52
8	C	82	8	E	89
9	B	87	9	B	83
10	E	86	10	C	85
11	D	83	11	D	76
12	D	66	12	D	52
13	E	38	13	E	51
14	D	35	14	E	38
15	C	27	15	A	26
16	B	20	16	B	25
17	B	72	17	E	34
18	E	76	18	C	77
19	A	52	19	D	45
20	B	48	20	A	36
21	A	46	21	A	92
22	C	79	22	D	83
23	B	73	23	A	79
24	C	47	24	E	59
25	E	32	25	B	40
26	D	47	26	C	75
27	B	59	27	D	55
28	B	94	28	A	96
29	A	88	29	D	82
30	B	80	30	C	92
31	A	82	31	E	63
32	C	76	32	D	34
33	A	42	33	B	37
34	D	36	34	B	38
35	D	23	35	A	37
36	C	26	36	D	31
37	C	27	37	E	27
38	A	20	38	A	26

QUANTITATIVE ABILITY

Section 2			Section 6		
Number	Answer	P+	Number	Answer	P+
1	B	80	1	A	82
2	D	82	2	C	89
3	A	78	3	B	77
4	D	80	4	A	86
5	B	81	5	C	79
6	A	76	6	B	70
7	B	72	7	B	66
8	A	62	8	D	72
9	D	59	9	A	65
10	A	56	10	B	77
11	C	36	11	C	61
12	B	38	12	D	47
13	D	34	13	A	61
14	B	27	14	D	39
15	C	22	15	C	30
16	D	94	16	E	92
17	D	79	17	C	88
18	C	78	18	A	80
19	B	74	19	E	71
20	D	72	20	B	53
21	A	82	21	C	78
22	D	75	22	B	81
23	B	69	23	D	62
24	E	52	24	A	21
25	B	40	25	C	42
26	C	61	26	C	52
27	A	52	27	E	52
28	C	48	28	A	27
29	E	40	29	D	35
30	E	39	30	C	20

ANALYTICAL ABILITY

Section 3			Section 7		
Number	Answer	P+	Number	Answer	P+
1	D	73	1	B	90
2	B	65	2	D	79
3	E	52	3	E	36
4	C	82	4	E	58
5	C	42	5	D	79
6	E	50	6	C	75
7	A	92	7	C	66
8	A	78	8	D	77
9	B	68	9	E	71
10	D	81	10	B	50
11	B	77	11	E	61
12	C	62	12	E	52
13	E	61	13	B	76
14	E	48	14	A	35
15	A	53	15	A	51
16	D	48	16	A	58
17	B	40	17	C	43
18	A	34	18	B	38
19	C	62	19	E	61
20	C	46	20	C	45
21	A	27	21	C	58
22	B	46	22	B	60
23	E	58	23	C	68
24	D	46	24	E	44
25	E	28	25	B	45

*Estimated P+ for the group of examinees who took the GRE General Test in a recent three-year period.

Score Conversions for GRE General Test GR92-2 Only and the Percents Below*

Raw Score	Verbal Scaled Score	Verbal % Below	Quantitative Scaled Score	Quantitative % Below	Analytical Scaled Score	Analytical % Below	Raw Score	Verbal Scaled Score	Verbal % Below	Quantitative Scaled Score	Quantitative % Below	Analytical Scaled Score	Analytical % Below
72-76	800	99					39	430	34	590	56	670	84
71	790	99					38	420	31	580	53	660	81
70	770	99					37	410	28	570	51	650	80
							36	400	25	560	49	630	75
69	760	99					35	390	23	550	46	620	73
68	740	98					34	380	20	540	44	610	70
67	730	97					33	370	18	520	39	600	67
66	720	96					32	360	15	510	37	580	62
65	710	95					31	350	13	500	34	570	59
64	700	94					30	350	13	490	32	550	53
63	680	93											
62	670	91					29	340	11	480	30	540	50
61	660	90					28	330	9	470	28	520	45
60	650	88	800	96			27	320	8	460	25	510	42
							26	310	7	440	21	500	38
59	640	87	800	96			25	310	7	430	19	480	33
58	630	85	800	96			24	300	5	420	17	470	30
57	610	82	790	95			23	290	4	410	16	450	26
56	600	80	780	93			22	280	3	400	14	440	23
55	590	78	770	92			21	280	3	380	11	420	19
54	580	75	750	88			20	270	2	370	10	410	17
53	570	73	740	87									
52	560	71	730	85			19	260	2	360	8	390	14
51	550	69	720	83			18	250	1	340	6	380	12
50	540	66	710	81	800	99	17	250	1	330	5	360	9
							16	240	1	310	3	340	7
49	530	63	700	79	800	99	15	230	1	300	3	330	6
48	520	60	690	77	800	99	14	220	1	280	2	320	5
47	510	58	680	75	790	98	13	210	1	270	1	300	3
46	500	55	670	73	770	97	12	200	1	250	1	290	3
45	480	50	660	71	750	95	11	200	1	240	1	280	2
44	470	47	650	69	740	94	10	200	1	220	1	260	1
43	460	43	640	67	720	92							
42	450	40	630	65	710	91	9	200	1	210	1	250	1
41	440	37	620	62	700	89	8	200	1	200	1	240	1
40	430	34	600	58	690	87	7	200	1	200	1	230	1
							6	200	1	200	1	210	1
							0-5	200	1	200	1	200	1

*Percent scoring below the scaled score is based on the performance of 954,995 examinees who took the General Test between October 1, 1987, and September 30, 1990. This percent below information is used for score reports during the 1991-92 testing year.

General Test Average Scores Classified by Intended Broad Graduate Major Field Based on Seniors and Nonenrolled College Graduates, 1987-1990

(Based on the performance of seniors and nonenrolled college graduates* who tested between October 1, 1987, and September 30, 1990)

Intended Broad Graduate Major Field	Number of Examinees	Verbal Ability	Quantitative Ability	Analytical Ability
Life Sciences	59,463	487	554	555
Physical Sciences	37,164	514	672	612
Engineering	42,889	489	697	594
Social Science	71,621	508	535	555
Humanities	43,297	560	536	573
Education	25,083	464	505	529
Business	7,318	460	543	534
Other	38,725	484	510	529

*Limited to those who earned their college degrees within two years of the test date. Note that this table does not include summary information on the 37,404 examinees whose response to the department code question was invalid (incorrect gridding, blanks, etc.) or the 61,468 examinees whose response was "Undecided."

DO NOT USE INK

Use only a pencil with soft, black lead (No. 2 or HB) to complete this answer sheet. Be sure to fill in completely the space that corresponds to your answer choice. Completely erase any errors or stray marks.

GRADUATE RECORD EXAMINATIONS® - GRE® - GENERAL TEST

SIDE 1

1. NAME Enter your last name, first name initial (given name), and middle initial if you have one. Omit spaces, apostrophes, Jr., II., etc.

Last Name only (Family or Surname) - first 15 letters | First Name Initial | Middle Initial

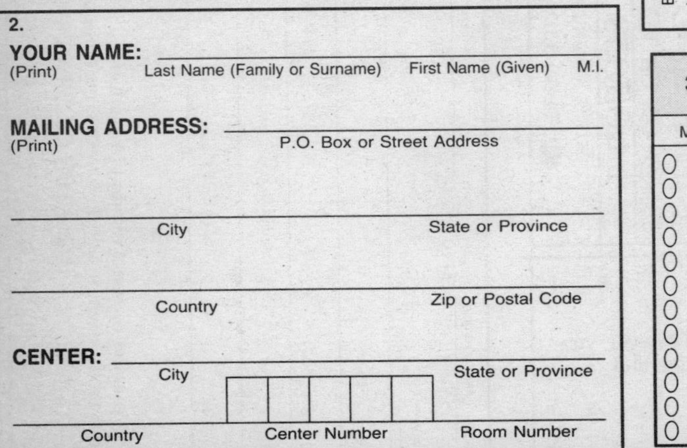

2. YOUR NAME: (Print) Last Name (Family or Surname) First Name (Given) M.I.

MAILING ADDRESS: (Print) P.O. Box or Street Address

City State or Province

Country Zip or Postal Code

CENTER: City State or Province

Country Center Number Room Number

BE SURE EACH MARK IS DARK AND COMPLETELY FILLS THE INTENDED SPACE AS ILLUSTRATED HERE: ●

YOU MAY FIND MORE RESPONSE SPACES THAN YOU NEED. IF SO, PLEASE LEAVE THEM BLANK.

SECTION 1 | SECTION 2 | SECTION 3

(Items 1–38 in each section, choices A B C D E)

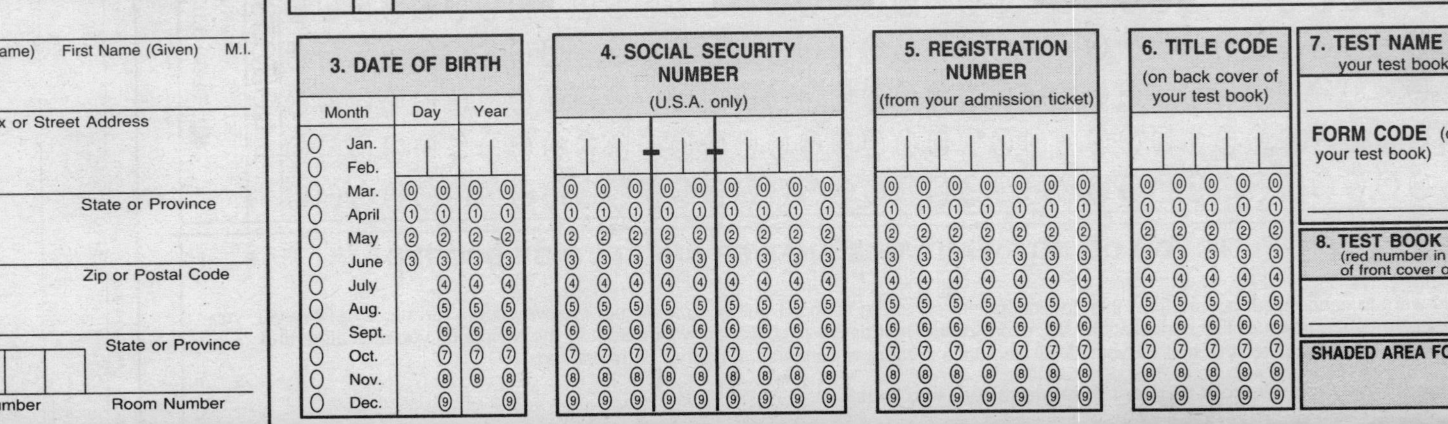

3. DATE OF BIRTH

Month: Jan. Feb. Mar. April May June July Aug. Sept. Oct. Nov. Dec.

Day | Year

4. SOCIAL SECURITY NUMBER (U.S.A. only)

5. REGISTRATION NUMBER (from your admission ticket)

6. TITLE CODE (on back cover of your test book)

7. TEST NAME (on back cover of your test book)

FORM CODE (on back cover of your test book)

8. TEST BOOK SERIAL NUMBER (red number in upper right corner of front cover of your test book)

SHADED AREA FOR ETS USE ONLY

SIDE 2

GENERAL TEST

CERTIFICATION STATEMENT

Please write the following statement below, DO NOT PRINT.
"I certify that I am the person whose name appears on this answer sheet. I al[so] agree not to disclose the contents of the test I am taking today to anyone." Sign and date where indicated.

SIGNATURE: ____________________ DATE: ___ / ___ / ___
Month Day Yea[r]

BE SURE EACH MARK IS DARK AND COMPLETELY FILLS THE INTENDED SPACE AS ILLUSTRATED HERE: ●.
YOU MAY FIND MORE RESPONSE SPACES THAN YOU NEED. IF SO, PLEASE LEAVE THEM BLANK.

	SECTION 4	SECTION 5	SECTION 6	SECTION 7
1	(A) (B) (C) (D) (E)	(A) (B) (C) (D) (E)	(A) (B) (C) (D) (E)	(A) (B) (C) (D) (E)
2	(A) (B) (C) (D) (E)	(A) (B) (C) (D) (E)	(A) (B) (C) (D) (E)	(A) (B) (C) (D) (E)
3	(A) (B) (C) (D) (E)	(A) (B) (C) (D) (E)	(A) (B) (C) (D) (E)	(A) (B) (C) (D) (E)
4	(A) (B) (C) (D) (E)	(A) (B) (C) (D) (E)	(A) (B) (C) (D) (E)	(A) (B) (C) (D) (E)
5	(A) (B) (C) (D) (E)	(A) (B) (C) (D) (E)	(A) (B) (C) (D) (E)	(A) (B) (C) (D) (E)
6	(A) (B) (C) (D) (E)	(A) (B) (C) (D) (E)	(A) (B) (C) (D) (E)	(A) (B) (C) (D) (E)
7	(A) (B) (C) (D) (E)	(A) (B) (C) (D) (E)	(A) (B) (C) (D) (E)	(A) (B) (C) (D) (E)
8	(A) (B) (C) (D) (E)	(A) (B) (C) (D) (E)	(A) (B) (C) (D) (E)	(A) (B) (C) (D) (E)
9	(A) (B) (C) (D) (E)	(A) (B) (C) (D) (E)	(A) (B) (C) (D) (E)	(A) (B) (C) (D) (E)
10	(A) (B) (C) (D) (E)	(A) (B) (C) (D) (E)	(A) (B) (C) (D) (E)	(A) (B) (C) (D) (E)
11	(A) (B) (C) (D) (E)	(A) (B) (C) (D) (E)	(A) (B) (C) (D) (E)	(A) (B) (C) (D) (E)
12	(A) (B) (C) (D) (E)	(A) (B) (C) (D) (E)	(A) (B) (C) (D) (E)	(A) (B) (C) (D) (E)
13	(A) (B) (C) (D) (E)	(A) (B) (C) (D) (E)	(A) (B) (C) (D) (E)	(A) (B) (C) (D) (E)
14	(A) (B) (C) (D) (E)	(A) (B) (C) (D) (E)	(A) (B) (C) (D) (E)	(A) (B) (C) (D) (E)
15	(A) (B) (C) (D) (E)	(A) (B) (C) (D) (E)	(A) (B) (C) (D) (E)	(A) (B) (C) (D) (E)
16	(A) (B) (C) (D) (E)	(A) (B) (C) (D) (E)	(A) (B) (C) (D) (E)	(A) (B) (C) (D) (E)
17	(A) (B) (C) (D) (E)	(A) (B) (C) (D) (E)	(A) (B) (C) (D) (E)	(A) (B) (C) (D) (E)
18	(A) (B) (C) (D) (E)	(A) (B) (C) (D) (E)	(A) (B) (C) (D) (E)	(A) (B) (C) (D) (E)
19	(A) (B) (C) (D) (E)	(A) (B) (C) (D) (E)	(A) (B) (C) (D) (E)	(A) (B) (C) (D) (E)
20	(A) (B) (C) (D) (E)	(A) (B) (C) (D) (E)	(A) (B) (C) (D) (E)	(A) (B) (C) (D) (E)
21	(A) (B) (C) (D) (E)	(A) (B) (C) (D) (E)	(A) (B) (C) (D) (E)	(A) (B) (C) (D) (E)
22	(A) (B) (C) (D) (E)	(A) (B) (C) (D) (E)	(A) (B) (C) (D) (E)	(A) (B) (C) (D) (E)
23	(A) (B) (C) (D) (E)	(A) (B) (C) (D) (E)	(A) (B) (C) (D) (E)	(A) (B) (C) (D) (E)
24	(A) (B) (C) (D) (E)	(A) (B) (C) (D) (E)	(A) (B) (C) (D) (E)	(A) (B) (C) (D) (E)
25	(A) (B) (C) (D) (E)	(A) (B) (C) (D) (E)	(A) (B) (C) (D) (E)	(A) (B) (C) (D) (E)
26	(A) (B) (C) (D) (E)	(A) (B) (C) (D) (E)	(A) (B) (C) (D) (E)	(A) (B) (C) (D) (E)
27	(A) (B) (C) (D) (E)	(A) (B) (C) (D) (E)	(A) (B) (C) (D) (E)	(A) (B) (C) (D) (E)
28	(A) (B) (C) (D) (E)	(A) (B) (C) (D) (E)	(A) (B) (C) (D) (E)	(A) (B) (C) (D) (E)
29	(A) (B) (C) (D) (E)	(A) (B) (C) (D) (E)	(A) (B) (C) (D) (E)	(A) (B) (C) (D) (E)
30	(A) (B) (C) (D) (E)	(A) (B) (C) (D) (E)	(A) (B) (C) (D) (E)	(A) (B) (C) (D) (E)
31	(A) (B) (C) (D) (E)	(A) (B) (C) (D) (E)	(A) (B) (C) (D) (E)	(A) (B) (C) (D) (E)
32	(A) (B) (C) (D) (E)	(A) (B) (C) (D) (E)	(A) (B) (C) (D) (E)	(A) (B) (C) (D) (E)
33	(A) (B) (C) (D) (E)	(A) (B) (C) (D) (E)	(A) (B) (C) (D) (E)	(A) (B) (C) (D) (E)
34	(A) (B) (C) (D) (E)	(A) (B) (C) (D) (E)	(A) (B) (C) (D) (E)	(A) (B) (C) (D) (E)
35	(A) (B) (C) (D) (E)	(A) (B) (C) (D) (E)	(A) (B) (C) (D) (E)	(A) (B) (C) (D) (E)
36	(A) (B) (C) (D) (E)	(A) (B) (C) (D) (E)	(A) (B) (C) (D) (E)	(A) (B) (C) (D) (E)
37	(A) (B) (C) (D) (E)	(A) (B) (C) (D) (E)	(A) (B) (C) (D) (E)	(A) (B) (C) (D) (E)
38	(A) (B) (C) (D) (E)	(A) (B) (C) (D) (E)	(A) (B) (C) (D) (E)	(A) (B) (C) (D) (E)

IF YOU DO NOT WANT THIS ANSWER SHEET TO BE SCORED

If you want to cancel your scores from this administration, complete A and B below. You will not receive scores for this test; however, you will receive confirmation of this cancellation. No record of this test or the cancellation will be sent to the recipients you indicated, and there will be no scores for this test on your GRE file. Once a score is canceled, it cannot be reinstated.

To cancel your scores from this test administration, you must:

FOR ETS USE ONLY	V1R	V2R	VTR	VCS	Q1R	Q2R	QTR	QCS	A1R	A2R	ATR	ACS

DO NOT USE INK

Use only a pencil with soft, black lead (No. 2 or HB) to complete this answer sheet. Be sure to fill in completely the space that corresponds to your answer choice. Completely erase any errors or stray marks.

GRADUATE RECORD EXAMINATIONS® - GRE® - GENERAL TEST

SIDE 1

1. NAME

Enter your last name, first name initial (given name), and middle initial if you have one. Omit spaces, apostrophes, Jr., II., etc.

Last Name only (Family or Surname) - first 15 letters

First Name Initial | Middle Initial

A B C D E F G H I J K L M N O P Q R S T U V W X Y Z –

2.

YOUR NAME: (Print) Last Name (Family or Surname) First Name (Given) M.I.

MAILING ADDRESS: (Print) P.O. Box or Street Address

City State or Province

Country Zip or Postal Code

CENTER: City State or Province

Country Center Number Room Number

BE SURE EACH MARK IS DARK AND COMPLETELY FILLS THE INTENDED SPACE AS ILLUSTRATED HERE: ●

YOU MAY FIND MORE RESPONSE SPACES THAN YOU NEED. IF SO, PLEASE LEAVE THEM BLANK.

SECTION 1		SECTION 2		SECTION 3	
1	A B C D E	1	A B C D E	1	A B C D E
2	A B C D E	2	A B C D E	2	A B C D E
3	A B C D E	3	A B C D E	3	A B C D E
4	A B C D E	4	A B C D E	4	A B C D E
5	A B C D E	5	A B C D E	5	A B C D E
6	A B C D E	6	A B C D E	6	A B C D E
7	A B C D E	7	A B C D E	7	A B C D E
8	A B C D E	8	A B C D E	8	A B C D E
9	A B C D E	9	A B C D E	9	A B C D E
10	A B C D E	10	A B C D E	10	A B C D E
11	A B C D E	11	A B C D E	11	A B C D E
12	A B C D E	12	A B C D E	12	A B C D E
13	A B C D E	13	A B C D E	13	A B C D E
14	A B C D E	14	A B C D E	14	A B C D E
15	A B C D E	15	A B C D E	15	A B C D E
16	A B C D E	16	A B C D E	16	A B C D E
17	A B C D E	17	A B C D E	17	A B C D E
18	A B C D E	18	A B C D E	18	A B C D E
19	A B C D E	19	A B C D E	19	A B C D E
20	A B C D E	20	A B C D E	20	A B C D E
21	A B C D E	21	A B C D E	21	A B C D E
22	A B C D E	22	A B C D E	22	A B C D E
23	A B C D E	23	A B C D E	23	A B C D E
24	A B C D E	24	A B C D E	24	A B C D E
25	A B C D E	25	A B C D E	25	A B C D E
26	A B C D E	26	A B C D E	26	A B C D E
27	A B C D E	27	A B C D E	27	A B C D E
28	A B C D E	28	A B C D E	28	A B C D E
29	A B C D E	29	A B C D E	29	A B C D E
30	A B C D E	30	A B C D E	30	A B C D E
31	A B C D E	31	A B C D E	31	A B C D E
32	A B C D E	32	A B C D E	32	A B C D E
33	A B C D E	33	A B C D E	33	A B C D E
34	A B C D E	34	A B C D E	34	A B C D E
35	A B C D E	35	A B C D E	35	A B C D E
36	A B C D E	36	A B C D E	36	A B C D E
37	A B C D E	37	A B C D E	37	A B C D E
38	A B C D E	38	A B C D E	38	A B C D E

3. DATE OF BIRTH

Month	Day	Year
Jan.		
Feb.		
Mar.	0 0	0 0
April	1 1	1 1
May	2 2	2 2
June	3 3	3 3
July	4	4 4
Aug.	5	5 5
Sept.	6	6 6
Oct.	7	7 7
Nov.	8	8 8
Dec.	9	9

4. SOCIAL SECURITY NUMBER

(U.S.A. only)

0 1 2 3 4 5 6 7 8 9

5. REGISTRATION NUMBER

(from your admission ticket)

0 1 2 3 4 5 6 7 8 9

6. TITLE CODE

(on back cover of your test book)

0 1 2 3 4 5 6 7 8 9

7. TEST NAME (on back cover of your test book)

FORM CODE (on back cover of your test book)

8. TEST BOOK SERIAL NUMBER

(red number in upper right corner of front cover of your test book)

SHADED AREA FOR ETS USE ONLY

SIDE 2

GENERAL TEST

CERTIFICATION STATEMENT

Please write the following statement below, DO NOT PRINT.
"I certify that I am the person whose name appears on this answer sheet. I a
agree not to disclose the contents of the test I am taking today to anyone."
Sign and date where indicated.

SIGNATURE: ____________________ **DATE:** ___/___/___
Month Day Ye

BE SURE EACH MARK IS DARK AND COMPLETELY FILLS THE INTENDED SPACE AS ILLUSTRATED HERE: ⬬.
YOU MAY FIND MORE RESPONSE SPACES THAN YOU NEED. IF SO, PLEASE LEAVE THEM BLANK.

SECTION 4		SECTION 5		SECTION 6		SECTION 7	
1	A B C D E	1	A B C D E	1	A B C D E	1	A B C D E
2	A B C D E	2	A B C D E	2	A B C D E	2	A B C D E
3	A B C D E	3	A B C D E	3	A B C D E	3	A B C D E
4	A B C D E	4	A B C D E	4	A B C D E	4	A B C D E
5	A B C D E	5	A B C D E	5	A B C D E	5	A B C D E
6	A B C D E	6	A B C D E	6	A B C D E	6	A B C D E
7	A B C D E	7	A B C D E	7	A B C D E	7	A B C D E
8	A B C D E	8	A B C D E	8	A B C D E	8	A B C D E
9	A B C D E	9	A B C D E	9	A B C D E	9	A B C D E
10	A B C D E	10	A B C D E	10	A B C D E	10	A B C D E
11	A B C D E	11	A B C D E	11	A B C D E	11	A B C D E
12	A B C D E	12	A B C D E	12	A B C D E	12	A B C D E
13	A B C D E	13	A B C D E	13	A B C D E	13	A B C D E
14	A B C D E	14	A B C D E	14	A B C D E	14	A B C D E
15	A B C D E	15	A B C D E	15	A B C D E	15	A B C D E
16	A B C D E	16	A B C D E	16	A B C D E	16	A B C D E
17	A B C D E	17	A B C D E	17	A B C D E	17	A B C D E
18	A B C D E	18	A B C D E	18	A B C D E	18	A B C D E
19	A B C D E	19	A B C D E	19	A B C D E	19	A B C D E
20	A B C D E	20	A B C D E	20	A B C D E	20	A B C D E
21	A B C D E	21	A B C D E	21	A B C D E	21	A B C D E
22	A B C D E	22	A B C D E	22	A B C D E	22	A B C D E
23	A B C D E	23	A B C D E	23	A B C D E	23	A B C D E
24	A B C D E	24	A B C D E	24	A B C D E	24	A B C D E
25	A B C D E	25	A B C D E	25	A B C D E	25	A B C D E
26	A B C D E	26	A B C D E	26	A B C D E	26	A B C D E
27	A B C D E	27	A B C D E	27	A B C D E	27	A B C D E
28	A B C D E	28	A B C D E	28	A B C D E	28	A B C D E
29	A B C D E	29	A B C D E	29	A B C D E	29	A B C D E
30	A B C D E	30	A B C D E	30	A B C D E	30	A B C D E
31	A B C D E	31	A B C D E	31	A B C D E	31	A B C D E
32	A B C D E	32	A B C D E	32	A B C D E	32	A B C D E
33	A B C D E	33	A B C D E	33	A B C D E	33	A B C D E
34	A B C D E	34	A B C D E	34	A B C D E	34	A B C D E
35	A B C D E	35	A B C D E	35	A B C D E	35	A B C D E
36	A B C D E	36	A B C D E	36	A B C D E	36	A B C D E
37	A B C D E	37	A B C D E	37	A B C D E	37	A B C D E
38	A B C D E	38	A B C D E	38	A B C D E	38	A B C D E

IF YOU DO NOT WANT THIS ANSWER SHEET TO BE SCORED

If you want to cancel your scores from this administration, complete A and B below. You will not receive scores for this test; however, you will receive confirmation of this cancellation. No record of this test or the cancellation will be sent to the recipients you indicated, and there will be no scores for this test on your GRE file. Once a score is canceled, it cannot be reinstated.

To cancel your scores from this test administration, you must:

FOR ETS USE ONLY	V1R	V2R	VTR	VCS	Q1R	Q2R	QTR	QCS	A1R	A2R	ATR	ACS

DO NOT USE INK

Use only a pencil with soft, black lead (No. 2 or HB) to complete this answer sheet.
Be sure to fill in completely the space that corresponds to your answer choice.
Completely erase any errors or stray marks.

GRADUATE RECORD EXAMINATIONS® - GRE® - GENERAL TEST

SIDE 1

1. NAME

Enter your last name, first name initial (given name), and middle initial if you have one.
Omit spaces, apostrophes, Jr., II., etc.

Last Name only (Family or Surname) - first 15 letters | First Name Initial | Middle Initial

A B C D E F G H I J K L M N O P Q R S T U V W X Y Z

2.

YOUR NAME: (Print) Last Name (Family or Surname) First Name (Given) M.I.

MAILING ADDRESS: (Print) P.O. Box or Street Address

City State or Province

Country Zip or Postal Code

CENTER: City State or Province

Country Center Number Room Number

BE SURE EACH MARK IS DARK AND COMPLETELY FILLS THE INTENDED SPACE AS ILLUSTRATED HERE:
YOU MAY FIND MORE RESPONSE SPACES THAN YOU NEED. IF SO, PLEASE LEAVE THEM BLANK.

	SECTION 1	SECTION 2	SECTION 3
1	A B C D E	A B C D E	A B C D E
2	A B C D E	A B C D E	A B C D E
3	A B C D E	A B C D E	A B C D E
4	A B C D E	A B C D E	A B C D E
5	A B C D E	A B C D E	A B C D E
6	A B C D E	A B C D E	A B C D E
7	A B C D E	A B C D E	A B C D E
8	A B C D E	A B C D E	A B C D E
9	A B C D E	A B C D E	A B C D E
10	A B C D E	A B C D E	A B C D E
11	A B C D E	A B C D E	A B C D E
12	A B C D E	A B C D E	A B C D E
13	A B C D E	A B C D E	A B C D E
14	A B C D E	A B C D E	A B C D E
15	A B C D E	A B C D E	A B C D E
16	A B C D E	A B C D E	A B C D E
17	A B C D E	A B C D E	A B C D E
18	A B C D E	A B C D E	A B C D E
19	A B C D E	A B C D E	A B C D E
20	A B C D E	A B C D E	A B C D E
21	A B C D E	A B C D E	A B C D E
22	A B C D E	A B C D E	A B C D E
23	A B C D E	A B C D E	A B C D E
24	A B C D E	A B C D E	A B C D E
25	A B C D E	A B C D E	A B C D E
26	A B C D E	A B C D E	A B C D E
27	A B C D E	A B C D E	A B C D E
28	A B C D E	A B C D E	A B C D E
29	A B C D E	A B C D E	A B C D E
30	A B C D E	A B C D E	A B C D E
31	A B C D E	A B C D E	A B C D E
32	A B C D E	A B C D E	A B C D E
33	A B C D E	A B C D E	A B C D E
34	A B C D E	A B C D E	A B C D E
35	A B C D E	A B C D E	A B C D E
36	A B C D E	A B C D E	A B C D E
37	A B C D E	A B C D E	A B C D E
38	A B C D E	A B C D E	A B C D E

3. DATE OF BIRTH

Month: Jan. Feb. Mar. April May June July Aug. Sept. Oct. Nov. Dec.

Day | Year

4. SOCIAL SECURITY NUMBER

(U.S.A. only)

5. REGISTRATION NUMBER

(from your admission ticket)

6. TITLE CODE

(on back cover of your test book)

7. TEST NAME (on back cover of your test book)

FORM CODE (on back cover of your test book)

8. TEST BOOK SERIAL NUMBER

(red number in upper right corner of front cover of your test book)

SHADED AREA FOR ETS USE ONLY

SIDE 2

GENERAL TEST

CERTIFICATION STATEMENT

Please write the following statement below, DO NOT PRINT.
"I certify that I am the person whose name appears on this answer sheet. I agree not to disclose the contents of the test I am taking today to anyone." Sign and date where indicated.

SIGNATURE: ______________________ DATE: ____/____/____
Month Day Y

BE SURE EACH MARK IS DARK AND COMPLETELY FILLS THE INTENDED SPACE AS ILLUSTRATED HERE: ●.
YOU MAY FIND MORE RESPONSE SPACES THAN YOU NEED. IF SO, PLEASE LEAVE THEM BLANK.

SECTION 4		SECTION 5		SECTION 6		SECTION 7	
1	Ⓐ Ⓑ Ⓒ Ⓓ Ⓔ	1	Ⓐ Ⓑ Ⓒ Ⓓ Ⓔ	1	Ⓐ Ⓑ Ⓒ Ⓓ Ⓔ	1	Ⓐ Ⓑ Ⓒ Ⓓ Ⓔ
2	Ⓐ Ⓑ Ⓒ Ⓓ Ⓔ	2	Ⓐ Ⓑ Ⓒ Ⓓ Ⓔ	2	Ⓐ Ⓑ Ⓒ Ⓓ Ⓔ	2	Ⓐ Ⓑ Ⓒ Ⓓ Ⓔ
3	Ⓐ Ⓑ Ⓒ Ⓓ Ⓔ	3	Ⓐ Ⓑ Ⓒ Ⓓ Ⓔ	3	Ⓐ Ⓑ Ⓒ Ⓓ Ⓔ	3	Ⓐ Ⓑ Ⓒ Ⓓ Ⓔ
4	Ⓐ Ⓑ Ⓒ Ⓓ Ⓔ	4	Ⓐ Ⓑ Ⓒ Ⓓ Ⓔ	4	Ⓐ Ⓑ Ⓒ Ⓓ Ⓔ	4	Ⓐ Ⓑ Ⓒ Ⓓ Ⓔ
5	Ⓐ Ⓑ Ⓒ Ⓓ Ⓔ	5	Ⓐ Ⓑ Ⓒ Ⓓ Ⓔ	5	Ⓐ Ⓑ Ⓒ Ⓓ Ⓔ	5	Ⓐ Ⓑ Ⓒ Ⓓ Ⓔ
6	Ⓐ Ⓑ Ⓒ Ⓓ Ⓔ	6	Ⓐ Ⓑ Ⓒ Ⓓ Ⓔ	6	Ⓐ Ⓑ Ⓒ Ⓓ Ⓔ	6	Ⓐ Ⓑ Ⓒ Ⓓ Ⓔ
7	Ⓐ Ⓑ Ⓒ Ⓓ Ⓔ	7	Ⓐ Ⓑ Ⓒ Ⓓ Ⓔ	7	Ⓐ Ⓑ Ⓒ Ⓓ Ⓔ	7	Ⓐ Ⓑ Ⓒ Ⓓ Ⓔ
8	Ⓐ Ⓑ Ⓒ Ⓓ Ⓔ	8	Ⓐ Ⓑ Ⓒ Ⓓ Ⓔ	8	Ⓐ Ⓑ Ⓒ Ⓓ Ⓔ	8	Ⓐ Ⓑ Ⓒ Ⓓ Ⓔ
9	Ⓐ Ⓑ Ⓒ Ⓓ Ⓔ	9	Ⓐ Ⓑ Ⓒ Ⓓ Ⓔ	9	Ⓐ Ⓑ Ⓒ Ⓓ Ⓔ	9	Ⓐ Ⓑ Ⓒ Ⓓ Ⓔ
10	Ⓐ Ⓑ Ⓒ Ⓓ Ⓔ	10	Ⓐ Ⓑ Ⓒ Ⓓ Ⓔ	10	Ⓐ Ⓑ Ⓒ Ⓓ Ⓔ	10	Ⓐ Ⓑ Ⓒ Ⓓ Ⓔ
11	Ⓐ Ⓑ Ⓒ Ⓓ Ⓔ	11	Ⓐ Ⓑ Ⓒ Ⓓ Ⓔ	11	Ⓐ Ⓑ Ⓒ Ⓓ Ⓔ	11	Ⓐ Ⓑ Ⓒ Ⓓ Ⓔ
12	Ⓐ Ⓑ Ⓒ Ⓓ Ⓔ	12	Ⓐ Ⓑ Ⓒ Ⓓ Ⓔ	12	Ⓐ Ⓑ Ⓒ Ⓓ Ⓔ	12	Ⓐ Ⓑ Ⓒ Ⓓ Ⓔ
13	Ⓐ Ⓑ Ⓒ Ⓓ Ⓔ	13	Ⓐ Ⓑ Ⓒ Ⓓ Ⓔ	13	Ⓐ Ⓑ Ⓒ Ⓓ Ⓔ	13	Ⓐ Ⓑ Ⓒ Ⓓ Ⓔ
14	Ⓐ Ⓑ Ⓒ Ⓓ Ⓔ	14	Ⓐ Ⓑ Ⓒ Ⓓ Ⓔ	14	Ⓐ Ⓑ Ⓒ Ⓓ Ⓔ	14	Ⓐ Ⓑ Ⓒ Ⓓ Ⓔ
15	Ⓐ Ⓑ Ⓒ Ⓓ Ⓔ	15	Ⓐ Ⓑ Ⓒ Ⓓ Ⓔ	15	Ⓐ Ⓑ Ⓒ Ⓓ Ⓔ	15	Ⓐ Ⓑ Ⓒ Ⓓ Ⓔ
16	Ⓐ Ⓑ Ⓒ Ⓓ Ⓔ	16	Ⓐ Ⓑ Ⓒ Ⓓ Ⓔ	16	Ⓐ Ⓑ Ⓒ Ⓓ Ⓔ	16	Ⓐ Ⓑ Ⓒ Ⓓ Ⓔ
17	Ⓐ Ⓑ Ⓒ Ⓓ Ⓔ	17	Ⓐ Ⓑ Ⓒ Ⓓ Ⓔ	17	Ⓐ Ⓑ Ⓒ Ⓓ Ⓔ	17	Ⓐ Ⓑ Ⓒ Ⓓ Ⓔ
18	Ⓐ Ⓑ Ⓒ Ⓓ Ⓔ	18	Ⓐ Ⓑ Ⓒ Ⓓ Ⓔ	18	Ⓐ Ⓑ Ⓒ Ⓓ Ⓔ	18	Ⓐ Ⓑ Ⓒ Ⓓ Ⓔ
19	Ⓐ Ⓑ Ⓒ Ⓓ Ⓔ	19	Ⓐ Ⓑ Ⓒ Ⓓ Ⓔ	19	Ⓐ Ⓑ Ⓒ Ⓓ Ⓔ	19	Ⓐ Ⓑ Ⓒ Ⓓ Ⓔ
20	Ⓐ Ⓑ Ⓒ Ⓓ Ⓔ	20	Ⓐ Ⓑ Ⓒ Ⓓ Ⓔ	20	Ⓐ Ⓑ Ⓒ Ⓓ Ⓔ	20	Ⓐ Ⓑ Ⓒ Ⓓ Ⓔ
21	Ⓐ Ⓑ Ⓒ Ⓓ Ⓔ	21	Ⓐ Ⓑ Ⓒ Ⓓ Ⓔ	21	Ⓐ Ⓑ Ⓒ Ⓓ Ⓔ	21	Ⓐ Ⓑ Ⓒ Ⓓ Ⓔ
22	Ⓐ Ⓑ Ⓒ Ⓓ Ⓔ	22	Ⓐ Ⓑ Ⓒ Ⓓ Ⓔ	22	Ⓐ Ⓑ Ⓒ Ⓓ Ⓔ	22	Ⓐ Ⓑ Ⓒ Ⓓ Ⓔ
23	Ⓐ Ⓑ Ⓒ Ⓓ Ⓔ	23	Ⓐ Ⓑ Ⓒ Ⓓ Ⓔ	23	Ⓐ Ⓑ Ⓒ Ⓓ Ⓔ	23	Ⓐ Ⓑ Ⓒ Ⓓ Ⓔ
24	Ⓐ Ⓑ Ⓒ Ⓓ Ⓔ	24	Ⓐ Ⓑ Ⓒ Ⓓ Ⓔ	24	Ⓐ Ⓑ Ⓒ Ⓓ Ⓔ	24	Ⓐ Ⓑ Ⓒ Ⓓ Ⓔ
25	Ⓐ Ⓑ Ⓒ Ⓓ Ⓔ	25	Ⓐ Ⓑ Ⓒ Ⓓ Ⓔ	25	Ⓐ Ⓑ Ⓒ Ⓓ Ⓔ	25	Ⓐ Ⓑ Ⓒ Ⓓ Ⓔ
26	Ⓐ Ⓑ Ⓒ Ⓓ Ⓔ	26	Ⓐ Ⓑ Ⓒ Ⓓ Ⓔ	26	Ⓐ Ⓑ Ⓒ Ⓓ Ⓔ	26	Ⓐ Ⓑ Ⓒ Ⓓ Ⓔ
27	Ⓐ Ⓑ Ⓒ Ⓓ Ⓔ	27	Ⓐ Ⓑ Ⓒ Ⓓ Ⓔ	27	Ⓐ Ⓑ Ⓒ Ⓓ Ⓔ	27	Ⓐ Ⓑ Ⓒ Ⓓ Ⓔ
28	Ⓐ Ⓑ Ⓒ Ⓓ Ⓔ	28	Ⓐ Ⓑ Ⓒ Ⓓ Ⓔ	28	Ⓐ Ⓑ Ⓒ Ⓓ Ⓔ	28	Ⓐ Ⓑ Ⓒ Ⓓ Ⓔ
29	Ⓐ Ⓑ Ⓒ Ⓓ Ⓔ	29	Ⓐ Ⓑ Ⓒ Ⓓ Ⓔ	29	Ⓐ Ⓑ Ⓒ Ⓓ Ⓔ	29	Ⓐ Ⓑ Ⓒ Ⓓ Ⓔ
30	Ⓐ Ⓑ Ⓒ Ⓓ Ⓔ	30	Ⓐ Ⓑ Ⓒ Ⓓ Ⓔ	30	Ⓐ Ⓑ Ⓒ Ⓓ Ⓔ	30	Ⓐ Ⓑ Ⓒ Ⓓ Ⓔ
31	Ⓐ Ⓑ Ⓒ Ⓓ Ⓔ	31	Ⓐ Ⓑ Ⓒ Ⓓ Ⓔ	31	Ⓐ Ⓑ Ⓒ Ⓓ Ⓔ	31	Ⓐ Ⓑ Ⓒ Ⓓ Ⓔ
32	Ⓐ Ⓑ Ⓒ Ⓓ Ⓔ	32	Ⓐ Ⓑ Ⓒ Ⓓ Ⓔ	32	Ⓐ Ⓑ Ⓒ Ⓓ Ⓔ	32	Ⓐ Ⓑ Ⓒ Ⓓ Ⓔ
33	Ⓐ Ⓑ Ⓒ Ⓓ Ⓔ	33	Ⓐ Ⓑ Ⓒ Ⓓ Ⓔ	33	Ⓐ Ⓑ Ⓒ Ⓓ Ⓔ	33	Ⓐ Ⓑ Ⓒ Ⓓ Ⓔ
34	Ⓐ Ⓑ Ⓒ Ⓓ Ⓔ	34	Ⓐ Ⓑ Ⓒ Ⓓ Ⓔ	34	Ⓐ Ⓑ Ⓒ Ⓓ Ⓔ	34	Ⓐ Ⓑ Ⓒ Ⓓ Ⓔ
35	Ⓐ Ⓑ Ⓒ Ⓓ Ⓔ	35	Ⓐ Ⓑ Ⓒ Ⓓ Ⓔ	35	Ⓐ Ⓑ Ⓒ Ⓓ Ⓔ	35	Ⓐ Ⓑ Ⓒ Ⓓ Ⓔ
36	Ⓐ Ⓑ Ⓒ Ⓓ Ⓔ	36	Ⓐ Ⓑ Ⓒ Ⓓ Ⓔ	36	Ⓐ Ⓑ Ⓒ Ⓓ Ⓔ	36	Ⓐ Ⓑ Ⓒ Ⓓ Ⓔ
37	Ⓐ Ⓑ Ⓒ Ⓓ Ⓔ	37	Ⓐ Ⓑ Ⓒ Ⓓ Ⓔ	37	Ⓐ Ⓑ Ⓒ Ⓓ Ⓔ	37	Ⓐ Ⓑ Ⓒ Ⓓ Ⓔ
38	Ⓐ Ⓑ Ⓒ Ⓓ Ⓔ	38	Ⓐ Ⓑ Ⓒ Ⓓ Ⓔ	38	Ⓐ Ⓑ Ⓒ Ⓓ Ⓔ	38	Ⓐ Ⓑ Ⓒ Ⓓ Ⓔ

IF YOU DO NOT WANT THIS ANSWER SHEET TO BE SCORED

If you want to cancel your scores from this administration, complete A and B below. You will not receive scores for this test; however, you will receive confirmation of this cancellation. No record of this test or the cancellation will be sent to the recipients you indicated, and there will be no scores for this test on your GRE file. Once a score is canceled, it cannot be reinstated.

To cancel your scores from this test administration, you must:

FOR ETS USE ONLY	V1R	V2R	VTR	VCS	Q1R	Q2R	QTR	QCS	A1R	A2R	ATR	ACS

DO NOT USE INK

Use only a pencil with soft, black lead (No. 2 or HB) to complete this answer sheet.
Be sure to fill in completely the space that corresponds to your answer choice.
Completely erase any errors or stray marks.

GRADUATE RECORD EXAMINATIONS® - GRE® - GENERAL TEST

SIDE 1

1. NAME

Enter your last name, first name initial (given name), and middle initial if you have one.
Omit spaces, apostrophes, Jr., II., etc.

Last Name only (Family or Surname) - first 15 letters | First Name Initial | Middle Initial

2.

YOUR NAME: (Print) ______ Last Name (Family or Surname) First Name (Given) M.I.

MAILING ADDRESS: (Print) ______ P.O. Box or Street Address

______ City State or Province

______ Country Zip or Postal Code

CENTER: ______ City State or Province

______ Country Center Number Room Number

BE SURE EACH MARK IS DARK AND COMPLETELY FILLS THE INTENDED SPACE AS ILLUSTRATED HERE: ●

YOU MAY FIND MORE RESPONSE SPACES THAN YOU NEED. IF SO, PLEASE LEAVE THEM BLANK.

SECTION 1	SECTION 2	SECTION 3
1 A B C D E	1 A B C D E	1 A B C D E
2 A B C D E	2 A B C D E	2 A B C D E
3 A B C D E	3 A B C D E	3 A B C D E
4 A B C D E	4 A B C D E	4 A B C D E
5 A B C D E	5 A B C D E	5 A B C D E
6 A B C D E	6 A B C D E	6 A B C D E
7 A B C D E	7 A B C D E	7 A B C D E
8 A B C D E	8 A B C D E	8 A B C D E
9 A B C D E	9 A B C D E	9 A B C D E
10 A B C D E	10 A B C D E	10 A B C D E
11 A B C D E	11 A B C D E	11 A B C D E
12 A B C D E	12 A B C D E	12 A B C D E
13 A B C D E	13 A B C D E	13 A B C D E
14 A B C D E	14 A B C D E	14 A B C D E
15 A B C D E	15 A B C D E	15 A B C D E
16 A B C D E	16 A B C D E	16 A B C D E
17 A B C D E	17 A B C D E	17 A B C D E
18 A B C D E	18 A B C D E	18 A B C D E
19 A B C D E	19 A B C D E	19 A B C D E
20 A B C D E	20 A B C D E	20 A B C D E
21 A B C D E	21 A B C D E	21 A B C D E
22 A B C D E	22 A B C D E	22 A B C D E
23 A B C D E	23 A B C D E	23 A B C D E
24 A B C D E	24 A B C D E	24 A B C D E
25 A B C D E	25 A B C D E	25 A B C D E
26 A B C D E	26 A B C D E	26 A B C D E
27 A B C D E	27 A B C D E	27 A B C D E
28 A B C D E	28 A B C D E	28 A B C D E
29 A B C D E	29 A B C D E	29 A B C D E
30 A B C D E	30 A B C D E	30 A B C D E
31 A B C D E	31 A B C D E	31 A B C D E
32 A B C D E	32 A B C D E	32 A B C D E
33 A B C D E	33 A B C D E	33 A B C D E
34 A B C D E	34 A B C D E	34 A B C D E
35 A B C D E	35 A B C D E	35 A B C D E
36 A B C D E	36 A B C D E	36 A B C D E
37 A B C D E	37 A B C D E	37 A B C D E
38 A B C D E	38 A B C D E	38 A B C D E

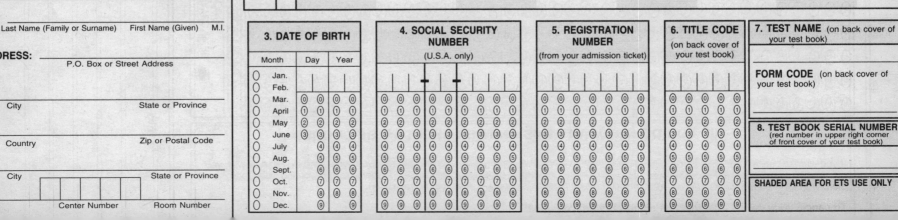

3. DATE OF BIRTH

Month: Jan. Feb. Mar. April May June July Aug. Sept. Oct. Nov. Dec. | Day | Year

4. SOCIAL SECURITY NUMBER

(U.S.A. only)

5. REGISTRATION NUMBER

(from your admission ticket)

6. TITLE CODE

(on back cover of your test book)

7. TEST NAME (on back cover of your test book)

FORM CODE (on back cover of your test book)

8. TEST BOOK SERIAL NUMBER

(red number in upper right corner of front cover of your test book)

SHADED AREA FOR ETS USE ONLY

SIDE 2

GENERAL TEST

CERTIFICATION STATEMENT

Please write the following statement below, DO NOT PRINT.
"I certify that I am the person whose name appears on this answer sheet. I a
agree not to disclose the contents of the test I am taking today to anyone."
Sign and date where indicated.

SIGNATURE: ______________________ DATE: ___/___/___
Month Day Ye

BE SURE EACH MARK IS DARK AND COMPLETELY FILLS THE INTENDED SPACE AS ILLUSTRATED HERE: ●.
YOU MAY FIND MORE RESPONSE SPACES THAN YOU NEED. IF SO, PLEASE LEAVE THEM BLANK.

	SECTION 4	SECTION 5	SECTION 6	SECTION 7
1	A B C D E	A B C D E	A B C D E	A B C D E
2	A B C D E	A B C D E	A B C D E	A B C D E
3	A B C D E	A B C D E	A B C D E	A B C D E
4	A B C D E	A B C D E	A B C D E	A B C D E
5	A B C D E	A B C D E	A B C D E	A B C D E
6	A B C D E	A B C D E	A B C D E	A B C D E
7	A B C D E	A B C D E	A B C D E	A B C D E
8	A B C D E	A B C D E	A B C D E	A B C D E
9	A B C D E	A B C D E	A B C D E	A B C D E
10	A B C D E	A B C D E	A B C D E	A B C D E
11	A B C D E	A B C D E	A B C D E	A B C D E
12	A B C D E	A B C D E	A B C D E	A B C D E
13	A B C D E	A B C D E	A B C D E	A B C D E
14	A B C D E	A B C D E	A B C D E	A B C D E
15	A B C D E	A B C D E	A B C D E	A B C D E
16	A B C D E	A B C D E	A B C D E	A B C D E
17	A B C D E	A B C D E	A B C D E	A B C D E
18	A B C D E	A B C D E	A B C D E	A B C D E
19	A B C D E	A B C D E	A B C D E	A B C D E
20	A B C D E	A B C D E	A B C D E	A B C D E
21	A B C D E	A B C D E	A B C D E	A B C D E
22	A B C D E	A B C D E	A B C D E	A B C D E
23	A B C D E	A B C D E	A B C D E	A B C D E
24	A B C D E	A B C D E	A B C D E	A B C D E
25	A B C D E	A B C D E	A B C D E	A B C D E
26	A B C D E	A B C D E	A B C D E	A B C D E
27	A B C D E	A B C D E	A B C D E	A B C D E
28	A B C D E	A B C D E	A B C D E	A B C D E
29	A B C D E	A B C D E	A B C D E	A B C D E
30	A B C D E	A B C D E	A B C D E	A B C D E
31	A B C D E	A B C D E	A B C D E	A B C D E
32	A B C D E	A B C D E	A B C D E	A B C D E
33	A B C D E	A B C D E	A B C D E	A B C D E
34	A B C D E	A B C D E	A B C D E	A B C D E
35	A B C D E	A B C D E	A B C D E	A B C D E
36	A B C D E	A B C D E	A B C D E	A B C D E
37	A B C D E	A B C D E	A B C D E	A B C D E
38	A B C D E	A B C D E	A B C D E	A B C D E

IF YOU DO NOT WANT THIS ANSWER SHEET TO BE SCORED

If you want to cancel your scores from this administration, complete A and B below. You will not receive scores for this test; however, you will receive confirmation of this cancellation. No record of this test or the cancellation will be sent to the recipients you indicated, and there will be no scores for this test on your GRE file. Once a score is canceled, it cannot be reinstated.

To cancel your scores from this test administration, you must:

FOR ETS USE ONLY	V1R	V2R	VTR	VCS	Q1R	Q2R	QTR	QCS	A1R	A2R	ATR	ACS

DO NOT USE INK

Use only a pencil with soft, black lead (No. 2 or HB) to complete this answer sheet. Be sure to fill in completely the space that corresponds to your answer choice. Completely erase any errors or stray marks.

GRADUATE RECORD EXAMINATIONS® - GRE® - GENERAL TEST

SIDE 1

1. NAME Enter your last name, first name initial (given name), and middle initial if you have one. Omit spaces, apostrophes, Jr., II., etc.

Last Name only (Family or Surname) - first 15 letters | First Name Initial | Middle Initial

A B C D E F G H I J K L M N O P Q R S T U V W X Y Z

2.

YOUR NAME: (Print) Last Name (Family or Surname) First Name (Given) M.I.

MAILING ADDRESS: (Print) P.O. Box or Street Address

City State or Province

Country Zip or Postal Code

CENTER: City State or Province

Country Center Number Room Number

BE SURE EACH MARK IS DARK AND COMPLETELY FILLS THE INTENDED SPACE AS ILLUSTRATED HERE: ●

YOU MAY FIND MORE RESPONSE SPACES THAN YOU NEED. IF SO, PLEASE LEAVE THEM BLANK.

	SECTION 1	SECTION 2	SECTION 3
1	A B C D E	A B C D E	A B C D E
2	A B C D E	A B C D E	A B C D E
3	A B C D E	A B C D E	A B C D E
4	A B C D E	A B C D E	A B C D E
5	A B C D E	A B C D E	A B C D E
6	A B C D E	A B C D E	A B C D E
7	A B C D E	A B C D E	A B C D E
8	A B C D E	A B C D E	A B C D E
9	A B C D E	A B C D E	A B C D E
10	A B C D E	A B C D E	A B C D E
11	A B C D E	A B C D E	A B C D E
12	A B C D E	A B C D E	A B C D E
13	A B C D E	A B C D E	A B C D E
14	A B C D E	A B C D E	A B C D E
15	A B C D E	A B C D E	A B C D E
16	A B C D E	A B C D E	A B C D E
17	A B C D E	A B C D E	A B C D E
18	A B C D E	A B C D E	A B C D E
19	A B C D E	A B C D E	A B C D E
20	A B C D E	A B C D E	A B C D E
21	A B C D E	A B C D E	A B C D E
22	A B C D E	A B C D E	A B C D E
23	A B C D E	A B C D E	A B C D E
24	A B C D E	A B C D E	A B C D E
25	A B C D E	A B C D E	A B C D E
26	A B C D E	A B C D E	A B C D E
27	A B C D E	A B C D E	A B C D E
28	A B C D E	A B C D E	A B C D E
29	A B C D E	A B C D E	A B C D E
30	A B C D E	A B C D E	A B C D E
31	A B C D E	A B C D E	A B C D E
32	A B C D E	A B C D E	A B C D E
33	A B C D E	A B C D E	A B C D E
34	A B C D E	A B C D E	A B C D E
35	A B C D E	A B C D E	A B C D E
36	A B C D E	A B C D E	A B C D E
37	A B C D E	A B C D E	A B C D E
38	A B C D E	A B C D E	A B C D E

3. DATE OF BIRTH

Month	Day	Year
Jan.		
Feb.		
Mar.	0 0	0 0
April	1 1	1 1
May	2 2	2 2
June	3 3	3 3
July	4	4 4
Aug.	5	5 5
Sept.	6	6 6
Oct.	7	7 7
Nov.	8	8 8
Dec.	9	9

4. SOCIAL SECURITY NUMBER (U.S.A. only)

0 1 2 3 4 5 6 7 8 9

5. REGISTRATION NUMBER (from your admission ticket)

0 1 2 3 4 5 6 7 8 9

6. TITLE CODE (on back cover of your test book)

0 1 2 3 4 5 6 7 8 9

7. TEST NAME (on back cover of your test book)

FORM CODE (on back cover of your test book)

8. TEST BOOK SERIAL NUMBER (red number in upper right corner of front cover of your test book)

SHADED AREA FOR ETS USE ONLY

SIDE 2

GENERAL TEST

CERTIFICATION STATEMENT

Please write the following statement below, DO NOT PRINT.
"I certify that I am the person whose name appears on this answer sheet. I a
agree not to disclose the contents of the test I am taking today to anyone."
Sign and date where indicated.

SIGNATURE: ______________________ DATE: ____/____/____
Month Day Ye

BE SURE EACH MARK IS DARK AND COMPLETELY FILLS THE INTENDED SPACE AS ILLUSTRATED HERE: ●.
YOU MAY FIND MORE RESPONSE SPACES THAN YOU NEED. IF SO, PLEASE LEAVE THEM BLANK.

	SECTION 4	SECTION 5	SECTION 6	SECTION 7
1	A B C D E	A B C D E	A B C D E	A B C D E
2	A B C D E	A B C D E	A B C D E	A B C D E
3	A B C D E	A B C D E	A B C D E	A B C D E
4	A B C D E	A B C D E	A B C D E	A B C D E
5	A B C D E	A B C D E	A B C D E	A B C D E
6	A B C D E	A B C D E	A B C D E	A B C D E
7	A B C D E	A B C D E	A B C D E	A B C D E
8	A B C D E	A B C D E	A B C D E	A B C D E
9	A B C D E	A B C D E	A B C D E	A B C D E
10	A B C D E	A B C D E	A B C D E	A B C D E
11	A B C D E	A B C D E	A B C D E	A B C D E
12	A B C D E	A B C D E	A B C D E	A B C D E
13	A B C D E	A B C D E	A B C D E	A B C D E
14	A B C D E	A B C D E	A B C D E	A B C D E
15	A B C D E	A B C D E	A B C D E	A B C D E
16	A B C D E	A B C D E	A B C D E	A B C D E
17	A B C D E	A B C D E	A B C D E	A B C D E
18	A B C D E	A B C D E	A B C D E	A B C D E
19	A B C D E	A B C D E	A B C D E	A B C D E
20	A B C D E	A B C D E	A B C D E	A B C D E
21	A B C D E	A B C D E	A B C D E	A B C D E
22	A B C D E	A B C D E	A B C D E	A B C D E
23	A B C D E	A B C D E	A B C D E	A B C D E
24	A B C D E	A B C D E	A B C D E	A B C D E
25	A B C D E	A B C D E	A B C D E	A B C D E
26	A B C D E	A B C D E	A B C D E	A B C D E
27	A B C D E	A B C D E	A B C D E	A B C D E
28	A B C D E	A B C D E	A B C D E	A B C D E
29	A B C D E	A B C D E	A B C D E	A B C D E
30	A B C D E	A B C D E	A B C D E	A B C D E
31	A B C D E	A B C D E	A B C D E	A B C D E
32	A B C D E	A B C D E	A B C D E	A B C D E
33	A B C D E	A B C D E	A B C D E	A B C D E
34	A B C D E	A B C D E	A B C D E	A B C D E
35	A B C D E	A B C D E	A B C D E	A B C D E
36	A B C D E	A B C D E	A B C D E	A B C D E
37	A B C D E	A B C D E	A B C D E	A B C D E
38	A B C D E	A B C D E	A B C D E	A B C D E

IF YOU DO NOT WANT THIS ANSWER SHEET TO BE SCORED

If you want to cancel your scores from this administration, complete A and B below. You will not receive scores for this test; however, you will receive confirmation of this cancellation. No record of this test or the cancellation will be sent to the recipients you indicated, and there will be no scores for this test on your GRE file. Once a score is canceled, it cannot be reinstated.

To cancel your scores from this test administration, you must:

FOR ETS USE ONLY	V1R	V2R	VTR	VCS	Q1R	Q2R	QTR	QCS	A1R	A2R	ATR	ACS

GRE® PUBLICATIONS ORDER FORM

1994-95

For credit card orders (VISA or MasterCard *only*), call 1-800-537-3160, Monday-Friday, 8:00 a.m. to 4:00 p.m. Eastern time. Outside the U.S. or Canada, call 609-771-7243.

Item Number	Publication	Price*	No. of Copies	Amount	Total
	Practice Test Books (540-01) †Available September 1994				
241278	Practicing to Take the GRE General Test — 9th Edition	$15.00			
241257	Practicing to Take the GRE Biology Test — 2nd Edition	11.00			
241242	Practicing to Take the GRE Chemistry Test — 2nd Edition	11.00			
241258	Practicing to Take the GRE Computer Science Test — 2nd Edition	11.00			
241249	Practicing to Take the GRE Economics Test — 2nd Edition	11.00			
241236	Practicing to Take the GRE Education Test — 2nd Edition	11.00			
241280	† Practicing to Take the GRE Engineering Test — 3rd Edition	13.00			
241254	Practicing to Take the GRE Geology Test — 2nd Edition	11.00			
241255	Practicing to Take the GRE History Test — 2nd Edition	11.00			
241261	Practicing to Take the GRE Literature in English Test — 2nd Edition	11.00			
241263	Practicing to Take the GRE Mathematics Test — 2nd Edition	11.00			
241265	Practicing to Take the GRE Music Test — 2nd Edition	11.00			
241256	Practicing to Take the GRE Physics Test — 2nd Edition	11.00			
241277	Practicing to Take the GRE Political Science Test	9.00			
241279	† Practicing to Take the GRE Psychology Test — 3rd Edition	13.00			
241264	Practicing to Take the GRE Sociology Test — 2nd Edition	11.00			
	Directory of Graduate Programs				
252035	Volume A — Natural Sciences	18.00			
252036	Volume B — Engineering • Business	18.00			
252037	Volume C — Social Sciences • Education	18.00			
252038	Volume D — Arts • Humanities • Other Fields	18.00			

* **Postage: In North America and U.S. Territories and for APO addresses,** postage and handling to a single address is included. **To all other locations (airmail only)** for postage and handling to a single address add $4 for the first book ordered and $2 for each additional book.

POSTAGE 540-52 ▶

Canada residents add 7% GST R131414468 ▶

In California add 8.25% sales tax ▶

TOTAL AMOUNT ENCLOSED

Make your remittance payable to **ETS-GRE**.

ETS use only

- Allow three to four weeks for delivery.
- Payment should be made by check or money order drawn on a U.S. or Canadian bank, U.S. Postal Money Order, or UNESCO Coupons.
- *Orders received without payment will be returned.*
- A returned practice book or *Directory of Graduate Programs* will be accepted for credit or full refund within 10 days of receipt only if currently in print and in salable condition.

TYPE OR PRINT CLEARLY YOUR NAME AND ADDRESS BELOW. DO NOT DETACH THIS MAILING LABEL.

Graduate Record Examinations
Educational Testing Service
P.O. Box 6014
Princeton, NJ 08541-6014

YOUR NAME: ______________________________

____

____

____